The Complete Gospels

The Scholars Version

Translation Panel

The Complete Gospels

Annotated Scholars Version

Revised and Expanded Edition

Robert J. Miller, editor

SONOMA, CALIFORNIA

 For information address Polebridge Press, P.O. Box 1526, Sonoma, California, 95476.

Library of Congress Cataloging-in-Publication Data

Bible, N.T. Gospels. English. Scholars. 1994.
The complete Gospels : annotated Scholars Version / Robert J. Miller, editor.—Rev. and expanded ed.
p. cm.
ISBN 0-944344-45-3 (casebound). - ISBN 0-944344-49-6 (pbk.)
I. Miller, Robert J. (Robert Joseph), 1954- . II. Title.
BS2553.S24 1994b
226'.05208—dc20 94-38279
CIP

94 95 96 97 98 RRD(H) 10 9 8 7 6 5 4 3 2 1

This edition is printed on acid-free paper that meets the American National Standards Institute Z39.48 Standard.

Contents

Illustrations and Cameo Essays

Robert W. Funk

Foreword

The Fellows of the Jesus Seminar have taken a bold step in gathering all the surviving gospels and gospel fragments into one volume in *The Complete Gospels.* So far as we know, it is the first time canonical and extracanonical gospels have been assembled under one cover.

The Seminar also decided to group the gospels by type—narrative gospels, sayings gospels, infancy gospels, and fragments. Since we believe the Gospel of Mark was written first and is the basis of both Matthew and Luke, we have placed Mark first among the narrative gospels. We have printed a reconstructed Signs Gospel as a separate text; many scholars believe the Signs Gospel is the precursor of the Gospel of John. The Sayings Gospel Q is also printed as a separate gospel, in both its Matthean and Lukan versions, with matched lines to make for easier comparison. The panel also decided to include three of the gospels found among the Nag Hammadi texts discovered in Egypt in 1945: the Gospel of Thomas, Secret James, and the Dialogue of the Savior. Another very interesting gospel that recently came to light is the Gospel of Mary, which, unfortunately, is missing several pages.

Although highly fanciful, the Fellows have included the two infancy gospels because they shed light on how the legends of Jesus' birth and childhood, and the birth and childhood of Mary, developed in the first two centuries of the common era.

The fragmentary gospels deserve far more attention than they have been given. The Gospel of Peter, the Egerton Gospel, and the gospels known as Oxyrhynchus 840 and 1224 are pieces of gospels lost until modern times. They preserve intriguing bits of lore and raise the hope that more fragments and manuscripts will turn up, whether in the sands of Egypt, the caves of the Jordan Valley, or museums in Europe. Meanwhile, *The Complete Gospels* makes all the gospel lore about Jesus available in a new, modern translation.

The Scholars Version—SV for short—is free of ecclesiastical and religious control, unlike other major translations into English, including the King James version and its descendants (Protestant) and the Douay-Rheims version and its progeny (Catholic). It also differs from most other English versions in that it is not a revision of a previous translation.

As the Fellows of the Jesus Seminar examined the Jesus tradition, they became increasingly dissatisfied with both the accuracy and style of the standard translations available for making their report to the public. (The Fellows themselves base their analyses on the original languages.) As a consequence, they decided to make their own translation into American English as it is spoken and written in North America.

In addition, traditional translations controlled by ecclesiastical bodies or groups and published by bible societies do not, as a rule, include gospels outside the four in the New Testament. The first challenge, then, was to produce readable renderings of those other gospels—sayings gospels, infancy gospels, fragmentary gospels, and a few stray sayings and stories. To historians and critical biblical scholars, these little known gospels are as important as canonical gospels. In other words, canonical boundaries are not real boundaries for those interested in the full story of how Christianity took its rise.

The translation panel (listed in the front of this book) adopted several guidelines.

The Scholars Version is a translation from the original languages, usually Greek but also Coptic, and occasionally Latin, Aramaic, or Hebrew.

We agreed that we would not translate anything we did not understand. When we agreed on what a text meant, we then endeavored to formulate that meaning in our own language. We adopted as our motto: A translation is artful to the extent that one can forget, while reading it, that it is a translation at all. Accordingly, rather than make SV a thinly disguised guide to the underlying original language, the translators attempted to recreate in the American reader an approximation of the experience the first readers (or listeners) had. It is worth mentioning that those who first encountered the gospels did so as listeners rather than as readers. With this in mind, we made listenability or readability the final test of every proposed phrase and sentence.

We have avoided "biblical language": gone are "It came to pass," "behold," "woe," and other legacies of the King James era. We have shunned euphemisms intended for polite company and liturgical usage. For example, in speaking of Joseph's relation to Mary during her pregnancy, the KJV translates: "And he knew her not until she had brought forth her firstborn son" (Matt 1:25), which in the New International Version becomes "But he had no union with her, . . ." and which the New Revised Standard Version renders, "but had no marital relations with her. . . ." SV is to the point: "He did not have sex with her until she had given birth to a son." In SV we have endeavored to employ the English idiom that corresponds to the Greek expression without dressing up the translation for the Victorian parlor.

"The first day of the week" has become "Sunday"—the term most Americans use. But we did not translate out archaic customs and practices. People still "recline at table" rather than "sit" because dining in the first-century world was done on couches rather than chairs. We left in distasteful references to slaves and caricatures of Pharisees and other stereotypes. But we avoided sexist language wherever possible. Jesus admitted women into his inner circle, as the Gospel of Mary shows, and he was especially fond of children. We have attempted to honor his inclusiveness by embracing women and children in the English pronoun.

The translation panel undertook to establish its own Greek text in the hundreds of places the handwritten manuscripts differ from each other. In these decisions we often depart from the Greek text underlying other translations.

When translating the words of Jesus, the panel attempted to make aphorisms sound like aphorisms and to put them into contemporary English at the same time. Instead of "You cannot serve God and mammon," SV renders "You can't be enslaved to God and a bank account." Instead of "For out of the abundance of the heart the mouth speaks," SV has "The mouth gives voice to what the heart is full of." At the end of a string of admonitions to love, in older translations Jesus is made to say, "Be perfect, therefore, as your heavenly Father is perfect." SV has translated the sense rather than the words: "Be as liberal in your love as your heavenly Father is." The reader does not need to consult a commentary to figure out what the words mean.

The translators believe that excessive capitalization gives the gospels an old-fashioned look. Pronouns referring to God are no longer capitalized as they once were. The term "son" is not capitalized when referring to Jesus. Rather than "Jesus Christ," SV uses the phrase "Jesus the Anointed" to avoid confusion: many readers take "Christ" to be the family name of Jesus when actually it means "messiah." The rationale in avoiding overcapitalization was the desire to desacralize terms that in the original were common and secular; English translators have given them an unwarranted sacred dimension by capitalizing them.

In other ways the translators have struggled to clarify. The "son of Man" has become the "son of Adam" and sometimes, when warranted, as "son of Adam and Eve" to indicate the link to the progenitors of humankind. We have avoided "kingdom of God"—a link to rascally King James—and used "God's imperial rule" or "God's domain" instead. Our intention was to wake the reader up to the force of the text by employing fresh, new language.

Preface

The Complete Gospels is the product of a uniquely collaborative effort. And it is a unique conception. It consists of fresh, new translations of *all* the gospels, which are then collected under one cover, together with introductions, notes, and cross references. All this was created by a team of scholars working toward a common goal.

The translation phase of the project began in the fall of 1988, when Robert W. Funk set four translators to work drafting renditions of the canonical gospels. Those four used the following New Year's holiday to gather and compare what they had produced. It was the first step in a three-year process of crafting the distinctive tone and style of the Scholars Version: the Gospels.

As work continued on the translations, other members of the growing Scholars Version (SV) team checked the accuracy of the drafts, compared parallel passages, and labored to make the English truly contemporary. Several revisions were circulated and further suggestions were exchanged. Adjustments to one passage often would ricochet into other passages where the wording was similar. Numerous passages were reworked repeatedly.

Gradually a common vision emerged. We refined the principles of translation which enabled us to progress toward the dual goal of being scrupulously faithful to the ancient texts while reflecting the way ordinary people actually speak English today. Yet few of us knew how difficult the task would be when we began.

Several important problems defied easy solution. Especially troublesome were a handful of phrases that are central to the gospels, such as the terms traditionally translated "Son of Man," "Kingdom of God," and "Lord." While we insisted on abandoning those misleading and anachronistic renderings, nevertheless it was not easy to arrive at fresh translations. Other issues, less central but no less thorny, also had to be resolved; for example: whether to translate the name *Petros* as "Peter" (its English equivalent) or as "Rock" (its literal meaning); how to handle the sexist bias inherent in English pronouns; and what to do with references to "the Jews," a term with modern ethnic and religious resonances quite foreign to our ancient texts.

Different solutions were proposed, and there were honest and vigorous disagreements. Several people changed their minds on certain issues—some more than once. Consenses eventually were found, though in some cases team members privately demurred. Such is the nature of collaboration in which individuals work together to produce something bigger and better than any could achieve alone and in which individuals submit their work to the collective judgment of the group, supporting the outcome of the process even if they must concede a point in honest debate along the way. The translations in the SV are the result of the work of some two dozen scholars, and are the collective responsibility of the entire SV panel. Individual authors undertook to produce original drafts. In some cases, these drafts were adopted with only modest changes; in others virtually nothing remains of the original proposals.

The Complete Gospels comes with introductions to each gospel, together with notes and cross references. These features provide readers with information necessary for the critical study of the gospels. They have been prepared by scholars each of whom is intimately familiar with his or her specific gospel—in most cases by the one responsible for the draft translation. As editor, I was gratified by the contributors' willingness to rethink and rewrite even where they were expert, in the interests of producing a volume more accessible to the general public and untutored student. As scholars who specialize in the study of these ancient texts, it is our goal to make them intelligible and inviting to all who are willing to invest the time and effort to work through this volume. For each gospel an *introduction* sets the text in its ancient historical and religious contexts, and discusses the overall structure and central themes. The *cross references* point out the numerous parallel passages, intratextual indicators, and thematic parallels so the reader can see how the individual passages of a gospel fit into the rich tapestry of Jewish and early Christian texts. The *notes* explain important translation issues, supply necessary background information, offer guidance in difficult passages, and honestly indicate problems in the texts or in our understanding of them. SV intentionally drops the pretense that scholars have all the answers. We strive to avoid both talking down to readers and talking over their heads; we hope rather to communicate with readers as partners in a common goal: understanding these fascinating documents.

The prime mover behind the collective effort was Robert Funk, general editor and publisher of Polebridge Press. He conceived the original idea of the SV, recruited the team of scholars, and prodded us along; he and other members of the panel "field tested" the translations with Westar associates and revised and refined our principles of translation. Funk also refereed the occasional debates and from time to time proposed solutions which the panel adopted. His office was the clearing house for the translation project, as a steady stream of drafts, revisions, memos, complaints, and critiques arrived on his desk via mail, phone, and fax, to be scrutinized and passed along for review. The SV is the collective product of all the participants, yet Robert Funk is the one person without whom it would not have come to be.

Char Matejovsky managed the production of the volume and devised the book's design, arranging the mass of information on the page in a way both friendly to the user and pleasing to the eye. Her endless patience, cheerful perseverance, and prevenient good sense have made the book what it is.

Contributors

Harold Attridge is Professor of Theology at the University of Notre Dame, Notre Dame, Indiana.

Infancy Gospel of Thomas: draft translation, introduction, notes

Ron Cameron is Associate Professor of Religion at Wesleyan University, Middletown, Connecticut.

Secret Book of James: draft translation
General Editor, apocryphal gospels

J. Dominic Crossan is Professor of Biblical Studies at DePaul University, Chicago, Illinois.

Oxyrhynchus Gospel 1224: draft translation, introduction, notes

Jon B. Daniels is Assistant Professor of Religious Studies at Defiance College, Defiance, Ohio.

Egerton Gospel: draft translation, introduction, notes

Arthur J. Dewey is Associate Professor of Theology at Xavier University, Cincinnati, Ohio.

Gospel of Peter: draft translation, introduction, notes

Robert T. Fortna is Professor of Religion at Vassar College, Poughkeepsie, New York.

Signs Gospel, Gospel of John: draft translation, introduction, notes

Robert W. Funk is director of the Westar Institute and publisher of Polebridge Press, Sonoma, California.

Oxyrhynchus Gospel 840: draft translation
Editor-in-Chief, The Scholars Version

Julian V. Hills is Associate Professor of Theology at Marquette University, Milwaukee, Wisconsin.

Dialogue of the Savior: draft translation, introduction, notes
Gospel of John: draft translation
General Editor, The Scholars Version

Ronald F. Hock is Associate Professor of Religion at the University of Southern California, Los Angeles.

Infancy Gospel of James: draft translation, introduction, notes
Infancy Gospel of Thomas: draft translation, introduction, notes

Arland D. Jacobson is the Director of the CHARIS Ecumenical Center at Concordia College, Moorhead, Minnesota.
Sayings Gospel Q: introduction, notes

Karen L. King is Associate Professor of Religious Studies at Occidental College, Los Angeles, California.
Gospel of Mary: draft translation, introduction, notes
General Editor, apocryphal gospels

John S. Kloppenborg is Associate Professor of New Testament at University of St. Michael's College, Toronto, Ontario.
Gospel of the Hebrews, Nazoreans, and Ebionites: draft translations, introductions, notes

Helmut Koester is Professor of New Testament Studies at Harvard Divinity School, Cambridge, Massachusetts.
Secret Gospel of Mark: draft translation, introduction, notes

Marvin W. Meyer is Associate Professor of Religion at Chapman College, Orange, California.
Gospel of Thomas: draft translation

Robert J. Miller teaches Religious Studies and Philosophy at Midway College, Midway, Kentucky.
Gospel of Luke: draft translation, introduction, notes
Gospel of John: notes
Gospels of the Hebrews, Nazoreans, and Ebionites: introductions, notes
Oxyrhynchus Gospel 1224: introduction, notes

Stephen J. Patterson is Associate Professor of New Testament at Eden Theological Seminary, St. Louis, Missouri.
Gospel of Thomas: draft translation, introduction, notes
Orphan Sayings & Stories: draft translations, introduction, notes
Secret Gospel of Mark: draft translation, introduction, notes

Donald Rappé is completing his Ph.D. in Theology at Marquette University, Milwaukee, Wisconsin
Secret Book of James: introduction, notes

Daryl D. Schmidt is Associate Professor of Religion at Texas Christian University, Fort Worth, Texas
Editor, Greek text of the gospels
General Editor, The Scholars Version

Bernard Brandon Scott is Professor of New Testament at Phillips Graduate Seminary, Tulsa, Oklahoma.
Gospel of Matthew: draft translation, introduction, notes

Philip Sellew is Associate Professor of Classical Studies at the University of Minnesota, Minneapolis.
Gospel of Mark: draft translation, introduction, notes
Oxyrhynchus Gospel 840: introduction, notes

Sigla

Used in the translation

⟨ ⟩ Pointed brackets indicate a subject, object, or other element implied by the original language and supplied by the translator.

[ ] Square brackets indicate words which have been restored from a lacuna or emended from a scribal error. (See the essay on *Emendation and restoration*, p. 334.)

[. . .] A lacuna or gap in the manuscript that cannot be satisfactorily restored.

( ) Parentheses are used in the usual sense, to indicate parenthetical remarks and narrative asides in the original text.

Used in cross references

Cross references are to passages in the canonical books of the Old and New Testaments and in the extracanonical works included in this volume. Occasionally, the notes refer to especially significant parallel passages in extracanonical texts not included in *The Complete Gospels*. In these cases, the passages referred to are quoted in the notes.

// Primary parallel: a pericope or saying with a significant degree of verbal similarity

Cf. Secondary parallel: a similar or comparable passage with a low degree of verbal similarity

▷ Old Testament reference: an Old Testament passage quoted or alluded to, or Old Testament laws or customs presupposed in a gospel passage

Ⓓ A doublet: a duplicate version of a story or saying within the same gospel

Ⓘ Narrative index: a reference to an earlier or later event narrated in the same gospel

Q The Sayings Gospel Q (found only in Matthew and Luke): a passage in Matthew or Luke also found in Q

Ⓢ Source reference (only in Infancy James): an Old Testament or New Testament passage whose wording or substance is used to create a new passage

Ⓣ Thematic parallel: a passage with a comparable theme or motif

How To Use This Book

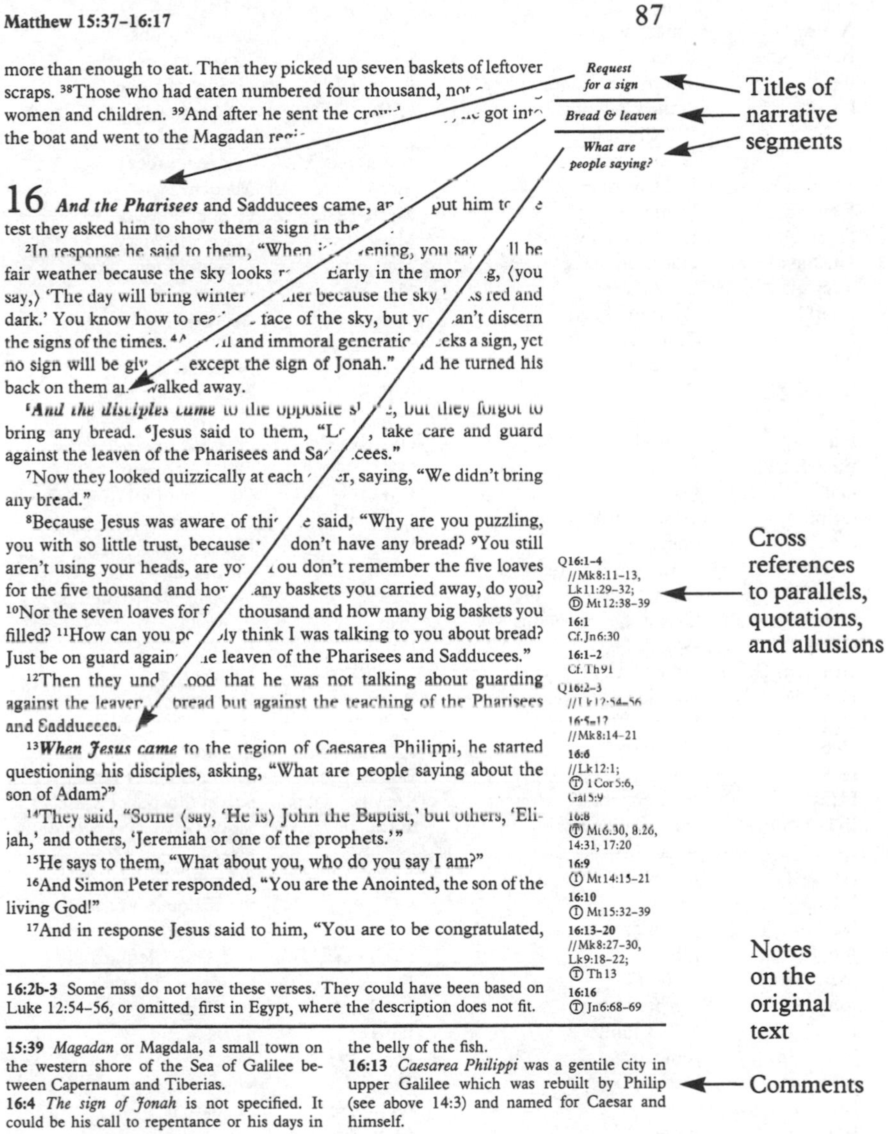

Matthew 15:37–16:17 87

more than enough to eat. Then they picked up seven baskets of leftover
scraps. 38Those who had eaten numbered four thousand, not ...
women and children. 39And after he sent the crowd ... he got into
the boat and went to the Magadan region.

Request for a sign

Bread & leaven

What are people saying?

Titles of narrative segments

16 ***And the Pharisees*** and Sadducees came, and ... put him to the
test they asked him to show them a sign in the ...
2In response he said to them, "When it's evening, you say, 'It'll be
fair weather because the sky looks red.' Early in the morning, ⟨you
say,⟩ 'The day will bring winter weather because the sky is red and
dark.' You know how to read the face of the sky, but you can't discern
the signs of the times. 4An evil and immoral generation seeks a sign, yet
no sign will be given it except the sign of Jonah." And he turned his
back on them and walked away.
5***And the disciples came*** to the opposite shore, but they forgot to
bring any bread. 6Jesus said to them, "Look, take care and guard
against the leaven of the Pharisees and Sadducees."
7Now they looked quizzically at each other, saying, "We didn't bring
any bread."
8Because Jesus was aware of this, he said, "Why are you puzzling,
you with so little trust, because you don't have any bread? 9You still
aren't using your heads, are you? You don't remember the five loaves
for the five thousand and how many baskets you carried away, do you?
10Nor the seven loaves for four thousand and how many big baskets you
filled? 11How can you possibly think I was talking to you about bread?
Just be on guard against the leaven of the Pharisees and Sadducees."
12Then they understood that he was not talking about guarding
against the leaven of bread but against the teaching of the Pharisees
and Sadducees.
13***When Jesus came*** to the region of Caesarea Philippi, he started
questioning his disciples, asking, "What are people saying about the
son of Adam?"
14They said, "Some ⟨say, 'He is⟩ John the Baptist,' but others, 'Elijah,' and others, 'Jeremiah or one of the prophets.'"
15He says to them, "What about you, who do you say I am?"
16And Simon Peter responded, "You are the Anointed, the son of the
living God!"
17And in response Jesus said to him, "You are to be congratulated,

Q16:1–4 //Mk8:11–13, Lk11:29–32; Ⓓ Mt12:38–39
16:1 Cf.Jn6:30
16:1–2 Cf.Th91
Q16:2–3 //Lk12:54–56
16:5–12 //Mk8:14–21
16:6 //Lk12:1; Ⓣ 1Cor5:6, Gal5:9
16:8 Ⓣ Mt6:30, 8:26, 14:31, 17:20
16:9 Ⓘ Mt14:15–21
16:10 Ⓘ Mt15:32–39
16:13–20 //Mk8:27–30, Lk9:18–22; Ⓣ Th13
16:16 Ⓣ Jn6:68–69

Cross references to parallels, quotations, and allusions

16:2b-3 Some mss do not have these verses. They could have been based on Luke 12:54–56, or omitted, first in Egypt, where the description does not fit.

Notes on the original text

15:39 *Magadan* or Magdala, a small town on the western shore of the Sea of Galilee between Capernaum and Tiberias.
16:4 *The sign of Jonah* is not specified. It could be his call to repentance or his days in the belly of the fish.
16:13 *Caesarea Philippi* was a gentile city in upper Galilee which was rebuilt by Philip (see above 14:3) and named for Caesar and himself.

Comments

Abbreviations

Acts	Acts
Amos, Am	Amos
Bar	Baruch
B.C.E.	before the Common Era
C.E.	of the Common Era
1–2 Chr	1–2 Chronicles
Col	Colossians
1–2 Cor	1–2 Corinthians
Dan, Dn	Daniel
Deut, Dt	Deuteronomy
DialSav, DSav	Dialogue of the Savior
Eccl	Ecclesiastes
EgerG	Egerton Gospel
Eph	Ephesians
2 Esd	2 Esdras
Esth, Est	Esther
Exod, Ex	Exodus
Ezek, Ez	Ezekiel
Ezra, Ezr	Ezra
Gal	Galatians
GEbi	Gospel of the Ebionites
Gen, Gn	Genesis
GHeb	Gospel of the Hebrews
GNaz	Gospel of the Nazoreans
GOxy 840	Gospel Oxyrhynchus 840
GOxy 1224	Gospel Oxyrhynchus 1224
GrThom,GrTh	Greek fragments of Thomas
Hab, Hb	Habakkuk
Hag, Hg	Haggai
Heb	Hebrews
Hos	Hosea
InJas	Infancy James
InThom	Infancy Thomas
Isa, Is	Isaiah
Jas	James
Jdt	Judith
Jer	Jeremiah
Job, Jb	Job
Joel	Joel
John, Jn	Gospel of John
1–2–3 John, Jn	1–2–3 John
Jonah, Jon	Jonah
Josh, Jos	Joshua
Jude	Jude
Judg, Jgs	Judges
1–2 Kgs	1–2 Kings
Lam	Lamentations
Lev, Lv	Leviticus
Luke, Lk	Gospel of Luke
LXX	the Septuagint, the Greek translation of the OT
1–2 Macc, Mc	1–2 Maccabees
Mal	Malachi
Mark, Mk	Gospel of Mark
Mary	Gospel of Mary
Matt, Mt	Gospel of Matthew
Mic, Mc	Micah
ms(s)	manuscript(s)
Nah, Na	Nahum
Neh	Nehemiah
NT	New Testament
Num, Nm	Numbers
Obad, Ob	Obadiah
OT	Old Testament
Pet	Gospel of Peter
1–2 Pet	1–2 Peter
Phil	Philippians
Phlm	Philemon
POxy	Papyrus Oxyrhynchus
Prov, Prv	Proverbs
Ps(s)	Psalms
Rev, Rv	Revelation
Rom	Romans
Ruth, Ru	Ruth
1–2 Sam, Sm	1–2 Samuel
SecJas, SJas	Secret Book of James
SecMk, SMk	Secret Gospel of Mark
SG	Signs Gospel
Sir	Sirach
Sus	Susanna
SV	the Scholars Version translation
1–2 Thess, Thes	1–2 Thessalonians
Thom, Th	Gospel of Thomas
1–2 Tim, Tm	1–2 Timothy
Titus, Ti	Titus
Tob	Tobit
Wis	Wisdom
Zech, Zec	Zechariah
Zeph, Zep	Zephaniah

Introduction

The Complete Gospels offers its readers several unique features. This volume is the premier publication of the Scholars Version translation of the gospels. SV, as it will be known, is a fresh translation of the original languages into idiomatic American English and is entirely free of ecclesiastical control.

The Complete Gospels is also the only publication including both the canonical gospels and their principal extracanonical counterparts under one cover. The other gospels are presented in fresh translations and with informative notes prepared for the general reader.

The Complete Gospels is the first publication for the general reader of the Signs Gospel, which many believe underlies the canonical Gospel of John. The Signs Gospel is thus older than John.

The Complete Gospels is also the first publication of the miscellaneous collection we call "Orphan Sayings and Stories"—anecdotes and sayings that never found a firm place in the manuscript tradition of any particular gospel, but which nevertheless survived as notes in one or more manuscripts.

The Complete Gospels also contains the Sayings Gospel Q laid out in parallel columns, with matched lines. By including both the Matthean and Lukan versions of the underlying Q text, the reader is able to see the basis on which scholars have reconstructed the Q gospel.

What is a gospel?

The word "gospel" translates the Greek *euangelion*, which literally means "good news." The term first appears in Christian literature in the letters of Paul, where it already has a technical sense, referring to the message about the death, resurrection, and return of Jesus Christ (e.g., 1 Cor 15:1–5). While two of the New Testament gospels use the word "gospel" (it is missing in Luke and John), they use it to indicate not the written works themselves, but rather the message preached either by Jesus (in Matthew) or about him (in Mark). Not until the middle of the second century are documents about the words and deeds of Jesus called gospels.

The New Testament gospels are complex works of literature that draw on a variety of oral and written sources of tradition, some from Jesus and some about him, such as miracle stories, collections of his parables and sayings, traditions about his birth and childhood, and stories about his death and resurrection. These different formats for preserving and transmitting Jesus traditions influenced the shape of the New Testament narrative gospels. But in addition, they each crystallized into distinct literary works in their own right, also called gospels, not all of which took the form of narratives.

The Complete Gospels presents examples of these different gospel forms. Besides the four New Testament gospels, there is what may be called a miracle gospel (the Signs Gospel), infancy gospels (the Infancy Gospels of Thomas and James), and a passion gospel (Gospel of Peter). There are sayings gospels: "Q" (the shorthand designation for the Synoptic Sayings Source), the Gospels of Thomas and Mary, the Secret Book of James, and the Dialogue of the Savior. Also included are fragments of gospels whose full character and ancient titles are unknown (the Gospels of the Hebrews, Nazoreans, and Ebionites, the Egerton Gospel and the Oxyrhynchus Gospels 840 and 1224), an esoteric edition of a New Testament gospel (Secret Gospel of Mark), and some free-floating Jesus traditions (our so-called Orphan Sayings and Stories).

What records have survived?

No manuscripts from the hands of the original authors of the gospels survive. All of our gospels, then, come to us at several removes from their authors. Mark, Matthew, Luke, and John are preserved in about 3,500 manuscripts. Best represented among these manuscripts is the Gospel of John, which was a favorite in the ancient Christian community as it is in modern times. The Greek texts behind our English translation is a reconstruction produced by patient and exacting comparison of thousands of differences in wording among the numerous copies. Most of the other gospels, however, come to us from the ancient world on the most meager of surviving records.

Of the sixteen other gospels in this volume, only two are amply represented by surviving manuscripts. They are the two infancy gospels, Thomas and James. The number of extant copies witnesses to the popularity of stories about the birth of Mary, Jesus, and the wondrous activities of the young Jesus.

Seven of our gospels are known to us on the basis of a single precious manuscript each: Gospel of Peter, Secret Book of James, Dialogue of the Savior, the Egerton Gospel, Secret Gospel of Mark, and the Oxyrhynchus Gospels 840 and 1224. The Gospel of Thomas is preserved in full form only in Coptic, but it has also survived in three important Greek fragments, which attest to the fact that it was originally written in Greek. The Gospel of Mary is known in both Coptic and Greek fragments.

Some of our gospels are not even preserved in their original language. All but one of them originally were written in Greek, but the Gospel of Thomas (except for the Greek fragments), the Secret Book of James, and the Dialogue of the Savior are known to us only in Coptic translation. Four gospels exist only in fragmentary form: Gospel of Peter, the Egerton Gospel, and the

Oxyrhynchus Gospels 840 and 1224. One gospel (Dialogue of the Savior) has numerous gaps in the manuscript and another one (Gospel of Mary) is missing about half of its pages. The Gospels of the Hebrews, Ebionites, and Nazoreans are preserved only in fragments, in the writings of the early Christian authors who quoted from them. The Secret Gospel of Mark is available only in a transcription made by an 18th-century scholar.

The other two gospels in this volume (the Signs Gospel and Q) are not even "texts" in the strict sense, since we have no manuscript copies of them at all. They have been reconstructed by being isolated from the larger texts in which they are embedded: the Signs Gospel from John, and Q from Matthew and Luke.

Beyond the holy four

Most who have sought to understand the words and deeds of Jesus and the traditions about him have confined their attention to the New Testament gospels. Those texts are readily available and have been intensively studied. Many interested in Jesus were not even aware of the existence of other gospels, or if they knew of them, did not know where to find them. While scholars had access to these documents—they are called extracanonical gospels because they were not included among the so-called canonical gospels—and could study them in the original languages, the vast majority tended to dismiss them as unimportant, on the hasty assumption that all of them were fanciful elaborations based on the New Testament gospels, or at least came from a much later period. However, research in the last several decades has significantly broadened our understanding of the diversity and complexity of the early Jesus traditions. Scholars now find it necessary to turn to the extracanonical gospels to learn about the development of even the earliest Jesus traditions. These texts disclose to us how Christian communities gathered, arranged, modified, embellished, interpreted, and created traditions about the teachings and deeds of Jesus. All of the intracanonical and extracanonical texts in this volume are witnesses to early Jesus traditions. All of them contain traditions independent of the New Testament gospels.

Authorized and canonical

During the first few centuries after Jesus, most Christian communities, if they were fortunate enough to possess written gospels at all, contented themselves with one or more of the four major gospels. These predominant narratives eventually gained formal ecclesiastical approval in the fourth century with a ruling by the Greek-speaking hierarchy that the only gospels authorized for official use—belonging to the rule or norm of the church and therefore canonical—were the texts attributed to Matthew, Mark, Luke, and John.

However, in earlier centuries many Christians had cherished other gospels, which they sincerely believed to carry the revealed truth about Jesus. It is only from the perspective of later centuries that these texts which nourished the faith of generations of Christians can be called non-canonical. The distinction between the canonical and the non-canonical gospels did not exist in the period of Christian origins, and therefore is not helpful for understanding the earliest centuries of Christianity in their rich diversity. Texts excluded from the canon of the New Testament nevertheless contain and disclose valuable historical information.

The Complete Gospels

The Complete Gospels now makes available to the general reader all the principal texts required for the critical study of the early gospel tradition. In addition to the four New Testament gospels, other gospels were selected with three considerations in mind. The extracanonical gospels selected are those which

1. date from the first and second centuries;
2. are more or less independent of the canonical gospels and contain significant material that is not derived from them; and
3. significantly contribute to our understanding of the developments in the Jesus traditions leading up to and surrounding the New Testament gospels.

The list of the gospels in this volume was determined after lengthy discussions by a panel of scholars who teach college and seminary courses on the gospels.

In *The Complete Gospels* each gospel is preceded by an introduction which provides basic information about that gospel. The New Testament gospels are sufficiently well known not to require an introduction here. But it may be helpful to summarize the value of the remaining texts.

The *Signs Gospel* is a source for most of the narrative in the Gospel of John, and may well be the earliest written account of the deeds of Jesus.

Q is a source for much of the teachings of Jesus in the Gospels of Matthew and Luke, and it witnesses to a very early stage of theological reflection in the Jesus tradition.

The *Gospel of Thomas* has core elements as old as the synoptic gospels which have proven a valuable source for the teachings of the historical Jesus; while in its later layer, Thomas is the record of a Christian community creatively accommodating influences from Gnosticism.

The *Secret Book of James* and the *Dialogue of the Savior* show the modulation in the form of the sayings gospel from the simple collection of sayings we see in Thomas to their composition into extended discourses and dialogues, a development in the use and interpretation of Jesus' sayings that is paralleled in the Gospel of John.

The *Gospel of Mary* is an historical window into the interpretation of the teaching of Jesus from the perspectives of Gnosticism and into the heated debate among early Christians about the role of women in the churches.

The *Infancy Gospels of Thomas and James* testify to the popular, if theologically unsophisticated, interest among early Christians in elaborating and embellishing the edifying biographical circumstances of Jesus' birth, childhood, and family background.

The *Gospel of Peter*, in the partial form in which we have it, is an early passion gospel with important differences from the other passion narratives. It may contain, in an embedded source document, the primary material for the passion and resurrection stories in the canonical gospels.

The *Egerton Gospel* and the *Oxyrhynchus Gospels 840* and *1224* are partial remnants of early, independent, and otherwise unknown gospels with some parallels to the canonical gospels.

The *Secret Gospel of Mark* consists of excerpts from a variant edition of the Gospel of Mark, and may represent an earlier version of Mark than the one in the New Testament.

The fragments of the *Gospels of the Hebrews, Nazoreans, and Ebionites* represent distinctive ways in which Jewish Christians interpreted the Jesus tradition.

The twenty gospels and gospel fragments in this volume, not including the orphan sayings and stories, are the principal texts needed for understanding the early Jesus traditions. There are, of course, other orthodox and heretical gospels that are required for tracing later developments. A complete anthology of extant gospels, along with detailed introductions and annotations, accompanied by extensive bibliographies, is available in a collection known as the *New Testament Apocrypha,* volume 1 (a new critical edition and translation is in preparation at Polebridge Press). *The Complete Gospels* is designed to serve the needs of the teacher, student, and lay reader at all but the most advanced level.

In keeping with the spirit of being a "complete" collection of gospels for the general reader, four new selections have been added in the third edition: the Greek fragments of the Gospel of Thomas and the remains of the three Jewish-Christian gospels. Also, in keeping with the character of the Scholars Version as a living translation that is periodically revised, numerous improvements have been made in the translation.

From John the Baptist to Nicea: Stages in the development of the early Christian tradition

1–30 C.E.

John the Baptist,
the precursor and mentor of Jesus
(died about 27 C.E.)

Jesus of Nazareth,
traveling sage and wonder-worker
(died about 30 C.E.)

30–60 C.E.

Paul of Tarsus,
chief founder of gentile Christianity
(letters written about 50–60 C.E.)

Sayings Gospel Q
(first edition, about 50 C.E.)

Gospel of Thomas
(first edition, about 50 C.E.)

60–80 C.E.

Signs Gospel
(eventually incorporated into John)

Gospel of Mark,
the first narrative gospel
(first edition, about 70 C.E.)

Didache, first believers' handbook
(first edition)

80–100 C.E.

Gospel of Matthew,
incorporating Mark and Q
(about 80 C.E.)

Gospel of Luke,
incorporating Mark and Q
(about 90 C.E.)

Dialogue of the Savior
(first edition, probably 50–100 C.E.)

Gospel of Peter
(first edition, probably 50–100 C.E.)

80–100 C.E., cont.

Egerton Gospel
(probably 50–100 C.E.)

Gospel of John,
incorporating the Signs Gospel
(about 90 C.E.)

Gospel of Mark, canonical edition
(about 100 C.E.)

100–150 C.E.

Gospel of John, third edition
(insertions and additions)

Secret Book of James, first edition
(found at Nag Hammadi)

Gospel of Mary
(found at Nag Hammadi)

Jewish-Christian Gospels
(preserved in patristic quotations)

Didache, second edition
(insertions and additions)

Gospel of Thomas, second edition
(surviving edition)

Surviving fragment of Gospel of John
(P^{52})

Surviving fragments of Egerton Gospel
($PEgerton^{2}$ and $PKöln^{255}$)

150–325 C.E.

Emergence of four "recognized" gospels

Emergence of an official collection of Christian writings ("New Testament")

Christianity becomes a legal religion
(313 C.E.)

Council of Nicea
(325 C.E.)

First official creeds

First surviving copies of "Bibles"
(about 325–350 C.E.)

Narrative Gospels

P^{52}, the earliest fragment of the gospels, dates to about 125 C.E. It contains a few words from John 18:31–33 and 18:37–38. *Reprinted with the permission of The John Rylands University Library of Manchester, England.*

The synoptic puzzle

The similarities between and among the three synoptic gospels, Matthew, Mark, and Luke, are striking. The three are called "synoptic," in fact, because they present a "common view" of Jesus. Most scholars believe that Matthew and Luke employed Mark as the basis of their gospels, to which they add other materials. There are powerful arguments to support this conclusion:

1. Agreement between Matthew and Luke begins where Mark begins and ends where Mark ends.

2. Matthew reproduces about 90% of Mark, Luke about 50%. They often reproduce Mark in the same order. When they disagree, either Matthew or Luke supports the sequence in Mark.

3. In segments the three have in common, verbal agreement averages about 50%. The extent of the agreement may be observed in the sample of the triple tradition reproduced below: the lines are matched for easy comparison.

4. In the triple tradition—segments all three have in common—Matthew and Mark often agree against Luke, and Luke and Mark often agree against Matthew, but Matthew and Luke rarely agree against Mark.

These facts and the close examination of agreements and disagreements in minute detail have led scholars to conclude that Mark is the adopted basis of Matthew and Luke.

This conclusion leads to further observations:

5. Mark is responsible for the chronological outline of the life of Jesus represented by the synoptics; Matthew and Luke do not have independent evidence for the order of events.

6. Mark is the earliest of the three.

Mark 2:16–17	**Matt 9:11–12**	**Luke 5:30–31**
[16]And whenever	[11]And whenever	
the Pharisees' scholars	the Pharisees	
saw him eating with	saw this,	
sinners and toll collectors,		
they	they	[30]The Pharisees
		and their scholars
would question	would question	would complain
his disciples:	his disciples:	to his disciples:
"What's he doing	"Why does your teacher	"Why do you people
eating with	eat with	eat and drink with
toll collectors and sinners?"	toll collectors and sinners?"	toll collectors and sinners?"
[17]When Jesus overhears,	[12]When Jesus overheard,	[31]In response,
he says to them:	he said,	Jesus said to them:
"Since when	"Since when	"Since when
do the able-bodied	do the able-bodied	do the healthy
need a doctor?	need a doctor?	need a doctor?
It's the sick who do."	It's the sick who do."	It's the sick who do."

The Gospel of Mark

Introduction

Story, structure, and narrative themes

In the Gospel of Mark we encounter a vivid and powerful telling of the story of Jesus. Through a rapid tumble of arresting scenes we watch Jesus emerge on the public stage, newly baptized and victorious over Satan, masterful yet oddly mysterious (chap. 1). A reluctant champion of the diseased and demon-possessed, Jesus does spiritual battle against the "unclean spirits" arrayed against him and his cause, "God's imperial rule." Larger and larger crowds of onlookers are soon drawn to Jesus' doings, crowds who form a chorus that is always curious, often sympathetic, but also frequently rather menacing in aspect (chaps. 2–3). What attracts these crowds is Jesus' quick success as faith healer and exorcist extraodinaire; soon Jesus turns to confront the crowds too with strange yet telling speech (4:1–34).

As Jesus and his small band of disciples move through the little towns, barren countryside, and stormy lake that make up of the gospel's controlling landscape, the sense of inevitable confrontation and foreboding grows stronger and stronger. Opposition to his practices and his disciples' habits comes from social and religious leaders, both those in Galilee and others summoned from Jerusalem (e.g., 3:19–22; 7:1–21). Eventually Jesus himself will lead his group to the capital city for the final confrontation that leads to his arrest and death.

Two dominant themes throughout the gospel are the question of Jesus' *identity* and the nature of *discipleship,* which Mark calls "following Jesus." At the midpoint of the narrative Jesus asks his followers "Who do people say I am? . . . What about you, who do *you* say I am?" (8:27–30). This scene serves as the story's fulcrum, as Peter's statement "You are God's Anointed!" leads to Jesus' puzzling and terrifying predictions about the divine necessity for "the son of Adam" to be punished and killed and yet to rise again (8:31; 9:31; 10:33–34). Those who want to "follow" Jesus are told to "pick up their cross!" (8:34). The disciples, already mystified about Jesus and his actions, are now left even more troubled and confused as they move on to Jerusalem. There Jesus engages in dramatic and dangerous debate with various authority figures and upsets the commerce of the temple (chaps. 11–12).

While contemplating the glory and beauty of the temple buildings, Jesus gives a second long speech, addressed within the story to his most intimate circle, but also to Mark's audience of Christian readers, about the troubles and distress in which they were caught up (chap. 13). After an unnamed woman signals Jesus' approaching death with a symbolic anointing, come a final meal and a wrenching scene of foreboding in Gethsemane (chap. 14). Jesus accepts his arrest and silently receives his punishment—flogging and tortuous death on the cross (chap. 15). The story ends when three faithful women go to minister to his body but instead encounter a mysterious, shining youth who tells them that Jesus has risen from the dead. Rather than report this astonishing news, the women run away with their speech frozen in fear (chap. 16).

Origins of the Gospel

Mark is generally thought to be the oldest surviving written gospel. The document itself never mentions its author, nor the place, time, or circumstances of its origin, but scholars have inferred that the gospel was composed at about the time of the Roman-Judean War (66–70 C.E.), perhaps in Greek-speaking Syria. Most scholars use the traditional name "Mark" as a convenient way to refer to the anonymous writer. The actual name and gender of the author are not known. Sometime in the second century the tradition grew up of connecting the unnamed author with the name "Mark," perhaps the "John Mark" mentioned in Luke's Acts of the Apostles (Acts 12:12, 25; 15:37–39). Another common tradition of the ancient church connected the gospel in various ways with the Apostle Peter, probably because a "Mark" is mentioned as a devoted follower of Peter at 1 Peter 5:13. This very indirect association may have helped lead to the further tradition that the book was written at Rome, the scene of Peter's martyrdom.

If Mark's is the first gospel, its "predecessors" would not have been evangelists in a literary sense, but instead prophets, teachers, missionaries, or community organizers, who passed along memories and stories of Jesus in their own particular social and church situations. When composing his text, Mark drew on many sorts of existing material for his own new purposes of narration. Identifying Mark's sources, and judging whether they were available in written or oral form, make a difficult enterprise. For a long time scholars have believed that there was a pre-Marcan "Passion Narrative" used not only by Mark but also by John (and perhaps also by the Gospel of Peter). Assurance on this point has been weakened with our growing awareness of Mark's own compositional work (on the basis of Hebrew Scriptures) in Jesus' trial and crucifixion scenes, as well as various suggestions about the independence of Gospel of Peter from the New Testament gospels. Confidence varies about our ability to isolate other sorts of pre-Marcan sources, such as a postulated series of miracle stories, or cycles of controversy dialogues, or collections of mysterious sayings coupled with explanations.

Notes on Mark's narrative style

The Gospel of Mark is written in a lively and direct story-teller's style. The Greek prose employed is the informal language of ordinary men and women who made up the common eastern Mediterranean culture in the first century. Instead of the polished literary style of an accomplished artistic writer, in this gospel we find an immediacy and simplicity of description; a certain harshness and awkwardness in expression; repetition of favored words and constructions; a sketchiness in characterization. These features have led scholars to believe that Mark's story is still close somehow, both stylistically and historically, to the oral preaching environment.

Most translations of the gospels flatten all their individual "voices" into one. The *Scholars Version* of Mark attempts to represent the writer's rushed, folksy, and vivid style in reasonably good English prose, while still leaving room for stylistic comparsion with the translations of other documents. For example, in Mark's story everything seems to happen "right away" or "right then," two of the phrases we use to translate the very frequent *euthus* (usually translated "immediately"). Matthew and Luke reduce the use of *euthus* considerably. Mark likes to use the present tense even when describing past events, something that gives his story a vivid but uncultivated tone: Luke changes about 150 of these "historic presents" into past tense verbs. Very many of Mark's sentences begin with the word "And . . . ," a word that we have usually omitted in the interests of better English style. Matthew and Luke had a similar interest, shown by their frequent replacements of Mark's parataxis ("and . . . and . . . and") with subordinate constructions.

Frequently Mark postpones providing some important details until well into the story when he tells his various episodes. Then, mostly using the Greek conjunction *gar* (meaning "for" or "since"), Mark will supply this sometimes crucial tidbit by way of a parenthetical aside ("You see, . . ." or "Keep in mind . . ."). The most famous example is the very last phrase of the Gospel story, when the women have turned and run in terror from the tomb and failed to inform others of Jesus' reported resurrection. Mark explains: "Talk about terrified . . . !" (16:8). Other instances are found at 2:15; 3:10, 21, 30; 5:28, 42; 6:14, 31, 52; 7:3–4; 9:6; 11:13; and the first mention of the "faithful women" only at 15:40–41.

Expansions in Mark's text

During the process of copying and recopying Mark's Gospel, Christian scribes introduced some major expansions into the text, most famously at the end of the story. Unsatisfied with the bleak conclusion showing the terrified women running away from the tomb (at 16:8), early copyists preferred to continue with additions of various length to portray the risen Jesus appearing to his disciples and commanding them to begin the work of evangelization. These additions are traditionally called the "Shorter Ending" and "Longer Ending" of Mark, though it would be more appropriate to term them shorter and longer "Supplements." Most of this material is closely patterned on other post-resurrection appearance stories, especially those in Luke's Gospel. For details see the textual notes at 16:8 and (16:9–10).

A recent discovery in the correspondence of Clement of Alexandria, a late second-century Christian theologian, has uncovered the existence of an alternative version of Mark, which Clement calls the "More Spiritual" or "Secret Mark." At two places Clement quotes additional material from this otherwise unknown edition of Mark (for details see the textual notes at 10:34–35 and 10:46).

God's imperial rule

The traditional translation of the Greek phrase *Basileia tou theou, Kingdom of God,* was more appropriate to the age of King James I (1603–25; King James translation: 1611) than it is to our own in which inherited monarchies are more symbolic than political. The SV panel went in search of a term or phrase that would satisfy three basic requirements: (1) the phrase had to function as both verb and noun, to denote both an activity and a region; (2) the phrase had to specify that God's activity was absolute; there could be no suggestion of democracy or shared governance; (3) the phrase should have feeling tones of the ominous, of ultimate threat, of tyranny—associations going with the end of the age and the last judgment, since it often appears in such contexts.

Some panel members proposed *empire* as an appropriate ancient and modern counterpart, since it called to mind both the Roman Empire and the evil empires of the nineteenth and twentieth centures. But empire could not serve as a verb; for this purpose something like *rule* or *reign* was required. And Jesus' own use of the phrase, particularly in connection with his parables, called for a phrase that was perhaps less ominous, yet no less absolute. The happy solution the panel reached was to combine "imperial" with "rule" to gain the nuances of both terms.

When a spatial term is required by the context, it was decided to utilize *domain* because of its proximity to *dominion:* in his domain God's dominion is supreme.

When Matthew subsitutes "Heaven" for "God," we translate "Heaven's imperial rule" or "Heaven's domain," as required by the context.

The Gospel of Mark

A voice in the wilderness

1 ***The good news*** of Jesus the Anointed begins 2with something
Isaiah the prophet wrote:

> Here is my messenger,
> whom I send on ahead of you
> to prepare your way!
> 3A voice of someone shouting in the wilderness:
> "Make ready the way of the Lord,
> make his paths straight."

4So, John the Baptizer appeared in the wilderness calling for baptism
and a change of heart that lead to forgiveness of sins. 5And everyone
from the Judean countryside and all the residents of Jerusalem
streamed out to him and got baptized by him in the Jordan river,
admitting their sins. 6And John wore a mantel made of camel hair and
had a leather belt around his waist and lived on locusts and raw honey.
7And he began his proclamation by saying:

"Someone more powerful than I will succeed me, whose sandal
straps I am not fit to bend down and untie. 8I have been baptizing you
with water, but he'll baptize you with holy spirit."

9During that same period Jesus came from Nazareth, Galilee, and
was baptized in the Jordan by John. 10And just as he got up out of the
water, he saw the skies torn open and the spirit coming down toward

1:2–6 //Mt 3:1–6, Lk 3:1–6, Jn 1:19–23, GEbi 3; cf. GEbi 1

1:2–3 ◊Mal 3:1, Is 40:3 (LXX), Ex 23:20

1:4 Ⓣ GHeb 2:1, GNaz 2:1

1:6 ◊2 Kgs 1:8 (LXX)

1:7–8 Cf. Q 3:16b–17; Mt 3:7, 11–12; Lk 3:16; Jn 1:26–27

1:9–11 Cf. Mt 3:13–17, Lk 3:21–22, Jn 1:29–34, GHeb 3, GEbi 4

1:1 Many mss add "son of God" after *Anointed.*

1:1 The opening line of the *good news* (or "Gospel") announces Jesus' identity to the reader, although the secret of his true identity will be hidden from most of the individuals that Jesus encounters as the story unfolds.

The Greek word *christos* is traditionally left untranslated and rendered as though part of Jesus' name ("Christ"), but this practice does not correspond with the use of the word within Mark's story. Its translation here as *the Anointed* reflects the meaning it would convey to a reader of Mark's time and also suggests its use as a title.

1:4–6 John's unusual dress characterizes him as a prophet at work in the *wilderness* (see Zech 13:4; 2 Kgs 1:8; Heb 11:37; cf. Q 7:24–25), linking him to the promise quoted in v. 3.

A time in the *wilderness* is a key event in many biblical heroes' careers (see, e.g., 1 Kings 19, Acts 21:38) and also reflects an Exodus typology prominent in the OT prophets (Hos 2:14; 12:9; and esp. Isaiah chaps. 40–51).

1:9 Jesus appears with even less biographical explanation than did John: the reader is expected to already know who these figures are. Jesus comes to John from *Galilee*, the northern region of biblical Israel in which his public career will center after his time of testing (see 1:14). This verse seems to imply that *Nazareth* is Jesus' hometown, a place mentioned without name in 6:1–6.

1:10–11 Mark relates the *tearing open* of the skies and the *voice* from above as Jesus' own experience, something apparently not seen

A voice in Galilee

him like a dove. 11There was also a voice from the skies: "You are my
favored son—I fully approve of you."

A day's work

12And right away the spirit drives him out into the wilderness,
13where he remained for forty days, being put to the test by Satan.
While he was living there among the wild animals, the heavenly messengers looked after him.

14***After John was locked up,*** Jesus came to Galilee proclaiming
God's good news. 15His message went:

"The time is up: God's imperial rule is closing in. Change your ways, and put your trust in the good news!"

16As he was walking along by the Sea of Galilee, he spotted Simon and Andrew, Simon's brother, casting ⟨their nets⟩ into the sea—since
they were fishermen—17and Jesus said to them: "Become my followers
and I'll have you fishing for people!"

18And right then and there they abandoned their nets and followed him.

19When he had gone a little farther, he caught sight of James, son of
Zebedee, and his brother John mending their nets in the boat. 20Right
then and there he called out to them as well, and they left their father Zebedee behind in the boat with the hired hands and accompanied him.

21***Then they come to Capernaum,*** and on the sabbath day he went

1:11 //GEbi 4:3, ◊Is 42:1, 44:2; Ps 2:7

1:12–13 Cf. Q 4:1–13, Mt 4:1–11, Lk 4:1–13, GHeb 4

1:14–15 //Mt 4:12, 17, Lk 4:14–15; cf. Jn 4:1–3, 43–46a

1:16–20 //Mt 4:18–22; cf. Lk 5:1–11, Jn 21:1–14, GEbi 2:3

1:21–28 //Mt 7:28–29, Lk 4:31–37

---

and heard by anyone else. Contrast Luke 3:21–22; John 1:31 and the transfiguration scene in Mark 9:7. The *voice from the skies* was a traditional Jewish way to describe public communication from God.

1:12–13 A period of *forty days* was traditional in biblical stories to mark significant transitions (e.g., Noah's rain in Genesis 7, Elijah's flight in 1 Kings 19, and cf. the forty years of Israel's wanderings in the Exodus).

1:14–15 A vivid summary of the main themes of Jesus' ministry. Mark uses summary statements to report Jesus' activities and their effect (as in 1:32–34; 3:7–12; 6:56).

God's imperial rule (or *domain*) is our translation of a Greek phrase that refers to God's ruling power rather than any particular geographical or spiritual place.

1:16 Mark usually begins a new episode with a brief mention of place or time, as here with *As he was walking along by the Sea of Galilee,* . . . Other examples in this chapter include 1:14; 1:21; 1:29; 1:32; and 1:35. With brief comments such as these, the narrator skillfully moves from one individual scene to another, which suggests that the author used the technique as a way to combine stories that earlier had been told separately.

1:16–20 Here Jesus calls as his first followers two pairs of brothers who will remain his closest companions (though Andrew plays a less prominent role). Their immediate response to Jesus' summons, apparently with no previous contact, emphasizes Jesus' spellbinding authority. (Contrast John 1:35–42 and Luke 5:1–11). We will see the close connection of these men with Jesus in the healing of the little girl in 5:37ff.; the scene of Jesus' transfiguration in 9:2–8; in the temple dialogue in 13:3ff; the Gethsemane scene in 14:32ff.; the ambitions of James and John in 10:35–40; and note also the sequence of the list of the twelve at 3:16–19.

1:21–28 Jesus performs his first exorcism at *Capernaum,* a town in Galilee that seems to be his main base of operations (see also 2:1; 3:19; 9:33). Here too we see a strong emphasis laid on Jesus' role as *teacher* (vv. 21, 22, 27). Jesus' actions on the sabbath day and in synagogues quickly arouse hostile notice (2:23–28; 3:1–6).

Stories of exorcisms display certain stock elements, including here a confrontation between Jesus and the demon (v. 24); Jesus' rebuke, silencing, and word of command for the unclean spirit to depart (v. 25); the performance of the cure (v. 26); the wonder of the bystanders (v. 27); and the effect of

right to the synagogue and started teaching. [22]They were astonished at
his teaching, since he would teach them on his own authority, unlike
the scholars.

[23]Now right there in their synagogue was a person possessed by an
unclean spirit, which shouted, [24]"Jesus! What do you want with us, you
Nazarene? Have you come to get rid of us? I know you, who you are:
God's holy man!"

[25]But Jesus yelled at it, "Shut up and get out of him!"

[26]Then the unclean spirit threw the man into convulsions, and
letting out a loud shriek it came out of him. [27]And they were all so
amazed that they asked themselves, "What's this? A new kind of
teaching backed by authority! He gives orders even to unclean spirits
and they obey him!"

[28]So his fame spread rapidly everywhere throughout Galilee and
even beyond.

[29]They left the synagogue right away and entered the house of
Simon and Andrew along with James and John. [30]Simon's mother-in-
law was in bed with a fever, and they told him about her right away.
[31]He went up to her, took hold of her hand, raised her up, and the fever
disappeared. Then she started looking after them.

[32]In the evening, at sundown, they would bring all the sick and
demon possessed to him. [33]And the whole town would crowd around
the door. [34]On such occasions he cured many people afflicted with
various diseases and drove out many demons. He would never let the
demons speak, because they realized who he was.

[35]And rising early, while it was still very dark, he went outside and
stole away to an isolated place, where he started praying. [36]Then Simon

1:29-31 //Mt8:14-15, Lk4:38-39
1:32-34 //Mt8:16-17, Lk4:40-41
1:35-38 //Lk4:42-43

---

increasing Jesus' fame (v. 28). A similar pattern is followed in the two other exorcisms that Mark will describe in full (5:1-20, esp. vv. 7-14; and 9:25-27).

1:23-24 The *unclean spirit* (Mark's favorite term for demons) knows who Jesus is and what his mission entails, though most onlookers remain confused. See further the notes at 1:1 and 1:43-45.

1:29-31 This is the first of many miraculous healings by Jesus described in Mark, and it unfolds in a conventional three-part structure: first a *description* of the ailment (v. 30); then Jesus' *performance* of a cure (v. 31a); finally a *demonstration* of the cure, through either an act of the healed person or the reaction of onlookers (v. 31b). The cure's effectiveness in this case is shown by Simon's mother-in-law being able to perform her socially prescribed duty of serving guests food. The same basic pattern is followed, though rarely so compactly, in several other healing stories (1:40-45; 2:3, 11-12; 3:1-6; 5:25-34, 35-42; 7:32-35; 8:22-25; 10:46-52).

1:32-34 This summary statement from Mark displays many aspects of his characteristic style: redundancy (*In the evening, at sundown, . . .*), hyperbole (*all the sick and demon possessed, the whole city*), and secrecy (*He would never let the demons speak*).

1:35-38 The first clear indication of the pressing effects of the crowds who are being drawn to Jesus by his great deeds. The overwhelming presence of crowds is a narrative theme repeatedly emphasized as the story develops (see also 1:45; 2:13; 3:7-10, 19b-20; 4:1; 5:21, 24; 6:54-56; 7:14; 8:1, 34; 9:14; 10:1, 46; 12:12). Jesus is often shown trying to avoid the presence of the crowds, sometimes seeking privacy in order to perform miracles or impart special instruction (e.g., 1:45; 5:37; 6:31; 7:17, 24, 33; 8:23; 9:28, 30; 10:10, 32b).

Jesus cures a leper

Jesus cures a paralytic

and those with him hunted him down. [37]When they had found him they say to him, "They're all looking for you."

[38]But he replies: "Let's go somewhere else, to the neighboring villages, so I can speak there too, since that's what I came for."

[39]So he went all around Galilee speaking in their synagogues and driving out demons.

[40]***Then a leper comes up*** to him, pleads with him, falls down on his knees, and says to him, "If you want to, you can make me clean."

[41]Although Jesus was indignant, he stretched out his hand, touched him, and says to him, "Okay—you're clean!"

[42]And right away the leprosy disappeared, and he was made clean. [43]And Jesus snapped at him, and dismissed him curtly [44]with this warning: "See that you don't tell anyone anything, but go, have a priest examine ⟨your skin⟩. Then offer for your cleansing what Moses commanded, as evidence ⟨of your cure⟩."

[45]But after he went out, he started telling everyone and spreading the story, so that ⟨Jesus⟩ could no longer enter a town openly, but had to stay out in the countryside. Yet they continued to come to him from everywhere.

2 ***Some days later*** he went back to Capernaum and was rumored to be at home. [2]And many people crowded around so there was no longer any room, even outside the door. Then he started speaking to them. [3]Some people then show up with a paralytic being carried by four of them. [4]And when they were not able to get near him on account of the crowd, they removed the roof above him. After digging it out, they lowered the mat on which the paralytic was lying. [5]When Jesus noticed their trust, he says to the paralytic, "Child, your sins are forgiven."

[6]Some of the scholars were sitting there and silently wondering:

1:39 //Mt 4:23; cf. Mt 9:35, Lk 4:44
1:40–44 //Mt 8:2–4, Lk 5:12–16, EgerG 2:1–4
2:1–12 //Mt 9:1–8, Lk 5:17–26; cf. Jn 5:2–9

1:41 Most mss read "And Jesus was moved" in place of *Although Jesus was indignant.*

1:40 *Lepers* were thought to be "dirty" or ritually impure. This sort of uncleanliness endangered the purity required of the people for proper worship of God. For the social and religious context see esp. Leviticus chaps. 13–14 and the note below at 2:15–17.

1:43–45 Jesus' anger (v. 41) and stern warning not to make him known, conveyed by *snapping* (literally "snorting") at the cured leper, is connected to a key narrative theme in Mark's gospel, the mandated "secret" of Jesus' true identity. Jesus repeatedly attempts to hide his actions, at least until he reaches Jerusalem, but usually without much apparent success (see also 1:25–28, 34; 3:12; 5:43; 7:36; 8:26).

It is an irony characteristic of Mark's story that while the demon possessed and the sick and even his opponents seem to recognize who Jesus is, his own followers display constant confusion or ignorance.

The command for silence is not always given, especially in the case of non-Israelites (5:20; 7:24–30; also 10:52).

2:4 The paralytic's friends *dig* through a flat mud roof, the typical construction for ordinary houses in ancient Palestine.

2:5 Jesus pronounces divine forgiveness for the paralyzed person and only heals him as a demonstration of his warrant to do so as son of Adam (for this title see note at 2:10). People frequently interpreted illness as punishment for sin (see, e.g., John 9 or the Book of Job).

7“Why does that fellow say such things? He’s blaspheming! Who can
forgive sins except the one God?”
8And right away, because Jesus sensed in his spirit that they were
raising questions like this among themselves, he says to them: “Why do
you entertain questions about these things? 9Which is easier, to say to
the paralytic, ‘Your sins are forgiven,’ or to say, ‘Get up, pick up your
mat and walk’?” 10But so that you may realize that on earth the son of
Adam has authority to forgive sins, he says to the paralytic, 11“You
there, get up, pick up your mat and go home!”
12And he got up, picked his mat right up, and walked out as
everyone looked on. So they all became ecstatic, extolled God, and
exclaimed, “We’ve never seen the likes of this!”
13***Again he went out*** by the sea. And, with a huge crowd gathered
around him, he started teaching.
14As he was walking along, he caught sight of Levi, the son of
Alphaeus, sitting at the toll booth, and he says to him, “Follow me!”
And Levi got up and followed him.
15***Then Jesus happens to recline*** at table in ⟨Levi’s⟩ house, along
with many toll collectors and sinners and Jesus’ disciples. (Remember,
there were many of these people and they were all following him.)
16And whenever the Pharisees’ scholars saw him eating with sinners

Levi becomes a follower

Jesus dines with sinners

2:11 //Jn 5:8–9
2:13–14 //Mt 9:9, Lk 5:27–28
2:14 Cf. GEbi 2:4
2:15–17 //Mt 9:10–13, Lk 5:29–32, GOxy 1224 5:1–2, cf. Lk 19:1–10

2:6–9 The confrontation between Jesus and *some of the scholars* opens a new theme in Mark’s narrative, that of opposition from the Jewish elite over questions of religious practice. This warning note sounds louder and louder as the story develops and helps to explain the rationale for the leadership’s actions later in Jerusalem. Jesus’ difficulties with the “scholars,” the “Pharisees,” or the aristocratic priestly establishment are featured throughout the story (see 2:16, 18, 24; 3:2, 6; 3:22; 7:1–2, 5; 8:11; 8:31; 10:2; 10:33–34; 11:15–19; 11:27–33; 12:12, 13–17; 12:38–40; 14:1–2, 10–11, 43–65; 15:1; 15:31–32).

2:10 Here for the first time Jesus refers to the enigmatic figure of *the son of Adam* (more literally, “son of the human being”). This title refers obliquely to a complex of apocalyptic traditions where a heavenly or angelic being in human form (as in Daniel 7 or *1 Enoch*) is honored in God’s court and comes to act as judge at the Final Judgment. In Christian usage, the son of Adam seems to be representative of God’s true intentions for humanity.

In Mark, as in the other gospels, the figure of *the son of Adam* is mentioned only by Jesus himself, and he often seems to use it as an indirect reference to himself in the third person.

2:14 Levi represents the class of *toll collectors* employed by big businessmen or “tax farmers,” who were contracted by the Roman authorities to raise government revenues in subjected territories through small tariffs and excise charges. Verse 15 equates toll collectors with *sinners*, meaning those who do not follow God’s law.

2:15–17 Jesus’ meals and his dinner companions are an important gospel theme, since questions of food and its preparation are a central concern in traditional Judaism. Some people, such as the Pharisees, considered it dangerous to eat with others who did not follow the same dietary customs. Often Jesus attracts notice and controversy by eating with those whom other Jews (here the oddly named Pharisees’ scholars) considered “unclean” (see note at 1:40–45). In Mark’s story, Jesus is portrayed as being less than fastidious in his dealings with people that more circumspect Jews considered suspect in terms of religious purity. Here in chapter 2 we see Jesus consorting with the sick, “sinners,” and toll collectors, as well as leading a group that didn’t fast and was rather careless about sabbath observance.

In passing Mark mentions that the group around Jesus includes his *disciples*, the conventional translation of a word meaning “student” or “trainee.” In Mark’s story Jesus teaches and his followers struggle to learn,

Fasting & feasting

Adam & Eve over the sabbath

and toll collectors, they would question his disciples: "What's he doing eating with toll collectors and sinners?"

17When Jesus overhears, he says to them: "Since when do the able-bodied need a doctor? It's the sick who do. I did not come to enlist religious folks but sinners!"

18***John's disciples and the Pharisees*** were in the habit of fasting, and they come and ask him, "Why do the disciples of John fast, and the disciples of the Pharisees, but your disciples don't?"

19And Jesus said to them: "The groom's friends can't fast while the groom is around, can they? So long as the groom is around, you can't expect them to fast. 20But the days will come when the groom is taken away from them, and then they will fast, on that day.

21"Nobody sews a piece of unshrunk cloth on an old garment, otherwise the new, unshrunk patch pulls away from the old and creates a worse tear.

22"And nobody pours young wine into old wineskins, otherwise the wine will burst the skins, and destroy both the wine and the skins. Instead, young wine is for new wineskins."

23***It so happened*** that he was walking along through the grainfields on the sabbath day, and his disciples began to strip heads of grain as they walked along. 24And the Pharisees started to argue with him: "See here, why are they doing what's not permitted on the sabbath day?"

25And he says to them: "Haven't you ever read what David did when he found it necessary, when both he and his companions were hungry? 26He went into the house of God, when Abiathar was high priest, and ate the consecrated bread, and even gave some to his men to eat. No one is permitted to eat this bread, except the priests!"

2:18–20 //Mt 9:14–15; Lk 5:33–35, Th 104; cf. Jn 3:25–30
2:21–22 //Mt 9:16–17, Lk 5:36–39, Th 47:3-5
2:23–28 //Mt 12:1–8, Lk 6:1–5; ◊1 Sm 21:1–7; Dt 5:14, 23:25–26; Ex 20:10
2:26 ◊Lv 24:5–9

2:26 Some mss omit *when Abiathar was high priest* (cf. 1 Sam 21:1–7).

not in the conventional school setting of rabbinic Judaism, but instead mostly in reaction to particular situations arising in their travels from place to place.

The customary Greek phrasing for "sitting down to a meal" was *to recline at table*, as Jesus does here, that is, to lie down on dining couches to be served.

2:17 Jesus' statement uses a well-known proverb to compare his actions to the work of a doctor. This is Mark's first example of how Jesus closes off debate with a striking word or pithy statement. His opponents are given no further chance to respond. Indeed the whole scene (perhaps v. 14 too) seems to function primarily to set up the punchline featuring Jesus' memorable words. The next two episodes (2:18–22, 23–28) are further instances of this formal type, which scholars have labelled variously the pronouncement story, chreia, or apophthegm.

2:18–20 This is the first of only two references in Mark to *John's disciples* (cf. 6:29; Q 7:18, 31–35; John 3:25–30). *Fasting* (usually accompanied by prayer) was a regular practice of pious Jews as a sign of mourning, contrition, or penitence. (For other comments in the gospel tradition see Matt 6:16; Luke 18:12; Thom 14:1; 27; 104.) Wedding imagery was favored in the gospels as a way to picture Jesus and his role: see Matt 22:1–14; 25:1–13; John 3:29; Thom 75; DialSav 50. In the Hebrew Scriptures, Israel is often portrayed as God's bride (e.g., Hosea 1–3; Isa 54:4; Jer 2:2; and cf. the frequent allegorical interpretation of the Song of Solomon).

2:21–22 The contrast and even incompatibility between what is *old* and what is *new* is used to highlight the great significance found in Jesus.

2:23–28 Jesus' followers are shown violating the observance of the sabbath rest, one of the central commandments of Judaism (featured in the Decalogue in Exod 20:8–11 and Deut

Man with a crippled hand

By the sea

The twelve

27And he continued:

The sabbath day was created for Adam and Eve,
not Adam and Eve for the sabbath day.
28So, the son of Adam lords it even over the sabbath day.

3 ***Then he went back*** to the synagogue, and a fellow with a crippled
hand was there. 2So they kept an eye on him, to see whether he would
heal the fellow on the sabbath day, so they could denounce him. 3And
he says to the fellow with the crippled hand, "Get up here in front of
everybody." 4Then he asks them, "On the sabbath day is it permitted to
do good or to do evil, to save life or to destroy it?"

But they maintained their silence. 5And looking right at them with
anger, exasperated at their obstinacy, he says to the fellow, "Hold out
your hand!"

He held it out and his hand was restored. 6Then the Pharisees went
right out with the Herodians and hatched a plot against him, to get rid
of him.

7***Then Jesus withdrew*** with his disciples to the sea, and a huge
crowd from Galilee followed. When they heard what he was doing, a
huge crowd from Judea, 8and from Jerusalem and Idumea and across
the Jordan, and from around Tyre and Sidon, collected around him.
9And he told his disciples to have a small boat ready for him on account
of the crowd, so they would not mob him. (10After all, he had healed so
many, that all who had diseases were pushing forward to touch him.)
11The unclean spirits also, whenever they faced him, would fall down
before him and shout out, "You son of God, you!"

12But he always warned them not to tell who he was.

13***Then he goes up*** on the mountain and summons those he wanted,
and they came to him. 14He formed a group of twelve to be his companions, and to be sent out to speak, 15and to have authority to drive out
demons.

2:27–28 Cf. Th 27
3:1–6 //Mt 12:9–14, Lk 6:6–11; cf. GNaz 4
3:7–12 //Lk 6:17–19; cf. Mt 4:23–25, 12:15–16
3:9 Ⓘ Mk 4:1
3:13–19 //Mt 10:1–4, Lk 6:12–16; cf. GEbi 2:3

3:14 Some mss insert "whom he also named apostles" after *twelve.*

5:12–15). In their defence, Jesus appeals to the example of how King David also violated a religious prohibition, though in his case because of real want. The story alluded to (found in 1 Samuel 21) mentions Ahimelech instead of his son Abiathar as the high priest (cf. Matt 12:4; Luke 6:4). The point for Mark, however, is that Jesus, acting as son of Adam, has authority comparable to David's to establish guidelines for proper religious behavior for his followers (vv. 27–28). Jesus as representative of true humanity has precedence over sabbath and its keeping.

3:1–6 This is the first clear statement in Mark's story of the malevolent intentions of Jesus' opponents. His fate had already been intimated in Jesus' picture of the groom "being taken away" (2:20).

3:7 Mark pictures Jesus as attracting huge multitudes who virtually empty out most of biblical Israel as well as the neighboring regions of Idumea, the Trans-Jordan, and even the regions surrounding the great port cities of Tyre and Sidon, which lay to the north in what today is Lebanon.

3:13–19 Jesus leads his group up an unnamed mountain. Mark creates an evocative landscape at will (empty places, a mountain, the seaside,"his home" or "the house"), without regard to narrative connection or plausibility. Simon is nicknamed *Peter*, meaning "Rock," a name that will eventually prove

Beelzebul controversy

True relatives

16 And to Simon he gave the nickname Rock, 17and to James, the son of Zebedee, and to John, his brother, he also gave a nickname, Boanerges, which means "Thunder Brothers"; 18and Andrew and Philip and Bartholomew and Matthew and Thomas and James, the son of Alphaeus; and Thaddeus and Simon the Zealot; 19and Judas Iscariot, who, in the end, turned him in.

20***Then he goes home,*** and once again a crowd gathers, so they could not even grab a bite to eat. 21When his relatives heard about it, they came to get him. (You see, they thought he was out of his mind.) 22And the scholars who had come down from Jerusalem would say, "He is under the control of Beelzebul" and "He drives out demons in the name of the head demon!"

23And after calling them over, he would speak to them in riddles: "How can Satan drive out Satan? 24After all, if a government is divided against itself, that government cannot endure. 25And if a household is divided against itself, that household won't be able to survive. 26So if Satan rebels against himself and is divided, he cannot endure but is done for.

27"No one can enter a powerful man's house to steal his belongings unless he first ties him up. Only then does he loot his house.

28"I swear to you, all offenses and whatever blasphemies humankind might blaspheme will be forgiven them. 29But whoever blasphemes against the holy spirit is never ever forgiven, but is guilty of an eternal sin."

(30Remember, it was they who had started the accusation, "He is controlled by an unclean spirit.")

31***Then his mother and his brothers*** arrive. While still outside, they send in and ask for him. 32A crowd was sitting around him, and they say to him, "Look, your mother and your brothers and sisters are outside looking for you."

33In response he says to them: "My mother and brothers—who ever are they?"

34And looking right at those seated around him in a circle, he says, "Here are my mother and my brothers. 35Whoever does God's will, that's my brother and sister and mother!"

3:22–26 //Q11:14–18; Mt9:35–38, 12:22–26; Lk11:14–18
3:27 //Q11:21–22, Mt12:19, Lk11:21–22, Th35
3:28–29 //Mt12:31–32, Lk12:10, Th44
3:31–35 //Mt12:46–50, Lk8:19–21, Th99, GEbi5
3:35 //GHeb4a

---

sadly ironic when even Simon "the Rock" wavers at the end.

3:21 The note on Jesus' relatives is interrupted by a new controversy over Jesus and the source of his power, with the topic of Jesus' true family relations then resumed in 3:31–35 (a case of Mark's interpolation or "sandwiching" technique; cf. 5:21–24a [24b–34], 35–43; 6:7–13 [14–29], 30; 14:1–2 [3–9], 10–11).

Mark often provides explanations in parenthetical asides inserted somewhere in the middle of an episode, as here (*You see, they thought he was out of his mind*). See also 3:10; 6:14, 31, 52; 7:3; 9:6; 11:13; 16:8.

3:22 *Beelzebul* is an obscure divine or spirit figure equated with Satan in v. 24.

3:23 Mark frequently portrays Jesus speaking in *riddles* or analogy or figurative speech, all of which Mark calls "parables."

3:31–35 Jesus' mother and other relations play only a minor and not very positive role in Mark's story (see also 6:3). Jesus' words about his true family strike a discordant note within the ancient value system that gave primacy to kinship relations. See also 10:28–

Sower, seeds, soils

Secret of God's imperial rule

4 ***Once again he started to teach*** beside the sea. An enormous crowd
gathers around him, so he climbs into a boat and sits there on the water
facing the huge crowd on the shore.
2 He would then teach them many things in parables. In the course
of his teaching he would tell them:

3 Listen to this! This sower went out to sow. 4 While he was sowing,
some seed fell along the path, and the birds came and ate it up.
5 Other seed fell on rocky ground where there wasn't much soil, and
it came up right away because the soil had no depth. 6 But when the
sun came up it was scorched, and because it had no root it withered.
7 Still other seed fell among thorns, and the thorns came up and
choked it, so that it produced no fruit. 8 Finally, some seed fell on
good earth and started producing fruit. The seed sprouted and grew:
one part had a yield of thirty, another part sixty, and a third part one
hundred.

9 And as usual he said: "Anyone here with two good ears had better
listen!"
10 ***Whenever he went off*** by himself, those close to him, together with
the twelve, would ask him about the parables. 11 And he would say to
them: "You have been given the secret of God's imperial rule; but to
those outside everything is presented in parables, 12 so that

They may look with eyes wide open
but never quite see,
and may listen with ears attuned
but never quite understand,
otherwise they might turn around and find forgiveness!"

4:1–2
//Mt13:1–3a, Lk8:4

4:3–8
//Mt13:3b–8, Lk8:5–8a, Th9; cf. SJas8:3

4:9
//Mt11:15, 13:9, 43b; Lk8:8b, 14:35b; Mary2.5, 3:14; Rev2:7a, 11a, 17a, 3:6, 13, 22, 13:9a; Th8.4, 21:10, 24:2, 63:4, 65:8, 96:3; Ⓓ Mk4:23 [7:16]

4:10–12
//Mt13:10–15, Lk8:9–10; ◊Is6:9–10, Jer5:21, Ez12:2

31.
4:1–2 The crowd forces Jesus onto the boat, from which he speaks his first of two major addresses in Mark's story. The parables here convey Jesus' commentary on the events of his own time as well as the time leading up to the crisis facing Mark's community. Jesus' other major address is the "apocalyptic discourse" spoken to a few chosen followers in chapter 13.

4:3–8 The parable of the Sower is actually concerned less with the actions of the human farmer than with the drama of natural processes: the fate of a series of seeds cast on various soils. The harvest obtained from the seed cast on good earth contrasts vividly with the losses experienced when other seeds fail to produce fruit.

Jesus introduces the story with a call to *listen*. The need for effective "listening" is stressed throughout this section (4:3, 9, 33–34).

Many scholars believe that the return of *thirty, sixty, or one hundred* seeds is intended to portray an extravagant harvest, though the point may simply be that though many seeds are lost in the process of sowing and growth, those that do bear fruit do so in great numbers.

4:10–12 Several times Mark shows Jesus moving into a private setting to explain his public speech or deeds to his chosen group (see also 7:17; 9:28; 10:10).

Here *the secret of God's imperial rule* is said to be given only to the insiders, while to others Jesus' meaning is obscured (see also vv. 33–34).

The prophetic words quoted from Isaiah 6 were a favorite passage for Christians as they tried to explain the lack of a positive response to Jesus and his followers from their fellow Jews (cf. e.g. Acts 28:25–28; John 12:40).

Understanding the sower

Lamp & bushel

Same standards

Seed & harvest

Mustard seed

4:13–20
//Mt13:18–23, Lk8:11–15; cf.SJas6:17
4:13
Cf.SJas5:5
4:21
//Q11:33; Mt5:15; Lk8:16, 11:33; Th33:2–3
4:22
//Q12:2; Mt10:26b; Lk8:17, 12:2; Th5:2, 6:5–6
4:23
//Mt11:15, 13:9, 43b; Lk8:8b, 14:35b; Mary2:5, 3:14; Rev2:7a, 11a, 17a, 3:6, 13, 22, 13:9a; Th8:4, 21:10, 24:2, 63:4, 65:8, 96:3; Ⓓ Mk4:9 [7:16]
4:24
//Q6:38c, Mt7:2b, Lk6:38c
4:25
//Q19:26; Mt13:12, 25:29; Lk8:18b, 19:26; Th41
4:26–29
Cf.Th21:9
4:30–32
//Q13:18–19, Mt13:31–32, Lk13:18–19, Th20; ◊Ez17:22–24; Dn4:10–12, 21; Ⓣ DSav36:1

13***Then he says to them:*** "You don't get this parable, so how are you going to understand other parables? 14The 'sower' is 'sowing' the message. 15The first group are the ones 'along the path': here the message 'is sown,' but when they hear, Satan comes right along and steals the message that has been 'sown' into them. 16The second group are the ones sown 'on rocky ground.' Whenever they listen to the message, right away they receive it happily. 17Yet they do not have their own 'root' and so are short-lived. When distress or persecution comes because of the message, such a person becomes easily shaken right away. 18And the third group are those sown 'among the thorns.' These are the ones who have listened to the message, 19but the worries of the age and the seductiveness of wealth and the yearning for everything else come and 'choke' the message and they become 'fruitless.' 20And the final group are the ones sown 'on good earth.' They are the ones who listen to the message and take it in and 'produce fruit, here thirty, there sixty, and there one hundred.' "

21***And he would say*** to them: "Since when is the lamp brought in to be put under the bushel basket or under the bed? It's put on the lampstand, isn't it?

22"After all, there is nothing hidden except to be brought to light, nor anything kept secret that won't be exposed.

23"If anyone here has two good ears, use them!"

24***And he went on to say*** to them: "Pay attention to what you hear! The standard you apply will be the standard applied to you, and then some.

25"In fact, to those who have, more will be given, and from those who don't have, even what they do have will be taken away!"

26***And he would say:***

> God's imperial rule is like this: Suppose someone sows seed on the ground, 27and sleeps and rises night and day, and the seed sprouts and matures, although the sower is unaware of it. 28The earth produces fruit on its own, first a shoot, then a head, then mature grain on the head. 29But when the grain ripens, all of a sudden ⟨that farmer⟩ sends for the sickle, because it's harvest time.

30***And he would say:***

> To what should we compare God's imperial rule, or what parable should we use for it? 31Consider the mustard seed: When it is sown

---

4:13–20 After a characteristic rebuke for their lack of understanding, Jesus proceeds to explain his symbolic story to his followers (cf. 7:14–23; 8:14–21). The key words of the parable are picked up and interpreted allegorically to explain the various failures and successes of the group's efforts at mission. The symbols shift from a focus on the soils and seeds to the fate of the plants that shoot up, and then are devoured, scorched, choked, or in some cases flourish in the difficult conditions of Jesus' work and Mark's community history.

4:26–32 In these brief symbolic pictures we have Jesus' continued prediction of the difficulties and apparent uncertainties at hand and to come. The workings of *God's imperial rule* are again likened to the inexplicable processes of nature, with the emphasis still lying on the contrast between unpromising

Only in parables

Rebuking wind & wave

The Demon of Gerasa

on the ground, though it is the smallest of all the seeds on the earth,
[32]—yet when it is sown, it comes up, and becomes the biggest of all
garden plants, and produces branches, so that the birds of the sky
can nest in its shade.

[33]***And with the help*** of many such parables he would speak his
message to them according to their ability to comprehend. [34]Yet he
would not say anything to them except by way of parable, but would
spell everything out in private to his own disciples.

[35]***Later in the day,*** when evening had come, he says to them,

"Let's go across to the other side."

[36]After sending the crowd away, they took him along since he was in
the boat, and other boats accompanied him. [37]Then a great squall
comes up and the waves begin to pound against the boat, so that the
boat suddenly began to fill up. [38]He was in the stern sleeping on a
cushion. And they wake him up and say to him, "Teacher, don't you
care that we are going to drown?"

[39]Then he got up and rebuked the wind and said to the sea, "Be
quiet, shut up!"

The wind then died down and there was a great calm.

[40]He said to them, "Why are you so cowardly? You still don't trust,
do you?"

[41]And they were completely terrified and would say to one another,
"Who can this fellow be, that even the wind and the sea obey him?"

5 ***And they came*** to the other side of the sea, to the region of the
Gerasenes. [2]And when he got out of the boat, suddenly a person controlled by an unclean spirit came from the tombs to accost him. [3]This
man made his home in the tombs, and nobody was able to bind him,
not even with a chain, [4]because, though he had often been bound with
fetters and with chains, he would break the fetters and pull the chains
apart, and nobody could subdue him. [5]And day and night he would

4:33–34 //Mt13:34
4:35–41 //Mt8:18, 23–27, Lk8:22–25; ◊Ps89:8–9, 93:3–4, 106:8–9; Is59.9–10, Jon1:4–5
5:1–20 //Mt8:28–34, Lk8:26–39

5:1 Some mss read *Gerasenes*, others "Gadarenes" or "Gergesenes."

beginnings and great endings.

4:35–41 Here Mark describes the first of several boat trips across the Galilean lake. Mark calls this lake the *sea*, using a word (*thalassa*) that most Greek writers reserve for the much larger Mediterranean (Luke uses the more proper term for a lake, *limnē*, in Luke 5:1; 8:22–23, 33).

The squall on the sea and Jesus' masterful silencing of the elements resonate powerfully within the biblical tradition of God's creative and redemptive control of the waters (e.g., Genesis 1; Exodus 14; Psalms 69; 89; 93; 104–107; Isaiah 43; 51:9–10). The story also helps Mark develop his theme of the faltering trust and faulty comprehension of Jesus' band of followers. Unwittingly they awaken Jesus with words elsewhere addressed to God (e.g., Ps 44:23). Jesus stills the storm with the formula for silencing a demon (see 1:25).

5:1–20 The placing of this episode in Gerasa, thirty miles from the lake, led to several "corrections" in the manuscript tradition. The story is one of Mark's longest and provides a good example of his rambling descriptive style (Matthew and Luke retell the story just as effectively with many fewer words).

Jairus' daughter

Jesus cures a woman

howl among the tombs and across the hills and keep bruising himself on the stones. 6And when he saw Jesus from a distance, he ran up and knelt before him 7and, shouting at the top of his voice, he says, "What do you want with me, Jesus, you son of the most high God? For God's sake, don't torment me!" 8—because he had been saying to it: "Come out of that fellow, you filthy spirit!"

9And ⟨Jesus⟩ started questioning him: "What's your name?"

"My name is Legion," he says, "for there are many of us."

10And it kept begging him over and over not to expel them from their territory.

11Now over there by the mountain a large herd of pigs was feeding. 12And so they bargained with him: "Send us over to the pigs so we may enter them!"

13And he agreed. And then the unclean spirits came out and entered the pigs, and the herd rushed down the bluff into the sea, about two thousand of them, and drowned in the sea. 14And the herdsmen ran off and reported it in town and out in the country.

And they went out to see what had happened. 15And they come to Jesus and notice the demoniac sitting with his clothes on and with his wits about him, the one who had harbored Legion, and they got scared. 16And those who had seen told them what had happened to the demoniac, and all about the pigs. 17And they started begging him to go away from their region. 18And as ⟨Jesus⟩ was getting into the boat, the ex-demoniac kept pleading with him to let him go along. 19And he would not let him, but says to him, "Go home to your people and tell them what your patron has done for you—how he has shown mercy to you."

20And he went away and started spreading the news in the Decapolis about what Jesus had done for him, and everybody would marvel.

21***When Jesus had again crossed over*** to the other side, a large crowd gathered around him, and he was beside the sea. 22And one of the synagogue officials comes, Jairus by name, and as soon as he sees him, he falls at his feet 23and pleads with him and begs, "My little daughter is on the verge of death, so come and put your hands on her so she may be cured and live!"

24And ⟨Jesus⟩ set out with him.

5:21–43 //Mt9:18–26, Lk8:40–56

And a large crowd started following and shoving against him. 25And there was a woman who had had a vaginal flow for twelve years, 26who

---

5:9 For Mark's audience the name of the demon, *Legion,* likely functioned as code language, making the story also refer to the desired expulsion of the Roman armies from the land.

5:20 The *Decapolis* was a league of ten cities mostly east of the Jordan, a predominantly Gentile region.

5:21–43 Here we find Mark relating two miraculous healings, one of which (vv. 24b–34) has been enclosed or "sandwiched" within the other (vv. 22–24a, 35–43; see note at 3:21). The interposing of the second story provides some dramatic suspense while Jairus' daughter lies on the verge of death.

5:22 Jairus (one of the few people given a name among the many who encounter Jesus in Mark's story) is a *synagogue official*, a wealthy patron of the local house of meeting and prayer.

had suffered much under many doctors, and who had spent everything she had, but hadn't been helped at all, but instead had gotten worse. [27]When ⟨this woman⟩ heard about Jesus, she came up from behind in the crowd and touched his cloak. ([28]No doubt she had been figuring, "If I could just touch his clothes, I'll be cured!") [29]And the vaginal flow stopped instantly, and she sensed in her body that she was cured of her illness.

Jairus' daughter dies

No respect at home

[30]And suddenly, because Jesus realized that power had drained out of him, he turned around and started asking the crowd, "Who touched my clothes?"

[31]And his disciples said to him, "You see the crowd jostling you around and you're asking, 'Who touched me?' "

[32]And he started looking around to see who had done this. [33]Although the woman got scared and started trembling—she realized what she had done—she came and fell down before him and told him the whole truth.

[34]He said to her, "Daughter, your trust has cured you. Go in peace, and farewell to your illness."

[35]***While he was still speaking,*** the synagogue official's people approach and say, "Your daughter has died; why keep bothering the teacher?"

[36]When Jesus overheard this conversation, he says to the synagogue official, "Don't be afraid, just have trust!"

[37]And he wouldn't let anyone follow along with him except Peter and James and John, James' brother. [38]When they come to the house of the synagogue official, he notices a lot of clamor and people crying and wailing, [39]and he goes in and says to them, "Why are you carrying on like this? The child hasn't died; she's sleeping."

[40]And they started laughing at him. But he runs everyone out and takes the child's father and her mother and his companions and goes in where the child is. [41]And he takes the child by the hand and says to her, "*talitha koum*" (which means, "Little girl," I say to you, "Get up!"). [42]And the little girl got right up and started walking around.

(Incidentally, she was twelve years old.)

And they were downright ecstatic. [43]And he gave them strict orders that no one should learn about this, and he told them to give her something to eat.

6 ***Then he left that place,*** and he comes to his hometown, and his disciples follow him. [2]When the sabbath day arrived, he started teaching in the synagogue; and many who heard him were astounded and

6:1–6a
//Mt 13:53–58, Lk 4:16–30

5:27–29 The woman's method of self-cure, by touching Jesus' garments, is reminiscent of the magical healing powers thought to be alive in the personal articles of holy people. (Cf. Paul's handkerchiefs in Acts 19:11–12).

6:1–6 This episode enacts the typical theme that one is not a hero to one's own family or neighbors. The *hometown* (literally, "native district") is unnamed but clearly lies somewhere in Galilee. If the note in 1:9 is meant to refer to Jesus' place of origin then the scene is located in Nazareth.

Instructions for the road

Herod beheads John

said so: "Where's he getting this?" and "What's the source of all this wisdom?" and "Who gave him the right to perform such miracles? [3]This is the carpenter, isn't it? Isn't he Mary's son? And who are his brothers, if not James and Judas and Simon? And who are his sisters, if not our neighbors?" And they were resentful of him.

[4]Jesus used to tell them: "No prophet goes without respect, except on his home turf and among his relatives and at home!"

[5]He was unable to perform a single miracle there, except that he did cure a few by laying hands on them, [6]though he was always shocked at their lack of trust. And he used to go around the villages, teaching in a circuit.

[7]***Then he summoned the twelve*** and started sending them out in pairs and giving them authority over unclean spirits. [8]And he instructed them not to take anything on the road, except a staff: no bread, no knapsack, no spending money, [9]but to wear sandals, and to wear no more than one shirt. [10]And he went on to say to them: "Wherever you enter someone's house, stay there until you leave town. [11]And whatever place does not welcome you or listen to you, get out of there and shake the dust off your feet in witness against them."

[12]So they set out and announced that people should turn their lives around, [13]and they often drove out demons, and they anointed many sick people with oil and healed ⟨them⟩.

[14]***King Herod heard about it***—by now, ⟨Jesus'⟩ reputation had become well known—and people kept saying that John the Baptizer had been raised from the dead and that, as a consequence, miraculous powers were at work in him. [15] Some spread the rumor that he was Elijah, while others reported that he was a prophet like one of the prophets.

[16]When Herod got wind of it, he started declaring, "John, the one I beheaded, has been raised!"

[17]Earlier Herod himself had sent someone to arrest John and put him in chains in a dungeon, on account of Herodias, his brother Philip's wife, because he had married her. [18]You see, John had said to Herod, "It is not right for you to have your brother's wife!"

[19]So Herodias nursed a grudge against him and wanted to eliminate

6:4 //Mt13:57, Lk4:24, Jn4:44, Th31
6:6b–13 //Mt9:35; 10:1, 7–11; Lk9:1–6; cf.Q10:1–12; Mt9:37–38, 10:7–15, Lk10:1–12
6:10–11 //Q10:5–12; Mt10:11–15; Lk9:4, 10:5–12; 1Cor10:27; Th14:4
6:14–29 //Mt14:3–13; cf.Lk3:19–20, 9:7–9; ◊Est5:3, 7:2

6:7–13 The disciples' journey of warning and spiritual healing is the only time in Mark's story where Jesus' followers have any success in carrying out his instructions (see their report at 6:30). The strange rules about the messengers' travel equipment emphasize the special meaning of their trip as a summons to heed Jesus' words about God's imperial rule.

6:11 *Shaking off a town's dust* is a gesture both of contempt and of warning.

6:14–29 Mark's narrative about the Baptist and King Herod (a son of Herod "the Great") is one of the Gospel's most gripping and effective stories. The scene is punctuated with the typical motifs of folktale (the comely dancing girl, the extravagant oath, the scheming wife). We get a rare example of the "flashback" technique as Herod wonders whether the stir aroused by the disciples' journey could be John's doing. We learn of John's fate just as the followers of Jesus are enjoying their first success, a combination which casts a troubling shadow on their future work.

6:30–44 Jesus' miracle of feeding evokes

him, but she couldn't manage it, 20because Herod was afraid of John.
He knew that he was an upright and holy man, and so protected him,
and, although he listened to him frequently, he was very confused, yet
he listened to him eagerly.
21Now a festival day came, when Herod gave a banquet on his
birthday for his courtiers, and his commanders, and the leading citizens of Galilee. 22And the daughter of Herodias came in and captivated
Herod and his dinner guests by dancing. The king said to the girl, "Ask
me for whatever you wish and I'll grant it to you!" 23Then he swore an
oath to her: "I'll grant you whatever you ask for, up to half my domain!"
24She went out and said to her mother, "What should I ask for?"
And she replied, "The head of John the Baptist!"
25She promptly hastened back and made her request: "I want you to
give me the head of John the Baptist on a platter, right now!"
26The king grew regretful, but, on account of his oaths and the
dinner guests, he didn't want to refuse her. 27So right away the king
sent for the executioner and commanded him to bring his head. And
he went away and beheaded ⟨John⟩ in prison. 28He brought his head
on a platter and presented it to the girl, and the girl gave it to her
mother. 29When his disciples heard about it, they came and got his
body and put it in a tomb.

The twelve report

30***Then the apostles regroup*** around Jesus and they reported to him
everything that they had done and taught.
31And he says to them, "You come privately to an isolated place and
rest a little."
(Remember, many were coming and going and they didn't even
have a chance to eat.)

Loaves & fish for 5,000

32So they went away in the boat privately to an isolated place. 33But
many noticed them leaving and figured it out and raced there on foot
from all the towns and got there ahead of them. 34When he came
ashore, he saw a huge crowd and was moved by them, because they
'resembled sheep without a shepherd,' and he started teaching them at
length.
35***And when the hour*** had already grown late, his disciples would
approach him and say, "This place is desolate and it's late. 36Send them
away so that they can go to the farms and villages around here to buy
something to eat."
37But in response he said to them, "Give them something to eat
yourselves!"
And they say to him, "Are we to go out and buy half a year's wages
worth of bread and donate it for their meal?!"
38So he says to them, "How many loaves do you have? Go look."
And when they find out, they say, "Five, and two fish."

6:30 //Lk 9:10a
6:32–44 //Mt 14:13–21, Lk 9:10b–17, Jn 6:1–13
6:34 ◊Num 27:17, 1 Kgs 22:17
6:35–44 Ⓓ Mk 8:1–9

God's care for the starving Israelites during the Exodus. The allusion is strengthened by Jesus' command to have the people arranged in groups of hundreds and fifties, reminiscent of the groupings of the wandering people of God.

Jesus departs

Jesus walks on the sea

Cure of the sick

Rules for handwashing

[39]Next he instructed them all to sit down and eat, some over here, some over there, on the green grass. [40]So they sat down group by group, in hundreds and in fifties. [41]And he took the five loaves and the two fish, looked up to the sky, gave a blessing, and broke the bread apart, and started giving it to his disciples to pass around to them, and even the two fish they shared with everybody. [42]Everybody had more than enough to eat. [43]Then they picked up twelve baskets full of leftovers, including some fish. [44]And the number of men who had some bread came to five thousand.

[45]***And right away*** he made his disciples embark in the boat and go ahead to the opposite shore toward Bethsaida, while he himself dispersed the crowd. [46]And once he got away from them, he went off to the mountain to pray.

[47]***When evening came,*** the boat was in the middle of the sea, and he was alone on the land. [48]When he saw they were having a rough time making headway, because the wind was against them, at about three o'clock in the morning he comes toward them walking on the sea and intending to go past them. [49]But when they saw him walking on the sea, they thought he was a ghost and they cried out. [50]By now they all saw him and were terrified. But right away he spoke with them and says to them, "Take heart, it's me! Don't be afraid." [51]And he climbed into the boat with them, and the wind died down. By this time they were completely dumbfounded. ([52]You see, they hadn't understood about the loaves; they were being obstinate.)

[53]***Once they had crossed over*** to land, they landed at Gennesaret and dropped anchor. [54]As soon as they had gotten out of the boat, people recognized him right away, [55]and they ran around over the whole area and started bringing those who were ill on mats to wherever he was rumored to be. [56]And wherever he would go, into villages, or towns, or onto farms, they would lay out the sick in the marketplaces and beg him to let them touch the fringe of his cloak. And all those who managed to touch it were cured!

6:42 ◊2 Kgs 4:42–44
6:45–52 //Mt 14:22–33, Jn 6:16–21
6:53–56 //Mt 14:34–36; cf. Jn 6:22–24
7:1–13 //Mt 15:1–9

7 ***The Pharisees gather*** around him, along with some of the scholars, who had come from Jerusalem. [2]When they notice some of his disciples eating their meal with defiled hands, that is to say, without washing their hands ([3]you see, the Pharisees and the Judeans generally

---

6:45–52 This brief tale confirms Jesus' mastery over the elements of nature as well as his followers' continued mystification.

6:52 The multiplication of the loaves should have disclosed Jesus' identity and divine authority to the disciples, but *they were being obstinate* (literally, "their hearts were hardened"), a biblical phrase suggesting a deliberate veiling on God's part for some larger purpose (e.g., Exod 4:21; 7:13; 14:17).

7:1–13 The stock characters of Pharisees and scholars continue to act as Jesus' main antagonists, while the disciples function as surrogates for the story's readers.

7:3–4 Mark addresses his audience directly, presuming that his readers will not understand or follow these ordinary Jewish rules of food preparation any more than the disciples

What comes out defiles

wouldn't think of eating without first washing their hands in a particular way, always observing the tradition of the elders, 4and they won't eat when they get back from the marketplace without washing again, and there are many other traditions they cherish, such as the washing of cups and jugs and kettles), 5the Pharisees and the scholars start questioning him: "Why don't your disciples live up to the tradition of the elders, instead of eating bread with defiled hands?"

6And he answered them, "How accurately Isaiah depicted you phonies when he wrote:

> This people honors me with their lips,
> but their heart stays far away from me.
> 7Their worship of me is empty,
> because they insist on teachings that are human commandments.

8You have set aside God's commandment and hold fast to human tradition!"

9Or he would say to them, "How expert you've become at putting aside God's commandment to establish your own tradition. 10For instance, Moses said, 'Honor your father and your mother' and 'Those who curse their father or mother will surely die.' 11But you say, 'If people say to their father or mother, "Whatever I might have spent to support you is *korban*"' (which means "consecrated to God"), 12you no longer let those persons do anything for their father or mother. 13So you end up invalidating God's word with your own tradition, which you then perpetuate. And you do all kinds of other things like that!"

14***Once again*** he summoned the crowd and would say to them: "Listen to me, all of you, and try to understand! 15What goes into you can't defile you; what comes out of you can. 16If anyone has two good ears, use them!"

17When he entered a house away from the crowd, his disciples started questioning him about the riddle. 18And he says to them: "Are you as dim-witted as the rest? Don't you realize that nothing from outside can defile by going into a person, 19because it doesn't get to the heart but passes into the stomach, and comes out in the outhouse?" (This is how everything we eat is purified.)

20And he went on to say, "It's what comes out of a person that

7:6–7 //EgerG 3:6; ◊ Is 29:13
7:10 ◊ Ex 20:12, 21:17; Lv 20:9; Dt 5.16
7:14–15 //Mt 15:10–11, Th 14.5
7:17–23 //Mt 15:15–20; Ⓣ Mk 4:10–20, 8:14–21, 9:28–30, 10:10–12

7:16 This entire verse is missing in some early mss.

---

did.
7:6 The word we translate as *phonies* (traditionally simply transliterated as *hypocrites*) means someone who acts a part in an insincere manner.
7:13 *Korban* is the Hebrew word for offerings made to God (see Lev 1:2; Num 7:13). The suggestion that dedications could be made to avoid one's obligation to care for needy parents is not known from other sources; rabbinic Jewish texts suggest that vows may be broken in such circumstances.
7:14–23 Mark counterposes the crowd with both Jesus' antagonists and followers. In chapter 4 the crowd is deliberately left confused while the disciples are given the secret to understanding (4:10–12, 33–34). Here in v. 18, and again after a second miracle of feeding (8:1–10, 14–21), Jesus reproaches the confused disciples in the same terms he had

Greek woman's daughter

Deaf mute

Loaves & fish for 4,000

defiles. [21]For from out of the human heart issue wicked intentions:
sexual immorality, thefts, murders, [22]adulteries, envies, wickedness,
deceit, promiscuity, an evil eye, blasphemy, arrogance, lack of good
sense. [23]All these evil things come from the inside out and defile the
person."

[24]***From there he got up*** and went away to the regions of Tyre.
Whenever he visited a house he wanted no one to know, but he could
not escape notice. [25]Instead, suddenly a woman whose daughter had an
unclean spirit heard about him, and came and fell down at his feet.
[26]The woman was a Greek, by race a Phoenician from Syria. And she
started asking him to drive the demon out of her daughter. [27]He
responded to her like this: "Let the children be fed first, since it isn't
good to take bread out of children's mouths and throw it to the dogs!"

[28]But as a rejoinder she says to him, "Sir, even the dogs under the
table get to eat scraps ⟨dropped by⟩ children!"

[29]Then he said to her, "For that retort, be on your way, the demon
has come out of your daughter."

[30]She returned home and found the child lying on the bed and the
demon gone.

[31]***Then he left the regions*** of Tyre and traveled through Sidon to the
Sea of Galilee, through the middle of the region known as the Decapolis.

[32]And they bring him a deaf-mute and plead with him to lay his
hand on him. [33]Taking him aside from the crowd in private, he stuck
his fingers into the man's ears and spat and touched his tongue. [34]And
looking up to the sky, he groaned and says to him, "*ephphatha*" (which
means, "Be opened!"). [35]And his ears opened up, and right away his
speech impediment was removed, and he started speaking properly.
[36]Then he ordered them to tell no one. But no matter how much he
enjoined them, they spread it around all the more.

[37]And they were completely dumbfounded. "He's done everything
and has done it quite well," they said; "he even makes the deaf hear and
the mute speak!"

7:24–30 //Mt15:21–28
7:31–37 Cf. Mt15:29–31
8:1–10 //Mt15:32–39; Ⓓ Mk6:35–44; ◊2Kgs4:42–44

8 ***And once again*** during that same period, when there was a huge
crowd without anything to eat, he calls the disciples aside and says to

---

used earlier for the uncomprehending crowds.

7:24–30 The Gentile woman wins Jesus over with a swift retort. This is Jesus' only miracle from a distance in Mark's story. On *Tyre and Sidon* see the note at 3:7.

7:31 Mark's geographical sense seems confused here, since Tyre is *south* of Sidon: to *return* to the Sea of Galilee from Tyre would not normally mean a journey *north* to Sidon, nor to the *southeast* through the region of the gentile cities of the Decapolis (cf. 5:20). What seems to be intended is a general indication of a trip through non-Israelite areas to the north and east of Galilee.

7:32–37 Jesus' cure of the deaf and mute man uses the techniques of magical healing: touching the ailing part, use of spittle, command in an exotic language (exotic to Mark's readers, that is).

8:1–9 This story is a doublet of the feeding

Demand for a sign

Bread & leaven

them, 2“I feel sorry for the crowd, because they have already spent
three days with me and now they’ve run out of food. 3If I send these
people home hungry, they will collapse on the road—in fact, some of
them have come from quite a distance.”
4And his disciples answered him, “How can anyone feed these
people bread out here in this desolate place?”
5And he started asking them, “How many loaves do you have?”
They replied, “Seven.”
6Then he orders the crowd to sit down on the ground. And he took
the seven loaves, gave thanks, and broke them into pieces, and started
giving ⟨them⟩ to his disciples to hand out; and they passed them
around to the crowd. 7They also had a few small fish. When he had
blessed them, he told them to hand those out as well. 8They had more
than enough to eat. Then they picked up seven big baskets of leftover
scraps. 9There were about four thousand people there. Then he started
sending them away.
10***And he got right into*** the boat with his disciples and went to the
Dalmanoutha district. 11The Pharisees came out and started to argue
with him. To test him, they demanded a sign in the sky. 12He groaned
under his breath and says, “Why does this generation insist on a sign? I
swear to God, this generation won’t get any sign!”
13And turning his back on them, he got back in the boat and crossed
over to the other side.
14***They forgot to bring any bread*** and had nothing with them in the
boat except one loaf. 15Then he started giving them directives: “Look,”
he says, “watch out for the leaven of the Pharisees and the leaven of
Herod!”
16They began looking quizzically at one another because they didn’t
have any bread. 17And because he was aware of this, he says to them:
“Why are you puzzling about your lack of bread? You still aren’t using
your heads, are you? You still haven’t got the point, have you? Are you
just dense? 18Though you have eyes, you still don’t see, and though you
have ears, you still don’t hear! Don’t you even remember 19how many
baskets full of scraps you picked up when I broke up the five loaves for
the five thousand?”
“Twelve,” they reply to him.
20“When I broke up the seven loaves for the four thousand, how
many big baskets full of scraps did you pick up?”
And they say, “Seven.”
21And he repeats, “You still don’t understand, do you?”

8:11–13 //Mt12:38–39; cf.Q11:29–30; Mt12:38–39, 16:1–4, Lk11:14–16, 29–30

8:14–21 //Mt16:5–12; ⓘ Mk6:35–44, 51–52, 7:14–21, 8:1–10

8:15 //Mt16:6, Lk12:1

8:18 ◊Jer5:21, Ez12:2

8:15 Some mss read “the Herodians” in place of *Herod*.

---

of five thousand men (6:35–44) with a few circumstantial details changed (seven loaves instead of five, big baskets in place of the ordinary baskets found in the first story).

8:13–21 Another scene of the disciples unable to understand Jesus’ meaning. Direct references are made to the two feeding miracles related in 6:30–44 and 8:1–10; the disciples are rebuked in terms reminiscent of 4:10–12 and 7:17.

A blind man receives his sight

What are people saying?

Son of Adam destined to suffer

Saving & losing life

[22]***They come to Bethsaida,*** and they bring him a blind person, and plead with him to touch him. [23]He took the blind man by the hand and led him out of the village. And he spat into his eyes, and placed his hands on him, and started questioning him: "Do you see anything?"

[24]When his sight began to come back, the first thing he said was: "I see human figures, as though they were trees walking around."

[25]Then he put his hands over his eyes a second time. And he opened his eyes, and his sight was restored, and he saw everything clearly. [26]And he sent him home, saying, "Don't bother to go back to the village!"

[27]***Jesus and his disciples*** set out for the villages of Caesarea Philippi. On the road he started questioning his disciples, asking them, "What are people saying about me?"

[28]In response they said to him, "⟨Some say, 'You are⟩ John the Baptist,' and others, 'Elijah,' but others, 'One of the prophets.'"

[29]But he continued to press them, "What about you, who do you say I am?"

Peter responds to him, "You are the Anointed!" [30]And he warned them not to tell anyone about him.

[31]***He started teaching them*** that the son of Adam was destined to suffer a great deal, and be rejected by the elders and the ranking priests and the scholars, and be killed, and after three days rise. [32]And he would say this openly. And Peter took him aside and began to lecture him. [33]But he turned, noticed his disciples, and reprimanded Peter verbally: "Get out of my sight, you Satan, you, because you're not thinking in God's terms, but in human terms."

[34]***After he called the crowd*** together with his disciples, he said to them, "If any of you wants to come after me, you should deny yourself, pick up your cross, and follow me! [35]Remember, by trying to save your own life, you're going to lose it, but by losing your life for the sake of the good news, you're going to save it. [36]After all, what good does it do to acquire the whole world and pay for it with life? [37]Or, what would you give in exchange for life?

8:27–30 //Mt16:13–20, Lk9:18–21; cf. Jn6:67–69, Th13

8:31–33 //Mt16:21–23, Lk9:22; Ⓣ Mk9:30–32, 10:32–34

8:34–35 Ⓣ SJas4:10–5:3

8:34–9:1 //Mt16:24–28, Lk9:23–27

8:34 Cf. Q14:17, Mt10:38, Th55:2; Ⓣ DSav11:4

8:35 Cf. Mt10:39, Lk17:33, Jn12:25

8:22–26 Mark concludes the first half of his story with this healing of a blind man. The cure's initial failure and the magical aspects of the healing may explain why the other Gospel writers fail to record this story.

Bethsaida is mentioned a few times in the gospel tradition as a scene of Jesus' work (Q 10)

8:27–33 A key juncture in Mark's story. Peter steps forward to assert Jesus' identity as God's Anointed One. Jesus meets this confession not with relief or approval but instead with a warning of impending suffering for the "son of Adam." Peter's disapproval of this prediction represents our own confusion as readers; he and we are rebuked for not seeing things from God's point of view.

Note that here as before Jesus and his band are in the villages or outskirts of a city, in this case the northern Caesarea Philippi: they are never seen actually entering a city or town of any size until they reach Jerusalem in chapter 11.

8:34–9:1 The crowd reenters as Jesus speaks his difficult words of self-sacrifice. The prediction made at 9:1 suggests that Mark's story arose at a time when some people from Jesus' time were still known to be alive, and God's imperial rule was expected to *set in with power* at any moment.

8:38 Rebuking God's people as *adulterous and sinful* is a theme of biblical prophets

Jesus transformed

Elijah must come

38"Moreover, if any of you are ashamed of me and my message in
this adulterous and sinful generation, of you the son of Adam will
likewise be ashamed when he comes in his Father's glory accompanied
by holy angels!"
9 1And he used to tell them, "I swear to you: Some of those standing
here won't ever taste death before they see God's imperial rule set in
with power!"

9 2***Six days later,*** Jesus takes Peter and James and John along and
leads them off by themselves to a lofty mountain. He was transformed
in front of them, 3and his clothes became an intensely brilliant white,
whiter than any laundry on earth could make them. 4Elijah appeared to
them, with Moses, and they were conversing with Jesus. 5Peter
responds by saying to Jesus, "Rabbi, it's a good thing we're here. In
fact, why not set up three tents, one for you, and one for Moses, and one
for Elijah!" (6You see, he didn't know how else to respond, since they
were terrified.)
7And a cloud moved in and cast a shadow over them, and a voice
came out of the cloud: "This is my favored son, listen to him!"
8Suddenly, as they looked around, they saw no one, but were alone
with Jesus.
9***And as they were walking*** down the mountain he instructed them
not to describe what they had seen to anyone, until the son of Adam
rise from the dead.
10And they kept it to themselves, puzzling over what this could
mean, this 'rising from the dead.' 11And they started questioning him:
"The scholars claim, don't they, that Elijah must come first?"
12He would respond to them, "Of course Elijah comes first to restore
everything. So, how does scripture claim that the son of Adam will
suffer greatly and be the object of scorn? 13On the other hand, I tell you
that Elijah in fact has come, and they had their way with him, just as
the scriptures indicate."

9:2–8 //Mt17:1–8, Lk9:28–36
9:7 //Mk1:11; ◊Is42:1, 44:2
9:9–13 //Mt17:9–13; ◊1Kgs19:2, 10

---

going back to Hosea, who charged that Israel's "going after other gods" was tantamount to committing adultery against their lawful master Yahweh.

9:2–8 The select group of three inner disciples privately see Jesus *transformed on a lofty mountain*. Again Mark provides his characters with a symbolic landscape appropriate to the moment, without having to get too specific about the geographical details.

Two significant heroes of faith also appear. *Moses'* burial place was never found (see Deut 34:6); *Elijah* was said to have been taken to heaven before death (2 Kings 2). Some people expected one or both to return in the last days.

This time God's voice is addressed to those around Jesus. The scene confirms for them (and for the reader) that Jesus has divine warrant for his work.

9:9 Jesus' remark about *the rising of the son of Adam* functions along with his predictions at 8:31–32; 9:31–32; 10:32–34 to strengthen the readers' confidence about Jesus' fate at the end of the story (see note at 16:8).

9:11–13 The Israelite prophet Elijah was seen in Mal 4:5–6 as a forerunner of the "coming of the day of the Lord," a time when peoples' hearts would be redirected to love of family and neighbor. Here Jesus explains that Elijah has come in the person of John the Baptist (Matthew makes the identifi-

The mute spirit [14]***When they rejoined the disciples,*** they saw a huge crowd sur-
Son of Adam will die & rise rounding them and scholars arguing with them. [15]And all of a sudden,
when the whole crowd caught sight of him, they were alarmed and
rushed up to meet him. [16]He asked them, "Why are you bothering to
argue with them?"
[17]And one person from the crowd answered him, "Teacher, I
brought my son to you, because he has a mute spirit. [18]Whenever it
takes him over, it knocks him down, and he foams at the mouth and
grinds his teeth and stiffens up. I asked your disciples to drive it out, but
they couldn't."
[19]In response he says, "You distrustful lot, how long must I associate
with you? How long must I put up with you? Bring him over to me!"
[20]And they brought him over to him. And when the spirit noticed
him, right away it threw him into convulsions, and he fell to the
ground, and kept rolling around, foaming at the mouth. [21]And ⟨Jesus⟩
asked his father, "How long has he been like this?"
He replied, "Ever since he was a child. [22]Frequently it has thrown
him into fire and into water to destroy him. So if you can do anything,
take pity on us and help us!"
[23]Jesus said to him, "What do you mean, 'If you can'? All things are
possible for the one who trusts."
[24]Right away the father of the child cried out and said, "I do trust!
Help my lack of trust!"
[25]When Jesus saw that the crowd was about to mob them, he
rebuked the unclean spirit, and commands it, "Deaf and mute spirit, I
command you, get out of him and don't ever go back inside him!"
[26]And after he shrieked and went into a series of convulsions, it
came out. And he took on the appearance of a corpse, so that the rumor
went around that he had died. [27]But Jesus took hold of his hand and
raised him, and there he stood.
[28]And when he had gone home, his disciples started questioning
him privately: "Why couldn't we drive it out?"
9:14–27 //Mt17:14–18, Lk9:37–43a [29]He said to them, "The only thing that can drive this kind out is
prayer."
9:28–30 //Mt17:19–20; Ⓣ Mk7:17–23, 10:10–12 [30]***They left there*** and started going through Galilee, and he did not
want anyone to know. [31]Remember, he was instructing his disciples
9:30–32 //Mt17:22–23, Lk9:43b–45; Ⓣ Mk8:31–33, 10:32–24 and telling them: "The son of Adam is being turned over to his
enemies, and they will end up killing him. And three days after he is
killed he will rise!" [32]But they never understood this remark, and
always dreaded to ask him ⟨about it⟩.

---

cation crystal clear to his readers at 17:13).

9:14–29 This episode combines elements of both an exorcism and a healing story. Jesus makes the cure depend on *trust.* His disciples (though without their leaders Peter, James, and John) had been unable to cure the boy. In a private scene at home at the end of the story (vv. 28–29) Jesus chooses not to rebuke them for failure but instead to give them some practical advice for the next time.

9:30–32 Jesus repeats his prediction about the approaching suffering, death, and rising of the son of Adam, again arousing fear and consternation in his followers.

Number one is last

For & against

Hand, foot & eye

33***And they came to Capernaum.*** When he got home, he started questioning them, "What were you arguing about on the road?" 34They fell completely silent, because on the road they had been bickering about who was greatest.

35He sat down and called the twelve and says to them, "If any of you wants to be 'number one,' you have to be last of all and servant of all!"

36And he took a child and had her stand in front of them, and he put his arm around her, and he said to them, 37"Whoever accepts a child like this in my name is accepting me. And whoever accepts me is not so much accepting me as the one who sent me."

38***John said to him,*** "Teacher, we saw someone driving out demons in your name, so we tried to stop him, because he wasn't one of our adherents."

39Jesus responded, "Don't stop him! After all, no one who performs a miracle in my name will turn around the next moment and curse me. 40In fact, whoever is not against us is on our side. 41By the same token, whoever gives you a cup of water to drink because you carry the name of the Anointed, I swear to you, such a person certainly won't go unrewarded!

42"***And any of you who misleads*** one of these little trusting souls would be better off if you had a millstone hung around your neck and were thrown into the sea!

43"And if your hand gets you into trouble, cut it off! It's better for you to enter life maimed than to wind up in Gehenna, in the unquenchable fire, with both hands!

45"And if your foot gets you into trouble, cut it off! It's better for you to enter life lame than to be thrown into Gehenna with both feet!

47"And if your eye gets you into trouble, rip it out! It's better for you to enter God's domain one-eyed than to be thrown into Gehenna with both eyes, 48where the worm never dies and the fire never goes out!

49"As you know, everyone there is salted by fire.

50"Salt is good ⟨and salty⟩—if salt becomes bland, with what will you renew it?

"Maintain 'salt' among yourselves and be at peace with one another."

9:33–37 //Mt 18:1–2, 5; Lk 9:46–48
9:37 Cf. Q 10:16; Mt 10:40; Lk 10:16; Jn 5:24, 12:43b–44, 13:20
9:38–40 //Lk 9:49–50
9:40 Cf. Q 11:23, Mt 12:30, Lk 11:23, GOxy 1224 6:1
9:41 Cf. Mt 10:42
9:42–48 //Mt 18:6–9
9:42 //Lk 17:1–2
9:48 ◊Is 66.24
9:50 //Q 14:34–35, Mt 5:13, Lk 14:34–35; ◊Lv 2:13

9:43, 45 Many mss repeat v. 48 at the end of vv. 43 and 45.

9:36–37 Using childhood as a symbol for the proper attitude of disciples and believers is a favorite theme in the gospel tradition. Cf. 10:13–16.
9:38–41 Jesus declares that in his fight "the foe of my foe is my friend." Elsewhere in the gospel tradition we find the more exclusive version of the saying, that "whoever is not with me is against me" (Q 11:23).
9:43 The word *Gehenna* derives from the name of the valley of Hinnom, adjacent to ancient Jerusalem. By Jesus' day the name had become synonymous with a place of fiery punishment after death, due perhaps to associations with stories of forbidden human sacrifices by fire in the valley (see 2 Chron 28:3; 33:6; Jer 7:31–32; 19:6; 32:35).
9:49–50 Striking but obscure statements, linking *salt* somehow to *fire, goodness*, and community *peace*.

Created male & female

Children in God's domain

Man with money

10 ***And from there he gets up*** and goes to the territory of Judea and
across the Jordan, and once again crowds gather around him. As usual,
he started teaching them. [2]And Pharisees approach him and, to test
him, they ask whether a husband is permitted to divorce his wife. [3]In
response he puts a question to them: "What did Moses command you?"
[4]They replied, "Moses allowed one to prepare a writ of abandon-
ment and thus to divorce the other party."
[5]Jesus said to them, "He gave you this injunction because you are
obstinate. [6]However, in the beginning, at the creation, 'God made
them male and female.' [7]'For this reason, a man will leave his father
and mother and be united with his wife, [8]and the two will become one
person,' so they are no longer two individuals but 'one person.' [9]There-
fore those God has coupled together, no one else should separate."
[10]And once again, as usual, when they got home, the disciples
questioned him about this. [11]And he says to them, "Whoever divorces
his wife and marries another commits adultery against her; [12]and if she
divorces her husband and marries another, she commits adultery."
[13]***And they would bring*** children to him so he could lay hands on
them, but the disciples scolded them. [14]Then Jesus grew indignant
when he saw this and said to them: "Let the children come up to me,
don't try to stop them. After all, God's domain belongs to people like
that. [15]I swear to you, whoever doesn't accept God's imperial rule the
way a child would, certainly won't ever set foot in ⟨his domain⟩!"
[16]And he would put his arms around them and bless them, and lay his
hands on them.
[17]***As he was traveling*** along the road, someone ran up, knelt before
him, and started questioning him: "Good teacher, what do I have to do
to inherit eternal life?"
[18]Jesus said to him, "Why do you call me good? No one is good
except for God alone. [19]You know the commandments: 'You must not

10:1–12 //Mt 19:1–12
10:4 ◊Dt 24:1
10:6–8 ◊Gn 1:27, 2:24
10:10–12 Ⓣ Mk 7:17–23, 9:28–20
10:11–12 //Mt 5:31–32, 19:9; Lk 16:18; 1 Cor 7:10
10:13–16 //Mt 19:13–15, Lk 18:15–17
10:15 //Mt 18:3; cf. Jn 3:1–10, Th 22
10:17–31 //Mt 19:16–30, Lk 18:18–30, GNaz 6
10:19 ◊Ex 20:12–16, Dt 5:16–20

10:1 Jesus begins his journey southward from Galilee towards his fate in Jerusalem. Again he is surrounded by crowds, religious antagonists, and disciples.

10:2–12 We are told that the Pharisees' question arises not from ignorance but from malice. Jesus engages in some scriptural jousting, overtrumping the Mosaic commandment (found in the fifth book of the Bible) with his own prooftexts from the opening chapters of Genesis. In v. 9 Jesus forbids divorce despite Moses' provisions. This leads to another private scene at home where Jesus forbids not divorce but remarriage.

10:13–16 Again children symbolize the proper approach to salvation, called *entering God's imperial domain*. The image of children is meant to evoke their condition of utter dependence and submission rather than "childlike" innocence.

10:17–22 Jesus is wary of accepting the eager praise of this man who runs up and kneels before him: *Why do you call me good?*. Throughout Mark's story the motives of those who approach Jesus are carefully scrutinized, with Jesus remaining indifferent to or suspicious of various ways in which people characterize him.

Salvation now is called *inheriting eternal life* (cf. 9:42–47). To the traditional biblical commandments Jesus adds the mandates of personal sacrifice and becoming his follower.

Needle's eye

Son of Adam will die & rise

murder, you are not to commit adultery, you are not to steal, you are not to give false testimony, you are not to defraud, and you are to honor your father and mother.' "

[20]He said to him, "Teacher, I have observed all these things since I was a child!"

[21]Jesus loved him at first sight and said to him, "You are missing one thing: make your move, sell whatever you have and give ⟨the proceeds⟩ to the poor, and you will have treasure in heaven. And then come, follow me!"

[22]But stunned by this advice, he went away dejected, since he possessed a fortune.

[23]***After looking around,*** Jesus says to his disciples, "How difficult it is for those who have money to enter God's domain!" [24]The disciples were amazed at his words.

In response Jesus repeats what he had said, "Children, how difficult it is to enter God's domain! [25]It's easier for a camel to squeeze through a needle's eye than for a wealthy person to get into God's domain!"

[26]And they were very perplexed, wondering to themselves, "Well then, who can be saved?"

[27]Jesus looks them in the eye and says, "For mortals it's impossible, but not for God; after all, everything's possible for God."

[28]Peter started lecturing him: "Look at us, we left everything to follow you!"

[29]Jesus said, "I swear to you, there is no one who has left home, or brothers, or sisters, or mother, or father, or children, or farms on my account and on account of the good news, [30]who won't receive a hundred times as much now, in the present time, homes, and brothers, and sisters, and mothers, and children, and farms—including persecutions—and in the age to come, eternal life.

[31]"Many of the first will be last, and of the last many will be first."

[32]***On the road*** going up to Jerusalem, Jesus was leading the way, they were apprehensive, and others who were following were frightened. Once again he took the twelve aside and started telling them what was going to happen to him:

[33]"Listen, we're going up to Jerusalem, and the son of Adam will be turned over to the ranking priests and the scholars, and they will sentence him to death, and turn him over to foreigners, [34]and they will

10:28
Cf. SJas 4:1
10:31
Cf. Mt 20:16, Lk 13:30, Th 4:2
10:32–34
// Mt 20:17–19, Lk 18:31–34; Ⓣ Mk 8:31–32, 9:30–32

10:23–27 The rich man's sorrow leads to one of Jesus' most memorable pronouncements, about *the camel and the needle's eye.* The image is both exaggerated and shocking, since most people presume that the wealthy already have God's favor and thus have *inheriting life* all taken care of.

10:28–31 In response to Peter's outburst (*We left everything to follow you*!) Jesus promises a replacement family made up of the group itself, though this transfer of affections will also involve harassment and pain. Jesus had made the same move himself in 3:31–35.

10:32–34 Jesus' third prediction of the approaching sufferings of the son of Adam is the most detailed yet. We will see precisely these items acted out in chapters 14–15.

Jesus' cup & baptism

make fun of him, and spit on him, and flog him, and put ⟨him⟩ to death. Yet after three days he will rise!"

Number one is slave

35 ***Then James and John,*** the sons of Zebedee, come up to him, and say to him, "Teacher, we want you to do for us whatever we ask!"

Blind Bartimaeus

36 He said to them, "What do you want me to do for you?"

37 They reply to him, "In your glory, let one of us sit at your right hand, and the other at your left."

38 Jesus said to them, "You have no idea what you're asking for. Can you drink the cup that I'm drinking, or undergo the baptism I'm undergoing?"

39 They said to him, "We can!"

Jesus said to them, "The cup I'm drinking you'll be drinking, and the baptism I'm undergoing you'll be undergoing, 40 but as for sitting at my right or my left, that's not mine to grant, but belongs to those for whom it has been reserved."

41 ***When they learned*** of it, the ten got annoyed with James and John. 42 So, calling them aside, Jesus says to them: "You know how those who supposedly rule over foreigners lord it over them, and how their strong men tyrannize them. 43 It's not going to be like that with you! With you, whoever wants to become great must be your servant, 44 and whoever among you wants to be 'number one' must be everybody's slave. 45 After all, the son of Adam didn't come to be served, but to serve, even to give his life as a ransom for many."

46 ***Then they come to Jericho.*** As he was leaving Jericho with his

---

10:34, 35 Between these verses Secret Mark continues: "And they come to Bethany, and a woman was there whose brother had died. She knelt down in front of Jesus and says to him, 'Son of David, have mercy on me.' But the disciples rebuked her.

"Jesus got angry and went with her into the garden where the tomb was. Just then a loud voice was heard from inside the tomb. Then Jesus went up and rolled the stone away from the entrance to the tomb. He went right in where the young man was, stuck out his hand, grabbed him by the hand, and raised him up. The young man looked at Jesus, loved him, and began to beg him to be with him. Then they left the tomb and went into the young man's house (incidentally, he was rich).

"Six days later Jesus gave him an order; and when evening had come, the young man went to him, dressed only in a linen cloth. He spent that night with him, because Jesus taught him the mystery of God's domain. From there ⟨Jesus⟩ got up and returned to the other side of the Jordan."

10:46 After *they come to Jericho* Secret Mark continues: "The sister of the young man whom Jesus loved was there, along with his mother and Salome, but Jesus refused to see them."

10:35–40 //Mt 20:20–23
10:41–45 //Mt 20:24–28, Lk 22:24–26; cf. Mt 23:11, Jn 13:1–20; Ⓣ Mk 9:35
10:46–52 //Mt 20:29–34, Lk 18:35–43

10:35–45 Jesus responds to James and John's request for preferential treatment with a promise of suffering and death, expressed in the church's sacramental language of *cup* and *baptism.* For the first time (v. 45) Jesus' own approaching death is explained in terms of its benefit for others: *as a ransom for many.*

10:46–52 Jesus' journey is framed with two healings of blind men, here and in 8:22–26. In this case the cured man is named *Bartimaeus* (with the Aramaic words being translated for Mark's readers). Instead of being sent home silent, this time the cured man follows Jesus on his way.

Bartimaeus shouts out that Jesus is *son of David*, a messianic title from which Jesus

disciples and a sizable crowd, Bartimaeus, a blind beggar, the son of Timaeus, was sitting alongside the road. 47When he learned that it was Jesus the Nazarene, he began to shout: "You son of David, Jesus, have mercy on me!"

48And many kept yelling at him to shut up, but he shouted all the louder, "You son of David, have mercy on me!"

49Jesus paused and said, "Tell him to come over here!"

They called to the blind man, "Be brave, get up, he's calling you!" 50So he threw off his cloak, and jumped to his feet, and went over to Jesus.

51In response Jesus said, "What do you want me to do for you?"

The blind man said to him, "Rabbi, I want to see again!"

52And Jesus said to him, "Be on your way, your trust has cured you." And right away he regained his sight, and he started following him on the road.

Jesus enters Jerusalem

11 ***When they get close*** to Jerusalem, near Bethphage and Bethany at the Mount of Olives, he sends off two of his disciples 2with these instructions: "Go into the village across the way, and right after you enter it, you'll find a colt tied up, one that has never been ridden. Untie it and bring it here. 3If anyone questions you, 'Why are you doing this?' tell them, 'Its master has need of it and he will send it back here right away.'"

4They set out and found a colt tied up at the door out on the street, and they untie it. 5Some of the people standing around started saying to them, "What do you think you're doing, untying that colt?" 6But they said just what Jesus had told them to say, so they left them alone.

7So they bring the colt to Jesus, and they throw their cloaks over it; then he got on it. 8And many people spread their cloaks on the road, while others cut leafy branches from the fields. 9Those leading the way and those following kept shouting,

11:1–10 //Mt21:1–9, Lk19:28–38; ◊Zec9:9

11:9–10 ◊Ps118:25–26

---

seems to distance himself in 12:34–37.

Jesus' odd entry and immediate exit from Jericho are supplemented in the shorter fragment from Secret Mark: "The sister of the young man whom Jesus loved was there, along with his mother and Salome, but Jesus refused to see them."

11:1–10 Entry into the great city is made with careful planning, with a scouting mission and even a staged reception. Within Mark's story world, this is Jesus' first visit to Jerusalem.

11:3–6 The mysterious instructions about the colt, and their immediate fulfillment in the narrative, increase the disciples' (and reader's) confidence about Jesus' mastery of the situation.

In Mark's Greek there is double entendre in the explanation that *its master (= the Lord) has need of the colt*—we know that the cultic title is meant.

11:8–9 The disciples shout words from Ps 118:25–26: *Hosanna* is a Greek transliteration of Hebrew words meaning "Save, we pray!" Waving of branches (called palm fronds only in John 12:13) is known in the ancient Feast of Tabernacles, but this was an autumn event.

Exactly how many people are involved in the entry scene is left rather vague – perhaps it is only Jesus' group that have stage managed the event. (Luke, Matthew, and especially John get larger crowds of bystanders involved.)

Fig tree without figs

Temple as hideout

Mountains into the sea

"Hosanna! Blessed is the one
who comes in the name of the Lord!"
[10]Blessed is the coming kingdom of our father David!
"Hosanna" in the highest!

[11]***And he went into Jerusalem*** to the temple area and took stock of everything, but, since the hour was already late, he returned to Bethany with the twelve.

[12]On the next day, as they were leaving Bethany, he got hungry. [13]So when he spotted a fig tree in the distance with some leaves on it, he went up to it expecting to find something on it. But when he got right up to it, he found nothing on it except some leaves. (You see, it wasn't 'time' for figs.) [14]And he reacted by saying: "May no one so much as taste your fruit again!" And his disciples were listening.

[15]***They come to Jerusalem.*** And he went into the temple and began chasing the vendors and shoppers out of the temple area, and he turned the bankers' tables upside down, along with the chairs of the pigeon merchants, [16]and he wouldn't even let anyone carry a container through the temple area. [17]Then he started teaching and would say to them: "Don't the scriptures say, 'My house is to be regarded as a house of prayer for all peoples'?—but you have turned it into 'a hideout for crooks'!"

[18]And the ranking priests and the scholars heard this and kept looking for a way to get rid of him. (The truth is that they stood in fear of him, and that the whole crowd was astonished at his teaching.) [19]And when it grew dark, they made their way out of the city.

[20]***As they were walking along*** early one morning, they saw the fig tree withered from the roots up. [21]And Peter remembered and says to him: "Rabbi, look, the fig tree you cursed has withered up!"

[22]In response Jesus says to them: "Have trust in God. [23]I swear to you, those who say to this mountain, 'Up with you and into the sea!' and do not waver in their conviction, but trust that what they say will happen, that's the way it will be. [24]This is why I keep telling you, trust that you will receive everything you pray and ask for, and that's the way it will turn out. [25]And when you stand up to pray, if you are holding anything against anyone, forgive them, so your Father in heaven may forgive your misdeeds."

11:11 //Mt21:10, 17
11:12–14 //Mt21:18–19
11:15–17 //Mt21:12–13, Lk19:45–46; cf. Jn2:14–16
11:17 ◊Is56:7, Jer7:11
11:18–19 //Lk19:47–48
11:20–25 //Mt21:20–22
11:23 Cf. Th48, 106
11:24 Cf. Q11:9–10; Mt7:7–8, 21:22; Lk11:9–10; Jn14:13–14; 15:7, 16; 16:23
11:25 Cf. Q6:37, Mt6:14–15, Lk6:37c

11:25 Many mss include a v. 26: "But if you do not forgive, neither will your father in heaven forgive your misdeeds."

11:11 Jesus himself now scouts out the territory around the temple, but rather than spend the night in the city, he slips back out of town after dark with his inner circle back to the neighboring village of *Bethany*. They will not spend the night in Jerusalem until Jesus' betrayal and arrest in Gethsemane.

11:13–25 Jesus creates havoc in the temple precincts. The critique of sales practices is both effective and provocative.

The story is framed by Jesus' curse of the unfortunate *fig tree*. The disciples and readers see a demonstration of Jesus' power and predictive abilities. The fig tree episode then becomes a memorable example for Jesus' instructions about confident prayer technique,

On whose authority?

Leased vineyard

27***Once again*** they come to Jerusalem. As he walks around in the
temple area, the ranking priests and scholars and elders come up to
him 28and start questioning him: "By what right are you doing these
things?" or, "Who gave you the authority to do these things?"
29But Jesus said to them: "I have one question for you. If you answer
me, then I will tell you by what authority I do these things. 30Tell me,
was the baptism of John heaven-sent or was it of human origin? Answer
me that."
31And they conferred among themselves, saying, "If we say 'heaven-
sent,' he'll say, 'Then why didn't you trust him?' 32But if we say 'Of
human origin . . . !'" They were afraid of the crowd. (You see, everybody considered John a genuine prophet.) 33So they answered Jesus by
saying, "We can't tell."

And Jesus says to them: "I'm not going to tell you by what authority I do these things either!"

12 ***And he began to speak*** to them in parables:

Someone planted a vineyard, put a hedge around it, dug a winepress,
built a tower, leased it out to some farmers, and went abroad. 2In due
time he sent a slave to the farmers to collect his share of the
vineyard's crop from them. 3But they grabbed him, beat him, and
sent him away empty-handed. 4So once again he sent another slave
to them, but they attacked him and abused him. 5Then he sent
another, and this one they killed; many others followed, some of
whom they beat, others of whom they killed.
6He still had one more, a son who was the apple of his eye. This
one he finally sent to them, with the thought, "They will show this
son of mine some respect."
7But those farmers said to one another, "This fellow's the heir!
Come on, let's kill him and the inheritance will be ours!" 8So they
grabbed him, and killed him, and threw him outside the vineyard.
9What will the owner of the vineyard do? He will come in person,
and do away with those farmers, and give the vineyard to someone
else.
10Haven't you read this scripture, "A stone that the builders
rejected has ended up as the keystone. 11 It was the Lord's doing and
is something you admire"?

11:27–33 //Mt21:23–27, Lk20:1–8

12:1–11 //Mt21:33–43, Lk20:9–18, Th65–66; ◊Is5:1–2

12:10 ◊Ps118:22–23

---

and perhaps also, in view of Mark's "sandwiching" technique, a symbolic sign about the fate of the temple.

11:27–33 Jesus returns to the city for a day of deadly serious banter and confrontation with religious authority figures. First Jesus silences his antagonists with a clever trick question, again linking his work with that of John. Verse 30 is a good example of the typical Jewish reticence in making direct mention of God: Jesus is asking: Did John's baptism have divine warrant?

12:1–12 Jesus addresses his symbolic story to his opponents. The imagery is taken from the picture of God's *vineyard* in Isaiah 5. The story's meaning is crystal clear to Jesus' opponents: they are plotting to do away with God's *son* (v. 6).

The emperor & God

Wife of seven brothers

12⟨His opponents⟩ kept looking for some opportunity to seize him, but they were still afraid of the crowd, since they realized that he had aimed the parable at them. So they left him there and went on their way.

13***And they send some*** of the Pharisees and the Herodians to him to trap him with a riddle. 14They come and say to him, "Teacher, we know that you are honest and impartial, because you pay no attention to appearances, but instead you teach God's way forthrightly. Is it permissible to pay the poll tax to the Roman emperor or not? Should we pay or should we not pay?"

15But he saw through their trap, and said to them, "Why do you provoke me like this? Let me have a look at a coin."

16They handed him a silver coin, and he says to them, "Whose picture is this? Whose name is on it?"

They replied, "The emperor's."

17Jesus said to them: "Pay the emperor what belongs to the emperor, and God what belongs to God!" And they were dumbfounded at him.

18***And some Sadducees***—those who maintain there is no resurrection—come up to him and they start questioning him. 19"Teacher," they said, "Moses wrote for our benefit, 'If someone's brother dies and leaves his widow childless, his brother is obligated to take the widow as his wife and produce offspring for his brother.' 20There were seven brothers; now the first took a wife but left no children when he died. 21So the second married her but died without leaving offspring, and the third likewise. 22In fact, all seven ⟨married her but⟩ left no offspring. Finally, the wife died too. 23In the resurrection, after they rise, whose wife will she be?" (Remember, all seven had her as wife.)

24Jesus said to them: "You've missed the point again, haven't you, all because you underestimate both the scriptures and the power of God. 25After all, when men and women rise from the dead, they do not marry, but resemble heaven's messengers. 26As for whether or not the dead are raised, haven't you read in the book of Moses in the passage about the bush, how God spoke to him: 'I am the God of Abraham and the God of Isaac and the God of Jacob'? 27This is not the God of the dead, only of the living—you're constantly missing the point!"

12:12 //Mt 21:45–46, Lk 20:19
12:13–17 //Mt 22:15–22, Lk 20:20–26, Th 100, EgerG 3:1–6
12:18–27 //Mt 22:23–32, Lk 20:27–38
12:19 ◊Gn 38:8, Dt 25:5–6
12:26 ◊Ex 3:6

12:13–17 Again Jesus outsmarts those setting out to trap him. Jesus *dumbfounds* them when he avoids sounding like a dangerous revolutionary, by not refusing to pay taxes to the Romans, but also avoids looking like a collaborator, when he points out the coin (which Mark calls by its Latin name, *denarius*), comes from the Roman emperor anyway.
12:18–27 The *Sadducees* argued against the Pharisees (and the Jesus movement) that there was no scriptural basis for belief in the *resurrection* of the dead. Their question to Jesus is the sort of logical dilemma they thought should confound those who held this "modern" or "unbiblical" belief. Jesus disposes of their exaggerated problem with sarcasm (*You've missed the point again!*), explanation of the angelic status of the resurrected, and an ingenious prooftext from the Torah: When God mentions the long-dead *Abraham, Isaac, and Jacob*, he must mean people who in some sense are still alive.
12:28–34 Jesus answers the scholar by reciting *Hear, Israel*, the *Shema*, the central con-

The greatest commandment | *David's lord & son* | *Scholars' privileges* | *Widow's pittance*

28 ***And one of the scholars*** approached when he heard them arguing, and because he saw how skillfully Jesus answered them, he asked him, "Of all the commandments, which is the most important?"

29 Jesus answered: "The first is,'Hear, Israel, the Lord your God is one Lord, 30 and you are to love the Lord your God with all your heart and all your soul and all your mind and with all your energy.' 31 The second is this: 'You are to love your neighbor as yourself.' There is no other commandment greater than these."

32 And the scholar said to him, "That's a fine answer, Teacher. You have correctly said that God is one and there is no other beside him. 33 And 'to love him with all one's heart and with all one's mind and with all one's energy' and 'to love one's neighbor as oneself' is greater than all the burnt offerings and sacrifices put together."

34 And when Jesus saw that he answered him sensibly, he said to him, "You are not far from God's domain."

And from then on no one dared question him.

35 ***And during the time*** Jesus was teaching in the temple area, he would pose this question: "How can the scholars claim that the Anointed is the son of David? 36 David himself said under the influence of the holy spirit, 'The Lord said to my lord, "Sit here at my right, until I make your enemies grovel at your feet."' 37 David himself calls him 'lord,' so how can he be his son?"

And a huge crowd would listen to him with delight.

38 ***During the course*** of his teaching he would say: "Look out for the scholars who like to parade around in long robes, and insist on being addressed properly in the marketplaces, 39 and prefer important seats in the synagogues and the best couches at banquets. 40 They are the ones who prey on widows and their families, and recite long prayers just to put on airs. These people will get a stiff sentence!"

41 ***And he would sit*** across from the treasury and observe the crowd dropping money into the collection box. And many wealthy people would drop large amounts in. 42 Then one poor widow came and put in two small coins, which is a pittance. 43 And he motioned his disciples over and said to them: "I swear to you, this poor widow has contributed more than all those who dropped something into the collection box! 44 After all, they were all donating out of their surplus, whereas she, out of her poverty, was contributing all she had, her entire livelihood!"

12:28–34 //Mt22:34–40, 46; Lk10:25–28, 20:39–40; ◊Dt6:4–5, Lv19:18, 1Sm15:22
12:35–37 //Mt22:41–46, Lk20:41–44; ◊Ps110:1
12:38–40 //Mt23:6, Lk20:45–47
12:41–44 //Lk21:1–4

---

fession and self-definition of Israelite belief. Pious Jews would often wear amulets containing these and similar phrases deriving from the opening words of the Decalogue.

12:35–37 With the crowds now properly impressed, Jesus poses his own riddle. He quotes the opening lines of Psalm 110, used in the coronation rituals of ancient Israelite and Judean kings. The (anointed) king referred to is taken by Jesus to mean the Messiah (the Hebrew word meaning "anointed"). This little story suggests that Mark does not agree with the tradition that Jesus was a *son of David* (a descendant of David's line), since otherwise Jesus' words mean that he is denying his own legitimacy to be considered God's Anointed.

Monumental buildings destroyed

Signs of final agonies

Days of distress

13 ***And as he was going out*** of the temple area, one of his disciples
remarks to him, "Teacher, look, what magnificent masonry! What
wonderful buildings!"
2And Jesus replied to him, "Take a good look at these monumental
buildings! You may be sure not one stone will be left on top of another!
Every last one will certainly be knocked down!"
3***And as he was sitting*** on the Mount of Olives across from the
temple, Peter would ask him privately, as would James and John and
Andrew: 4"Tell us, when are these things going to happen, and what
will be the sign to indicate when all these things are about to take
place?"
5And Jesus would say to them, "Stay alert, otherwise someone might
just delude you! 6You know, many will come using my name and
claim, 'I'm the one!' and they will delude many people. 7When you
hear of wars and rumors of wars, don't be afraid. These are inevitable,
but it is not yet the end. 8For nation will rise up against nation and
empire against empire; there will be earthquakes everywhere; there
will be famines. These things mark the beginning of the final agonies.
9"But you look out for yourselves! They will turn you over to
councils, and beat you in synagogues, and haul you up before governors and kings, on my account, so you can make your case to them.
10Yet the good news must first be announced to all peoples. 11And
when they arrest you to lock you up, don't be worried about what you
should say. Instead, whatever occurs to you at the moment, say that.
For it is not you who are speaking but the holy spirit. 12And one brother
will turn in another to be put to death, and a father his child, and
children will turn against their parents and kill them. 13And you will be
universally hated because of me. Those who hold out to the end will be
saved!
14"***When you see*** the 'devastating desecration' standing where it
should not (the reader had better figure out what this means), then the

13:1–2 //Mt 24:1–2, Lk 21:5–6

13:3–8 //Mt 24:3–8, Lk 21:7–11

13:5 //Mary 4:3

13:9–13 //Mt 24:9, 10:17–22; Lk 21:12–17

13:14–20 //Mt 24:15–22, Lk 21:20–24; cf. Lk 17:31

13:14 ◊Dn 9:27, 11:31, 12:11; 1 Mc 1:54

13:1–2 Jesus gives an apocalyptic edge to his followers' admiration of the temple area, which had been greatly enlarged and adorned by Herod the Great. Many of his subjects resented paying the heavy taxes that Herod exacted for this and other large-scale building projects.

13:3–37 In another private scene, this time set on a ridge facing the temple mount across the Kidron valley, Jesus' inner circle asks him to explain his outburst about the temple's impending destruction. In response, Jesus delivers his second long speech in Mark's story, this time addressing the turbulent experiences to come.

In good apocalyptic style, Jesus' predictions are in effect a resumé of the group's recent history. Picking their way through the confusion and disorder to come will be a dangerous task.

13:14 Here is the most obvious instance of Mark breaking through his narrative conventions to speak directly to the reader—even though in the story Jesus is apparently still speaking to his inner group. (See also 7:3–4.)

The *devastating desecration* alludes to the apocalyptic Book of Daniel (Dan 9:27; 11:31; 12:11), where attempts by Hellenistic rulers to convert the Jerusalem temple into a shrine of Zeus in the early second century B.C.E. were interpreted as a sign of the near approach of the end (1 Macc 1:54). Mark's readers are meant to connect this "prophecy" with a desecration or the threat of one sometime closer to their own day, perhaps the emperor Caligula's attempt to place his own

Son of Adam comes on clouds

No one knows the day or minute

people in Judea should head for the hills; [15]no one on the roof should
go downstairs; no one should enter the house to retrieve anything;
[16]and no one in the field should turn back to get a coat. [17]It'll be too bad
for pregnant women and nursing mothers in those days! [18]Pray that
none of this happens in winter! [19]For those days will see distress the
likes of which has not occurred since God created the world until now,
and will never occur again. [20]And if the Lord had not cut short the
days, no human being would have survived! But he did shorten the
days for the sake of the chosen people whom he selected. [21]And then if
someone says to you, 'Look, here is the Anointed,' or 'Look, there he
is!' don't count on it! [22]After all, counterfeit messiahs and phony
prophets will show up, and they will provide portents and miracles so
as to delude, if possible, even the chosen people. [23]But you be on your
guard! Notice how I always warn you about these things in advance.
[24]"***But in those days,*** after that tribulation,

the sun will be darkened,
and the moon will not give off her glow,
[25]and the stars will fall from the sky,
and the heavenly forces will be shaken!

[26]And then they will see the son of Adam coming on the clouds with
great power and splendor. [27]And then he will send out messengers and
will gather the chosen people from the four winds, from the ends of the
earth to the edge of the sky!
[28]"Take a cue from the fig tree. When its branch is already in bud
and leaves come out, you know that summer is near. [29]So, when you
see these things take place, you ought to realize that he is near, just
outside your door. [30]I swear to you, this generation certainly won't pass
into oblivion before all these things take place! [31]The earth will pass
into oblivion and so will the sky, but my words will never be obliterated!
[32]"***As for that exact day*** or minute: no one knows, not even heaven's
messengers, nor even the son, no one, except the Father.
[33]"Be on guard! Stay alert! For you never know what time it is. [34]It's
like a person who takes a trip and puts slaves in charge, each with a
task, and enjoins the doorkeeper to be alert. [35]Therefore, stay alert! For
you never know when the landlord returns, maybe at dusk, or at
midnight, or when the rooster crows, or maybe early in the morning.

13:21–23 //Mt24:23–25, Th113; ◊Dt13:2–4
13:21 //Mary4:4
13:24 ◊Is13:10, 34:4
13:24–27 //Mt24:29–31, Lk21:25–28, Rev1:7
13:26 ◊Dn7:13–14, 4Ezr13:1–3
13:28–32 //Mt24:32–36, Lk21:29–33
13:33–37 //Mt24:42; cf.Mt25:13–15, Lk19:12–13

---

statue in the temple (in 40/41 C.E.), or perhaps the disturbances surrounding the great revolt against the Romans in 66–70.

13:21–23 The warning about *counterfeit messiahs* and *phony prophets* evokes Moses' warnings in Deut 13:2–4, but probably also describes the confusion of Mark's own day.

13:24–32 The heavenly disturbances that usher in the arrival of *the son of Adam on the clouds* resonate with the imagery of cosmic catastrophe found in biblical prophecy and apocalyptic (compare, e.g., Isa 13:10; 34:4; Dan 7:13–14; also 2 Esdras 13:1–3).

13:33–37 Jesus ends his apocalyptic speech with a brief similitude about the return of one's *landlord* or master at an unexpected time. At the end Jesus turns once again from his inner group to address Mark's readers directly: *What I'm telling you, I say to everyone: Stay alert!*

Woman anoints Jesus

Priests promise to pay

Jesus celebrates Passover

36He may return suddenly and find you asleep. 37What I'm telling you,
I say to everyone: Stay alert!"

14 ***Now it was two days*** until Passover and the feast of Unleavened
Bread. And the ranking priests and the scholars were looking for some
way to arrest him by trickery and kill him. 2For their slogan was: "Not
during the festival, otherwise the people will riot."

3When he was in Bethany at the house of Simon the leper, he was
just reclining there, and a woman came in carrying an alabaster jar of
myrrh, of pure and expensive nard. She broke the jar and poured ⟨the
myrrh⟩ on his head.

4Now some were annoyed ⟨and thought⟩ to themselves: "What good
purpose is served by this waste of myrrh? 5For she could have sold the
myrrh for more than three hundred silver coins and given ⟨the money⟩
to the poor." And they were angry with her.

6Then Jesus said, "Let her alone! Why are you bothering her? She
has done me a courtesy. 7Remember, there will always be poor around,
and whenever you want you can do good for them, but I won't always
be around. 8She did what she could—she anticipates in anointing my
body for burial. 9So help me, wherever the good news is announced in
all the world, what she has done will also be told in memory of her!"

10***And Judas Iscariot,*** one of the twelve, went off to the ranking
priests to turn him over to them. 11When they heard, they were
delighted, and promised to pay him in silver. And he started looking
for some way to turn him in at the right moment.

12***On the first day*** of Unleavened Bread, when they would sacrifice
the Passover lamb, his disciples say to him, "Where do you want us to
go and get things ready for you to celebrate Passover?"

13He sends two of his disciples and says to them, "Go into the city,
and someone carrying a waterpot will meet you. Follow him, 14and
whatever place he enters say to the head of the house, 'The teacher
asks, "Where is my guest room where I can celebrate Passover with my
disciples?"' 15And he'll show you a large upstairs room that has been
arranged. That's the place you're to get ready for us."

14:1–2
//Mt26:2–5, Lk22:1–2; cf.Jn11:55–57
14:3–9
//Mt26:6–13; cf.Lk7:36–50, Jn12:1–8
14:10–11
//Mt26:17–19, Lk22:3–6
14:12–16
//Mt26:17–19, Lk22:7–13
14:12
//GEbi7:1

14:1–2 With the approach of the *Passover* festival the threat of violence to Jesus becomes even stronger. Major feast days attracted huge crowds of pilgrims to the holy city. Mark's crowds again play a shifting role, here shielding Jesus from the malevolent intentions of the city aristocracy, perhaps unwittingly; soon their mood will turn ugly (15:8).

14:3–9 Mark "sandwiches" a story about a private meal in Bethany into his larger theme about the Jewish leaders looking for a way to get rid of Jesus (resumed in vv. 10–11). Here an unnamed woman pours out a vessel of expensive ointment on Jesus' head. The disciples miss the point, which Jesus makes clear: the woman has signalled his impending death and burial.

It must be unintentional irony when Mark has Jesus predict that this story will always be *told in memory* of a woman whose very name escapes him.

14:10–11 As Judas Iscariot seeks a way to betray Jesus, Mark reminds us again that he was *one of the twelve* (see also 3:19; 14:20, 43).

14:12–16 The story of the Passover feast resumes as Jesus sends two disciples to make

Peter takes an oath

Jesus in Gethsemane

16 And the disciples left, went into the city, and found it exactly as he
had told them; and they got things ready for Passover.
17 When evening comes, he arrives with the twelve. 18 And as they
reclined at table and were eating, Jesus said, "So help me, one of you
eating with me is going to turn me in!"
19 They began to fret and to say to him one after another, "I'm not the
one, am I?"
20 But he said to them, "It's one of the twelve, the one who is dipping
into the bowl with me. 21 The son of Adam departs just as the scriptures
predict, but damn the one responsible for turning the son of Adam in!
It would be better for that man had he never been born!"
22 And as they were eating, he took a loaf, gave a blessing, broke it
into pieces and offered it to them. And he said, "Take some; this is my
body!" 23 He also took a cup, gave thanks and offered it to them, and
they all drank from it. 24 And he said to them: "This is my blood of the
covenant, which has been poured out for many! 25 So help me, I
certainly won't drink any of the fruit of the vine again until that day
when I drink it for the first time in God's domain!"
26 And they sang a hymn and left for the Mount of Olives.
27 ***And Jesus says to them,*** "You will all lose faith. Remember,
scripture says, 'I will strike the shepherd and the sheep will be
scattered!' 28 But after I'm raised I'll go ahead of you to Galilee."
29 Peter said to him, "Even if everyone else loses faith, I won't!"
30 And Jesus says to him, "So help me, tonight before the rooster
crows twice you will disown me three times!"
31 But he repeated it with more bluster: "If they condemn me to die
with you, I will never disown you!" And they took the same oath—all
of them.
32 ***And they go to a place*** the name of which was Gethsemane, and
he says to his disciples, "Sit down here while I pray."
33 And he takes Peter and James and John along with him, and he
grew apprehensive and full of anguish. 34 He says to them, "I'm so sad I
could die. You stay here and be alert!"

14:17–21 //Mt26:20–25; Lk22:14, 21–23; cf.Jn13:21–26
14:22–25 //Mt26:26–29, Lk22:15–20; cf.Jn6:48–58, 1Cor11:23–25
14:22 Cf.GHeb9:4
14:24 ◊Ex24:8, Jer31:31, Zec9:11
14:25 Cf.GHeb9:2
14:26–31 //Mt26:30–35; cf.Lk22:31–34, Jn13:36–38
14:27 ◊Zec13:7
14:28 ① Mk16:7
14:32–42 //Mt26:36–46, Lk22:39–46
14:34 Cf.Jn12:27; ◊Ps42:5–6, 11–12; 43:5

---

preparations for the only meal he will eat in Jerusalem. Jesus' detailed instructions are followed exactly; his control and foreknowledge give the readers confidence that Jesus is master of his destiny.

14:22–25 The scene narrating the passing of bread and wine is told simply, with little or no explanation of Jesus' surprising words. Presumably Mark's readers knew all about this last meal and what it signified from their own customary remembrances (cf. 1 Cor 11:23–26; Luke 22:19b).

14:24 The *blood of the covenant* alludes to biblical language of the propitiatory sacrificial cult (e.g., Exod 24:8), redirected by Israelite prophecy in a spiritual or moralizing fashion (Jer 31:31). The language is that of the church celebrating its sacrament: Jesus says his blood *has been poured out for many*, to seal a new redemptive covenant, though in Mark's story the death is still a day ahead.

14:28 Jesus predicts his resurrection and appearance *in Galilee*, something the reader is meant to remember when hearing the young man's words from the tomb in 16:7.

14:32–42 Mark gives us a rare glimpse of Jesus' inner thoughts when we overhear his prayer to his father while his closest followers sleep. The contrast between Jesus' resolve and the disciples' weakness is powerfully

Judas turns Jesus in

Trial before the Council

35And he would move on a little, fall on the ground, and pray that he
might avoid the crisis, if possible. 36And he would say, "*Abba* (Father),
all things are possible for you! Take this cup away from me! But it's not
what I want ⟨that matters⟩, but what you want."
37And he returns and finds them sleeping, and says to Peter, "Simon,
are you sleeping? Couldn't you stay awake for one hour? 38Be alert and
pray that you won't be put to the test! Though the spirit is willing, the
flesh is weak."
39And once again he went away and prayed, saying the same thing.
40And once again he came and found them sleeping, since their eyes
had grown very heavy, and they didn't know what to say to him.
41And he comes a third time and says to them, "You may as well
sleep on now and get your rest. It's all over! The time has come! Look,
the son of Adam is being turned over to foreigners. 42Get up, let's go!
See for yourselves! Here comes the one who is going to turn me in."
43***And right away,*** while he was still speaking, Judas, one of the
twelve, shows up, and with him a crowd, dispatched by the ranking
priests and the scholars and the elders, wielding swords and clubs.
44Now the one who was to turn him in had arranged a signal with
them, saying, "The one I'm going to kiss is the one you want. Arrest
him and escort him safely away!" 45And right away he arrives, comes
up to him, and says, "Rabbi," and kissed him.
46And they seized him and held him fast. 47One of those standing
around drew his sword and struck the high priest's slave and cut off his
ear. 48In response Jesus said to them, "Have you come out to take me
with swords and clubs as though you were apprehending a rebel? 49I
was with you in the temple area day after day teaching and you didn't
lift a hand against me. But the scriptures must come true!"
50And they all deserted him and ran away. 51And a young man was
following him, wearing a shroud over his nude body, and they grab
him. 52But he dropped the shroud and ran away naked.
53***And they brought Jesus*** before the high priest, and all the ranking
priests and elders and scholars assemble.
54Peter followed him at a distance until he was inside the courtyard
of the high priest, and was sitting with the attendants and keeping
warm by the fire.
55The ranking priests and the whole Council were looking for evi-

14:41 Ⓣ EgerG 1:9
14:43–50 //Mt 26:47–56; cf. Lk 22:47–53, Jn 18:2–12
14:51–52 Ⓣ SecMark
14:53–54 //Mt 26:57–58, Lk 22:54–55, Jn 18:13–15
14:55–65 //Mt 26:59–68; cf. Lk 22:67–71, 63–65; Jn 18:19–24

---

drawn.

14:51–52 The nameless *young man* who watches Jesus' arrest from afar has long puzzled interpreters. One suggestion is that for Mark the youth symbolizes all of Jesus' followers, both in Jesus' "then" and in Mark's "now," *running away* in terror from the prospect of Jesus' (and their) fate. A young man with a robe also appears in 16:5–7 and in the longer Secret Mark fragment.

14:53–72 The trial before the Jewish Council is artfully portrayed, with an especially poignant Marcan "sandwich" showing Peter skulking in the courtyard all the while (vv. 54, 66–72).

Mark tells a frightening story of official malevolence. It is difficult to reconcile much of Mark's picture with known Jewish judicial procedures: a secret court session, at night, with trumped-up and contradictory evidence. Jesus' initial refusal to speak is no defense. Finally Jesus' avowal of his messiahship

dence against Jesus in order to issue a death sentence, but they couldn't find any. 56Although many gave false evidence against him, their stories didn't agree. 57And some people stood up and testified falsely against him: 58"We have heard him saying, 'I'll destroy this temple made with hands and in three days I'll build another, not made with hands!'" 59Yet even then their stories did not agree.

A rooster crows

60And the high priest got up and questioned Jesus: "Don't you have some answer to give? Why do these people testify against you?"

61But he was silent and refused to answer.

Once again the high priest questioned him and says to him, "Are you the Anointed, the son of the Blessed One?"

62Jesus replied, "I am! And you will see the son of Adam sitting at the right hand of Power and coming with the clouds of the sky!"

63Then the high priest tore his vestments and says, "Why do we still need witnesses? 64You have heard the blasphemy! What do you think?" And they all concurred in the death penalty.

65And some began to spit on him, and to put a blindfold on him, and punch him, and say to him, "Prophesy!" And the guards abused him as they took him into custody.

66***And while Peter was below*** in the courtyard, one of the high priest's slave women comes over, 67and sees Peter warming himself; she looks at him closely, then speaks up: "You too were with that Nazarene, Jesus!"

68But he denied it, saying, "I haven't the slightest idea what you're talking about!" And he went outside into the forecourt.

69And when the slave woman saw him, she once again began to say to those standing nearby, "This fellow is one of them!"

70But once again he denied it.

And a little later, those standing nearby would again say to Peter, "You really are one of them, since you also are a Galilean!"

71But he began to curse and swear, "I don't know the fellow you're talking about!" 72And just then a rooster crowed a second time, and Peter remembered what Jesus had told him: "Before a rooster crows twice you will disown me three times!" And he broke down and started to cry.

Trial before Pilate

15 ***And right away,*** at daybreak, the ranking priests, after consulting with the elders and scholars and the whole Council, bound Jesus and led him away and turned him over to Pilate. 2And Pilate questioned him: "*You* are 'the King of the Judeans'?"

14:58
Cf. Th 71, Jn 2:19

14:62
Ⓣ Mk 13:26;
▷ Dn 7:13,
4 Ezr 13:1–3

14:63–64
▷ Lv 24:16

14:65
Cf. Pet 3:4

14:66–72
// Mt 26:69–75;
Lk 22:56–62;
Jn 18:17, 25–27

15:1
// Mt 27:1–2,
Lk 22:66–23:1;
cf. Jn 18:28

(14:62) provokes the desired verdict.

15:1–15 The portrayal of Jesus' trial before *Pilate* is more in keeping with what we know of ancient judicial procedure than his nighttime Council appearance, though the supposed custom of freeing a dangerous criminal at the festival (v. 6) is unknown outside the gospels and would in fact be highly unlikely in such a volatile situation.

Roman governors had enormous discretion in matters of public order. Their power is difficult to reconcile with Mark's portrait of Pilate as a helpless tool of the Jewish leaders, submissive to the demands of a bloodthirsty

Soldiers make fun of Jesus

Soldiers crucify Jesus

And in response he says to him, "If you say so."
[3]And the ranking priests started a long list of accusations against
him. [4]Again Pilate tried questioning him: "Don't you have some
answer to give? You see what a long list of charges they bring against
you!"
[5]But Jesus still did not respond, so Pilate was baffled.
[6]At each festival it was the custom for him to set one prisoner free for
them, whichever one they requested. [7]And one called Barabbas was
being held with the insurgents who had committed murder during the
uprising. [8]And when the crowd arrived, they began to demand that he
do what he usually did for them.
[9]And in response Pilate said to them, "Do you want me to set 'the
King of the Judeans' free for you?" [10]After all, he realized that the
ranking priests had turned him over out of envy.
[11]But the ranking priests incited the crowd to get Barabbas set free
for them instead.
[12]But in response ⟨to their request⟩ Pilate would again say to them,
"What do you want me to do with the fellow you call 'the King of the
Judeans'?"
[13]And they in turn shouted, "Crucify him!"
[14]Pilate kept saying to them, "Why? What has he done wrong?"
But they shouted all the louder, "Crucify him!" [15]And because
Pilate was always looking to satisfy the crowd, he set Barabbas free for
them, had Jesus flogged, and then turned him over to be crucified.
[16]***And the soldiers led him away*** to the courtyard of the governor's
residence, and they called the whole company together. [17]And they
dressed him in purple and crowned him with a garland woven of
thorns. [18]And they began to salute him: "Greetings, 'King of the
Judeans'!" [19]And they kept striking him on the head with a staff, and
spitting on him; and they would get down on their knees and bow down
to him. [20]And when they had made fun of him, they stripped off the
purple and put his own clothes back on him. And they lead him out to
crucify him.
[21]***And they conscript someone*** named Simon of Cyrene, who was
coming in from the country, the father of Alexander and Rufus, to
carry his cross.
[22]And they bring him to the place Golgotha (which means "Place of

15:2–5
//Mt27:11–14, Lk23:3; cf. Jn18:33–37
15:6–14
//Mt27:15–23, Lk23:17–23, Jn18:39–40
15:7
Cf. GNaz9
15:15
//Mt27:26, Lk23:24–25; cf. Jn19:16a
15:16–20a
//Mt27:27–31a, Jn19:2–3; cf. Pet2:3b–3:4
15:20b–21
//Mt27:31b–32, Lk23:26; cf. Jn19:16b–17a
15:22–26
//Mt27:33–37; Lk23:33–34; Jn19:17b–19, 24; Pet4:1–2

---

mob. Nonetheless a Roman magistrate would not shrink from using summary punishment to preserve order in such an uncertain situation.

15:16–39 Jesus' maltreatment and execution by the soldiers highlight the ironies in describing the death of a submissive and suffering *king*. The Roman legionnaires have unwittingly furthered God's secret purposes by dressing Jesus up as a king (vv. 17–20) and labelling his cross with his royal title (v. 26).

15:21 Mentioning *Simon of Cyrene* by name is unusual, since bystanders and bit players usually remain anonymous in Mark's story (cf. also Jairus in 5:22; Bartimaeus in 10:46; Joseph of Arimathea in 15:42).

15:22–32 The scene of Jesus' crucifixion is studded with scriptural allusions and quotations, chiefly from the Psalms (see the cross references).

the Skull"). 23And they tried to give him wine mixed with myrrh, but he didn't take it. 24And they crucify him, and they divide up his garments, casting lots to see who would get what. 25It was 9 o'clock in the morning when they crucified him. 26And the inscription, which identified his crime, read, 'The King of the Judeans.' 27And with him they crucify two rebels, one on his right and one on his left. [28]

29Those passing by kept taunting him, wagging their heads, and saying, "Ha! You who would destroy the temple and rebuild it in three days, 30save yourself and come down from the cross!"

31Likewise the ranking priests had made fun of him to one another, along with the scholars; they would say, "He saved others, but he can't save himself! 32'The Anointed,' 'the King of Israel,' should come down from the cross here and now, so that we can see and trust for ourselves!"

Even those being crucified along with him would abuse him.

Jesus breathes his last

33***And when noon came,*** darkness blanketed the whole land until mid-afternoon. 34And at 3 o'clock in the afternoon Jesus shouted at the top of his voice, "*Eloi, Eloi, lema sabachthani*" (which means "My God, my God, why did you abandon me?").

35And when some of those standing nearby heard, they would say, "Listen, he's calling Elijah!" 36And someone ran and filled a sponge with sour wine, stuck it on a pole, and offered him a drink, saying, "Let's see if Elijah comes to rescue him!"

37But Jesus let out a great shout and breathed his last.

38And the curtain of the temple was torn in two from top to bottom! 39When the Roman officer standing opposite him saw that he had died like this, he said, "This man really was God's son!"

40Now some women were observing this from a distance, among whom were Mary of Magdala, and Mary the mother of James the younger and Joses, and Salome. 41⟨These women⟩ had regularly followed and assisted him when he was in Galilee, along with many other women who had come up to Jerusalem in his company.

Joseph buries Jesus

42***And when it had already grown dark,*** since it was preparation day (the day before the sabbath), 43Joseph of Arimathea, a respected

15:23 ◊Ps69:22
15:24 ◊Ps22:18
15:27–32a //Mt27:38–42; Lk23:33b, 35, 17
15:27 //Pet4:1
15:29 ◊Ps22:8
15:32b //Mt27:44; cf.Lk23:39–43, Pet4:4
15:33–39 //Mt27:45–54, Lk23:44–48, Jn19:28–30; cf.Pet5:1–6
15:33 ◊Am8:9
15:34 ◊Ps22:2
15:36 ◊Ps69:22
15:38 Cf.GNaz10a
15:40–41 //Mt27:55–56, Lk23:49; cf.Jn19.25b–27, ◊Ps37:12

15:39 Mark's theme of Jesus' hidden identity reaches its ironic climax when the *Roman officer* offers as Jesus' epitaph a remark that was presumably meant as sarcasm, not an indication of a sudden change of heart: *This man really was God's son.* We readers are privileged to realize that those soldiers knew even more than they thought they did.

15:40–41 The sudden and unprepared mention of these three women, *Mary of Magdala, Mary the mother of James and Joses, and Salome*, who Mark now tells us *had regularly followed and assisted* Jesus during his public work in Galilee, is an extreme example of the narrator's tendency to withhold apparently important information until we are far into a story (on this see the Introduction to Mark).

15:42–47 In this scene about Joseph and Pilate, Mark skillfully establishes that Jesus really died and that the women really knew where he was buried. Jesus' quick death and burial provide a motivation for the women to visit Jesus' tomb as soon as would be proper. All these points could otherwise be questioned by those doubting reports of Jesus' resurrection.

Joseph of Arimathea has not previously been mentioned and his care and concern here are quite unexpected. Affluent families would purchase *tombs hewn out of rock* large

Three women at the tomb

council member, who himself was anticipating God's imperial rule,
appeared on the scene, and dared to go to Pilate to request the body of
Jesus. [44]And Pilate was surprised that he had died so soon. He summoned the Roman officer and asked him whether he had been dead for
long. [45]And when he had been briefed by the Roman officer, he
granted the body to Joseph. [46]And he bought a shroud and took him
down and wrapped him in the shroud, and placed him in a tomb that
had been hewn out of rock, and rolled a stone up against the opening of
the tomb. [47]And Mary of Magdala and Mary the mother of Joses noted
where he had been laid to rest.

16 ***And when the sabbath day*** was over, Mary of Magdala and Mary
the mother of James and Salome bought spices so they could go and
embalm him. [2]And very early on Sunday they got to the tomb just as
the sun was coming up. [3]And they had been asking themselves, "Who
will help us roll the stone away from the opening of the tomb?" [4]Then
they look up and discover that the stone has been rolled away! (For in
fact the stone was very large.)

[5]And when they went into the tomb, they saw a young man sitting
on the right, wearing a white robe, and they grew apprehensive.

[6]He says to them, "Don't be alarmed! You are looking for Jesus the
Nazarene who was crucified. He was raised, he is not here! Look at the
spot where they put him! [7]But go and tell his disciples, including
'Rock,' 'He is going ahead of you to Galilee! There you will see him,
just as he told you.'"

[8]And once they got outside, they ran away from the tomb, because
great fear and excitement got the better of them. And they didn't
breathe a word of it to anyone: talk about terrified . . .

15:42–47
//Mt 27:57–61,
Lk 23:50–55,
Jn 19:38–42;
cf. Pet 2:1–3a,
6:1–4;
◊ Dt 21:22–23,
Jos 10:26–27
16:1–8
Cf. Mt 28:1–8,
Lk 24:1–9,
Pet 12:1–13:3,
Jn 20:1–10
16:7
Ⓘ Mk 14:28

16:8 The best ancient mss conclude the Gospel of Mark with this verse. Other mss supply lengthier narrative endings. See "The endings of the Gospel of Mark," pp. 453–55.

---

enough for the eventual burial of several generations. Is Joseph in effect bringing Jesus into his family? Jesus' own relatives seem to be far out of the picture.

16:1–8 When the women so recently introduced (15:40, 47) approach Jesus' tomb, their worry as to *who will roll away the stone* is unexplained until Mark adds, again a bit late, that *the stone was very large* (v. 4).

The women's fright does not necessarily remain the readers' final thought: *the young man* in the dazzling clothes, while terrifying the women into silence, confirms the readers' expectations, based on Jesus' frequent predictions of his fate (esp. 10:33–34; 14:28).

The mystery of the double tradition

In addition to the verbal agreements Matthew and Luke share with Mark, they also have striking verbal agreements in passages where Mark offers nothing comparable. There are about 200 verses that fall into this category. Virtually all of the material in the double tradition, as it is known, consists of sayings or parables. Verbal agreement is sometimes very high; at other times it is difficult to determine whether Matthew and Luke are copying from a common source because the agreement is so minimal.

The material Matthew and Luke take from this hypothetical common source is not arranged in their own gospels in the same way. It appears that Matthew and Luke have inserted material from the sayings source into the outline they have borrowed from Mark, but they have distributed that sayings material in very different ways.

A sample of the double tradition is laid out in matching lines below. In this segment, Matt 3:7–10//Luke 3:7–9, verbal agreement is 99%: only in the choice of one verb and whether or not one noun is singular or plural do they differ, except for the transitional remarks in v. 7 in both gospels.

The German scholar who first proposed a written document to explain the striking agreements of the double tradition simply referred to that document as a *Quelle,* which means "source" in German. The abbreviation "Q" was later adopted as its name. Scholars now refer to this hypothetical document as the Sayings Gospel Q.

Matt 3:7–10	**Luke 3:7–9**
7 When he saw that many	
of the Pharisees and Sadducees	
were coming for baptism,	
⟨John⟩ said to them,	7 So ⟨John⟩ would say to the crowds
	that came out to get baptized by him,
"You spawn of Satan!	"You spawn of Satan!
Who warned you to flee	Who warned you to flee
from the impending doom?	from the impending doom?
8 Well then, start producing fruit	8 Well then, start producing fruit*s*
suitable for a change of heart,	suitable for a change of heart,
9 and don't even *think of*	and don't even *start*
saying to yourselves,	saying to yourselves,
'We have Abraham for our father.'	'We have Abraham for our father.'
Let me tell you,	Let me tell you,
God can raise up children for	God can raise up children for
Abraham right out of these rocks.	Abraham right out of these rocks.
10 Even now the axe is aimed	9 Even now the axe is aimed
at the root of the trees.	at the root of the trees.
So every tree not producing	So every tree not producing
choice fruit gets cut down	choice fruit gets cut down
and tossed into the fire."	and tossed into the fire."

THE TWO SOURCE THEORY

Q

MARK

MATTHEW

LUKE

The Two Source Theory is the view that Matthew and Luke made use of two written sources—Mark and the Sayings Gospel Q—in composing their gospels.

THE FOUR SOURCE THEORY

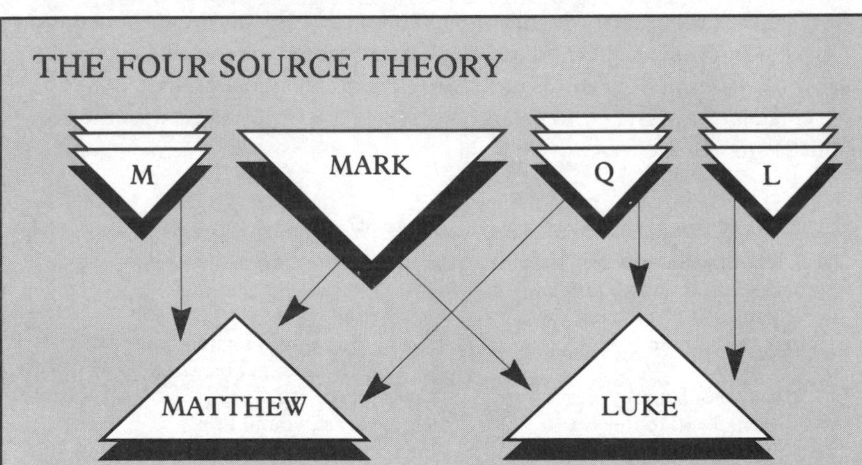

The Four Source Theory is a common explanation of the relationships found in the Synoptic Gospels. Matthew used Mark, Q, and his own special source called M. Luke also used Mark and Q, but had another source called L, that Matthew did not have. The material in M and L probably comes from oral tradition.

Introduction

The most quoted and influential of the synoptic gospels until modern times was the Gospel of Matthew. The earliest commentaries were on this gospel, and the large number of surviving fragments suggest that it was copied more frequently than the other synoptic gospels. The popularity of Matthew can be explained by three factors: (1) the author was allegedly Matthew, one of the first followers of Jesus; (2) it came first in the New Testament canon; (3) it contained virtually all of Mark, making Mark all but superfluous.

Sources & plot

The Gospel of Matthew is based on the Gospel of Mark and the Sayings Gospel Q.

The outline of Mark's Gospel is evident in Matthew. Matthew employs the same basic plot as Mark:

1. Jesus' baptism and initial ministry in Galilee
2. Peter's confession at Caesarea Philippi and the transfiguration
3. Journey to Jerusalem and debates in the temple
4. Concluding tragic death and resurrection.

However, Matthew does not simply repeat Mark's story. While Mark begins with John the Baptist's preaching, Matthew launches his gospel with a genealogy and birth narrative that shows Jesus to be the son of David and thus both king and the Anointed. At the gospel's conclusion the author appends a commissioning scene in which the risen Jesus sends the eleven out to baptize the whole world.

Five sermons

By far the most notable additions to Mark's outline are the five sermons. Each has a distinctive theme and all conclude with the formula, "now when Jesus had finished . . ." Much of the material in these sermons is derived from the Sayings Gospel Q (see the cameo essay, *Establishing the Text of Q*, p. 248).

The famous Sermon on the Mount (chaps. 5–7) sets forth a Christian interpretation of the Law. The second sermon (chap. 10) deals with the sending out of the disciples and by implication with the practice of Christian missionaries. The third sermon (chap. 13) derives its core from Mark 4, but

Matthew's version is composed of parables and interpretations that expose the mixed nature of the congregation: it is made up of wheat and weeds, the good and the bad. The next sermon (chap. 18) also advances the theme of the congregation by addressing those responsible for the community's order. Yet the guiding principle is not authority but forgiveness. The final sermon (chaps. 24–25) deals with events to occur at the end of history (eschatology). The first part copies Jesus' preaching about the end from Mark 13; the second part focuses on the last judgment in which the standard to be applied is how each person has treated the least of his or her fellow humans.

Author

The early church tradition held that the author of this gospel was the apostle Matthew. Papias, one of the early authorities of the church (about 150 C.E.), claimed that "Matthew organized the sayings in the Hebrew language, but everyone has translated them as best he could." Papias knew the Gospel of Matthew only in its current form and had not seen a version in a Semitic language. Even though later church authorities accepted Papias' assertions, modern scholars have rejected them for a variety of reasons. First, there is no evidence that the gospel was originally composed in Hebrew. It is written in good Koine Greek of the period. Moreover, it is dependent on Q and Mark, both of which existed only in Greek. Finally, the Gospel is not a collection of sayings, like Q, but a narrative with an ordered plot. To refer to the author as Matthew is only a convention.

Date & community

Since the Gospel refers to the destruction of Jerusalem in the parable of the banquet, when the king sends his troops to destroy "their city" (22:7), it must have been composed after 70 C.E. It is generally thought to have been written before the end of the first century.

The picture of the Matthean community that emerges from a study of the gospel is this: the community is engaged in intense debate with rabbinic Judaism that is itself creating new institutions to replace the destroyed temple. Both groups are trying to define themselves. This is the only gospel in which the Greek word *ekklesia*, meaning church or congregation, appears. Prior to the temple's destruction there were many different competing interpretations of what it meant to be an Israelite. But the destruction of Jerusalem set in motion for Judaism and Christianity a long process of consolidation and self-definition that reached its first definitive form around the beginning of the third century. In Judaism this process received a powerful impetus with the triumph of Pharisaism and rabbinic Judaism. In Christianity this process eventuated in what was to become the orthodoxy reflected in the early creeds and institutions.

The Matthean group, recently expelled from the synagogue (5:11), is contesting with the synagogue over who is the true Israel. The Christians and Jesus stand in the line of John the Baptist and the prophets. For this reason the summary of Jesus' message is the same as that of John the Baptist (3:2; 4:17), and John, the last of the prophets, baptizes Jesus. The Pharisees erected the tombs of the prophets (23:29) and they persecute the Christians who follow the prophets (5:12). The line of true Israel is, then, the prophets, John the Baptist, Jesus, and the Matthean community.

This forging of a self-definition over and against emerging rabbinic Judaism is important to remember in reading Matthew's gospel. The debate is not between Judaism and Christianity, nor between Jew and Gentile, but between two parties within Judaism. Both groups are withdrawing and consolidating into antagonistic camps.

The rejection of the Pharisees in Matthew implies neither the rejection of Judaism nor the Law. Even though the Pharisees sit in the chair of Moses (23:2), yet the standard epithet for them is "phonies" or "impostors." Both Jesus and John the Baptist address them as "spawn of Satan" (3:7; 12:34; 23:33) and John prophesies that their end is near. As "phonies" they practice their religion in public (6:1–2); they cleanse the outside of the cup, but inside they are "full of greed and dissipation" (23:25).

As for the Law, not even the smallest part will pass away (5:18). Matthew portrays Jesus as the true and authoritative interpreter of the Law. He restores it to its original meaning: "As you know, our ancestors were told . . . But I tell you" (5:21).

Use of scripture

At important moments in the story, the narrator quotes from the scriptures, using the standard formula: "All this has happened so the prediction of the Lord given by the prophet would come true" (1:22; 2:15, 18, 23, 25; 4:14–16; 5:17; 8:17; 12:17–21; 13:14–15, 35; 21:4–5; 26:56; 27:9). Normally such citations are employed to resolve conflict in the story or buttress especially important positions. Matthew even changes several items in Mark's stories to make the narrative fit the quotations. For example, he has Jesus ride into Jerusalem on both a donkey and a colt (21:7), a somewhat confusing and odd picture when compared with Mark's simple colt. But the prophecy from Zechariah 9:9, which is composed in Semitic parallelism, reads:

> Look, your king is coming to you.
> He is triumphant, victorious,
> Yet humble, riding on a donkey,
> On a colt foaled by a donkey.

Matthew takes the two lines quite literally and has Jesus ride two animals, rather than understanding the second line as a poetic repetition of the first.

Beyond that, Matthew has blended Zechariah with Isaiah 62:11 and created a unique version. Close attention to Matthew's use of quotations from scripture is a sure guide to distinctive features of the Matthean gospel.

Self-portrait

The author has left what seems to be self-portrait in 13:52: "every scholar who is schooled in Heaven's imperial rule is like some proprietor who produces from his storeroom treasures old and new." This suggests how the Matthean community understands itself: it pores over the records of the past, the scriptures, but it produces something new and original—a new understanding of the Law.

The scholar evidently plays an important role in this community. Jesus is regularly pictured as teaching. Yet as important as scholarship and teaching is to this community, Jesus is addressed as "teacher" or "Rabbi" only by outsiders. The disciples and believers refer to him as "Master" or "Lord."

Scholar

A *scholar* is someone who can read and write. Since that ability was not altogether common in the ancient world, scholars functioned as secretaries in writing letters, framing petitions, and copying documents for ordinary people who could not read or write.

The term was also frequently used to refer to those who were learned in other respects. Scholars served as high government officials, royal viceroys, or assistants to sages and prophets, as in the case of Baruch's relationship to Jeremiah (Jer 36:32). The traditional translation, "scribe," seems archaic to users of English today, so the SV translators decided to employ a more colloquial word.

In the gospels, the scholars are usually represented as opposing Jesus. They are sometimes associated with the high priest and elders, sometimes with Pharisees. They were probably versed in the Law and rhetoric, so they knew how to conduct an argument over fine points in the Law in public debate. Jesus is pictured as sparring with them on numerous occasions. Once Jesus says, "Damn you, scholars," and calls them impostors and phonies (Matt 23:13).

Since scholars are responsible for the Scholars Version and are versed in the language and interpretation of the gospels, it seems appropriate that they should bear part of the brunt of Jesus' criticism. After all, those exempt from criticism have risked nothing and so have gained nothing.

The Gospel of Matthew

1 ***This is the family tree*** of Jesus the Anointed, who was a descen- *Jesus' family tree*
dant of David and Abraham.
2Abraham was the father of Isaac, Isaac of Jacob, Jacob of Judah and
his brothers, 3and Judah and Tamar were the parents of Perez and
Zerah. Perez was the father of Hezron, Hezron of Ram, 4Ram of
Amminadab, Amminadab of Nahshon, Nahshon of Salmon, 5and
Salmon and Rahab were the parents of Boaz. Boaz and Ruth were the
parents of Obed. Obed was the father of Jesse, 6and Jesse of David the
king.
David and Uriah's wife were the parents of Solomon. 7Solomon was
the father of Rehoboam, Rehoboam of Abijah, Abijah of Asaph,
8Asaph of Jehoshaphat, Jehoshaphat of Joram, Joram of Uzziah,
9Uzziah of Jotham, Jotham of Ahaz, Ahaz of Hezekiah, 10Hezekiah of
Manasseh, Manasseh of Amos, Amos of Josiah, 11and Josiah was the 1:1–17 //Lk3:23–38
father of Jechoniah and his brothers at the time of the exile to Babylon. 1:2–6 ◊1Chr2:1–15
12After the Babylonian exile, Jechoniah was the father of Salathiel,
Salathiel of Zerubbabel, 13Zerubbabel of Abiud, Abiud of Eliakim, 1:3–6 ◊Ru4:18–22
Eliakim of Azor, 14Azor of Zadok, Zadok of Achim, Achim of Eliud, 1:3 ◊Gn38
15Eliud of Eleazar, Eleazar of Matthan, Matthan of Jacob. 16And Jacob
was the father of Joseph, the husband of Mary, who was the mother of 1:5 ◊Jos 2, Ru4:13–17
Jesus. Jesus is known as the Anointed.
17In sum, the generations from Abraham to David come to fourteen, 1:7–12 ◊1Chr 3:10–19

1:1–11 The first two sections of genealogy are based on the genealogies of 1 Chronicles 1–3 and Ruth 4:18–22. It is impossible to reconcile this genealogy with the one in Luke (3:23–38).
1:1 *Anointed* is the literal meaning of the Greek title often transliterated in English as "Christ." *David* establishes the royal line and *Abraham* the line of Israel.
1:3 *Judah* was *Tamar's* father-in-law (Genesis 38).
1:5 *Rahab* was the prostitute of Jericho who helped the Israelites overtake Jericho (Joshua 2). She is nowhere mentioned as the mother of Boaz. *Ruth*, a gentile, was the great-grandmother of David (Ruth 4:18–22).
1:6 *Uriah's wife* was Bathsheba. After David had raped her, he had her husband killed in battle (2 Samuel 11).
1:7 *Asaph* is probably a confusion for Asa, the fifth king in David's line. Asaph was psalm singer appointed by David (1 Chr 6:39). A number of psalms are also attributed to him (e.g., Psalm 50).
1:8 According to 1 Chr 3:11–12, *Joram* was the great-great-grandfather of *Uzziah* (called Azariah in 1 Chronicles).
1:10 The actual successor of Manasseh was Amon, not *Amos*. Some manuscripts make the correction.
1:11 According to 1 Chr 3:15–16, *Josiah* was the grandfather of *Jeconiah*.
1:13 *Abiud* is not mentioned among the sons of Zerubbabel (1 Chr 3:19).
1:15 With *Matthan*, Joseph's grandfather, the genealogy no longer follows 1 Chronicles.
1:16 The fact that this is Joseph's genealogy and not Mary's looks forward to his adoption of Jesus in the birth story (vv. 21, 25).
1:17 Matthew has arranged this genealogy

Birth of Jesus

Astrologers from the East

those from David to the Babylonian exile number fourteen, and those from the Babylonian exile to the Anointed amount to fourteen also.

[18]***The birth of Jesus*** the Anointed took place as follows: While his mother Mary was engaged to Joseph, but before they slept together, she was found to be pregnant by the holy spirit. [19]Since Joseph her husband was a decent man and did not wish to expose her publicly, he planned to break off their engagement quietly.

[20]While he was thinking about these things, a messenger of the Lord surprised him in a dream with these words: "Joseph, descendant of David, don't hesitate to take Mary as your wife, since the holy spirit is responsible for her pregnancy. [21]She will give birth to a son and you will name him Jesus—the name means 'he will save his people from their sins.'" [22]All of this has happened so the prediction of the Lord given by the prophet would come true:

> [23]Behold, a virgin will conceive a child
> and she will give birth to a son,
> and they will name him Emmanuel

(which means "God with us").

[24]Joseph got up and did what the messenger of the Lord told him: he took ⟨Mary as⟩ his wife. [25]He did not have sex with her until she had given birth to a son. Joseph named him Jesus.

2 ***Jesus was born*** at Bethlehem, Judea, when Herod was king. Astrologers from the East showed up in Jerusalem just then. [2]"Tell us," they said, "where the newborn king of the Judeans is. We have observed his star in the east and have come to pay him homage."

1:18–25 //Lk 2:1–7
1:20 Ⓣ Mt 2:12, 19, 22; 27:19
1:23 ◊Is 7:14 (LXX); Is 8:8, 10 (LXX); Ⓣ Mt 18:20, 28:20
2:1–6 //Lk 2:8–14
2:2 Ⓣ Mt 2:8, 11, 8:2, 9:18, 14:33, 15:25, 18:26, 20:20, 28:9, 17

1:18 A few mss omit *Jesus*. **1:25** Some mss read "her firstborn" *son*.

around the number 14. This number in Hebrew forms David's name. There are only 13 generations in the last group from the Babylonian exile to the Anointed.

1:19 Joseph's dilemma involves the conflicting demands of justice—he is not the father and so cannot claim the child as his own, and his desire not to humiliate Mary by a public act of breaking the engagement.

1:20 *Dreams* are often occasions for revelations, e.g., Jacob's dreams (Gen 20:12), Joseph's dreams (Gen 37), or Daniel's interpretations of dreams (Dan 2).

1:21 The Greek name *Jesus* is derived from the Hebrew "Joshua" which according to popular etymology means "Yahweh is salvation." This multilingual wordplay is echoed in this verse.

1:23 The quotation is from the Greek translation (the Septuagint) of the Hebrew Bible, as is normal in Matthew. The Hebrew Bible refers to a "young woman" rather than the *virgin* of the LXX. This is the first of a number of distinctive quotations introduced by a nearly identical formula.

1:25 The act of naming the child is tantamount to adoption, claiming the child as his own. Thus Jesus is a legal son of Joseph.

2:1 *Bethlehem*, a few miles south of Jerusalem, was the ancestral home of David (1 Sam 16:1), as well as the burial place of Rachel (Gen 35:19), whose lament is mentioned in 2:18. The city also figures prominently in the story of Ruth, who is mentioned in the genealogy.

Herod the king is Herod the Great who ruled both Judea and Galilee from 37–4 B.C.E.

Astrologers were also involved in magic, the observation of the stars, and wisdom.

Flight to Egypt

Murder of the babies

3When this news reached King Herod, he was visibly shaken, and all
Jerusalem along with him. 4He called together all the ranking priests
and local experts, and pressed them for information: "Where is the
Anointed supposed to be born?"
5They replied, "At Bethlehem, Judea. This is how it is put by the
prophet:

6And you, Bethlehem, in the province of Judah,
you are by no means least among the leaders of Judah.
Out of you will come a leader
who will shepherd my people, Israel."

7Then Herod called the astrologers together secretly and ascertained from them the precise time the star became visible. 8Then he
sent them to Bethlehem with these instructions: "Go make a careful
search for the child. When you find him, report back to me, so I can
also go and pay him homage."
9They listened to what the king had to say and continued on their
way.

And there guiding them on was the star that they had observed in
the East: it led them on until it came to a standstill above where the
child lay. 10Once they saw the star, they were beside themselves with
joy. 11And they arrived at the house and saw the child with his mother
Mary. They fell down and paid him homage. Then they opened their
treasure chests and presented him with gifts—gold, pure incense, and
myrrh. 12And because they had been advised in a dream not to return to
Herod, they journeyed back to their own country by a different route.
13***After*** ⟨***the astrologers***⟩ had departed, a messenger of the Lord appeared in a dream to Joseph, saying, "Get ready, take the child and his
mother and flee to Egypt. Stay there until I give you instructions. You
see, Herod is determined to hunt the child down and destroy him."
14So Joseph got ready and took the child and his mother under cover
of night and set out for Egypt. 15There they remained until Herod's
death. This happened so the Lord's prediction spoken by the prophet
would come true: "Out of Egypt I have called my son."
16***When Herod realized*** he had been duped by the astrologers, he
was outraged. He then issued instructions to kill all the children two

2:3 Ⓣ Mt 21:10
2:6 Cf. Jn 7:42; ◊Mi 5:2, 2 Sm 5:2
2:7–9a See 2:2
2:9b-12 //Lk 2:15–20
2:11 ◊Ps 72:10–11, Is 60:6; see 2:2
2:12 Mt 1:20; 2:19, 22; 27:19
2:13 ◊Ex 2:15
2:15 Cf. GNaz 1; ◊Hos 11:1

2:2 *Star*: Despite numerous attempts to identify a specific stellar event as the Bethlehem star, no effort has proven successful.

Pay homage is a very frequent term in Matthew's gospel. See the cross references.

2:4 The *ranking priests* were those who held positions of authority in the temple hierarchy.

The *local experts* were usually employed in the bureaucracy. In the gospels they are frequently linked with the Pharisees. But in Matt 13:52 "scholar schooled in Heaven's imperial rule" refers to the Matthean community.

2:11 The *gifts* were most likely picked for their expensiveness.

2:13 The flight into *Egypt* and the eventual return recalls the captivity and exodus themes so prominent in Israel's history.

2:16 Historians are unable to find any evidence of the murder of the children.

Return to Nazareth

A voice in the wilderness

years old and younger in Bethlehem and the surrounding region. This
corresponded to the time ⟨of the star⟩ that he had learned from the
astrologers. [17]With this event the prediction made by Jeremiah the
prophet came true:

> [18]In Ramah the sound of mourning
> and bitter grieving was heard:
> Rachel weeping for her children.
> She refused to be consoled:
> They were no more.

[19]***After Herod's death,*** a messenger of the Lord appeared in a dream
to Joseph in Egypt: [20]"Get ready, take the child and his mother, and
return to the land of Israel; those who were seeking the child's life are
dead."

[21]So he got ready, took the child and his mother, and returned to the
land of Israel. [22]He heard that Archelaus was the king of Judea in the
place of his father Herod; as a consequence, he was afraid to go there.
He was instructed in a dream to go to Galilee; [23]so he went there and
settled in a town called Nazareth. So the prophecy uttered by the
prophets came true: "He will be called a Nazorean."

3 ***In due course*** John the Baptist appears in the wilderness of Judea,
[2]calling out: "Change your ways because Heaven's imperial rule is
closing in."

[3]No doubt this is the person described by Isaiah the prophet:

> A voice of someone shouting in the wilderness:
> "Make ready the way of the Lord;
> make his paths straight."

[4]Now this same John wore clothes made of camel hair and had a
leather belt around his waist; his diet consisted of locusts and raw
honey. [5]Then Jerusalem, and all Judea, and all the region around the
Jordan streamed out to him, [6]and got baptized in the Jordan river by
him, admitting their sins.

2:18 ◊Jer 31:15
2:19 Ⓣ Mt 1:20; 2:12, 22; 27:19
2:22 Ⓣ Mt 1:20; 2:12, 19; 27:19
2:23 Cf. GNaz 1; ◊Jgs 13:5
3:1–12 //Mk 1:2–8, Lk 3:1–20; cf. Jn 1:19–28
3:2 //Mk 1:15; Ⓣ Mt 4:17, 10:7
3:3 ◊Is 40:3
3:4–7 //GEbi 3; cf. GEbi 1
3:4 ◊2 Kgs 1:8

2:18 Some mss read *the sound of* "dirges and" *mourning.* This appears to be an effort of early scribes to bring the quote into conformity with the Septuagint of Jer 31:15.

2:18 *Ramah* of Benjamin is about five miles north of Jerusalem. It was the place from which the Israelites were sent into exile in Babylon.

Rachel was the wife of Jacob whose name was also "Israel" (Gen 32:28).

2:22 *Archelaus*, the son of Herod the Great, ruled as ethnarch of Judea, Samaria, and Idumea from 4 B.C.E. until 6 C.E., when Rome banished him and made Judea a Roman province.

2:23 In this story Jesus is a Judean who after the sojourn in Egypt moves to *Nazareth* in Galilee, while in Luke Jesus is a Galilean whose parents must travel to Bethlehem in Judea (Lk 2:4).

Nazorean: This quote may be dependent upon the Septuagint of Judg 13:5 or 16:17. Matthew's spelling of the word differs form Mark's "Nazarene" (e.g., 1:24).

John baptizes Jesus

Jesus is tested

7When he saw that many of the Pharisees and Sadducees were coming for baptism, ⟨John⟩ said to them, "You spawn of Satan! Who warned you to flee from the impending doom? 8Well then, start producing fruit suitable for a change of heart, 9and don't even think of saying to yourselves, 'We have Abraham for our father.' Let me tell you, God can raise up children for Abraham right out of these rocks. 10Even now the axe is aimed at the root of the trees. So every tree not producing choice fruit gets cut down and tossed into the fire."

11"I baptize you with water to signal a change of heart, but someone more powerful than I will succeed me. I am not fit to carry his sandals. He'll baptize you with holy spirit and fire. 12His pitchfork is in his hand, and he'll make a clean sweep of his threshing floor, and gather his wheat into the granary, but the chaff he'll burn in a fire that can't be put out."

13***Then Jesus comes*** from Galilee to John at the Jordan to get baptized by him. 14And John tried to stop him with these words: "I'm the one who needs to get baptized by you, yet you come to me?"

15In response, Jesus said to him, "Let it go for now. After all, in this way we are doing what is fitting and right." Then John deferred to him.

16After Jesus had been baptized, he got right up out of the water, and—amazingly—the skies opened up, he saw God's spirit coming down on him like a dove, perching on him, 17and—listen!—there was a voice from the skies, which said, "This is my favored son —I fully approve of him!"

4 ***Then Jesus was guided*** into the wilderness by the spirit to be put to the test by the devil. 2And after he had fasted 'forty days and forty nights,' he was famished.

Q3:7–10 //Lk3:7–9
3:7 Ⓣ Mt12:24, 23:33
3:10 Ⓣ Mt7:19
3:11 //Acts 1:5, 11:16, 13:24–25
3:13–17 //Mk1:9–11, Lk3:21–22, Jn1:29–34, GHeb3, GEbi4
3:14–15 //GEbi4:7–8; cf.GHeb2:2, GNaz2:2
3:15 Ⓣ Mt5:17
3:17 //GEbi4:6; Ⓣ Mt12:18, 17:5; ◊Ps2:7, Is42:1, 44:2
Q4:1–11 //Mk1:12–13, Lk4:1–13
4:1 Ⓣ Heb 4:15; cf.GHeb4
4:2 ◊Ex34:28, Dt9:9, 1Kgs19:8

3:7 Many mss read "his" *baptism.*

3:7 *Sadducees* were one of the main groups of Jewish society. They were mostly priests and belonged to the upper class. Many of their members served in the Council. Theologically they were very conservative, accepting only the Pentateuch and rejecting the resurrection. While in the gospels they are frequently allied with the Pharisees, in rabbinic literature they are the Pharisees' opponents.

Pharisees were likewise one of the principal groups of first century Judaism and were generally popular among the ordinary people. They were interpreters of the Law and made an effort to make it applicable to all aspects of life. In the post-70 period they became the principal Jewish opponents of Christianity, which accounts for the strident opposition to them in the gospels.

3:15 John the Baptist's dilemma parallels Joseph's. To do what is just he should not baptize Jesus, just as Joseph should not marry Mary.

3:16 Unlike Mark (1:10) Matthew seems to envision the coming of the spirit as a physical event (see likewise Luke 3:22).

4:1 *Devil* is a translation for the Greek word *diabolos* meaning "accuser" or "slanderer." In the Septuagint it is used to translate the Hebrew word *satan,* which means "adversary." In the New Testament, Devil and Satan mean the same thing. In the Hebrew Bible, Satan is a member of God's court (Job 1:1; Zech 3:1–2; 1 Chr 21:1) and is not the embodiment of evil. That notion develops after 200 B.C.E.

4:2 *Forty days and forty nights* recalls the fasting of Moses and Elijah.

A voice in Galilee

[3]And the tester confronted him and said, "To prove you're God's son, order these stones to turn into bread."

[4]He responded, "It is written, 'Human beings are not to live on bread alone, but on every word that comes out of God's mouth.'"

[5]Then the devil conducts him to the holy city, sets him on the pinnacle of the temple, [6]and says to him, "To prove you're God's son, jump off; remember, it is written, 'To his heavenly messengers he will give orders about you,' and 'with their hands they will catch you, so you won't even stub your toe on a stone.'"

[7]Jesus said to him, "Elsewhere it is written, 'You are not to put the Lord your God to the test.'"

[8]Again the devil takes him to a very high mountain and shows him all the empires of the world and their splendor, [9]and says to him, "I'll give you all these, if you will kneel down and pay homage to me."

[10]Finally Jesus says to him, "Get out of here, Satan! Remember, it is written, 'You are to pay homage to the Lord your God, and you are to revere him alone.'"

[11]Then the devil leaves him, and heavenly messengers arrive out of nowhere and look after him.

[12]***When Jesus heard*** that John had been locked up, he headed for Galilee. [13]He took leave of Nazareth to go and settle down in Capernaum-by-the-sea, in the territory of Zebulun and Naphtali, [14]so that the word spoken through Isaiah the prophet would come true:

[15]Land of Zebulun and of Naphtali,
the way to the sea,
across the Jordan,
Galilee of the pagans!
[16]You who languished in darkness have seen a great light,
you who have wasted away in the shadow of death,
for you a light has risen.

[17]From that time on Jesus began to proclaim: "Change your ways because Heaven's imperial rule is closing in."

[18]As he was walking by the Sea of Galilee, he spotted two brothers, Simon, also known as Peter, and Andrew his brother, throwing their net in the sea, since they were fishermen. [19]And Jesus says to them, "Become my followers and I'll have you fishing for people!" [20]So right then and there they abandoned their nets and followed him.

[21]When he had gone on a little farther, he caught sight of two other brothers, James, Zebedee's son, and his brother John, in the boat with Zebedee their father, mending their nets, and he also called out to

4:4 ◊Dt 8:3
4:6 ◊Ps 91:11–12
4:7 ◊Dt 6:16
4:8–10 Cf. GHeb 4
4:10 ◊Dt 6:13
4:11 Ⓣ Jn 1:51
4:12–17 //Mk 1:14–15, Lk 4:14–15
4:12 Ⓘ Mt 14:3
4:15–16 ◊Is 9:1–2
4:17 Ⓘ Mt 16:21, 26:16; //Mt 3:2, 10:7
4:18–20 //Mk 1:16–18, Lk 5:1–3, Jn 1:40–42; cf. GEbi 2:3
4:21–22 //Mk 1:19–20, Lk 5:4–11

4:10 Some mss conform Jesus' dismissal of Satan to his dismissal of Peter in 16:23: "Get out of my sight." **4:17** A few mss omit *Change your ways.*

4:5 *Pinnacle* probably refers to the highest point of the temple, although technically the temple did not have a pinnacle.

4:13 *Capernaum* is a town on the northwest shore of the Sea of Galilee.

4:23 Matthew generally refers to *their syna-*

Congratulations!

them. 22They abandoned their boat and their father right then and
there and followed him.
23And he toured all over Galilee, teaching in their synagogues, proclaiming the news of ⟨Heaven's⟩ imperial rule, and healing every disease and every ailment the people had. 24And his reputation spread
through the whole of Syria. They brought him everyone who was ill,
who suffered from any kind of disease or was in intense pain, who was
possessed, who was epileptic, or a paralytic, and he cured them. 25And
huge crowds followed him from Galilee and the Decapolis and Jerusalem and Judea and from across the Jordan.

5 ***Taking note*** of the crowds, he climbed up the mountain, and when
he had sat down, his disciples came to him. 2He then began to speak,
and this is what he would teach them:

3Congratulations to the poor in spirit!
Heaven's domain belongs to them.
4Congratulations to those who grieve!
They will be consoled.
5Congratulations to the gentle!
They will inherit the earth.
6Congratulations to those who hunger and thirst for justice!
They will have a feast.
7Congratulations to the merciful!
They will receive mercy.
8Congratulations to those with undefiled hearts!
They will see God.
9Congratulations to those who work for peace!
They will be known as God's children.
10Congratulations to those who have suffered persecution for the
sake of justice!
Heaven's domain belongs to them.

11"Congratulations to you when they denounce you and persecute you
and spread malicious gossip about you because of me. 12Rejoice and be
glad! In heaven you will be more than compensated. Remember, this is
how they persecuted the prophets who preceded you.

4:23–25 //Mk1:35–39, Lk4:42–44
4:23 Ⓣ Mt9:35; Mary4:8
5:1–12 //Lk6:17–26
5:1 Ⓣ Mk3:13, Lk6:12–14, Jn6:3
Q5:3 //Lk6:20, Th54; Ⓣ Mt11:5; Ⓣ Jas2:5
Q5:4 //Lk6:21; ◊Is61:2
5:5 ◊Ps 37:11
Q5:6 //Lk6:21, Th69:2
5:8 ◊Ps 24:3–4
5:10 //Th69:1
Q5:11 //Lk6:22, Th68:1

5:11 A few mss add "tell lies" to the triad of *denounce, persecute and spread malicious gossip.*

gogues which indicates that the gospel was written after the separation of the church from the synagogue.
4:24 *Syria* is the major Roman province in the East which includes Galilee, Judea, Samaria. Its capital was Antioch. Here it may refer to the area around Damascus.
4:25 *The Decapolis* was a confederation of ten Hellenistic cities in the area east of Samaria and Galilee.
5:1 *The mountain* may be an allusion to Moses ascending Mount Sinai. This gospel ends with Jesus on the mountain with his disciples.

Salt & light

[13]"***You are*** the salt of the earth. But if salt loses its zing, how will it be made salty? It then has no further use than to be thrown out and stomped on. [14]You are the light of the world. A city sitting on top of a mountain can't be concealed. [15]Nor do people light a lamp and put it under a bushel basket but rather on a lampstand, where it sheds light for everyone in the house. [16]That's how your light is to shine in the presence of others, so they can see your good deeds and acclaim your Father in the heavens.

Law & prophets

[17]"***Don't imagine*** that I have come to annul the Law or the Prophets. I have come not to annul but to fulfill. [18]I swear to you, before the world disappears, not one iota, not one serif, will disappear from the Law, until that happens. [19]Whoever ignores one of the most trivial of these regulations, and teaches others to do so, will be called trivial in Heaven's domain. But whoever acts on ⟨these regulations⟩ and teaches ⟨others to do so⟩, will be called great in Heaven's domain. [20]Let me tell you: unless your religion goes beyond that of the scholars and Pharisees, you won't set foot in Heaven's domain.

On anger

[21]"***As you know,*** our ancestors were told, 'You must not kill' and 'Whoever kills will be subject to judgment.' [22]But I tell you: those who are angry with a companion will be brought before a tribunal. And those who say to a companion, 'You moron,' will be subject to the sentence of the court. And whoever says, 'You idiot,' deserves the fires of Gehenna. [23]So, even if you happen to be offering your gift at the altar and recall that your friend has some claim against you, [24]leave your gift there at the altar. First go and be reconciled with your friend, and only then return and offer your gift. [25]You should come to terms quickly with your opponent while you are both on the way ⟨to court⟩, or else your opponent will hand you over to the judge, and the judge ⟨will turn you over⟩ to the bailiff, and you are thrown in jail. [26]I swear to you, you'll never get out of there until you've paid the last dime.

On lust

[27]"***As you know,*** we once were told, 'You are not to commit adultery.' [28]But I tell you: Those who leer at a woman and desire her have

Q5:13
//Mk9:50, Lk14:34–35
5:14
Ⓣ Th32
Q5:15
//Mk4:21, Lk8:16, Lk11:33, Th33:2–3
5:17
Cf. GEbi6
Q5:18
//Lk16:17
5:21
◊Ex20:13, Dt5:17
5:23–24
Cf. Mk11:25
Q5:25–26
//Lk12:58–59
5:27
◊Ex20:13, Dt5:17

5:22 To mitigate the rigor of the statement, some mss add "without cause" after *a companion.* **5:25** The translators of SV felt compelled for the sake of English style to fill in the ellipses ⟨*will turn you over*⟩ as did some mss.

5:13 *Salt* was the most commonly used seasoning and preservative in the ancient world. If it was overcooked in its manufacture, it would be tasteless.

5:16 *Father in the heavens* or "heavenly Father" is a distinctive Matthean phrase.

5:17 *Law* and *Prophets* refer to the first two parts of the Hebrew Bible: Law, Prophets and Writings. "The Law" can stand for the whole of the Hebrew Bible as well as for the first five books (The Pentateuch).

5:18 *Iota* is the smallest Greek letter and a *serif* is the "hook" on a Hebrew letter.

5:22 For *moron* the text uses an Aramaic word *raka*, which is a mild phrase of abuse.

Gehenna is derived from the Hebrew meaning "valley of Hinnon," which ran southwest of Jerusalem. At one time human sacrifice was practiced there (2 Chr 28:3; Jer 7:32). In the NT it is a metaphor for Hell.

On divorce

On oaths

Eye for an eye

Love of enemies

already committed adultery with her in their hearts. 29And if your right
eye gets you into trouble, rip it out and throw it away! You would be
better off to lose a part of your body, than to have your whole body
thrown into Gehenna. 30And if your right hand gets you into trouble,
cut it off and throw it away! You would be better off to lose a part of
your body, than to have your whole body wind up in Gehenna.

31"***We once were told,*** 'Whoever divorces his wife should give her a
bill of divorce.' 32But I tell you: Everyone who divorces his wife (except
in the case of infidelity) makes her the victim of adultery; and whoever
marries a divorced woman commits adultery.

33"***Again,*** as you know, our ancestors were told, 'You must not break
an oath,' and 'Oaths sworn in the name of God must be kept.' 34But I
tell you: Don't swear at all. Don't invoke heaven, because it is the
throne of God, 35and don't invoke earth, because it is God's footstool,
and don't invoke Jerusalem, because it is the city of the great king.
36You shouldn't swear by your head either, since you aren't able to turn
a single hair either white or black. 37Rather, your responses should be
simply 'Yes' and 'No.' Anything that goes beyond this is inspired by the
evil one.

38"***As you know,*** we once were told, 'An eye for an eye' and 'A tooth
for a tooth.' 39But I tell you: Don't react violently against the one who is
evil: when someone slaps you on the right cheek, turn the other as
well. 40If someone is determined to sue you for your shirt, let that
person have your coat along with it. 41Further, when anyone conscripts
you for one mile, go along an extra mile. 42Give to the one who begs
from you; and don't turn away the one who tries to borrow from you.

43"***As you know,*** we once were told, 'You are to love your neighbor'
and 'You are to hate your enemy.' 44But I tell you: Love your enemies
and pray for your persecutors. 45You'll then become children of your
Father in the heavens. ⟨God⟩ causes the sun to rise on both the bad
and the good, and sends rain on both the just and the unjust. 46Tell me,
if you love those who love you, why should you be commended for
that? Even the toll collectors do as much, don't they? 47And if you greet
only your friends, what have you done that is exceptional? Even the
pagans do as much, don't they? 48To sum up, you are to be as liberal in
your love as your heavenly Father is."

5:29–30 Ⓓ Mt 18:8–9
Q**5:31–32** //Mk 10:10–12, Lk 16:18; Ⓓ Mt 19:7–9
5:31 ◇Dt 24:1–4
5:32 Ⓣ 1 Cor 7:10–11
5:33 ◇Lv 19:12
5:34 Ⓣ Mt 23:16–22
5:34–35 ◇Is 66:1
5:35 ◇Ps 48:2
5:38 ◇Ex 21:23–25, Lv 24:19–20, Dt 19:21
Q**5:39–42** //Lk 6:27–31
Q**5:43–48** //Lk 6:27–36
5:43 ◇Lv 19:18
5:48 ◇Dt 18:13, Lv 19:2; Ⓣ 1 Cor 14:20

5:47 Many mss read "toll collectors" instead of *pagans.*

5:32 The except clause is similar to 19:9.
5:41 *Conscription* was a common and oppressive way of raising troops.
5:43 *Hate your enemy* does not occur in the Hebrew Bible. It may be a reference to the Community Rule of Qumran: "They may love all that He has chosen and hate all that he has rejected."
5:48 To be *liberal in your love* means to follow all the demands of the Torah without any reduction. See 1 Cor 14:20 where Christians are urged by Paul not to be babies but mature. The same Greek word is used to translate "perfect" and "mature."

Piety in public

Prayer in public

On fasting

6 "***Take care*** that you don't flaunt your religion in public to be noticed by others. Otherwise, you will have no recognition from your Father in the heavens. [2]For example, when you give to charity, don't bother to toot your own horn as some phony pietists do in houses of worship and on the street. They are seeking human recognition. I swear to you, their grandstanding is its own reward. [3]Instead, when you give to charity, don't let your left hand in on what your right hand is up to, [4]so your acts of charity may remain hidden. And your Father, who has an eye for the hidden, will applaud you.

[5]"***And when you pray,*** don't act like phonies. They love to stand up and pray in houses of worship and on street corners, so they can show off in public. I swear to you, their prayers have been answered! [6]When you pray, go into a room by yourself and shut the door behind you. Then pray to your Father, the hidden one. And your Father, with his eye for the hidden, will applaud you. [7]And when you pray, you should not babble on as the pagans do. They imagine that the length of their prayers will command attention. [8]So don't imitate them. After all, your Father knows what you need before you ask. [9]Instead, you should pray like this:

> Our Father in the heavens,
> your name be revered.
> [10]Impose your imperial rule,
> enact your will on earth as you have in heaven.
> [11]Provide us with the bread we need for the day.
> [12]Forgive our debts
> to the extent that we have forgiven those in debt to us.
> [13]And please don't subject us to test after test,
> but rescue us from the evil one.

[14]"For if you forgive others their failures and offenses, your heavenly Father will also forgive yours. [15]And if you don't forgive the failures and mistakes of others, your Father won't forgive yours.

[16]"***When you fast,*** don't make a spectacle of your remorse as the pretenders do. As you know, they make their faces unrecognizable so their

6:1–4 //Th 14:1–3
6:3 //Th 62:2
Q**6:5–15** //Lk 11:1–4
6:6 ▷Is 26:20
6:11 //GNaz 3
6:15 Cf. Mk 11:25
6:16–18 Ⓣ Th 6; 14:1–3
6:16 ▷Is 58:5

6:12 Many mss read "we forgive." **6:13** At the end of the verse, many mss insert "for yours is the kingdom, the power, and the glory. Amen." This reflects an adaptation of the prayer for liturgical use (see 1 Chr 29:10–11).

6:2 The Greek word transliterated into English as "hypocrite" and here translated *phony* (and *pretender* in v. 16) means in classical and Hellenistic Greek an actor in a play. Only in Hellenistic Judaism and early Christianity does the word have an exclusively negative sense. Thirteen times in Matthew it refers to the Pharisees.

6:7 Gentile prayers were noted for their piling up of epithets.

6:11 The meaning of the Greek translated *we need for the day* is very debated. Origen, a church author of the third century and one of the greatest early Christian scholars, thought that the word was coined by the evangelists. Its only certain occurrence in the Greek language is in the Lord's prayer.

On possessions

Eye & light

Two masters

On anxieties

On judging

fasting may be publicly recognized. I swear to you, they have been paid in full. [17]When you fast, comb your hair and wash your face, [18]so your fasting may go unrecognized in public. But it will be recognized by your Father, the hidden one, and your Father, who has an eye for the hidden, will applaud you.

[19]"***Don't acquire possessions*** here on earth, where moths and insects eat away and where robbers break in and steal. [20]Instead, gather your nest egg in heaven, where neither moths nor insects eat away and where no robbers break in or steal. [21]As you know, what you treasure is your heart's true measure.

[22]"***The eye is*** the body's lamp. It follows that if your eye is clear, your whole body will be flooded with light. [23]If your eye is clouded, your whole body will be shrouded in darkness. If, then, the light within you is darkness, how dark that can be!

[24]"***No one can*** be a slave to two masters. No doubt that slave will either hate one and love the other, or be devoted to one and disdain the other. You can't be enslaved to both God and a bank account!

[25]"***That's why I tell you:*** Don't fret about your life—what you're going to eat and drink—or about your body—what you're going to wear. There is more to living than food and clothing, isn't there? [26]Take a look at the birds of the sky: they don't plant or harvest, or gather into barns. Yet your heavenly Father feeds them. You're worth more than they, aren't you? [27]Can any of you add one hour to life by fretting about it? [28]Why worry about clothes? Notice how the wild lilies grow: they don't slave and they never spin. [29]Yet let me tell you, even Solomon at the height of his glory was never decked out like one of them. [30]If God dresses up the grass in the field, which is here today and tomorrow is thrown into an oven, won't ⟨God care for⟩ you even more, you who don't take anything for granted? [31]So don't fret. Don't say, 'What am I going to eat?' or 'What am I going to drink?' or 'What am I going to wear?' [32]These are all things pagans seek. After all, your heavenly Father is aware that you need them. [33]You are to seek ⟨God's⟩ domain, and his justice first, and all these things will come to you as a bonus. [34]So don't fret about tomorrow. Let tomorrow fret about itself. The troubles that the day brings are enough.

7 "***Don't pass judgment,*** so you won't be judged. [2]Don't forget, the judgment you hand out will be the judgment you get back. And the standard you apply will be the standard applied to you. [3]Why do you notice the sliver in your friend's eye, but overlook the timber in your

Q6:19–21 //Lk12:33–34
6:19 //Th76:3; ▷Is51:8
6:21 //Mary7:4
Q6:22–23 //Lk11:34–36, Th24:3, DSav6
Q6:24 //Lk16:13, Th47:2
Q6:25–34 //Lk12:22–34
6:25 //Th36
6:27 //GrTh36:3–4
6:28 //GrTh36:2
6:30 Ⓣ Mt8:26; 14:31, 16:8; 17:20
6:31 //Th36
6:34 //DSav20:1
Q7:1–5 //Lk6:37–42
7:1 //Mary9:12
7:2 //Mk4:24–25
7:3–5 //Th26

6:25 Some mss omit *and drink,* to extend the parallel with v. 31. **6:33** A few very early mss do not have *God's*. It is more likely that this was added since it is implied in the phrase.

6:24 *Bank account*: The Greek uses the Aramaic word *mammon*, meaning wealth.

Pearls to pigs

Ask, seek, knock

Golden rule

Two gates

By their fruit

Invocation without obedience

Foundations

own? 4How can you say to your friend, 'Let me get the sliver out of your eye,' when there is that timber in your own? 5You phony, first take the timber out of your own eye and then you'll see well enough to remove the sliver from your friend's eye.

6"***Don't offer to dogs*** what is sacred, and don't throw your pearls to pigs, or they'll trample them underfoot and turn and tear you to shreds.

7"***Ask—it'll be given to you;*** seek—you'll find; knock—it'll be opened for you. 8Rest assured: everyone who asks receives; everyone who seeks finds; and for the one who knocks it is opened. 9Who among you would hand a son a stone when it's bread he's asking for? 10Again, who would hand him a snake when it's fish he's asking for? Of course no one would! 11So if you, worthless as you are, know how to give your children good gifts, isn't it much more likely that your Father in the heavens will give good things to those who ask him?

12"***Consider this:*** Treat people in ways you want them to treat you. This sums up the whole of the Law and the Prophets.

13"***Try to get in*** through the narrow gate. Wide and smooth is the road that leads to destruction. The majority are taking that route. 14Narrow and rough is the road that leads to life. Only a minority discover it.

15"***Be on the lookout*** for phony prophets, who make their pitch disguised as sheep; inside they are really voracious wolves. 16You'll know who they are by what they produce. Since when do people pick grapes from thorns or figs from thistles? 17Every healthy tree produces choice fruit, but the rotten tree produces spoiled fruit. 18A healthy tree cannot produce spoiled fruit, any more than a rotten tree can produce choice fruit. 19Every tree that does not produce choice fruit gets cut down and tossed on the fire. 20Remember, you'll know who they are by what they produce.

21"***Not everyone*** who addresses me as 'Master, master,' will get into Heaven's domain—only those who carry out the will of my Father in heaven. 22On that day many will address me: 'Master, master, didn't we use your name when we prophesied? Didn't we use your name when we exorcised demons? Didn't we use your name when we performed all those miracles?' 23Then I will tell them honestly: 'I never knew you; get away from me, you subverters of the Law!'

24"***Everyone who pays*** attention to these words of mine and acts on them will be like a shrewd builder who erected a house on bedrock. 25Later the rain fell, and the torrents came, and the winds blew and pounded that house, yet it did not collapse, since its foundation rested on bedrock. 26Everyone who listens to these words of mine and doesn't act on them will be like a careless builder, who erected a house on the sand. 27When the rain fell, and the torrents came, and the winds blew and pounded that house, it collapsed. Its collapse was colossal."

7:6 //Th93
Q7:7–11 //Lk11:9–13
7:7 //Th92:1; 94; cf. Th2
7:7–8 Ⓣ Mt21:22
7:8 //Mary4:7, GHeb6b
Q7:12 //Lk6:31
Q7:13–14 //Lk13:22–30
Q7:15–20 //Lk6:43–45
7:15 Ⓣ Mk13:22, Mt24:24
7:16 //Th45:1
7:17 //Mt12:33–37
7:19 //Mt3:10
7:21–23 Ⓣ Mt25:31–46
Q7:21 //Lk6:46; cf. EgerG3:5
Q7:22–23 //Lk13:26–27
7:22 Ⓣ Mk9:38–40
7:23 ◊ Ps 6:8
Q7:24–27 //Lk6:47–49

7:15 *Phony prophets* is a reference to Christian prophets.

7:21 *Master* can also be translated "Lord." A double meaning is surely intended here.

[28]And so, when Jesus had finished this discourse, the crowds were astonished at his teaching, [29]since he had been teaching them on his own authority, unlike their ⟨own⟩ scholars.

Jesus cures a leper

Officer's servant

Peter's mother-in-law

At day's end

8

When he came down from the mountain, huge crowds followed him. [2]Just then a leper appeared, bowed down to him, and said, "Sir, if you want to, you can make me clean."

[3]And he stretched out his hand, touched him, and says, "Okay—you're clean!" At once his leprosy was cleansed away. [4]Then Jesus warns him: "See that you don't tell anyone, but go, have a priest examine ⟨your skin⟩. Then offer the gift that Moses commanded, as evidence ⟨of your cure⟩."

[5]***When he had entered*** Capernaum, a Roman officer approached him and pleaded with him: [6]"Sir, my servant boy was struck down with paralysis and is in terrible pain."

[7]And he said to him, "I'll come and cure him."

[8]And the Roman officer replied, "Sir, I don't deserve to have you in my house, but only say the word and my boy will be cured. [9]After all, I myself am under orders, and I have soldiers under me. I order one to go, and he goes; I order another to come, and he comes; and ⟨I order⟩ my slave to do something, and he does it."

[10]As Jesus listened he was amazed and said to those who followed, "I swear to you, I have not found such trust in a single Israelite! [11]I predict that many will come from east and west and dine with Abraham and Isaac and Jacob in Heaven's domain, [12]but those who think Heaven's domain belongs to them will be thrown where it is utterly dark. There'll be weeping and grinding of teeth out there."

[13]And Jesus said to the Roman officer, "Be on your way. Your trust will be the measure of the results." And the boy was cured at that precise moment.

[14]***And when Jesus came*** to Peter's house, he noticed his mother-in-law lying sick with a fever. [15]He touched her hand and the fever disappeared. Then she got up and started looking after him.

[16]***In the evening,*** they brought many who were demon-possessed to him. He drove out the spirits with a command, and all those who were ill he cured. [17]In this way Isaiah's prophecy came true:

> He took away our illnesses
> and carried off our diseases.

7:28 Ⓘ Mt11:1, 13:53, 19:1, 26:1
7:29 Ⓣ Mk1:21–22, Mt13:54, Lk4:32
8:1–4 //Mk1:40–45, Lk5:12–16; Ⓣ EgerG2:1–4
8:2 See 2:2
8:4 ◊Lv14:2–20
Q**8:5–13** //Lk7:1–10, Jn4:45–54
Q**8:11–12** //Lk13:28–30
8:12 Cf. Mt13:42, 50, 22:13, 24:51, 25:30, Lk13:28
8:14–15 //Mk1:29–31, Lk4:38–39
8:16–17 //Mk1:32–34, Lk4:40–41
8:17 ◊Is53:4

8:13 Several mss add: "The Roman official returned to his house and found at that very moment that the boy was in good health."

7:28 The formulaic phrase *And so when Jesus had finished* occurs at the end of each of the five speeches in Matthew (7:28, 11:1, 13:53, 19:1, 26:1).

8:12 *Weeping and grinding of teeth* occurs six times in Matthew and only once in Luke.

Foxes have dens

Rebuking wind & wave

Demons of Gadara

18 ***When Jesus saw*** the crowds around him, he gave orders to cross over to the other side. 19 And one scholar came forward and said to him, "Teacher, I'll follow you wherever you go."

20 And Jesus says to him, "Foxes have dens, and birds of the sky have nests, but the son of Adam has nowhere to rest his head."

21 Another of his disciples said to him, "Master, first let me go and bury my father."

22 But Jesus says to him, "Follow me, and leave it to the dead to bury their own dead."

23 ***When he got*** into a boat, his disciples followed him. 24 And just then a great storm broke on the sea, so that the boat was swamped by the waves; but he was asleep. 25 And they came and woke him up, and said to him, "Master, save us! We are going to drown!"

26 He says to them, "Why are you so cowardly? Don't you trust me at all?" Then he got up and rebuked the winds and the sea, and there was a great calm.

27 And everyone marveled, saying, "What kind of person is this, that even the winds and the sea obey him?"

28 ***And when he came*** to the other side, to the region of the Gadarenes, he was met by two demoniacs who came out from the tombs. They were so hard to deal with that no one could pass along that road. 29 And just then they shouted, "What do you want with us, you son of God? Did you come here ahead of time to torment us?" 30 And a large herd of pigs was feeding off in the distance. 31 And the demons kept bargaining with him: "If you drive us out, send us into the herd of pigs."

32 And he said to them, "Get out ⟨of him⟩!"

And they came out and went into the pigs, and suddenly all the herd rushed down the bluff into the sea and drowned in the water. 33 The herdsmen ran off, and went into town and reported everything, especially about the demoniacs. 34 And what do you know, the whole town came out to meet Jesus. And when they saw him, they begged him to move on from their district.

Q8:18–22 //Lk9:57–62
8:20 //Th86
8:23–27 //Mk4:35–41, Lk8:22–25
8:24 ◊Jon1:4
8:26 Ⓣ Mt6:30, 14:31, 16:8, 17:20
8:28–34 //Mk5:1–20, Lk8:26–39

8:18 Most mss report that "huge" *crowds* surrounded Jesus. While only several very early mss have the simple *crowds,* it is most likely that the scribes elaborated the size. **8:28** Some mss spell the name of people in the region "Gerasenes," while other mss spell it "Gergesenes."

8:18 To *cross over to the other side* is a generic note indicating narrative motion, not a specific place.

8:20 This is the first occurrence of the title *son of Adam* in Matthew's Gospel. It is only used in the speech of Jesus; never in reference to him. Matthew uses the title in three ways: Jesus refers to (1) his present activity, as in this verse; (2) his passion and resurrection (17:22); (3) coming activity of the *son of Adam* as judge (16:27).

8:21 To *bury* the dead is one of the most important tasks of the living towards the dead, although the touching of a corpse caused defilement (Num 19:11).

8:25 There may be a double meaning in *Master*, which can also mean "Lord."

8:28 Gadara is the city of the *Gadarenes*. It is one of the Hellenistic cities which belongs to the Decapolis (the ten cities) and is situated southeast of the Sea of Galilee (see note at 4:25).

8:31 *Pigs* were unclean for Jews (Lev 11:7; Deut 14:8).

9 ***After he got*** on board the boat, he crossed over and came to his
own town. 2The next thing you know, some people were bringing him
a paralytic lying on a bed. When Jesus noticed their trust, he said to the
paralytic, "Take courage, child, your sins are forgiven."
3At that some of the scholars said to themselves, "This fellow blasphemes!"
4Because he understood the way they thought, Jesus said, "Why do
you harbor evil thoughts? 5Which is easier: to say, 'Your sins are
forgiven,' or to say, 'Get up and walk'?" 6But so that you may realize
that on earth the son of Adam has authority to forgive sins, he then says
to the paralytic, "Get up, pick up your bed and go home."
7And he got up and went to his home. 8When the crowds saw this,
they became fearful, and extolled God for giving such authority to
humans.
9***As Jesus was walking*** along there, he caught sight of a man sitting
at the toll booth, one named Matthew, and he says to him, "Follow
me!" And he got up and followed him.
10***And it so happened*** while he was dining in ⟨Matthew's⟩ house
that many toll collectors and sinners showed up just then and dined
with Jesus and his disciples.
11And whenever the Pharisees saw this, they would question his disciples: "Why does your teacher eat with toll collectors and sinners?"
12When Jesus overheard, he said, "Since when do the able-bodied
need a doctor? It's the sick who do. 13Go and learn what this means,
'It's mercy I desire instead of sacrifice.' After all, I did not come to
enlist religious folks but sinners!"
14***Then the disciples*** of John come up to him, and ask: "Why do we
fast, and the Pharisees fast, but your disciples don't?"
15And Jesus said to them, "The groom's friends can't mourn as long
as the groom is around, can they? But the days will come when the
groom is taken away from them, and then they will fast. 16Nobody puts
a piece of unshrunk cloth on an old garment, since the patch pulls
away from the garment and creates a worse tear. 17Nor do they pour
young wine into old wineskins, otherwise the wineskins burst, the wine
gushes out, and the wineskins are destroyed. Instead, they put young
wine in new wineskins and both are preserved."
18***Just as he was*** saying these things to them, one of the officials
came, kept bowing down to him, and said, "My daughter has just died.
But come and put your hand on her and she will live." 19And Jesus got
up and followed him, along with his disciples.
20***And just then*** a woman who had suffered from vaginal bleeding for
twelve years came up from behind and touched the hem of his cloak.
21She had been saying to herself, "If I only touch his cloak, I'll be
cured." 22When Jesus turned around and saw her, he said, "Take cour-

Jesus cures a paralytic

Matthew becomes a follower

Jesus dines with sinners

Fasting & feasting

Official's daughter

Jesus cures a woman

9:1–8
//Mk 2:1–12, Lk 5:17–26

9:6
Ⓣ Jn 5:8

9:9–13
//Mk 2:14–17, Lk 5:27–32, GOxy 1224 5:1–2

9:9
Cf. GEbi 2:4

9:13
Ⓘ Mt 12:7; cf. GEbi 6; ◊ Hos 6:6

9:14–17
//Mk 2:18–22, Lk 5:33–39

9:14
Ⓣ Mt 11:18–19

9:15
Cf. Th 27, 104

9:16–17
//Th 47:3–5

9:18–26
//Mk 5:21–43, Lk 8:40–56

9:18
See 2:2

9:20
◊ Lv 15:25, Dt 22:29

9:1 *His own city* refers to Capernaum.

Official's daughter dies | *Two blind men* | *Jesus cures a mute* | *Good crop, few workers* | *The twelve* | *Instructions for the twelve*

age, daughter, your trust has cured you." And the woman was cured right then and there.

[23]***And when Jesus came*** into the home of the official and saw the mourners with their flutes, and the crowd making a disturbance, [24]he said, "Go away; you see, the girl hasn't died; she's sleeping." And they started laughing at him. [25]When the crowd had been thrown out, he came in and took her by the hand and raised the little girl up. [26]And his reputation spread all around that region.

[27]***And when Jesus left there,*** two blind men followed him, crying out, "Have mercy on us, son of David."

[28]When ⟨Jesus⟩ arrived home, the blind men came to him. Jesus says to them, "Do you trust that I can do this?"

They reply to him, "Yes, master."

[29]Then he touched their eyes, saying, "Your trust will be the measure of your cure." [30]And their eyes were opened. Then Jesus scolded them, saying, "See that no one finds out about it." [31]But they went out and spread the news of him throughout that whole territory.

[32]***Just as they were leaving,*** they brought to him a mute who was demon-possessed. [33]And after the demon had been driven out, the mute started to speak. And the crowd was amazed and said, "Nothing like this has ever been seen in Israel."

[34]But the Pharisees would say, "He drives out demons in the name of the head demon."

[35]***And Jesus went*** about all the towns and villages, teaching in their synagogues and proclaiming the gospel of ⟨Heaven's⟩ imperial rule and healing every disease and ailment. [36]When he saw the crowd, he was moved by them because they were in trouble and helpless, like sheep without a shepherd. [37]Then he said to his disciples, "Although the crop is good, still there are few to harvest it. [38]So beg the harvest boss to dispatch workers to the fields."

10 ***And summoning his twelve*** disciples he gave them authority to drive out unclean spirits and to heal every disease and every ailment. [2]The names of the twelve apostles were these: first, Simon, also known as Rock, and Andrew his brother, and James the son of Zebedee and John his brother, [3]Philip and Bartholomew, Thomas, and Matthew the toll collector, James the son of Alphaeus, and Thaddaeus, [4]Simon the Zealot, and Judas of Iscariot, the one who, in the end, turned him in.

[5]***Jesus sent out*** these twelve after he had given them these instructions: "Don't travel foreign roads and don't enter a Samaritan town, [6]but go rather to the lost sheep of the house of Israel.

9:27–31 Ⓓ Mt 20:29–34; //Mk 10:46–52, Lk 18:35–43
Q**9:32–34** Ⓓ Mt 12:22–24; //Mk 3:22, Lk 11:14–15
9:35 Cf. Mk 1:39, 6:6b, Lk 8:1; Ⓣ Mary 4:8; Ⓘ Mt 4:23
9:36 Ⓣ Mk 6:34; ◊Nm 27:16–17, 1 Kgs 22:17, Zec 10:27, Jdt 11:19
Q**9:37–38** //Lk 10:2, Th 73
9:37 Ⓣ Jn 4:35
10:1–4 //Mk 3:13–19, Lk 6:12–16; cf. GEbi 2:3
10:1 //Mk 6:7, Lk 9:1
Q**10:5–15** //Mk 6:6–13, Lk 9:1–6, 10:1–15

9:34 A few mss omit this verse. **10:3** A few mss have "Lebbaeus" instead of *Thaddaeus.* Many mss have "Lebbaeus who is called Thaddaeus."

9:23 *Flutes* were used by professional mourners.
10:2 *Rock* is a translation of Greek *Petros* which was a nickname (4:18) but was taken as a proper name later in the tradition.
10:5 This is the beginning of the second of five major sermons in Matthew (see 7:28).

Fate of the disciples

[7]"Go and announce: 'Heaven's imperial rule is closing in.'

[8]"Heal the sick, raise the dead, cleanse the lepers, drive out demons. You have received freely, so freely give. [9]Don't get gold or silver or copper coins for spending money, [10]don't take a knapsack for the road, or two shirts, or sandals, or a staff; for 'the worker deserves to be fed.'

[11]"Whichever town or village you enter, find out who is deserving; stay there until you leave. [12]When you enter a house, greet it. [13]And if the house is deserving, give it your peace blessing, but if it is unworthy, withdraw your peace blessing. [14]And if anyone does not welcome you, or listen to your words, as you are going out of that house or town shake the dust off your feet. [15]I swear to you, the land of Sodom and Gomorrah will be better off on judgment day than that town.

[16]"***Look,*** I'm sending you out like sheep to a pack of wolves. Therefore you must be as sly as a snake and as simple as a dove. [17]And beware of people, for they will turn you over to the Council and in the synagogues they will scourge you. [18]And you will be hauled up before governors and even kings on my account so you can make your case to them and to the nations. [19]And when they lock you up, don't worry about how you should speak or what you should say. It will occur to you at that moment what to say. [20]For it is not you who are speaking but your Father's spirit speaking through you. [21]One brother will turn in another to be put to death, and a father his child, and children will turn against their parents and kill them. [22]And you will be universally hated because of me. But those who hold out to the end will be saved. [23]When they persecute you in this town, flee to another. I swear to you, you certainly won't have exhausted the towns of Israel before the son of Adam comes.

Student & teacher

[24]"***Students are not*** above their teachers, nor slaves above their masters. [25]It is appropriate for students to be like their teachers and slaves to be like their masters. If they have dubbed the master of the house 'Beelzebul,' aren't they even more likely to malign the members of his household?

Have no fear

[26]"***So don't be afraid*** of them. After all, there is nothing veiled that won't be unveiled, or hidden that won't be made known. [27]What I say to you in darkness, say in the light, and what you hear whispered in your ear, announce from the rooftops.

[28]"Don't fear those who kill the body but cannot kill the soul; instead, you ought to fear the one who can destroy both the soul and the body in Gehenna. [29]What do sparrows cost? A penny apiece? Yet not one of them will fall to the earth without the consent of your Father. [30]As for you, even the hairs on your head have all been counted. [31]So, don't be so timid: you're worth more than a flock of

10:6 //Mt15:24
10:7 //Mt3:2, 4:17
10:10 //1Tm5:18; Ⓣ 1Cor9:14
10:15 ◊Gn19:24
10:16–23 //Mk13:9–13, Lk21:12–19
10:16 //Lk10:3, Th39:3
10:17 Ⓓ Mt24:9
Q**10:19–20** //Lk12:11–12; cf. Jn14:26
10:21 ◊Mi7:6
10:22 Ⓓ Mt24:13; cf. Jn15:18
Q**10:24** //Lk6:40; cf. Jn13:16, 15:20
10:25 Cf. Mt9:34, 12:24, Lk11:15
Q**10:26–33** //Lk12:1–12
10:26 //Mk4:22, Th5:2, 6:5–6, Lk8:17
10:27 Cf. Th33:1
10:30 //Lk21:18; ◊1Sm14:45, 2Sm14:11

10:23 In the middle of the verse, a few mss add: "And when they persecute you in another, flee to yet another one."

10:25 In 2 Kgs 1:2–16 Beelzebul is a god of the Philistines. By the time of the New Testament it was used as one of several names for the devil.

Way of the cross

John queries Jesus

Jesus praises John

sparrows. [32]Everyone who acknowledges me in public, I too will acknowledge before my Father in the heavens. [33]But the one who disowns me in public, I too will disown before my Father in the heavens.

[34]"***Don't get the idea*** that I came to bring peace on earth. I did not come to bring peace but a sword. [35]After all, I have come

> to pit a man against his father,
> a daughter against her mother,
> and a daughter-in-law against her mother-in-law.
> [36]Your enemies live under your own roof.

[37]"If you love your father and mother more than me, you're not worthy of me, and if you love your son or daughter more than me, you're not worthy of me. [38]Unless you take your cross and come along with me, you're not worthy of me. [39]By finding your life, you'll lose it, and by losing your life for my sake, you'll find it.

[40]"The one who accepts you accepts me, and the one who accepts me accepts the one who sent me. [41]The one who accepts a prophet as a prophet will be treated like a prophet; and the one who accepts a virtuous person as a virtuous person will be treated like a virtuous person. [42]And whoever gives so much as a cup of cool water to one of these little ones, because the little one is a follower of mine, I swear to you, such a person certainly won't go unrewarded."

11 And so when Jesus had finished instructing his twelve disciples, he moved on from there to teach and proclaim in their towns.

[2]***While John was in prison*** he heard about what the Anointed had been doing and he sent his disciples [3]to ask, "Are you the one who is to come or are we to wait for another?"

[4]And so Jesus answered them, "Go report to John what you have heard and seen:

> [5]The blind see again and the lame walk;
> lepers are cleansed and the deaf hear;
> the dead are raised,
> and the poor have the good news preached to them.
> [6]Congratulations to those who don't take offense at me."

[7]***After ⟨John's disciples⟩*** had departed, Jesus began to talk about John to the crowds: "What did you go out to the wilderness to gawk at? A reed shaking in the wind? [8]What did you really go out to see? A man dressed in fancy ⟨clothes⟩? But wait! Those who wear fancy ⟨clothes⟩ are found in regal quarters. [9]Come on, what did you go out to see? A prophet? Yes, that's what you went out to see, yet someone more than a prophet.

[10]"This is the one about whom it was written:

10:33 //Mk8:38, Lk9:26
Q**10:34–36** //Lk12:49–53, Th16, cf.GNaz11
10:35–36 ◊Mi7:5–6
Q**10:37–39** //Lk14:25–27
10:37–38 //Th55; cf.Th101:1–2
10:38–39 //Mk8:34–35, Mt16:24–25, Lk9:23–24; cf.Jn12:25
10:39 //Lk17:33
Q**10:40** //Lk10:16
10:42 //Mk9:41
Q**11:1–6** //Lk7:18–23
11:1 ① Mt7:28, 13:53, 19:1, 26:1
11:5 ◊Is35:6, 29:18
Q**11:7–15** //Lk7:24–30
11:7–8 //Th78

11:9 Ancient mss have no punctuation, so Jesus' question could also be translated, "Why did you go out? To see a prophet?" (see Thom 78).

Here is my messenger,
whom I send on ahead of you
to prepare your way before you.

11"I swear to you, among those born of women no one has arisen who is greater than John the Baptist; yet the least in Heaven's domain is greater than he. 12From the time of John the Baptist until now Heaven's imperial rule has been breaking in violently, and violent men are attempting to gain it by force. 13You see, the Prophets and even the Law predicted everything that was to happen prior to John's time. 14And if you are willing to admit it, John is the Elijah who was to come. 15Anyone here with two ears had better listen!

16"***What does this generation*** remind me of? It is like children sitting in marketplaces who call out to others:

17We played the flute for you,
but you wouldn't dance;
we sang a dirge
but you wouldn't mourn.

18Just remember, John appeared on the scene neither eating nor drinking, and they say, 'He is demented.' 19The son of Adam appeared on the scene both eating and drinking, and they say, 'There's a glutton and a drunk, a crony of toll collectors and sinners!' Indeed, wisdom is vindicated by her deeds."

20***Then he began*** to insult the towns where he had performed most of his miracles, because they had not changed their ways: 21"Damn you, Chorazin! Damn you, Bethsaida! If the miracles done in you had been done in Tyre and Sidon, they would have ⟨sat⟩ in sackcloth and ashes and changed their ways long ago. 22So I tell you, Tyre and Sidon will be better off on judgment day than you. 23And you, Capernaum, you don't think you'll be exalted to heaven, do you? No, you'll go to Hell. Because if the miracles done among you had been done in Sodom, Sodom would still be around. 24So I tell you, the land of Sodom will be better off on judgment day than you."

25***At that point,*** Jesus responded: "I praise you, Father, Lord of heaven and earth, because you have hidden these things from the wise and the learned but revealed them to the untutored; 26yes indeed, Father, because this is the way you want it. 27My Father has turned everything over to me. No one knows the son except the Father, nor

Children in marketplaces

Damn you Chorazin

Father & son

11:10 Cf. Mk 1:2; ◊Mal 3:1
11:11 //Th 46
Q11:12–13 //Lk 16:16
11:14 Cf. Mk 9:13, Jn 1:21; ◊Mal 4:5
Q11:16–19 //Lk 7:31–35
11:18 Ⓣ Mt 9:14
Q11:20–24 //Lk 10.12–15
11:23 ◊Is 14:13–15
11:24 Ⓓ Mt 10:15
Q11:25–30 //Lk 10:21–22
11:27 Cf. Jn 3:35, 7:29

11:12 The Greek grammar here is very difficult. The more traditional translation would be "Heaven's imperial rule is suffering violence." Such a translation has been justified by the notion that Heaven's imperial rule must be peaceful. However, the normal use of the verb in Greek is not passive but active: Heaven's imperial rule breaks in violently.

11:16 The *marketplace* was the normal place where *children* recited their lessons for their tutors.

11:21 *Chorazin* was a Jewish town just north of Capernaum. *Bethsaida* was most probably situated at the mouth of the Jordan river as it entered the north end of the Sea of Galilee. In Hebrew the name means "House of the fisherman."

Tyre and *Sidon* were the two leading cities of ancient Phoenicia.

Son of Adam over the sabbath

Man with a crippled hand

Jesus withdraws

does anyone know the Father except the son—and anyone to whom the son wishes to reveal him. [28]All you who labor and are overburdened come to me, and I will refresh you. [29]Take my yoke upon you and learn from me, because I am meek and modest and your lives will find repose. [30]For my yoke is comfortable and my load is light."

12 ***On that occasion*** Jesus walked through the grainfields on the sabbath day. His disciples were hungry and began to strip heads of grain and chew them. [2]When the Pharisees saw this, they said to him, "See here, your disciples are doing what's not permitted on the sabbath day."

[3]He said to them, "Haven't you read what David did when he and his companions were hungry? [4]He went into the house of God, and ate the consecrated bread, which no one is permitted to eat—not even David or his companions—except the priests alone! [5]Or haven't you read in the Law that during the sabbath day the priests violate the sabbath in the temple and are held blameless? [6]Yet I say to you, someone greater than the temple is here. [7]And if you had known what this means, 'It's mercy I desire instead of sacrifice,' you would not have condemned those who are blameless. [8]Remember, the son of Adam lords it over the sabbath day."

[9]***And when he had*** moved on, he went into their synagogue. [10]Just then a fellow with a crippled hand appeared, and they asked him, "Is it permitted to heal on the sabbath day?" so they could discredit him.

[11]He asked them, "If you had only a single sheep, and it fell into a ditch on the sabbath day, wouldn't you grab it and pull it out? [12]A person is worth considerably more than a sheep. So, it is permitted to do good on the sabbath day!"

[13]Then he says to the fellow, "Hold out your hand!" He held it out and it was restored to health like the other.

[14]The Pharisees went out and hatched a plot against him to get rid of him.

[15]***Aware of this,*** Jesus withdrew from there, and huge crowds followed him, and he healed all of them. [16]And he warned them not to disclose his identity, [17]so what was spoken through Isaiah the prophet would come true:

[18]Here is my servant whom I have selected,
my favored of whom I fully approve.
I will put my spirit upon him,
and he will announce judgment for foreigners.
[19]He will not be contentious,
nor loud-mouthed,

11:28–29 ◊Sir 51:23–27
11:28–30 //Th90
11:29 ◊Jer 6:16
12:1–8 //Mk2:23–28, Lk6:1–5
12:1 ◊Dt23:25
12:3–4 ◊1Sm21:1–6
12:4 ◊Lv24:5–9
12:7 Ⓘ Mt9:13; cf. GEbi6; ◊Hos 6:6
12:9–14 //Mk3:1–6, Lk6:6–11; cf. GNaz4
12:11–12 //Lk14:5; cf. Lk13:15
12:15–21 //Mk3:7–12, Lk6:17–19
12:18–21 ◊Is42:1–4

12:15 Some mss read "many" instead of *huge crowds*.

11:29 *Yoke* is not viewed negatively in the ancient world, but is a beneficent symbol of the discipline and resulting good life produced by following the Law or the teaching of Jesus.

nor will anyone hear his voice on main street.
[20]He is not about to break a crushed reed,
and he's not one to snuff out a smoldering wick,
until he brings forth a decisive victory,
[21]and foreigners will center their hope on him.

Beelzebul controversy

[22]***Then they brought*** to him a blind and mute person who was demon-possessed, and he cured him so the mute was able both to speak and to see. [23]And the entire crowd was beside itself and would say, "This fellow can't be the son of David, can he?"

[24]But when the Pharisees heard of it, they said, "This fellow drives out demons only in the name of Beelzebul, the head demon."

[25]But he knew how they thought, and said to them: "Every government divided against itself is devastated, and every town or household divided against itself won't survive. [26]So if Satan drives out Satan, he is divided against himself. In that case, how will his domain endure?

[27]"Even if I drive out demons in Beelzebul's name, in whose name do your own people drive ⟨them⟩ out? In that case, they will be your judges. [28]But if by God's spirit I drive out demons, then for you God's imperial rule has arrived.

[29]"Or how can someone enter a powerful man's house and steal his belongings, unless he first ties him up? Only then does he loot his house.

[30]"The one who isn't with me is against me, and the one who doesn't gather with me scatters. [31]That's why I tell you: Every offense and blasphemy will be forgiven humankind, but the blasphemy of the spirit won't be forgiven. [32]And the one who speaks a word against the son of Adam will be forgiven; but the one who speaks a word against the holy spirit won't be forgiven, either in this age or in the one to come.

[33]"If you make the tree choice, its fruit will be choice; if you make the tree rotten, its fruit will be rotten. After all, the tree is known by its fruit. [34]You spawn of Satan, how can your speech be good when you are corrupt? As you know, the mouth gives voice to what the heart is full of. [35]The good person produces good things out of a fund of good; and the evil person produces evil things out of a fund of evil. [36]Let me tell you: On judgment day people will have to account for every thoughtless word they utter. [37]Your own words will vindicate you, and your own words will condemn you."

Request for a sign

[38]***Then some of the scholars*** and Pharisees responded to him, "Teacher, we would like to see a sign from you."

[39]In response he said to them, "An evil and immoral generation insists on a sign, and no sign will be given it, except the sign of Jonah the prophet. [40]You see, just as 'Jonah was in the belly of a sea monster for three days and three nights,' so the son of Adam will be in the bowels of the earth for three days and three nights. [41]At judgment time, the citizens of Nineveh will come back to life along with this generation and condemn it, because they had a change of heart in response to Jonah's message. Yet take note: what is right here is greater than Jonah.

Q12:22–37
//Mk 3:20–30, Lk 11:14–23
12:22–24
(D) Mt 9:32–34
12:29
//Th 35
12:30
Cf. Mk 9:40, Lk 9:50
12:31–32
//Th 44
Q12:32
//Lk 12:10
12:33–35
//Th 45
Q12:33
//Lk 6:43–44; cf. Mt 7:20
Q12:34–35
//Lk 6:45
12:34
Cf. Mt 15:18; (I) Mt 3:7, 23:33
Q12:38–42
//Mk 8:11–13, Lk 11:29–32
12:38
Cf. Jn 2:18, 6:30
12:38–39
(D) Mt 16:1–4
12:40
◊Jon 1:17
12:41
◊Jon 3:5

Return of an unclean spirit

True relatives

Sower, seeds, soils

In parables

42“At judgment time, the queen of the south will be brought back to life along with this generation, and she will condemn it, because she came from the ends of the earth to listen to Solomon's wisdom. Yet take note: what is right here is greater than Solomon.

43“***When an unclean spirit*** leaves a person, it wanders through waterless places in search of a resting place. When it doesn't find one, 44it then says, ‘I will return to the home I left.’ It then returns and finds it empty, swept, and refurbished. 45Next, it goes out and brings back with it seven other spirits more vile than itself, who enter and settle in there. So that person ends up worse off than when he or she started. That's how it will be for this perverse generation.”

46***While he was still speaking*** to the crowds, his mother and brothers showed up outside; they had come to speak to him. 47Someone said to him, “Look, your mother and your brothers are outside wanting to speak to you.”

48In response he said to the one speaking to him, “My mother and my brothers—who ever are they?” 49And he pointed to his disciples and said, “Here are my mother and my brothers. 50For whoever does the will of my Father in heaven, that's my brother and sister and mother.”

13 ***That same day,*** Jesus left the house and sat beside the sea. 2Huge crowds gathered around him, so he climbed into a boat and sat down, while the entire crowd stood on the sea shore. 3He told them many things in parables:

> This sower went out to sow. 4While he was sowing, some seed fell along the path, and the birds came and ate it up. 5Other seed fell on rocky ground where there wasn't much soil, and it came up right away because the soil had no depth. 6When the sun came up it was scorched, and because it had no roots it withered. 7Still other seed fell among thorns, and the thorns came up and choked them. 8Other seed fell on good earth and started producing fruit: one part had a yield of one hundred, another a yield of sixty, and a third a yield of thirty.
>
> 9Anyone here with two ears had better listen!

10***And his disciples*** came up and said to him, “Why do you instruct them only in parables?”

11In response he said to them, “You have been given the privilege of knowing the secrets of Heaven's imperial rule, but that privilege has not been granted to anyone else. 12In fact, to those who have, more will

12:42 ◊ 1 Kgs 10:1–13
Q **12:43–45** //Lk 11:24–26
12:46–50 //Mk 3:31–35, Lk 8:19–21, Th 99, GEbi 5
12:50 //GHeb 4a
13:1–9 //Mk 4:1–9, Lk 8:4–8, Th 9; cf. SJas 8:2–3
13:10–17 //Mk 4:10–12, Lk 8:9–10
13:12 Ⓓ Mt 25:29; //Mk 4:25; Lk 8:18, 19:26; Th 41

12:47 In Greek both vv. 46 and 47 end with the same word. This led many mss to skip over and omit v. 47.

13:3 This marks the beginning of the third Sermon (see 7:28).

be given, and then some; and from those who don't have, even what they do have will be taken away! 13That is why I tell them parables, because

Understanding the sower

When they look they don't really see
and when they listen they don't really hear or understand.

14Moreover, in them the prophecy of Isaiah comes true, the one which says,

You listen closely, yet you won't ever understand,
and you look intently but won't ever see.
15For the mind of this people has grown dull,
and their ears are hard of hearing,
and they have shut their eyes,
otherwise they might actually see with their eyes,
and hear with their ears,
and understand with their minds,
and turn around
and I would heal them.

16How privileged are your eyes because they see, and your ears because they hear. 17I swear to you, many prophets and righteous ones have longed to see what you see and didn't see it, and to hear what you hear and didn't hear it.

18"***You there,*** pay attention to the interpretation of the sower. 19When anyone listens to the message of ⟨Heaven's⟩ imperial rule and does not understand it, the evil one comes and steals away what was sown in the heart: this is the one who is sown 'along the path.' 20The one who is sown 'on rocky ground' is the one who listens to the message and right away receives it happily. 21However, this one lacks its own 'root' and so is short-lived. When distress or persecution comes because of the message, such a person becomes easily shaken right away. 22And the one sown 'into the thorns' is the one who listens to the message, but the worries of the age and the seductiveness of wealth 'choke' the message and it becomes 'fruitless.' 23The one who is sown 'on the good earth' is the one who listens to the message and understands, who really 'produces fruit and yields here a hundred, there sixty, and there thirty.'"

Weeds in the field

24***He spun out*** another parable for them:

Heaven's imperial rule is like someone who sowed good seed in his field. 25And while everyone was asleep, his enemy came and scattered weed seed around in his wheat and stole away. 26And when the crop sprouted and produced heads, then the weeds also appeared. 27The owner's slaves came and asked him, "Master, didn't you sow good seed in your field? Then why are there weeds everywhere?" 28He replied to them, "Some enemy has done this." The slaves said to him, "Do you want us then to go and pull the weeds?" 29He

13:13–15
◊Is6:9–10
Q**13:16–17**
//Lk10:23–24
13:18–23
//Mk4:13–20, Lk8:11–15
13:24–30
//Th57

Mustard seed & leaven

Understanding the weeds in the field

More parables

replied, "No, otherwise you'll root out the wheat at the same time as you pull the weeds. 30Let them grow up together until the harvest, and at harvest time I'll say to the harvesters, 'Gather the weeds first and bind them in bundles to burn, but gather the wheat into my granary.' "

31***He put another parable*** before them with these words:

Heaven's imperial rule is like a mustard seed that a man took and sowed in his field. 32Though it is the smallest of all seeds, yet, when it has grown up, it is the largest of garden plants, and becomes a tree, so that the birds of the sky come and roost in its branches.

33He told them another parable:

Heaven's imperial rule is like leaven that a woman took and concealed in fifty pounds of flour until it was all leavened.

34Jesus spoke all these things to the crowds in parables. And he would not say anything to them 35except by way of parable, so what was spoken through the prophet would come true:

I will open my mouth in parables,
I will utter matters kept secret since the foundation of the world.

36***Then he left*** the crowds and went into the house. His disciples came to him with this request: "Explain the parable of the weeds in the field to us."

37This was his response: "The one who 'sows the good seed' is the son of Adam; 38'the field' is the world; and 'the good seed' are those to whom Heaven's domain belongs, but 'the weeds' represent progeny of the evil one. 39'The enemy' who sows ⟨the weeds⟩ is the devil, and 'the harvest' is the end of the present age; 'the harvesters' are the heavenly messengers. 40Just as the weeds are gathered and destroyed by fire—that's how it will be at the end of the age. 41The son of Adam will send his messengers and they will gather all the snares and the subverters of the Law out of his domain 42and throw them into the fiery furnace. People in that place will weep and grind their teeth. 43Then those who are vindicated will be radiant like the sun in my Father's domain. Anyone here with two ears had better listen!

44***Heaven's imperial rule*** is like treasure hidden in a field: when someone finds it, that person covers it up again, and out of sheer joy goes and sells every last possession and buys that field.

Q13:31–32
//Mk 4:30–32, Lk 13:18–19, Th 20
13:32
◊Ez 17:23, 31:69; Dn 4:20–22
Q13:33
//Lk 13:20, Th 96; ◊Ex 12:15, Ⓣ Mt 16:6, 1 Cor 5:6, Gal 5:9
13:35
◊Ps 78:2–3; cf. SJas 6:15
13:41
Cf. Mt 24:31
13:42
Cf. Mt 8:12, 13:50, 22:13, 24:51, 25:30; ◊Dn 3:6
13:44
//Th 109

13:35 A few mss have supplied the prophet Isaiah's name. Some mss do not have *of the world.* Scribes may have copied it here from the parallel in 25:34. *Foundation* then means "beginning."

13:31 *The mustard seed's* smallness was proverbial, but it hardly grows up to become a *tree.*
13:33 The ancients viewed the process of leaven as corrupting the loaf, like a corpse, causing it to swell up. Therefore leaven is unclean, something to be avoided (16:11). Leaven is the symbol of the unholy (Exod

No respect at home

Herod beheads John

[45]Again, Heaven's imperial rule is like some trader looking for beautiful pearls. [46]When that merchant finds one priceless pearl, he sells everything he owns and buys it.

[47]Once more: Heaven's imperial rule is like a net that is cast into the sea and catches all kinds of fish. [48]When the net is full, they haul it ashore. Then they sit down and collect the good fish into baskets, but the worthless fish they throw away. [49]This is how the present age will end. God's messengers will go out and separate the evil from the righteous [50]and throw the evil into the fiery furnace. People in that place will weep and grind their teeth.

[51]"Do you understand all these things?"

"Of course," they replied.

[52]He said to them, "That's why every scholar who is schooled in Heaven's imperial rule is like some proprieter who produces from his storeroom treasures old and new."

[53]And so when Jesus had finished these parables, he moved on from there.

[54]***And he came to his hometown*** and resumed teaching them in their synagogue, so they were astounded and said so: "What's the source of this wisdom and these miracles? [55]This is the carpenter's son, isn't it? Isn't his mother called Mary? And aren't his brothers James and Joseph and Simon and Judas? [56]And aren't all his sisters neighbors of ours? So where did he get all this?" [57]And they were resentful of him. Jesus said to them, "No prophet goes without respect, except on his home turf and at home!" [58]And he did not perform many miracles there because of their lack of trust.

14 ***On that occasion*** Herod the tetrarch heard the rumor about Jesus [2]and said to his servants, "This is John the Baptizer. He's been raised from the dead; that's why miraculous powers are at work in him."

[3]Herod, remember, had arrested John, put him in chains, and thrown him in prison, on account of Herodias, his brother Philip's wife. [4]John, for his part, had said to him, "It is not right for you to have her."

[5]And while ⟨Herod⟩ wanted to kill him, he was afraid of the crowd because they regarded ⟨John⟩ as a prophet. [6]On Herod's birthday, the daughter of Herodias danced for them and captivated Herod, [7]so he swore an oath and promised to give her whatever she asked.

13:45–46 //Th 76
13:47–50 //Th 8
13:50 ◊Dn 3:6
13:53–58 //Mk 6:1–6, Lk 4:16–30
13:53 ① Mt 7:28, 11:1, 19:1, 26:1
13:57 //Jn 4:44, Th 31
14:1–12 //Mk 6:14–29, Lk 9:7–9
14:3 Cf. Lk 3:19–20
14:4 ◊Lv 18:16, 20:21

12:15).

13:55 A *carpenter* in this period would also have been skilled in stone work.

14:1 *Herod the Tetrach* is Herod Antipas, a son of Herod of the Great. He ruled Galilee and Perea from 4 B.C.E.–39 C.E.

14:3 *Herodias* was the niece of Herod Antipas and was married to Herod *Philip* his half brother. In order to marry Herodias he had to divorce the daughter of the powerful king of the Nabateans, Aretas.

Loaves & fish for 5,000

Jesus departs

Jesus walks on the sea

8Prompted by her mother, she said, "Give me the head of John the Baptist right here on a platter."

9The king was sad, but on account of his oath and his dinner guests, he ordered that it be done. 10And he sent and had John beheaded in prison. 11⟨John's⟩ head was brought on a platter and presented to the girl, and she gave it to her mother. 12Then his disciples came and got his body and buried him. Then they went and told Jesus.

13***When Jesus got word*** of ⟨John's death⟩, he sailed away quietly to an isolated place. The crowds got wind of ⟨his departure⟩ and followed him on foot from the towns. 14When he stepped ashore, he saw this huge crowd, took pity on them, and healed their sick.

15When it was evening the disciples approached him, and said, "This place is desolate and it's already late. Send the crowd away so that they can go to the villages and buy food for themselves."

16Jesus said to them, "They don't need to leave; give them something to eat yourselves!"

17But they say to him, "We have nothing here except five loaves of bread and two fish."

18He said, "Bring them here to me." 19And he told the crowd to sit down on the grass, and he took the five loaves and two fish, and looking up to the sky he gave a blessing, and breaking it apart he gave the bread to the disciples, and the disciples ⟨gave it⟩ to the crowd.

20And everybody had more than enough to eat. Then they picked up twelve baskets full of leftovers. 21The number of people who had eaten came to about five thousand, not counting women and children.

22***And right away*** he made the disciples get in a boat and go ahead of him to the other side, while he dispersed the crowds. 23After he had dispersed the crowds, he went up to the mountain privately to pray. He remained there alone well into the evening.

24***By this time*** the boat was already some distance from land and was being pounded by waves because the wind was against them. 25About three o'clock in the morning he came toward them walking on the sea. 26But when the disciples saw him walking on the sea, they were terrified. "It's a ghost," they said, and cried out in fear.

27Right away Jesus spoke to them, saying, "Take heart, it's me! Don't be afraid."

28In response Peter said, "Master, if it's really you, order me to come across the water to you."

29He said, "Come on."

And Peter got out of the boat and walked on the water and came toward Jesus. 30But with the strong wind in his face, he started to panic. And when he began to sink, he cried out, "Master, save me."

31Right away Jesus extended his hand and took hold of him and says

14:13–14
//Mk6:30–34, Lk9:10–11
14:15–21
//Mk6:35–44, Lk9:12–17, Jn6:1–15; Ⓓ Mt15:32–39, Mk8:1–10; ◊ 1 Kgs4:42–44
14:19
Cf. Mt26:26
14:22–23
//Mk6:45–46, Jn6:15
14:24–33
//Mk6:47–52, Jn6:16–21
14:26
Ⓣ Lk24:37
14:31
Ⓣ Mt6:30, 8:26, 16:8, 17:20

14:30 There is perhaps a double meaning in Peter's reply. It could be translated "Master, rescue me," or, in a religious sense, "Lord, save me."

to him, "You don't have enough trust! Why did you hesitate?" 32And by the time they had climbed into the boat, the wind had died down.

33Then those in the boat paid homage to him, saying, "You really are God's son."

Cure of the sick

34***Once they had crossed*** over they landed at Gennesaret. 35And the local people recognized him and sent word into the whole surrounding area and brought him all who were ill. 36And they begged him just to let them touch the fringe of his cloak. And all those who managed to touch ⟨it⟩ were cured!

Rules for handwashing

15

Then the Pharisees and scholars from Jerusalem come to Jesus, and say, 2"Why do your disciples deviate from the traditions of the elders? For instance, they don't wash their hands before they eat bread."

3In response he asked them, "Why do you also break God's commandment because of your tradition? 4You remember God said, 'Honor your father and mother' and 'Those who curse their father or mother will surely die.' 5But you say, 'If people say to their father or mother, "Whatever I might have spent to support you has been consecrated to God," 6they certainly should not honor their father or mother.' So you end up invalidating God's word because of your tradition. 7You phonies, how accurately Isaiah depicted you when he said,

> 8This people honors me with their lips,
> but their heart strays far away from me.
> 9Their worship of me is empty,
> because they insist on teachings that are human regulations."

What comes out defiles

10***And he summoned*** the crowd and said to them, "Listen and try to understand. 11What goes into your mouth doesn't defile you; what comes out of your mouth does."

12The disciples came and said to him, "Don't you realize that the Pharisees who heard this remark were offended by it?"

13He responded: "Every plant which my heavenly Father does not plant will be rooted out. 14Never mind them. They are blind guides of blind people! If one blind person guides another, both will end up in some ditch."

15Then Peter replied, "Explain the riddle to us."

16He said, "Are you still as dim-witted as the rest? 17Don't you realize that everything that goes into the mouth passes into the stomach and comes out in the outhouse? 18But the things that come out of the

14:33 See 2:2
14:34–36 //Mk6:53–56; Ⓣ Mt4:23, 8:16–17
15:1–9 //Mk7:1–13
15:4 ◊Ex20:12, 21:17; Lv20:9, Dt5:16
15:7–9 Ⓣ EgerG 3:6
15:8–9 ◊Is29:13
15:10–20 //Mk7:14–23
15:11 //Th14:5
15:13 //Th40
Q**15:14** //Lk6:39, Th34

15:14 Some mss omit *of blind people.*

15:5 *If people say . . .* is an example of case law reasoning.

Canaanite woman's daughter

Loaves & fish for 4,000

mouth come from the heart, and those things defile a person. [19]For out of the heart emerge evil intentions: murders, adulteries, sexual immorality, thefts, false witnesses, blasphemies. [20]These are the things that defile a person. However, eating with unwashed hands doesn't defile anybody."

[21]***So Jesus left there,*** and withdrew to the district of Tyre and Sidon.

[22]And this Canaanite woman from those parts appeared and cried out, "Have mercy on me, sir, you son of David. My daughter is severely possessed."

[23]But he did not respond at all.

And his disciples came and began to complain: "Get rid of her, because she is badgering us."

[24]But in response he said, "I was sent only to the lost sheep of the house of Israel."

[25]She came and bowed down to him, saying, "Sir, please help me."

[26]In response he said, "It's not right to take bread out of children's mouths and throw it to the dogs."

[27]But she said, "Of course, sir, but even the dogs eat the scraps that fall from their master's table."

[28]Then in response Jesus said to her, "My good woman, your trust is enormous! Your wish is as good as fulfilled." And her daughter was cured at that moment.

[29]***Then Jesus left*** there and went to the sea of Galilee. And he climbed up the mountain and sat there. [30]And huge crowds came to him and brought with them the lame, the blind, the maimed, the mute, and many others, and they crowded around his feet and he healed them. [31]As a result, the crowd was astonished when they saw the mute now speaking, the maimed made strong, and the lame walking and the blind seeing. And they gave all the credit to the God of Israel.

[32]Then Jesus called his disciples aside and said: "I feel sorry for the crowd because they have already spent three days with me and now they've run out of food. And I don't want to send these people away hungry, for fear they'll collapse on the road."

[33]And the disciples say to him, "How can we get enough bread here in this desolate place to feed so many people?"

[34]Jesus says to them, "How many loaves do you have?"

They replied, "Seven, plus a few fish."

[35]And he ordered the crowd to sit down on the ground.

[36]And he took the seven loaves and the fish and gave thanks and broke them into pieces, and started giving ⟨them⟩ to the disciples, and the disciples ⟨started giving them⟩ to the crowds. [37]And everyone had

15:21–28 //Mk7:24–30
15:24 //Mt10:6
15:25 See 2:2
15:29–31 //Mk7:31–37
15:32–39 //Mk8:1–10, Lk9:12–27, Jn6:1–15, Ⓣ Mt14:15–21, Mk6:35–44; ◊2Kgs4:42–44
15:36 Cf. Mt26:26

15:26 Many mss read "it's not good" instead of *it's not right.*

15:21 For *Tyre* and *Sidon* see the note to 14:21.

15:22 A *Canaanite* is a gentile, and the Canaanites were ancient enemies of Israel.

15:25 *Sir, please help me* can also be understood as "Lord, help me."

more than enough to eat. Then they picked up seven baskets of leftover scraps. 38Those who had eaten numbered four thousand, not counting women and children. 39And after he sent the crowds away, he got into the boat and went to the Magadan region.

Request for a sign

Bread & leaven

What are people saying?

16 ***And the Pharisees*** and Sadducees came, and to put him to the test they asked him to show them a sign in the sky.

2In response he said to them, "When it's evening, you say, 'It'll be fair weather because the sky looks red.' 3Early in the morning, ⟨you say,⟩ 'The day will bring winter weather because the sky looks red and dark.' You know how to read the face of the sky, but you can't discern the signs of the times. 4An evil and immoral generation seeks a sign, yet no sign will be given it except the sign of Jonah." And he turned his back on them and walked away.

5***And the disciples came*** to the opposite shore, but they forgot to bring any bread. 6Jesus said to them, "Look, take care and guard against the leaven of the Pharisees and Sadducees."

7Now they looked quizzically at each other, saying, "We didn't bring any bread."

8Because Jesus was aware of this, he said, "Why are you puzzling, you with so little trust, because you don't have any bread? 9You still aren't using your heads, are you? You don't remember the five loaves for the five thousand and how many baskets you carried away, do you? 10Nor the seven loaves for four thousand and how many big baskets you filled? 11How can you possibly think I was talking to you about bread? Just be on guard against the leaven of the Pharisees and Sadducees."

12Then they understood that he was not talking about guarding against the leaven in bread but against the teaching of the Pharisees and Sadducees.

13***When Jesus came*** to the region of Caesarea Philippi, he started questioning his disciples, asking, "What are people saying about the son of Adam?"

14They said, "Some ⟨say, 'He is⟩ John the Baptist,' but others, 'Elijah,' and others, 'Jeremiah or one of the prophets.'"

15He says to them, "What about you, who do you say I am?"

16And Simon Peter responded, "You are the Anointed, the son of the living God!"

17And in response Jesus said to him, "You are to be congratulated,

Q16:1–4 //Mk8:11–13, Lk11:29–32; Ⓓ Mt12:38–39
16:1 Cf. Jn6:30
16:1–2 Cf. Th91
Q16:2–3 //Lk12:54–56
16:5–12 //Mk8:14–21
16:6 //Lk12:1; Ⓣ 1Cor5:6, Gal5:9
16:8 Ⓣ Mt6:30, 8:26, 14:31, 17:20
16:9 Ⓘ Mt14:15–21
16:10 Ⓘ Mt15:32–39
16:13–20 //Mk8:27–30, Lk9:18–22; Ⓣ Th13
16:16 Ⓣ Jn6:68–69

16:2b-3 Some mss do not have these verses. They could have been based on Luke 12:54–56, or omitted, first in Egypt, where the description does not fit.

15:39 *Magadan* or Magdala, a small town on the western shore of the Sea of Galilee between Capernaum and Tiberias.
16:4 *The sign of Jonah* is not specified. It could be his call to repentance or his days in the belly of the fish.
16:13 *Caesarea Philippi* was a gentile city in upper Galilee which was rebuilt by Philip (see above 14:3) and named for Caesar and himself.

Jesus destined to suffer

Saving & losing life

Jesus transformed

Simon son of Jonah, because flesh and blood did not reveal this to you
but my Father who is in heaven. 18Let me tell you, you are Peter, 'the
Rock,' and on this very rock I will build my congregation, and the gates
of Hades will not be able to overpower it. 19I shall give you the keys of
Heaven's domain, and whatever you bind on earth will be considered
bound in heaven, and whatever you release on earth will be considered
released in heaven."

20Then he ordered the disciples to tell no one that he was the
Anointed.

21***From that time on*** Jesus started to make it clear to his disciples that
he was destined to go to Jerusalem, and suffer a great deal at the hands
of the elders and ranking priests and scholars, and be killed and, on the
third day, be raised.

22And Peter took him aside and began to lecture him, saying, "May
God spare you, master; this surely can't happen to you."

23But he turned and said to Peter, "Get out of my sight, you Satan,
you. You are dangerous to me because you are not thinking in God's
terms, but in human terms."

24***Then Jesus said*** to his disciples, "If any of you wants to come after
me you should deny yourself, pick up your cross, and follow me!

25"Remember, by trying to save your own life, you are going to lose
it, but by losing your own life for my sake, you are going to find it.
26After all, what good will it do if you acquire the whole world but
forfeit your life? Or what will you give in exchange for your life?

27"Remember, the son of Adam is going to come in the glory of his
Father with his messengers, and then he will reward everyone according to their deeds. 28I swear to you: Some of those standing here won't
ever taste death before they see the son of Adam's imperial rule arriv-
ing."

17

Six days later, Jesus takes Peter and James and his brother John
along and he leads them off by themselves to a lofty mountain. 2He was
transformed in front of them and his face shone like the sun, and his
clothes turned as white as light. 3The next thing you know, Moses and
Elijah appeared to them and were conversing with Jesus.

4Then Peter responded by saying to Jesus, "Master, it's a good thing

16:19 Ⓓ Mt18:18; Ⓣ Jn20:22–23
16:21–23 //Mk8:31–33, Lk9:18–22
16:21 Ⓘ Mt4:17, 26:16; Ⓣ Mt17:22–23, 20:17–19
16:24–28 //Mk8:34–9:1, Lk9:23–27
16:24–25 Ⓓ Mt10:38–39
16:24 //Th55
16:25 //Jn12:25
16:31 Ⓣ Mt24:30, 25:31
17:1–13 //Mk9:2–13, Lk9:28–36

16:21 A few mss have *Jesus* "the Anointed."

16:17 *Son of Jonah:* John 1:42 calls Simon the son of John.
16:18 *Peter* is an Aramaic nickname meaning "Rock," thus producing the word play.

Here and Matt 18:17 are the only two verses in which the word *congregation* (frequently translated "church") appear in the Gospels. It is a term of Greek-speaking Christianity. In secular Greek it refers to a popular assembly. Early Greek-speaking Christians borrowed the term from their Bible, the Septuagint, where it frequently is used to translate the Hebrew term for the community of God (e.g., Deut 23:2).
16:19 To *bind* and to *release* refers to the power to announce a command as binding at present or not binding.
17:3 *Moses* represents the Law and *Elijiah* the Prophets, the first two divisions of the Hebrew Bible (see 5:17).

The epileptic

Son of Adam will die & rise

Temple tax

we're here. If you want, I'll set up three tents here, one for you, one for
Moses, and one for Elijah!"
5While he was still speaking, there was a bright cloud that cast a
shadow over them. And just then a voice spoke from the cloud: "This is
my favored son of whom I fully approve. Listen to him!"
6And as the disciples listened, they prostrated themselves, and were
frightened out of their wits.
7And Jesus came and touched them and said: "Get up; don't be
afraid." 8Looking up they saw no one except Jesus by himself.
9And as they came down from the mountain, Jesus ordered them:
"Don't tell anyone about this vision until the son of Adam has been
raised from the dead."
10And the disciples questioned him: "Why, in the light of this, do
the scholars claim that Elijah must come first?"
11In response he said, "Elijah does indeed come and will restore
everything. 12But I tell you that Elijah has already come, and they did
not recognize him but had their way with him. So the son of Adam is
also going to suffer at their hands."
13Then the disciples understood that he had been talking to them
about John the Baptist.
14***And when they rejoined*** the crowd, a person approached and knelt
before him 15and said, "Master, have mercy on my son, because he is
epileptic and suffers great ⟨pain⟩. For instance, he often falls into the
fire and just as often into the water. 16So I brought him to your disciples, but they couldn't heal him."
17In response Jesus said, "You distrustful and perverted lot, how
long must I associate with you? How long must I put up with you?
Bring him here to me!" 18And Jesus rebuked him and the demon came
out of him and the child was healed at that precise moment.
19Later the disciples came to Jesus privately and asked, "Why
couldn't we drive it out?"
20So he says to them, "Because of your lack of trust. I swear to you,
even if you have trust no larger than a mustard seed, you will say to this
mountain, 'Move from here to there,' and it will move. And nothing
will be beyond you."
22***And when they had*** been reunited in Galilee, Jesus said to them,
"The son of Adam is about to be turned over to his enemies, 23and they
will end up killing him, and on the third day he'll be raised." And they
were very sad.
24***And when they came*** to Capernaum, those who collect the temple
tax came to Peter and said, "Your teacher pays his temple tax, doesn't
he?" 25He said, "That's right."

17:20 Some mss add a v. 21, "This kind does not come out except with prayer and fasting." It was copied here from Mark 9:29.

17:5 Ⓣ Mt3:16–17; ◊Ps 2:7
17:10–11 ◊Mal4:5–6
17:14–20 //Mk9:14–27, Lk9:37–43
Q**17:20** //Lk17:6; Ⓣ Mt6:30, 8:26, 14:31, 16:8
17:22–23 //Mk9:30–32, Lk9:43–45; Ⓣ Mt16:21, 20:17–19
17:24 ◊Ex30:13

17:24 At this time custom required that the temple tax be paid with two drachmas from Tyre, which is why money changers were required at the temple. That would be the equivalent of two days labor for a peasant of the period.

Children in God's domain

Hand, foot & eye

Lost sheep

Discipline & forgiveness

And when he got home, Jesus anticipated what was on Peter's mind:
"What are you thinking, Simon? On whom do secular rulers levy taxes
and tolls? Do they levy them on their own people or on aliens?"
26Peter said, "On aliens."
Jesus responded to him, "Then their own people are exempt. 27Still,
we don't want to get in trouble with them, so go down to the sea, cast
your line in, and take the first fish that rises. Open its mouth and you
will find a coin. Take it and pay them for both of us."

18 ***At that moment*** the disciples approached Jesus with the question: "Who is greatest in Heaven's domain?"
2And he called a child over, had her stand in front of them, 3and
said, "I swear to you, if you don't do an about-face and become like
children, you'll never enter Heaven's domain. 4Therefore those who
put themselves on a level with this child are greatest in Heaven's
domain. 5And whoever accepts one such child in my name is accepting
me. 6Any of you who misleads one of these little souls who trusts me
would be better off to have a millstone hung around your neck and be
drowned in the deepest part of the sea!
7"***Damn the world*** for the snares it sets! Even though it's inevitable
for snares to be set, nevertheless, damn the person who sets such
snares. 8If your hand or your foot gets you into trouble, cut it off and
throw it away! It's better for you to enter life maimed or lame than to be
thrown into the eternal fire with both hands and both feet. 9And if your
eye gets you into trouble, rip it out and throw it away! After all, it's
better for you to enter life one-eyed than to be thrown into Gehenna's
fire with both eyes. 10See that you don't disdain one of these little ones.
For I tell you, their guardian angels constantly gaze on the face of my
Father in heaven.
12"***What do you think*** about this? If someone has a hundred sheep
and one of them wanders off, won't that person leave the ninety-nine in
the hills and go look for the one that wandered off? 13And if he should
find it, you can bet he'll rejoice over it more than over the ninety-nine
that didn't wander off. 14And so it is the intention of your Father in
heaven that not one of these little souls be lost.
15"***And if some*** companion does wrong, go have it out between the
two of you privately. If that person listens to you, you have won your
companion over. 16And if he or she doesn't listen, take one or two
people with you so that 'every fact may be supported by two or three

18:1–10
//Mk9:33–37, 9:42–50; Lk9:46–50
18:3–4
Cf. Mk10:13–16, Lk18:15–17
18:3
Cf. Th22; Ⓣ Jn3:3–5
Q**18:6–7**
//Lk17:1–2
18:8–9
Ⓓ Mt5:29–30
Q**18:12–14**
//Lk15:3–7, Th107; ◊Ez34:6–12, Ps119:176
Q**18:15**
//Lk17:3
18:16
◊Dt19:15

18:10 Some mss add a v. 11, "The son of Adam came to save the lost." This was copied from Luke 19:10. **18:14** Many mss have "my" *Father*.
18:15 Some mss made the condition more specific by inserting a "you:" *if some companion does* "you" *wrong.*

17:27 The coin here is a *stater*, worth about 4 drachmas.

18:1 This is the beginning of the fourth sermon.

witnesses.' [17]Then if he or she refuses to listen to them, report it to the congregation. If he or she refuses to listen even to the congregation, treat that companion like you would a pagan or toll collector. [18]I swear to you, whatever you bind on earth will be considered bound in heaven, and whatever you release on earth will be considered released in heaven. [19]Again I assure you, if two of you on earth agree on anything you ask for, it will be done for you by my Father in heaven. [20]In fact, wherever two or three are gathered together in my name, I will be there among them."

The unforgiving slave

[21]Then Peter came up and asked him, "Master, how many times can a companion wrong me and still expect my forgiveness? As many as seven times?"

[22]Jesus replies to him, "My advice to you is not seven times, but seventy-seven times.

[23]***This is why*** Heaven's imperial rule should be compared to a secular ruler who decided to settle accounts with his slaves. [24]When the process began, this debtor was brought to him who owed ten million dollars. [25]Since he couldn't pay it back, the ruler ordered him sold, along with his wife and children and everything he had, so he could recover his money.

[26]At this prospect, the slave fell down and groveled before him: 'Be patient with me, and I'll repay every cent.' [27]Because he was compassionate, the master of that slave let him go and canceled the debt.

[28]As soon as he got out, that same fellow collared one of his fellow slaves who owed him a hundred dollars, and grabbed him by the neck and demanded: 'Pay back what you owe!'

[29]His fellow slave fell down and begged him: 'Be patient with me and I'll pay you back.'

[30]But he wasn't interested; instead, he went out and threw him in prison until he paid the debt.

[31]When his fellow slaves realized what had happened, they were terribly distressed and went and reported to their master everything that had taken place.

[32]At that point, his master summoned him: 'You wicked slave,' he says to him, 'I canceled your entire debt because you begged me. [33]Wasn't it only fair for you to treat your fellow slave with the same consideration as I treated you?' [34]And the master was so angry he handed him over to those in charge of punishment until he paid back everything he owed. [35]That's what my heavenly Father will do to you, unless you find it in your heart to forgive each one of your brothers and sisters."

18:18
Ⓓ Mt 16:19; cf. Jn 20:23
18:20
Ⓘ Mt 1:23, 28:20; cf. Th 30:2
Q18:21–22
//Lk 17:4, GNaz 5:1; ◊Gen 4:24
18:26
See 2:2
18:35
Ⓣ Mt 6:14–15

18:22 *Seventy-seven times* can also be understood as seventy times seven.

18:24 *Ten million dollars* translates "ten thousand talents," an almost fantastic amount. The total yearly taxation for Judea during this period was 600 talents. Some have suggested that the story involves the taxation practices of the Roman Empire.

Jesus leaves Galilee

Created male & female

Celibacy

Children in Heaven's domain

Man with money

19 ***And so when*** Jesus had finished this instruction, he took leave of Galilee and went to the territory of Judea across the Jordan. [2]And large crowds followed him and he healed them there.

[3]***And the Pharisees*** approached him and, to test him, they ask, "Is ⟨a husband⟩ permitted to divorce his wife for any reason?"

[4]In response he puts a question to them: "Have you not read that in the beginning the Creator 'made them male and female,' [5]and that further on it says, 'for this reason, a man will leave his father and mother and be united with his wife, and the two will be one body'? [6]Consequently, from then on they are one body instead of two. Therefore those whom God has coupled together, no one else should separate."

[7]They say to him, "Then why did Moses order 'a written release and separation'?"

[8]He says to them, "Because you are obstinate Moses permitted you to divorce your wives, but it wasn't like that originally. [9]Now I say to you, whoever divorces his wife, except for infidelity, and marries another commits adultery."

[10]***The disciples say to him,*** "If this is how it is in the case of a man and his wife, it's better not to marry."

[11]Then he said to them, "Not everyone will be able to accept this advice, only those for whom it was intended. [12]After all, there are castrated men who were born that way, and there are castrated men who were castrated by others, and there are castrated men who castrated themselves because of Heaven's imperial rule. If you are able to accept this ⟨advice⟩, do so."

[13]***Then little children*** were brought to him so he could lay his hands on them and pray, but the disciples scolded them.

[14]Now Jesus said, "Let the children alone. Don't try to stop them from coming up to me. After all, Heaven's domain belongs to people like that." [15]And he laid his hands on them and left that place.

[16]***And just then*** someone came and asked him, "Teacher, what good do I have to do to have eternal life?"

[17]He said to him, "Why do you ask me about the good? There is only One who is good. If you want to enter life, observe the commandments."

[18]He says to him, "Which ones?"

Jesus replied, "'You must not murder, you are not to commit adultery, you are not to steal, you are not to give false testimony, [19]you are to honor your father and mother, and you are to love your neighbor as yourself.'"

[20]The young man says to him, "I have observed all these; what am I missing?"

19:1–9 //Mk 10:1–12
19:1 Ⓘ Mt 7:28, 11:1, 13:53, 26:1
19:4 ◊Gn 1:27
19:5 ◊Gn 2:24
19:7 ◊Dt 24:1–4
19:9 Ⓓ Mt 5:31–32; cf. Lk 16:18; Ⓣ 1 Cor 7:10–11
19:12 Cf. Th 22:4–7
19:13–15 //Mk 10:13–16, Lk 18:15–17; cf. Th 22:1–3
19:16–22 //Mk 10:17–22, Lk 18:18–25, GNaz 6:1–4
19:18–19 ◊Ex 20:12–16, Dt 5:16–20
19:19 Cf. Th 25; ◊Lv 19:18

19:9 Only Matthew modifies the absolute prohibition against divorce otherwise attributed to Jesus. The Greek term is not very specific but means sexual immorality of any kind, although it is frequently associated with prostitution.

Needle's eye

Vineyard laborers

21 Jesus said to him, "If you wish to be perfect, make your move, sell your belongings and give ⟨the proceeds⟩ to the poor and you will have treasure in heaven. And then come, follow me!"

22 When the young man heard this advice, he went away dejected since he possessed a fortune.

23 ***Jesus said*** to his disciples, "I swear to you, it's difficult for the rich to enter Heaven's domain. 24 And again I tell you, it's easier for a camel to squeeze through a needle's eye than for a wealthy person to get into God's domain."

25 When the disciples heard this, they were quite perplexed and said, "Well then, who can be saved?"

26 Jesus looked them in the eye, and said to them, "For mortals this is impossible; for God everything's possible."

27 In response Peter said to him, "Look at us, we left everything to follow you! What do we get out of it?"

28 Jesus told them, "I swear to you, you who have followed me, when the son of Adam is seated on his throne of glory in the renewal ⟨of creation⟩, you also will be seated on twelve thrones and sit in judgment on the twelve tribes of Israel. 29 And everyone who has left homes or brothers or sisters or father or mother or children or farms, on my account, will receive a hundred times as much and inherit eternal life. 30 Many of the first will be last, and of the last many will be first.

20 ***For Heaven's imperial rule*** is like a proprietor who went out the first thing in the morning to hire workers for his vineyard. 2 After agreeing with the workers for a silver coin a day he sent them into his vineyard.

3 And coming out around nine A.M. he saw others loitering in the marketplace 4 and he said to them, 'You go into the vineyard too, and I'll pay you whatever is fair.' 5 So they went.

Around noon he went out again, and at three P.M. he repeated the process. 6 About five P.M. he went out and found others loitering about and says to them, 'Why did you stand around here idle the whole day?'

7 They reply, 'Because no one hired us.'

He tells them, 'You go into the vineyard as well.'

8 When evening came the owner of the vineyard tells his foreman: 'Call the workers and pay them their wages starting with those hired last and ending with those hired first.'

9 Those hired at five P.M. came up and received a silver coin each. 10 Those hired first approached thinking they would receive more. But they also got a silver coin apiece. 11 They took it and began to

19:23–30
//Mk10:23–31, Lk18:26–30
19:24
//GNaz6:5
Q**19:28**
Cf. Lk22:28–30
19:30
Ⓓ Mt20:16; //Mk10:31, Lk13:30, Th4:2

19:24 The *needle's eye* refers to a sewing needle, not, as some have maintained, a twisting door in the city walls. The aphorism is a paradox.

20:2 This *silver coin* is a *denarius*, a subsistence wage for a laborer.

Son of Adam will die & rise

Jesus' cup

Number one is slave

Two blind men

grumble against the proprietor: 12‘These guys hired last worked only an hour but you have made them equal to us who did most of the work during the heat of the day.’

13In response he said to one of them, ‘Look, pal, did I wrong you? You did agree with me for a silver coin, didn't you? 14Take your wage and get out! I intend to treat the one hired last the same way I treat you. 15Is there some law forbidding me to do as I please with my money? Or is your eye filled with envy because I am generous?’

16The last will be first and the first last.”

17***On the way up*** to Jerusalem Jesus took the twelve aside privately and said to them as they walked along: 18“Listen, we're going up to Jerusalem, and the son of Adam will be turned over to the ranking priests and scholars, and they will sentence him to death, 19and turn him over to foreigners to make fun of, and flog, and crucify. Yet on the third day he will be raised.”

20***Then the mother*** of the sons of Zebedee came up to him with her sons, bowed down before him, and asked him for a favor.

21He said to her, “What do you want?”

She said to him, “Give me your word that these two sons of mine may sit one at your right hand and one at your left in your domain.”

22In response Jesus said, “You have no idea what you're asking for. Can you drink the cup that I'm about to drink?”

They said to him, “We can!”

23He says to them, “You'll be drinking my cup, but as for sitting at my right or my left, that's not mine to grant, but belongs to those for whom it's been reserved by my Father.”

24***And when they learned*** of it, the ten became annoyed with the two brothers. 25And calling them aside, Jesus said, “You know how foreign rulers lord it over their subjects, and how their strong men tyrannize them. 26It's not going to be like that with you! With you, whoever wants to become great will be your slave, 27and whoever among you wants to be ‘number one’ is to be your slave. 28After all, the son of Adam didn't come to be served but to serve, even to give his life as a ransom for many.”

29***And as they were*** leaving Jericho, a huge crowd followed him. 30There were two blind men sitting beside the road. When they learned that Jesus was going by, they shouted, “Have mercy on us, Master, you son of David.”

Q**20:16** Ⓓ Mt19:30; //Mk10:31, Lk13:30, Th4:2
20:17–19 //Mk10:32–34, Lk18:31–34; Ⓣ Mt16:21, 17:22–23
20:20–28 //Mk10:35–45, Lk22:24–47
20:20 See 2:2
20:24–28 Ⓣ Mt18:1–4, Mk9:33–37, Lk9:46–50
20:26–27 Cf.Mt23:11–12
20:29–34 //Mk10:46–52, Lk18:35–43; Ⓓ Mt9:27–31

20:30 Some mss omit *Master* from the blind men's shout, while a few mss substitute “Jesus.”

20:15 The master accuses the laborers of giving him the “evil eye,” an expression for putting a curse on someone, still common in the Mediterranean world.

20:28 *Ransom* usually has to do with the manumission of a slave.

20:29 *Jericho* was one of the more important cities of the Jordan Valley. It was an extremely ancient city, on a major ford of the Jordan river and thus important in both trade and agriculture. The valley was fertile in contrast to the surrounding barren mountains.

[31]The crowd yelled at them to shut up, but they shouted all the louder, "Have mercy on us, Master, you son of David."

[32]Jesus paused and called out to them, "What do you want me to do for you?"

[33]They said to him, "Master, open our eyes!"

[34]Then Jesus took pity on them, touched their eyes, and right away they regained their sight and followed him.

Jesus enters Jerusalem

Temple as hideout

21

When they got close to Jerusalem, and came to Bethphage at the Mount of Olives, then Jesus sent two disciples ahead [2]with these instructions: "Go into the village across the way, and right away you will find a donkey tied up, and a colt alongside her. Untie ⟨them⟩ and bring ⟨them⟩ to me. [3]And if anyone says anything to you, you are to say, 'Their master has need of them and he will send them back right away.'" [4]This happened so the word spoken through the prophet would come true:

> [5]Tell the daughter of Zion,
> Look, your king comes to you in all modesty
> mounted on a donkey and on a colt,
> the foal of a pack animal.

[6]Then the disciples went and did as Jesus instructed them, [7]and brought the donkey and colt and they placed their cloaks on them, and he sat on top of them. [8]The enormous crowd spread their cloaks on the road, and others cut branches from the trees and spread them on the road. [9]The crowds leading the way and those following kept shouting,

> "Hosanna" to the son of David!
> "Blessed is the one who comes in the name of the Lord!"
> "Hosanna" in the highest.

[10]And when he entered into Jerusalem the whole city trembled, saying, "Who is this?" [11]The crowds said, "This is the prophet Jesus from Nazareth, Galilee!"

[12]***And Jesus went*** into God's temple and chased all the vendors and shoppers out of the temple area and he turned the bankers' tables upside down, along with the chairs of the pigeon merchants.

21:1–11 //Mk11:1–11, Lk19:28–40, Jn12:12–19
21:5 ◊Zec9:9
21:9 ◊Ps118:26
21:12–17 //Mk11:15–19, Lk19:45–48, Jn2:13–22

21:12 Some mss omit *God's* as a modifier of *temple*, removing a rare expression not found elsewhere.

20:33 *Master* can also mean "Lord." This double meaning occurs a number of times in Matthew.
21:1 *Bethphage's* exact location has never been determined. It was apparently on the side of the Mount of Olives.
21:7 Jesus is here pictured as astride both animals in literal fulfillment of the prophecy in Zechariah.
21:9 *Hosanna* is a Hebrew expression from Psalm 118 meaning "Help, I pray!" The psalm was part of Passover celebration, and pilgrims coming to Jerusalem for the festival would have shouted this like "Hurrah!" Later it was used in early Christian liturgies as an expression of joy.

Children cheer Jesus

Fig tree without figs

On whose authority?

Two sons

13Then he says to them, "It is written, 'My house is to be regarded as a house of prayer,' but you're turning it into 'a hideout for crooks'!"

14***And some blind*** and lame people came to him in the temple area, and he healed them. 15Then the ranking priests and scholars saw the remarkable feats he performed, and the children who kept cheering in the temple area, shouting, "Hosanna to the son of David," and they were infuriated. 16And they said to him, "Do you hear what these people are saying?"

Jesus says to them, "Of course. Have you never read 'You have produced praise for yourselves out of the mouths of babies and infants at breast'?"

17And leaving them behind, he went outside the city to Bethany and spent the night there.

18***Early in the morning,*** as he was returning to the city, he got hungry. 19And so when he spotted a single fig tree on the way, he went up to it, and found nothing on it except some leaves, and he says to it, "You are never to bear fruit again!" And the fig tree withered instantly.

20And when the disciples saw this, they expressed amazement: "How could the fig tree wither up so quickly?"

21In response Jesus said to them, "I swear to you, if you have trust and do not doubt, not only can you do this to a fig tree but you can even say to this mountain, 'Up with you and into the sea!' and that's what will happen; 22and everything you ask for in prayer you'll get if you trust."

23***And when he came*** to the temple area, the ranking priests and elders of the people approached him while he was teaching, and asked, "By what right are you doing these things?" and "Who gave you this authority?"

24In response Jesus said to them, "I also have one question for you. If you answer me, I'll tell you by what authority I do these things. 25The baptism of John, what was its origin? Was it heaven-sent or was it of human origin?"

And they conferred among themselves, saying, "If we say 'heaven-sent,' he'll say to us, 'Why didn't you trust him?' 26And if we say 'Of human origin . . .!' We are afraid of the crowd." (Remember, everybody considered John a prophet.) 27So they answered Jesus by saying, "We can't tell."

He replied to them in kind: "I'm not going to tell you by what authority I do these things either!

28***Now what*** do you think? A man had two children. He went to the first, and said, 'Son, go and work in the vineyard today.'

21:13
◊Is56:7, Jer7:11
21:16
◊Ps8:1–2
21:18–22
//Mk11:12–25
21:21
Ⓣ Mt18:19; //Th48, 106; Lk17:5–7
21:23–27
//Mk11:27–33, Lk20:1–8

21:17 *Bethany* is a village on the side of the Mount of Olives, about two miles east of Jerusalem.

Leased vineyard

29He responded, 'I'm your man, sir,' but he didn't move.
30Then he went to the second and said the same thing.
He responded, 'I don't want to,' but later on he thought better of it and went ⟨to work⟩.
31'Which of the two did what the father wanted?'
They said, 'The second.'"

Jesus said to them,

I swear to you, the toll collectors and prostitutes will get into God's
domain, but you will not. 32After all, John came to you advocating
justice, but you didn't believe him; yet the toll collectors and prostitutes believed him. Even after you observed ⟨this⟩, you didn't think better of it later and believe him.

33"***Listen to*** another parable:

There once was a landlord who 'planted a vineyard, put a hedge around it, dug a winepress in it, built a tower,' leased it out to some
farmers, and went abroad. 34Now when it was about harvest time, he
sent his slaves to the farmers to collect his crop. 35And the farmers
grabbed his slaves, and one they beat and another they killed, and another they stoned.
36Again he sent other slaves, more than the first group, and they did the same thing to them.
37Then finally he sent his son to them, with the thought, 'They will show this son of mine some respect.'
38But when the farmers recognized the son they said to one another, 'This fellow's the heir! Come on, let's kill him and we'll have
his inheritance!' 39And they grabbed him, dragged him outside the
vineyard, and killed him.

40"When the owner of the vineyard comes, what will he do to those farmers then?"
41They say to him, "He'll get rid of these wicked villains and lease the vineyard out to other farmers who will deliver their produce to him at the proper time."
42Jesus says to them, "Haven't you read in the scriptures,

A stone that the builders rejected
has ended up as the keystone.
It was the Lord's doing
and is something you admire?

21:29–31 The textual transmission of the parable is very confusing. Some mss adopt the version printed above; many mss had the first son say "no," but then change his mind, while the second son says "yes," and then doesn't go. In this case the audience responds "the first." A few mss even have the first son say "no," but change his mind; the second say "yes," but not go; and the audience answer the "the second."

21:32
Ⓣ Lk7:29–30
21:33–46
//Mk12:1–12, Lk20:9–19, Th65–66
21:33
◊Is5:1–2
21:42
◊Ps118:22–23

Royal wedding feast

The emperor & God

[43]Therefore I say to you, God's domain will be taken away from you and given to a people that bears its fruit."

[45]And when the ranking priests and Pharisees heard his parable, they realized that he was talking about them. [46]They wanted to seize him, but were afraid of the crowds, because everyone regarded him as a prophet.

22 ***Jesus again responded*** to them and told them parables:

[2]Heaven's imperial rule is like a secular ruler who gave a wedding celebration for his son. [3]Then he sent his slaves to summon those who had been invited to the wedding, but they declined to attend.

[4]He sent additional slaves with the instructions: "Tell those invited, 'Look, the feast is ready, the oxen and fat calves have been slaughtered, and everything is set. Come to the wedding!'"

[5]But they were unconcerned and went off, one to his own farm, one to his business, [6]while the rest seized his slaves, attacked and killed them.

[7]Now the king got angry and sent his armies to destroy those murderers and burn their city. [8]Then he tells his slaves: "The wedding celebration is ready but those we've invited didn't prove deserving. [9]So go to the city gates and invite anybody you find to the wedding."

[10]Those slaves then went out into the streets and collected everybody they could find, the good and bad alike. And the wedding hall was full of guests.

[11]The king came in to see the guests for himself and noticed this man not properly attired. [12]And he says to him, "Look pal, how'd you get in here without dressing for the occasion?"

And he was speechless.

[13]Then the king ordered his waiters: "Bind him hand and foot and throw him where it is utterly dark. They'll weep and grind their teeth out there. [14]After all, many are called but few are chosen."

[15]***Then the Pharisees*** went and conferred on how to entrap him with a riddle. [16]And they send their disciples to him along with the Herodians to say, "Teacher, we know that you are honest and that you teach God's way forthrightly, and are impartial, because you pay no attention to appearances. [17]So tell us what you think: Is it permissible to pay the poll tax to the Roman emperor or not?"

Q22:1–14 //Lk 14:15–24, Th 64
22:6 Ⓣ Mt 21:35, 23:37
22:13 Cf. Mt 8:12, 13:42, 13:50, 24:51, 25:30
22:15–22 //Mk 12:13–17, Lk 20:20–26, Th 100; cf. EgerG 3:1–6

21:43 Many mss add a v. 44: "The one who falls over this stone will be smashed to pieces, and anyone on whom it falls will be crushed." It is most probably an interpolation from Luke 20:18.

22:7 *Burned their city* may be a reference to the destruction of Jerusalem by Titus in 70 C.E. The arch celebrating his victory still stands in Rome.

Wife of seven brothers

The greatest commandment

David's lord & son

[18]Jesus knew how devious they were, and said, "Why do you provoke me, you pious frauds? [19]Let me see the coin used to pay the poll tax."

And they handed him a silver coin.

[20]And he says to them, "Whose picture is this? Whose name is on it?"

[21]They say to him, "The emperor's."

Then he says to them, "Pay the emperor what belongs to the emperor, and God what belongs to God!"

[22]Upon hearing his reply, they were dumbfounded. And they withdrew from him and went away.

[23]***That same day,*** some Sadducees—who maintain there is no resurrection—came up to him and questioned him. [24]"Teacher," they said, "Moses said, 'If someone dies without children, his brother is obligated to marry the widow and produce offspring for his brother.' [25]There were seven brothers we knew; now the first married and died. And since he left no children, he left his widow to his brother. [26]The second brother did the same thing, and the third, and so on, through the seventh brother. [27]Finally the wife died. [28]So then, in the resurrection whose wife, of the seven, will she be?" (Remember, they had all married her.)

[29]In response Jesus said to them, "You have missed the point again, all because you underestimate both the scriptures and the power of God. [30]After all, at the resurrection people do not marry but resemble heaven's messengers. [31]As for the resurrection of the dead, haven't you read God's word to you: [32]'I am the God of Abraham and the God of Isaac and the God of Jacob.' This is not the God of the dead, only of the living."

[33]And when the crowd heard, they were stunned by his teaching.

[34]***When the Pharisees*** learned that he had silenced the Sadducees, they conspired against him. [35]And one of them, a legal expert, put him to the test: [36]"Teacher, which commandment in the Law is the greatest?"

[37]He replied to him, "'You are to love the Lord your God with all your heart and all your soul and all your mind.' [38]This commandment is first and foremost. [39]And the second is like it: 'You are to love your neighbor as yourself.' [40]On these two commandments hangs everything in the Law and the Prophets."

[41]***When the Pharisees*** gathered around, Jesus asked them, [42]"What do you think about the Anointed? Whose son is he?"

They said to him, "David's."

22:22–33 //Mk 12:18–27, Lk 20:27–40

22:24 ◊ Dt 25:5–6

22:32 ◊ Ex 3:6

22:34–40 //Mk 12:28–31, Lk 10:25–28

22:37 ◊ Dt 6:5

22:39 ◊ Lv 19:18; Cf. Th 25; Ⓓ Mt 19:19; Ⓣ Rom 13:8–10, Gal 5:13–15

22:41–46 //Mk 12:35–37, Lk 20:41–44

22:23 Many mss read this verse differently: "That same day, Sadducees came up to him and said, 'There is no resurrection.'"

22:24 This debate involves the so-called Levirate law in which a brother was obliged to take his brother's wife if she had not borne a son. This was to ensure the family line. See Deut 25:5–6.

Scholars' privileges

Damn you, scholars & Pharisees

[43]He said to them, "Then how can David call him 'lord,' while speaking under the influence of the spirit: [44]'The Lord said to my lord, "Sit here at my right, until I make your enemies grovel at your feet"'? [45]If David actually called him 'lord,' how can he be his son?"

[46]And no one could come up with an answer to his riddle. And from that day on no one dared ask him a question.

23 ***Then Jesus said*** to the crowds and to his disciples, [2]"The scholars and Pharisees occupy the chair of Moses. [3]This means you're supposed to observe and follow everything they tell you. But don't do what they do; after all, they're all talk and no action. [4]They invent heavy burdens and lay them on folks' shoulders, but they themselves won't lift a finger to move them. [5]Everything they do, they do for show. So they widen their phylacteries and enlarge their tassels. [6]They love the best couches at banquets and prominent seats in synagogues [7]and respectful greetings in marketplaces, and they like to be called 'Rabbi' by everyone. [8]But you are not to be called 'Rabbi'; after all, you only have one teacher, and all of you belong to the same family. [9]And don't call anyone on earth 'father,' since you have only one Father, and he is in heaven. [10]You are not to be called 'instructors,' because you have only one instructor, the Anointed. [11]Now whoever is greater than you will be your slave. [12]Those who promote themselves will be demoted and those who demote themselves will be promoted.

[13]"***You scholars*** and Pharisees, you impostors! Damn you! You slam the door of Heaven's domain in people's faces. You yourselves don't enter, and you block the way of those trying to enter.

[15]"You scholars and Pharisees, you impostors! Damn you! You scour land and sea to make one convert, and when you do, you make that person more of a child of Hell than you are.

22:44 ◊Ps 110:1
22:46 Cf. Mk 12:34, Lk 20:40
Q**23:4** //Lk 11:46
23:5 ◊Nm 15:37–39
23:6–7 //Mk 12:38–40, Lk 20:45–47
Q**23:6** //Lk 11:43
23:11 //Mk 9:35, 10:43; Lk 22:26; Mt 20:26
Q**23:13** //Lk 11:52; cf. Th 39, 102

23:4 Some mss add "that are hard to bear" after *heavy burdens*. This is part of an effort of early scribes to intensify Jesus' sayings. The interpolation is based on 11:47. **23:13** Some mss add a v. 14: "Damn you, you scholars and Pharisees, impostors! You prey on widows and their families, and recite long prayers for appearance sake. Therefore, you you will get a stiff sentence." This verse is clearly derived from Mark 12:40 and Luke 20:47.

23:2 *The chair of Moses* probably refers to the seat next to the arch in the synagogue where the scroll of the Law was kept. Sometimes the scroll was apparently enthroned on the seat and teachers also would teach from the seat. It represents the teaching authority of the scholars.

23:5 *Phylacteries* are amulets worn on the forehead and arm during prayer. The amulet was a little box in which there was a small piece of paper containing a verse from scripture. The amulet with its scripture verse was probably used for protection against demons.

23:15 From about the 2nd century B.C.E. until the the reign of Constantine, it appears that Judaism engaged in a strong program of conversion. Monotheism, strict sexual morality, and sabbath practice were very attractive to pagans. The "God Fearers" mentioned in Acts (10:2, 13:26) suggests a group of pagans attracted to Judaism but who have not officially joined, perhaps because of circumcision. However, there is no other evidence of such a group.

16“Damn you, you blind guides who claim: ‘When you swear by the
temple, it doesn’t matter, but when you swear by the treasure in the
temple, it is binding.’ 17You blind fools, which is greater, the treasure
or the temple that makes the gold sacred? 18You go on: ‘When you
swear by the altar, it doesn’t matter, but when you swear by the offering
that lies on the altar, it is binding.’ 19You sightless souls, which is
greater, the offering or the altar that makes the offering sacred? 20So
when you swear by the altar, you swear by the altar and everything on
it. 21And anyone who swears by the temple, swears by the temple and
the one who makes it home, 22and anyone who swears by heaven
swears by the throne of God and the one who occupies it.

23“You scholars and Pharisees, you impostors! Damn you! You pay
tithes on mint and dill and cumin too, but ignore the really important
matters of the Law, such as justice and mercy and trust. You should
have attended to the last without ignoring the first. 24You blind leaders!
You strain out a gnat and gulp down a camel.

25“You scholars and Pharisees, you impostors! Damn you! You wash
the outside of cups and plates, but inside they are full of greed and
dissipation. 26You blind Pharisee, first clean the inside of the cup and
then the outside will be clean too.

27“You scholars and Pharisees, you impostors! Damn you! You are
like whitewashed tombs: on the outside they look beautiful, but inside
they are full of dead bones and every kind of decay. 28So you too look
like decent people on the outside, but on the inside you are doing
nothing but posturing and subverting the Law.

29“You scholars and Pharisees, you impostors! Damn you! You erect
tombs to the prophets and decorate the graves of the righteous 30and
claim: ‘If we had lived in the days of our ancestors, we wouldn’t have
joined them in spilling the prophets’ blood.’ 31So, you witness against
yourselves: You are descendants of those who murdered the prophets,
32and you’re the spitting image of your ancestors. 33You serpents! You
spawn of Satan! How are you going to escape Hell’s judgment? 34Look,
that is why I send you prophets and sages and scholars. Some you’re
going to kill and crucify, and some you’re going to beat in your synagogues and hound from town to town. 35As a result there will be on
your heads all the innocent blood that has been shed on the earth, from
the blood of innocent Abel to the blood of Zechariah, son of Baruch,
whom you murdered between the temple and the altar. 36I swear to
you, all these things are going to rain down on this generation.

Q23:23 //Lk 11:42
Q23:25–26 //Lk 11:39–41, Th 89; cf. GOxy 840 2:8
Q23:27 //Lk 11:44
Q23:29–31 //Lk 11:47–48
23:33 (T) Mt 3:17
Q23:34–36 //Lk 11:49–51
23:35 Cf. GNaz 7; ◊Gn 4:8, Zec 1:1, 2 Chr 24:20–21

23:30 *Spilling the prophets’ blood* is an accusation that is not borne out historically. Actually very few of the prophets were murdered.

23:34 *Prophets and sages and scholars* appears to be a description of the Christian community.

23:35 *Abel* to *Zechariah the son of Baruch* would seem to be a reference from the first of the prophets to the last. Abel was killed by his brother Cain (Gen 4:8); Zechariah, the last of the prophets, was killed for prophesying that God had abandoned his people. But according to 2 Chr 24:20 he is not the son of Baruch but of Jehoiada. Matthew may have confused this Zechariah with that of Zech 1:1.

Lament over Jerusalem

37“***Jerusalem, Jerusalem,*** you murder the prophets and stone those
sent to you! How often I wanted to gather your children as a hen
gathers her chicks under her wings, but you wouldn't let me. 38Can't
you see, your house is being abandoned as a ruin? 39I tell you, you
certainly won't see me from now on until you say, ‘Blessed is the one
who comes in the name of the Lord.’”

Monumental buildings destroyed

24

24 ***And Jesus was*** leaving the temple area on his way out, when his
disciples came to him and called his attention to the sacred buildings.
2In response he said to them, “Yes, take a good look at all this! I
swear to you, you may be sure not one stone will be left on top of
another! Every last one will certainly be knocked down!”

Signs of final agonies

3***As he was sitting*** on the Mount of Olives, the disciples came to him
privately, and said, “Tell us, when are these things going to happen,
and what will be the sign of your coming and the end of the age?”
4And in response Jesus said to them: “Stay alert, otherwise someone
might just delude you! 5You know, many will come using my name,
and claim, ‘I am the Anointed!’ and they will delude many people.
6You are going to hear about wars and rumors of wars. See that you are
not afraid. For these are inevitable, but it is not yet the end. 7For nation
will rise up against nation and empire against empire; and there will be
famines and earthquakes everywhere. 8Now all these things mark the
beginning of the final agonies.
9“At that time they will turn you over for torture, and will kill you,
and you will be universally hated because of me. 10And then many will
suffer a loss of faith, and they will betray one another and hate each
other. 11And many false prophets will appear and will delude many.
12And as lawlessness spreads, mutual love will grow cool. 13Those who
hold out to the end will be saved! 14And this good news of Heaven's
imperial rule will have been proclaimed in the whole inhabited world,
so you can make your case to all peoples. And then the end will come.

Days of distress

15“***So when you see*** the ‘devastating desecration’ (as described by
Daniel the prophet) standing ‘in the holy place’ (the reader had better
figure out what this means), 16then the people in Judea should head for
the hills; 17no one on the roof should go downstairs to retrieve anything; 18and no one in the field should turn back to get a coat. 19It'll be
too bad for pregnant women and nursing mothers in those days! 20Pray
that you don't have to flee during the winter or on the sabbath day.
21For there will be great distress, the likes of which has not occurred
since the world began until now, and will never occur again. 22And if

Q**23:37–39** //Lk13:34–35
23:37 ◊Is31:5
23:39 ◊Ps 118:26
24:1–2 //Mk13:1–2, Lk21:5–6
24:3–14 //Mk13:3–13, Lk21:5–19
24:4 //Mary4:3
24:5 Cf. Mt24:23–26, Mk13:21–23, Lk17:23
24:7 ◊Is19:2
24:13 Ⓓ Mt10:22
24:14 Ⓣ Mt28:19
24:15–28 //Mk13:14–23, Lk21:20–24
24:15 ◊Dn11:31, 12:11; 1 Mc1:54
24:17–18 //Lk17:31
24:19 Cf. Th 79:3
24:21 ◊Joel 2:2; Dn12:1

24:15 *Devastating desecration*, as Matthew makes evident, is a reference to Dan 9:27 in which the prophet in veiled language refers to the desecration of the temple by the Syrian king Antiochus Epiphanes in 167 B.C.E. 1 Macc 1:54 refers to this same event in a direct fashion. In the style of apocalyptic literature, the author of the gospel is referring to some recent event in the original readers experience. It may be either Titus's setting up of the Roman shields in the temple area after the conquest of Jerusalem in 70 C.E. or the zealots' activity in the temple area during the preceding two years.

Son of Adam comes on clouds

No one knows the day or minute

those days had not been cut short, no human being would have survived. But for the sake of the chosen people, those days will be cut short.

[23]"Then if someone says to you, 'Look, here is the Anointed' or 'over here,' don't count on it! [24]After all, counterfeit messiahs and phony prophets will show up, and they'll offer great portents and miracles to delude, if possible, even the chosen people. [25]Look, I have warned you in advance. [26]In fact, if they should say to you, 'Look, he's in the wilderness,' don't go out there; 'Look, he's in one of the secret rooms,' don't count on it. [27]For just as lightning comes out of the east and is visible all the way to the west, that's what the coming of the son of Adam will be like. [28]For wherever there's a corpse, that's where vultures gather.

[29]"***Immediately after*** the tribulation of those days

the sun will be darkened,
and the moon will not give off her glow,
and the stars will fall from the sky,
and the heavenly forces will be shaken!

[30]And then the son of Adam's sign will appear in the sky, and every tribe of the earth will lament, and they'll see the son of Adam coming on clouds of the sky with great power and splendor. [31]And he'll send out his messengers with a blast on the trumpet, and they'll gather his chosen people from the four winds, from one end of the sky to the other!

[32]"Take a cue from the fig tree. When its branch is already in bud and leaves come out, you know that summer is near. [33]So, when you see all these things, you ought to realize that he is near, just outside your door. [34]I swear to God, this generation certainly won't pass into oblivion before all these things take place! [35]The earth will pass into oblivion and so will the sky, but my words will never be obliterated!

[36]"***As for that*** exact day and minute: no one knows, not even heaven's messengers, nor even the son—no one, except the Father alone.

[37]"The son of Adam's coming will be just like the days of Noah. [38]This is how people behaved then before the flood came: they ate and drank, married and were given in marriage, until the day 'Noah boarded the ark,' [39]and they were oblivious until the flood came and swept them all away. This is how it will be when the son of Adam comes. [40]Then two men will be in the field; one will be taken and one will be left. [41]Two women will be grinding at the mill; one will be taken and one left. [42]So stay alert! You never know on what day your lord returns.

[43]"Mark this well: if the homeowner had known when the burglar was coming, he would have been on guard and not have allowed

---

24:36 *Nor even the son* is omitted by many mss, but it is present in the best early mss. The doctrinal difficulty caused by the phrase indicates why later copyists would drop the phrase.

24:23–25
Cf. Mt 24:5
24:23
//Lk 17:23;
Mary 4:4;
cf. Th 113, Lk 17:21
Q**24:26–27**
//Lk 17:23–24
Q**24:28**
//Lk 17:37
24:29–36
//Mk 13:24–32,
Lk 21:25–33
24:29
◊ Is 13:10
24:30–31
Ⓣ 1 Thes 4:15–16
24:30
Ⓓ Mt 26:64;
Ⓘ Mt 25:31–46;
◊ Dn 7:13–14;
Ⓣ Rv 1:7
24:34
Cf. Mt 16:28,
Mk 9:1, Lk 9:27
Q**24:37–39**
//Lk 17:26–30
Q**24:40–41**
//Lk 17:34–35
24:42–43
Ⓣ 1 Thes 5:2,
Rv 16:15
24:42
//Mk 13:35

Ten maidens

The money in trust

anyone to break into his house. 44By the same token, you too should be prepared. Remember, the son of Adam is coming when you least expect it.

45"Who then is the reliable and shrewd slave to whom the master assigns responsibility for his household, to provide them with food at the right time? 46Congratulations to the slave who's on the job when his master arrives. 47I swear to you, he'll put him in charge of all his property. 48But suppose that worthless slave says to himself, 'My master is taking his time,' 49and begins to beat his fellow slaves, and starts eating and drinking with drunkards, 50that slave's master will show up on the day he least expects and at an hour he doesn't suspect. 51He'll cut him to pieces, and assign him a fate fit for the other impostors. ⟨Those who share this fate⟩ will moan and grind their teeth.

25 ***When the time comes,*** Heaven's imperial rule will be like ten maidens who took their lamps and went out to meet the bridegroom. 2Five of them were foolish and five were sensible. 3You see, the foolish maidens took their lamps but failed to take oil with them, 4while the sensible ones took flasks of oil along with their lamps. 5When the bridegroom didn't come, they all dozed off and fell asleep.

6Then in the middle of the night there was a shout: 'Look, the bridegroom is coming! Let's go out to meet him.' 7Then the maidens all got up and trimmed their lamps.

8The foolish said to the sensible ones, 'Let us have some of your oil because our lamps are going out.'

9But the prudent maidens responded, 'We can't do that in case there isn't enough for both of us. Instead, you had better go to the merchants and buy some for yourselves.'

10While they were gone to get some, the bridegroom arrived and those who had come prepared accompanied him to the wedding; then the door was closed.

11The other maidens finally come and say, 'Master, master, open the door for us.'

12He responded, 'I swear to you, I don't recognize you.'

13So stay alert because you don't know either the day or the hour.

14***You know,*** it's like a man going on a trip who called his slaves and turned his valuables over to them. 15To the first he gave thirty thousand silver coins, to the second twelve thousand, and to the third six thousand, to each in relation to his ability, and he left.

Q24:43–44
//Lk12:39–40, Th21, cf.Th103
Q24:45–51
//Lk12:42–46; cf.GNaz8
24:51
Cf.Mt8:12, 13:42, 13:50, 22:13, 25:30
25:1–13
Ⓣ Lk12:35–36
Q25:14–30
//Lk19:11–27; cf.GNaz8

24:46 The return of the *master* is a reference to the coming of the son of Adam and his judgment of the nations (see also 25:5).
25:1 This parable describes a custom not otherwise attested in Jewish practice.
25:5 *When the bridegroom didn't come* is probably a reference to the delay of the coming of the son of Adam.
25:15 These amounts are astronomical. The smallest one (*six thousand silver coins*) represents nearly twenty years' wages for a laborer.

Sheep & goats

[16]Immediately the one who had received thirty thousand silver coins went out and put the money to work; he doubled his investment.

[17]The second also doubled his money.

[18]But the third, who had received the smallest amount, went out, dug a hole, and hid his master's silver.

[19]After a long absence, the slaves' master returned to settle accounts with them. [20]The first, who had received thirty thousand silver coins, came and produced an additional thirty thousand, with this report: 'Master, you handed me thirty thousand silver coins; as you can see, I have made you another thirty thousand.'

[21]His master commended him: 'Well done, you competent and reliable slave! You have been trustworthy in small amounts; I'll put you in charge of large amounts. Come celebrate with your master!'

[22]The one with twelve thousand silver coins also came and reported: 'Master, you handed me twelve thousand silver coins; as you can see, I have made you another twelve thousand.'

[23]His master commended him: 'Well done, you competent and reliable slave! You have been trustworthy in small amounts; I'll put you in charge of large amounts. Come celebrate with your master!'

[24]The one who had received six thousand silver coins also came and reported: 'Master, I know that you drive a hard bargain, reaping where you didn't sow and gathering where you didn't scatter. [25]Since I was afraid, I went out and buried your money in the ground. Look, here it is!'

[26]But his master replied to him, 'You incompetent and timid slave! So you knew that I reap where I didn't sow and gather where I didn't scatter, did you? [27]Then you should have taken my money to the bankers. Then when I returned I would have received my capital with interest. [28]So take the money away from this fellow and give it to the one who has the greatest sum. [29]In fact, to everyone who has, more will be given and then some; and from those who don't have, even what they do have will be taken away. [30]And throw this worthless slave where it is utterly dark. Out there they'll weep and grind their teeth.'

[31]***When the son*** of Adam comes in his glory, accompanied by all his messengers, then he will occupy his glorious throne. [32]Then all peoples will be assembled before him, and he will separate them into groups, much as a shepherd segregates sheep from goats. [33]He'll place the sheep to his right and the goats to his left. [34]Then the king will say to those at his right, 'Come, you who have the blessing of my Father, inherit the domain prepared for you from the foundation of the world. [35]You may remember, I was hungry and you gave me something to eat; I was thirsty and you gave me something to drink;

25:29
//Mt13:12, Lk8:18, Th41

25:30
Cf. Mt8:12, 13:42, 13:50, 22:13, 24:51

25:31
Ⓣ Mt16:27, 24:30; ◊Dn7:13–14

25:34
Ⓣ Mt13:35

25:15–16 Some mss by the insertion of "and" interpret the action differently: *he left immediately.* "And" *the one who.*

Woman anoints Jesus

I was a foreigner and you offered me hospitality; 36I was naked and
you clothed me; I was ill and you visited me; I was in prison and you
came to see me.'

37Then the virtuous will say to him, 'Lord, when did we see you
hungry and feed you or thirsty and give you a drink? 38When did we
notice that you were a foreigner and offer you hospitality? Or naked
and clothe you? 39When did we find you ill or in prison and come to
visit you?'

40And the king will respond to them: 'I swear to you, whatever
you did for the most inconspicuous members of my family, you did
for me as well.'

41Next, he will say to those at his left, 'You, condemned to the
everlasting fire prepared for the devil and his messengers, get away
from me! 42You too may remember, I was hungry and you didn't
give me anything to eat; I was thirsty and you refused me a drink; 43I
was a foreigner and you failed to offer me hospitality; naked and you
didn't clothe me; ill and in prison and you didn't visit me.'

44Then they will give him a similar reply: 'Lord, when did we
notice that you were hungry or thirsty or a foreigner or naked or ill
or in prison and did not attempt to help you?'

45He will then respond: 'I swear to you, whatever you didn't do for
the most inconspicuous members of my family, you didn't do for
me.'

46The second group will then head for everlasting punishment,
but the virtuous for everlasting life."

26:1 ① Mt 7:28, 11:1, 13:53, 19:1
26:2 //Mk 14:1–2, Lk 22:1–2
26:3–5 //Jn 11:47–53, 55–57; Ⓣ Mk 11:18, 12:12; Lk 19:47–48, 20:19
26:6–13 //Mk 14:3–9; cf. Lk 7:36–50, Jn 12:1–8

26 And so when Jesus had concluded his discourse, he told his disciples, 2"You know that Passover comes in two days, and the son of
Adam will be turned over to be crucified."

3***Then the ranking priests*** and elders of the people gathered in the
courtyard of the high priest, whose name was Caiaphas, 4and they conspired to seize Jesus by trickery and kill him. 5Their slogan was: "Not
during the festival, so there won't be a riot among the people."

6While Jesus was in Bethany at the house of Simon the leper, 7a
woman who had an alabaster jar of very expensive myrrh came up to
him and poured it over his head while he was reclining ⟨at table⟩.

25:40 Some scholars think that *my family* refers only to the Christian community. But it should also be noted that since by the time of judgment the gospel is to be preached to all the nations, there is a correlation between the church and the world. See the interpretation of the parable of the Wheat and Weeds where the field is the world (13:38) and in the parable stands for the church (13:24).

26:3 *Caiaphas* was the high priest from 18 C.E. until he was deposed by Vitellius, Pontius Pilate's successor, in 36 or 37 C.E. He was himself the successor of Annas, who was his father-in-law. But see Luke 3:2 and Acts 4:6 for a somewhat different assumption.

26:7 *Myrrh* is an aromatic gum with a slightly bitter taste that comes from Arabia and parts of Africa. It is used for anointing the body much like a perfume, but is also used in the preparation of a corpse for burial.

Priests promise to pay

Jesus celebrates Passover

Peter takes an oath

8When they saw this, the disciples were annoyed, and said, "What good purpose is served by this waste? 9After all, she could have sold it for a good price and given ⟨the money⟩ to the poor."

10But Jesus saw through ⟨their complaint⟩ and said to them, "Why are you bothering this woman? After all, she has done me a courtesy. 11Remember, there will always be poor around; but I won't always be around. 12After all, by pouring this myrrh on my body she has made me ready for burial. 13So help me, wherever this good news is announced in all the world, what she has done will be told in memory of her."

14***Then one of the twelve,*** Judas Iscariot by name, went to the ranking priests 15and said, "What are you willing to pay me if I turn him over to you?" They agreed on thirty silver coins. 16And from that moment he started looking for the right occasion to turn him in.

17***On the first ⟨day⟩*** of Unleavened Bread the disciples came to Jesus, and said, "Where do you want us to get things ready for you to celebrate Passover?"

18He said, "Go into the city to so-and-so and say to him, 'The teacher says, "My time is near, I will observe Passover at your place with my disciples."'" 19And the disciples did as Jesus instructed them and they got things ready for Passover.

20When it was evening, he was reclining ⟨at table⟩ with his twelve followers. 21And as they were eating, he said, "So help me, one of you is going to turn me in."

22And they were very upset and each one said to him in turn, "I'm not the one, am I, Master?"

23In response he said, "The one who dips his hand in the bowl with me—that's who's going to turn me in! 24The son of Adam departs just as the scriptures predict, but damn the one responsible for turning the son of Adam in. It would be better for that man had he never been born!"

25Judas, who was to turn him in, responded, "You can't mean me, can you, Rabbi?"

He says to him, "You said it."

26As they were eating, Jesus took a loaf, gave a blessing, and broke it into pieces. And he offered it to the disciples, and said, "Take some and eat; this is my body."

27And he took a cup and gave thanks and offered it to them, saying, "Drink from it, all of you, 28for this is my blood of the covenant, which has been poured out for many for the forgiveness of sins. 29Now I tell you, I certainly won't drink any of this fruit of the vine from now on, until that day when I drink it for the first time with you in my Father's domain!"

30And they sang a hymn and left for the Mount of Olives.

31***Then Jesus says*** to them, "All of you will lose faith in me this night. Remember, it is written, 'I will strike the shepherd and the sheep of his flock will be scattered!' 32But after I'm raised, I'll go ahead of you to Galilee."

26:11
◊Dt15:11

26:14–16
//Mk14:10–11, Lk23:3–6

26:15
Ⓘ Mt4:17, 16:21, 27:3, 27:9; ◊Zec11:12

26:17–30
//Mk14:12–26, Lk22:7–23

26:17
//GEbi 7:1; ◊Ex12:14–20

26:20–25
//Jn13:21–30

26:26–28
//1Cor11:23–25; cf. Jn6:48–58

26:26
Cf. GHeb9:4

26:28
◊Ex24:8, Zec9:11

26:29
Cf. GHeb9:2

26:30
//Lk22:39

26:31–35
//Mk14:27–31

26:31
Cf. Jn16:32; ◊Zec13:7

Jesus in Gethsemane

Judas turns Jesus in

33In response Peter said to him, "If everyone else loses faith in you, I
never will."
34Jesus said to him, "So help me, tonight before the rooster crows
you will disown me three times!"
35Peter says to him, "Even if they condemn me to die with you, I will
never disown you!" And all of the disciples took the same oath—all of
them.
36***Then Jesus goes*** with them to a place called Gethsemane, and he
says to the disciples, "Sit down here while I go over there and pray."
37And taking Peter and the two sons of Zebedee, he began to feel
dejected and full of anguish. 38He says to them, "I'm so sad I could die.
You stay here with me and be alert!"
39And he went a little farther, lay facedown, and prayed, "My Father,
if it is possible, take this cup away from me! Yet it's not what I want
⟨that matters⟩, but what you want."
40And he returns to the disciples and finds them sleeping, and says to
Peter, "Couldn't you stay awake with me for one hour? 41Be alert, and
pray that you won't be put to the test! Though the spirit is willing, the
flesh is weak."
42Again for a second time he went away and prayed, "My Father, if it
is not possible for me to avoid this ⟨cup⟩ without drinking it, your will
must prevail!"
43And once again he came and found them sleeping, since their eyes
had grown heavy. 44And leaving them again, he went away and prayed,
repeating the same words for a third time.
45Then he comes to the disciples and says to them, "Are you still
sleeping and taking a rest? Look, the time is at hand! The son of Adam
is being turned over to foreigners. 46Get up, let's go! See for yourselves!
Here comes the one who is going to turn me in."
47***And while he was*** still speaking, suddenly Judas, one of the twelve,
arrived and with him a great crowd wielding swords and clubs, dispatched by the ranking priests and elders of the people.
48Now the one who was to turn him in had arranged a sign with
them, saying, "The one I'm going to kiss is the one you want. Arrest
him!"
49And he came right up to Jesus, and said, "Hello, Rabbi," and
kissed him.
50But Jesus said to him, "Look friend, what are you doing here?"
Then they came and seized him and held him fast. 51At that moment
one of those with Jesus lifted his hand, drew his sword, struck the high
priest's slave, and cut off his ear.
52Then Jesus says to him, "Put your sword back where it belongs.

26:33–34 //Lk22:31–34, Jn13:36–38
26:34 Ⓘ Mt26:75
26:35 Cf. Jn11:16
26:36–46 //Mk14:32–42, Lk22:39–46
26:36 Cf. Jn18:1
26:38–39 Cf. Jn12:27
26:39 Cf. Jn18:11
26:42 Ⓣ Mt6:10
26:47–56 //Mk14:43–52, Lk22:47–54, Jn18:1–12
26:50 Cf. EgerG1:8
26:52 ◊Gn9:6

26:36 *Gethsamane* means "oil press" and its exact location is unknown.

26:39 *Cup* is frequently used in the Hebrew Bible as a metaphor for suffering (e.g., Ps 11:6; 75:9).

26:48 The fact that Judas needs to use a *sign* indicates that Jesus was not known by face in Jerusalem.

Kissing is the equivalent of a handshake in our culture.

Trial before the council

A rooster crows

For everyone who takes up the sword will be done in by the sword. 53Or do you suppose I am not able to call on my Father, who would put more than twelve legions of heavenly messengers at my disposal? 54How then would the scriptures come true that say these things are inevitable?"

55At that moment Jesus said to the crowds, "Have you come out to take me with swords and clubs as though you were apprehending a rebel? I used to sit there in the temple area day after day teaching, and you didn't lift a hand against me."

56All of this happened so the writings of the prophets would come true. Then all the disciples deserted him and ran away.

57***Those who had arrested*** Jesus brought him before Caiaphas the high priest, where the scholars and elders had assembled. 58But Peter followed him at a distance as far as the courtyard of the high priest. He went inside and sat with the attendants to see how things would turn out.

59The ranking priests and the whole Council were looking for false testimony against Jesus so they might issue a death sentence; 60but they couldn't find many perjurers to come forward. Finally, two persons came forward 61and said, "This fellow said, 'I'm able to destroy the temple of God and rebuild it within three days.'"

62Then the high priest got up, and questioned him: "Don't you have something to say? Why do these people testify against you?"

63But Jesus was silent.

And the high priest said to him, "I adjure you by the living God: Tell us if you are the Anointed, the son of God!"

64Jesus says to him, "If you say so. But I tell you, from now on you will see the son of Adam sitting at the right hand of Power and coming on the clouds of the sky."

65Then the high priest tore his vestment, and said, "He has blasphemed! Why do we still need witnesses? See, now you have heard the blasphemy. 66What do you think?"

In response they said, "He deserves to die!" 67Then they spit in his face, and punched him and hit him, 68saying, "Prophesy for us, you Anointed, you! Guess who hit you!"

69***Meanwhile Peter*** was sitting outside in the courtyard, and one slave woman came up to him, and said, "You too were with Jesus the Galilean."

70But he denied it in front of everyone, saying, "I don't know what you're talking about!"

71After ⟨Peter⟩ went out to the entrance, another slave woman saw him and says to those there, "This fellow was with Jesus of Nazareth."

26:57–58 //Mk14:53–54, Lk22:54–55
26:59–68 //Mk14:55–65; Lk22:63–71, Jn18:13–14, 19–24
26:60 ◊Dt17:6
26:61 //Jn2:19, Th71
26:64 Ⓓ Mt24:30; ◊Dn7:13–14, Ps110:1
26:65–66 ◊Lv24:16
26:65 Ⓘ Mt9:3
26:67 //Pet3:4
26:69–75 //Mk14:66–72; Lk22:54–62; Jn18:15–18, 25–27

26:56 It is not clear which *writings of the prophets* are being fulfilled.
26:60 In Jewish legal practice *two* witnesses are required for a conviction.
26:61 Nowhere in Matthew's Gospel is it reported that Jesus is going to *destroy the temple.*
26:65 It is not clear why what Jesus said is *blasphemy.*

Trial before Pilate

Judas repents

Trial before Pilate continues

72And again he denied it with an oath: "I don't know the man!"

73A little later those standing about came and said to Peter, "You really are one of them; even the way you talk gives you away!"

74Then he began to curse and swear: "I don't know the fellow."

And just then the rooster crowed. 75And Peter remembered what Jesus had said: "Before the rooster crows you will disown me three times." And he went outside and wept bitterly.

27 ***When morning came,*** all the ranking priests and elders of the people plotted against Jesus to put him to death. 2And they bound him and led him away and turned him over to Pilate the governor.

3***Then Judas,*** who had turned him in, realizing that he had been condemned, was overcome with remorse and returned the thirty silver coins to the ranking priests and elders 4with this remark, "I have made the grave mistake of turning in this blameless man."

But they said, "What's that to us? That's your problem!"

5And hurling the silver into the temple he slunk off, and went out and hanged himself.

6The ranking priests took the silver and said, "It wouldn't be right to put this into the temple treasury, since it's blood money."

7So they devised a plan and bought the Potter's Field as a burial ground for foreigners. 8As a result, that field has been known as the Bloody Field even to this day. 9So the prediction Jeremiah the prophet made came true: "And they took the thirty silver coins, the price put on a man's head (this is the price they put on him among the Israelites), 10and they donated it for the Potter's Field, as my Lord commanded me."

11***Jesus stood*** before the governor, and the governor questioned him: "You are 'the King of the Judeans'?"

Jesus said, "If you say so."

12And while he was being accused by the ranking priests and elders, he said absolutely nothing.

13Then Pilate says to him, "Don't you have something to say to the long list of charges they bring against you?" 14But he did not respond to him, not to a single charge, so the governor was baffled.

15At each festival it was the custom for the governor to set one prisoner free for the crowd, whichever one they wanted. 16They were

26:75 Ⓘ Mt26:34
27:1–2 //Mk15:1, Lk23:1, Jn18:28
27:2 Cf.GHeb1:6
27:3–10 Cf.Acts1:15–20
27:3 Ⓘ Mt26:15–16
27:6 ◊Dt23:19
27:9–10 ◊Zec11:12–13
27:11–14 //Mk15:2–5, Lk23:1–7, Jn18:29–38a

27:4 A few mss have "righteous" *man*. This phrase is synonymous with *blameless man* which translates an unusual expression derived from the Greek Bible. It is associated with the violent death of God's agents (Deut 27:25 LXX, Jer 19:14). Righteousness is a favorite word of Matthew's, so it is difficult to decide what the reading should be.

27:2 *Pilate* was the fifth governor of Judea and his term was the second longest (26–36 C.E.). He was a very controversial governor, according to the contemporary Jewish historian Josephus.

27:9 The quote is not from *Jeremiah* but Zechariah.

27:15 This exchange practice is otherwise unattested for the period.

then holding a notorious prisoner named Jesus Barabbas. [17]When the
crowd had gathered, Pilate said to them, "Do you want me to set Jesus
Barabbas free for you or Jesus who is known as 'the Anointed'?" [18]After
all, he knew that they had turned him in out of envy.
[19]While he was sitting on the judgment seat, his wife sent a message
to him: "Don't have anything to do with that innocent man, because I
have agonized a great deal today in a dream on account of him."
[20]The ranking priests and the elders induced the crowds to ask for
Barabbas but to execute Jesus. [21]In response ⟨to their request⟩ the
governor said to them, "Which of the two do you want me to set free for
you?"
They said, "Barabbas!"
[22]Pilate says to them, "What should I do with Jesus known as 'the
Anointed'?"
Everyone responded, "Have him crucified!"
[23]But he said, "Why? What has he done wrong?"
But they would shout all the louder, "Have him crucified!"
[24]Now when Pilate could see that he was getting nowhere, but
rather that a riot was starting, he took water and washed his hands in
full view of the crowd, and said, "Don't blame me for this fellow's
blood. Now it's your business!"
[25]In response all the people said, "So, smear his blood on us and on
our children."
[26]Then he set Barabbas free for them, but had Jesus flogged, and
then turned him over to be crucified.

Soldiers make fun of Jesus

[27]***Then the governor's*** soldiers took Jesus into the governor's residence and surrounded him with the whole company. [28]They stripped
him and dressed him in a crimson cloak, [29]and they wove a crown out
of thorns and put it on his head. They placed a staff in his right hand,
and bowing down before him, they made fun of him, saying, "Greetings, 'King of the Judeans'!" [30]And spitting on him, they took a staff
and hit him on the head. [31]And when they had made fun of him, they
stripped off the cloak and put his own clothes back on him and led him
out to crucify him.

27:15–26 //Mk15:6–15, Lk23:13–25, Jn18:38–19:16
27:16 Cf.GNaz9
27:19 Ⓣ Mt1:20; 2:12, 19, 22
27:24 ◊Dt21:6–9
27:25 ◊2Sm1:16
27:27–31 //Mk15:16–20, Jn19:1–3, Pet2:3b–3:4

27:16; 17 Many texts omit *Jesus,* but it is probably the original reading of Matthew and was omitted because of the reverence shown to the name of Jesus. The early church authority Origen (early third century) knows of mss with and without the double name, but thinks it cannot be original because "in all of the scriptures we know of no one who is a sinner called Jesus."

27:16 *Barabbas* means in Aramaic "Son of the father."
27:19 The word translated as *good* also means innocent or righteous. Matthew has Pilate's wife join Judas (see 27:4 textual note) and Pilate (27:24) in declaring Jesus guiltless.
27:25 This cry by the crowd has been used to justify the pogroms against the Jews. But it should be noted that it only occurs in this gospel and so its historicity is highly doubtful. Moreover, if the original readers of Matthew's Gospel were Jewish, they would also be implicating themselves in the death of Jesus.
27:28 *Crimson* is the color of the Roman warrior. Jesus who entered Jerusalem as a king of peace and modesty (21:5) is now clothed as a warrior.

Soldiers crucify Jesus

Jesus breathes his last

32***As they were*** going out, they came across a Cyrenian named Simon. This fellow they conscripted to carry his cross.

33And when they reached the place known as Golgotha (which means "Place of the Skull"), 34they gave him a drink of wine mixed with something bitter, and once he tasted it, he didn't want to drink it. 35After crucifying him, they divided up his garments by casting lots. 36And they sat down there and kept guard over him. 37And over his head they put an inscription that identified his crime: "This is Jesus the King of the Judeans."

38Then they crucified two rebels with him, one on his right and one on his left.

39Those passing by kept taunting him, wagging their heads, and saying, 40"You who would destroy the temple and rebuild it in three days, save yourself; if you're God's son, come down from the cross!"

41Likewise the ranking priests made fun of him along with the scholars and elders; they would say, 42"He saved others, but he can't even save himself! He's the King of Israel; he should come down from the cross here and now and we'll trust him. 43He trusted God, so God should rescue him now if he holds him dear. After all, he said, 'I'm God's son.'"

44In the same way the rebels who were crucified with him would abuse him.

45***Beginning at noon*** darkness blanketed the entire land until mid-afternoon. 46And about 3 o'clock in the afternoon Jesus shouted at the top of his voice, "*Eli, Eli, lema sabachthani*" (which means, "My God, my God, why did you abandon me?")

47When some of those standing there heard, they would say, "This fellow's calling Elijah!" 48And immediately one of them ran and took a sponge filled with sour wine and stuck it on a pole and offered him a drink.

49But the rest would say, "Wait! Let's see if Elijah comes to rescue him."

50Jesus again shouted at the top of his voice and stopped breathing.

51And suddenly the curtain of the temple was torn in two from top to bottom, and the earth quaked, rocks were split apart, 52and the tombs were opened and many bodies of sleeping saints came back to life. 53And they came out of the tombs after his resurrection and went into the holy city, where they appeared to many. 54The Roman officer and those keeping watch over Jesus with him witnessed the sign and what had happened, and were terrified, and said, "This man really was God's son."

27:32 //Mk15:21, Lk23:26
27:33–44 //Mk15:22–32, Lk23:33–43, Jn19:17–24, Pet4:1–5
27:34 ◊Ps 69:21
27:35 ◊Ps 22:18
27:39 ◊Ps 22:7
27:40 Ⓘ Mt26:61; //Jn2:19, Th71
27:43 ◊Ps22:8
27:45–56 //Mk15:33–41, Lk23:44–49, Jn19:25–37, Pet5:1–6
27:46 ◊Ps22:1
27:48 ◊Ps69:21
27:51 Cf.GNaz10a; ◊Ex26:31

27:32 *Cyrene* was a city in north Africa (modern Libya) that had a large Jewish population. They had a synagogue in Jerusalem.

27:34 The *something bitter* was gall, a drug used to deaden the senses.

27:35 To *cast lots* involves either pebbles or sticks or straw.

27:46 *Eli, Eli* is Hebrew; Mark has Jesus speak Aramaic. This makes the word play with on Elijah's name easier in Greek.

27:51–52 *Earthquakes* and *the opening of tombs* are probably apocalyptic signs of the end times.

Joseph buries Jesus

The tomb is secured

Two Marys at the tomb

Jesus meets the two women

Priests and elders bribe the guard

55Many women were there observing this from a distance—those who had followed Jesus from Galilee to assist him, 56among whom were Mary of Magdala, and Mary the mother of James and Joseph, and the mother of the sons of Zebedee.

57***When it had*** grown dark, a rich man from Arimathea, by the name of Joseph, who himself was a follower of Jesus, appeared, 58and went to Pilate and requested the body of Jesus. Then Pilate ordered it to be turned over ⟨to him⟩. 59And taking the body, Joseph wrapped it in a clean linen shroud 60and put it in his new tomb, which had been cut in the rock. He rolled a huge stone in the opening of the tomb and went away. 61But Mary of Magdala and the other Mary stayed there, sitting opposite the tomb.

62***On the next day,*** which is the day after Preparation, the ranking priests and the Pharisees met with Pilate: 63"Your Excellency, we remember what that impostor said while he was still alive: 'After three days I am going to be raised up.' 64So order the tomb sealed for three days so his disciples won't come and steal his body and tell everyone, 'He has been raised from the dead,' in which case, the last deception will be worse than the first."

65Pilate replied to them, "You have a guard; go and secure it the best way you know how."

66They went and secured the tomb by sealing ⟨it with a⟩ stone and posting a guard.

28 ***After the sabbath day,*** at first light on Sunday, Mary of Magdala and the other Mary came to inspect the tomb. 2And just then there was a strong earthquake. You see, a messenger of the Lord had come down from the sky, arrived ⟨at the tomb⟩, rolled away the stone, and was sitting on it. 3The messenger gave off a dazzling light and wore clothes as white as snow. 4Now those who kept watch were paralyzed with fear and looked like corpses themselves.

5In response the messenger said to the women, "Don't be frightened! I know you are looking for Jesus who was crucified. 6He is not here! You see, he was raised, just as he said. Come, look at the spot where he was lying. 7And run, tell his disciples that he has been raised from the dead. Don't forget, he is going ahead of you to Galilee. There you will see him. Now I have told you so."

8***And they hurried*** away from the tomb, full of apprehension and an overpowering joy, and ran to tell his disciples.

9And then Jesus met them saying, "Hello!"

They came up and took hold of his feet and paid him homage.

10Then Jesus says to them, "Don't be afraid. Go tell my companions so they can leave for Galilee, where they will see me."

11***While they were*** on their way, some of the guards returned to the city and reported to the ranking priests everything that had happened. 12They met with the elders and hatched a plan: they bribed the soldiers with an adequate amount of money 13and ordered them: "Tell every-

27:55–56 ◊Ps38:11
27:57–61 //Mk15:42–47, Lk23:50–56, Jn19:38–42
27:57–58 //Pet2:1–3a
27:58 ◊Dt21:22–23
27:59–60 //Pet6:1–4
27:62–66 Cf. Pet8:1–9:1
27:66 ◊Dn6:17
28:1–8 //Mk16:1–8, Lk24:1–11, Jn20:1–10, Pet12:1–13:3
28:9 See 2:2

On a mountain in Galilee

body that his disciples came at night and stole his body while we were
asleep. [14]If the governor should hear about this, we will deal with him;
you need have no worries." [15]They took the money and did as they had
been instructed. And this story has been passed around among the Jews
until this very day.

[16]***The eleven disciples*** went to the mountain in Galilee where Jesus
had told them to go. [17]And when they saw him, they paid him homage;
but some were dubious.

[18]And Jesus approached them and spoke these words: "All authority
has been given to me in heaven and on earth. [19]You are to go and make
followers of all peoples. You are to baptize them in the name of the
Father and the son and the holy spirit. [20]Teach them to observe everything I commanded. I'll be with you day in and day out, as you'll see, so
long as this world continues its course."

28:17 See 2:2
28:18 Ⓘ Mt9:6, 11:27
28:19 Ⓘ Mt10:5–6
28:20 Ⓘ Mt1:23, 18:20

28:16 The disciples had been instructed by the messengers to go to Galilee but no *mountain* was mentioned.

28:19 *The Father and the son and the holy spirit* is the earliest Trinitarian formula in the New Testament.

The Gospel of Luke

Introduction

Luke opens his two-volume narrative with a statement of his motive and purpose (1:1–4). Luke tactfully expresses dissatisfaction with previous narratives about Jesus and implies that his gospel will set the record straight and assure readers (addressed through Theophilus) of the integrity of their tradition. The Acts of the Apostles begins with an address to Theophilus which refers to the gospel as "the first book." The author therefore intends both works to be read together (scholars usually refer to Luke's work as "Luke-Acts.")

The narrative

Luke-Acts comprises over one-fourth of the total text of the New Testament. Its sprawling narrative begins in Jerusalem before the birth of Jesus and ends with Paul preaching the gospel in Rome. It is nothing less than a story of the working out of God's plan to offer salvation to humankind. This salvation was anticipated by Israel, definitively announced by Jesus, and continues to be offered through the church. Luke-Acts carefully connects what God does in Jesus and through the church to the promises made to Israel through its prophets (examples are found at 4:16–21; 18:31–34; 24:44–49; Acts 13:32–41; and 26:22–23).

Luke sets the story of Jesus within this larger story. In Luke, unlike the other gospels, Jesus is not the prime mover of the narrative, though he is, of course, its central figure. It is God who determines the course of events in the story. Luke expresses this by describing certain events as predetermined (e.g., 2:25; 22:22; Acts 2:23; 4:27–28) or directed by the Holy Spirit (e.g., 3:22; 4:1, 14, 18; 12:12). Although God directs the story, He does so from "off-stage." God speaks directly only twice to certify the divine mandate of Jesus' mission (3:22; 9:35).

Luke's portrait of Jesus

These two divine interventions in the story underline the fundamental aspect of Luke's portrayal of Jesus: he is the divinely commissioned agent who announces and promotes God's will for Israel: Jesus is a prophet. In his first public speech (4:16–30), Jesus predicts that his mission will fulfill the words of the prophets and will meet the same reception as the prophets met before him.

Another central aspect of Luke's Jesus is his solicitude for the poor and the outcast. Jesus claims that his outreach to them constitutes his messianic credentials (7:18–22). Jesus congratulates them for belonging to God's kingdom (6:20–21), which he envisions as a great banquet full of the poor and the outcast (14:12–24). Conversely, Jesus warns often about the spiritual dangers of wealth (6:24–25; 8:11–15; 12:13–21; 16:13–15, 19–31; 18:18–25). Among the outcasts are sinners, to whom Jesus' mission is especially directed (5:32, 19:10). Jesus befriends "toll collectors and sinners" (5:30; 7:34; 15:1–2). He uses the despised toll collectors and Samaritans as examples of positive religious behavior (10:29–37; 17:11–19; 18:10–14; 19:2–10). Some of the more memorable passages in the gospel feature Jesus' compassion for sinners or his teaching about God's compassion for them (7:36–50; 15:1–32; 23:34, 39–43).

Tradition and sources

In his preface, Luke acknowledges that there already was a tradition of gospel writing before he began his project. Among the works to which he alludes, at least two served as his literary sources: the Gospel of Mark, from which Luke takes his narrative framework, and the Sayings Gospel Q, an important fund of teachings ascribed to Jesus. In addition, about one-third of the material in Luke's Gospel has no known literary source (and so is called special Lukan material). Some of it is traditional (indeed a portion of it may well have originated with Jesus himself) and some of it is composed by Luke. Within the special Lukan material are some of the most famous teachings in the gospel tradition: the stories about Martha and Mary (10:38–39), the ten lepers (17:11–19), and Zacchaeus (19:1–10); and the parables: the Two Debtors (7:41–43), the Good Samaritan (10:29–37), the Prodigal Son (15:11–32), the Dishonest Manager (16:1–13), Lazarus and the Rich Man (16:19–31), and the Unjust Judge (18:1–8).

Structure

The Gospel is not a tightly structured narrative. Luke derives his basic story outline from Mark:

1. John the Baptist setting the stage for Jesus,
2. Jesus' baptism, temptation, announcement of his message, and gathering of disciples,
3. teaching and healing in Galilee,
4. journey to Jerusalem, culminating in a symbolic action in the temple,
5. preaching in the temple, culminating in an eschatological discourse,
6. arrest, trial, and crucifixion,
7. discovery of the empty tomb.

Luke extends the Markan outline in both directions, adding stories of the birth and infancy of John and Jesus (chapters 1 and 2) and accounts of Jesus' resurrection appearances (chapter 24). Luke also greatly expands the journey to Jerusalem, making it a major vehicle for his exposition of Jesus' teachings. Often called the "Travel Narrative" (9:51–19:46), it contains most of the special Lukan material. It has minimal narrative structure and is almost entirely taken up with teaching.

Eschatology

In contrast to Mark, Luke downplays the belief in the imminence of the return of Jesus and the end of the world. The first words of Mark's Jesus are, "The time is up, God's imperial rule is closing in" (Mark 1:15). The parallel verse in Luke merely reports that Jesus "taught in their synagogues" (4:15). Luke's Jesus corrects the idea that the Kingdom is in the near future (19:11), pointing instead to its presence among believers (17:20–21). In 21:8 he explicitly warns against those who declare that the End is near (contrast the parallel Mark 13:6).

Luke's audience

Luke shows a strong interest in the universalism of the Christian message. Jesus' offer of salvation comes first to Israel, but is meant for the whole world (2:30–32; 3:6; 13:28–29). Acts tells how and why the gospel spreads beyond Israel to all peoples.

Luke's writing shows sensitivity for a gentile audience. He regularly translates or omits Aramaic terms in his sources, and often substitutes Greek names for Semitic ones. He omits Mark's story about the Syro-Phoenician woman (Mark 7:24–30), the one story most likely to offend gentiles. He depicts Jesus freely interacting with non-Jews and using them as positive examples in his teaching (4:25, 27; 7:1–10; 10:29–37; 17:11–19).

Luke presents Jesus so as to be intelligible to Greco-Roman readers. He sets Jesus' birth in the context of world history (2:1) and traces his genealogy (3:23–38) all the way to Adam (not simply to the Jewish progenitor Abraham, as in the genealogy offered by Matthew). Although Luke affirms that Jesus is the Jewish Messiah foretold in the scriptures (e.g., 4:21), Luke is the only synoptic writer to present Jesus also as a "savior" (2:11; Acts 3:13–15), a Hellenistic title for divine deliverers.

Luke's doubts about the imminence of Jesus' return and his emphasis on universalism point to his concept of the Christian movement (which is called "the Way" in Acts) as both international in membership and indefinite in duration. In this light, Luke-Acts can be seen as a charter document for a church taking stock for the long haul: showing it how to understand its past (its Jewish roots) and how to live in an open-ended present, by following the teachings of Jesus (in his gospel) as modelled by the earliest disciples (in Acts), and by a continual openness to the guidance of the Holy Spirit.

The Gospel of Luke

Prologue

Forecast of John's birth

1 ***Since so many*** have undertaken to compile an orderly narrative of the events that have run their course among us, [2]just as the original eyewitnesses and ministers of the word transmitted them to us, [3]it seemed good that I, too, after thoroughly researching everything from the beginning, should set them systematically in writing for you, Theophilus, [4]so that Your Excellency may realize the reliability of the teachings in which you have been instructed.

[5]***In the days of Herod,*** king of Judea, there happened to be this priest named Zechariah, who belonged to the priestly clan of Abijah. His wife, a descendant of Aaron, was named Elizabeth. [6]They were both scrupulous in the sight of God, obediently following all the commandments and ordinances of the Lord. [7]But they had no children, because Elizabeth was infertile, and both were well along in years. [8]While he was serving as priest before God when his priestly clan was on temple duty, [9]it so happened that he was chosen by lot, according to the custom of the priesthood, to enter the sanctuary of the Lord and burn incense.

[10]At the hour of incense, while a huge crowd was praying outside, [11]there appeared to him a messenger of the Lord standing to the right of the altar of incense. [12]When he saw him, Zechariah was shaken and overcome by fear. [13]But the heavenly messenger said to him, "Don't be afraid, Zechariah, for your prayer has been heard, and your wife Elizabeth will bear you a son, and you are to name him John. [14]And you will be joyful and elated, and many will rejoice at his birth, [15]because he will be great in the sight of the Lord; he will drink no wine or beer, and he will be filled with holy spirit from the very day of his birth. [16]And he will cause many of the children of Israel to turn to the Lord their God. [17]He will precede him in the spirit and power of Elijah: he will turn the hearts of the parents back towards their children, and the disobedient back towards the ways of righteousness, and will make people ready for their Lord."

1:1–4 (I) Acts 1:1–2
1:5 Cf. GEbi 1:1–2
1:13 ◊Gn 17:19, Jgs 13:2–5
1:15 ◊Num 6:1–4
1:16–17 ◊Mal 4:5–6, Sir 48:10

1:5 Herod the Great ruled 37–4 B.C.E.
1:8 Priests were divided into 24 units, each unit serving in the Temple twice a year for one week.
1:9 *It so happened* (*kai egeneto*) is a deliberate imitation of the style of the LXX. Its frequent use is apparently meant to make the Gospel sound like the Jewish Bible. Most modern English translations (e.g., RSV, NAB, NEB) omit this phrase.
1:15 Abstention from alcohol was a mark of special consecration to God practiced by Nazirites (Num 6:1–4). The LXX describes Samuel as "drinking no wine or liquor"

Announcement to Mary

[18]But Zechariah said to the heavenly messenger, "How can I be sure of this? For I am an old man and my wife is well along in years."

[19]And the messenger answered him, "I am Gabriel, the one who stands in the presence of God. I was sent to speak to you, and to bring you this good news. [20]Listen to me: you will be struck silent and speechless until the day these things happen, because you did not trust my words, which will come true at the appropriate time."

[21]Meanwhile, the people were waiting for Zechariah, wondering why he was taking so long in the sanctuary. [22]And when he did come out and was unable to speak to them, they realized that he had seen a vision inside. And he kept making signs to them, since he could not speak. [23]And it so happened, when his time of official service was completed, that he went back home.

[24]Afterwards, his wife Elizabeth conceived, and went into seclusion for five months, telling herself: [25]"This is how the Lord has seen fit to deal with me in his good time in taking away the public disgrace ⟨of my infertility⟩."

[26]***In the sixth month*** the heavenly messenger Gabriel was sent from God to a town in Galilee called Nazareth, [27]to a virgin engaged to a man named Joseph, of the house of David. The virgin's name was Mary. [28]He entered and said to her, "Greetings, favored one! The Lord is with you."

[29]But she was deeply disturbed by the words, and wondered what this greeting could mean.

[30]The heavenly messenger said to her, "Don't be afraid, Mary. You see, you have found favor with God. [31]Listen to me: you will conceive in your womb and give birth to a son, and you will name him Jesus. [32]He will be great, and will be called son of the Most High. And the Lord God will give him the throne of David, his father. [33]He will rule over the house of Jacob forever; and his dominion will have no end."

[34]And Mary said to the messenger, "How can this be, since I've not had sex with any man."

[35]The messenger replied, "The holy spirit will come over you, and the power of the Most High will cast its shadow on you. This is why the child to be born will be holy, and be called son of God. [36]Further, your relative Elizabeth has also conceived a son in her old age. She who was said to be infertile is already six months along, [37]since nothing is impossible with God."

[38]And Mary said, "Here I am, the Lord's slave. I pray that all you've told me comes true." Then the heavenly messenger left her.

1:18 ◊Gn15:8, 18:11
1:25 ◊Gn30:23
1:28 ◊Jdt13:18
1:31 Cf. Mt1:21–23; ◊Is7:14
1:32–33 Ⓣ Acts2:30, 13:23; ◊2Sm7:12–16, Is9:6–7
1:37 ◊Gn18:14(LXX)

1:28 Some mss add "Blessed are you among women" to the end of the verse.

(1 Sam 1:11).

1:25 Infertility was interpreted as a sign of God's disapproval.

1:26 *In the sixth month*: of Elizabeth's pregnancy.

1:32 It is unclear how Jesus can be descended from David if Joseph is not his father. The only information on Mary's lineage is that she is a relative of Elizabeth, a descendant of Aaron (1:5, 36).

Mary visits Elizabeth

[39]***At that time*** Mary set out in haste for a town in the hill country of Judah, [40]where she entered Zechariah's house and greeted Elizabeth.

Birth & childhood of John

[41]And it so happened, when Elizabeth heard Mary's greeting, that the baby jumped in her womb. Elizabeth was filled with holy spirit [42]and proclaimed at the top of her voice, "Blessed are you among women, and blessed is the fruit of your womb! [43]Who am I that the mother of my lord should visit me? [44]You see, when the sound of your greeting reached my ears, the baby jumped for joy in my womb. [45]Congratulations to her who trusted that what the Lord promised her would come true."

[46]And Mary said, "My soul extols the Lord, [47]and my spirit rejoices in God my Savior, [48]for he has shown consideration for the lowly status of his slave. As a consequence, from now on every generation will congratulate me; [49]the Mighty One has done great things for me, and holy is his name, [50]and his mercy will come to generation after generation of those who fear him. [51]He has shown the strength of his arm, he has put the arrogant to rout, along with their private schemes; [52]he has pulled the mighty down from their thrones, and exalted the lowly; [53]he has filled the hungry with good things, and sent the rich away empty. [54]He has come to the aid of his servant Israel, remembering his mercy, [55]as he spoke to our ancestors, to Abraham and to his descendants forever." [56]And Mary stayed with her about three months, and then returned home.

[57]***The time came*** for Elizabeth to give birth and she had a son. [58]Her neighbors and relatives heard that the Lord had shown her great mercy, and they rejoiced with her. [59]And so on the eighth day they came to circumcise the child; and they were going to name him Zechariah after his father.

[60]His mother spoke up and said, "No; he is to be called John."

[61]But they said to her, "No one in your family has this name." [62]So they made signs to his father, asking what he would like him to be called.

[63]He asked for a writing tablet and to everyone's astonishment he wrote, "His name is John." [64]And immediately his mouth was opened and his tongue loosed, and he began to speak, blessing God.

[65]All their neighbors became fearful, and all these things were talked about throughout the entire hill country of Judea. [66]And all who heard about these things took them to heart and wondered: "Now what is this child going to be?" You see, the hand of the Lord was with him.

[67]Then his father Zechariah was filled with holy spirit and prophesied: [68]"Blessed be the Lord, the God of Israel, for he has visited and ransomed his people. [69]He has raised up for us a horn of salvation in the house of David his servant. [70]This is what he promised in the words of his holy prophets of old: [71]deliverance from our enemies, and from the hands of all who hate us; [72]mercy to our ancestors, and the remem-

1:46–55 ◊1 Sm 2:1–10
1:47 ◊Hab 3:18
1:48 ◊1 Sm 1:11
1:49 ◊Dt 10:21, Ps 111:9
1:50 ◊Ps 103:17
1:51–52 ◊2 Sm 22:28
1:52 ◊1 Sm 2:4, 7; Sir 10:14; Jb 5:11, 12:19
1:53 ◊Ps 107:9, 2 Sm 2:5, Jb 22:9
1:54 ◊Is 41:8–9, Ps 98:3
1:55 ◊Mi 7:20, 2 Sm 22:51
1:59 ◊Lv 12:3
1:68 ◊Ps 41:13
1:69 ◊Ps 18:2
1:71 ◊Ps 106:10

1:69 *horn*: a symbol of strength (see e.g., Ps 89:17; 92:10).

2:1 This census is attested nowhere else in ancient sources.

Birth of Jesus

brance of his holy covenant. [73]This is the oath he swore to Abraham our ancestor: [74]to grant that we be rescued from the hands of our enemies, to serve him without fear, [75]in holiness and righteousness before him all our days. [76]And you, child, will be called a prophet of the Most High; for you will go before the Lord to prepare his way, [77]to give his people knowledge of salvation through the forgiveness of their sins. [78]In the heartfelt mercy of our God, the dawn from on high will visit us, [79]to shine on those sitting in darkness, in the shadow of death, to guide our feet to the way of peace."

[80]And the child grew up and became strong in spirit. He was in the wilderness until the day of his public appearance to Israel.

2 ***In those days*** it so happened that a decree was issued by Emperor Augustus that a census be taken of the whole civilized world. [2]This first census was taken while Quirinius was governor of Syria. [3]Everybody had to travel to their ancestral city to be counted in the census. [4]So Joseph too went up from Galilee, from the town of Nazareth, to Judea, to the town of David called Bethlehem, because he was a descendant of David, [5]to be counted in the census with Mary, to whom he was engaged; Mary was pregnant. [6]It so happened while they were there that the time came for her to give birth; [7]and she gave birth to a son, her firstborn. She wrapped him in strips of cloth and laid him in a feeding trough, because the travelers' shelter was no place for that.

Visit of the shepherds

[8]***Now in the same area*** there were shepherds living outdoors. They were keeping watch over their sheep at night, [9]when a messenger of the Lord stood near them and the glory of the Lord shone around them. They became terrified. [10]But the messenger said to them, "Don't be afraid: I bring you good news of a great joy, which is to benefit the whole nation; [11]today in the city of David, the Savior was born to you—he is the Anointed, the Lord. [12]And this will be a sign for you: you will find a baby wrapped in strips of cloth and lying in a feeding trough."

[13]And suddenly there appeared with the messenger a whole troop of the heavenly army praising God:

> [14]Glory to God in the highest,
> and on earth peace to people whom he has favored!

[15]It so happened when the messengers left and returned to heaven that the shepherds said to one another, "Come on! Let's go over to Bethlehem and see what has happened, the event the Lord has told us about." [16]And they hurried away, and found Mary and Joseph, and the

1:72 ◊Ps 105:8, 106:45
1:73 ◊Mi 7:20, Gn 26:3
1:75 ◊Jos 24:14, Is 38:20
1:76 ◊Is 40:3, Mal 3:1
1:78 ◊Is 9:2
1:79 ◊Ps 107:10, Is 59:8
2:11 ◊2 Sm 5:7,9 (LXX)
2:15–20 Cf. Mt 2:1–12

2:14 Some mss read "peace, good will among people."

2:2 Quirinius was governor of Syria in 6–7 C.E. The problem of how to reconcile the chronology of 2:2 with 1:5 (Herod died in 4 B.C.E.) has defied solution.
2:3–4 This procedure for a census is unattested in ancient sources.
2:7 The *travelers' shelter* was a caravansary. The sense of *no place* seems to be that they wanted privacy, not that there was no vacancy.

Circumcision of Jesus

Presentation of Jesus

baby lying in a feeding trough. [17]And when they saw it they reported what they had been told about this child. [18]Everyone who listened was astonished at what the shepherds told them. [19]But Mary took all this in and reflected on it. [20]And the shepherds returned, glorifying and praising God for all they had heard and seen; everything turned out just as they had been told.

[21]***Now eight days later,*** when the time came to circumcise him, they gave him the name Jesus, the name assigned him by the heavenly messenger before he was conceived in the womb.

[22]***Now when the time came*** for their purification according to the Law of Moses, they brought him up to Jerusalem to present him to the Lord—[23]as it is written in the Law of the Lord, "Every male that opens the womb is to be considered holy to the Lord"— [24]and to offer sacrifice according to what is dictated in the Law of the Lord: "A pair of turtledoves or two young pigeons."

[25]Now there was a man in Jerusalem, named Simeon, a decent and devout man who was waiting for the consolation of Israel, and the holy spirit was with him. [26]It had been disclosed to him by the holy spirit that he would not see death before he had laid eyes on the Lord's Anointed. [27]And so he was guided by the spirit to the temple area. When the parents brought in the child Jesus, to perform for him what was customary according to the Law, [28]he took him in his arms and blessed God: [29]"Now, Lord, you can dismiss your slave in peace, according to your word, [30]now that my eyes have seen your salvation, [31]which you have prepared in the sight of all the peoples—[32]a revelatory light for foreigners, and glory for your people Israel."

[33]His father and mother were astonished at what was being said about him.

[34]Then Simeon blessed them and said to Mary his mother, "This child is linked to the fall and rise of many in Israel, and is destined to be a sign that is rejected. [35]You too will have your heart broken—and the schemes of many minds will be exposed."

[36]A prophetess was also there, Anna, daughter of Phanuel, of the tribe of Asher. She was well along in years, since she had married as a young girl and lived with her husband for seven years, [37]and then alone as a widow until she was eighty-four. She never left the temple area, and she worshiped day and night with fasting and prayer. [38]Coming on the scene at that very moment, she gave thanks to God, and began to speak about the child to all who were waiting for the liberation of Jerusalem.

2:19
Ⓓ Lk 2:51
2:22
◊ Lv 12:6
2:23
◊ Ex 13:2, 12, 15
2:24
◊ Lv 12:8
2:30
◊ Is 40:5
2:31
◊ Is 52:10
2:32
Ⓣ Acts 13:47, 26:23; ◊ Is 49:6

2:22 *Their* refers grammatically to Mary and Joseph. Lev 12:2–8 prescribes a ritual purification for a mother forty days after childbirth. There is no known ritual which involved the purification of both parents.
2:22–23 Such a custom of presenting a firstborn to God in the temple is unknown in Jewish tradition.
2:23 The Law (Num 3:47–48) required a firstborn son to be redeemed by payment of a fee, about which Luke is silent.
2:24 This is part of the maternal purification ritual.

Jesus in the temple at twelve

A voice in the wilderness

[39]And when they had carried out everything required by the Law of
the Lord, they returned to Galilee, to Nazareth, their own city. [40]And
the boy grew up and became strong, and was filled with wisdom; and
God regarded him favorably.

[41]***Now his parents*** used to go to Jerusalem every year for the Passover festival. [42]And when he was twelve years old, they went up for the
festival as usual. [43]When the festival was over and they were returning
home, the young Jesus stayed behind in Jerusalem, without his parents
knowing about it. [44]Assuming that he was in the traveling party, they
went a day's journey, and then began to look for him among their
relatives and acquaintances. [45]When they did not find him, they returned to Jerusalem to search for him.

[46]And after three days it so happened that they found him in the
temple area, sitting among the teachers, listening to them and asking
them questions. [47]Everyone who listened to him was astounded at his
understanding and his responses.

[48]And when ⟨his parents⟩ saw him they were overwhelmed.
"Child," his mother said to him, "why have you done this to us? Don't
you see, your father and I have been worried sick looking for you."

[49]"Why were you looking for me?" he said to them. "Didn't you
know that I have to be in my Father's house?"

[50]But they did not understand what he was talking about. [51]Then he
returned with them to Nazareth, and was obedient to them. His mother
took careful note of all these things. [52]And Jesus, precocious as he was,
continued to excel in learning and gain respect in the eyes of God and
others.

3 ***In the fifteenth year*** of the rule of Emperor Tiberius, when Pontius Pilate was governor of Judea, Herod tetrarch of Galilee, his brother
Philip tetrarch of the district of Iturea and Trachonitis, and Lysanias
tetrarch of Abilene, [2]during the high-priesthood of Annas and Caiaphas, the word of God came to John, son of Zechariah, in the wilderness. [3]And he went into the whole region around the Jordan, calling
for baptism and a change of heart that lead to forgiveness of sins. [4]As is
written in the book of the sayings of Isaiah the prophet,

> The voice of someone shouting in the wilderness:
> "Make ready the way of the Lord,
> make his paths straight.

2:40 Ⓣ Lk 1:80; Ⓓ Lk 2:52
2:51 Ⓓ Lk 2:19
2:52 Ⓓ Lk 2:40; ◊ 1 Sm 2:26
3:1–17 //Mk 1:2–8, Mt 3:1–12, Jn 1:19–28
3:1–3 Cf. GEbi 1
3:3 Ⓣ Acts 2:38, 13:24; GHeb 2:1; GNaz 2:1
3:4–6 ◊ Is 40:3–5
3:4 Ⓣ Lk 1:76

3:1 *The fifteenth year of Tiberius* probably points to 28 or 29 C.E. This synchronizes with the reign of the other rulers, though nothing is known about Lysanius.

Herod: Antipas, son of Herod the Great (1:5).

3:2 There was only one high priest at a time. Perhaps it was customary for former high priests (Annas was deposed in 15 C.E.) to retain their title.

The word of God came to . . . is an OT phrase denoting a divine call to prophecy (see Isa 38:4; Jer 1:1; 13:3). Luke identifies John as a prophet in 1:76 and 7:26.

John baptizes Jesus

[5]Every valley will be filled,
and every mountain and hill leveled.
What is crooked will be made straight,
and the rough ways smooth.
[6]Then the whole human race will see the salvation of God."

[7]So ⟨John⟩ would say to the crowds that came out to get baptized by him, "You spawn of Satan! Who warned you to flee from the impending doom? [8]Well then, start producing fruits suitable for a change of heart, and don't even start saying to yourselves, 'We have Abraham for our father.' Let me tell you, God can raise up children for Abraham right out of these rocks. [9]Even now the axe is aimed at the root of the trees. So every tree not producing choice fruit gets cut down and tossed into the fire."

[10]The crowds would ask him, "So what should we do?"

[11]And he would answer them, "Whoever has two shirts should share with someone who has none; whoever has food should do the same." [12]Toll collectors also came to get baptized, and they would ask him, "Teacher, what should we do?" [13]He told them, "Charge nothing above the official rates." [14]Soldiers also asked him, "And what about us?" And he said to them, "No more shakedowns! No more frame-ups either! And be satisfied with your pay."

[15]The people were filled with expectation and everyone was trying to figure out whether John might be the Anointed.

[16]John's answer was the same to everyone: "I baptize you with water; but someone more powerful than I is coming. I am not fit to untie his sandal straps. He'll baptize you with holy spirit and fire. [17]His pitchfork is in his hand, to make a clean sweep of his threshing floor and to gather his wheat into the granary, but the chaff he'll burn in a fire that can't be put out."

[18]And so, with many other exhortations he preached to the people. [19]But Herod the tetrarch, who had been denounced by John over the matter of Herodias, his brother's wife, [20]topped off all his other crimes by shutting John up in prison.

[21]***And it so happened,*** when all the people were baptized, and after Jesus had been baptized and while he was praying, that the sky opened up, [22]and the holy spirit came down on him in bodily form like a dove,

Q**3:7–9**
//Mt3:7–10;
Ⓣ SJas6:28–30
3:7
//Mt23:33
3:8
Cf. Jn8:39
3:9
//Mt7:19
Q**3:16–17**
//Mt3:11–12
3:16
Ⓣ Acts1:5, 11:16, 13:25, 19:1–7
3:19–20
//Mk6:17–18, Mt14:3–4
3:21–22
//Mk1:9–11, Mt3:13–17, Jn1:32–34, GHeb3, GEbi4
3:22
//GEbi4:3–4;
Ⓣ Lk9:35;
◊ Ps2:7, Is42:1

3:16 Untying sandal straps was the task of a slave.

3:19 Herod left his first wife to marry the wife of his half-brother. Such a marriage violates the Law (Lev 18:16).

3:20–21 Luke puts John's imprisonment before Jesus' baptism, reversing the Markan order of events. Thus Jesus is baptized, but not by John. This contradicts not only the other gospels, but Luke's own resumé of Jesus' career in Acts 1:21–22. Luke's probable motive for this unusual sequencing of events is to remove John from the scene before Jesus appears in public, thus clearly demarcating their careers. (See also Luke 16:16 and Acts 13:25.)

3:21 Luke often portrays Jesus *praying* at significant moments in his life (6:12; 9:18, 28; 11:2; 22:32, 41; 23:46).

3:24–38 The genealogy lists 77 generations

Jesus' family tree

Jesus is tested

and a voice came from the sky, "You are my son; today I have become your father."

[23]***Jesus was about thirty*** years old when he began his work. He was supposedly the son of Joseph, son of Eli, [24]son of Matthat, son of Levi, son of Melchi, son of Jannai, son of Joseph, [25]son of Mattathias, son of Amos, son of Nahum, son of Hesli, son of Naggai, [26]son of Maath, son of Mattathias, son of Semein, son of Josech, son of Joda, [27]son of Johanan, son of Rhesa, son of Zerubbabel, son of Salathiel, son of Neri, [28]son of Melchi, son of Addi, son of Cosam, son of Elmadam, son of Er, [29]son of Joshua, son of Eliezer, son of Jorim, son of Matthat, son of Levi, [30]son of Simeon, son of Judah, son of Joseph, son of Jonam, son of Eliakim, [31]son of Melea, son of Menna, son of Mattatha, son of Nathan, son of David, [32]son of Jesse, son of Obed, son of Boaz, son of Sala, son of Nahshon, [33]son of Amminadab, son of Admin, son of Arni, son of Hezron, son of Perez, son of Judah, [34]son of Jacob, son of Isaac, son of Abraham, son of Terah, son of Nahor, [35]son of Serug, son of Reu, son of Peleg, son of Eber, son of Shelah, [36]son of Cainan, son of Arphachshad, son of Shem, son of Noah, son of Lamech, [37]son of Methuselah, son of Enoch, son of Jared, son of Mahalalel, son of Kenan, [38] son of Enosh, son of Seth, son of Adam, son of God.

4 ***Jesus departed*** from the Jordan full of the holy spirit and was guided by the spirit into the wilderness, [2]where he was put to the test by the devil for forty days. He ate nothing that whole time; and when it was all over, he was famished.

[3]The devil said to him, "To prove you're God's son, order this stone to turn into bread."

[4]Jesus responded to him, "It is written, 'Human beings are not to live on bread alone.'"

[5]Then he took Jesus up, and in an instant of time showed him all the empires of the civilized world. [6]The devil said to him, "I'll bestow on you authority over all this and the glory that comes with it; understand, it has been handed over to me, and I can give it to anyone I want. [7]So, if you will pay homage to me, it will all be yours."

[8]Jesus responded, "It is written, 'You are to pay homage to the Lord your God, and you are to revere him alone.'"

[9]Then he took him to Jerusalem, set him on the pinnacle of the temple, and said to him, "To prove you're God's son, jump off from here; [10]remember, it is written, 'To his heavenly messengers he will give orders about you, to protect you,' [11]and 'with their hands they will catch you, so you won't even stub your toe on a stone.'"

3:23–38 //Mt 1:1–17
3:23 Cf. GEbi 2:1
3:27–34 ◊1 Chr 1–3
3:34–38 ◊Gn 5:1–32, 11:10–26
Q4:1–13 //Mt 4:1–11; cf. GHeb 4
4:1–2 //Mk 1:12–13
4:4 ◊Dt 8:3
4:8 ◊Dt 6:13
4:10–11 ◊Ps 91:11–12

3:22 Most mss read "You are my beloved son—of you I fully approve" (as in Mark 1:11).

from Adam to Jesus and cannot be reconciled with the genealogy in Matthew 1. The names between Joseph (v. 23) and Zerubabbel (v. 27) are otherwise unknown.

A voice in Galilee

[12]And in response Jesus said to him, "It is said, 'You are not to put
the Lord your God to the test.'"
[13]So when the devil had tried every kind of test, he let him alone for
the time being.
[14]***Then Jesus returned*** in the power of the spirit to Galilee. News
about him spread throughout all the surrounding area. [15]He used to
teach in their synagogues, and was acclaimed by everyone.
[16]When he came to Nazareth, where he had been brought up, he
went to the synagogue on the sabbath day, as was his custom. He stood
up to do the reading [17]and was handed the scroll of the prophet Isaiah.
He unrolled the scroll and found the place where it was written:

> [18]The spirit of the Lord is upon me,
> because he has anointed me
> to bring good news to the poor.
> He has sent me to announce pardon for prisoners
> and recovery of sight to the blind;
> to set free the oppressed,
> [19]to proclaim the year of the Lord's amnesty.

[20]After rolling up the scroll, he gave it back to the attendant, and sat
down; and the attention of everyone in the synagogue was riveted on
him.
[21]He began by saying to them, "Today this scripture has come true
as you listen."
[22]And they all began voicing approval of him, and marveling at the
pleasing speech that he delivered; and would remark, "Isn't this
Joseph's son?"
[23]And he said to them, "No doubt you will quote me that proverb,
'Doctor, cure yourself,' and you'll tell me, 'Do here in your hometown
what we've heard you've done in Capernaum.'"
[24]Then he said, "The truth is, no prophet is welcome on his home
turf. [25]I can assure you, there were many widows in Israel in Elijah's
time, when the sky was dammed up for three and a half years, and a
severe famine swept through the land. [26]Yet Elijah was not sent to any
of them, but instead to a widow in Zarephath near Sidon. [27]In addition,
there were many lepers in Israel in the prophet Elisha's time; yet none
of them was made clean, except Naaman the Syrian."
[28]Everyone in the synagogue was filled with rage when they heard
this. [29]They rose up, ran him out of town, and led him to the brow of
the hill on which their town was built, intending to hurl him over it.
[30]But he slipped away through the throng and went on his way.

4:12
◊Dt 6:16
4:14–15
//Mk 1:14–15, Mt 4:12–17
4:16–30
Cf. Mk 6:1–6, Mt 13:53–58
4:18–19
◊Is 61:1–2
4:18
Ⓣ Lk 7:22
4:24
//Jn 4:44, Th 31
4:25–26
◊1 Kgs 17:1–16
4:27
◊2 Kgs 5:1–14

4:13 *for the time being* (*kairos*): until 22:3, 31–32.

4:23 In Mark this scene (6:1–6) occurs after the miracles at Capernaum. By relocating this scene to the beginning of Jesus' public ministry, Luke creates an inconsistency in his narrative, for Jesus has not yet been to Capernaum. Luke narrates his feats there at 4:31–41 and 7:1–10.

4:29 Nazareth is not built on or near a cliff face. Luke generally seems poorly informed about Palestinian geography. Aspects of his geography may therefore be fictive.

An unclean spirit

Peter's mother-in-law

At day's end

Fishing for people

[31]***He went down to Capernaum,*** a town in Galilee, and he would teach them on the sabbath day. [32]They were astonished at his teaching because his message carried authority.

[33]Now in the synagogue there was a person who had an unclean demon, which screamed at the top of its voice, [34]"Hey Jesus! What do you want with us, you Nazarene? Have you come to get rid of us? I know you, who you are: God's holy man."

[35]But Jesus yelled at it, "Shut up and get out of him!"

Then the demon threw the man down in full view of everyone and came out of him without doing him any harm. [36]And so amazement came over them all and they would say to one another, "What kind of message is this? With authority and power he gives orders to unclean spirits, and they leave." [37]So rumors about him began to spread to every corner of the surrounding region.

[38]***He got up*** from the synagogue and entered the house of Simon. Simon's mother-in-law was suffering from a high fever, and they made an appeal to him on her behalf. [39]He stood over her, rebuked the fever, and it disappeared. She immediately got up and started looking after them.

[40]***As the sun was setting,*** all those who had people sick with various diseases brought them to him. He would lay his hands on each one of them and cure them. [41]Demons would also come out of many of them screaming, and saying, "You son of God, you!" But he would rebuke them and not allow them to speak, because they knew that he was the Anointed.

[42]The next morning he went outside and withdrew to an isolated place. Then the crowds came looking for him, and when they got to him they tried to keep him from leaving them. [43]He said to them, "I must declare God's imperial rule to the other towns as well; after all, this is why I was sent." [44]And he continued to speak in the synagogues of Judea.

5 ***On one occasion,*** when the crowd pressed him to hear the word of God, he was standing by the lake of Gennesaret. [2]He noticed two boats moored there at the shore; the fishermen had left them and were washing their nets. [3]He got into one of the boats, the one belonging to Simon, and asked him to put out a little from the shore. Then he sat down and began to teach the crowds from the boat.

[4]When he had finished speaking, he said to Simon, "Put out into deep water and lower your nets for a catch."

[5]But Simon replied, "Master, we've been hard at it all night and haven't caught a thing. But if you insist, I'll lower the nets."

4:31–37 //Mk 1:21–28
4:32 Cf. Mt 7:28–29
4:38–39 //Mk 1:29–31, Mt 8:14–15
4:40–41 //Mk 1:32–34, Mt 8:16–17
4:42–44 //Mk 1:35–39, Mt 4:23–25; cf. Acts 10:36–38
5:1–11 //Mk 1:16–20, Mt 4:18–22; cf. GEbi 2:3

4:44 Instead of Judea, some mss read "Galilee," which makes more sense, since 4:42–43 and 5:1 occur there.

5:1 *lake of Gennesaret*: usually called the Sea of Galilee.

Jesus cures a leper

Paralyzed person forgiven

6So they did and netted such a huge number of fish that their nets began to tear apart. 7They signaled to their partners in the other boat to come and lend a hand. They came and loaded both boats until they nearly sank.

8At the sight of this, Simon Peter fell to his knees in front of Jesus and said, "Have nothing to do with me, Master, heathen that I am." 9For he and his companions were stunned at the catch of fish they had taken, 10as were James and John, sons of Zebedee and partners of Simon.

Jesus said to Simon, "Don't be afraid; from now on you'll be catching people." 11They then brought their boats to shore, abandoned everything, and followed him.

12***And it so happened*** while he was in one of the towns, there was this man covered with leprosy. Seeing Jesus, he knelt with his face to the ground and begged him, "Sir, if you want to, you can make me clean."

13Jesus stretched out his hand, touched him, and says, "Okay—you're clean!"

And at once the leprosy disappeared. 14He ordered him to tell no one. "But go, have a priest examine ⟨your skin⟩. Then make an offering, as Moses commanded, for your cleansing, as evidence ⟨of your cure⟩."

15Yet the story about him spread around all the more. Great crowds would gather to hear him and to be healed of their sicknesses. 16But he would withdraw to isolated places and pray.

17***And it so happened*** one day, as he was teaching, that the Lord's healing power was with him. Now Pharisees and teachers of the Law, who had come from every village of Galilee and Judea and from Jerusalem, were sitting around. 18The next thing you know, some men appeared, carrying a paralyzed person on a bed. They attempted to bring him in and lay him before ⟨Jesus⟩. 19But finding no way to get him in on account of the crowd, they went up onto the roof and lowered him on his pallet through the tiles into the middle of the crowd in front of Jesus.

20When Jesus noticed their trust, he said, "Mister, your sins have been forgiven you."

21And the scholars and the Pharisees began to raise questions: "Who is this that utters blasphemies? Who can forgive sins except God alone?"

22Because Jesus was aware of their questions, he responded to them, "Why do you entertain such questions? 23Which is easier: to say, 'Your sins have been forgiven you,' or to say, 'Get up and walk'?" 24But so that you may realize that on earth the son of Adam has authority to

5:4–10
Cf. Jn 21:1–14
5:12–16
// Mk 1:40–45, Mt 8:1–4; cf. EgerG 2:1–4
5:14
◊ Lv 14:2–32
5:17–26
// Mk 2:1–12, Mt 9:1–8
5:20–21
Ⓣ Lk 7:48–49

5:12 Prostration was a gesture of submission and respect. *clean*: recovered from leprosy, which rendered one *unclean*.

Levi

Fasting & wedding

Son of Adam over the sabbath

forgive sins, he said to the paralyzed man, "You there, get up, pick up
your pallet and go home!"
25And immediately he stood up in front of them, picked up what he
had been lying on, and went home praising God. 26They all became
ecstatic, and they began to extol God, but they were also filled with fear
and exclaimed, "We saw some incredible things today!"
27***After these events*** he went out and observed a toll collector named
Levi sitting at the toll booth. He said to him, "Follow me!" 28Leaving
everything behind, he got up, and followed him.
29And Levi gave him a great banquet in his house, and a large group
of toll collectors and others were dining with them.
30The Pharisees and their scholars would complain to his disciples:
"Why do you people eat and drink with toll collectors and sinners?"
31In response Jesus said to them: "Since when do the healthy need a
doctor? It's the sick who do. 32I have not come to enlist religious folks
to change their hearts, but sinners!"
33***They said to him,*** "The disciples of John are always fasting and
offering prayers, and so are those of the Pharisees, but yours just eat and
drink."
34And Jesus said to them, "You can't make the groom's friends fast
as long as the groom is around, can you? 35But the days will come when
the groom is taken away from them, and then they will fast, in those
days."
36He then gave them a proverb: "Nobody tears a piece from a new
garment and puts it on an old one, since the new one will tear and the
piece from the new will not match the old. 37And nobody pours young
wine into old wineskins, otherwise the young wine will burst the wineskins, it will gush out, and the wineskins will be destroyed. 38Instead,
young wine must be put into new wineskins. 39Besides, nobody wants
young wine after drinking aged wine. As they say, 'Aged wine is just
fine!'"

6 ***It so happened*** that he was walking through grainfields on a sabbath day, and his disciples would strip some heads of grain, husk them
in their hands, and chew them. 2Some of the Pharisees said, "Why are
you doing what's not permitted on the sabbath day?"
3And Jesus answered them, "Haven't you read what David did when
he and his companions were hungry? 4He went into the house of God,
took and ate the consecrated bread himself, and gave some to his men
to eat. No one is permitted to eat this bread except the priests alone!"

5:27–32 //Mk 2:14–17, Mt 9:9–13

5:27–28 Cf. GHeb 5, GEbi 2:4

5:29–30 //GOxy 1224 5 Ⓣ Lk 7:34, 15:2, 19:7

5:33–39 //Mk 2:18–22, Mt 9:14–17

5:35 Cf. Th 104

5:36–39 //Th 47:3–5

6:1–5 //Mk 2:23–28, Mt 12:1–8

6:4 ◊ Lv 24:5–9, 1 Sm 21:1–6

5:30 To eat with someone implied social approval and established a bond of friendship.

5:37 New wine produces gas bubbles as it ferments, which will burst an old wineskin.

6:2 The Law permits taking grain from someone else's field (Deut 23:25). What is unlawful is working (i.e., picking grain) on the sabbath.

Man with a crippled hand

The twelve

Congratulations!

[5]And he used to say to them, "The son of Adam lords it over the sabbath day."

[6]***On another sabbath day,*** it so happened that he entered the synagogue and taught. A man was there whose right hand was crippled. [7]And the scholars and the Pharisees watched him carefully, to see if he would heal on the sabbath day, so they could find some excuse to denounce him. [8]However, he knew their motives, and he said to the fellow with the crippled hand, "Get up and stand here in front of everybody." And he got to his feet and stood there.

[9]Then Jesus queried them: "I ask you, on the sabbath day is it permitted to do good or to do evil, to save life or to destroy it?" [10]And he looked right at all of them, and said to him, "Hold out your hand!" He did and his hand was restored.

[11]But they were filled with rage and discussed among themselves what to do with Jesus.

[12]***During that time,*** it so happened that he went out to the mountain to pray, and spent the night in prayer to God. [13]The next day, he called his disciples and selected twelve of them, whom he named apostles: [14]Simon, whom he nicknamed Rock, and Andrew his brother, and James and John, and Philip, and Bartholomew, [15]and Matthew, and Thomas, and James the son of Alphaeus, and Simon who was called the Zealot, [16]and Judas the son of James, and Judas Iscariot, who turned traitor.

[17]***On the way down*** with them, Jesus stopped at a level place. There was a huge crowd of his disciples and a great throng of people from all Judea and Jerusalem and the coast of Tyre and Sidon. They came to hear him and to be healed of their diseases. [18]Those who were tormented by unclean spirits were cured. [19]And everyone in the crowd tried to touch him, since power would flow out from him and heal them all.

[20]Then he would look squarely at his disciples and say:

Congratulations, you poor!
God's domain belongs to you.
[21]Congratulations, you hungry!
You will have a feast.
Congratulations, you who weep now!
You will laugh.

6:6–11 //Mk 3:1–6, Mt 12:9–14; Cf. GNaz 4
6:9 Ⓣ Lk 14:3
6:12–16 //Mk 3:13–19, Mt 10:1–4; cf. GEbi 2:3
6:17–19 //Mk 3:7–12, Mt 12:15–21
Q**6:20–26** //Mt 5:3–12
6:20 //Th 54
6:21 //Th 69:2; Ⓣ DSav 8:1

6:7 Sabbath regulations forbad a physician to treat patients on the sabbath, except in emergencies.

6:15 The Zealots were a militaristic Jewish independence movement which precipitated the war against Roman occupation in 66–70 C.E. However, their existence during Jesus' lifetime is highly doubtful.

6:17 *A level place* contrasts with the setting for the parallel "Sermon on the Mount" in Matt 5:1. Luke's version of this speech is often called the "Sermon on the Plain."

Tyre and *Sidon* are Gentile areas outside Palestine.

6:20 *Congratulations* (*makarios*): traditionally translated "blessed." "Congratulations" better expresses the performative language of the Beatitudes, which grant the recipient recognition of good fortune. (See the essay on p. 448).

Love of enemies

Golden rule

On judging

[22]"Congratulations to you when people hate you, and when they ostracize you and denounce you and scorn your name as evil, because of the son of Adam! [23]Rejoice on that day, and jump for joy! Just remember, your compensation is great in heaven. Recall that their ancestors treated the prophets the same way.

[24]Damn you rich!
You already have your consolation.
[25]Damn you who are well-fed now!
You will know hunger.
Damn you who laugh now!
You will learn to weep and grieve.

[26]"Damn you when everybody speaks well of you! Recall that their ancestors treated the phony prophets the same way.

[27]"***But to you who listen*** I say, love your enemies, do favors for those who hate you, [28]bless those who curse you, pray for your abusers.

[29]"When someone strikes you on the cheek, offer the other as well. If someone takes away your coat, don't prevent that person from taking your shirt along with it.

[30]"Give to everyone who begs from you; and when someone takes your things, don't ask for them back.

[31]"***Treat people*** the way you want them to treat you.

[32]"If you love those who love you, what merit is there in that? After all, even sinners love those who love them. [33]And if you do good to those who do good to you, what merit is there in that? After all, even sinners do as much. [34]If you lend to those from whom you hope to gain, what merit is there in that? Even sinners lend to sinners, in order to get as much in return. [35]But love your enemies, and do good, and lend, expecting nothing in return. Your reward will be great, and you'll be children of the Most High. As you know, the Most High is generous to the ungrateful and the wicked.

[36]"***Be as compassionate*** as your Father is. [37]Don't pass judgment, and you won't be judged; don't condemn, and you won't be condemned; forgive, and you'll be forgiven. [38]Give, and it will be given to you: they'll put in your lap a full measure, packed down, sifted and overflowing. For the standard you apply will be the standard applied to you."

[39]And he posed a riddle for them: "Can one blind person guide another? Won't they both end up in some ditch?

[40]"Students are not above their teachers. But those who are fully taught will be like their teachers. [41]Why do you notice the sliver in your

6:22
//Th 68:1;
cf. Th 69:1;
Ⓣ 1 Pet 3:14,
4:13–14
6:23
Ⓣ Acts 7:52
6:24
Cf. Jas 5:1
Q6:27–36
//Mt 5:38–48
6:27
//GOxy 1224 6:1
6:28
Ⓣ Rom 12:14,
1 Pet 3:9
6:31
//Mt 7:12;
cf. Tob 4:15
6:34–35
Cf. Th 95
Q6:37–42
//Mt 7:1–5
6:37
//Mary 9:12
6:38
//Mk 4:24
Q6:39
//Mt 15:14, Th 34
Q6:40
//Mt 10:24–25,
Jn 13:16, 15:20;
cf. DSav 20
6:41–42
//Th 26

6:22 *your name*: not one's personal name, but the name of "Christian," a title attested in the NT only by Acts 11:26; 26:28; 1 Pet 4:16.
6:24 *Damn you*: traditionally translated as "Woe to you." (See the essay on p. 448).

6:29 The *coat* and *shirt* are the full-length outer and under garments worn in the ancient world. One who lacked both garments would be nearly nude.

By their fruit

Foundations

Officer's slave

friend's eye, but overlook the timber in your own? 42How can you say to
your friend, 'Friend, let me get the sliver in your eye,' when you don't
notice the timber in your own? You phony, first take the timber out of
your own eye, and then you'll see well enough to remove the sliver in
your friend's eye.

43"***A choice tree*** does not produce rotten fruit, any more than a
rotten tree produces choice fruit; 44for each tree is known by its fruit.
Figs are not gathered from thorns, nor are grapes picked from bram-
bles. 45The good person produces good from the fund of good in the
heart, and the evil person produces evil from the evil within. As you
know, the mouth gives voice to what the heart is full of.

46"***Why do you call me*** 'Master, master,' and not do what I tell you?
47Everyone who comes to me and pays attention to my words and acts
on them—I'll show you what such a person is like: 48That one is like a
person building a house, who dug deep and laid the foundation on
bedrock; when a flood came, the torrent slammed against that house,
but could not shake it, because it was well built. 49But the one who
listens ⟨to my words⟩ and doesn't act ⟨on them⟩ is like a person who
built a house on the ground without a foundation; when the torrent
slammed against it, it collapsed immediately. And so the ruin of that
house was total."

7 ***After he had completed*** all he had to say to his audience, he went
into Capernaum.

2A Roman officer had a slave he was very fond of but who was sick
and about to die. 3So when he heard about Jesus, the Roman officer
sent some Jewish elders to him, and asked him to come and cure his
slave. 4When they came to Jesus, they pleaded with him urgently,
saying, "He deserves to have you do this for him. 5As you probably
know, he loves our people, and even built a synagogue for us."

6So Jesus went with them.

When he got close to the house, the Roman officer dispatched
friends to say to him, "Don't trouble yourself, sir, for I don't deserve to
have you in my house; 7that's why I didn't presume to come to you in
person. Just say the word, and let my boy be cured. 8After all, I myself
am under orders, and I have soldiers under me. I order one to go, and
he goes; I order another to come, and he comes; and ⟨I order⟩ my slave
to do something, and he does it."

9As Jesus listened to this he was amazed at him. He turned and said
to the crowd that followed, "Let me tell you, not even in Israel have I
found such trust."

10And when the emissaries returned to the house, they found the
slave in good health.

Q6:43–45 //Mt 7:15–20, 12:33–35, Th 45
6:44 Cf. Jas 3:12
Q6:46–49 //Mt 7:21, 24–27; SJas 6:15c
6:46 //Mt 7:21, EgerG 3:5
Q7:1–10 //Mt 8:5–13, Jn 4:46–54

7:6 Entering the home of a Gentile would render a Jew unclean (see Acts 10:28).

7:7 *boy*: The Greek word *pais* can refer either to a child or to a servant.

Widow's son at Nain

John queries Jesus

Jesus praises John

[11]***And it so happened*** soon afterward that he went to a town called Nain, and his disciples and a large crowd accompanied him. [12]As he neared the town gate, just then a dead man was being carried out, the only son of his mother, who was herself a widow. And a considerable crowd from the town was with her.

[13]When the Lord saw her, his heart went out to her and he said to her, "Don't cry." [14]And he went up and touched the bier. The bearers paused, and he said, "Young man, I tell you, get up."

[15]And the dead man sat up and began to speak; then ⟨Jesus⟩ gave him back to his mother.

[16]Fear gripped them all; and they gave God the glory, saying, "A great prophet has been raised up among us!" and "God has visited his people!"

[17]And this story about him spread throughout Judea and all the surrounding area.

[18]***The disciples of John*** brought reports of all these things to him. [19]John summoned a couple of his disciples and sent them to the Lord to ask: "Are you the one who is to come, or are we to wait for someone else?"

[20]And when the men came to ⟨Jesus⟩, they said, "John the Baptist sent us to you to ask: 'Are you the one who is to come, or are we to wait for someone else?'"

[21]Jesus had just cured many of their diseases and plagues and evil spirits, and restored sight to many who were blind. [22]And so he answered them, "Go report to John what you have seen and heard:

> the blind see again,
> the lame walk,
> lepers are cleansed,
> the deaf hear,
> the dead are raised,
> and the poor have the good news preached to them.

[23]Congratulations to those who don't take offense at me."

[24]***After John's messengers*** had left, ⟨Jesus⟩ began to talk about John to the crowds: "What did you go out to the wilderness to gawk at? A reed shaking in the wind? [25]What did you really go out to see? A man dressed in fancy clothes? But wait! Those who dress fashionably and live in luxury are found in palaces. [26]Come on, what did you go out to see? A prophet? Yes, that's what you went out to see, yet someone more than a prophet. [27]This is the one about whom it was written:

> Here is my messenger,
> whom I send on ahead of you
> to prepare your way before you.

7:11–17 ◊1 Kgs 17:17–24
7:15 ◊1 Kgs 17:23
7:16 Ⓣ Lk 1:68, 19:44
Q7:18–23 //Mt 11:2–6
7:22 Ⓘ Lk 4:18; ◊Is 35:5–6, 61:1
Q7:24–28 //Mt 11:7–14
7:24–25 //Th 78
7:27 Cf. Mk 1:2; Ⓘ Lk 3:4; ◊Mal 3:1, Ex 23:20

7:11 Some mss read "on the next day" in place of *soon afterward.*

7:11–16 This miracle closely resembles that of Elijah's in 1 Kgs 17:17–24.

Children in the marketplace

[28]I tell you, among those born of women none is greater than John; yet the least in God's domain is greater than he." ([29]All the people, even the toll collectors, who were listening and had been baptized by John, vindicated God's plan; [30]but the Pharisees and the legal experts, who had not been baptized by him, subverted God's plan for themselves.)

A woman anoints Jesus' feet

[31]"***What do members*** of this generation remind me of? What are they like? [32]They are like children sitting in the marketplace and calling out to one another:

We played the flute for you,
but you wouldn't dance;
we sang a dirge,
but you wouldn't weep.

[33]"Just remember, John the Baptist appeared on the scene, eating no bread and drinking no wine, and you say, 'He is demented.' [34]The son of Adam appeared on the scene both eating and drinking, and you say, 'There's a glutton and a drunk, a crony of toll collectors and sinners!' [35]Indeed, wisdom is vindicated by all her children."

[36]***One of the Pharisees*** invited him to dinner; he entered the Pharisee's house, and reclined at the table. [37]A local woman, who was a sinner, found out that he was having dinner at the Pharisee's house. She suddenly showed up with an alabaster jar of myrrh, [38]and stood there behind him weeping at his feet. Her tears wet his feet, and she wiped them dry with her hair; she kissed his feet, and anointed them with the myrrh.

[39]The Pharisee who had invited him saw this and said to himself, "If this man were a prophet, he would know who this is and what kind of woman is touching him, since she is a sinner."

[40]And Jesus answered him, "Simon, I have something to tell you."

"Teacher," he said, "speak up."

[41]"This moneylender had two debtors; one owed five hundred silver coins, and the other fifty. [42]Since neither one of them could pay, he wrote off both debts. Now which of them will love him more?"

[43]Simon answered, "I would imagine, the one for whom he wrote off the larger debt."

And he said to him, "You're right." [44]Then turning to the woman, he said to Simon, "Do you see this woman? I walked into your house and you didn't offer me water for my feet; yet she has washed my feet with her tears and dried them with her hair. [45]You didn't offer me a kiss, but she hasn't stopped kissing my feet since I arrived. [46]You didn't anoint my head with oil, but she has anointed my feet with myrrh. [47]For this reason, I tell you, her sins, many as they are, have been

7:28
//Th46
7:29–30
Ⓣ Lk20:46, Mt21:32
7:29
Ⓘ Lk3:12
7:30
Cf. EgerG 1:10
Q7:31–35
//Mt11:16–19
7:34
Ⓣ Lk5:30, 15:2, 19:7;
▷Dt21:20
7:36–38
//Mk14:3–9, Mt26:6–13, Jn12:1–8
7:36
Ⓣ Lk11:37, 14:1

7:38 *stood behind him weeping at his feet*: Jesus was reclining to eat and so his feet would be behind him.

forgiven, as this outpouring of her love shows. But the one who is forgiven little shows little love."

48And he said to her, "Your sins have been forgiven."

49Then those having dinner with him began to mutter to themselves, "Who is this who even forgives sins?"

50And he said to the woman, "Your trust has saved you; go in peace."

8 ***And it so happened*** soon afterward that he traveled through towns and villages, preaching and announcing the good news of God's imperial rule. The twelve were with him, 2and also some women whom he had cured of evil spirits and diseases: Mary, the one from Magdala, from whom seven demons had taken their leave, 3and Joanna, the wife of Chuza, Herod's steward, and Susanna, and many others, who provided for them out of their resources.

4***Since a huge crowd*** was now gathering, and people were making their way to him from town after town, he told them some such parable as this:

> 5A sower went out to sow his seed; and while he was sowing, some seed fell along the path, and was trampled under foot, and the birds of the sky ate it up. 6Other seed fell on the rock; when it grew, it withered because it lacked moisture. 7Still other seed fell among thorns; the thorns grew with it and choked it. 8Other seed fell on fertile earth; and when it matured, it produced fruit a hundredfold.

During his discourse, he would call out, "Anyone here with two good ears had better listen!"

9***His disciples asked him*** what this parable was all about. 10He replied, "You have been given the privilege of knowing the secrets of God's imperial rule; but the rest get only parables, so that

> They may look but not see,
> listen but not understand.

11"***Now this is the interpretation*** of the parable. The 'seed' is God's message. 12Those 'along the path' are those who have listened to it, but then the devil comes and steals the message from their hearts, so they won't trust and be saved. 13Those 'on the rock' are those who, when they listen to the message, receive it happily. But they 'have no root': they trust for the moment but fall away when they are tested. 14What 'fell into the thorns' represents those who listen, but as they continue on, they are 'choked' by the worries and wealth and pleasures of life, and they do not come to maturity. 15But the seed 'in good earth' stands for those who listen to the message and hold on to it with a good and fertile heart, and 'produce fruit' through perseverance.

16"***No one lights a lamp*** and covers it with a pot or puts it under a bed; rather, one puts it on a lampstand, so that those who come in can

Traveling around

Sower, seeds, soils

In parables

Understanding the sower

Lamp & bed

7:48–49
Ⓣ Lk5:20–21
7:50
Ⓣ Lk8:48, 17:19, 18:42
8:4–8
//Mk4:1–9, Mt13:3–9, Th9; cf.SJas8:3
8:9–10
//Mk4:10–12, Mt13:10–15; cf.SJas6:5–6
8:10
Ⓣ Acts28:26–27; ◊Is6:9–10
8:11–15
//Mk4:13–20, Mt13:18–23; cf.SJas6:17
8:16–17
//Mk4:21–23
8:16
//Mt5:15, Th33:2–3; Ⓓ Lk11:33

True relatives

Rebuking wind & wave

Demon of Gerasa

see the light. [17]After all, there is nothing hidden that won't be brought to light, nor kept secret that won't be made known and exposed.

[18]"So pay attention to how you're listening; in fact, to those who have more will be given, and from those who don't have, even what they seem to have will be taken away."

[19]***Then his mother*** and his brothers came to see him, but they could not reach him because of the crowd. [20]When he was told, "Your mother and your brothers are outside and want to see you," [21]he replied to them, "My mother and my brothers are those who listen to God's message and do it."

[22]***One day*** Jesus and his disciples happened to get into a boat, and he said to them, "Let's cross to the other side of the lake."

So they shoved off, [23]and as they sailed he fell asleep. A squall descended on the lake; they were being swamped, and found themselves in real danger. [24]And they came and woke him up, saying, "Master, master, we are going to drown!"

He got up and rebuked the wind and the rough water; and they settled down, and there was a calm. [25]Then he said to them, "Where is your trust?"

Although they were terrified, they marveled, saying to one another, "Who can this fellow be, that he commands even winds and water and they obey him?"

[26]***They sailed*** to the region of the Gerasenes, which lies directly across from Galilee. [27]As he stepped out on land, this man from the town who was possessed by demons met him. For quite some time he had been going without clothes and hadn't lived in a house but stayed in the tombs instead.

[28]When he saw Jesus, he screamed and fell down before him, and said at the top of his voice, "What do you want with me, Jesus, you son of the most high God? I beg you, don't torment me." ([29]You see, he was about to order the unclean spirit to get out of the man. It seems, the demon had taken control of him many times; the man had been kept under guard, bound with chains and fetters, but he would break the bonds and be driven by the demon into the wilderness.)

[30]Jesus questioned him: "What is your name?"

"Legion," he said, because many demons had entered him. [31]They kept begging him not to order them to depart into the abyss.

[32]Now over there a large herd of pigs was feeding on the mountain; and they bargained with him to let them enter those pigs. And he agreed. [33]Then the demons came out of the fellow and entered

8:17 //Mt 10:26, Th 5:2, 6:5–6; (D) Lk 12:2
8:18 //Mk 4:25; Mt 13:12, 25:29; Th 41; (D) Lk 19:26
8:19–21 //Mk 3:31–35, Mt 12:46–50, Th 99, GEbi 5
8:21 //GHeb 4a; Cf. DSav 41:4; Lk 11:27–28
8:22–25 //Mk 4:35–41, Mt 8:23–27
8:26–39 //Mk 5:1–20, Mt 8:28–34

8:26 Some mss read either "Gergesenes" or "Gadarenes."

8:26 *Gerasenes*: probably a Gentile area.
8:30 *Legion* is a Latin word. There were 6000 soldiers in a Roman legion.
8:31 *abyss*: the final prison of Satan and his demons (see Rev 20:3). In popular belief, demons prowled the earth seeking dwelling places, usually in tombs, deserted places, or human souls (see Luke 11:24–26).

Jairus' daughter

Jesus cures a woman

Jairus' daughter revived

the pigs, and the herd rushed down the bluff into the lake and was drowned.

[34]When the herdsmen saw what had happened, they ran off and reported it in town and out in the country. [35]And people came out to see what had happened. They came to Jesus and found the fellow from whom the demons had gone, sitting at the feet of Jesus, with his clothes on and his wits about him; and they got scared. [36]Those who had seen it explained to them how the demoniac had been cured. [37]Then the entire populace of the Gerasene region asked him to leave them; for they were gripped by a great fear.

So he got into a boat and went back. [38]The man from whom the demons had departed begged to go with him; but he dismissed him, saying, [39]"Return home, and tell the story of what God has done for you." And he went his way, spreading the news throughout the whole town about what Jesus had done for him.

[40]***Now when Jesus returned,*** the crowd welcomed him, for they were all waiting for him. [41]Just then a man named Jairus, a synagogue official, came up to Jesus. He fell at Jesus' feet and begged him to come to his house, [42]because his only child, a twelve-year-old daughter, was dying.

As ⟨Jesus⟩ was walking along, the crowd milled around him. [43]A woman who had had a vaginal flow for twelve years, and had found no one able to heal her, [44]came up behind him, and touched the hem of his cloak. Immediately her flow of blood stopped.

[45]Then Jesus said, "Who touched me?"

When everyone denied it, Peter said, "Master, the crowds are pressing in and jostling you!"

[46]But Jesus insisted: "Someone touched me; I can tell that power has drained out of me."

[47]And when the woman saw that she had not escaped notice, she came forward trembling, and fell down before him. In front of all the people she explained why she had touched him, and how she had been immediately healed.

[48]Jesus said to her, "Daughter, your trust has cured you; go in peace."

[49]***While he is still speaking,*** someone from the synagogue official's house comes and says, "Your daughter is dead; don't bother the teacher further."

[50]When Jesus heard this, he answered him, "Don't be afraid; just have trust, and she'll be cured."

[51]When he arrived at the house, he wouldn't allow anyone to go in with him except Peter and John and James, and the child's father and

8:40–56 //Mk5:21–43, Mt9:18–26

8:48 Ⓣ Lk7:50, 17:19, 18:42

8:43 Many mss add "and had spent her life savings on physicians" after *twelve years.*

8:43 According to the Law (Lev 15:25–27), an untimely menstrual flow renders a woman unclean and cuts her off from social interaction.

Instructions for the road

Herod is curious about John

The apostles report

Loaves & fish for 5,000

mother. 52Everyone was crying and grieving over her, but he said, "Don't cry; she hasn't died; she's sleeping."

53But they started laughing at him, certain that she had died. 54He took her by the hand and called out, "Child, get up!" 55Her breathing returned and she immediately got up. He ordered them to give her something to eat.

56Her parents were quite ecstatic; but he commanded them not to tell anyone what had happened.

9 ***He called the twelve*** together and gave them power and authority over all demons and to heal diseases. 2He sent them out to announce God's imperial rule and to heal the sick. 3He said to them, "Don't take anything for the road: neither staff nor knapsack, neither bread nor money; no one is to take two shirts. 4And whichever house you enter, stay there and leave from there. 5And wherever they do not welcome you, leave the town and shake the dust from your feet in witness against them."

6And they set out and went from village to village, bringing good news and healing everywhere.

7***Now Herod the tetrarch*** heard about everything that was happening. He was perplexed because some were saying that John had been raised from the dead, 8some that Elijah had appeared, and others that one of the ancient prophets had come back to life. 9Herod said, "John I beheaded; but this one about whom I hear such things—who is he?" And he was curious to see him.

10***On their return*** the apostles reported to him what they had done. Taking them along, Jesus withdrew privately to a town called Bethsaida. 11But the crowds found this out and followed him. He welcomed them, spoke to them about God's imperial rule, and cured those in need of treatment.

12***As the day*** began to draw to a close, the twelve approached him and said, "Send the crowd away, so that they can go to the villages and farms around here and find food and lodging; for we are in a desolate place here."

13But he said to them, "Give them something to eat yourselves."

They said, "All we have are five loaves and two fish—unless we go ourselves and buy food for all these people." (14There were about five thousand men.)

He said to his disciples, "Have them sit down in groups of about fifty." 15They did so, and got them all seated. 16Then he took the five loaves and two fish, looked up to the sky, gave a blessing, and broke them, and started handing them out to the disciples to pass around to the crowd.

9:1–6 //Mk6:7–13, Mt10:1, 9–14
9:1 //Mk3:14–15
9:5 (T) Lk10:11; Acts13:51, 18:6
9:7–9 //Mk6:14–16, Mt14:1–2
9:7–8 (T) Lk9:19
9:9 (I) Lk23:8
9:10–11 //Mk6:30–34, Mt14:13–14
9:12–17 //Mk6:35–44, Mt14:15–21, Jn6:1–14; ◊2Kgs4:42–44
9:16 (T) Lk22:19, 24:30

9:7 A *tetrarch* was the client ruler of a minor state in the Roman Empire.

9:8 It was believed that Elijah would return before the Day of the Lord (Mal 3:1; 4:5).

What are the crowds saying?

Son of Adam destined to suffer

Saving & losing life

Jesus transformed

[17]And everybody had more than enough to eat. Then the leftovers were collected, twelve baskets full.

[18]***And on one occasion*** when Jesus was praying alone the disciples were with him; and he questioned them asking: "What are the crowds saying about me?"

[19]They said in response, "⟨Some say, 'You are⟩ John the Baptist,' while others, 'Elijah,' and still others, 'One of the ancient prophets has come back to life.'"

[20]Then he said to them, "What about you, who do you say I am?"

And Peter responded, "God's Anointed!"

[21]***Then he warned them,*** and forbade them to tell this to anyone, [22]adding, "The son of Adam is destined to suffer a great deal, be rejected by the elders and ranking priests and scholars, and be killed and, on the third day, be raised."

[23]***He would say*** to everyone, "If any of you wants to come after me, you should deny yourself, pick up your cross every day, and follow me! [24]Remember, by trying to save your own life, you're going to lose it, but by losing your life for my sake, you're going to save it. [25]After all, what good does it do you to acquire the whole world and lose or forfeit yourself? [26]Moreover, if any of you are ashamed of me and of my message, of you will the son of Adam be ashamed when he comes in his glory and the glory of the Father and of the holy messengers. [27]I swear to you, some of those standing here won't ever taste death before they see God's imperial rule."

[28]***About eight days after*** these sayings, Jesus happened to take Peter and John and James along with him and climbed up the mountain to pray. [29]And it so happened as he was praying that his face took on a strange appearance, and his clothing turned dazzling white. [30]The next thing you know, two figures were talking with him, Moses and Elijah, [31]who appeared in glory and were discussing his departure, which he was destined to carry out in Jerusalem.

[32]Now Peter and those with him were half asleep at the time. But they came wide awake when they saw his glory and the two men standing next to him. [33]And it so happened as the men were leaving him that Peter said to Jesus, "Master, it's a good thing we're here. In fact, why not set up three tents, one for you, one for Moses, and one for Elijah!" (He didn't know what he was saying).

[34]While he was still speaking, a cloud moved in and cast a shadow over them. And their fear increased as they entered the cloud. [35]And out of the cloud a voice spoke: "This is my son, my chosen one. Listen

9:18–22 //Mk8:27–33, Mt16:13–23
9:22 Ⓣ Lk17:25, 22:22, 24:6–8, 26, 46
9:23–27 //Mk8:34–9:1, Mt16:24–28
9:23 Cf.Th55, SJas4:10 5:3; Ⓓ Lk14:27
9:24 //Jn12:25; Ⓓ Lk17:33
9:26 Ⓣ 2Tim 2:11–13; Ⓓ Lk12:9
9:27 Ⓣ Lk21:32
9:28–36 //Mk9:2–8, Mt7:1–8
9:35 Ⓣ Lk3:22; ◊Ps2:7, Is42:1

9:35 Many mss read "my beloved" in place of *my chosen one.*

9:18 Jesus *was alone,* yet *the disciples were with him*: a baffling anomaly.
9:23 Note the *every day* in Luke's version of the saying (compare Mark 8:34–35).
9:31 *Departure* translates the Greek word *exodos* (which is also the title of the second book of the LXX), thus associating Jesus with Moses.
9:34 Clouds are OT symbols of the presence of God (e.g., Exodus 19).

Son with an unclean spirit

Son of Adam to be turned in

Dispute about greatness

Jesus leaves for Jerusalem

to him!" [36]When the voice had spoken, Jesus was perceived to be alone. And they were speechless and told no one back then anything of what they had seen.

[37]***On the following day,*** when they came down from the mountain, a huge crowd happened to meet him. [38]Suddenly a man from the crowd shouted, "Teacher, I beg you to take a look at my son, for he is my only child. [39]Without warning a spirit gets hold of him, and all of a sudden he screams; it throws him into convulsions, causing him to foam at the mouth; and it leaves him only after abusing him. [40]I begged your disciples to drive it out, but they couldn't."

[41]In response Jesus said, "You distrustful and perverted lot, how long must I associate with you and put up with you? Bring your son here."

[42]But as the boy approached, the demon knocked him down and threw him into convulsions. Jesus rebuked the unclean spirit, healed the boy, and gave him back to his father.

[43]And everybody was astounded at the majesty of God.

While they all were marveling at everything he was doing, he said to his disciples, [44]"Mark well these words: the son of Adam is about to be turned over to his enemies."

[45]But they never understood this remark. It was couched in veiled language, so they would not get its meaning. And they always dreaded to ask him about this remark.

[46]***Now an argument*** broke out among them over which of them was greatest. [47]But Jesus, knowing what was on their minds, took a child and had her stand next to him. [48]He said to them, "Whoever accepts this child in my name is accepting me. And whoever accepts me accepts the one who sent me. Don't forget, the one who has a lower rank among you is the one who is great."

[49]John said in response, "Master, we saw someone driving out demons in your name, and we tried to stop him, because he isn't one of us."

[50]But he said to him, "Don't stop him; in fact, whoever is not against you is on your side."

[51]***It so happened*** as the days were drawing near for him to be taken up that he was determined to go to Jerusalem. [52]He sent messengers on ahead of him. They entered a Samaritan village, to get things ready for him. [53]But the Samaritans would not welcome him, because he had made up his mind to go on to Jerusalem. [54]When his disciples James and John realized this, they said, "Lord, do you want us to call down

9:37–43a
//Mk9:14–27, Mt17:14–18
9:43b-45
//Mk9:30–32, Mt17:22–23
9:44
Ⓣ Lk17:25, 18:31–33, 22:22, 24:6–8, 26, 46
9:45
Ⓣ Lk18:34
9:46–48
//Mk9:33–37, Mt18:1–5; Ⓣ Lk22:24–27
9:48a
Ⓓ Lk10:16
9:48b
//Mt23:11
9:49–50
//Mk9:38–40
9:50
//Lk11:23, GOxy1224 6:1
9:54
▷2Kgs1:9–12

9:54 Many mss add "as Elijah did" to the end of the verse.

9:51 *taken up:* the Greek word *analēmpsis* also means "ascension" (see Luke 24:51).
9:53 Samaritans would not offer hospitality to those travelling to the temple in Jerusalem, which the Samaritans regarded as an illegitimate rival to their own temple on Mount Gerasim (see John 4:20).

Foxes have dens

fire from heaven and annihilate them?" 55But he turned and reprimanded them. 56Then they continued on to another village.
57***As they were going along*** the road, someone said to him, "I'll
follow you wherever you go."
58And Jesus said to him, "Foxes have dens, and birds of the sky have
nests; but the son of Adam has nowhere to rest his head."
59To another he said, "Follow me."
But he said, "First, let me go and bury my father."
60Jesus said to him, "Leave it to the dead to bury their own dead; but
you, go out and announce God's imperial rule."
61Another said, "I'll follow you, sir; but let me first say good-bye to
my people at home."
62Jesus said to him, "No one who puts his hand to the plow and
looks back is qualified for God's imperial rule."

Instructions for the seventy

10 ***After this*** the Lord appointed seventy-two others and sent them
on ahead of him in pairs to every town and place that he himself
intended to visit. 2He would say to them, "Although the crop is good,
still there are few to harvest it. So beg the harvest boss to dispatch
workers to the fields. 3Get going; look, I'm sending you out like lambs
into a pack of wolves. 4Carry no purse, no knapsack, no sandals. Don't
greet anyone on the road. 5Whenever you enter a house, first say,
'Peace to this house.' 6If peaceful people live there, your peace will rest
on them. But if not, it will return to you. 7Stay at that one house, eating
and drinking whatever they provide, for workers deserve their wages.
Do not move from house to house. 8Whenever you enter a town and
they welcome you, eat whatever is set before you. 9Cure the sick there
and tell them, 'God's imperial rule is closing in.' 10But whenever you
enter a town and they do not receive you, go out into its streets and say,
11'Even the dust of your town that sticks to our feet, we wipe off against
you. But know this: God's imperial rule is closing in.' 12I tell you, on
that day Sodom will be better off than that town.
13"Damn you, Chorazin! Damn you, Bethsaida! If the miracles done
in you had been done in Tyre and Sidon, they would have sat in
sackcloth and ashes and changed their ways long ago. 14But Tyre and
Sidon will be better off at the judgment than you. 15And you, Capernaum, you don't think you'll be exalted to heaven, do you? No, you'll
go to Hell.

Q9:57–62 //Mt 8:18–22
9:58 //Th 86
9:61–62 ◊ 1 Kgs 19:19–21
Q10:1–12 //Mt 10:5–15; Mk 6:7–13; Ⓓ Lk 9:2–6
10:1 Ⓣ Lk 9:52
Q10:2 //Mt 9:37, Th 73; cf. Jn 4:35
Q10:3 //Mt 10:16
10:7 Cf. 1 Cor 9:14, 1 Tm 5:18, DSav 20
10:8 //Th 14:4; cf. 1 Cor 10:27
10:11 Ⓣ Acts 13:51, 18:6
10:12 Ⓣ Jude 7; ◊ Gn 19:24–28
Q10:13–15 //Mt 11:20–24
10:15 ◊ Is 14:13–15

10:1 Many mss read "seventy" rather than *seventy-two.*

9:59–60 Burying one's parent was the highest filial duty.

10:13 Bethsaida is a town in Galilee. The location of Chorazin is unknown, but it was presumably also in Galilee. Tyre and Sidon were two Gentile cities in what is now Lebanon. There was a history of enmity between them and Israel (e.g., Joel 3:4–8).

10:15 Jesus had performed healings in Capernaum (4:23; 7:1–10), but Luke does not report that the city rejected Jesus or his disciples.

Hell: literally, *Hades*, the realm of the dead.

The seventy report

Father & son

Privileged eyes

Good Samaritan

16“Whoever hears you hears me, and whoever rejects you rejects me, and whoever rejects me rejects the one who sent me.”

17***The seventy-two returned*** with joy, saying, “Lord, even the demons submit to us when we invoke your name!”

18And he said to them, “I was watching Satan fall like lightning from heaven. 19Look, I have given you authority to step on snakes and scorpions, and over all the power of the enemy; and nothing will ever harm you. 20However, don’t rejoice that the spirits submit to you; rejoice instead that your names have been inscribed in heaven.”

21***At that moment*** Jesus was overjoyed by the holy spirit and said, “I praise you, Father, Lord of heaven and earth, because you have hidden these things from the wise and the learned but revealed them to the untutored; yes indeed, Father, because this is the way you want it. 22My Father has turned everything over to me. No one knows who the son is except the Father, or who the Father is except the son—and anyone to whom the son wishes to reveal him.”

23***Turning to the disciples*** he said privately, “How privileged are the eyes that see what you see! 24I tell you, many prophets and kings wanted to see what you see, and didn’t see it, and to hear what you hear, and didn’t hear it.”

25***On one occasion,*** a legal expert stood up to put him to the test with a question: “Teacher, what do I have to do to inherit eternal life?”

26He said to him, “How do you read what is written in the Law?”

27And he answered, “You are to love the Lord your God with all your heart, with all your soul, with all your energy, and with all your mind; and your neighbor as yourself.”

28Jesus said to him, “You have given the correct answer; do this and you will have life.”

29But with a view to justifying himself, he said to Jesus, “But who is my neighbor?”

30Jesus replied:

> This fellow was on his way from Jerusalem down to Jericho when he fell into the hands of robbers. They stripped him, beat him up, and went off, leaving him half dead. 31Now by coincidence a priest was going down that road; when he caught sight of him, he went out of his way to avoid him. 32In the same way, when a Levite came to the place, he took one look at him and crossed the road to avoid him.

Q10:16 //Mt 10:40; Jn 12:44–45, 13:20; Ⓓ Lk 9:48
10:19 Cf. Mk 16:17–18; ◊Ps 91:13
10:20 Ⓣ Phil 4:3, Heb 12:23, Rv 3:5, 13:8
Q10:21–22 //Mt 11:25–27
10:21 Cf. Th 4:1
10:22 //Jn 3:35, 10:15, 17:25–26; Ⓣ SJas 6:24–26
Q10:23–24 //Mt 13:16–17
10:24 Cf. Th 38
10:25–28 //Mk 12:28–34, Mt 22:35–40
10:25 Ⓓ Lk 18:18
10:27 Cf. Th 25; Ⓣ Rom 13:8–10, Gal 5:14, Jas 2:8; ◊Dt 6:5, Lv 19:18

10:17 Many mss read “seventy” rather than *seventy-two*.

10:19 The *snake* and the *scorpion* are symbols of evil in the OT (e.g., Deut 8:15).

10:20 *Inscribed in heaven* reflects an OT idea that a book in heaven contains the names of all who belong to God’s people (see Exod 32:32–33; Dan 12:1).

10:23 The Greek word *makarios*, elsewhere translated *congratulations*, is here rendered *privileged* because it is addressed to parts of the body.

10:31–32 Contact with corpses made one unclean, so priests and levites would have good reason to avoid what seemed to be a corpse.

10:32 *Levite*: a layman with special religious duties and privileges in teaching and worship.

Mary & Martha

On prayer

Friend at midnight

33But this Samaritan who was traveling that way came to where he was and was moved to pity at the sight of him. 34He went up to him and bandaged his wounds, pouring olive oil and wine on them. He hoisted him onto his own animal, brought him to an inn, and looked after him. 35The next day he took out two silver coins, which he gave to the innkeeper, and said, "Look after him, and on my way back I'll reimburse you for any extra expense you have had."

36"Which of these three, in your opinion, acted like a neighbor to the man who fell into the hands of the robbers?"

37He said, "The one who showed him compassion."

Jesus said to him, "Then go and do the same yourself."

38***Now as they went along,*** he came to this village where a woman named Martha welcomed him into her home. 39And she had a sister named Mary, who sat at the Lord's feet and listened to his words. 40But Martha kept getting distracted because she was doing all the serving. So she went up ⟨to Jesus⟩ and said, "Lord, doesn't it matter to you that my sister has left me with all the serving? Tell her to give me a hand."

41But the Lord answered her, "Martha, Martha, you are worried and upset about a lot of things. 42But only one thing is necessary. Mary has made the better choice and it is something she will never lose."

11

On one occasion he happened to be praying somewhere. When he had finished, one of his disciples said to him, "Lord, teach us how to pray, just as John taught his disciples."

2He said to them, "When you pray, you should say:

Father, your name be revered.
Impose your imperial rule.
3Provide us with the bread we need day by day.
4Forgive our sins, since we too forgive everyone in debt to us.
And please don't subject us to test after test."

5***Jesus said to them,*** "Suppose you have a friend who comes to you in the middle of the night and says to you, 'Friend, lend me three loaves, 6for a friend of mine on a trip has just shown up and I have nothing to offer him.' 7And suppose you reply, 'Stop bothering me. The door is already locked and my children and I are in bed. I can't get up to give you anything'—8I tell you, even though you won't get up and give the friend anything out of friendship, yet you will get up and give the other whatever is needed because you'd be ashamed not to.

Q11:2–4 //Mt6:9–15
11:3 //GNaz3
11:4 //Mk11:25; cf.SJas4:2
11:5–8 Ⓣ Lk18:1–5

10:42 Some mss read "few things are necessary, or only one."

10:35 The *silver coins* are *denarii*, each worth a day's wage for a laborer.

11:3 The meaning of the Greek word *epiousios* is disputed. Possible translations are "daily," "for subsistence," and "for the future." Its only certain occurrence in the Greek language is in the Lord's Prayer.

11:8 By the standards of the time, it was

Ask, seek, knock

Beelzebul controversy

Return of an unclean spirit

Privileged is the womb

9"***So I tell you,*** ask—it'll be given to you; seek—you'll find; knock—it'll be opened for you. 10Rest assured: everyone who asks receives; everyone who seeks finds; and for the one who knocks it is opened. 11Which of you fathers would hand his son a snake when it's fish he's asking for? 12Or a scorpion when it's an egg he's asking for? 13So if you, worthless as you are, know how to give your children good gifts, isn't it much more likely that the heavenly Father will give holy spirit to those who ask him?"

14***Jesus was driving out*** a demon that was mute, and when the demon had departed the mute man spoke. And the crowds were amazed. 15But some of them said, "He drives out demons in the name of Beelzebul, the head demon."

16Others were testing him by demanding a sign from heaven.

17But he knew what they were thinking, and said to them: "Every government divided against itself is devastated, and a house divided against a house falls. 18If Satan is divided against himself—since you claim I drive out demons in Beelzebul's name—how will his domain endure? 19If I drive out demons in Beelzebul's name, in whose name do your own people drive ⟨them⟩ out? In that case, they will be your judges. 20But if by God's finger I drive out demons, then for you God's imperial rule has arrived.

21"When a strong man is fully armed and guards his courtyard, his possessions are safe. 22But when a stronger man attacks and overpowers him, he takes the weapons on which he was relying and divides up his loot.

23"The one who isn't with me is against me, and the one who doesn't gather with me scatters."

24"***When an unclean spirit*** leaves a person, it wanders through waterless places in search of a resting place. When it doesn't find one, it says, 'I will go back to the home I left.' 25It then returns, and finds it swept and refurbished. 26Next, it goes out and brings back seven other spirits more vile than itself, who enter and settle in there. So that person ends up worse off than when he or she started."

27***And so just*** as he was making these remarks, a woman from the crowd raised her voice and addressed him, "How privileged is the womb that carried you and the breasts that nursed you!"

28"Rather," he replied, "privileged are those who hear the word of God and keep it."

Q11:9–13 //Mt7:7–11
11:9 //Th94; cf.Th2:1, 92:1; DSav7:2, 11:5
11:10 //Mary4:7, GHeb6b
Q11:14–23 //Mt12:22–30, Mk3:22–27
Q11:15 //Mt9:34
11:20 ◊Ex8:19
11:21–22 Cf.Th35
11:23 //Lk9:50, GOxy1224 6:2
11:24–26 //Mt12:43–45
11:27–28 //Th79:1–2
11:28 Cf.Lk8:21

11:11 Some mss insert "stone, if he asks for bread, or give him a" before *snake.*

considered shameful to refuse a friend's request for help in offering hospitality.

11:15 The name *Beelzebul* is derived from an old Canaanite god (Baalzebul), used here presumably as another name for Satan (see v. 18).

Sign of Jonah

[29]***As more and more people*** were crowding around him, he began to say, "This generation is an evil generation. It insists on a sign, but it will be given no sign except the sign of Jonah. [30]You see, just as Jonah became a sign for the Ninevites, so the son of Adam will be a sign for this generation. [31]At judgment time, the queen of the south will be brought back to life along with members of this generation, and she will condemn them, because she came from the ends of the earth to listen to Solomon's wisdom. Yet take note: what is right here is greater than Solomon. [32]At judgment time, the citizens of Nineveh will come back to life, along with this generation, and condemn it, because they had a change of heart in response to Jonah's message. Yet take note: what is right here is greater than Jonah.

Lamp & bushel

[33]"***No one lights a lamp*** and then puts it in a cellar or under a bushel basket, but rather on a lampstand so that those who come in can see the light. [34]Your eye is the body's lamp. When your eye is clear, your whole body is flooded with light. When your eye is clouded, your body is shrouded in darkness. [35]Take care, then, that the light within you is not darkness. [36]If then your whole body is flooded with light, and no corner of it is darkness, it will be completely illuminated as when a lamp's rays engulf you."

Damn you Pharisees & legal experts

[37]***While he was speaking,*** a Pharisee invites him to dinner at his house. So he came and reclined at the table. [38]The Pharisee was astonished to see that he did not first wash before the meal.

[39]But the Lord said to him, "You Pharisees clean the outside of cups and dishes, but inside you are full of greed and evil. [40]You fools! Did not the one who made the outside also make the inside? [41]Still, donate what is inside to charity, and then you'll see how everything comes clean for you.

[42]"Damn you, Pharisees! You pay tithes on mint and rue and every herb, but neglect justice and the love of God. You should have attended to the last without neglecting the first.

[43]"Damn you, Pharisees! You're so fond of the prominent seat in synagogues and respectful greetings in marketplaces. [44]Damn you! You are like unmarked graves that people walk on without realizing it."

[45]One of the legal experts says to him in reply, "Teacher, when you say these things you are insulting us, too."

[46]And he said, "Damn you legal experts too! You load people down with crushing burdens, but you yourselves don't lift a finger to help

Q11:29–32 //Mt 12:38–42
Q11:29 //Mt 16:4, Mk 8:11–12; Cf. Jn 6:30; Ⓣ 1 Cor 1:22
11:31 ◊ 1 Kgs 10:1–10
11:32 ◊ Jon 3:5
Q11:33 //Mt 5:15, Mk 4:21, Th 33:2–3; Ⓓ Lk 8:16
Q11:34–36 //Mt 6:22–23; cf. Th 24:3, DSav 6
11:37–52 //Mt 23:1–36
11:37 Ⓣ Lk 7:36, 14:1
Q11:39–41 //Mt 23:25–26, Th 89; cf. GOxy 840 2:8
Q11:42 //Mt 23:23; ◊ Mi 6:8
Q11:43 //Mt 23:6–7, Mk 12:38–39; Ⓓ Lk 20:46–47
Q11:44 //Mt 23:27–28
Q11:46 //Mt 23:4

11:33 A few mss omit *or under a bushel basket*.

11:29–30 *sign of Jonah*: a prophet preaching repentance.
11:31 *queen of the south*: see 1 Kgs 10:1–29.
11:32 Nineveh was the capital of Assyria, a bitter and brutal enemy of the Israelites in the 8th century B.C.E.
11:38 See the explanation in Mark 7:3.
11:41 *donate to charity*: traditionally translated as "give alms," an expression rarely now used in common English.
11:44 Contact with a grave renders one unclean (see Num 19:16).

Leaven of the Pharisees

Have no fear

Acknowledgement & defense

carry them. 47Damn you! You erect monuments to the prophets whom your ancestors murdered. 48You are therefore witnesses to and approve of the deeds of your ancestors: they killed ⟨the prophets⟩ and you erect ⟨monuments⟩ to them. 49That is why the wisdom of God has said, 'I will send them prophets and apostles, and some of them they are always going to kill and persecute. 50So, this generation will have to answer for the blood of all the prophets that has been shed since the world was founded, 51from the blood of Abel to the blood of Zechariah, who perished between the altar and the sanctuary.' Yes, I tell you, this generation will have to answer for it.

52"You legal experts, damn you! You have taken away the key of knowledge. You yourselves haven't entered and you have blocked the way of those trying to enter."

53By the time he had left there, the scholars and Pharisees began to resent him bitterly and to harass him with all kinds of questions, 54conspiring to trap him with his own words.

12 ***Meanwhile,*** a crowd of many thousands had thronged together and were trampling each other.

He began to speak first to his disciples: "Guard against the leaven of the Pharisees, which is to say, their hypocrisy. 2There is nothing veiled that won't be unveiled, or hidden that won't be made known. 3And so whatever you've said in the dark will be heard in the light, and what you've whispered behind closed doors will be announced from the rooftops.

4"***I tell you,*** my friends, don't fear those who kill the body, and after that can do no more. 5I'll show you whom you ought to fear: fear the one who can kill and then has authority to cast into Gehenna. Believe me, that's the one you should fear! 6What do sparrows cost? A dime a dozen? Yet not one of them is overlooked by God. 7In fact, even the hairs of your head have all been counted. Don't be so timid: You're worth more than a flock of sparrows.

8"***I tell you,*** everyone who acknowledges me in public, the son of Adam will acknowledge in front of God's messengers. 9But whoever disowns me in public will be disowned in the presence of God's messengers. 10And everyone who utters a word against the son of Adam will be forgiven; but whoever blasphemes against the holy spirit won't

Q11:47–51 //Mt23:29–36; Ⓣ Lk13:33–34, Acts7:51–52, Neh9:26
Q11:52 //Mt23:13, Th39:1–2; cf.Th102
Q12:1–10 //Mt10:26–33
12:1 //Mk8:15, Mt16:6
12:2 //Mk4:22; Th5:2, 6:5–6; Ⓓ Lk8:17
12:3 //Th33:1
12:7 //Lk21:18, Acts27:34
12:8–9 Ⓣ 2 Tm2:11–13; Ⓓ Lk9:26
Q12:10 //Mt12:32, Mk3:28–29, Th44

11:51 Abel was a son of Adam who was murdered by his brother (Gen 4:8–10). Zechariah was a priest who was murdered in the Temple (2 Chr 24:20–22). Neither of these men are identified as prophets in the OT.

12:1 *Leaven* was a metaphor for a pervasive evil influence. See Paul's use of it in 1 Cor 5:6–7 and Gal 5:9.

12:5 *Gehenna*: the valley of Hinnom, a place outside Jerusalem associated with idolatry and fire in the OT and later used as a rubbish dump. In the first century, it symbolized the place of punishment for sinners after the final judgment.

12:6 *Sparrows* were sold for food. *A dime* translates the Greek *assarion*, which was a coin worth 1/16 of a denarius.

Rich fool

On anxieties

be forgiven. [11]And when they make you appear in synagogues and haul you up before rulers and authorities, don't worry about how or in what way you should defend yourself or what you should say. [12]The holy spirit will teach you at that very moment what you ought to say."

[13]***Someone in the crowd*** said to him, "Teacher, tell my brother to divide the inheritance with me."

[14]But Jesus said to him, "Mister, who appointed me your judge or arbiter?"

[15]Then he said to them, "Watch out! Guard against greed in all its forms; after all, possessions, even in abundance, don't guarantee someone life."

[16]Then he told them a parable:

> There was a rich man whose fields produced a bumper crop. [17]"What do I do now?" he asked himself, "since I don't have any place to store my crops. [18]I know!" he said, "I'll tear down my barns and build larger ones so I can store all my grain and my goods. [19]Then I'll say to myself, 'You have plenty put away for years to come. Take it easy; eat, drink, and enjoy yourself.'" [20]But God said to him, "You fool! This very night your life will be demanded back from you. All this stuff you've collected—whose will it be now?" [21]That's the way it is with those who save up for themselves, but aren't rich where God is concerned.

[22]***He said to his disciples,*** "That's why I tell you: Don't fret about life—what you're going to eat—or about your body—what you're going to wear. [23]Remember, there is more to living than food and clothing. [24]Think about the crows: they don't plant or harvest, they don't have storerooms or barns. Yet God feeds them. You're worth a lot more than the birds! [25]Can any of you add an hour to life by fretting about it? [26]So if you can't do a little thing like that, why worry about the rest? [27]Think about how the lilies grow: they don't slave and they never spin. Yet let me tell you, even Solomon at the height of his glory was never decked out like one of them. [28]If God dresses up the grass in the field, which is here today and tomorrow is tossed into an oven, it is surely more likely ⟨that God cares for⟩ you, you who don't take anything for granted! [29]And don't be constantly on the lookout for what you're going to eat and what you're going to drink. Don't give it a thought. [30]These are all things the world's pagans seek, and your Father is aware that you need them. [31]Instead, you are to seek ⟨God's⟩ domain, and these things will come to you as a bonus.

Q12:11–12 //Mt10:19–20, Lk21:14–15, Mk13:9–11
12:13–14 //Th72
12:14 ◊Ex2:14
12:16–21 //Th63
12:19–20 ◊Sir 11:19
12:19 Cf. 1Cor15:32; ◊Is22:13, Ecc18.15
Q12:22–31 //Mt6:25–33
12:22 //Th36
12:25 //GrTh 36:3–4
12:27 //GrTh 36:2

12:20, 22, 23 *Psychē* is the principle of life and can mean both "life" and "soul." Here the contexts require *life*. *Psychē* is to be distinguished from *zōē*, which refers to the mere state of being alive, as in v. 15.

12:25 *hour:* The Greek can mean either "life span/age" or "stature" (see 2:52 and 19:3, where it means stature or maturity). The present context favors taking it metaphorically as a reference to increasing one's length of life, rather than literally as increasing one's height.

Heart's true measure

Unexpected return

Not peace, but conflict

32“***Don't be afraid,*** little flock, for it has delighted your Father to
give you his domain. 33Sell your belongings, and donate to charity;
make yourselves purses that don't wear out, with inexhaustible wealth
in heaven, where no robber can get to it and no moth can destroy it.
34As you know, what you treasure is your heart's true measure.
35“***Keep your belts fastened*** and your lamps lighted. 36Imitate those
who are waiting for their master to come home from a wedding, ready
to open the door for him as soon as he arrives and knocks. 37Those
slaves the master finds alert when he arrives are to be congratulated. I
swear to you, he will put on an apron, have them recline at the table,
and proceed to wait on them. 38If he gets home around midnight, or
even around 3 a.m., and finds them so, they are to be congratulated!
39Mark this well: if the homeowner had known what time the burglar
was coming, he would not have let anyone break into his house. 40You
too should be prepared. Remember, the son of Adam is coming when
you least expect it.”
41Peter said, “Lord, are you telling this parable just for us or for the
benefit of everyone?”
42The Lord said, “Who then is the reliable and shrewd manager to
whom the master assigns responsibility for his household staff, to dole
out their food allowance at the right time? 43Congratulations to the
slave who's on the job when his master arrives. 44I'm telling you the
truth: he'll put him in charge of all his property. 45But suppose that
slave says to himself, ‘My master is taking his time getting here,’ and
begins to beat the servants and the maids, and to eat and drink and get
drunk, 46that slave's master will show up on the day he least expects
and at an hour he doesn't suspect. He'll cut him to pieces and assign
him a fate fit for the faithless. 47And the slave who knew what his
master wanted, but didn't get things ready or act properly, will be
flogged severely. 48On the other hand, the slave who didn't know what
his master wanted, yet did things that deserve punishment, will be
flogged lightly. A great deal will be required of everyone to whom
much is given; yet even more will be demanded from the one to whom
a great deal has been entrusted.
49“***I came*** to set the earth on fire, and how I wish it were already
ablaze! 50I have a baptism to be baptized with, and what pressure I'm
under until it's over! 51Do you suppose I came here to bring peace on
earth? No, I tell you, on the contrary: conflict. 52As a result, from now
on in any given house there will be five in conflict, three against two
and two against three. 53Father will be pitted against son and son
against father, mother against daughter and daughter against mother,

Q**12:33–34** //Mt 6:19–21
12:33 //Th 76:3; Ⓓ Lk 18:22
12:34 //Mary 7:4
12:35–40 //Mk 13:33–37
Q**12:39–48** //Mt 24:43–51
12:39 //Th 21:5; cf. Th 103
12:40 Ⓣ 1 Thes 5:2, 2 Pet 3:10, Rv 16:15
Q**12:49–53** //Mt 10:34–36
12:49 //Th 10
12:51–53 //Th 16; cf. GNaz 11

12:39 Many mss insert “he would have watched and” after *coming.*

12:42 A *manager* (*oikonomos*) is one who administers the affairs of a wealthy household, which includes the extended family and the slaves and their families.

12:45 *My master is taking his time getting here* probably reflects the belief that Jesus is not returning any time soon.

12:50 *baptism*: probably a figurative refer-

mother-in-law against daughter-in-law and daughter-in-law against mother-in-law."

54***He would also say*** to the crowds, "When you see a cloud rising in the west, right away you say that it's going to rain; and so it does. 55And when the wind blows from the south, you say we're in for scorching heat; and we are. 56You phonies! You know the lay of the land and can read the face of the sky, so why don't you know how to interpret the present time?

57"***Why can't you decide*** for yourselves what is right? 58When you are about to appear with your opponent before the magistrate, do your best to settle with him on the way, or else he might drag you up before the judge, and the judge turn you over to the jailer, and the jailer throw you in prison. 59I tell you, you'll never get out of there until you've paid every last red cent."

Signs of the times

Settle with opponent

Change of heart or doom

Fig tree without figs

Afflicted woman

13

Some who were there at the time told him about the Galileans, about how Pilate had mixed their blood with their sacrifices. 2He answered them, "Do you suppose that these Galileans were the worst sinners in Galilee, because they suffered this? 3Hardly. However, let me tell you, if you don't have a change of heart, you'll all meet your doom in the same way. 4Or how about those eighteen in Siloam, who were killed when the tower fell on them—do you suppose that they were any guiltier than the whole population of Jerusalem? 5Hardly. However, let me tell you, if you don't have a change of heart, all of you will meet your doom in a similar fashion."

6***Then he told this parable:*** "A man had a fig tree growing in his vineyard; he came looking for fruit on it but didn't find any.

7"So he said to the vinekeeper, 'See here, for three years in a row I have come looking for fruit on this tree, and haven't found any. Cut it down. Why should it suck the nutrients out of the soil?'

8"In response he says to him, 'Let it stand, sir, one more year, until I get a chance to dig around it and work in some manure. 9Maybe it will produce next year; but if it doesn't, we can go ahead and cut it down.'"

10***Now he was teaching*** in one of the synagogues on the sabbath day. 11A woman showed up who for eighteen years had been afflicted by a spirit; she was bent over and unable to straighten up even a little. 12When Jesus noticed her, he called her over and said, "Woman, you are freed from your affliction." 13He laid hands on her, and immediately she stood up straight and began to praise God.

12:53 ▷Mi 7:6
Q12:54–56 //Mt 16:2–3, Th 91
Q12:57–59 //Mt 5:25–26

---

ence to his death.

12:59 *Cent* translates the Greek *lepton*, a coin worth 1/128 of a denarius.

13:1 This atrocity is nowhere else attested in ancient sources.

13:11 Physical abnormalities were often attributed to demons. As in this case, there was considerable overlap between the notions of healing and exorcism. Even though Jesus heals her without casting out the spirit, in v. 16 he refers to the healing as *releasing her from Satan's bonds*.

Mustard seed & leaven

Narrow door

Warning & lament

14The leader of the synagogue was indignant, however, because Jesus had healed on the sabbath day. He lectured the crowd: "There are six days which we devote to work; so come on one of those days and be healed, but not on the sabbath day."

15But the Lord answered him, "You phonies! Every last one of you unties your ox or your donkey from the feeding trough on the sabbath day and leads it off to water, don't you? 16This woman, a daughter of Abraham whom Satan has kept in bondage for eighteen long years—should she not be released from these bonds just because it is the sabbath day?" 17As he said this, all his adversaries were put to shame, but most folks rejoiced at all the wonderful things he was doing.

18***Then he would say:***

> What is God's imperial rule like? What does it remind me of? 19It is like a mustard seed that a man took and tossed into his garden. It grew and became a tree, and the birds of the sky roosted in its branches.

20He continued:

> What does God's imperial rule remind me of? 21It is like leaven that a woman took and concealed in fifty pounds of flour until it was all leavened.

22***On his journey,*** he passed through towns and villages, teaching and making his way toward Jerusalem.

23And someone asked him, "Sir, is it true that only a few are going to be saved?"

He said to them, 24"Struggle to get in through the narrow door; I'm telling you, many will try to get in, but won't be able. 25Once the master of the house gets up and bars the door, you'll be left standing outside and knocking at the door: 'Sir, open up for us.' But he'll answer you, 'I don't know where you come from.' 26Then you'll start saying, 'We ate and drank with you, and you taught in our streets.' 27But he'll reply, 'I don't know where you come from; get away from me, all you evildoers!' 28There'll be weeping and grinding teeth out there when you see Abraham and Isaac and Jacob and all the prophets in God's domain and yourselves thrown out. 29And people will come from east and west, from north and south, and dine in God's domain. 30And remember, those who will be first are last, and those who will be last are first."

31***About that time*** some Pharisees approached and warned him, "Get out of here! Herod wants to kill you."

32He replied to them, "Go tell that fox, 'Look here, today and tomorrow I'll be driving out demons and healing people, and the third day I'll be finished. 33Still, today and tomorrow and the day after, I have to

13:14
◊Ex 20:9
Q13:18–19
//Mt 13:31–32, Th 20, Mk 4:30–32
Ⓣ DSav 36:1
13:19
◊Dn 4:20–21
Q13:20–21
//Mt 13:33, Th 96; SJas 6:15g
Q13:24
Cf. Mt 7:13–14
13:25
Cf. Mt 25:10–12
Q13:26–27
Cf. Mt 7:21–23; ◊Ps 6:8
Q13:28–29
//Mt 8:11–12; Ⓣ DSav 8:8; ◊Ps 107:3
Q13:30
//Mt 19:30, 20:16; Th 4:2, Mk 10:31

13:19 Jewish law prohibited the growing of mustard seed in a garden. Mustard is a shrub, not a tree.

13:21 *leaven*: See the note on 12:1.

Man with dropsy

Places of honor

Choice of guests

Dinner party

move on, because it is impossible for a prophet to die outside of Jerusalem.' [34]Jerusalem, Jerusalem, you murder the prophets and stone those sent to you! How often I wanted to gather your children as a hen ⟨gathers⟩ her own chicks under her wings, but you wouldn't let me. [35]Can't you see, your house is being abandoned? I tell you, you certainly won't see me until the time comes when you say, 'Blessed is the one who comes in the name of the Lord.'"

14 ***And so one sabbath day,*** when Jesus happened to have dinner at the house of a prominent Pharisee, they were keeping an eye on him. [2]This man who had dropsy suddenly showed up.

[3]Jesus addressed the legal experts and Pharisees: "Is it permitted to heal on the sabbath day, or not?"

[4]But they were silent.

So he took the man, healed him, and sent him on his way.

[5]Then he said to them, "Suppose your son or your ox falls down a well, would any of you hesitate for a second to pull him out on the sabbath day?"

[6]And they had no response to this.

[7]***Or he would tell a parable*** for those who had been invited, when he noticed how they were choosing the places of honor.

He said to them, [8]"When someone invites you to a wedding banquet, don't take the place of honor, in case someone more important than you has been invited. [9]Then the one who invited you both will come and say to you, 'Make room for this person,' and you'll be embarrassed to have to take the lowest place. [10]Instead, when you are invited, go take the lowest place, so when the host comes he'll say to you, 'Friend, come up higher.' Then you'll be honored in front of all those reclining around the table with you.

[11]"Those who promote themselves will be demoted, and those who demote themselves will be promoted."

[12]***Then he said*** also to his host, "When you give a lunch or a dinner, don't invite your friends, or your brothers and sisters, or relatives, or rich neighbors. They might invite you in return and so you would be repaid. [13]Instead, when you throw a dinner party, invite the poor, the crippled, the lame, and the blind. [14]In that case, you are to be congratulated, since they cannot repay you. You will be repaid at the resurrection of the just."

[15]***When one of his fellow guests*** heard this, he said to him, "Congratulations to those who will eat bread in God's domain!"

[16]Jesus told him:

13:33–34
Cf. Lk 11:49, Acts 7:51–52

Q**13:34–35**
//Mt 23:37–39

13:34
◊ Is 31:5

13:35
Ⓘ Lk 19:37–38; ◊ Ps 118:26, Jer 22:5

14:1–6
//Lk 6:6–11

14:5
//Mt 12:11–12

14:8–10
◊ Prv 25:6–7

Q**14:11**
//Mt 23:12; Ⓓ Lk 18:14

14:5 Some mss read "donkey" in place of *son*.

13:32 *Fox* is a metaphor for a devious and deceitful person. (See Ezek 13:4, where false prophets are called foxes.)

13:35 *House* is most likely a reference to the temple.

Way of the cross

Lost sheep

Someone was giving a big dinner and invited many guests. [17]At the dinner hour the host sent his slave to tell the guests: "Come, it's ready now." [18]But one by one they all began to make excuses. The first said to him, "I just bought a farm, and I have to go and inspect it; please excuse me." [19]And another said, "I just bought five pairs of oxen, and I'm on my way to check them out; please excuse me." [20]And another said, "I just got married, and so I cannot attend." [21]So the slave came back and reported these ⟨excuses⟩ to his master. Then the master of the house got angry and instructed his slave: "Quick! Go out into the streets and alleys of the town, and usher in the poor, and crippled, the blind, and the lame."

[22]And the slave said, "Sir, your orders have been carried out, and there's still room."

[23]And the master said to the slave, "Then go out into the roads and the country lanes, and force people to come in so my house will be filled. [24]Believe you me, not one of those who were given invitations will taste my dinner."

[25]***Once when hordes of people*** were traveling with him, he turned and addressed them: [26]"If any of you comes to me and does not hate your own father and mother and wife and children and brothers and sisters—yes, even your own life—you're no disciple of mine. [27]Unless you carry your own cross and come along with me—you're no disciple of mine.

[28]"Consider this: Don't those who plan to build a tower first sit down and calculate whether they can afford to complete it? [29]Otherwise they might lay the foundation and not be able to finish, and all the onlookers would begin to make fun of them: [30]'Those people started to build but couldn't finish.'

[31]"Or what king would go to war against another king and not first sit down and figure out whether he would be able with ten thousand men to engage an enemy coming against him with twenty thousand? [32]If he decided he could not, he would send an envoy to ask for terms of peace while the enemy was still a long way off.

[33]"On these analogies, then, if you don't say good-bye to everything that belongs to you, you're no disciple of mine.

[34]"Salt is good ⟨and salty⟩. But if salt loses its zing, how will it be renewed? [35]It's no good for either earth or manure. It just gets thrown away. Anyone here with two good ears had better listen!"

15 ***Now the toll collectors*** and sinners kept crowding around Jesus so they could hear him. [2]But the Pharisees and the scholars would complain to each other: "This fellow welcomes sinners and eats with them."

[3]So he told them this parable:

Q14:16–24 //Mt22:1–10, Th64
Q14:26–27 //Mt10:37–38, Th55, 101
14:27 //Mk8:34, Mt16:24; Ⓓ Lk9:23
Q14:34–35 //Mt5:13, Mk9:50
15:2 Ⓣ Lk5:30, 7:34, 19:7; GOxy1224 5:1

14:24 *You* is plural in the Greek.

Lost coin

Prodigal son

[4]Is there any one of you who owns a hundred sheep and one of them gets lost, who wouldn't leave the ninety-nine in the wilderness, and go after the one that got lost until he finds it? [5]And when he finds it, he lifts it up on his shoulders, happy. [6]Once he gets home, he invites his friends and his neighbors over, and says to them, "Celebrate with me, because I have found my lost sheep."

[7]"I'm telling you it'll be just like this in heaven: there'll be more celebrating over one sinner who has a change of heart than over ninety-nine virtuous people who have no need to change their hearts.

[8]***Or again,*** is there any woman with ten silver coins, who if she loses one, wouldn't light a lamp and sweep the house and search carefully until she finds it? [9]When she finds it, she invites her friends and neighbors over and says, 'Celebrate with me, because I have found the silver coin I had lost.'

[10]"I'm telling you, it's just like this among God's messengers: they celebrate when one sinner has a change of heart."

[11]***Then he said:***

Once there was this man who had two sons. [12]The younger of them said to his father, "Father, give me the share of the property that's coming to me." So he divided his resources between them.

[13]Not too many days later, the younger son got all his things together and left home for a faraway country, where he squandered his property by living extravagantly. [14]Just when he had spent it all, a serious famine swept through that country, and he began to do without. [15]So he went and hired himself out to one of the citizens of that country, who sent him out to his farm to feed the pigs. [16]He longed to satisfy his hunger with the carob pods, which the pigs usually ate; but no one offered him anything. [17]Coming to his senses he said, "Lots of my father's hired hands have more than enough to eat, while here I am dying of starvation! [18]I'll get up and go to my father and I'll say to him, 'Father, I have sinned against heaven and affronted you; [19]I don't deserve to be called a son of yours any longer; treat me like one of your hired hands.'" [20]And he got up and returned to his father.

But while he was still a long way off, his father caught sight of him and was moved to compassion. He went running out to him, threw his arms around his neck, and kissed him. [21]And the son said to him, "Father, I have sinned against heaven and affronted you; I don't deserve to be called a son of yours any longer."

Q15:3–7 //Mt18:12–14, Th107; SJas6:15a
15:8–10 //SJas6:15f

15:21 Some mss add "treat me like one of your hired hands" to the end of the verse.

15:8 The coin here is a *drachma*, worth approximately a day's wage for a laborer.
15:12 In asking for his share of the inheritance, the son acts as if his father were dead.
15:15 To work with pigs would be the ultimate degradation for a Jew.

Dishonest manager

[22]But the father said to his slaves, "Quick! Bring out the finest robe and put it on him; put a ring on his finger and sandals on his feet. [23]Fetch the fat calf and slaughter it; let's have a feast and celebrate, [24]because this son of mine was dead and has come back to life; he was lost and now is found." And they started celebrating.

[25]Now his elder son was out in the field; and as he got closer to the house, he heard music and dancing. [26]He called one of the servant-boys over and asked what was going on.

[27]He said to him, "Your brother has come home and your father has slaughtered the fat calf, because he has him back safe and sound."

[28]But he was angry and refused to go in. So his father came out and began to plead with him. [29]But he answered his father, "See here, all these years I have slaved for you. I never once disobeyed any of your orders; yet you never once provided me with a kid goat so I could celebrate with my friends. [30]But when this son of yours shows up, the one who has squandered your estate with prostitutes —for him you slaughter the fat calf."

[31]But ⟨the father⟩ said to him, "My child, you are always at my side. Everything that's mine is yours. [32]But we just had to celebrate and rejoice, because this brother of yours was dead, and has come back to life; he was lost, and now is found."

16 ***Or Jesus would say*** to the disciples:

There was this rich man whose manager had been accused of squandering his master's property. [2]He called him in and said, "What's this I hear about you? Let's have an audit of your management, because your job is being terminated."

[3]Then the manager said to himself, "What am I going to do? My master is firing me. I'm not able to dig ditches and I'm ashamed to beg. [4]I've got it! I know what I'll do so doors will open for me when I'm removed from management."

[5]So he called in each of his master's debtors. He said to the first, "How much do you owe my master?"

[6]He said, "Five hundred gallons of olive oil."

And he said to him, "Here is your invoice; sit down right now and make it two hundred and fifty."

[7]Then he said to another, "And how much do you owe?"

He said, "A thousand bushels of wheat."

He says to him, "Here is your invoice; make it eight hundred."

[8]The master praised the dishonest manager because he had acted shrewdly; for the children of this world exhibit better sense in dealing with their own kind than do the children of light.

16:6–7 The manager is probably defrauding his master. However, the discounts may represent kickbacks to the customers of his own exorbitant commissions.

Slave with two masters

9"I tell you, make use of your ill-gotten gain to make friends for yourselves, so that when the bottom falls out they are there to welcome you into eternal dwelling places.

10"***The one who can be trusted*** in trivial matters can also be trusted with large amounts; and the one who cheats in trivial matters will also cheat where large amounts are concerned. 11So if you couldn't be trusted with ill-gotten gain, who will trust you with real wealth? 12And if you can't be trusted with something that belongs to another, who will let you have property of your own? 13No servant can be a slave to two masters. No doubt that slave will either hate one and love the other, or be devoted to one and disdain the other. You can't be enslaved to both God and a bank account."

14The Pharisees, who were money grubbers, heard all this and sneered at him. 15But he said to them, "You're the type who justify yourselves to others, but God reads your hearts: what people rank highest is detestable in God's estimation.

Law & Prophets

16"***Right up to John's time*** you have the Law and the Prophets; since then God's domain has been proclaimed as good news and everyone is breaking into it violently. 17But it is easier for the world to disappear than for one serif of one letter of the Law to drop out.

On divorce

18"***Everyone who divorces*** his wife and marries another commits adultery; and the one who marries a woman divorced from her husband commits adultery.

Rich man & Lazarus

19***There was this rich man,*** who wore clothing fit for a king and who dined lavishly every day. 20This poor man, named Lazarus, languished at his gate, all covered with sores. 21He longed to eat what fell from the rich man's table. Dogs even used to come and lick his sores. 22 It so happened that the poor man died and was carried by the heavenly messengers to be with Abraham. The rich man died too, and was buried.

23From Hades, where he was being tortured, he looked up and saw Abraham a long way off and Lazarus with him. 24He called out, "Father Abraham, have pity on me! Send Lazarus to dip the tip of his finger in water and cool my tongue, for I am in torment in these flames."

25But Abraham said, "My child, remember that you had good fortune in your lifetime, while Lazarus had it bad. Now he is being comforted here, and you are in torment. 26And besides all this, a

Q16:13 //Mt 6:24, Th 47:1–2
Q16:16 //Mt 11:12–13; cf. SJas 6:2–4
Q16:17 //Mt 5:18
Q16:18 //Mt 5:31–32, 19:9; Mk 10:11–12; cf. 1 Cor 7:10–11

16:8 The *master* probably refers to the rich man of v. 1. The manager calls him "master" in vv. 3 and 5.

16:9, 13 *Gain* (v. 9) and *bank account* (v. 13) translate *mammon*, an Aramaic word often left untranslated in English Bibles.

16:15 *Detestable* (traditionally translated "abomination") is a term from the Law which designates ritual and moral practices incompatible with membership in the covenant community (see e.g., Lev 11:10–23; 18:22; Deut 12:31; 27:15).

16:16 *John*: the Baptist.

16:19 *Fit for a king* translates the Greek word for purple, a color associated with the clothing of royalty.

16:20 *Lazarus* is not to be identified with the character in John 11.

Millstone award

On faith

Miserable slaves

Ten lepers

great chasm has been set between us and you, so that even those who want to cross over from here to you cannot, and no one can cross over from that side to ours."

27But he said, "Father, I beg you then, send him to my father's house 28—after all, I have five brothers—so he can warn them not to wind up in this place of torture."

29But Abraham says, "They have Moses and the prophets; why don't they listen to them?"

30"But they won't do that, father Abraham," he said. "But, if someone appears to them from the dead, they'll have a change of heart."

31⟨Abraham⟩ said to him, "If they won't listen to Moses and the prophets, they won't be convinced even if someone were to rise from the dead."

17 ***He said to his disciples,*** "It's inevitable that snares will be set; nevertheless, damn the one who sets them! 2You'd be better off if you had a millstone hung around your neck and were dumped into the sea than to mislead one of these little ones. 3So be on your guard. If your companion does wrong, scold that person; if there is a change of heart, forgive the person. 4If someone wrongs you seven times a day, and seven times turns around and says to you, 'I'm sorry,' you should forgive that person."

5***The apostles said*** to the Lord, "Make our trust grow!"

6And the Lord said, "If you had trust no larger than a mustard seed, you could tell this mulberry tree, 'Uproot yourself and plant yourself in the sea,' and it would obey you.

7"***If you had a slave*** plowing or herding sheep and he came in from the fields, would any of you tell him, 'Come right in and recline at the table'? 8 Wouldn't you say to him instead, 'Get my dinner ready, put on your apron, and serve me while I eat and drink. You can eat and drink later'? 9He wouldn't thank the slave because he did what he was told to do, would he? 10The same goes for you: when you've done everything you've been told to do, say, 'We're miserable slaves; we've only done our job.'"

11***And on the way to Jerusalem*** he happened to pass between Samaria and Galilee. 12As he was coming into this village, he was met by ten lepers, who kept their distance. 13They shouted: "Jesus, Master, have mercy on us!"

14When he saw them, he said to them, "Go show yourselves to the priests."

And as they departed they happened to be made clean.

Q17:1–2 //Mt18:6–7, Mk9:42
Q17:3 //Mt18:15
Q17:4 //Mt18:21–22, GNaz5:1
Q17:5–6 //Mt17:20, 21:21; Mk11:22–23
17:6 Cf. Th48, 106
17:14 Cf. EgerG2:4

17:14 *show yourselves to the priests*: in accord with the Law in Leviticus 13–14.

Not with signs

Days of the son of Adam

[15]Then one of them, realizing that he had been healed, came back. He praised God out loud, [16]prostrated himself at Jesus' feet, and thanked him. (Incidentally, this man was a Samaritan.)

[17]But Jesus said, "Ten were cured, weren't they? What became of the other nine? [18]Didn't any of them return to praise God besides this foreigner?"

[19]And he said to him, "Get up and be on your way; your trust has cured you."

[20]***When asked by the Pharisees*** when God's imperial rule would come, he answered them, "You won't be able to observe the coming of God's imperial rule. [21]People are not going to be able to say, 'Look, here it is!' or 'Over there!' On the contrary, God's imperial rule is right there in your presence."

[22]***And he said to the disciples,*** "There'll come a time when you will yearn to see one of the days of the son of Adam, and you won't see it. [23]And they'll be telling you, 'Look, there it is!' or 'Look, here it is!' Don't rush off; don't pursue it. [24]For just as lightning flashes and lights up the sky from one end to the other, that's what the son of Adam will be like in his day. [25]But first it is necessary that he suffer many things and be rejected by this present generation. [26]And just as it was in the days of Noah, that's how it will be in the days of the son of Adam. [27]They ate, drank, got married, and were given in marriage, until the day 'Noah boarded the ark.' Then the flood came and destroyed them all. [28]That's also the way it was in the days of Lot. Everyone ate, drank, bought, sold, planted, and built. [29]But on the day Lot left Sodom, fire and sulfur rained down from the sky and destroyed them all. [30] It will be like that on the day the son of Adam is revealed. [31]On that day, if any are on the roof and their things are in the house, they had better not go down to fetch them. The same goes for those in the field: they had better not turn back for anything left behind. [32]Remember Lot's wife. [33]Whoever tries to hang on to life will forfeit it, but whoever forfeits life will preserve it. [34]I tell you, on that night there will be two on one couch: one will be taken and the other left. [35]There will be two women grinding together: one will be taken and the other left." [37]Then they asked him, "Taken where, Lord?" And he said to them, "Vultures collect wherever there's a carcass."

17:19
Ⓣ Lk 7:50, 8:48, 18:42
17:20–21
//Th 3:1–3; 113; cf. DSav 9:3; Mary 4:4–5
Q17:23–24
//Mt 24:26–27
17:23
//Mk 13:21, Mt 24:23, Mary 4:4
Q17:26–30
//Mt 24:37–39
17:27
◊Gn 7:7
17:29
◊Gn 19:24
17:31
//Mk 13:15–16, Mt 24:17–18
17:32
◊Gn 19:26
Q17:33
//Mt 10:39, 16:25; Mk 8:35; cf. SJas 4:10–5:3, Ⓓ Lk 9:24
Q17:34–35
//Mt 24:40–41, Th 61:1
Q17:37
//Mt 24:28

17:24 Some mss omit *in his day*. **17:35** Some mss add another verse, traditionally numbered 17:36: "Two will be in the fields; one will be taken, the other left."

17:21 *In your presence* translates the Greek *entos humōn. Entos* is an unusual word which can mean either "within" or "among." The traditional translation "within you" suggests within each individual. However, Greek distinguishes singular from plural "you," and this "you" is plural. A better translation is thus *in your presence.*

17:31 Most houses in this part of the world had flat roofs, where people would go in the course of daily activities.

17:37 Greek uses the same word (*aetos*) to refer to vultures and eagles.

Judge & widow

Pharisee & toll collector

Children in God's domain

18 ***He told them a parable*** about the need to pray at all times and
never to lose heart. 2This is what he said:

Once there was a judge in this town who neither feared God nor
cared about people.

3In that same town was a widow who kept coming to him and
demanding: "Give me a ruling against the person I'm suing."

4For a while he refused; but eventually he said to himself, "I'm
not afraid of God and I don't care about people, 5but this widow
keeps pestering me. So I'm going to give her a favorable ruling, or
else she'll keep coming back until she wears me down."

6And the Lord said, "Don't you hear what that corrupt judge says?
7Do you really think God won't hand out justice to his chosen ones—
those who call on him day and night? Do you really think he'll put
them off? 8I'm telling you, he'll give them justice and give it quickly.
Still, when the son of Adam comes, will he find trust on the earth?"

9***Then for those who were confident*** of their own moral superiority
and who held everyone else in contempt, he had this parable:

10Two men went up to the temple to pray, one a Pharisee and the
other a toll collector.

11The Pharisee stood up and prayed silently as follows: "I thank
you, God, that I'm not like everybody else, thieving, unjust, adulterous, and especially not like that toll collector over there. 12I fast
twice a week, I give tithes of everything that I acquire."

13But the toll collector stood off by himself and didn't even dare to
look up, but struck his chest, and muttered, "God, have mercy on
me, sinner that I am."

14Let me tell you, the second man went back home acquitted but
the first one did not. For those who promote themselves will be
demoted, but those who demote themselves will be promoted.

15***They would even bring him*** their babies so he could lay hands on
them. But when the disciples noticed it, they scolded them. 16Jesus
called for the infants and said, "Let the children come up to me, and
don't try to stop them. After all, God's domain belongs to people like
that.

18:1–8 Ⓣ Lk 11:5–8
18:1 Ⓣ Rom 12:12
Q**18:14** //Mt 23:12; Ⓓ Lk 14:11
18:15–17 //Mk 10:13–16, Mt 19:13–15
18:16 Cf. Th 22:1–2

18:11 Some mss read "the Pharisee stood and prayed thus to himself;" a few mss read "the Pharisee stood and prayed thus."

18:3 The widow demands that he not allow her opponent to exploit her vulnerable social status.

18:5 The Greek word *hypōpiazō* (literally, "to hit under the eye") was a boxing term, also used figuratively in the sense of "to wear down."

18:13 Striking one's chest was a ritual gesture of repentance.

Man with money

17“I swear to you, whoever doesn’t accept God’s imperial rule the way a child would, certainly won’t ever set foot in ⟨his domain⟩!”

18***Someone from the ruling class*** asked him, “Good teacher, what do I have to do to inherit eternal life?”

19Jesus said to him, “Why do you call me good? No one is good except God alone. 20You know the commandments: ‘You are not to commit adultery; you must not murder, or steal, and you are not to give false testimony; you are to honor your father and mother.’ ”

21And he said, “I have observed all these since I was a child.”

22When Jesus heard this, he said to him, “You are still short one thing. Sell everything you have and distribute ⟨the proceeds⟩ among the poor, and you will have treasure in heaven. And then come, follow me!”

23But when he heard this, he became very sad, for he was extremely rich.

Needle’s eye

24***When Jesus observed*** that he had become very sad, he said, “How difficult it is for those with real money to enter God’s domain! 25It’s easier for a camel to squeeze through a needle’s eye than for a wealthy person to get into God’s domain.”

26Those who heard this spoke up: “Well then, who can be saved?”

27But he said, “What’s humanly impossible is perfectly possible for God.”

28Then Peter said, “Look at us! We have left what we had to follow you!”

29And he told them, “I swear to you, there is no one who has left home, or wife, or brothers, or parents, or children, for the sake of God’s imperial rule, 30who won’t receive many times as much in the present age, and in the age to come, eternal life.”

Son of Adam will die & rise

31⟨***Jesus***⟩ ***took the twelve aside*** and instructed them: “Listen, we’re going up to Jerusalem, and everything written by the prophets about the son of Adam will come true. 32For he will be turned over to the foreigners, and will be made fun of and insulted. They will spit on him, 33and flog him, and put him to death. Yet after three days he will rise.” 34But they did not understand any of this; this remark was obscure to them, and they never did figure out what it meant.

Blind man of Jericho

35***One day*** as he was coming into Jericho, this blind man was sitting along the roadside begging. 36Hearing a crowd passing through, he asked what was going on.

37They told him, “Jesus the Nazarene is going by.”

38Then he shouted, “Jesus, you son of David, have mercy on me!”

39Those in the lead kept yelling at him to shut up, but he kept shouting all the louder, “You son of David, have mercy on me!”

18:17 Cf.Mt18.3 Ⓣ SJas2:6
18:18–30 //Mk10:17–31, Mt19:16–30, GNaz6
18:18 Ⓓ Lk10:25
18:20 ◊Ex20:12–16
18:22 Ⓣ Lk12:33
18:28 Ⓣ Lk5:11, 28, cf.SJas4:1
18:31–34 //Mk10:32–34, Mt20:17–19
18:31–33 Ⓣ Lk9:44, 17:25, 22:22, 24:6–8
18:34 Ⓣ Lk9:45, 24:25–27, 44–45
18:35–43 //Mk10:46–52, Mt9:27–31, 20:29–34

18:25 The camel was the largest animal in Palestine; the eye of a needle was the smallest known opening.

Rich Zacchaeus

The money in trust

[40]Jesus paused and ordered them to guide the man over. When he came near, ⟨Jesus⟩ asked him, [41]"What do you want me to do for you?" He said, "Master, I want to see again."

[42]Jesus said to him, "Then use your eyes; your trust has cured you."

[43]And right then and there he regained his sight, and began to follow him, praising God all the while. And everyone who saw it gave God the praise.

19 ***Then he entered Jericho*** and was making his way through it. [2]Now a man named Zacchaeus lived there who was head toll collector and a rich man. [3]He was trying to see who Jesus was, but couldn't, because of the crowd, since he was short. [4]So he ran on ahead to a point Jesus was to pass and climbed a sycamore tree to get a view of him.

[5]When Jesus reached that spot, he looked up at him and said, "Zacchaeus, hurry up and climb down; I have to stay at your house today."

[6]So he scurried down, and welcomed him warmly.

[7]Everyone who saw this complained: "He is going to spend the day with some sinner!"

[8]But Zacchaeus stood his ground and said to the Lord, "Look, sir, I'll give half of what I own to the poor, and if I have extorted anything from anyone, I'll pay back four times as much."

[9]Jesus said to him, "Today salvation has come to this house. This man is a real son of Abraham. [10]Remember, the son of Adam came to seek out and to save what was lost."

[11]***While they were still paying attention*** to this exchange, he proceeded to tell a parable, because he was near Jerusalem and people thought that God's imperial rule would appear immediately. [12]So he said:

> A nobleman went off to a distant land intending to acquire a kingship for himself and then return. [13]Calling ten of his slaves, he gave them each one hundred silver coins, and told them: "Do business with this while I'm away."
>
> [14]His fellow citizens, however, hated him and sent a delegation right on his heels, with the petition: "We don't want this man to rule us."
>
> [15]As it turned out, he got the kingship and returned. He had those slaves summoned to whom he had given the money, in order to find out what profit they had made.
>
> [16]The first came in and reported, "Master, your investment has increased ten times over."

18:42
Ⓣ Lk7:50, 8:48, 17:19
19:7
Ⓣ Lk5:30, 7:34, 15:2
19:8
◊Ex22:1
19:10
◊Ez34:16
Q**19:11–27**
//Mt25:14–30

19:13 *one hundred silver coins* was about three months wages for a laborer. Compare Luke's amount to that of Matt 25:15.

17He said to him, "Well done, you excellent slave! Because you have been trustworthy in this small matter, you are to be in charge of ten towns."

18The second came in and reported, "Master, your investment has increased five times over."

19And he said to him, "And you are to be in charge of five towns."

20Then the last came in and said, "Master, here is your money. I kept it tucked away safe in a handkerchief. 21You see, I was afraid of you, because you're a demanding man: you withdraw what you didn't deposit, and reap what you didn't sow."

22He said to him, "You incompetent slave! Your own words convict you. So you knew I was demanding, did you? That I withdraw what I didn't deposit and reap what I didn't sow? 23So why didn't you put my money in the bank? Then I could have collected it with interest when I got back."

24Then he said to his attendants, "Take the money away from this fellow and give it to the one who has ten times as much."

25"But my lord," they said to him, "he already has ten times as much."

26He replied, "I tell you, to everyone who has, more will be given; and from those who don't have, even what they do have will be taken away. 27But now, about those enemies of mine, the ones who didn't want me to rule them: bring them here and execute them in front of me."

Jesus enters Jerusalem

28***When he had finished*** the parable, he walked on ahead, on his way up to Jerusalem. 29And it so happened as he got close to Bethphage and Bethany, at the mountain called Olives, that he sent off two of the disciples, 30with these instructions: "Go into the village across the way. As you enter it, you will find a colt tied there, one that has never been ridden. Untie it and bring it here. 31If anyone asks you, 'Why are you untying it?' Just tell them: 'Its master has need of it.'" 32So those designated went off and found it exactly as he had described.

33Just as they were untying the colt, its owners challenged them: "What are you doing untying that colt?"

34So they said, "Its master needs it."

35So they brought it to Jesus. They threw their cloaks on the colt and helped Jesus mount it. 36And as he rode along, people would spread their cloaks on the road. 37As he approached the slope of the Mount of Olives, the entire throng of his disciples began to cheer and shout praise to God for all the miracles they had seen. 38They kept repeating,

19:26 //Mk4:25, Mt13:12, Th41; Ⓓ Lk8:18

19:28–40 //Mk11:1–10, Mt21:1–9, Jn12:12–19

19:30–31 This seems to be a pre-arranged password. Alternatively, the story may intend to emphasize Jesus' foreknowledge.

19:31 *Master* here translates *kyrios*. Some confusion is created by the use of this term in v. 33 (in the plural, *owners*) and again in v. 34.

19:36 The garments on the road may be an allusion to the honor shown the new king Jehu in 2 Kgs 9:13.

Lament over Jerusalem

Temple as hideout

On whose authority?

Leased vineyard

Blessed is the king who comes in the name of the Lord!
Peace in heaven and glory in the highest!

[39]But some of the Pharisees, also in the crowd, said to him, "Teacher, restrain your followers."

[40]But he responded, "I tell you, if these folks were to keep quiet, these stones would break into cheers."

[41]***When he got close enough*** to catch sight of the city, he wept over it: [42]"If you—yes, you—had only recognized the path to peace even today! But as it is, it is hidden from your eyes. [43]The time will descend upon you when your enemies will throw up a rampart against you and surround you, and hem you in on every side, [44]and then smash you to the ground, you and your children with you. They will not leave one stone upon another within you, because you failed to recognize the time of your visitation."

[45]***Then he entered the temple area*** and began chasing the vendors out. [46]He says to them, "It is written, 'My house is to be a house of prayer'; but you have turned it into 'a hideout for crooks'!"

[47]Every day he would teach in the temple area. The ranking priests and the scholars, along with the leaders of the people, kept looking for some way to get rid of him. [48]But they never figured out how to do it, because all the people hung on his every word.

20 ***One day*** as he was teaching the people in the temple area and speaking of the good news, the ranking priests and the scholars approached him along with the elders, [2]and put this question to him: "Tell us, by what right are you doing these things? Who gave you this authority?"

[3]In response Jesus said to them, "I also have a question for you: tell me, [4]was John's baptism heaven-sent or was it of human origin?"

[5]And they started conferring among themselves, reasoning as follows: "If we say, 'Heaven-sent,' he'll say, 'Why didn't you trust him?' [6]But if we say, 'Of human origin,' the people will all stone us." Remember, ⟨the people⟩ were convinced John was a prophet. [7]So they answered that they couldn't tell where it came from.

[8]And Jesus said to them, "Neither am I going to tell you by what authority I do these things!"

[9]***Then he began*** to tell the people this parable:

Someone planted a vineyard, leased it out to some farmers, and went abroad for an extended time. [10]In due course he sent a slave to the farmers, so they could pay him his share of the vineyard's crop. But the farmers beat him and sent him away empty-handed. [11]He repeated his action by sending another slave; but they beat him up

19:38
Ⓣ Lk13:35;
◊ Ps118:26
19:44
Ⓣ Lk21:6
19:45–48
//Mk11:15–19, Mt21:12–13, Jn2:13–22
19:46
◊ Is56:7, Jer7:11
20:1–8
//Mk11:27–33, Mt21:23–27
20:2
Cf. Jn2:18
20:4
Cf. DSav36:1–2
20:5–6
Ⓣ Lk7:29–30
20:9–19
//Mk12:1–12, Mt21:33–46, Th65
20:9
◊ Is5:1–2
20:10–12
◊ 2Chr36:15–16, Neh9:25–26

19:43 This describes seige tactics used by ancient armies.

20:9 The *farmers* here are sharecroppers.

too, and humiliated him, and sent him away empty-handed. [12]And he sent yet a third slave; but they injured him and threw him out.

[13]Then the owner of the vineyard asked himself, "What should I do now? I know, I will send my son, the apple of my eye. Perhaps they will show him some respect."

[14]But when the farmers recognized him, they talked it over, and concluded: "This fellow's the heir! Let's kill him so the inheritance will be ours!" [15]So they dragged him outside the vineyard and killed him.

What will the owner of the vineyard do to them as a consequence? [16]He will come in person, do away with those farmers, and give the vineyard to someone else.

When they heard this, they said, "God forbid!"

[17]But ⟨Jesus⟩ looked them straight in the eye and said, "What can this scripture possibly mean: 'A stone that the builders rejected has ended up as the keystone'? [18]Everyone who falls over that stone will be smashed to bits, and anyone on whom it falls will be crushed."

[19]The scholars and the ranking priests wanted to lay hands on him then and there, but they were afraid of the people, since they realized he had aimed this parable at them. [20]So they kept him under surveillance, and sent spies, who feigned sincerity, so they could twist something he said and turn him over to the authority and jurisdiction of the governor.

The emperor & God

[21]***They asked him,*** "Teacher, we know that what you speak and teach is correct, that you show no favoritism, but instead teach God's way forthrightly. [22]Is it permissible for us to pay taxes to the Roman emperor or not?"

[23]But he saw through their duplicity, and said to them, [24]"Show me a coin. Whose likeness does it bear? And whose name is on it?"

They said, "The emperor's."

[25]So he said to them, "Then pay the emperor what belongs to the emperor, and God what belongs to God!"

[26]And so they were unable to catch him in anything he said in front of the people; they were dumbfounded at his answer and fell silent.

Wife of seven brothers

[27]***Some of the Sadducees***—those who argue there is no resurrection—came up to him [28]and put a question to him. "Teacher," they said, "Moses wrote for our benefit, 'If someone's brother dies, leaving behind a wife but no children, his brother is obligated to take the widow as his wife and produce offspring for his brother.' [29]Now let's say there were seven brothers; the first took a wife, and died childless. [30]Then the second [31]and the third married her, and so on. All seven

20:13
Ⓣ Lk 3:22
20:17
Ⓣ Acts 20:17, Th 66; ◊ Ps 118:22
20:19
Ⓣ Lk 19:47–48, 22:2
20:20–26
//Mk 12:13–17, Mt 22:15–22, Th 100, EgerG 3:1–6
20:21
Cf. Jn 3:2
20:25
Ⓣ Rom 13:7
20:27–40
//Mk 12:18–27, Mt 22:23–33
20:28
◊ Dt 25:5–10, Gn 38:8

20:13, 15 *Owner* here translates *kyrios*.

20:28 The allusion here is to levirate marriage (see Deut 25:5). This was a strategy to produce an heir for the dead man, in order to continue his lineage and keep his property within the family. Legally, children born of such a marriage are children of the dead man, not of the brother who physically fathered them.

David's lord & son

Scholars' privileges

Widow's two coins

Monumental buildings destroyed

Signs of final agonies

⟨married her but⟩ left no children when they died. [32]Finally, the wife died too. [33]So then, in the 'resurrection' whose wife will the woman be?" (Remember, all seven had her as wife.)

[34]And Jesus said to them, "The children of this age marry and are given in marriage; [35]but those who are considered worthy of participating in the coming age, which means 'in the resurrection from the dead,' do not marry. [36]They can no longer die, since they are the equivalent of heavenly messengers; they are children of God and children of the resurrection. [37]That the dead are raised, Moses demonstrates in the passage about the bush: he calls the Lord 'the God of Abraham, the God of Isaac, and the God of Jacob.' [38]So this is not the God of the dead, only of the living, since to him they are all alive."

[39]And some of the scholars answered, "Well put, Teacher." [40]You see, they no longer dared to ask him about anything else.

[41]***Then he asked them,*** "How can they say that the Anointed is the son of David? [42]Remember, David himself says in the book of Psalms, 'The Lord said to my lord, "Sit here at my right, [43]until I make your enemies grovel at your feet."' [44]Since David calls him 'lord,' how can he be his son?"

[45]***Within earshot*** of the people Jesus said to the disciples, [46]"Be on guard against the scholars who like to parade around in long robes, and who love to be addressed properly in the marketplaces, and who prefer important seats in the synagogues and the best couches at banquets. [47]They are the ones who prey on widows and their families, and recite long prayers just to put on airs. These people will get a stiff sentence!"

21 ***He looked up*** and observed the rich dropping their donations into the collection box. [2]Then he noticed that a needy widow put in two small coins, [3]and he observed: "I swear to you, this poor widow has contributed more than all of them! [4]After all, they all made donations out of their surplus, whereas she, out of her poverty, was contributing her entire livelihood, which was everything she had."

[5]***When some were remarking*** about how the temple was adorned with fine masonry and ornamentation, he said, [6]"As for these things that you now admire, the time will come when not one stone will be left on top of another! Every last one will be knocked down!"

[7]***And they asked him,*** "Teacher, when are these things going to happen? What sort of portent will signal when these things are about to occur?"

20:36 Ⓣ Gal 4:5–7
20:37 ◗Ex 3:6
20:41–44 //Mk 12:35–37, Mt 22:41–46
20:42–43 Ⓓ Acts 2:34–35; ◗Ps 110:1
20:45–47 //Mk 12:38–40
20:46 //Mt 23:6; Ⓣ Lk 11:43
21:1–4 //Mk 12:41–44
21:5–19 //Mk 13:3–13, Mt 24:3–14
21:6 Ⓣ Lk 19:44

20:36 *Children* (literally, "sons") *of God* is a title unique to Luke's version of this pericope. Elsewhere "son of God" is a title reserved for Jesus, while here it is applied to all who participate in the resurrection.

20:47 The interpretation of *prey on widows* (literally, "devour the houses of widows") is difficult. It may refer to the scribes' embezzlement of revenue from estates left to widows in their husbands' wills and entrusted to scribes to manage on their behalf.

21:2 The coins are *leptons*, the least valuable coins in use at the time.

21:7 *These things* refers to the destruction of

Days of distress

Son of Adam comes on clouds

[8]He said, "Stay alert! Don't be deluded. You know, many will come
using my name and claim, 'I'm the one!' and 'The time is near!' Don't
go running after them! [9]And when you hear of wars and insurrections,
don't panic. After all, it's inevitable that these things take place first,
but it doesn't mean the end is about to come."
[10]Then he went on to tell them, "Nation will rise up against nation,
and empire against empire; [11]there will be major earthquakes, and
famines and plagues all over the place; there will be dreadful events
and impressive portents from heaven. [12]But before all these things
⟨take place⟩, they will manhandle you, and persecute you, and turn
you over to synagogues and deliver you to prisons, and you will be
hauled up before kings and governors on account of my name. [13]This
will give you a chance to make your case. [14]So make up your minds not
to rehearse your defense in advance, [15]for I will give you the wit and
wisdom which none of your adversaries will be able to resist or refute.
[16]You will be turned in, even by parents and brothers and relatives and
friends; and they will put some of you to death. [17]And you will be
universally hated because of me. [18]Yet not a single hair on your head
will be harmed. [19]By your perseverance you will secure your lives.
[20]"***When you see Jerusalem*** surrounded by armies, know then that
its destruction is just around the corner. [21]Then the people in Judea
should head for the hills, and those inside the city flee, and those out in
the countryside not re-enter. [22]For these are days of retribution, when
everything that was predicted will come true. [23]It'll be too bad for
pregnant women and for nursing mothers in those days! For there will
be utter misery throughout the land and wrath ⟨will fall⟩ upon this
people. [24]They will fall by the edge of the sword, and be taken prisoner
⟨and scattered⟩ in all the foreign countries, and Jerusalem will be
overrun by pagans, until the period allotted to the pagans has run its
course.
[25]"***And there will be portents*** in the sun and moon and stars, and on
the earth nations will be dismayed in their confusion at the roar of the
surging sea. [26]People will faint from terror at the prospect of what is
coming over the civilized world, for the heavenly forces will be shaken!
[27]And then they will see the son of Adam coming on clouds with great
power and splendor. [28]Now when these things begin to happen, stand

21:8 //Mary 4:3
21:10 ◊2Chr 15:6, Is 19:2
21:12–19 //Mt 10:16–23
21:14–15 Ⓣ Lk 12:11–12
21:18 Ⓣ Lk 12:7, Acts 27:34; ◊1 Sm 14:45, 2Sm 14:11, 1Kgs 1:52
21:20–24 //Mk 13:14–23, Mt 24:15–28
21:22 ◊Jer 46:10, Hos 9:7
21:23 Cf. Th 79; Ⓣ Lk 23:27–31
21:24 ◊Jer 21:7, Dt 28:64
21:25–33 //Mk 13:24–32, Mt 24:29–36
21:26 ◊Is 34:4
21:27 ◊Dn 7:13

---

the temple, not the end of the world (as in Mark 13:4).

21:9 *the end*: of the temple.

21:11 Earthquakes are standard apocalyptic imagery (see Hag 2:6).

impressive portents: See 2 Macc 5:2–3 for portents which preceded the invasion of Jerusalem in 169 B.C.E. Josephus describes two signs at the destruction of the temple in 70 C.E.: "a star resembling a sword, which stood over the city, and a comet, which lasted a whole year" (*War* 6.5.3).

21:16 *put to death*: This happens to Stephen and James in Acts 7:54–60 and 12:1–2.

21:19 *lives*: The Greek word *psyche* can also mean "soul."

21:22 *days of retribution*: It is not clear what the retribution is for.

21:25 These signs are standard apocalyptic imagery (e.g., Joel 2:30–31; Isa 13:10; 34:4) and are possible allusions to Ps 46:2–3 and LXX Isa 24:19.

21:26 *Heavenly forces* are the celestial bodies mentioned in v. 25.

Guard yourselves

Priests promise to pay

Jesus celebrates Passover

tall and hold your heads high, because your deliverance is just around the corner!"

[29]Then he told them a parable: "Observe the fig tree, or any tree, for that matter. [30]Once it puts out foliage, you can see for yourselves that summer is at hand. [31]So, when you see these things happening, you ought to realize that God's imperial rule is near. [32]I swear to you, this generation certainly won't pass into oblivion before it all takes place! [33]The earth will pass into oblivion and so will the sky, but my words will never be obliterated!

[34]"***So guard yourselves*** so your minds won't be dulled by hangovers and drunkenness and the worries of everyday life, and so that day won't spring upon you suddenly like some trap you weren't expecting. [35]It will descend for sure on all who inhabit the earth. [36]Stay alert! Pray constantly that you may have the strength to escape all these things that are about to occur and stand before the son of Adam."

[37]During the day he would teach in the temple area, and in the evening he would go and spend the night on the mountain called Olives. [38]And all the people would get up early to come to the temple area to hear him.

22 ***The feast of Unleavened Bread,*** known as Passover, was approaching. [2]The ranking priests and the scholars were still looking for some way to get rid of Jesus. But remember, they feared the people.

[3]Then Satan took possession of Judas, the one called Iscariot, who was a member of the twelve. [4]He went off to negotiate with the ranking priests and officers on a way to turn Jesus over to them. [5]They were delighted, and consented to pay him in silver. [6]And Judas accepted the deal, and began looking for the right moment to turn him over to them when a crowd was not around.

[7]***The feast of Unleavened Bread*** arrived, when the Passover ⟨lambs⟩ had to be sacrificed. [8]So ⟨Jesus⟩ sent Peter and John, with these instructions: "Go get things ready for us to eat the Passover."

[9]They said to him, "Where do you want us to get things ready?"

[10]He said to them, "Look, when you enter the city, someone carrying a waterpot will meet you. Follow him into the house he enters, [11]and say to the head of the house, 'The Teacher asks you, "Where is the guest room where I can celebrate Passover with my disciples?"' [12]And he will show you a large upstairs room that's been arranged; that's the place you're to get things ready."

[13]They set off and found things exactly as he had told them; and they got things ready for Passover.

21:32 Cf. Mk 9:1, Mt 16:28, Lk 9:27
21:33 Ⓣ Lk 16:17
21:34–36 //Mk 13:33–37, Mt 24:37–51
21:34 Ⓣ Lk 12:45–46
22:1–2 //Mk 14:1–2, Mt 26:1–5
22:2 Ⓣ Lk 19:47–48, 20:19
22:3–6 //Mk 14:10–11, Mt 26:14–16; cf. Acts 1:16–20
22:3 Cf. Jn 13:2
22:7–13 //Mk 14:12–16, Mt 26:17–19
22:8–9 //GEbi 7:1

21:28 Note how Luke connects redemption (*deliverance*) to Christ's second coming instead of to his death.

22:3 This is the time (*kairos*) the devil has waited for since 4:13.

22:10 This is probably a pre-arranged signal, since carrying water was women's work. The Greek *anthropos* does not connote a male, but this seems implied since a woman carrying water would not be an unusual sight.

Servant is greatest

Peter takes an oath

Two swords

[14]When the time came, he took his place ⟨at table⟩, and the apostles joined him. [15]He said to them, "I have looked forward with all my heart to celebrating this Passover with you before my ordeal begins. [16]For I tell you, I certainly won't eat it again until everything comes true in God's domain."

[17]Then he took a cup, gave thanks, and said, "Take this and share it among yourselves. [18]For I tell you, I certainly won't drink any of the fruit of the vine from now on until God's domain is established!"

[19]And he took a loaf, gave thanks, broke it into pieces, offered it to them, and said, "This is my body which is offered for you. Do this as my memorial."

[20]And, in the same manner, ⟨he took⟩ the cup after dinner and said, "This cup is the new covenant in my blood, which is poured out for you. [21]Yet look! Here with me at this very table is the one who is going to turn me in. [22]The son of Adam goes to meet his destiny; yet damn the one responsible for turning him in."

[23]And they began to ask one another which of them could possibly attempt such a thing.

[24]***Then a feud broke out*** among them over which of them should be considered the greatest. [25]He said to them, "Among the foreigners, it's the kings who lord it over everyone, and those in power are addressed as 'benefactors.' [26]But not so with you; rather, the greatest among you must behave as a beginner, and the leader as one who serves. [27]Who is the greater, after all: the one reclining at a banquet or the one doing the serving? Isn't it the one who reclines? Among you I am the one doing the serving.

[28]"You are the ones who have stuck by me in my ordeals. [29]And I confer on you the right to rule, just as surely as my Father conferred that right on me, [30]so you may eat and drink at my table in my domain, and be seated on thrones and sit in judgment on the twelve tribes of Israel.

[31]"***Simon, Simon,*** look out, Satan is after all of you, to winnow you like wheat. [32]But I have prayed for you that your trust may not give out. And once you have recovered, you are to shore up these brothers of yours."

[33]He said to him, "Master, I'm prepared to follow you not only to prison but all the way to death."

[34]He said, "Let me tell you, Peter, the rooster will not crow tonight until you disavow three times that you know me."

[35]***And he said to them,*** "When I sent you out with no purse or knapsack or sandals, you weren't short of anything, were you?"

22:14–20 //Mk14:22–25, Mt26:26–29; cf. 1Cor11:23–25
22:18 Cf. GHeb9:2, GEbi7:2
22:19 Cf. GHeb9:4; Ⓣ Lk9:16, 24:30
22:20 ◊Ex24:8, Jer31:31, Zec9:11
22:21–23 //Mk14:18–21, Mt26:21–25, Jn13:21–30
22:22 Ⓣ Lk9:22, 44, 17:25, 18:31, 24:7, 26, 46
22:24–30 //Mk10:14–15, Mt20:24–28
22:26 Cf. Mk9:35, Mt23:11–12, Lk9:48
Q**22:28–30** //Mt19:28
22:31–34 //Mk14:26–31, Mt26:30–35, Jn13:36–38
22:33 Ⓣ Acts21:13
22:35–36 Ⓘ Lk9:3, 10:4

22:19–20 A few mss omit *which is offered for you* and all of v. 20.

22:25 *Benefactor* was an honorific title often bestowed on gods and rulers.
22:28 The reference to *ordeals* is unclear. The only event Luke calls an *ordeal* is Jesus' temptation, at which the disciples were not present.
22:31 The *you* is plural in Greek. To *winnow like wheat* is to separate wheat from chaff.

Jesus in Gethsemane

Judas turns Jesus in

A rooster crows

They said, "Not a thing."

36He said to them, "But now, if you have a purse, take it along; and the same goes for a knapsack. And if you don't have a sword, sell your coat and buy one. 37For I tell you, this scripture must come true where I am concerned: 'And he was treated like a criminal'; for what is written about me is coming true."

38And they said, "Look, Master, here are two swords."

And he said to them, "That's enough."

39***Then he left*** and walked, as usual, over to the Mount of Olives; and the disciples followed him. 40When he arrived at his usual place, he said to them, "Pray that you won't be put to the test."

41And he withdrew from them about a stone's throw away, fell to his knees and began to pray, 42"Father, if you so choose, take this cup away from me! Yet not my will, but yours, be done." [43, 44]

45And when he got up from his prayer and returned to the disciples, he found them asleep, weary from grief. 46He said to them, "What are you doing asleep? Get up and pray that you won't be put to the test."

47***Suddenly,*** while he was still speaking, a crowd appeared with the one called Judas, one of the twelve, leading the way. He stepped up to Jesus to give him a kiss.

48But Jesus said to him, "Judas, would you turn in the son of Adam with a kiss?"

49And when those around him realized what was coming next, they said, "Master, now do we use our swords?" 50And one of them struck the high priest's slave and cut off his right ear.

51But Jesus responded, "Stop! That will do!" And he touched his ear and healed him.

52Then Jesus addressed the ranking priests and temple officers and elders who had come out after him: "Have you come out with swords and clubs as though you were apprehending a rebel? 53When I was with you day after day in the temple area, you didn't lay a hand on me. But this is your hour, and the authority darkness confers is yours."

54They arrested him and marched him away to the house of the high priest.

Peter followed at a distance. 55When they had started a fire in the middle of the courtyard and were sitting around it, Peter joined them.

56Then a slave woman noticed him sitting there in the glow of the fire. She stared at him, then spoke up, "This fellow was with him, too."

57He denied it, "My good woman," he said, "I don't know him."

22:37
◊Is 53:12
22:39–46
//Mk 14:32–42, Mt 26:36–46
22:42
Cf. Jn 18:11
22:47–53
Mk 14:43–52, Mt 26:47–56, Jn 18:1–11
22:54–62
//Mk 14:53–54, 66–72; Mt 26:57–58, 69–75; Jn 18:13–18, 25–27

22:42 Many mss add another two verses, traditionally numbered 22:43–44: "43 An angel from heaven appeared to him and gave him strength. 44 In his anxiety he prayed more fervently, and it so happened that his sweat fell to the ground like great drops of blood." (It is very doubtful that these verses were part of the original text.)

22:42 *Cup* is a biblical metaphor for one's destiny (see e.g., Jer 25:15).

[58]A little later someone else noticed him and said, "You are one of
them, too."
"Not me, mister," Peter replied.
[59]About an hour went by and someone else insisted, "No question
about it; this fellow's also one of them; he's even a Galilean!"
[60]But Peter said, "Mister, I don't know what you're talking about."
And all of a sudden, while he was still speaking, a rooster crowed.
[61]And the Lord turned and looked straight at Peter. And Peter remembered what the master had told him: "Before the rooster crows tonight,
you will disown me three times." [62]And he went outside and wept
bitterly.

Guards make fun of Jesus

[63]***Then the men*** who were holding ⟨Jesus⟩ in custody began to make
fun of him and rough him up. [64]They blindfolded him and demanded:
"Prophesy! Guess who hit you!" [65]And this was only the beginning of
their insults.

Trial before the Council

[66]***When day came,*** the elders of the people convened, along with the
ranking priests and scholars. They had him brought before their Council, where they interrogated him: [67]"If you are the Anointed, tell us."
But he said to them, "If I tell you, you certainly won't believe me.
[68]If I ask you a question, you certainly won't answer. [69]But from now on
the son of Adam will be seated at the right hand of the power of God."
[70]And they all said, "So you, are you the son of God?"
He said to them, "You're the ones who say so."
[71]And they said, "Why do we still need witnesses? We have heard it
ourselves from his own lips."

Trial before Pilate

23 ***At this point*** the whole assembly arose and took him before
Pilate. [2]They introduced their accusations by saying, "We have found
this man to be a corrupting influence on our people, opposing the
payment of taxes to the Roman emperor and claiming that he himself
is an anointed king."
[3]Pilate questioned him, "You are 'the King of the Judeans'?"
In response he said to him, "If you say so."
[4]And Pilate said to the ranking priests and the crowds, "In my judgment there is no case against this man."
[5]But they persisted, saying, "He foments unrest among the people by
going around teaching everywhere in Judea, and as far away as Galilee
and everywhere between."
[6]When Pilate heard this, he asked whether the man were a Galilean.
[7]And once he confirmed that he was from Herod's jurisdiction, he sent
him on to Herod, who happened to be in Jerusalem at the time.

Trial before Herod

[8]***Now Herod was delighted*** to see Jesus. In fact, he had been eager
to see him for quite some time, since he had heard so much about him,
and was hoping to see him perform some sign. [9]So ⟨Herod⟩ plied him
with questions; but ⟨Jesus⟩ would not answer him at all. [10]All this time
the ranking priests and the scholars were standing around, hurling

22:61
Ⓘ Lk22:34
22:63–65
Mk14:65, Mt26:67–68
22:66–71
Mk14:55–64, Mt26:59–66, Jn18:19–24
22:69
Ⓣ Lk21:27, Acts7:55–56; ◊Dn7:13, Ps110:1
23:1–5
// Mk15:1–5; Mt27:1–2, 11–14; Jn18:28–38

Trial before Pilate resumed

Jesus is led away

accusation after accusation against him. 11 Herod and his soldiers
treated him with contempt and made fun of him; they put a magnificent robe around him, then sent him back to Pilate. 12 That very day
Herod and Pilate became fast friends, even though beforehand they
had been constantly at odds.

13 ***Pilate then called together*** the ranking priests, the rulers, and the
people, 14 and addressed them: "You brought me this man as one who
has been corrupting the people. Now look, after interrogating him in
your presence, I have found in this man no grounds at all for your
charges against him. 15 Nor has Herod, since he sent him back to us.
Indeed, he has done nothing to deserve death. 16 So I will teach him a
lesson and set him free."[17]

18 But they all cried out in unison, "Do away with this man, and set
Barabbas free." (19 This man had been thrown into prison for murder
and for an act of sedition carried out in the city.)

20 But Pilate, who wanted to set Jesus free, addressed them again,
21 but they shouted out, "Crucify, crucify him!"

22 For the third time he said to them, "Why? What has he done
wrong? In my judgment there is no capital case against him. So, I will
teach him a lesson and set him free."

23 But they kept up the pressure, demanding with loud cries that he
be crucified. And their cries prevailed. 24 So Pilate ruled that their
demand should be carried out. 25 He set free the man they had asked
for, who had been thrown into prison for sedition and murder; but
Jesus he turned over to them to do with as they pleased.

26 ***And as they were marching him away,*** they grabbed someone
named Simon, a Cyrenian, as he was coming in from the country. They
loaded the cross on him, to carry behind Jesus. 27 A huge crowd of the
people followed him, including women who mourned and lamented
him. 28 Jesus turned to them and said, "Daughters of Jerusalem, do not
weep for me. Weep instead for yourselves and for your children.
29 Look, the time is coming when they will say, 'Congratulations to
those who are sterile, to the wombs that never gave birth, and to the
breasts that never nursed an infant!'

> 30 Then they will beg the mountains:
> "Fall on us";
> and the hills:
> "Bury us."

31 If they behave this way when the wood is green, what will happen
when it dries out?"

32 Two others, who were criminals, were also taken away with him to
be executed.

23:13–25
// Mk 15:6–15, Mt 27:15–26, Jn 18:39–19:16; Ⓘ Acts 3:13–15
23:18–19
Cf. GNaz 9
23:26
// Mk 15:21, Mt 27:32
23:29
Cf. Lk 21:23, Th 79
23:30
◊ Hos 10:8

23:16 Many mss add another verse, traditionally numbered 23:17: "He was required to release one man to them during the festival." A few mss place this verse after verse 19.

33***And when they reached*** the place called "The Skull," they crucified him there along with the criminals, one on his right and the other
on his left. 34They divided up his garments after they cast lots. 35And
the people stood around looking on.

And the rulers kept sneering at him: "He saved others; he should
save himself if he is God's Anointed, the Chosen One!"

36The soldiers also made fun of him: They would come up and offer
him sour wine, 37and they would say, "If you are the King of the
Judeans, why not save yourself?"

38There was also this sign over him: "This is the King of the
Judeans."

39One of the criminals hanging there kept cursing and taunting him:
"Aren't you supposed to be the Anointed? Save yourself and us!"

40But the other ⟨criminal⟩ rebuked the first: "Don't you even fear
God, since you are under the same sentence? 41We are getting justice,
since we are getting what we deserve. But this man has done nothing
improper."

42And he implored, "Jesus, remember me when you come into your
domain."

43And ⟨Jesus⟩ said to him, "I swear to you, today you'll be with me
in paradise."

44***It was already about noon,*** and darkness blanketed the whole land
until mid-afternoon, 45during an eclipse of the sun. The curtain of the
temple was torn down the middle.

46Then Jesus cried out at the top of his voice, "Father, into your
hands I entrust my spirit!" Having said this he breathed his last.

47Now when the Roman officer saw what happened, he praised God
and said, "This man was completely innocent!"

48And when the throng of people that had gathered for this spectacle
observed what had transpired, they all returned home beating their
chests. 49And all his acquaintances and the women who had followed
him from Galilee were standing off at a distance watching these events.

50***There was a man*** named Joseph, a Council member, a decent and
upright man, 51who had not endorsed their decision or gone along with
their action. He was from the town of Arimathea in Judea, and he lived
in anticipation of God's imperial rule. 52This man went to Pilate and
asked for the body of Jesus. 53Then he took it down and wrapped it in a

Soldiers crucify Jesus

Jesus breathes his last

Joseph buries Jesus

23:33–43 // Mk 15:22–32, Mt 27:33–44, Jn 19:17–24, Pet 4:1–4
23:34a // Acts 7:60
23:34b ◊ Ps 22:18
23:35 ◊ Ps 22:7
23:36 // Mk 15:35–36, Mt 27:47–48, Jn 19:29; Pet 5:2; ◊ Ps 69:21
23:44–49 // Mk 15:33–41, Mt 27:45–56, Jn 19:28–30
23:44–45 ◊ Am 8:9
23:44 Cf. Pet 5:1, 6:2
23:46 // Acts 7:59; ◊ Ps 31:5
23:48 Cf. Pet 7:1
23:49 ① Lk 8.2–3, ◊ Ps 38:11
23:50–56 // Mk 15:42–47, Mt 27:57–61, Jn 19:38–42
23:50–52 // Pet 2:1
23:53 // Pet 6:1–4

23:34 Many mss add "And Jesus said, 'Father, forgive them because they don't know what they're doing'" at the beginning of the verse.
23:38 Many mss add that the inscription "was written in Greek, Latin, and Hebrew." **23:42** Many mss read "with" instead of *into.*

23:36 *Sour wine* is not vinegar, but the cheap, dry wine from the soldiers' rations (ordinary wine being sweet).
23:43 *paradise*: a Greek word meaning a shaded garden, used in LXX for the garden of Eden. It was used in contemporary Judaism for the abode of the souls of the just.
23:45 This seems to refer to a solar eclipse. However, a solar eclipse is physically impossible at Passover, which always falls at the time of a full moon.

The women discover the empty tomb

shroud, and laid him in a tomb cut from the rock, where no one had ever been buried. [54]It was the day of preparation, and the sabbath was about to begin. [55]The women who had come with him from Galilee tagged along. They kept an eye on the tomb, to see how his body was laid to rest. [56]Then they went home to prepare spices and ointments. On the sabbath day they rested in accordance with the commandment.

24 ***On Sunday***, at daybreak, they made their way to the tomb, bringing the spices they had prepared. [2]They found the stone rolled away from the tomb, [3]but when they went inside they did not find the body of the Lord Jesus.

[4]And so, while they were still uncertain about what to do, two figures in dazzling clothing suddenly appeared and stood beside them. [5]Out of sheer fright they prostrated themselves on the ground; the men said to them, "Why are you looking for the living among the dead? [6]He is not here—he was raised. Remember what he told you while he was still in Galilee: [7]'The son of Adam is destined to be turned over to heathen, to be crucified, and on the third day to rise.'" [8]Then they recalled what he had said.

[9]And returning from the tomb, they related everything to the eleven and to everybody else. [10]The group included Mary of Magdala and Joanna and Mary the mother of James, and the rest of the women companions. They related their story to the apostles; [11]but their story seemed nonsense to them, so they refused to believe the women.

[12]But Peter got up and ran to the tomb. He peeped in and saw only the linen wrappings, and returned home, marveling at what had happened.

Two on the road to Emmaus

[13]***Now, that same day*** two of them were traveling to a village named Emmaus, about seven miles from Jerusalem. [14]They were engaged in conversation about all that had taken place. [15]And it so happened, during the course of their discussion, that Jesus himself approached and began to walk along with them. [16]But they couldn't recognize him.

[17]He said to them, "What were you discussing as you walked along?"

Then they paused, looking depressed. [18]One of them, named Cleopas, said to him in reply, "Are you the only visitor to Jerusalem who doesn't know what's happened there these last few days?"

[19]And he said to them, "What are you talking about?"

And they said to him, "About Jesus of Nazareth, who was a prophet powerful in word and deed in the eyes of God and all the people, [20]and

23:54
◊ Dt21:22–23
24:1–12
// Mk16:1–8, Mt28:1–10, Jn20:1–18, Pet12:1–13:3
24:7
(I) Lk9:44, 18:32
24:19
(T) Acts2:22, 10:38

24:3 A few mss omit *of the Lord Jesus.* **24:6** A few mss omit *He is not here—he was raised.* **24:12** A few mss omit this verse.

23:54 The *day of preparation* is the day before the sabbath, which begins at sunset on Friday.

24:12 Not only is this verse textually doubtful, it is implausible, for Peter's home was in Capernaum.

24:13 The location of *Emmaus* is disputed.

In Emmaus

In Jerusalem

about how our ranking priests and rulers turned him in to be sentenced to death, and crucified him. 21We were hoping that he would be the one who was going to ransom Israel. And as if this weren't enough, it's been three days now since all this happened. 22Meanwhile, some women from our group gave us quite a shock. They were at the tomb early this morning 23and didn't find his body. They came back claiming even to have seen a vision of heavenly messengers, who said that he was alive. 24Some of those with us went to the tomb and found it exactly as the women had described; but nobody saw him."

25And he said to them, "You people are so slow-witted, so reluctant to trust everything the prophets have said! 26Wasn't the Anointed One destined to undergo these things and enter into his glory?" 27Then, starting with Moses and all the prophets, he interpreted for them every passage of scripture that referred to himself.

28***They had gotten close*** to the village to which they were going, and he acted as if he were going on. 29But they entreated him, saying, "Stay with us; it's almost evening, the day is practically over." So he went in to stay with them.

30And so, as soon as he took his place at table with them, he took a loaf, and gave a blessing, broke it, and started passing it out to them. 31Then their eyes were opened and they recognized him; and he vanished from their sight. 32They said to each other, "Weren't our hearts burning within us while he was talking to us on the road, and explaining the scriptures to us?" 33And they got up at once and returned to Jerusalem.

And when they found the eleven and those with them gathered together, 34they said, "The Lord really has been raised, and has appeared to Simon!" 35Then they described what had happened on the road, and how they came to recognize him in the breaking of the bread.

36While they were talking about this, he himself appeared among them and says to them, "Peace be with you." 37But they were terrified and frightened, and figured that they were seeing a ghost.

38And he said to them, "Why are you upset? Why do such thoughts run through your minds? 39You can see from my hands and my feet that it's really me. Touch me and see—a ghost doesn't have flesh and bones as you can see that I have."

41And while for sheer joy they still didn't know what to believe and were bewildered, he said to them, "Do you have anything here to eat?"

24:21
Ⓣ Lk 1:68, 2:38
24:36–49
// Jn 20:19–23; cf. Mt 28:16–20, Mk 16:14–18
24:38
Cf. Mary 3:2

24:32 Several mss omit *within us.* **24:36** A few mss omit *and says to them, "Peace be with you."* **24:39** Many mss add a v. 40, "As he said this, he showed them his hands and his feet," taken from John 20:20.

24:19 Moses is similarly described in Acts 7:22, 36, 38.

24:21 Moses is similarly described in Acts 7:35.

24:26 No Jewish text earlier than the NT (including the OT) contains the idea of a suffering Messiah and no other NT author explicitly speaks of Jesus in these terms.

Bethany: Jesus ascends

[42]They offered him a piece of grilled fish, [43]and he took it and ate it in
front of them.
[44]Then he said to them, "This is the message I gave you while I was
still with you: everything written about me in the Law of Moses and the
Prophets and the Psalms is destined to come true."
[45]Then he prepared their minds to understand the scriptures. [46]He
said to them, "This is what is written: the Anointed will suffer and rise
from the dead on the third day. [47] And all peoples will be called on to
undergo a change of heart for the forgiveness of sins, beginning from
Jerusalem. [48] You are witnesses to this. [49]And be prepared: I am
sending what my Father promised down on you. Stay here in the city
until you are invested with power from on high."
[50]***Then he led them out*** as far as Bethany, and lifting up his hands he
blessed them. [51]And while he was blessing them, it so happened that
he parted from them, and was carried up into the sky. [52]And they paid
homage to him and returned to Jerusalem full of joy, [53]and were
continually in the temple blessing God.

24:45
(I) Lk9:45, 18:34, 24:25
24:46
(T) Lk9:22, 44; 17:25; 18:31–33; 22:22; 24:6–8, 26
24:50–53
(T) Acts1:9–12, SJas10:1–3

24:51 Some mss omit *and was carried up into the sky.* **24:52** A few mss omit *paid homage to him and.*

24:48 A very important theme in Acts (see, e.g., Acts 1:8, 22, 2:32, 3:15, 5:32).
24:50 *Bethany* is about 1½ miles from Jerusalem, on the Mount of Olives.
24:53 *in the temple*: The Gospel ends where it began (1:8–9).

Heavenly messenger

The traditional translation of the Greek term *angelos* is *angel,* which is actually an English version of the Greek term. An angel is a messenger or envoy dispatched by God or the gods to carry messages to humankind. Angels are therefore intermediaries between the divine and human realms. In order to avoid popular associations with the standard word and to refurbish the concept in English, the translators decided to employ the phrase, *heavenly messenger.*

Introduction

A *hypothetical text*

As with "Q"—an early collection of Jesus' sayings widely believed to underlie Matthew and Luke—many scholars are convinced that a good deal of the narrative in John comes from a document now lost. If so, this was not a collection of Jesus' words, as in Q, but rather an account of his deeds—principally his miracles, perhaps seven of them. These were meant to be understood as "signs" (that is, demonstrations) that Jesus was the Jewish Messiah, the Anointed. (This point is elaborated in the note on 2:11.) Like Q, the existence of this document is hypothetical; we have no manuscript copies of it. It survives only embedded within the text of John and must be reconstructed, by trying to read backward from John, just as Q is recovered by working backward from Matthew and Luke.

The Signs Gospel is reconstructed chiefly by looking for points in John where obvious literary seams appear; such seams often indicate inconsistencies and even contradictions in the text of the completed gospel. These rough spots are infrequent in the synoptic gospels, even where Matthew or Luke reproduces material from Mark or Q. But they are common in John and seem to suggest that when using the hypothetical "source," the author of John quoted it practically verbatim; the author simply allowed the rough connections and inconsistencies to stand. Perhaps the document was so familiar and revered by John's audience that it could not be rewritten or even paraphrased, although it had undoubtedly become in some way obsolete. It could be reinterpreted or corrected only by adding brief comments, rearranging it, or interpolating new material.

Both Q and the Signs Gospel have until recently been important chiefly as sources for the later New Testament gospels. But in this volume we explore Q and the Signs Gospel not as sources for the later writings, but rather as documents in their own right. Neither was written in order to be a source for a later writer, but as a distinctive presentation of the Christian claim.

The fact that these documents happened later to be employed as sources led not only to their *disappearance* but also in a way to their *preservation*, buried in the later gospels that used them as literary sources. Mark also was used as a source by Matthew and Luke, and it was probably only by chance that Mark survived on its own; it was almost discarded, since virtually all of it is now to be found, somewhat reworded, in either Matthew or Luke, or in both.

A rudimentary gospel

This document was a *gospel*—as perhaps, in an altogether different way, was Q. Though rudimentary, it announces the single message of early Christianity: the good news that at last the Messiah has come. It presents Jesus' miracles as self-evident and self-sufficient proofs of this news, and calls on its readers to believe it—to perceive the miracles as signs—just as the original disciples are shown to have done. Because of this singular focus on Jesus' signs, this "book" (John 20:30) can be called the Signs Gospel.

"Proof" that Jesus was Messiah

Jesus, it seems clear, had healed people—as portrayed in two or three of the episodes in the Signs Gospel—but not in order to make any claim, still less to expect belief in himself. Yet perhaps twenty years or more before Mark, the earliest extant gospel, stories recounting these characteristic acts of Jesus—supplemented with still more impressive feats such as walking on the sea, turning a few loaves into enough to feed a huge crowd, or water into wine—had been transformed by the Signs Gospel into theological proofs. How did this happen? In what context?

Answering the latter question is easier, and helps us solve the former: The context was evidently a Greek-speaking synagogue whose members believed that Jesus was the Messiah. The religion of these believers was Judaism. They were "Christians" only in the literal sense of the word, that is, believers in Jesus as the Christ, the Messiah. A more precise name for these Christian Jews would be *Messianists*. These Messianists collected stories about his wonders to serve a missionary purpose. As to the first question: The model for reshaping these miracle stories as messianic proofs was the series of "signs" that Moses had worked in Exodus. Over the centuries it had been expected that the future Messiah would be the Prophet that Moses had promised, who would be, like himself, the representative of Israel's God (see Deut 18:15–18). Elijah also had performed miracles, and his reappearance was another way of imagining the Messiah. (See further the notes on 1:20–21 and 41, [43], 45, below.) So a Signs Gospel would have been, for a time at least, a most effective way of presenting the Christian message to fellow Jews, both as announcement and as claim.

But before long, tension arose between Christian Jews and Jews who did not accept that Jesus was the Anointed, tension that led ultimately to a separation. For some time prior to the schism that was gradually taking place among Jews throughout the Roman empire, the collected sign stories proved to be less and less effective in convincing Jews that Jesus was the Anointed.

Apology for Jesus' death

A reason for this growing failure, perhaps the chief one, was the question: How could the one depicted by these miracles as the Anointed have come to the shameful death Jesus experienced at the hand of the Roman governor? How, in fact, could the Messiah have died at all? This objection was a serious weakness in the case for Jesus' messiahship, and it seems to have troubled Christian Jews as well. To answer it, an "apology," a defense, was developed, one parallel to the account underlying Mark 14–16. It showed that Jesus' suffering, death, and resurrection had been occasioned, indeed foreordained, by God. Evidence for this could be found in the prophecies of scripture, by rereading them in the light of Christian beliefs, much as the Qumran community reread the scriptures as prophecies for its own time. Prooftexts were gathered and, together with such memories and suppositions as had circulated in the tradition about Jesus, were worked into a continuous account of Jesus' passion and, whether immediately or later, appended to the original Signs Gospel. Such proof-texts appear explicitly in 2:17; 12:38, 40; 12:15; 19:24, (28), 36, 37. Allusions to such proof texts also occur, for example, at 18:2 (Ps 109:3; also at Jn 19:1, 3); 19:18 (Isa 53:12); 19:29 (Ps 69:21). Virtually all of these OT references are in the passion account. (See also the note on 2:14–19.)

The earlier form of the Signs Gospel had been no haphazard collection of miracle stories. It was a book containing a connected account of how Jesus' activity began with John the Baptist and of the signs he performed, first in Galilee, then in Jerusalem. In time, as just now noted, the passion and resurrection story were added, probably after a transitional summary of how the account only of Jesus' signs had in the end met with disbelief: the Council's plot to have Jesus killed, Jesus' provocative act in the temple, and a justification for that death from scripture.

The earliest gospel?

From this narrative combining Jesus' signs with his death and resurrection was born what ever since has been thought essential to a book that could be called a "gospel." The Signs Gospel and Mark developed much the same format for telling the good news, and probably did so quite independently. Mark differs from this format only by the introduction of some of Jesus' teaching, a development meager in Mark compared to Matthew, Luke, and John, but noticeable in comparison with the Signs Gospel's almost total lack of sayings. In the Signs Gospel, then, we have perhaps the earliest, certainly the most rudimentary of gospels. Even in its original, shorter form without passion and resurrection stories, the Signs Gospel had proclaimed the good news, as in their own way did many of the other extra-canonical gospels brought together in this volume.

The reconstructed text

What follows is an attempt to recreate what a Signs Gospel would have looked like. It is based largely on the work of R. T. Fortna, *The Fourth Gospel and its Predecessor* (1988), which to some degree is overlapped by U. C. von Wahlde's reconstruction, *The Earliest Version of John's Gospel* (1989). The reconstructed text set out below uses the Scholars Version of John, but translates a number of words and phrases differently, in order to reflect how the Greek in question would have had a somewhat distinct meaning in its earlier context. Differences in the Signs Gospel are printed in *italic*. For example, *signs* in the Signs Gospel is translated *miracles* in John. Three types of passages are enclosed in square brackets—[ ]: (a) those questionably assigned to the Signs Gospel, (b) those whose placement within it suggests Johannine rearrangement or is not certain, and (c) those involving hypothetical reconstruction.

The reader comparing this reconstruction with John will notice that the evident order of individual narrative units in the Signs Gospel differs from that in John, as reflected by the chapter and verse numbers. In John the units have been greatly rearranged from their order in the Signs Gospel (see its outline below) and interpolated with later material. A comparison will also show that only some of the parenthetical remarks now dotting that gospel are thought to have been original to the Signs Gospel. Those that translate a Greek term or name back into its Semitic original (e.g., 19:13) belong to the source. Those that do the reverse (see the note, e.g., on 1:38)—evidently for the benefit of readers who knew only Greek, among them probably some non-Jews—are attributable to the later Johannine redaction. Creating the Gospel according to John involved supplementing the Signs Gospel, which was necessitated by the final and bitter split in the community out of which an early stage of this source arose.

In a few passages, the Johannine redactor's reinterpretation has been sufficiently extensive that recreation of the pre-Johannine text is more uncertain than usual. This is especially true in the following sections: John the Baptist's witness to Jesus and to his disciples (1:23–36), the resurrection of Lazarus (11:1–45), and Jesus' trials before the high priest and Pilate (18:13, 19–24 and 18:33–19:16a).

There are several points in John where an older account very likely underlies the Johannine gospel but is not recoverable, namely, other material about John the Baptist (3:22–30; 10:40–42), Jesus and Nicodemus (3:1–2), and Jesus and the Samaritan woman (4:1–42). To this list belongs above all the last supper (chap. 13; 14:30b), including in particular Jesus' prediction (13:38) that Peter will disown him (as in 18:16b-27) and perhaps also that the disciples present at the meal will abandon him (14:35). The latter is not fulfilled in John, unless it is implied by the presence only of women disciples at Jesus' execution and finally at the burial, and by the fact that Mary of Magdala went alone to the tomb on Sunday and was the first to find it empty. Whether any of this material listed above was part of the Signs Gospel is a matter of debate; perhaps in the meantime it was redacted more than once, making the recovery of its earliest written form virtually impossible.

A purely narrative gospel

What is quite clear, however, is that Jesus' lengthy and lofty teaching about himself as "the Son" and his relation to his "Father," together with his instruction to (clearly future) followers, had no place in the Signs Gospel. This manner of speech is most distinctive of the Johannine portrayal of Jesus and reaches its fullest expression in the so-called farewell discourse during the last supper (13:31–17:26). But already in early chapters, besides minor interpolations, a number of the signs stories serve now only as the pretext for extended dialogue between Jesus and "the Judeans."

Outline of the Signs Gospel

The Opening
John's announcement (1:6–7, 19–34)
John's disciples & the Messiah (1:35–49)

Jesus' Signs in Galilee
Water into wine (2:1–11)
An official's son healed (2:12a, 4:46b–54)
A huge catch of fish (21:1–14)
Loaves & fish for 5,000;
Jesus walks on the sea (6:1–25)

Jesus' Signs in Jerusalem
Lazarus raised (11:1–45)
A blind man given sight (9:1–8)
A crippled man healed (5:2–9)

The Culmination of Jesus' Signs
The Council's plan (11:47–53)
Jesus in the temple (2:14–19)
The Anointed must die (12:37–40)

The Prelude to Jesus' Passion
Mary anoints Jesus (12:1–8)
Jesus enters Jerusalem (12:12–15)

Jesus' Passion
Judas turns Jesus in (18:1–11)
Trial before the high priest;
Peter's denials (18:12–27)
Trial before Pilate (18:28–19:16a)
Jesus is crucified (19:16b–37)
Joseph buries Jesus (19:38–42)

Jesus' Resurrection
Mary & Peter at the tomb (20:1–10)
Mary meets Jesus (20:11–18)
Behind locked doors (20:19–22)

The Closing
Conclusion (20:30–31ab)

The Signs Gospel

John's announcement

The Opening

1:6–7, 19–34/1:35–49

1 [6]**There appeared a man** sent from God named John. [7]He came *to*
make announcement, so that everyone would believe through him.
[19]This is what John *announced*: When priests and Levites [came] to
him from Jerusalem to ask him, "Who are you?" [20]he *declared*, "I'm not
the Anointed." [21]*So* they asked him, "Then what are you? Are you
Elijah?" And he replies, "I am not." "Are you the Prophet?" He
answered, "No." [22]*Then* they said to him, "Who are you? What have
you got to say of yourself?" [23]He replied, "I am

> the voice of *the one who is shouting* in the wilderness,
> 'Make the way of the Lord straight,'

as Isaiah the prophet *predicted*. [26b]I baptize, yes, but only with water.
Right there with you is *the one* [27]who is to be my successor. I don't even
deserve to untie his sandal straps. [31bc]I came so he would be revealed to

1:19–34 Cf. Mk 1:2–11, Mt 3:1–2, 13–17, Lk 3:1–22
1:21 Ⓣ Mt 11:13–14; D Mal 4:5
1:23 // Mk 1:2–3, Mt 3:3, Lk 3:4–6; D Is 40:3
1:26b–27 // Q 3:16, Mt 3:11, Lk 3:16
1:32b // Mk 1:10, Mt 3:16, Lk 3:22

1:6–7, 19–34 As in a few other scenes, here the author of the canonical Gospel of John has considerably altered the Signs Gospel (SG), making its recovery, both its original wording and its order, uncertain at points. The pre-Johannine context of SG has sometimes required a slight change in translation from John (Scholars Version). Most of these instances (printed in *italics*) will be self-evident; a few will receive comment.

1:6–7 The natural beginning of a narrative. The hymn to the "divine word and wisdom" (vv. 1–5, 8–18), later made to surround this opening, has encapsulated and almost overpowered it.

1:7 *to make announcement*: The later Johannine atmosphere of an official interrogation (and that John "came to testify") is missing; also in vv. 19–20.

Unlike the later insertion—"to testify to the light"—there is no indication yet whom or what John will announce.

everyone: that is, all of Israel (see v. 31).

would believe: Namely, that Jesus was the Messiah (vv. 40–49)—the major theme of this early Gospel.

1:19 Evidently they came not as spies for the religious authorities (as now, John 1:19, 22, 24) but perhaps out of expectant hope.

1:20 *declared*: This is no concession as in the Johannine redaction, but a claim. See the note on v. 7.

1:20–21 *the Anointed . . . Elijah . . . the Prophet*: Various ways of designating the savior whom many in Israel were awaiting. John denies for himself the three titles applied to Jesus in the next section (vv. 41–45).

1:23 *as Isaiah the prophet predicted*: In Isa 40:3, the first use of Hebrew Scriptures, frequent in SG.

1:26b *I baptize, yes, but only with water*: John acknowledges, in fact volunteers, that the chief activity associated with him in the tradition is merely another way of announcing his successor.

1:27 *successor*: that is, John's superior, his supplanter.

1:31bc *I came so he would be revealed to Israel*: Re-emphasizing (after v. 7) John's single role in SG as announcer. Given the intended audience of SG (see the Introduction), it is expected that all of Israel will acknowledge the revelation.

John's disciples & the Messiah

Israel. [32b]I have seen the spirit coming down like a dove out of the sky *upon* him. [33d]*He's* the one who baptizes with holy spirit. [34c]I have seen and now have *announced*: This is God's son."

[35]**John was standing there** with two of his disciples, [36]When he saw Jesus walking by he says, "Look, the lamb of God!" [37]His two disciples heard him ⟨say this⟩ , and they followed Jesus. [38]Jesus turned, saw them following, and says to them, "What are you looking for?" They said to him, "Rabbi, where are you staying?" [39]He says to them, "Come and see." So they went and saw where he was staying and spent the day with him. It was about four in the afternoon.

[40]Andrew was one of the two who followed Jesus after hearing John ⟨speak about him⟩. [41]First he goes and finds his brother Simon and tells him, "We have found the Messiah," [42]and he took him to Jesus. When Jesus laid eyes on him, he said, "You're Simon, John's son; you're to be called Kephas."

[43b]Then he finds Philip and [says to him, "We've found Elijah." And he led him to Jesus. And Jesus] says to him, "Follow me. " [44]Philip was from Bethsaida, the hometown of Andrew and Peter.

[45]Philip finds Nathanael and tells him, "We've found the one Moses wrote about in the Law—and the prophets mention too: Jesus, Joseph's son, from Nazareth." [46]"From Nazareth?" Nathanael said to him. "Can anything good come from that place?" Philip replies to him,

1:33d
Ⓣ Acts 1:5, 11:16, 19:1–7
1:41
Ⓣ Mk 8:29, Mt 16:16, Lk 9:20
1:42
Ⓣ Mk 3:16, Mt 10:2, Lk 6:14

1:34 *God's son*: Still another title, and the first John explicitly applies to Jesus; by it he makes the announcement he came for.
1:36 *the lamb of God*: Whatever it means, John announces still another title for Jesus.
1:38 *Rabbi*: There is no need to translate the Semitic word into Greek, as in the present gospel; evidently SG's original audience was bilingual. Similarly, *Messiah* in v. 41 and *Kephas* in v. 42.
1:43b The story continues without the interruption of v. 43a. The words bracketed are a hypothetical reconstruction of material evidently omitted by the author of John, perhaps because calling Jesus *Elijah* would remind the reader that Elijah had "gone up to heaven" (2 Kgs 2:1–12) and thus seem to contradict the important assertion in John (possibly directed against local synagogue leaders) that "no has gone up to heaven . . . except the son of Adam" (3:13). If this title is restored, the balance between the titles denied by John for himself in vv. 20–21 and those applied to Jesus here is restored.

It was not clear in SG who it is that calls Philip here (see the next note), and so after the insertion of 43a in John it is taken to mean Jesus, breaking the pattern of the spreading good news.

Follow me: Only here does Jesus in some sense call the disciples, as in the synoptic gospels; otherwise he invites them to "come and see" (v. 39), and they spread the news that "[they] have found the Messiah."
1:44 This kind of datum is common in SG (see the hour of the day in v. 39 and many other instances) but odd alongside the abstract quality of Johannine elements. Here, apparently it explains how it happened that *Philip* was the next to hear the spreading news—whether from Andrew, completing the otherwise forgotten *first* in v. 41, or Peter, in a kind of chain reaction.

Peter: The original, bilingual reader (see the note on v. 38) would recognize that both *Kephas* (v. 42) and its Greek equivalent here refer to Andrew's brother, Simon (v. 41).
1:45 *the one Moses wrote about in the Law*: After *Messiah* in v. 41 and, apparently, *Elijah* in 43b, this designation, which clearly refers to Deut 18:15, 18, ascribes to Jesus the last of the three titles John denied for himself (vv. 20–21).

and the prophets mention too: Perhaps referring indirectly to the prediction in Mal 4:5 that Elijah would return.

Water into wine

An official's son healed

"Come and see." [47]Jesus saw Nathanael coming toward him, and he
remarks about him: "There's a genuine Israelite." [48]"Where do you
know me from?" Nathanael asks him. Jesus replied, "I saw you under
the fig tree before Philip invited you ⟨to join us⟩." [49]Nathanael
responded to him, "Rabbi, you are God's son! You are king of Israel!"

Jesus' Signs in Galilee
2:1–11/2:12a, 4:46b–54/21:1–14/6:1–14/6:15b–25

2 [1]***Now [on a Tuesday]*** there was a wedding in Cana, Galilee. Jesus'
mother was there. [2]Jesus was also invited to the wedding, along with
his disciples. [3a]When the wine had run out, Jesus' mother says [5b]to the
servants, "Whatever he tells you, do it." [6]Six stone water-jars were
standing there, and each could hold twenty or thirty gallons. [7]"Fill the
jars with water," Jesus tells them. So they filled them to the brim.
[8]Then he tells them, "Now dip some out and take it to the caterer."
And they did so. [9]When the caterer tasted the water, now changed into
wine, he calls the groom aside [10]and says to him, "Everyone serves the
best wine first and only later, when people are drunk, the cheaper wine.
But you've held back the good wine till now." [11]*This ⟨was⟩ the
beginning of the signs Jesus did, and he showed ⟨himself⟩*, and his
disciples believed in him.

2 [12a]**Then he *set out*** for Capernaum, he and his mother and brothers and disciples. 4 [46b]In Capernaum there was an official whose son

1:49
Ⓣ Mt16:16
2:12a
Cf. Mk1:21, Mt4:12–13, Lk4:31

1:49 *God's son . . . king of Israel*: Nathanael reiterates John's acclamation (v. 34c), extends it, and addresses it directly to Jesus.

2:1–11 The site of the preceding sections is unspecified, apart from Isaiah's "wilderness" (1:23). Beginning with this episode Jesus works only in Galilee until the Feeding story (6:1–14) is complete.

2:1 *Tuesday* evidently was a common day for weddings. Literally, "on the third day," and if that translation is the better, the phrase has been added to SG by the author of John, as completion of the temporal sequence that has been introduced at 1:29, 35, 43.

2:2 *along with his disciples*: Jesus' newly acquired followers, at least two of them having changed their allegiance from John to Jesus, are present at all the "signs" Jesus now begins to perform.

2:3a,5b Without the later Johannine insertion of vv. 3b–5a, Jesus' mother rightly assumes that he knows of the need for wine and will provide it.

2:6 *Six stone water-jars were standing there*: SG's Christian Jewish audience would not need to be told (as in John) that this was "for use in the Jewish rite of purification."

2:11 *This ⟨was⟩ the beginning of the signs Jesus did*: Such a nearly literal translation expresses SG's singular focus on the miracles of Jesus. This sign (see the following note) was not merely the first of many—it will appear in the Closing (21:30) that Jesus worked many signs—but the opening of Jesus' public ministry, depicted simply as the working of signs.

signs: The wondrous deeds Jesus accomplishes, in the completed text of John, are better understood there as "miracles"—acts that sometimes merely astound (4:48), or on the other hand may have no effect (2:18, 6:26). But in SG they were demonstrations; by them Jesus *showed* who he was.

his disciples believed in him: the immediate effect, and the intended one.

2:12a *Then he set out for Capernaum*: A natural transition to Jesus' second sign. In John, with the intervention of 2:13–4:46a, the statement is left hanging and continues, literally, "and they did not stay there many days."

A huge catch of fish

was sick. 47When he heard that Jesus *was coming*, he approached him
and pleaded with him: 49b"Sir, please come down before my child
dies." 50acJesus says, "Go, your son *will live*." And *the man* departed.
51While he was still on his way home, his slaves met him and told him
that his boy was alive. 52So he asked them when he had begun to
recover, and they told him, "Yesterday at one o'clock the fever broke."
53Then the father realized that one o'clock was precisely the time Jesus
had said to him, "Your son will live." And he believed, as did all his
household. 54*This ⟨was the⟩ second sign ⟨that⟩* Jesus performed.

[21 1**Jesus *showed himself*** again to his disciples by the Sea of Tiberias. This is how he did it: 2When Simon Peter and Thomas were
together, along with Nathanael from Cana, the sons of Zebedee, and
two other disciples, 3Simon Peter says to them, "I'm going to go
fishing." "We're coming with you," they reply. They went down and
got into the boat, but that night they didn't catch a thing. 4aIt was
getting light *and* Jesus *was standing* on the shore. 5"Lads, you haven't
caught any fish, have you?" Jesus asks them. "No," they replied. 6He
tells them, "Cast your net on the right side of the boat and you'll have
better luck." They do as he instructs them and now they can't haul it in
for the huge number of fish. 7b*So* Simon Peter tied his clothes around
himself, since he was stripped for work, and *leapt* into the water. 8The
rest of them came in the boat, dragging the net full of fish. They were
not far from land, only about a hundred yards offshore. 11*So* he went
ashore and hauled *in* the net full of large fish—one hundred fifty-three

4:46b–54
Cf. Q7:1–10, Mt8:5–13, Lk7:1–10

21:1–8
Cf. Lk5:4–11

4:47 *was coming*: In SG Jesus is on his way from Cana, not—as in the present arrangement of John—returning from Judea.

4:50ac *the man departed*: In SG his belief is not at Jesus' word (as in the Johannine v. 50b) but comes only at the end of the episode, and as its climax (v. 53b).

4:54 *This ⟨was the⟩ second sign ⟨that⟩ Jesus performed*: That is, in its own right, not only "after he had returned from Judea to Galilee."

21:1–14 The assignment of this story to SG (as well as its placement here) is more hypothetical than is the case for most other episodes.

21:1 *showed himself*: Not the risen Lord appearing to them, as later in John, but demonstrating once again by his signs that he is the Anointed. The verb is the same as at 2:11b.

21:2 *Thomas*: SG need not explain to its readers that in Greek this disciple is "known as The Twin"—the Semitic name means just that.

21:4a *was standing*: This more literal translation fits SG better than "appeared." That Jesus was at first unrecognizable to the disciples (4b) seems a later addition; in 6:19 (Jesus walking on the sea) such a lack of recognition, leading to fear, is implied, but the point is only that by identifying himself Jesus calms their fear.

21:5 This leads solely to the miracle—not also to an Easter appearance by the risen Jesus and a meal with him, as in John.

21:7 *leapt into the water*: Here Peter does not desperately "throw himself," as in John 21, presumably out of shame for his recent denials of Jesus in chap. 18, but only hurries to wade ashore to help land the catch.

21:11 The original sign story continues.

So: Here, as in v. 7b, the Greek word (*oun*), that can be left untranslated or mean simply "next," has the other meaning of causal connection.

he went ashore and hauled in . . .: The word usually taken to mean "went aboard [the boat]" equally can mean "went onto land." The disciples are just landing the boat and are still aboard; Peter helps pull the net, unmanageably heavy, up onto the shore.

one hundred fifty-three of them: The detail demonstrates the miracle's magnitude and is

Loaves & fish for 5000

of them. Even though there were so many of them, the net still did not tear. 14This was the third time Jesus showed himself to his disciples.]

Jesus walks on the sea

6 1**After these events,** Jesus crossed the Sea of Tiberias. 3Jesus climbed up the mountain, and he sat down there with his disciples. 5⟨He⟩ looks up and sees a big crowd approaching him, and he says to Philip, "Where are we going to get enough bread to feed this mob?" 7"Half a year's wages wouldn't buy enough bread for everyone to have a bite," Philip said. 8One of his disciples, Andrew, Simon Peter's brother, says to him, 9"There's a lad here with five loaves of barley bread and two fish; but what does that amount to for so many?" 10Jesus said, "Have the people sit down." (They were in a grassy place.) So they sat down; the men alone numbered about five thousand. 11Jesus took the loaves, gave thanks, and passed them around to the people sitting there, along with the fish, and all of them had as much as they wanted. 12abAnd when they had eaten their fill, he says to his disciples, "Gather up the leftovers so nothing goes to waste." 13So they gathered them up. And they filled twelve baskets with scraps from the five barley loaves—from what was left over. 14When these folks saw the *sign* he had performed they would say, "Yes indeed! This is undoubtedly *the Prophet* who is to come into the world."

15b**Jesus *went away*** once again to the mountain by himself. 16As evening approached, his disciples went down to the sea. 17They boarded a boat and were trying to cross the lake to Capernaum. It had already gotten dark, and Jesus still had not joined them. 18A strong wind began to blow and the sea was getting rough. 19When they had rowed about three or four miles, they catch sight of Jesus walking on the lake and coming towards the boat. They were frightened, 20but he says to them, "Don't be afraid! It's me." 21Then they would have taken him on board, but the boat instantly arrived at the shore they had been making for. [22The crowd, which was still on the other side of the lake,

6:1–14
//Mk6:30–44, 8:1–10; Mt14:13–21, 15:32–39; Lk9:10–17; ◊2Kgs4:42–44
6:14
◊Dt18:15–18
6:16–21
//Mk6:45–52, Mt14:22–33
6:22–25
//Mk6:53–56, Mt14:34–36

---

an instance of SG's interest in verisimilitude; see the note on 1:44.

21:14 *the third time Jesus showed himself to his disciples*: Or possibly, *the third [sign by which]* . . . .

6:5 *Where are we going to get enough bread?*: In contrast to the synoptic version of this story, Jesus takes the initiative in working this miracle, here a "sign." The question to Philip is not merely rhetorical here, intended "to test" him, as now in v. 6 of John.

6:14 *saw the sign he had performed*: Unlike the first three signs, from this episode on the signs are no longer numbered. Perhaps some such notices were original to SG and necessarily omitted with their rearrangement in John.

the Prophet: one of the messianic titles used in 1:21.

6:15b *went away*: Without v. 15a, Jesus does not next "retreat" but simply goes farther up into the hill country, this time *by himself.*

6:19 See the note on 21:4a (p. 183).

6:21 *the boat instantly arrived*: Another miracle, but probably secondary to Jesus' walking on the water.

6:22 The story continues, not divided by "And the next day," added here and at a number of other points in John.

saw that Jesus had not gotten into that boat with the disciples. [25]They found him on the other side of the lake and asked him, "Rabbi, when did you get here?"]

Lazarus raised

A blind man given sight

Jesus' Signs in Jerusalem
11:1–45/9:1–8/5:2–9

11 [1]**Now someone named Lazarus** had fallen ill; he was from Bethany, the village of Mary. ([2]This was the Mary who anointed the Master with oil and wiped his feet with her hair; it was her brother Lazarus who was sick.) [3]So [she] sent for ⟨Jesus⟩: "Master, the one you love is sick." [4]But when Jesus heard this he said, [14]"Lazarus is dead. [15c]Now let's go to him." [17]When Jesus arrived, he found that ⟨Lazarus⟩ had been buried four days earlier. [32]When Mary got to where Jesus was and saw him, she fell down at his feet. "Master," she said, "if you'd been here, my brother wouldn't have died." [33ac]When Jesus saw her crying, he was agitated and deeply disturbed; [34]he said, "Where have you put him?" "Master," they say, "come and see." [[35]Then Jesus cried.] [38bc]Jesus arrives at the tomb; it was a cave, and a stone lay up against the opening. [39a]Jesus says, "Take the stone away." [41a]So they took the stone away. [43]Then he shouted at the top of his voice, "Lazarus, come out!" [44]The dead man came out, his hands and feet bound in strips of burying cloth, and his face covered with a cloth. Jesus says to them, "Free him ⟨from the burying cloth⟩ and let him go." [45]As a result, many who had come to Mary and observed what Jesus had done came to believe in him.

11:2
Ⓘ SG 12:3
11:35
Ⓣ Lk 19:41

9 [1]**As he was leaving** he saw a man who had been blind from birth. [6]He spat on the ground, made mud with his spit, and treated the man's

---

6:25 *Rabbi, when did you get here?*: The crowd's astonished question serves as a kind of confirmation of Jesus' miraculous crossing of the lake.

11:1–45 This story is the most difficult of the original signs to reconstruct since it has been repeatedly interpolated with later material. Further, it is only tentatively assigned this place in SG. The reason for thinking it may have come here is that it occasions Jesus' coming to Jerusalem (see the note on 11:17). In John this episode has become the event precipitating the Judean leaders' formal plot to kill Jesus, which in SG was occasioned by the apparently unfailing belief Jesus' signs evoked.

11:3 *she sent*: In John, "they sent," after Martha has been introduced into the story.

11:17 *buried four days earlier*: Presumably it took at least two days for Mary's message to reach Jesus in Galilee, sent when Lazarus was still alive, and so two or more for his journey to Bethany, a village just outside Jerusalem.

11.32 *got to where Jesus was*: Here Mary is not summoned by Martha, as in John.

11:35 *Then Jesus cried*: This human side of Jesus is as unexpected in SG as in John. But perhaps it is one of the details often used in SG to lend a sense of factuality.

9:1–8 This very brief story (of only three or four verses) may no longer contain all of its original material—particularly the transition between vv. 1 and 6, perhaps simply displaced by the material later inserted. Its placement in SG, like the episodes before and after it, is based on the natural but unobtrusive itinerary it affords. See the notes on 9:1 and 5:2, below.

9:1 *As he was leaving*: That is, perhaps, leaving Bethany and on the way to the city. The pool of Siloam is just outside Jerusalem.

A crippled man healed

The Council's plan

eyes with the mud. [7]Then ⟨Jesus⟩ said to him, "Go, rinse off in the
pool of Siloam." So he went over, rinsed ⟨his eyes⟩ off, and came back
with his sight restored. [[8]Then his neighbors, and those who recognized him as the one who had been a beggar before, would say, "Isn't
this the fellow who used to sit and beg?"]

5 [2]**In Jerusalem,** by the Sheep ⟨Gate⟩, there is a pool called Bethzatha in Hebrew. It has five colonnades, [3a]among which numerous
invalids were usually lying around—blind, lame, paralyzed. [5a]One
man had been crippled for thirty-eight years. [6]Jesus observed him lying
there and realized he had been there a long time. "Do you want to get
well?" he asks him. [7]The crippled man replied, "Sir, I don't have
anyone to put me in the pool when the water is agitated; while I'm
trying to get in someone else beats me to it." [8]"Get up, pick up your
mat and *start walking,*" Jesus tells him. [9]And at once the man
recovered; he picked up his mat and started walking.

The Culmination of Jesus' Signs
11:47–53/2:14–19/12:37–40

5:2–9
Cf. Mk 2:1–12,
Mt 9:1–8,
Lk 5:17–26

11 [47ac]**So the ranking priests** called the Council together and *said,*
"This fellow performs many *signs*. [48]If we let him go on like this,
everybody will come to believe in him. Then the Romans will come

---

9:8 This verse is possibly part of the original ending; or something has been lost here, too. Otherwise, there is none of the typical reaction to the sign.

5:2 *In Jerusalem, by the Sheep ⟨Gate⟩*: Jesus has now come into the city's center, perhaps to one of the very gates of the temple precinct. See the note on 9:1 above.

It has five colonnades: The present text here (taken over into John, which usually retains the wording of the source verbatim) suggests that the source, but not the completed John, was written before the destruction of the Jerusalem temple in 70 C.E.

5:7 *when the water is agitated*: Apparently it was believed to be curative only then. (This bare notice must have given rise to the vivid and elaborate legend that was later interpolated into John, as vv. 3b–4.)

5:8 *start walking*: The Greek here is precisely repeated in the man's compliance in v. 9—a common feature in SG.

11:47–53 If, as is probable, SG did not at first contain a passion narrative, it would probably have ended here—that is, after the healing of the blind man—with the concluding words of 20:30–31a. It seems likely, however, that by the time it served (according to the hypothesis) as basis for much of the narrative in John it would already have been joined with, or extended to include, the account of Jesus' arrest, trial, execution, and burial. This so-called Passion Source would have had a distinct origin from a purely "Signs Source," each serving a quite different purpose; the earlier sought to prove Jesus' messiahship, the later to account for his death.

This episode, interrupting the account of Jesus' public activity, provides the turning point. Jesus' signs now complete and the people's response to them patent, the authorities would have reacted, citing the very danger Jesus' popularity posed.

11:48 *everybody will come to believe in him*: In each of the signs, as SG presents them, *to believe in* Jesus was the purpose—and often the expressed result.

The Romans will come and destroy our nation: The Council fears that belief in Jesus as the Anointed will be seen as support for a leader who is challenging Roman rule and

and destroy our nation." 49abThen one of them, Caiaphas, that year's
high priest, addressed them as follows: 50bc"It's to your advantage to
have one person die for the people and not have the whole nation
wiped out." 53So from that day on they began plotting how to kill him.

2 14**In the temple precincts** ⟨Jesus⟩ came upon people selling oxen
and sheep and doves, and bankers were doing business there too. 15He
made a whip out of rope and drove them all out of the temple area,
sheep, oxen, and all; then he knocked over the bankers' tables, and set
their coins flying. 16And to the dove merchants he said, "Get these
birds out of here! How dare you use my Father's house as a public
market." 17b*For it says in* scripture:

> Zeal for your house is eating me *up*.

18To this the [people] responded, "What *justification* can you show us
⟨for⟩ doing all this?" 19Jesus replied, "Destroy this temple and I'll
resurrect it in three days."

Jesus in the temple

11:53 Cf. Mk 3:6, Mt 12:14, Mk 11:18, Lk 19:47–48, Mk 14:1–2, Mt 26:3–5, Lk 22:1–2

2:14–17 //Mk 11:15–17, Mt 21:12–13, Lk 19:45–46

2:17b ◊Ps 69:9

2:18–19 Cf. Mk 11:27–33, Mt 21:23–27, Lk 20:1–8

2:19 //Mk 14:57–58, 15:29; Mt 26:60–61, 27:40; cf. Th 71

---

thus lead to the loss of such nationhood as Israel is allowed.

11:53 Jesus' fate is sealed, an outcome altogether out of keeping with the expectations his signs have raised. This inconsistency will be explained in 12:37–40.

2:14–19 Whatever its origin, the passion story underlying John 18–19 (as well as parts of chaps. 11–12 and including this story, now in John 2) serves the purpose of an *apology*—a "defense" of Jesus' crucifixion. It does this by a single device: showing that the Anointed's death was foreordained in Scripture and therefore happened by divine necessity. This device appears here for the first time (v. 17), the explicit fulfillment of a specific passage from the Hebrew scriptures. This episode, before it was removed to John 2, furthers the transition to an account of Jesus' end: The unfailing belief that the signs evoked gives way to the people's suspicion of Jesus' right to take decisive steps in the temple. See the Introduction.

2:14 *In the temple precincts*: In resuming Jesus' activity, after the Council's secret decision, the narrative flow from the healing of the lame man—most likely near a gate into the temple area (see the note on 5:2, above)—is smooth.

Oxen and sheep and doves were required for Jewish sacrifices.

bankers: That is, money-changers, those who exchanged—no doubt for profit—Roman money for Jewish shekels, which were required for paying the temple tax and perhaps to purchase the sacrificial animals.

2:17b This sentence is evidently not a continuation of Jesus' words but the explanation provided by SG's author.

For it says in scripture: That is, Jesus did this *because* of the passage in Ps 69:10. See below, on 12:38.

Eating me up is ambiguous and appropriately so, as the passion story begins. It accounts for the vehemence of Jesus' act; it is meant also to foreshadow the deadly consequence this act will have.

2:18 *people*: Or, "authorities."

Justification: Literally, "sign," but here Jesus is asked to show by what authority he has purged the temple area. Any such retroactive demonstration would be only a response to their lack of faith in him, not a miracle that was to be perceived as a sign of his messiahship.

2:19 *Destroy this temple and . . .*: Meaning, as now also in John, "If you kill me . . . ."

I'll resurrect it in three days: Instead of displaying another sign on the spot, Jesus promises one—it will be his greatest and will give the best apology imaginable for his death. That he is to accomplish his own resurrection is virtually unique in the NT. If there was any doubt that he had been alluding to his own death (and resurrection), it is dispelled by the formula, *in three days*.

The Anointed must die

Mary anoints Jesus

12 [37]**Although he had performed** so many miracles before their eyes, they did not believe in him, [38]so that the word the prophet Isaiah spoke would come true:

Lord, who has believed our message?
To whom is God's might revealed?

[39]So they were unable to believe, for Isaiah also said:

[40]He has blinded their eyes,
he has turned their hearts to stone,
so their eyes are sightless
and their hearts closed to understanding,
or they would do an about-face
for me to heal them.

The Prelude to Jesus' Passion
12:1–8/12:12–15

12 [1]**Six days before Passover** Jesus came to Bethany, where Lazarus lived, the one Jesus had brought back from the dead. [2]There they gave a dinner for him; Martha did the serving, and Lazarus was one of those who ate with him. [3]Mary brought in a pound of expensive lotion and anointed Jesus' feet and wiped them with her hair. And the house was filled with the lotion's fragrance. [4]Judas Iscariot, the disciple who was going to turn him in, says, [5]"Why wasn't this lotion sold? It would bring a year's wages, and the proceeds could have been given to the poor." [[6]He didn't say this because he cared about the poor, but because he was a thief. He was in charge of the common purse and now and again would pilfer money put into it.] [7]"Let her alone," Jesus said. "Let her keep it for the time I am to be embalmed. [8]There will always be poor around; but I won't always be around."

12:37–40 Cf. Mk4:10–12, Mt13:10–17, Lk8:9–10
12:38 ◊Is53:1
12:40 ◊Is6:9–10
12:1–8 //Mk14:3–9, Mt26:6–13; cf. Lk7:36–50
12:8 ◊Dt15:11

12:37–40 This interpretive comment by SG's author brings the recital of Jesus' public activity formally to a close, admits its failure (at least for the people's leaders), and explains how this contradiction was inevitable (see on v. 38, below).

12:37 *miracles*: They could not see them as the *signs* they were.

12:38 *so that ⟨scripture⟩ would come true*: The first instance of this formula, making explicit the divine necessity, and therefore acceptability, of Jesus' death.

who has believed . . . : In Isa 53:1 the prophet expresses the same defeat that author and reader of SG now feel.

our message: Here, of course, that Jesus is the Anointed.

God's might revealed: Clearly, in Jesus' signs.

12:40 Indeed, as God had once hardened Pharaoh's heart, it is by God's design that the leaders did not, could not, believe. The story of Jesus' passion can now proceed with neither anxiety nor incomprehension on the reader's part.

12:3 *anointed*: Jesus has been the Anointed from the beginning of SG, so at most this anointing only recognizes the fact; but primarily it points forward to Jesus' burial (v. 7).

12:4 Judas' fateful role is recognized from his first appearance.

12:5 *A year's wages*: Judas uses an outlandish figure.

12:6 Unless added to SG in its revision as John, this explanation represents an intermediate stage in the tendency to heighten Judas' blame. Note John 6:70, 13:10.

[12]**The next day** the huge crowd that had come for the celebration
heard that Jesus was coming into Jerusalem. [13]They got palm fronds
and went out to meet him. They began to shout, "Hosanna! Blessed is
the one who comes in the name of the Lord! ⟨Blessed is⟩ the King of
Israel!" [14]Then Jesus found a young donkey and rode on it, as scripture
puts it:

Jesus enters Jerusalem

Judas turns Jesus in

Trial before the high priest

> [15]Calm your fears, daughter of Zion.
> Look, your king comes riding on a donkey's colt!

Jesus' Passion
18:1–11/18:12–27/18:28–19:16a/19:16b–37/19:38–42

18 [1]**Jesus went out** with his disciples across the Kidron valley. There
was a garden there where he and his disciples went. [2]But because Jesus
had often gone there with his disciples, Judas, who was about to turn
him in, knew the place too. [3]So it wasn't long before Judas arrives,
bringing with him the detachment ⟨of Roman soldiers⟩ and some of
the police from the ranking priests, armed and with their lamps and
torches. [4b]So Jesus went right up to them and says, "Who is it you're
looking for?" [5]"Jesus the Nazarene," was their reply. "That's me," says
Jesus. And all the while Judas, who was turning him in, was standing
there with them. [10]Simon Peter had brought along a sword, and now he
drew it, slashed at the high priest's slave, who was called Malchus, and
cut off his right ear. [11]"Put the sword back in its scabbard," Jesus told
Peter. "Am I not to drink from the cup my Father has given me?"

[12]***So* the detachment** and their captain, with the Judean police,
arrested Jesus and put him under constraint.[13]They took him first to

12:12–15 //Mk11:1–10, Mt21:1–11, Lk19:28–40
12:13 ◊Ps118:26
18:1–11 //Mk14:43–52, Mt26:47–56, Lk22:47–54
18:1 //Mk14:32, Mt26:36
18:11 Ⓣ Mk14:36, Mt26:39, Lk22:42

12:13 *Blessed is the one who comes in the name of the Lord*: Jesus is given the traditional welcome as for any festal pilgrim, but here it is far more; *the crowd that had come for the celebration* acclaim Jesus as *King of Israel*, just as Nathanael had done at the beginning of SG (1:49).
12:14 *as scripture puts it*: Jesus' preordained role continues (see above, on 2:17), as Zech 9:9 requires.
12:15 *your king comes riding on a donkey's colt*: Jesus' humility hints already at his otherwise inconceivable submission to the abasement and execution that lie before him.
18:1–11 Between this passage and the preceding (Jesus' entry into Jerusalem, 12:12–15) there was probably a brief account of Jesus' supper with his disciples, including his prediction that one of them would betray him and that Peter would disown him.
18:1 *Jesus went out with his disciples*: Presumably from the place of their last supper.
18:4b–5 Jesus virtually offers himself to the arresting posse; what is about to occur must happen.
18:11 *drink from the cup my Father has given me*: A reiteration that what awaits him is determined by God.
18:12–27 SG's simple successive arrangement of these two scenes has evidently been reordered in John, as a number of redundancies suggest; the two are interwoven in John into a double scene, perhaps to heighten the irony of Jesus' being condemned simultaneously with Peter's denying him. And what was apparently a single Jewish hearing has become two in John (by the delay of v. 24). The attempt here to restore the original order requires slight changes in translation as the context has changed.

Peter's denials

Trial before Pilate

Annas. Annas was the father-in-law of that year's high priest, Caiaphas. [[24]*So* Annas sent him, *still* under constraint, to the high priest, Caiaphas.] [15]Simon Peter and another disciple continued to trail along behind Jesus. This other disciple, somehow known to the high priest, went in with Jesus to the high priest's court. [16a]*But* Peter was [left] standing outside the door. [19]Now the high priest interrogated Jesus [about his disciples and about his teaching. [20b]Jesus replied, "I've always taught in synagogues and in the temple area, in places where all gather. [21a]Why are you asking me?"] [22]No sooner had he said this than one of the police on duty there slapped Jesus. "So this is how you talk back to the high priest!" he said.

[[16b]**So this other disciple,** the one acquainted with the high priest, went out, had a word with the woman who kept the door, and got Peter in. [17]The woman who kept watch at the door says to Peter, "You're not one of this man's disciples too, are you?" "No, I'm not," he replies. [18]Meanwhile, since it was cold, the slaves and police had made a charcoal fire and were standing around it, trying to keep warm. Peter was standing there too, warming himself.] [25b]The others there said to him,"You're not one of his disciples too, are you?" He denied it: "No, I'm not," he said. [26]One of the high priest's slaves, a relative of the one whose ear Peter had cut off, says,"I saw you in the garden with him, didn't I?" [27]Once again Peter denied it. At that moment a rooster crowed.

[28a]**They then take Jesus** from Caiaphas' place to the governor's residence. By now it was early morning. [29]Pilate says to them, "What charge are you bringing against this man?" . . . [33]Then Pilate summoned Jesus and asked him,"*You* are 'the King of the Judeans'?" [37b]"You're the one who says I'm a king," responded Jesus. [38c]And he says to them, "In my judgment there is no case against him. [39]But it's your privilege at Passover to have me free one prisoner for you. So, do you want me to free 'the King of the Judeans' for you?" [40]At this they shouted out, "Not him, but Barabbas!" (Barabbas was a rebel.) 19[6a]The ranking priests and the police screamed, "Crucify him! Crucify him!" [13]*So* Pilate brought Jesus out and sat *down* on the judge's seat

18:15–27
//Mk14:55–72; Mt26:55–75; Lk22:58–62, 66–71

18:20b
Cf. Mk14:49, Mt26:55, Lk22:53

18:28a–40
//Mk15:1–15; Mt27:1–2, 11–26; Lk23:1–7, 13–25

18:33–38
Cf. Mk15:2, Mt27:1, Lk23:2–3

19:6–16a
//Mk15:1–15; Mt27:11–26; Lk23:1–7, 13–25

18:19b–21a There is reason to think that the substance of this interrogation, in John, has been removed to chap. 10 and there been expanded. The bracketed material here is a rough attempt to reconstruct part of what may have been removed.

18:28–19:16a In John the Roman trial is a drama of seven scenes, but in SG it was probably rather brief; its reconstruction is unclear at several points.

18:29 *"What charge are you bringing against this man?" . . .*: An original answer has perhaps been replaced by the leaders' arrogant reply (now 18:30). But from Pilate's question to Jesus in what follows (v. 33) it is clear enough that Jesus is being charged with insurrection.

19:13 *sat down on the judge's seat*: Because of an ambiguity in the Greek this can be translated in John as a kind of enthronement of Jesus by Pilate ("sat *him* on the judge's seat"); here it can only mean that Pilate will now sentence Jesus, having cynically abandoned a fleeting attempt to release him (18:38). In SG there seems to be no interest in exonerating Pilate so as to incriminate the Jewish leaders.

Jesus is crucified

in the place called Stone Pavement (Gabbatha in Hebrew). [14a]It was
now the day of preparation, about twelve noon. [[1]Then Pilate had Jesus
taken away and beaten. [2]And the soldiers wove a crown out of thorns
and put it on his head; they also dressed him up in a purple robe. [3]They
began marching up to him: "Greetings, 'King of the Judeans,'" they
would say, as they slapped him in the face.] [16a]And so, in the end,
⟨Pilate⟩ turned him over to them to be crucified.

So they took Jesus, [17]who carried the cross for himself, out to the
place called Skull (known in Hebrew as Golgotha). [18]There they crucified him, and with him two others—one on each side, with Jesus in the
middle. [19]Pilate also had a notice written and posted it on the cross; it
read: "Jesus the Nazarene, the King of the Judeans," [20b]and it was
written in Hebrew, Latin, and Greek. [23]When the soldiers had crucified Jesus, they took his clothes and divided them into four shares, one
share for each soldier. But his shirt was woven continuously without
seam. [24]So they said to each other, "Let's not tear it, but toss to see who
gets it." This happened so that the scripture would come true that says,

> They divided my garments among them,
> and for my clothes they cast lots.

So while the soldiers did this, [25]Jesus' mother, his mother's sister, Mary
the wife of Clopas, and Mary of Magdala stood by his cross. [28]Then, so
the scripture would come true, Jesus says, "I'm thirsty." [29]A bowl of
sour wine was sitting there, and so they filled a sponge with wine, put it
on some hyssop, and held it to his mouth. [30]When Jesus had taken
some wine, he said,"It's all over." His head sank and he breathed his
last.

[[31]Since it was the day of preparation, *they* asked Pilate to have the
legs of the three broken and the bodies taken away. Otherwise their
bodies would remain on the cross during the sabbath day. That sabbath
was a high holy day.] [32]*So* the soldiers came and broke the legs of the
first man, and then of the other who had been crucified with him. [33]But
when they came to Jesus, they could see that he was already dead, so
they didn't break his legs. [34]Instead, one of the soldiers jabbed him in
the side with his spear, and right away blood and water came pouring
out. [36]This happened so the scripture that says,

19:1–3 //Mk15:16–20, Mt27:27–31, Pet2:3b–3:4
19:16b–30 //Mk15:22–37, Mt27:33–50, Lk22:32–46, Pet4:1–5
19:24 ◊Ps22:18
19:28–30 Cf.Pet5:1–5
19:28–29 ◊Ps69:21
19:31 ◊Dt21:22–23
19:36 ◊Ps34:20

19:14a *the day of preparation*: For Passover, or the sabbath day, or both; see also 19:31, 42.

19:1–3 The ritual scourging of a condemned man would most naturally come here in the story. In John, where it is placed earlier, as its verse numbers show, it has a different function.

19:24 *This happened so that the scripture would come true*: A reiteration of the rationale that all this is happening—here in precise detail—by divine necessity. The quotation is from Ps 22:18.

19:28 *so the scripture would come true*: The by now familiar formula, evidently with Ps 22:15 or 69:21 in mind.

19:31 This request, with its evident concern chiefly for Israelite law, may be a later addition to SG. Otherwise we are left uncertain who makes it: the women standing nearby? the disciples—if they are still present?

Joseph buries Jesus

Mary & Peter at the tomb

Mary meets Jesus

No bone of his shall be broken,

would come true, [37]as well as another scripture that says,

They shall look at the one they have pierced.

[38]**After all this,** Joseph of Arimathea, a disciple of Jesus, asked
Pilate's permission to take Jesus' body down. Pilate agreed, so
⟨Joseph⟩ came and took his body down, [40b]wound it up in strips of
burial cloth along with spices. [41]Now there was a garden in the place
where he had been crucified, and a new tomb in the garden where no
one had yet been laid to rest. [42]Since this tomb was handy and because
of the day of preparation, it was here that ⟨he⟩ laid Jesus.

Jesus' Resurrection
20:1–10/20:11–18/20:19–22

20 [1]**On Sunday, by the half-light** of the early morning, Mary of Magdala comes to the tomb—and sees that the stone has been moved away.
[2]So she runs and comes to Simon Peter and tells [him], "They've taken
the Master from the tomb, and we don't know where they've put him."
[3]So Peter went out, and they make their way to the tomb, [6b]and Simon
Peter went in and sees the strips of burial cloth there, [7]and also the
cloth they had used to cover his head, not lying with the strips of burial
cloth but rolled up by itself. [9]But since neither of them yet understood
the prophecy that he *must* rise from the dead, [10][Peter] went back
home.

[11]**Mary, however, stood** crying outside, and in her tears she stooped
to look into the tomb, [12]and she sees two heavenly messengers in white
seated where Jesus' body had lain, one at the head and the other at the
feet. [13]"Woman, why are you crying?" they ask her. "They've taken my
Master away," she tells them, "and I don't know where they've put
him." [14]No sooner had she said this than she turned around and sees
Jesus standing there. [15]"Woman," Jesus says to her, "why are you
crying? Who is it you're looking for?" She could only suppose that it
was the gardener, and so she says to him,"Please, mister, if you've
moved him, tell me where you've put him so I can take him away."

19:37
◊Zec 12:10
19:38–42
//Mk 15:42–47; Mt 27:57–61; Lk 23:50–56; Pet 2:1–3a, 6:1–4
20:1–10
//Mk 16:1–6, Mt 28:1–6, Lk 24:1–7; cf. Pet 12:1–13:3
20:11–18
//Mt 28:7–9, Lk 24:9–10

19:36–37 SG's justification of Jesus' death culminates in a double proof-text, with the usual formula. The first seems to be a combination of Ps 34:20 with passages from Torah about the paschal lamb (Exod 12:46; Num 9:12); the second quotes Zech 12:10.

20:1 No *stone* was mentioned at Jesus' burial, but it was a common practice to close a tomb in this way (see 11:38–39).

20:2 *tells him*: With the later addition of "the disciple that Jesus loved most" to this scene, this would have been changed to "them," as now in John. Similarly SG would read *Peter* in v. 10.

20:15 *so I can take him away*: Perhaps to give Jesus a less hasty burial, or at least—now that his body has evidently been removed—to re-bury him. Her original intent in coming to the tomb (v.1) is not explained.

16"Mary," says Jesus. She turns around and exclaims in Hebrew,
"Rabbi!" 17 ac"Don't touch me," Jesus tells her, "but go to my brothers
and tell them." 18Mary of Magdala goes and reports to the disciples, "I
have seen the Master!"

Behind locked doors

19**That Sunday evening,** the disciples had locked the doors but Jesus
came and stood in front of them and he greets them: "Peace." 20Then
he showed them his hands and his side. The disciples were delighted
to see the Master. 22And at this he breathed over them and says,
"Here's holy spirit. Take it."

Conclusion

The Closing
20:30–31ab

30**Although Jesus performed** many more *signs* for his disciples to see
than could be written down in this book, 31 abthese are written down so
you will come to believe that Jesus is the Anointed, God's son.

20:17
Ⓣ SJas6:13
20:19–22
//Lk24:33–49; cf.Mk16:14–18

20:22 *Here's holy spirit. Take it*: Fulfilling the promise the Baptist had implied at 1:33, having himself just seen Jesus receive the spirit (1:32).

20:30–31ab Perhaps this once was the ending of a Signs Source in the narrow sense, without a passion narrative. Here these words—because of Jesus' greatest sign, his own resurrection (see 2:19)—properly conclude the Signs Gospel, a Signs Source expanded to include Jesus' death and resurrection.

20:31ab *believe that Jesus is the Anointed, God's son*: From the start, the chief purpose of SG (1:6, 41, 49).

The Judeans

The religious tradition known today as Judaism—the religion practiced by Jews—has a long history, which may be divided into three major periods:

The religion of the first temple (ca. 950–586 B.C.E.)
The religion of the second temple (ca.520 B.C.E.–70 C.E.)
The religion of rabbis and synagogue (ca. 90 C.E. and continuing)

By convention, scholars refer to the religion of the first temple as Israelite religion. The first temple was constructed in Jerusalem by King Solomon in the mid-tenth century B.C.E. and became the center of Israelite national life. The first temple was destroyed by the Babylonians, who completed their conquest of Judah—the southern kingdom—in 586 B.C.E.

The temple was reconstructed about seventy years later, around 520 B.C.E., under the leadership of Zerubbabel, the local governor commissioned by the Persians. The second temple was renovated and extended by Herod the Great (37–4 B.C.E.). It was the second temple in its new splendor that Jesus and his contemporaries visited when they came to Jerusalem.

In determining what to call the religion of the second temple, it is necessary to recall some important earlier history.

The people of Israel had become a nation by the tenth century under Kings Saul, David, and Solomon. When Solomon died, the nation divided into a northern and a southern kingdom; the northern kingdom alone was known as Israel, the southern as Judah. The northern kingdom ceased to exist when its capital, Samaria, fell after a long siege by the Assyrians in 721 B.C.E. Citizens of the northern kingdom were deported by the thousands, and the northern monarchy never recovered.

The restoration that began around 520 B.C.E. was focused in Judah and Jerusalem. The central part of the northern kingdom, meanwhile, had become peopled by Samaritans, who were of mixed ethnic background, and who worshiped at their temple on Mt. Gerizim. They preserved their own version of the Torah (the five books ascribed to Moses) and claimed the legacy of northern Israelite religion as their own. The southern legacy passed exclusively into the hands of citizens of Judah, who came to be known as Judeans and their territory as Judea.

The religion of the second temple should be termed Judean religion, just as the people who practiced this religion (even outside Judea) were known as Judeans. The religion of the second temple centered in the sacrificial cult connected with Jerusalem and dominated by a priestly caste. That would make it possible to refer to the religion of the third major period as Judaism, the religion practiced by Jews, whose religious leaders are rabbis and whose worship is centered in the synagogue rather than the temple. In current terminology, scholars find it necessary to add the qualifier "rabbinic" to Judaism to distinguish the third period from the religion of the second temple.

The Scholars Version, accordingly, has adopted the following terminology for the three phases of the religion practiced by the Israelites, the Judeans, and the Jews:

(1) Israel, Israelites and Israelite religion: first temple
(2) Judea, Judeans and Judean religion: second temple
(3) Jews and Judaism: religion of the rabbis, talmud, and synagogue

In the Scholars Version, the placard placed on the cross reads: "King of the Judeans," and those stereotyped opponents of Jesus in the Gospel of John are regularly "Judeans." This terminological adjustment has been a long time in coming. The failure to observe crucial transitions in the history of Judaism has contributed to the tragic history of anti-semitism among Christians, which the new terminology will help put to an end. Further, it will set the historical record straight.

Introduction

John and the Synoptics

From early times Christians have recognized that "the Gospel according to John" is dramatically different from the synoptic gospels (Mark, Matthew, Luke). In John there is nothing of Jesus' teaching in parables or his associating with the outcast. He performs no exorcisms and barely gives ethical teaching. He speaks of God's imperial rule on only one occasion (3:3, 5) but claims a rule ("government") of his own (18:36). Virtually nothing is found here of the synoptic eschatology (see the notes on 5:24; 8:51; and 14:3). We hear of ranking priests and Pharisees (perhaps reflecting the author's own experience more than Jesus' time), but nothing of Sadducees, Zealots, scholars, elders, toll collectors, prostitutes, rich and poor. Jesus accomplishes miracles but in the Greek they are called "signs"—just what the synoptics' Jesus refuses to give—and are done solely to prove that Jesus is the incarnate Son of God. This focus on Jesus' divinity—established not by birth narratives as in Matthew and Luke but by the sonorous theological language of the hymn to the eternal divine word become human (1:1–18)—is both more prominent and at the same time simply taken for granted. Jesus speaks not like the first-century itinerant teacher that he in fact was but as if he were from heaven, revealing the nature of God ("my Father"—see especially 5:18). All the gospels paint a Christian, that is, a post-resurrection, portrait of Jesus, but this gospel far more than the others. The later Christian creeds were based on the theological language of John's gospel much more than on that of the synoptic gospels.

This gospel's uniqueness does not stem, apparently, from a deliberate intent to differ from the synoptic gospels, for it was probably independent of them literarily. It overlaps with them in the *narratives*—of Jesus' miracles and of his "passion" and resurrection—but this overlap is probably due to common sources underlying the various gospels.

Jesus' teaching

It is the *discourses* of Jesus, his long monologues on truth, life, light, that distinguish this gospel's portrait of him. There is virtually nothing of this teaching in the synoptics, and it seems to be the expression partly of a Jesus tradition unique to this gospel and partly of the interpretation given that tradition within the gospel's Christian Jewish community, in the light of what that community has experienced. This discourse tradition may be rooted in the teaching of the shadowy figure known as "the disciple Jesus loved most," perhaps the founder of the distinctive Christian community out of which this gospel arises. But despite what is claimed in the comment inserted in 21:24, there is in this gospel very little of the historical Jesus' actual teaching (see further the notes on that verse). And it is not altogether certain that this Beloved Disciple, as he has usually been known, was in fact a real person.

The words of the Johannine Jesus are often ambiguous—even deliberately confusing his listeners (e.g., 3:3), conveying two levels of meaning at once. Thus, Jesus frequently says "I am," which at face value means only something like "It's me" (e.g., 6:20) but equally expresses the divine I AM of the Hebrew Scriptures. He cryptically refers to his "time," points out how frequently his hearers do not understand what he is saying, and announces his solemn declarations with the formula, "As God is my witness" or "I swear to God," and with its double preface (literally, "Amen Amen") the formula is still more mysterious than in the synoptics. He refers to himself as "the son of Adam," just as in the other gospels, but here it means something closer to "the true human being," as expressed by Pilate when he presents Jesus to the hostile crowd in 19:5.

A Jewish Christian gospel

The ideological milieu of this gospel is thoroughly Jewish: even the abstract and dualistic symbolism (such as light/darkness) comes from a world that has very little to do with Gentile culture. Nevertheless, this document is ardently anti-Jewish. Only here are the Jewish people spoken of monolithically and from the outside; in the other gospels Pilate alone uses the phrase "the Jews." The explanation appears to be that this group of Christian Jews has recently been expelled from the synagogue (9:22, 34; 12:42; 16:2) and therefore has a highly ambivalent, and frequently hostile, attitude toward *Ioudaioi*. Traditionally translated into English as "Jews," the term is indistinguishable in Greek from "Judeans"; at the time, "Jews" were simply those who survived the fall of the Kingdom of Judah and had their spiritual base, and in many cases their actual residence, in what Rome called Judea. This gospel has given rise, still more than Matthew, to savage Christian anti-Semitism down the subsequent centuries. For this, and other reasons (see the cameo essay "Jews and Judeans," pp. 193–94), in almost every case the phrase is here translated by the more neutral term, "the Judeans."

Despite its utter Jewishness, the so-called Fourth Gospel has a mentality quite different from that of Jesus, and from Matthew too, the most Jewish of the synoptics. Instead of portraying God's imperial rule breaking into human history for the sake of redeeming or judging Israel, this gospel thinks on a cosmic scale. The very term "world" (*kosmos*) is fundamental in the Johannine vocabulary, and it is used negatively to speak of the nationalistic realms of Roman and Jew alike—7:7 (see the note there) is only one instance of many—as well as positively, affirming all of creation and humanity. This broadened world view is probably due both to the "wisdom" tradition that has informed the Johannine version of Jesus' teaching and to the fact that the Christians for whom the gospel was written could no longer think of themselves in nationalist terms. The universality that Paul espoused and that of "John" are arrived at by rather different paths, but both contribute to early Christianity's growing awareness of itself as a religion separate from and more inclusive than Judaism.

Thus, the Jesus of this gospel argues with the Jewish scholars, sometimes about arcane matters of biblical interpretation (e.g., 3:13), sometimes about the ultimate issues of salvation and truth and authentic life. As the incarnate son of God, savior of the world, this Jesus both appeals to the authority of the Jewish ancestors Abraham and Moses and presents himself as anterior and superior to them. The interlocking themes of continuity and discontinuity run like tapestry threads through the theological debates that comprise so much of this gospel. Indeed, he says, "I existed before there was an Abraham," and dares to speak the divine "I AM," which breaks upon its hearers with shock and rage.

If the synoptics' Jesus appeals to the "trust" of those who hear and would follow him, for our gospel the same term (*pistis*) means "belief"—in Jesus' divine sonship and in the rescue from the world's stranglehold that he offers. Jesus' miracles, along with all that he has said and done, are written "so you will come to believe that Jesus is the Anointed, God's son—and by believing this have life in his name" (20:30–31).

Origin

Where and when was this gospel written? It is addressed: to an audience of whom part are (or until recently were) bilingual, thinking in both Greek and "Hebrew"; to a city having a substantial and effective Jewish presence, over against which those "who were born from God" and "have believed in his name" understand themselves as a beleaguered but divinely vindicated minority; and to a perspective not far removed from that of Galilee and Judea. A small city in Syria is perhaps the best informed guess. And the date would be within the decade or two following the centralized Jewish decision to expel believers in Jesus from the synagogue, that is, during the last fifteen years or so of the first century—roughly contemporary with, but evidently independent of, the writing of Matthew and Luke-Acts. The author, like the three other "evangelists," is anonymous and only a century later was identified with John, the son of Zebedee (and he with "the disciple Jesus loved most").

The work divides, at the beginning of chap. 13, roughly into two halves: (1) the account of Jesus' public career, with its miracles and the discourses they occasion, and (2) the last supper (consisting mostly of Jesus' farewell instructions to "his own"), followed immediately by his arrest, trial, and execution, and finally the resurrection. Chapter 21 appears to be a later appendix to the original gospel.

The Gospel of John

The divine word and wisdom

1 ***In the beginning*** there was the divine word and wisdom.

The divine word and wisdom was there with God,
and it was what God was.
2It was there with God from the beginning.
3Everything came to be by means of it;
nothing that exists came to be without its agency.
4In it was life,
and this life was the light of humanity.
5Light was shining in darkness,
and darkness did not master it.

6There appeared a man sent from God named John. 7He came to
testify—to testify to the light—so everyone would believe through
him. 8He was not the light; he came only to attest to the light.

9Genuine light—the kind that provides light for everyone
—was coming into the world.
10Although it was in the world,
and the world came about through its agency,
the world did not recognize it.
11It came to its own place,
but its own people were not receptive to it.
12But to all who did embrace it,
to those who believed in it,
it gave the right to become children of God.
13They were not born from sexual union,
not from physical desire,
and not from male willfulness:
they were born of God.

1:1 Cf. Gn 1:1
1:9–11 Ⓣ Th 24:3

1:1–18 With the exception of vv. 6–8 and 15, which seem to be interruptions, this prologue is in the form of Semitic poetry.

1:1 *the divine word and wisdom:* This double phrase attempts to express for the moment the complex and difficult Greek term *Logos*, whose various meanings include *concept*, *pattern*, *reason*, *speech*, and *revelation*. Its precise function here will become clearer as this prologue unfolds.

there with: or "facing," difficult to express in English.

it: Not until v. 14 will it emerge that "the divine word and wisdom" is to be identified with a person, God's *only son*.

1:5 *did not master:* A deliberate ambiguity, meaning both "did not overcome" and "did not understand."

1:6–8 See the note on vv. 1–18.

1:9 *Genuine light . . . into the world:* Or, *There was genuine light providing light for everyone who comes into the world.*

A voice in the wilderness

[14]The divine word and wisdom became human
and made itself at home among us.
We have seen its majesty,
majesty appropriate
to a Father's only son,
brimming with generosity and truth.

[15]John testifies on his behalf and has called out, "This is the one I was talking about when I said, 'He who is to come after me is actually my superior, because he was there before me.'"

[16]From his richness
all of us benefited—
one gift after another.
[17]Law was given through Moses;
mercy and truth came through Jesus the Anointed.
[18]No one has ever seen God;
the only son, an intimate of the Father—he has disclosed ⟨him⟩.

[19]***This is what John had to say*** when the Judeans sent priests and Levites from Jerusalem to ask him, "Who are you?"
[20]He made it clear—he wouldn't deny it—"I'm not the Anointed."
[21]And they asked him, "Then what are you? Are you Elijah?"
And he replies, "I am not."
"Are you the Prophet?"
He answered, "No."
[22]So they said to him, "Tell us who you are so we can report to those who sent us. What have you got to say for yourself?"
[23]He replied, "I am the voice of someone shouting in the wilderness, 'Make the way of the Lord straight'—that's how Isaiah the prophet put it."
([24]It was the Pharisees who had sent them.)

1:14 Ⓣ Th 28:1, SJas 6:23, DSav 2
1:15 Cf. Q 7:19, Mt 11:2–3, Lk 7:19
1:18 ◊ Ex 33:20
1:19–28 Cf. Mk 1:2–8, Mt 3:1–2, Lk 3:1–20
1:21 Ⓣ Mt 11:13–14; ◊ Mal 4:5
1:23 //Mk 1:2–3, Mt 3:3, Lk 3:4–6; ◊ Is 40:3

1:18 Some mss read "only begotten God" in place of *only son.*

1:14 *generosity*: The same word (*charis*—usually rendered "grace") is translated *gift* in v. 16 and *mercy* in v. 17.
1:15 See the note on vv. 1–18.
testifies: Greek narrative alternates between past and present tense, rather like our use in story telling ("When I told her, do you know what she says to me?") but in Greek more acceptably written than in English. Other translations usually render these "historic presents" in the past tense, depriving the Greek narration of its immediacy and freshness. Sometimes, as here and, e.g., 1:29, the present calls attention to a new element in the story.
when I said: This refers to an event still to come, in 1:30.
1:17 There is no conjunction logically connecting the two clauses of this verse. To supply either "but" or "and" would do violence to what is very likely meant to be ambiguous; the gospel affirms both the contrast and the continuity between Judaism and Christianity—represented here respectively by Moses and Christ.
1:21 *the Prophet:* Probably the one like himself promised by Moses (Deut 18:15); this was another figure like *the Anointed*, who as with *Elijah*, was expected by some at the beginning of the new age.
1:24 *who had sent them:* or, *who had been sent.*

John's testimony

[25]"So," they persisted, "why are you baptizing if you're not the Anointed, not Elijah, and not the Prophet?"

Andrew & Peter

[26]John answered them, "I baptize, yes, but only with water. Right there with you is someone you don't yet recognize; [27]he's the one who is to be my successor. I don't even deserve to untie his sandal straps."

[28]All this took place in Bethany on the far side of the Jordan, where John was baptizing.

[29]***The next day*** John sees Jesus approaching and says, "Look, the lamb of God, who does away with the sin of the world. [30]This is the one I was talking about when I said, 'Someone is coming after me who is actually my superior, because he was there before me.' [31]I didn't know who he was, although I came baptizing with water so he would be revealed to Israel."

[32]And John continued to testify: "I have seen the spirit coming down like a dove out of the sky, and it hovered over him. [33]I wouldn't have recognized him, but the very one who sent me to baptize with water told me, 'When you see the spirit come down and hover over someone, that's the one who baptizes with holy spirit.' [34]I have seen this and I have certified: This is God's son."

[35]The next day John was standing there again with two of his disciples. [36]When he noticed Jesus walking by, he says, "Look, the lamb of God."

[37]His two disciples heard him ⟨say this⟩, and they followed Jesus. [38]Jesus turned around, saw them following, and says to them, "What are you looking for?"

They said to him, "Rabbi" (which means Teacher), "where are you staying?"

[39]He says to them, "Come and see."

They went and saw where he was staying and spent the day with him. It was about four in the afternoon.

[40]***Andrew, Simon Peter's brother,*** was one of the two who followed Jesus after hearing John ⟨speak about him⟩. [41]First he goes and finds his brother Simon and tells him, "We have found the Messiah" (which is translated, Anointed), [42]and he took him to Jesus.

When Jesus laid eyes on him, he said "You're Simon, John's son; you're going to be called Kephas" (which means Peter ⟨or Rock⟩).

1:26–27 //Q3:16, Mt3:11, Lk3:16
1:29–34 Cf. Mk1:9–11, Mt3:13–17, Lk3:21–22, GHeb3
1:30 Ⓘ Jn1:15
1:32 //Mk1:10, Mt3:16, Lk3:22
1:33 Ⓣ Acts1:5, 11:16, 19:1–7
1:41 Ⓣ Mk8:29, Mt16:16, Lk9:20
1:42 Ⓣ Mk3:16, Mt10:2, Lk6:14

1:28 Some mss read "Bethabara" in place of *Bethany.*

1:27 *To untie sandal straps* was a slave's task.
1:28 *Bethany on the far side of the Jordan:* A place otherwise unknown, possibly intended to balance the Bethany of 11:1 (see 10:40).
1:29 *the world:* Possibly this phrase here lacks the negative meaning it often has in this gospel; see the note on 7:7.
1:41 *First:* A sequel to this word is missing.

Messiah: In the NT, only here and at 4:29 is found the Aramaic original behind the Greek word *Christ.*

Kephas: From *kepha*, the Aramaic word for *rock.*

Peter: From *petra*, the Greek word for *rock.*

Philip & Nathanael

43 ***The next day*** Jesus decided to leave for Galilee. He finds Philip and says to him, "Follow me."

44 Philip was from Bethsaida, the hometown of Andrew and Peter. 45 Philip finds Nathanael and tells him, "We've found the one Moses wrote about in the Law, and the prophets mention too: Jesus, Joseph's son, from Nazareth."

46 "From Nazareth?" Nathanael said to him. "Can anything good come from that place?"

Philip replies to him, "Come and see."

47 Jesus saw Nathanael coming toward him, and he remarks about him: "There's a genuine Israelite—not a trace of deceit in him."

48 "Where do you know me from?" Nathanael asks him.

Jesus replied, "I saw you under the fig tree before Philip invited you ⟨to join us⟩."

49 Nathanael responded to him, "Rabbi, you are God's son! You are King of Israel!"

50 Jesus replied, "Do you believe just because I told you I saw you under the fig tree? You're going to see far more than that."

51 Then he adds, "As God is my witness before you all: You'll see the sky split open and God's messengers traveling to and from the son of Adam."

Miracle at Cana

2 ***Three days later*** there was a wedding in Cana, Galilee. Jesus' mother was there. 2 Jesus was also invited to the wedding along with his disciples. 3 When the wine had run out, Jesus' mother says to him, "They're out of wine."

4 Jesus replies to her, "Woman, what is it with you and me? It's not my time yet."

5 His mother says to the servants, "Whatever he tells you, do it."

6 Six stone water-jars were standing there—for use in the Jewish rite of purification—and each could hold twenty or thirty gallons.

7 "Fill the jars with water," Jesus tells them.

So they filled them to the brim.

8 Then he tells them, "Now dip some out and take it to the caterer."

And they did so. 9 When the caterer tasted the water, now changed into wine—he had no idea where it had come from, even though the servants who had taken the water out knew—he calls the groom aside 10 and says to him, "Everyone serves the best wine first and only later,

1:43
Cf. Mk 1:14, Mt 4:12, Lk 4.14
1:49
Ⓣ Mt 16:16
1:51
Cf. Mk 14:62, Mt 26:64, Lk 22:68
2:4
Cf. Mk 5:7, Lk 8:28

1:51 *to and from:* Greek, *up and down*, like the angels on the ladder in Jacob's dream (Gen 28:12).

2:4 *Woman, what is it with you and me?:* A strangely hostile way for a man to address his mother; *Woman* is abrupt and disrespectful, and the question is the same as that used by demons to address Jesus in Mark 1:24 and Luke 4:34 (see 1 Kgs 17:18).

my time: Jesus' *time* has a special significance in this gospel; see 4:21; 5:25; 13:1. That he seems to object to his mother's implied request and then proceeds to work the miracle is puzzling; evidently there is something improper about wanting a miracle. See 2:18; 20:29, and the note on 6:26.

Jesus in Jerusalem

Conversation with Nicodemus

when people are drunk, the cheaper wine. But you've held back the
good wine till now."
[11]Jesus performed this miracle, the first, in Cana, Galilee; it displayed his majesty, and his disciples believed in him.
[12]Then he went down to Capernaum, he and his mother and brothers and disciples; but they stayed there only a few days.
[13]***It was almost time*** for the Jewish Passover celebration, so Jesus
went up to Jerusalem. [14]In the temple precincts he came upon people
selling oxen and sheep and doves, and bankers were doing business
there too. [15]He made a whip out of rope and drove them all out of the
temple area, sheep, oxen, and all; then he knocked over the bankers'
tables, and set their coins flying. [16]And to the dove merchants he said,
"Get these birds out of here! How dare you use my Father's house as a
public market."
([17]His disciples were reminded of the words of scripture: "Zeal for
your house is eating me alive.")
[18]To this the Judeans responded, "What miracle can you show us ⟨to
justify⟩ doing all this?"
[19]Jesus replied, "Destroy this temple and I'll resurrect it in three
days."
[20]"It has taken forty-six years to build this temple," the Judeans said,
"and you can reconstruct it in three days?"
([21]However, he was referring to his body as a temple. [22]When he had
been raised from the dead his disciples remembered that he had made
this remark, and so they came to believe both the written word and the
word Jesus had spoken.)
[23]When he was in Jerusalem at the Passover celebration, many
believed in him once they saw with their own eyes the miracles he
performed. [24]But Jesus didn't trust himself to them, because he understood them all too well. [25]He didn't need to know more about humanity; he knew what people were really like.

2:12 Cf. Mk 1:21, Mt 4:12–13, Lk 4:31
2:13–17 //Mk 11:15–17, Mt 21:12–13, Lk 19:45–46
2:17 ◊Ps 69:9
2:18–22 Cf. Mk 11:27–33, Mt 21:23–27, Lk 20:1–8
2:19 //Mk 14:57–58, 15:29; Mt 26:60–61, 27:40; cf. Th 71
3:2 Cf. Mk 12:14, Mt 22:16, Lk 20:21, EgerG 3:2

3 ***A Pharisee named Nicodemus,*** a Judean leader, [2]came to ⟨Jesus⟩
during the night and said, "Rabbi, we know that you've come as a
teacher from God; after all, nobody can perform the miracles you do
unless God is with him."

2:11 *it displayed:* or *he displayed.*
2:17 *is eating me alive:* There may be a wordplay here, meaning both "demanding all my attention" and "leading to my destruction."
2:20 *forty-six years:* Herod's reconstruction of the temple was evidently begun in 20/19 B.C.E., so this datum, if it is accurate, would suggest the year 27/28 C.E. as the date for such a statement as this, or its origin. Some have suggested consequently that Jesus' age is to be taken as 46 years (see 8:57—"You're not even 50 years old"), but a factual concern such as this does not appear to be any more important in this gospel than in the others, with the possible exception of Luke.
2:23 *believed in him:* literally, "believed in his name" (as in 1:12 and 3:18), perhaps a formula meaning "became a Christian."
3:2 *during the night:* See the note on 13:30.

John's final testimony

[3]Jesus replied to him, "As God is my witness: No one can experience God's imperial rule without being reborn from above."

[4]Nicodemus says to him, "How can an adult be reborn? Can you reenter your mother's womb and be born a second time?"

[5]Jesus replied, "As God is my witness: No one can enter God's domain without being born of water and spirit. [6]What is born of the human realm is human, but what is born of the spiritual realm is spirit. [7]Don't be surprised that I told you, 'Every one of you must be reborn from above.' [8]The spirit blows every which way, like wind: you hear the sound it makes but you can't tell where it's coming from or where it's headed. That's how it is with everyone reborn of the spirit."

[9]"How can that be possible?" Nicodemus retorted.

[10]Jesus replied, "You are a teacher of Israel, and you don't understand this? [11]As God is my witness: We tell what we know, and we give evidence about what we've seen, but none of you accepts our evidence. [12]If I tell you about what's mundane and you don't believe, how will you believe if I tell you about what's heavenly? [13]No one has gone up to heaven except the one who came down from there—the son of Adam."

[14]In the wilderness Moses elevated the snake; in the same way the son of Adam is destined to be elevated, [15]so every one who believes in him can have real life. [16]This is how God loved the world: God gave up an only son, so that every one who believes in him will not be lost but have real life. [17]After all, God sent this son into the world not to condemn the world but to rescue the world through him. [18]Those who believe in him are not condemned. Those who don't believe in him are already condemned: they haven't believed in God's only son. [19]This is the verdict ⟨on them⟩: Light came into the world but people loved darkness instead of light. Their actions were evil, weren't they? [20]All those who do evil things hate the light and don't come into the light—otherwise their deeds would be exposed. [21]But those who do what is true come into the light so the nature of their deeds will become evident: their deeds belong to God.

[22]***After this*** Jesus and his disciples went to Judea, and he extended his stay with them there and began to baptize. [23]John was baptizing too, in Aenon near Salim, since there was plenty of water around; and people kept coming to be baptized. ([24]Remember, John hadn't yet been thrown in prison.)

3:3–8 Cf. Th 22
3:3–5 Ⓣ SJas 2:6
3:3 Cf. Mk 10:15, Mt 18:3, Lk 18:17
3:6 Ⓣ Th 112
3:14 Nm 21:9

3:13 Some mss add "who is in heaven" after *son of Adam.*

3:3 *reborn from above:* An attempt to capture both senses in Jesus' ambiguous phrase (literally meaning either "reborn" or "born from above"), a Johannine wordplay that Nicodemus fails to grasp (v. 4).

3:11 *As God is my witness:* Addressed to Nicodemus, but from this point he fades from view and Jesus addresses his audience (presumably the Judeans in general) with the second person plural.

3:13 Under the constraints of modern punctuation, it is usual to end Jesus' words either here or at v. 21. No such problem faced the ancient writer; Jesus' words merge into those of the evangelist—or perhaps no such distinction is to be made.

3:22 *to Judea:* or, *into the Judean countryside*; in Jerusalem, Jesus is of course already in Judea.

The one from above

The woman at the well

[25]A dispute over purification broke out between John's disciples and
one of the Judeans. [26]They came to John and reported: "Rabbi, that
fellow who was with you across the Jordan—you spoke about him
earlier—guess what! He's now baptizing and everyone is flocking to
him."
[27]John answered, "You can't lay claim to anything unless it's a gift
from heaven. [28]You yourselves can confirm this: I told you I was not
the Anointed but had been sent on ahead of him. [29]The bride belongs
to the groom, and the best man stands with him and is happy enough
just to be close at hand. So I am content. [30]He can only grow in
importance; my role can only diminish."
[31]***The one who comes from above*** is superior to everyone. Earthly
things are simply earthly and give voice to their earthliness. The one
who comes from heaven [32]testifies to what he has seen and heard—
little wonder that no one accepts his testimony! [33]Whoever does accept
his testimony can guarantee that God is truthful. [34]In other words, the
one God sent speaks God's language, since the spirit does not give by
half measures. [35]The Father loves the son and has entrusted everything
to him. [36]Those who entrust themselves to the son have real life, but
those who refuse the son will not see life; no, they remain the object of
God's wrath.

4 ***Jesus was aware*** of the rumor that had reached the Pharisees:
Jesus is recruiting and baptizing more disciples than John. ([2]Actually,
Jesus himself didn't baptize anyone; his disciples did the baptizing.)
[3]So he left Judea again for Galilee. [4]His route took him through
Samaria.
[5]He came to a Samaritan town called Sychar, near the field Jacob
had given to his son Joseph— [6]that's where Jacob's well was. Jesus was
exhausted from traveling, so he sat down on the edge of the well. It was
about noon. [7]When a Samaritan woman comes to get water, Jesus asks
her, "Give me a drink." ([8]In fact, his disciples had already gone off to
town to buy food and drink.)
[9]The woman replies to him, "You are a Judean; how can you ask a
Samaritan woman for a drink?" (You see, Judeans don't associate with
Samaritans.)

3:35 Cf. Q 10:22, Mt 11:27, Lk 10:22, Th 61:3; Ⓣ Jn 13:3
4:5 ◊ Gn 33:18–19

4:1 Some mss read "the Lord" in place of *Jesus*. **4:9** A few mss lack the sentence in parentheses.

3:31–36 It is unclear who speaks here. See the note on 3:13.

4:2 *Jesus himself didn't baptize* contradicts the obvious sense of 3:22. Perhaps 4:2 is a late gloss, added to accentuate the difference between Jesus and John the Baptist.

4:9 *associate with:* The antipathy of Jews/Judeans toward Samaritans was, among other things, based on the fact that Samaritans were considered neither pure nor ritually "clean"; since the fall of the Northern kingdom of Israel there had been intermarriage in the territory of Samaria, and the Samaritans did not follow the rabbinic interpretation and practical application of Torah that was developing in Judaism.

[10]Jesus answered her, "If you knew what God can give you, and who
just said to you, 'Give me a drink,' you would ask him and he would
give you lively, life-giving water."
[11]"Mister, you don't have anything to draw water with," she says,
"and the well is deep; where will you get this 'lively, life-giving water'?
[12]Can you do better than our patriarch Jacob? He left us this well,
which used to quench his thirst and that of his family and his live-
stock."
[13]Jesus responded to her, "Whoever drinks this water will get thirsty
again; [14]but all who drink the water I'll provide them with will never
get thirsty again; it will be a source of water within them, a fountain of
real life."
[15]The woman says to him, "Sir, give me some of this water, so I'll
never be thirsty or have to keep coming back here for water."
[16]Jesus says to her, "Go, call your husband and come back."
[17]"I don't have a husband," she answered.
"You're right to say that you don't have a husband," Jesus says. [18]"In
fact, you've had five husbands, and the man you are now living with is
not your husband; you've told the truth."
[19]"Master," she exclaims, "I can tell you're a prophet. [20]Our ancestors worshiped on this mountain; you people claim Jerusalem is the
only place for worship."
[21]Jesus says to her, "Woman, believe me, the time is coming when
you won't worship the Father either on this mountain or in Jerusalem.
[22]You people worship God-knows-what; we worship what we know—
'Judeans are the agents of salvation,' and all that. [23]But the time is
coming—in fact, it's already here—for true worshipers to worship the
Father as he truly is, without regard to place. It's worshipers of this sort
that the Father is looking for. [24]God is not tied to place, and those who
worship God must worship him as he truly is, without regard to place."
[25]The woman continues, "All I know is that the Messiah, the one
called Anointed, is going to come; when he does he'll tell us everything." **4:13–15** Cf. Th 13:5
[26]Jesus says to her, "You've been talking to ⟨the Anointed⟩ all along; **4:13–14**
I am he." Ⓣ Th 108:1

4:10–11 *Lively, life-giving:* There is a wordplay here; "living water" is flowing water, as opposed to water in a cistern, but the term soon gains a metaphoric meaning as well (v. 14). The gospel uses the verb "live" and the noun "life" in many important ways.

4:11 *Mister:* The same word (*kyrie*) is translated *sir* in v. 15 and *master* in v. 19, as the woman gradually gains first respect and then devotion toward Jesus.

the well is deep: The word used here (*phrear*) denotes only a deep shaft, not necessarily an underground spring; but in v. 6 this "well" was referred to as also a water source (*pēgē*), an important distinction in that part of the world. The woman assumes that Jesus speaks of "living" water only at the bottom of such a good, deep well; Jesus, however, as so often in this gospel, is speaking on another level of meaning.

4:20 The Samaritan temple on Mt. Gerizim, the most prominent sight from Sychar and Jacob's well, was regarded as a direct competitor and even affront to the temple in Jerusalem, for Jews *the only place for worship.*

4:26 *I am he:* Greek, simply *I am*, used

Real food

Samaritans believe

Official's son

27***But just then*** his disciples returned. They were puzzled that he was talking with a woman, but no one said, "What are you trying to do? Why are you talking with her?" 28At this the woman left her water jar, hurried off to town, and tells everyone, 29"Come, see someone who told me everything I ever did. Could he be the Anointed?"

30They set out from their town and made their way to him.

31Meanwhile the disciples pleaded with him, "Rabbi, eat something."

32He replied to them, "I have food to eat, food you know nothing about."

33The disciples queried each other: "Has someone already brought him food?"

34"Doing the will of the one who sent me and completing his work—that's my food," Jesus tells them. 35"You have a saying: 'It's still four months till harvest.' Yet I tell you: Look at the fields, they're ripe for harvesting. 36The harvester is already getting his pay; he is gathering the crop ⟨that sustains⟩ real life, so planter and harvester can celebrate together. 37Here too the proverb holds true: 'One plants, another harvests.' 38I sent you to harvest what you haven't labored over; others have labored, and you've benefited from their work."

39***Many Samaritans from that town*** had believed in him because of the woman's testimony: "He told me everything I ever did." 40So when those Samaritans got to him they kept begging him to stay with them. And he stayed there for two days. 41And many more believed because of what he said. 42They told the woman, "We no longer believe because of what you said. Now we've listened to him ourselves and we realize that he really is the savior of the world."

43Two days later Jesus left there for Galilee. (44Remember, ⟨Jesus⟩ himself had observed, "A prophet gets no respect on his own turf.")

45So when he came to Galilee, the Galileans welcomed him, since they had seen everything he had done at the celebration in Jerusalem. (They had gone to the celebration too.) 46Then he came back to Cana, Galilee, where he had turned the water into wine.

In Capernaum there was an official whose son was sick. 47When he heard that Jesus had returned to Galilee from Judea, he approached him and pleaded with him to come down and cure his son, who was about to die.

48Jesus said to him, "You people refuse to believe unless you see 'portents and miracles.'"

4:35 Cf. Q10:2, Mt9:38, Lk10:2, Th73
4:44 //Mk6:4, Mt13:57, Lk4:24, Th31
4:46–54 Cf. Q7:1–10, Mt8:5–13, Lk7:1–10
4:48 ◊Ex11:10(LXX)

frequently in the gospel in this everyday sense but often with divine resonance as well, since "I AM" is a version of God's name in the Hebrew Bible (see Exod 3:14–15).

4:27 It was considered indecent in Jewish culture for a man to talk alone with a woman, even in a public place.

4:43 *Two days later:* That is, at the end of his stay (v. 40).

4:44–45 Despite the datum that Jesus is from Nazareth (1:45) or a Nazarene (19:19), in this gospel Jesus' homeland is evidently to be understood as Judea, not Galilee (see 1:11). This differs from the synoptic gospels.

[49]The official responds, "Sir, please come down before my child dies."

Crippled man

[50]Jesus says, "Go, your son is alive and well."

The man believed what Jesus told him and departed. [51]While he was
still on his way home, his slaves met him and told him that his boy was
alive. [52]So he asked them when he had begun to recover, and they told
him, "Yesterday at one o'clock the fever broke."

[53]Then the father realized that one o'clock was precisely the time
Jesus had said to him, "Your son is alive." And he believed, as did all
his household. [54]Jesus performed this second miracle after he had returned from Judea to Galilee.

5 ***After these events,*** on the occasion of a Jewish celebration, Jesus
went up to Jerusalem. [2]In Jerusalem, by the Sheep ⟨Gate⟩, there is a
pool, called *Bethzatha* in Hebrew. It has five colonnades, [3]among
which numerous invalids were usually lying around—blind, lame,
paralyzed. [5]One man had been crippled for thirty-eight years. [6]Jesus
observed him lying there and realized he had been there a long time.

"Do you want to get well?" he asks him.

[7]The crippled man replied, "Sir, I don't have anyone to put me in
the pool when the water is agitated; while I'm trying to get in someone
else beats me to it."

[8]"Get up, pick up your mat and walk around," Jesus tells him.

[9]And at once the man recovered; he picked up his mat and started
walking.

Now that was a sabbath day. [10]So the Judeans said to the man who
had been cured, "It's the sabbath day; you're not permitted to carry
your mat around."

[11]But he explained, "The man who cured me told me, 'Pick up your
mat and walk around.'"

[12]They asked him, "Who is this man who said to you, 'Pick it up and
walk'?"

[13]Now the man who'd been cured had no idea who it was, since
Jesus had withdrawn because people were crowding around.

[14]Later, Jesus finds him in the temple area and said to him, "Look,
you are well now. Don't sin any more, or something worse could
happen to you."

5:2–9 Cf. Mk 2:1–12, Mt 9:1–8, Lk 5:17–26
5:10 ◊Jer 17:21, Neh 13:19
5:14 Cf. EgerG 2:4

5:2 *Bethzatha:* The name varies considerably among mss, *Bethesda* being the most widely attested alternative. **5:3** At the end of this verse, many mss add the following explanatory gloss: "waiting for some movement of the water. ([4]Remember, a heavenly messenger would descend into the pool from time to time and agitate the water; when that happened the first one ⟨into the pool⟩ would be cured of whatever disease he or she had.)"

5:2 *the Sheep ⟨Gate⟩:* There is no noun in Greek; on the basis of archeological evidence this is the best guess.

in Hebrew: The term explained here (as frequently in the gospel) is not actually in Hebrew but in the cognate Aramaic.

Son & father

15The man went and told the Judeans it was Jesus who had cured him. 16And this is the reason the Judeans continued to hound Jesus: he would do things like this on the sabbath day.

17⟨Jesus⟩ would respond to them: "My Father never stops laboring, and I labor as well."

18So this is the reason the Judeans then tried even harder to kill him: Not only did he violate the sabbath day; worse still, he would call God his Father and make himself out to be God's equal.

19***This is how Jesus would respond:*** "As God is my witness, the son can't do anything on his own; ⟨he can only do⟩ what he sees the Father doing. Whatever ⟨the Father⟩ does, the son does as well. 20The Father loves the son, and shows him everything he does. He is going to show him even greater works, so that you'll be amazed. 21Just as the Father raises the dead and gives them life, the son also gives life to everyone he wants. 22Not that the Father condemns anyone; rather, he has turned all such decisions over to the son, 23so that everyone will honor the son, just as they honor the Father. Whoever does not honor the son does not honor the Father who sent him.

24"As God is my witness: Those who hear my word and believe the one who sent me have real life and do not come up for trial. No, they have passed through death into life. 25I swear to God: The time is coming—in fact, it's already here—for the dead to hear the voice of God's son and, because they've heard it, to live. 26Just as the Father is himself the source of life, he has also made the son to be the source of life. 27And he has given him the authority to do the judging, because he is the son of Adam. 28Don't be surprised; the time is coming when all who are in their graves will hear his voice 29and come out—those who have done good will be raised to life, and those who have done vile acts raised to stand trial.

30"I can do nothing on my own authority. I base my decision on what I hear; and my decision is the right one, because I don't consider what I want but what the one who sent me wants. 31If I give evidence on my own behalf, my testimony is not reliable. 32Someone else testifies on my behalf, and I am certain the evidence he gives about me is reliable.

5:19–20
Ⓣ SJas 6:24–26
5:23
Cf. Q 10:16, Mt 10:40, Lk 10:16; Jn 12:44, 13:20
5:29
Ⓣ Mt 25:46, Lk 14:14;
◊ Dn 12:2

5:15 The very person Jesus has cured becomes informer, perhaps a common enough occurrence in the late-first century conflict between Christians and "Judeans" that underlies the gospel.

5:19 *the son:* Typically of this gospel, Jesus speaks of himself in the language of late first-century Christians.

what he sees the Father doing: Because of the intimacy and mutual knowledge between Father and son implied already in 1:1–18.

5:23 *honor the son, just as they honor the Father:* Evidently justifying the Judeans' objection in v. 18 that Jesus *would . . . make himself out to be God's equal* (see Introduction).

5:24 *they have passed through death into life:* Despite some hints of an eventual Last Judgment when finally the dead will be raised and the righteous awarded a place in the new age, this gospel mostly declares that as believers Christians have already undergone that transformation. See the combination of both views in the following verse (*the time is coming—in fact, it's already here—for the dead to hear the voice of God's son*) and the statements that Jesus' followers will *never die* (8:51; 11:26).

Loaves & fish for 5,000

[33]You've sent ⟨messengers⟩ to John, and he has provided reliable testimony. [34]I'm not interested in evidence from a human source; rather, I make these statements so you will be rescued. [35]⟨John⟩ was a bright shining light, and you were willing to bask in that light of his for a while. [36]But I have given evidence that is even weightier than John's: the tasks the Father gave me to carry out. These very tasks I am performing are evidence that the Father has sent me. [37]The one who sent me has himself also given evidence on my behalf. You've never heard his voice, you've never seen his image, [38]and his message doesn't find a home in you, since you don't believe the one he has sent.

[39]"You pore over the ⟨sacred⟩ writings, because you imagine that in them there's real life to be had. They do indeed give evidence on my behalf, [40]yet you refuse to come to me to have life. [41]I'm not interested in any human praise; [42]but I ⟨also⟩ know that you have none of God's love in you. [43]I've come in my Father's name, and you don't welcome me; if others come in their own name, you'll welcome them. [44]How can you believe, since you accept praise from each other but don't even consider the praise that comes from the only God? [45]Don't suppose that I'll be your accuser before the Father. You have an accuser, and it's Moses—the one you thought you could trust. [46]But if you really believed Moses, you'd believe me; after all, I'm the one he wrote about. [47]But since you don't really believe what he wrote, how are you going to believe what I say?"

6 ***After these events,*** Jesus crossed to the far side of the Sea of Galilee, ⟨also known as the Sea of⟩ Tiberias. [2]A huge crowd was following him, because they wanted to see the miracles he was performing on the sick. [3]Jesus climbed up the mountain, and he sat down there with his disciples. [4]It was about time for the Jewish celebration of Passover. [5]Jesus looks up and sees a big crowd approaching him, and he says to Philip, "Where are we going to get enough bread to feed this mob?" ([6]He was saying this to test him; you see, Jesus already knew what he was going to do.)

[7]"Half a year's wages wouldn't buy enough bread for everyone to have a bite," Philip said.

[8]One of his disciples, Andrew, Simon Peter's brother, says to him, [9]"There's a lad here with five loaves of barley bread and two fish; but what does that amount to for so many?"

[10]Jesus said, "Have the people sit down." (They were in a grassy place.) So they sat down; the men alone numbered about five thousand.

5:37 ◊Dt4:12
5:39 //Th52:1, EgerG1:2
5:45 //EgerG1:3
5:46 Cf. EgerG1:6
6:1–15 //Mk6:30–44, 8:1–10; Mt14:13–21, 15:32–39; Lk9:10–17; ◊2Kgs4:42–44

5:45–47 The comparison of Jesus with Moses (1:17) reappears. His writings—the five books of the Law—testify to Jesus (see 1:45) and his actions prefigure what Jesus does (3:14); therefore Moses himself judges those who don't believe in Jesus. The Judeans are pictured as not even believing their own scriptures.

6:1 *the Sea of Galilee, ⟨also known as the Sea of⟩ Tiberias:* or, *the Galilean Sea of Tiberias.* In modern terms this body of water is more a lake than, as traditionally rendered, a "sea."

Jesus walks on the sea

Crowds pursue Jesus

[11]Jesus took the loaves, gave thanks, and passed them around to the people sitting there, along with the fish, and all of them had as much as they wanted. [12]And when they had eaten their fill, he says to his disciples, "Gather up the leftovers so that nothing goes to waste."

[13]So they gathered them up and filled twelve baskets with scraps from the five barley loaves—from what was left over. [14]When these folks saw the miracle he had performed they would say, "Yes indeed! This is undoubtedly the Prophet who is to come into the world." [15]Jesus perceived that they were about to come and make him king by force, so he retreated once again to the mountain by himself.

[16]***As evening approached,*** his disciples went down to the sea. [17]They boarded a boat and were trying to cross the lake to Capernaum. It had already gotten dark, and Jesus still had not joined them. [18]A strong wind began to blow and the sea was getting rough. [19]When they had rowed about three or four miles, they catch sight of Jesus walking on the lake and coming towards the boat. They were frightened, [20]but he says to them, "Don't be afraid! It's me." [21]Then they would have taken him on board, but the boat instantly arrived at the shore they had been making for.

[22]***The next day,*** the crowd, which was still on the other side of the lake, remembered that there had been only one boat there, and that Jesus had not gotten into that boat with the disciples, but that his disciples had set off alone. [23]Other boats came out from Tiberias, near the place where they had eaten bread. [24]So when the crowd saw that neither Jesus nor his disciples were there, they, too, got into boats and set out for Capernaum to look for Jesus.

[25]They found him on the other side of the lake and asked him, "Rabbi, when did you get here?"

[26]"I swear to God," Jesus replied, "you're looking for me only because you ate the bread and had all you wanted, not because you witnessed miracles. [27]Don't work for food that goes to waste, but for food that lasts—food for real life—which the son of Adam will give you; on him God the Father has put his stamp of approval."

[28]So they asked him, "What must we do to set about what God wants done?"

[29]"What God wants you to do," Jesus answered, "is to believe in the one God has sent."

6:14
◊Dt 18:15–18
6:16–21
//Mk 6:45–52, Mt 14:22–33
6:22–24
//Mk 6:53–56, Mt 14:34–36
6:27
◊Is 55:2
6:28–29
Ⓣ DSav 41:4

6:23 At the end of this verse, many mss add "after the Lord had given thanks."

6:14 *the Prophet who is to come into the world:* see the note on 1:21.
6:20 *It's me:* See the note on 4:26.
6:26 Evidently really to *witness miracles* involves more than seeing and even benefitting from them.
6:29 Christian belief is especially important in this gospel: It is presented as fulfilling God's chief wish for humanity.

My mortal flesh

[30]They asked him, "What miracle are you going to perform so we can see it and come to believe in you? What 'labor' are you going to perform? [31]Our ancestors had manna to eat in the wilderness. As the scripture puts it, 'He gave them bread from heaven to eat.'"

[32]Jesus responded to them: "I swear to God, it was not Moses who gave you bread from heaven to eat; rather, it is my Father who gives you real bread from heaven. [33]I mean this: God's bread comes down from heaven and gives life to the world."

[34]"Sir," they said to him, "give us this bread every time."

[35]Jesus explained to them: "I am the bread of life. Anyone who comes to me will never be hungry again, and anyone who believes in me will never again be thirsty. [36]But I told you this: You have even seen me, yet you still refuse to believe. [37]Every one the Father gives me will come to me, and I would never reject anyone who comes to me. [38]Understand, I have come down from heaven, not to do what I want, but to do what the one who sent me wants. [39]What the one who sent me wants is this: that I lose nothing put in my care, but that I resurrect it on the last day. [40]My Father's intent is that all those who see the son and believe in him will have real life, and I'll resurrect them on the last day."

[41]***The Judeans then began*** to grumble about him because he had said, "I am the bread that came down from heaven." [42]They would say things like, "Isn't this Jesus, Joseph's son? Don't we know both his father and his mother? How can he now say, 'I have come down from heaven'?"

[43]Jesus replied, "Don't grumble under your breath. [44]People cannot come to me unless the Father who sent me takes them in, and I will resurrect them on the last day. [45]As the prophets put it: 'And they will all be informed by God.'

"Everyone who listens to the Father and learns from him comes to me. [46]Not that anyone has seen the Father; the only one who has seen the Father is the one who is from God. [47]I swear to God, the believer has real life. [48]I am the bread of life. [49]Your ancestors ate the manna in the desert, but they still died. [50]This is the bread that comes down from heaven: anyone who eats it never dies. [51]I am the life-giving bread that

6:30
Ⓣ Mk8:11, Mt12:38, 16:1; Lk11:16

6:31
▷Neh 9:15; Ps78:24, 105:40; Ex16:14

6:37
Ⓣ SJas9:6

6:42
Cf. Mk6:2–3, Mt13:55–57, Lk4:22

6:45
▷Is54:13

6:48–58
Cf. Mk14:22–25, Mt26:26–29, Lk22:17–20, 1 Cor 11:23–25

6:36 A few mss omit *me.*

6:30 *What miracle are you going to perform?:* Jesus has just worked a miracle, which provoked this very conversation. The questioners' blindness is obvious.

6:30–31 The crowd, in requesting a miracle—and after a miraculous feeding of a multitude with bread—ironically imply that Moses' miracle of feeding the multitude of their *ancestors* with *manna* is greater than anything Jesus can do, thereby falling into their own argumentative trap.

6:32 Just as Jesus claims that he only executes what the Father in fact does, he robs Moses of any credit in the giving of *bread from heaven* in the wilderness. And he shifts attention from what God did in the past to what God is doing now (*gives you real bread from heaven*).

6:46 See 1:18.

6:49 *but they still died:* Again the comparison of Moses and Jesus only shows the former's inferiority.

Disciples grumble

came down from heaven. Anyone who eats this bread will live forever.
And the bread that I will give for the world's life is my mortal flesh."
52At this point the Judeans began quarreling among themselves:
"How can this fellow give us his mortal flesh to eat?"
53So Jesus told them: "I swear to God, if you don't eat the son of
Adam's mortal flesh and drink his blood, you don't possess life.
54Everyone who feeds on my mortal flesh and drinks my blood possesses real life, and I will resurrect them on the last day. 55For my
mortal flesh is real food, and my blood real drink. 56Those who feed on
my mortal flesh and drink my blood are part of me, and I am part of
them. 57The Father of life sent me, and I have life because of the
Father. Just so, anyone who feeds on me will have life because of me.
58This is the bread that comes down from heaven. Unlike your ancestors who ate ⟨manna⟩ and then died, anyone who feeds on this bread
will live forever."
59He said these things while he was teaching in the synagogue at
Capernaum.
60***When the disciples heard this,*** many responded, "This teaching is
offensive. Who can take it seriously?"
61Jesus knew his disciples were grumbling about it and said to them:
"Does this shock you, then? 62What if you should see the son of Adam
going back up to where he was to begin with? 63The spirit is life-giving;
mortal flesh is good for nothing. The words I have used are 'spirit' and
'life.' 64Yet some of you still don't believe." (Jesus was aware from the
outset which ones were not believers, and he knew who would turn
him in.) 65And so he would say, "This is why I told you: People cannot
come to me unless the Father has granted it to them."
66As a result, many of his disciples pulled out and would no longer
travel about with him.
67Jesus then said to the twelve, "Do you want to leave too?"
68Simon Peter replied to him, "Lord, is there anyone else we can
turn to? You have the words of real life! 69We have become believers
and are certain that you are God's holy one."
70Jesus responded to them, "Isn't this why I chose you twelve? Even
so, one of you is a devil." (71He was of course referring to Judas, son of
Simon Iscariot, one of the twelve, who was going to turn him in.)

6:61 Ⓣ Mt 13:57
6:63 Ⓣ SJas 7:7
6:68–69 Cf. Mk 8:29, Mt 16:16, Lk 9:20; Ⓣ Mk 1:24, Lk 4:34
6:70–71 Ⓘ Jn 13:2, 27

6:52 Some mss omit *his*. **6:71** *Iscariot:* Here and elsewhere many mss have variants of this obscure name.

6:53–58 Just as this gospel lacks any depiction of Jesus' actual baptism, so also (at the last supper in chap. 13) Jesus does not "institute" the other great Christian sacrament, the eucharist or Lord's supper. It is debated whether these are deliberate omissions of the traditions firmly imbedded in the synoptic gospels. The present passage reflects an elevated understanding of the Christian eucharist, but even here it is not clear that the reader is to think of the communion bread.

6:63 *mortal flesh:* The Greek term underlying this phrase, used so exaltedly in 1:14 and just above (vv. 51–56), here contrasts with that usage, applying only to Jesus, and means what is ordinary, earthly, material, natural.

To Jerusalem or not?

7 ***After this,*** Jesus moved around in Galilee; he decided not to go
into Judea, because the Judeans were looking for a chance to kill him.
2The Jewish celebration of Sukkoth was coming, 3so his brothers said
to him, "Get out of here; go to Judea so your disciples can see the
miracles you're doing. 4No one who wants public recognition does
things in secret. If you are going to do these ⟨miracles⟩, let the world
see you." (5Evidently, even his brothers didn't have any confidence in
him.)

6Jesus replies, "It's not my time yet. It's always your time. 7The
world can never hate you, but it hates me, because I provide evidence
that its actions are evil. 8You go ahead to the celebration; I'm not going
to this celebration because my time hasn't yet arrived."

9With this piece of advice, he stayed behind in Galilee.

10After his brothers had left for the celebration, he went too; he
didn't go openly but traveled incognito. 11So the Judeans kept an eye
out for him at the celebration, inquiring repeatedly, "Where is that
fellow?" 12and there was a good deal of wrangling about him in the
crowd. Some were claiming, "He's a good man," but others dissented,
"No, he's just hoodwinking the public." 13Yet no one spoke openly
about him for fear of the Judeans.

Teaching in the temple

14***When the celebration was half over,*** Jesus went up to the temple
area and started teaching. 15The Judeans were taken aback, saying,
"This man is uneducated; how come he's so articulate?"

16To this Jesus responded, "What I'm teaching does not originate
with me but with the one who sent me. 17Anyone who sets out to do
what God wants knows well enough whether this teaching originates
with God or whether I'm speaking solely on my own authority. 18All
who speak on their own authority are after praise for themselves. But as
for him who is concerned with the praise of the one who sent him—he
is truthful; there is nothing false about him.

19"Moses gave you the Law, didn't he? (Not that any of you observes
the Law!) Why are you bent on killing me?"

20The crowd answered, "You're out of your mind! Who's trying to
kill you?"

7:15 Ⓣ Mk 6:2, Mt 13:54–56
7:20 Ⓣ Mk 3:22; Jn 8:48, 52, 10:20

7:8 Some mss read "not yet" in place of *not.*

7:2 *Sukkoth:* Also known as the Feast of Booths, or Tabernacles.

7:4 *let the world see you:* Either Galilee is not *the world*, but only Jerusalem, or Jesus' brothers express a stereotyped view of rural unsophistication.

7:7 In contrast to his brothers (v. 4), Jesus speaks of *the world* here in a negative sense, expressing all that is organized against God and therefore against Jesus, deliberately or not.

7:13 The risk in speaking about Jesus that evidently prevailed when this gospel was written is read back into Jesus' lifetime.

7:19 *Not that any of you observes the Law!:* Jesus' hearers are shown as guilty not only of failing to believe the Law (5:47) but of disobeying its commandments; they are unworthy representatives of Judaism.

21“I do one miracle,” Jesus replied, “and you’re stunned! 22That’s why Moses gave you circumcision—not that it really came from Moses, but from our ancestors—and you can circumcise someone on the sabbath day. 23If someone can be circumcised on the sabbath day without breaking Moses’ Law, can you really be angry with me for making someone completely well on the sabbath day? 24Don’t judge by appearances; judge by what is right.”

25Some of the Jerusalemites began to say, “Isn’t this the one they are trying to kill? 26Look, here he is, speaking in public, and they say nothing to him. You don’t suppose the authorities have now concluded that he is the Anointed? 27But wait—we know where this fellow’s from. When the Anointed comes, no one is supposed to know where he’s from.”

28As a consequence, while he was teaching in the temple area, Jesus shouted out: “It’s true, you know me; it’s true, you know where I’m from. But I haven’t come on my own—the one who sent me is authentic, and you don’t have any idea who that is. 29I know who he is, because I came from him and he is the one who sent me.”

30They would have arrested him then and there, but no one laid a hand on him, because his time had not yet come.

31Many people in the crowd believed in him and would ask, “When the Anointed comes, is he likely to perform any more miracles than this man?”

32The Pharisees heard the crowd wrangling about him; so the ranking priests and the Pharisees sent deputies to arrest him.

33Then Jesus said, “I’ll be with you a little longer; then I’ll return to the one who sent me. 34You’ll look for me, but you won’t find me: where I am you can’t come.”

35So the Judeans reflected aloud, “Where is this man going to go, that we won’t find him? Will he go to the Greek Diaspora, to teach the Greeks? 36What is this spiel he’s giving us—‘You’ll look for me, but you won’t find me: where I am you can’t come’?”

37On the last and most important day of the celebration, Jesus stood up and shouted out, “Anyone who’s thirsty must come to me and drink. 38The one who believes in me—as scripture puts it—‘will be the source of rivers of life-giving water.’ ”

7:29 Ⓣ Jn 13:3
7:30–32 Cf. EgerG 1:8
7:33–34 Cf. Th 38:2, 59
7:33 Ⓣ SJas 2:4
7:36 Cf. Th 38:2
7:37 Cf. Th 108:1
7:38–39 ◊ Is 44:3

7:21 *one miracle:* Evidently the healing of the lame man in chap. 5; the debate over this action *on the sabbath day*, last heard of in 5:18, is resumed.

7:28 *you don’t have any idea who that is:* Jesus’ hearers are almost accused of not knowing God.

7:30 Causality is not in the hands of humans, not even the most powerful Judean leaders; they will only occasion Jesus’ death, and not until *his time* comes.

7:32 *The Pharisees heard the crowd wrangling about him:* This may reflect as much the situation in which the gospel was written as Jesus’ lifetime.

7:34 *where I am:* presumably after the resurrection.

7:35 *the Greek Diaspora:* Greek-speaking Jews living outside of Judea.

Jesus' discourse in Jerusalem

([39]He was talking about the spirit that those who believed in him were about to receive. You realize, of course, that there was no spirit as yet, since Jesus hadn't been glorified.)

[40]When they heard this declaration, some in the crowd said, "This man has to be the Prophet." [41]"The Anointed!" others said. Still others objected: "Is the Anointed to come from Galilee? [42]Doesn't scripture teach that the Anointed is to be descended from David and come from the village of Bethlehem, where David lived?" ([43]As you can see, the crowd was split over who he was.)

[44]Some were in favor of arresting him, but no one laid a hand on him. [45]Then the deputies came back to the ranking priests and the Pharisees, who said to them, "Why haven't you brought him in?"

[46]The deputies answered, "No one ever talked like this!"

[47]The Pharisees came back at them, "Don't tell us you've been duped too! [48]None of the authorities or the Pharisees have believed in him, have they? [49]As for this rabble, they are ignorant of the Law! Damn them!"

[50]Then Nicodemus, who was one of their number—he had earlier paid Jesus a visit—challenges them: [51]"Since when does our Law pass judgment on a person without first letting him or her speak for themselves, and without establishing the facts?"

[52]They retorted, "You wouldn't be from Galilee too, now would you? Check for yourself: no prophet has ever come from Galilee."

8 [12]***Jesus spoke out again,*** saying to them, "I am the light of the world. My followers won't ever have to walk in the dark; no, they'll have the real light."

[13]The Pharisees came back at him: "You're giving evidence on your own behalf; your evidence is invalid."

[14]Jesus answered them, "Even if I give evidence on my own behalf, my evidence is valid, because I know where I came from and where I'm going. You, on the other hand, don't know where I come from or where I'm headed. [15]You judge by human standards; I pass judgment on no one. [16]But if I do render judgment, my decisions are valid because I do not render these judgments alone; rather, the Father who sent me joins me in them. [17]Your Law stipulates that the testimony of

7:42 Ⓣ Mk 12:35–37, Mt 22:41–45, Lk 20:41–44, ◊ Mi 5:2
7:43–44 Cf. Lk 19:47–48, 20:19; EgerG 1:9
7:46 Ⓣ Mk 1:22; Mt 7:28–29; Lk 4:32, 36
8:12 Cf. Mt 5:14, Th 77:1; Ⓓ Jn 9:5
8:17 ◊ Dt 19:15

7:39 A few mss read "the spirit had not yet been given" in place of *there was no spirit as yet.* **7:53—8:11** Some mss insert here the story of the woman caught in adultery. See p. 453 in Orphan Sayings and Stories. **8:16** A few mss read "the one" in place of *the Father.*

7:39 *there was no spirit as yet:* See 14:16.
7:40 *the Prophet:* See the note on 1:21.
7:41 *from Galilee:* Despite the implication at 4:43–45 that Jesus' *own turf* (or "homeland") was Judea, it is known that he was *a Nazarene* (18:5), that is, *from Nazareth* in Galilee (1:45).
7:52 *You wouldn't be from Galilee too, now would you?:* Here to be *from Galilee* seems to mean virtually to "believe in Jesus."

two is valid. [18]I offer evidence on my own behalf and the Father who sent me offers evidence on my behalf."

[19]So they asked him, "Where is your father?"

Jesus replied, "You don't recognize me or my Father. If you recognized me, you would recognize my Father too."

[20]He made these remarks while he was teaching near the collection box in the temple area. But no one arrested him because his time had not yet come.

[21]He spoke to them again: "I am going away. You'll try to find me, but you'll die in your sin. Where I'm going you can't come."

[22]The Judeans then said, "Does he intend to kill himself—is that what he means when he says, 'Where I'm going you can't come'?"

[23]So he would respond to them, "You belong down here, I belong up above. You're right at home in this world, I'm not at home in this world. [24]I told you you would die in your sins. If you don't believe that I am ⟨what I say I am⟩, you will die in your sins."

[25]So they countered, "Who are you?"

"What I told you from the start," Jesus replied. [26]"There's a lot I could say about you and judge you for; but the one who sent me is the real authority, so I'll tell the world what I've heard from him."

([27]They didn't realize that he was talking to them about the Father.)

[28]Then Jesus continued, "When you elevate the son of Adam, then you'll know that I am ⟨what I say⟩, and that I don't act on my own. Rather, I say what my Father taught me. [29]The one who sent me is with me. ⟨The Father⟩ hasn't left me on my own, because I always do what pleases ⟨the Father⟩."

[30]Many believed in him because he was saying this.

[31]Then Jesus began to tell the Judeans who had come to believe in him, "If you adhere to my teaching you really are my disciples, [32]and you'll know the truth, and the truth will liberate you."

[33]They protested: "We're Abraham's descendants, and we've never been slaves to anyone; how ⟨can⟩ you say, 'You'll be liberated'?"

[34]Jesus answered them, "I swear to God, everyone who commits sin is a slave. [35]No slave is ever a permanent member of the family; but a son is. [36]So if the son liberates you, you'll really be free.

[37]"I recognize that you are Abraham's descendants, yet you're trying to kill me because my teaching gets nowhere with you. [38]I'm telling you what I saw ⟨when I was⟩ with the Father, and you do ⟨only⟩ what you learned from ⟨your own⟩ father."

[39]"Our father is Abraham," they ⟨repeated⟩.

Jesus says, "If you ⟨really⟩ are children of Abraham, act as Abraham did. [40]As it is, you're trying to kill me, even though I've told you the

8:20 Cf. EgerG 1:9
8:21 Cf. Th 59
8:32 Ⓣ DSav 41:6
8:35 ◊Gn 21:10
8:39 Ⓣ Q 3:8, Mt 3:8, Lk 3:8

8:34 Many mss add "to sin" after *slave.*

8:20 *But no one arrested him:* See the note on 7:30.

8:23 *this world:* See the note on 7:7.

truth I heard from God. Abraham never did that. [41]No, you're doing
what ⟨your real⟩ father does."
They replied, "We're not bastards; we have only one father—God."
[42]Jesus responded, "If in fact God were your father, you'd love me,
since I've come from God and here I am—not on my own initiative;
⟨God⟩ sent me. [43]Why don't you understand what I'm saying? ⟨It's⟩
because you can't hear what I'm saying. [44]You are your father's children all right—children of the devil. And you intend to accomplish
your father's desires. He was a murderer from the start; he is far from
truth, ⟨in fact,⟩ there's no truth in him at all. When he tells his lies, he
is expressing his nature, because he is a liar and breeds lying. [45]But
since I tell the truth, you don't ⟨want to⟩ believe me. [46]Which of you
can implicate me in sin? If I speak truthfully, why don't you believe
me? [47]Everyone who belongs to God ⟨can⟩ hear God's words. That's
why you don't listen: you don't belong to God."
[48]The Judeans replied, "Aren't we right to say, 'You're a Samaritan
and out of your mind'?"
[49]"I'm not out of my mind," Jesus replied. "What I do is simply
honor my Father; you ⟨on the other hand⟩ dishonor me. ([50]Not that
I'm looking to be honored; there is one who seeks that ⟨for me⟩ and
who acquits ⟨me⟩.) [51]I swear to God, all who obey my teaching will
certainly never die."
[52]To this the Judeans retorted, "Now we're certain you're out of
your mind! ⟨Even⟩ Abraham died, and so did the prophets, and here
you are claiming, 'All who obey my teaching will certainly never taste
death.' [53]Are you greater than our father Abraham? He died, and so did
the prophets. What do you make yourself out to be?"
[54]Jesus replied, "If I were to glorify myself, that glory of mine would
mean nothing. But in fact my Father glorifies me—the one you call
your God, [55]though you've never known God. But I know him; if I
were to say I don't know ⟨God⟩ I would be a liar like you. I do know
God, and I obey God's teaching. [56]Your father Abraham would have
been overjoyed to see my day; in fact, he did see it and he rejoiced."
[57]The Judeans said to him, "You aren't even fifty years old and
you've seen Abraham!"
[58]Jesus said to them, "As God is my witness, I existed before there
was an Abraham."
[59]They picked up stones to hurl at him, but Jesus disappeared from
the temple area.

8:47 Ⓣ SJas 6:33
8:48 Ⓣ Mk 3:22; Jn 7:20, 10:20
8:51 Cf. Th 1, 111:2
8:52 Ⓣ Mk 3:22; Jn 7:20, 10:20
8:59 Cf. Lk 4:28–30, EgerG 1:7

8:53 A few mss omit *our father*.

8:41 *We're not bastards:* In Greek "we" is emphasized. The suggestion is that by contrast Jesus' birth was illegitimate; is this because he claims God as his Father?

8:44 *children of the devil:* One of the several extreme expressions of anti-Judaism in this gospel; see also v. 47, for example, and Introduction.

8:48 *a Samaritan:* That is, an enemy of the Judeans.

8:51 *never die:* See the note on 5:24–25 and Introduction.

Man born blind

9 ***As he was leaving*** he saw a man who had been blind from birth. 2His disciples asked him, "Rabbi, was it this man's wrongdoing or his parents' that caused him to be born blind?"

3Jesus responded, "This fellow did nothing wrong, nor did his parents. Rather, ⟨he was born blind⟩ so God could display his work through him. 4We must carry out the work of the one who sent me while the light lasts. Nighttime is coming and then no one will be able to undertake any work. 5So long as I am in the world I am the light of the world."

6With that he spat on the ground, made mud with his spit and treated the man's eyes with the mud. 7Then ⟨Jesus⟩ said to him, "Go, rinse off in the pool of Siloam" (the name means "Emissary"). So he went over, rinsed ⟨his eyes⟩ off, and came back with his sight restored.

8Then his neighbors, and those who recognized him as the one who had been a beggar before, would say, "Isn't this the fellow who used to sit and beg?"

9Some would agree, "It's him"; others would say, "No, it only looks like him."

He kept saying, "It's me."

10So they asked him, "How were your eyes opened?"

11He answered, "Someone called Jesus made some mud and treated my eyes; he told me, 'Go to Siloam and rinse off.' So I went, and when I had rinsed off, I could see."

12They said to him, "Where is this man?"

He says, "I don't know."

13They take the man who had been blind to the Pharisees. (14It was the sabbath day when Jesus made mud and opened his eyes.) 15So the Pharisees asked him again how he could see.

9:2
◊ Ex 20:5
9:5
Cf. Mt 5:14, Th 77:1; Ⓓ Jn 8:12

9:4 Many mss read "I" in place of *we*. Some mss read "us" in place of *me*.

9:2 *this man's wrongdoing:* It was often believed that all misfortune was deserved, the result of some someone's "sin." In the case of a congenital disability there arose the question whether the victim had *caused it* or—perhaps because such sin was hard to attribute to an unborn baby—the victim's parents.

9:3 *so God could display his work:* Jesus cuts through the disciples' speculation and, as common in this gospel, interprets special events, particularly those done through him, as having an essentially theological purpose, that is, to show what God is like. This purpose overclouds any concern for the victim such as Jesus displays in the synoptic gospels.

9:4–5 The anomalous mixture of plural and singular personal pronouns (but see the text-critical note) is perhaps to be explained as a combination of an affirmation of the Johannine community (*we*) with a saying from its tradition of Jesus' teaching (*me, I*).

9:7 *the name means Emissary:* probably a fanciful etymology. Either it is meant simply to suggest the aptness of Jesus' sending the blind man to this pool or it subtly reminds the reader that Jesus is himself the emissary of God.

9:8–12 The *neighbors* and others display the inability of many witnesses of Jesus' deeds to see them as "miracles" (6:26), and perhaps the responses reflect the varying effect of these stories on their hearers at the time the gospel was written. Even those who accept the miracle display mainly curiosity.

"He put mud on my eyes, I washed, and I can see," he told them.

[16]Then some of the Pharisees said, "That man is not from God, because he does not keep the sabbath day." But others said, "How can a sinner do such miracles?" And there was a rift among them. [17]So they ask the blind man again, "What do you have to say about him, since it was your eyes he opened?"

He said, "He's a prophet."

[18]The Judeans wouldn't believe that he had been blind and got his sight until they called in the parents of this man who had recovered his sight. [19]They asked them, "Is this your son that you claim was born blind? So how come he can see now?"

[20]His parents replied, "We know this is our son; we know he was born blind; [21]but we don't know how he can see now or who opened his eyes. Ask him, he's an adult; he'll speak for himself." ([22]His parents said this because they were afraid of the Judeans, for the Judeans had already agreed that anyone who acknowledged ⟨Jesus⟩ as the Anointed would be banned from the synagogue. [23]That's why his parents said, "He's an adult, ask him.")

[24]So for a second time they called in the man who had been blind, and said to him, "Give God the credit. We know this man is a sinner."

[25]He replied, "Whether he's a sinner I don't know; the one thing I do know is that I was blind, and now I can see."

[26]They asked him, "What did he do to you? How did he open your eyes?"

[27]He answered them, "I told you already and you wouldn't listen to me. Why do you want to hear it again? You don't want to become his disciples too, do you?"

[28]They hurled insults at him: "You may be his disciple; we're disciples of Moses. [29]We know God spoke to Moses; we don't even know where this man came from."

[30]"Now isn't that wonderful," he responded. "You don't know where he's from and yet he opened my eyes! [31]God doesn't listen to sinners; we know that. But if someone is devout and does God's will, ⟨God⟩ listens. [32]It's unheard of that anyone ever opened the eyes of someone born blind. [33]If this man were not from God, he couldn't do anything at all."

[34]"You're a born sinner and you're going to teach us?" they replied. And they threw him out.

[35]Jesus heard they had thrown him out; so he found him and said, "Do you believe in the son of Adam?"

9:29
//EgerG 1:4

9:17 *a prophet:* Like the Samaritan woman in chap. 4, the man healed of his blindness only gradually recognizes what Jesus is. See vv. 33, 38.

9:22 *banned from the synagogue:* See Introduction.

9:34 *they threw him out:* The consequence his parents feared (v. 22) now applies to this new convert, as apparently to Christians generally in the circumstances where the gospel was written.

Sheep & the shepherd

36He replied, "Master, who is he, so I can believe in him?"
37Jesus said to him, "You've already seen him; he's speaking with
you right now."
38He said, "Master, I believe," and paid him homage.
39Jesus said, "I came into this world to hand down this verdict: the
blind are to see and those with sight are to be blind."
40When some of the Pharisees around him heard this, they said to
him, "We're not blind, are we?"
41Jesus said to them, "If you really were blind, you would be free of
sin; but now ⟨since⟩ you say, 'We see,' your sin is confirmed."

10 "***I swear to God,*** anyone who does not enter the sheep pen
through the gate, but climbs in some other way, is nothing but a thief
and a robber. 2But the one who comes through the gate is the shepherd. 3The gatekeeper lets him in. The sheep recognize his voice; he
calls his own sheep by name and leads them out. 4When he has driven
out the last of his own sheep, he walks in front of them, and the sheep
follow him, because they know his voice. 5They would never follow a
stranger, but would run away from him, since they don't know the
voice of strangers."
6Jesus used this figure of speech with them, but they didn't understand what he was talking about.
7Jesus went on to say, "As God is my witness, I am that gate for the
sheep. 8All who came before me are nothing but thieves and robbers,
but the sheep haven't paid any attention to them. 9I am the gate;
whoever comes in through me will be safe and will go in and out and
find pasture. 10The thief comes only to steal and sacrifice and
slaughter. I came so they can have life and have it to the full.
11"I am the good shepherd. The good shepherd gives his life for his
sheep. 12A hired hand, who isn't a shepherd and doesn't own the
sheep, would see the wolf coming and run off, abandoning the sheep;
then the wolf ⟨could⟩ attack the sheep and scatter them. 13He would
run off because he's a hired hand and the sheep don't matter to him. 14I
am the good shepherd; I know my sheep and my sheep know me, 15just
as the Father knows me and I know the Father: so I give my life for my

9:39
Cf. Mk 4:10–12, 8:17–18; Mt 13:10–17; Lk 8:9–10; ◊ Is 6:9–10
9:40–41
Ⓣ Mt 15:14, 23:16, 17, 19, 24, 26; GOxy 840 2:7
10:6
Ⓣ SJas 6:5
10:8
◊ Ez 34:2
10:14–15
Ⓣ Q 10:22, Mt 11:27, Lk 10:22
10:15
Ⓣ Jn 15:13, 1 Jn 3:16

10:1–38 The extended *figure of speech* (v. 6) of the Good Shepherd is the closest parallel in this gospel to the parables Jesus so characteristically tells in both the synoptic gospels and Thomas. Like some of them, in their present form, this metaphor becomes allegorical (see the note on v. 8).

10:1 The words of Jesus continue, but they can hardly be taken as addressed simply to the Pharisees of chapter 9.

10:8 *All who came before me:* The allegorical meaning of aspects of the Good Shepherd metaphor like this (and, for example, the *hired hand* or the *wolf* in v. 12) was undoubtedly apparent to this gospel's original audience but probably a matter of guesswork for later readers. They may refer either to the Jewish leaders in conflict with the Christians to whom this gospel is addressed or, just possibly, to some conflict among Christian leaders, as in 1 John.

Jesus at the Festival of Lights

sheep. [16]Yet I have sheep from another fold, and I must lead them too.
They'll recognize my voice, and there'll be one flock, one shepherd.
[17]"This is the reason my Father loves me: I am giving up my life so I
can take it back again. [18]No one can take it away from me; I give it up
freely. I have the power to give it up and the power to take it back again.
I have been charged with this responsibility by my Father."

[19]Once more there was a rift among the Judeans because he made
these claims. [20]Many of them were saying, "He's out of his mind and
crazy. Why pay any attention to him?" [21]Others would say, "These
aren't the words of someone who is demon-possessed. A demon can't
open the eyes of the blind, can it?"

[22]***It was then*** the Festival of Lights in Jerusalem, and it was winter-
time. [23]Jesus was walking about in the temple area, in Solomon's
Colonnade. [24]Judeans surrounded him. "How long are you going to
keep us in suspense?" they kept asking. "If you are the Anointed, just
say so."

[25]Jesus answered them, "I did tell you, and you don't believe. The
things I am achieving in my Father's name are evidence on my behalf.
[26]But you don't believe me, because you're not my sheep. [27]My sheep
recognize my voice; I know them and they follow me, [28]and I provide
them with real life; they'll never be lost, nor will anyone snatch them
away from me. [29]What my Father has given me is greatest of all, and no
one can wrest it from the Father. [30]What goes for the Father, goes for
me too."

[31]Again the Judeans took stones in hand to stone him. [32]Jesus
responded, "I showed you many wonderful works that were really the
Father's. Which of these works makes you want to stone me?"

[33]The Judeans answered him, "We're not stoning you for some
wonderful work, but for blasphemy—you, a mere human, make yourself out to be God."

[34]Jesus answered them, "Isn't it written in your Law: 'I said, You are
gods'? [35]The scripture can't be wrong: if God has called them gods—
those who got the word of God—[36]do you mean to say about the one
the Father set apart and sent to earth, 'You're blaspheming,' just
because I said, 'I am God's son'? [37]If I don't do my Father's works,

10:16 ▷Is 56:8
10:20 Ⓣ Mk 3:22; Mt 12:24; Lk 11:5; Jn 7:20, 8:48, 52
10:24–25 Cf. Mk 14:61, Mt 26:63, Lk 22:66–68
10:25–26 Ⓣ SJas 6:33
10:30 Cf. EgerG 6:1
10:31 Cf. EgerG 1:7
10:33 ▷Lv 24:16
10:34 ▷Ps 82:6

10:29 Some mss have one or another variant of "my Father, who has given ⟨them⟩ to me" in place of *what my Father has given me.*

10:16 *one flock:* On the matter of unity among Jesus' followers, see further chap. 17.
10:22 *Festival of Lights:* That is, *Hanukkah*, the feast celebrating the rededication of the Temple in 164 B.C.E.
10:25 *I did tell you, and you don't believe:* Perhaps the common experience of Christian evangelists among the Judeans in the author's own time.

10:30 Literally, "I and the Father are one." While this can mean that Jesus believes himself to be in perfect harmony with God's will, it can also be taken as Jesus' claim to be divine, which is how the Judeans understand it in v. 33.
10:33 *make yourself out to be God:* See v. 30 and 5:18.

Many believe

don't believe me; [38]if I do, even if you can't believe in me, believe in the works, so that you'll fully understand that the Father is in me and I am in the Father."

[39]Again they tried to arrest him, but he escaped.

[40]***He went away once more,*** to the place across the Jordan where John had first baptized, and there he stayed. [41]Many people came to him; they kept repeating, "John didn't perform any miracle, but everything John said about this man was true." [42]And many believed in him there.

Lazarus

11 ***Now someone named Lazarus*** had fallen ill; he was from Bethany, the village of Mary and her sister Martha. ([2]This was the Mary who anointed the Master with oil and wiped his feet with her hair; it was her brother Lazarus who was sick.) [3]So the sisters sent for ⟨Jesus⟩: "Master, the one you love is sick."

[4]But when Jesus heard this he said, "This illness is not fatal; it is to show God's majesty, so God's son also will be honored by it."

[5]Jesus loved Martha and her sister and Lazarus. [6]When he heard that ⟨Lazarus⟩ was sick, he lingered two more days where he was; [7]then he says to the disciples, "Let's go to Judea again."

[8]The disciples say to him, "Rabbi, just now the Judeans were looking for the opportunity to stone you; are you really going back there?"

[9]"Aren't there twelve hours in the day?" Jesus responded. "Those who walk during the day won't stumble; they can see by this world's light. [10]But those who walk at night are going to stumble, because they have no light to go by."

[11]He made these remarks, and then he tells them, "Our friend Lazarus has fallen asleep, but I am going to wake him up."

[12]"Master, if he's only fallen asleep," said the disciples, "he'll revive." ([13]Jesus had been speaking of death but they thought that he meant ⟨he was⟩ only asleep.)

[14]Then Jesus told them plainly, "Lazarus is dead; [15]and I'm happy for you that I wasn't there, so you can believe. Now let's go to him."

[16]Then Thomas, called "the Twin," said to his fellow disciples, "Let's go along too, so we can die with him."

10:39 //EgerG 1:10; cf. Lk 4:29–30
11:2 Ⓘ Jn 12:3
11:9–10 Cf. Jn 12:35

10:38 Some mss read "know and believe" in place of *fully understand.*

10:40 *the place across the Jordan where John had first baptized:* See 1:28.

11:1 *Bethany:* Not the Bethany of 1:28, but the well-known village just outside of Jerusalem (v. 18).

11:2 *the Mary who anointed the Master with oil:* A reference to what will be depicted in 12:1–8.

11:6 *where he was:* Presumably the place (also named Bethany) of 10:40.

11:16 *called the Twin:* Or *called Didymus* or *which means Twin.* The name *Thomas* is derived from the Hebrew word for twin; *Didymus*, a Greek personal name, is from the Greek word for twin. The phrase is used at every appearance of Thomas except 14:5 (i.e., 20:24 and 21:2).

die: The first of several allusions in this story—also the tomb covered by a stone, the head cloth, etc.—to the account of Jesus'

[17]When Jesus arrived, he found that ⟨Lazarus⟩ had been buried four days earlier. [18]Bethany was near Jerusalem, about two miles away, [19]and many of the Judeans had come to Martha and Mary to console them about their brother. [20]When Martha heard that Jesus was coming, she went to meet him; Mary stayed at home. [21]"Master," said Martha, "if you'd been here, my brother wouldn't have died. [22]Still I know that whatever you ask of God, God will grant you."

[23]Jesus says to her, "Your brother will be resurrected."

[24]Martha responds, "I know he'll be raised in the resurrection on the last day."

[25]Jesus said to her, "I am resurrection and life; those who believe in me, even if they die, will live; [26]but everyone who is alive and believes in me will never die. Do you believe this?"

[27]"Yes, Master," she says, "I believe that you are the Anointed, God's son, who is to come to earth."

[28]At this point she went to call her sister Mary, telling her privately, "The Teacher is here and is asking for you." [29]When she heard that, she got up quickly and went to him.

([30]Jesus hadn't yet arrived at the village; he was still where Martha had met him.)

[31]When the Judeans, who hovered about her in the house to console her, saw Mary get up and go out quickly, they followed her, thinking she was going to the tomb to grieve there. [32]When Mary got to where Jesus was and saw him, she fell down at his feet. "Master," she said, "if you'd been here, my brother wouldn't have died."

[33]When Jesus saw her crying, and the Judeans who accompanied her crying too, he was agitated and deeply disturbed; [34]he said, "Where have you put him?"

"Master," they say, "come and see."

[35]Then Jesus cried.

[36]So the Judeans observed, "Look how much he loved him." [37]But some wondered: "He opened the blind man's eyes; couldn't he have kept this man from dying?"

[38]Again greatly agitated, Jesus arrives at the tomb; it was a cave, and a stone lay up against the opening. [39]Jesus says, "Take the stone away."

Martha, sister of the dead man, replies, "But Master, by this time the body will stink; it's been four days."

[40]Jesus says to her, "Didn't I tell you, if you believe you'll see God's majesty?" [41]So they took the stone away, and Jesus looked upwards and said, "Father, thank you for hearing me. [42]I know you always hear me,

11:35
Ⓣ Lk19:41

11:25 A few mss omit *and life.*

own death and resurrection (which is, as here, a demonstration that Jesus himself accomplishes—see 2:19).

11:24 *the resurrection on the last day:* Many first-century Jews believed that at the "Last Judgment" God would raise the just to life in the Age to Come.

11:26 *never die:* See the note on 5:24.

Deliberations of the Council

Mary anoints Jesus

but I say this because of the people standing here, so they'll believe that you sent me." 43Then he shouted at the top of his voice, "Lazarus, come out!" 44The dead man came out, his hands and feet bound in strips of burying cloth, and his face covered with a cloth. Jesus says to them, "Free him ⟨from the burying cloth⟩ and let him go."

45***As a result,*** many of the Judeans who had come to Mary and observed what Jesus had done came to believe in him. 46But some of them went to the Pharisees and reported what Jesus had done.

47So the ranking priests and Pharisees called the Council together and posed this question to them: "What are we going to do now that this fellow performs many miracles? 48If we let him go on like this, everybody will come to believe in him. Then the Romans will come and destroy our ⟨holy⟩ place and our nation."

49Then one of them, Caiaphas, that year's high priest, addressed them as follows: "Don't you know anything? 50Don't you realize that it's to your advantage to have one person die for the people and not have the whole nation wiped out?"

(51He didn't say this on his own authority, but since he was that year's high priest he could foresee that Jesus would die for the nation. 52In fact, ⟨he would die⟩ not only for the nation, but to gather together all God's dispersed children and make them one ⟨people⟩.)

53So from that day on they began plotting how to kill him. 54As a consequence, Jesus no longer moved about among the Judeans publicly, but withdrew to a region bordering the wilderness, to a town called Ephraim, and there he stayed with the disciples.

55It was almost time for the Jewish Passover, and many of the country people went up to Jerusalem before Passover to purify themselves. 56They were on the lookout for Jesus, and as they stood around in the temple area, they were saying to one another, "What do you think? He certainly won't come to the celebration, will he?" (57The ranking priests and the Pharisees had given orders that anyone who knew his whereabouts was to report it, so they could arrest him.)

11:53 Cf. Mk 3:6, Mt 12:14; Mk 11:18, Lk 19:47–48; Mk 14:1–2, Mt 26:3–5, Lk 22:1–2

12:1–8 // Mk 14:3–9, Mt 26:6–13; cf. Lk 7:36–50

12 ***Six days before Passover*** Jesus came to Bethany, where Lazarus lived, the one Jesus had brought back from the dead. 2There they gave a dinner for him; Martha did the serving, and Lazarus was one of those who ate with him. 3Mary brought in a pound of expensive lotion and

---

11:47 *the Council:* the ruling body of the Judeans.

11:48 ⟨*holy*⟩ *place:* the temple.

11:50 *for the people:* The preposition used here can mean simply "in place of" or "for the benefit of." The irony that Caiaphas *could foresee* this is made explicit in the following comment by the author (vv. 51–52).

11:52 *to gather together all God's dispersed children and make them one* ⟨*people*⟩*:* what the Messiah would do, according to widespread expectations.

11:53 Before this there have been several official attempts to kill Jesus. Perhaps this represents the first concerted plan to get rid of him.

12:3 Mary's act would ordinarily be considered both brazen and indecent in that

Entry into Jerusalem

anointed Jesus' feet and wiped them with her hair. And the house was filled with the lotion's fragrance. [4]Judas Iscariot, the disciple who was going to turn him in, says, [5]"Why wasn't this lotion sold? It would bring a year's wages, and the proceeds could have been given to the poor." ([6]He didn't say this because he cared about the poor, but because he was a thief. He was in charge of the common purse and now and again would pilfer money put into it.)

[7]"Let her alone," Jesus said. "Let her keep it for the time I am to be embalmed. [8]There will always be poor around; but I won't always be around."

[9]When the huge crowd of Judeans found out he was there, they came not only because of Jesus but also to see Lazarus, the one he had brought back from the dead. [10]So the ranking priests planned to put Lazarus to death, too, [11]since because of him many of the Judeans were defecting and believing in Jesus.

[12]***The next day*** the huge crowd that had come for the celebration heard that Jesus was coming into Jerusalem. [13]They got palm fronds and went out to meet him. They began to shout,

> Hosanna! Blessed is the one who comes in the name of the Lord!
> ⟨Blessed is⟩ the King of Israel!

[14]Then Jesus found a young donkey and rode on it, as scripture puts it,

> [15]Calm your fears, daughter of Zion.
> Look, your king comes riding on a donkey's colt!

([16]His disciples didn't understand these matters at the time, but when Jesus had been glorified, they then recalled that what had happened to him matched the things written about him.)

[17]The people who were with ⟨Jesus⟩ when he had summoned Lazarus from his tomb and brought him back from the dead kept repeating ⟨this story⟩. ([18]That's why the crowd went out to meet him: they heard that he had performed this miracle.)

[19]So the Pharisees remarked under their breath, "You see, you can't win; look, the world has gone over to him."

12:8 ◊Dt 15:11
12:12–15 //Mk 11:1–10, Mt 21:1–11, Lk 19:28–40
12:13 ◊Ps 118:26
12:15 ◊Zec 9:9

12:8 A few mss lack this verse. **12:17** Some mss read "kept repeating that he had summoned Lazarus from his tomb" in place of *when he had summoned Lazarus . . . kept repeating ⟨this story⟩*.

---

cultural context. It will naturally provoke objection, and it does so in all versions of this story. Except for Luke 7:39, the objection takes the form of the disciples' (here only Judas') criticizing the woman's extravagance. Jesus justifies her action as percipiently pointing to his approaching death (v. 7).

12:8 *There will always be poor around:* Not an acceptance of poverty's inevitability, as this saying (along with Deut 15:11) is usually understood. Jesus wryly comments, perhaps, on the inaptness of Judas' objection: "It's interesting that you should mention the poor just now."

12:9 *the huge crowd:* apparently the same as in 11:55–56.

12:13 *Hosanna!:* This Hebrew word, once a prayer meaning "Save ⟨us⟩," has evidently become, as in the other gospels, an expression of praise.

The time has come

[20]***There were some Greeks*** among those who had come up to worship at the celebration. [21]These people came to Philip, who was from Bethsaida, Galilee, and requested of him, "Sir, we want to meet Jesus."

[22]Philip goes and tells Andrew, and both Andrew and Philip go and tell Jesus. [23]And Jesus responds: "The time has come for the son of Adam to be glorified. [24]I swear to God, unless the kernel of wheat falls to the earth and dies, it remains a single seed; but if it dies, it produces a great harvest. [25]Those who love life lose it, but those who hate life in this world will preserve it for unending, real life. [26]Whoever serves me must follow me, for wherever I am, my servant must be there also. Whoever serves me, the Father will honor.

[27]"Now my life is in turmoil, but should I say, 'Father, rescue me from this moment'? No, it was to face this moment that I came. [28]Father, glorify your name!" Then a voice spoke out of the sky: "I have glorified it and I will glorify it further."

[29]The crowd there heard this, and some people remarked that it had thundered, others that an angel had spoken to him.

[30]"That voice did not come for me but for you," Jesus rejoined. [31]"Now sentence is passed on this world; now the ruler of this world will be expelled. [32]And if I'm elevated from the earth, I'll take everyone with me." ([33]He said this to show what kind of death he was going to die.)

[34]The crowd replied to him, "We've learned from the Law that the Anointed will stay forever, so how can you say that the son of Adam is destined to be elevated? Who is this son of Adam anyway?"

[35]So Jesus said to them, "The light is still with you for a while. Walk while you have light, so darkness won't overpower you. Those who walk in the dark don't know where they're going. [36]Since you have the light, believe in the light, so you will become children of light." When Jesus had said this, he left and went into hiding.

[37]Although he had performed ever so many miracles before their eyes, they did not believe in him, [38]so that the word the prophet Isaiah spoke would come true:

> Lord, who has believed our message?
> To whom is God's might revealed?

12:24 Ⓣ SJas6:9–11
12:25 //Mk8:35; Mt10:39, 16:25; Lk9:24, 17:33
12:26 Cf. Q12:8, Mt10:32, Lk12:8
12:27 Ⓣ Mk14:34–36, Mt26:38–39, Lk22:41–42
12:31 Ⓣ EgerG1:5, Lk10:18
12:34 ▷Is9:7
12:35–36 Ⓣ SJas8:5
12:35 Cf. Th24:3, Ⓣ DSav8:3
12:37–40 Cf. Mk4:10–12, Mt13:10–17, Lk8:9–10
12:38 ▷Is53:1

12:32 A few mss read "everything" in place of *everyone.*

12:20 *Greeks:* See the note on 7:35.
12:23 *The time has come:* Beginning with 2:4 there have been a number of references to Jesus' *time*, until now always in the future. Here at last it begins. See also 13:1.

to be glorified: Jesus' *time* is understood not so much as his death, which nevertheless is central to it, as his vindication and exaltation.
12:31 *the ruler of this world:* Either Satan (13:27), or a human representative such as the emperor.
12:32–33 Jesus' word about being *elevated from the earth* is taken to refer to his crucifixion.
12:37 *ever so many miracles:* or, *so many miracles ⟨as have been reported in this gospel⟩.*
12:38–40 These passages in Isaiah, and especially the second of them, helped the Christian movement explain why so few Jews accepted Jesus as the Messiah.

The footwashing

39So they were unable to believe, for Isaiah also said:

40He has blinded their eyes,
he has turned their hearts to stone,
so their eyes are sightless
and their hearts closed to understanding,
or they would do an about-face
for me to heal them.

41Isaiah said these things because he saw God's majesty, and spoke
about it.
42Nevertheless, many did believe in him, even many of the ruling
class, but because of the Pharisees they did not acknowledge it, so they
wouldn't be thrown out of the synagogue. (43You see, they were more
concerned with human approval than with God's endorsement.)
44Then Jesus proclaimed aloud: "Those who believe in me do not
believe only in me, but in the one who sent me. 45And those who see
me see the one who sent me. 46I am light come into the world, so all
who believe in me need not remain in the dark. 47I won't pass judgment on those who hear my message but don't keep it. You see, I didn't
come to pass judgment on the world; I've come to save the world. 48But
those who reject me and don't accept my message have a judge: the
message I've spoken will itself be their judge on the last day. 49For I
don't speak on my own authority, but the Father who sent me ordered
me to say what I have said and will say, 50and I know that his commandment is unending, real life. Therefore, I say just exactly what the
Father told to me to say."

13 ***Before the Passover celebration*** Jesus knew that the time had
come for him to leave this world and return to the Father. He had
loved his own in the world and would love them to the end. 2Now that
the devil had planted it in the mind of Judas, Simon Iscariot's son, to
turn him in, at supper 3Jesus could tell that the Father had left everything up to him and that he had come from God and was going back to
God. 4So he got up from the meal, took off his clothing, put it aside,
and wrapped a towel around himself. 5Then he put water in a basin and
began to wash the disciples' feet and to wipe them off with the towel
around his waist. 6He comes to Simon Peter.
Peter says to him, "Master, you're going to wash my feet?"
7Jesus replied, "Right now you don't understand what I'm doing,
but later you will."

12:40
◊Is 6:9–10
12:44–45
Cf. Mk 9:37;
Q 10:16, Mt 10:40,
Lk 10:16; 9:48;
Jn 5:23, 13:20
13:2
Ⓣ Jn 6:70–71,
13:27; Lk 22:3
13:3–4
Cf. Th 61:3
13:3
Ⓣ Jn 3:35,
Q 10:22, Mt 11:27,
Lk 10:22

12:41 *God's majesty:* Literally, "his glory." This could refer instead to Jesus' glory.
12:42 See Introduction.
12:43 *God's endorsement:* Strictly, *honor from God*, or possibly *God's majesty*.
12:47 *the world:* See the note on 7:7.
13:1 *to the end*: This highly ambiguous phrase can mean "until his death," "fully," or "to the end of the age."
13:4 *took off his clothing:* that is, his shirt, so that he is as scantily dressed as a slave.

Forecast of Judas' act

8“You'll never, ever wash my feet,” Peter says.

Jesus answered him, “Unless I wash you, you won't have anything in common with me.”

9“In that case, Master,” Peter says, “⟨wash⟩ not only my feet but my hands and my head too.”

10Jesus says, “People who have bathed need only to wash their feet; nevertheless, they're clean all over. And you are clean—but not quite all of you.”

(11He knew, of course, who was going to turn him in; that's why he said, “You're not all clean.”)

12When he had washed their feet, he put his clothes back on and sat down at the table again. “Do you realize what I've done?” he asked. 13“You call me Teacher and Master, and you're right: that's who I am. 14So if I am your master and teacher and have washed your feet, you ought to wash each other's feet. 15In other words, I've set you an example: you are to do as I've done to you. 16I swear to God, slaves are never better than their masters; messengers are never superior to their senders. 17If you understand this, congratulations if you can do it. 18I'm not talking about all of you: I know the ones I've chosen. But scripture has to come true: ‘The one who has shared my food has turned on me.’ 19I tell you this now, before it happens, so that when it does happen you'll know that I am ⟨what I say I am⟩. 20I swear to God, if they welcome the person I send, they welcome me; and if they welcome me, they welcome the one who sent me.”

21***When he had said all this,*** Jesus became deeply disturbed. He declared: “I swear to God, one of you will turn me in.”

22The disciples stole glances at each other, at a loss to understand who it was he was talking about. 23One of them, the disciple Jesus loved most, was sitting at Jesus' right. 24So Simon Peter leans over to ask that disciple who it was ⟨Jesus⟩ was talking about. 25He, in turn, leans over to Jesus and asks him, “Master, who is it?”

26Jesus answers: “I am going to dunk this piece of bread, and the one I give it to is the one.” So he dunks the piece of bread and gives it to Judas, Simon Iscariot's son. 27The moment ⟨he had given Judas⟩ the piece of bread, Satan took possession of him. Then Jesus says to him, “Go ahead and do what you're going to do.”

28Of course no one at dinner understood why Jesus had made this remark. 29Some had the idea that because Judas kept charge of the funds, Jesus was telling him, “Buy whatever we need for the celebration,” or to give something to the poor. 30In any case, as soon as ⟨Judas⟩ had eaten the piece of bread he went out. It was nighttime.

13:14
Ⓣ Mk9:35, Mt23:11, Lk9:48; Mk10:42–45, Mt20:25–28, Lk22:25–27
13:15–17
Ⓣ Mk10:43–44, Mt20:26–27, Lk22:26–27
13:16
//Q6:40, Mt10:24–25, Lk6:40, DSav20:1
13:17
Cf. Lk11:28, Th79:2; Ⓣ Jas1:25
13:18
◊Ps41:9
13:20
Cf. Mk9:37; Q10:16, Mt10:40, Lk10:16; 9:48; Jn5:23, 12:44–45
13:21–30
//Mk14:18–21, Mt26:21–25, Lk22:21–22
13:27
Ⓣ Jn6:70–71, 13:2

13:19 *I am ⟨what I say I am⟩:* See the note on 4:26.

13:23 *the disciple Jesus loved most:* The identity of this nameless figure, appearing here for the first time, is perhaps the most puzzling element in the gospel. See Introduction and note on 21:23.

13:30 *It was nighttime:* Undoubtedly this is not intended as a mere matter of fact but is symbolic, as perhaps at 3:2. See what Jesus

[31]***When ⟨Judas⟩ had gone,*** Jesus says, "Now the son of Adam is
glorified, and God is glorified through him. [32]If God is glorified
through him, God in turn will glorify him through himself, and will
glorify him at once. [33]My children, I'm going to be with you only a
little while longer. You'll look for me, but, as I told the Judeans, I'm
going where you can't come; it's to you that I say this now. [34]I am
giving you a new directive: Love each other. Just as I've loved you, you
are to love each other. [35]Then everyone will recognize you as my
disciples—if you love each other."

[36]***Simon Peter says to him,*** "Master, where are you going?"

Jesus answered, "For now you can't follow me where I'm going;
you'll follow later."

[37]Peter says to him, "Master, why can't I follow you now? I'd give my
life for you."

[38]Jesus responded, "You'd give your life for me? I swear to God: The
rooster won't crow before you disown me three times."

A new directive

Forecast of Peter's denial

The way

14 ***"Don't give in*** to your distress. You believe in God, then believe
in me too. [2]There are plenty of places to stay in my Father's house. If it
weren't true, I would have told you; I'm on my way to make a place
ready for you. [3]And if I go to make a place ready for you, I'll return and
embrace you. So where I am you can be too. [4]You know where I'm
going and you know the way."

[5]Thomas says to him, "Master, we don't know where you're going.
How can we possibly know the way?"

[6]"I am the way, and I am truth, and I am life," replies Jesus. "No one
gets to the Father unless it is through me. [7]If you do recognize me, you
will recognize my Father also. From this moment on you know him
and you've even seen him."

13:33 Cf. Th 59
13:36–38 Cf. Mk 14:26–31, Mt 26:30–35, Lk 22:31–34
13:36 Ⓣ SJas 2:4
14:2 Ⓣ SJas 8:7
14:3–5 Ⓣ SJas 2:4
14:3 Ⓣ SJas 6:23
14:4–7 Cf. Th 24:1
14:5 Ⓣ DSav 28:1
14:7–9 Ⓣ DSav 16.5

13:32 Several mss omit *if God is glorified through him.* **13:37** A few mss omit *Master.* **14:4** Some mss read "the way where I am going" in place of *where I'm going and you know the way.*

has said about the *night* in 9:4; 11:10.

13:34 *Love each other:* The ethic in this gospel has been reduced from the synoptic ethic of love of neighbor, even of enemy, and is restricted to love within the Christian community.

13:36 *For now you can't follow . . . ; you'll follow later:* This is spoken to Peter alone and perhaps refers to Jesus' death and the possibility that Peter would also be crucified (21:19). Or it is clarified by Jesus' promise to all the disciples in 14:2 that they would eventually join him in his *Father's house.*

14:1 *You believe in God:* Or, *Believe in God.* *then believe:* Or, *then you believe.*

14:3 *if I go . . . I'll return:* Usually these two predictions are taken to refer to the synoptic view of Jesus' resurrection and his eventual coming again, but in the context of this Farewell Address (chaps. 14–17) at the last supper, they probably refer instead to his approaching death and resurrection.

14:6 *No one gets to the Father unless it is through me:* This may state the rhetoric of Jewish/Christian conflict that occasions this gospel—or one side of it—as much as the absolute claim it is usually taken to be. Perhaps Jesus here speaks mainly positively, to reassure his followers, as v. 7 shows.

The advocate

8“Let us see the Father,” Philip says to him, “and we’ll be satisfied.”

9“I’ve been around you all this time,” Jesus replies, “and you still don’t know me, do you, Philip? Anyone who has seen me has seen the Father. So how can you say, ‘Let us see the Father’? 10Don’t you believe that I’m in the Father and the Father is in me? I don’t say what I say on my own. The Father is with me constantly, and I perform his labors. 11You ought to believe that I’m in the Father and the Father is in me. If not, at least you ought to believe these labors in and of themselves. 12I swear to God, anyone who believes in me will perform the works I perform and will be able to perform even greater feats, because I’m on my way to the Father. 13In addition, I’ll do whatever you request in my name, so the Father can be honored by means of the son. 14If you request anything using my name, I’ll do it.”

15“***If you love me,*** you’ll obey my instructions. 16At my request the Father will provide you with yet another advocate, the authentic spirit, who will be with you forever. 17The world is unable to accept ⟨this spirit⟩ because it neither perceives nor recognizes it. You recognize it because it dwells in you and will remain in you.

18“I won’t abandon you as orphans; I’ll come to you. 19In a little while the world won’t see me any longer, but you’ll see me because I’m alive as you will be alive. 20At that time you will come to know that I’m in my Father and that you’re in me and I’m in you. 21Those who accept my instructions and obey them—they love me. And those who love me will be loved by my Father; moreover, I will love them and make myself known to them.”

22Judas (not Iscariot) says to him, “Master, what has happened that you are about to make yourself known to us but not to the world?”

23Jesus replied to him, “Those who love me will heed what I tell them, and my Father will love them, and we’ll come to them and make our home there. 24Those who don’t love me won’t follow my instructions. Of course, the things you heard me say are not mine but come from the Father who sent me.

25“I have told you these things while I am still here with you. 26Yet the advocate, the holy spirit the Father will send in my stead, will teach you everything and remind you of everything I told you. 27Peace is what I leave behind for you; my peace is what I give you. What I give you is not a worldly gift. Don’t give in to your distress or be overcome by terror. 28You heard me tell you, ‘I’m going away and I’m going to return to you.’ If you loved me, you’d be glad that I’m going to the

14:9
Ⓣ SJas 9:2
14:10–11
Ⓣ DSav 41:4
14:13–14
Cf. Mk 11:24; Mt 21:22; Q 11:9–10, Mt 7:7–8, Lk 11:9–10; Th 2, 92:1, 94; Ⓓ Jn 15:7, 16; 16:23
14:16–17
Ⓣ Jn 15:26–27, 16:13
14:21–23
Ⓣ SJas 6:7
14:23
Ⓣ SJas 4:4, 6:23
14:25
Ⓣ SJas 9:7
14:26
Ⓣ Mk 13:11, Mt 10:20, Lk 12:12
14:27
Cf. Mary 3:12, 7:2

14:15 Some mss read “obey” in place of *you’ll obey*.

14:16 *yet another advocate:* That is, beside Jesus himself.

14:17 *The world:* See the note on 7:7.

it . . . will remain in you: A major element of the comfort that this gospel seeks to provide the beleaguered community it addresses is the reassurance of permanence and dependability in otherwise unreliable circumstances. The word for *remain* (or “stay”) consequently appears many times (e.g., 6:27, 8:35).

Father, because the Father is greater than I am. [29]So I have now told you all this ahead of time so you will believe when it happens.

[30]"Time does not permit me to tell you much more; you see, the ruler of this world is already on the way. [31]However, so the world may know I love the Father, I act exactly as my Father instructed me. Come on, let's get out of here."

The authentic vine

World's hatred

15

"***I am the authentic vine*** and my Father does the cultivating. [2]He prunes every cane of mine that does not bear fruit, and every cane that does bear fruit he dresses so it will bear even more fruit. [3]You have already been 'dressed up' by the things I have told you. [4]You must stay attached to me, and I ⟨must stay attached⟩ to you. Just as a cane cannot bear fruit in and of itself—if it is detached from the trunk—so you ⟨can't bear fruit⟩ unless you stay attached to me. [5]I am the trunk, you are the canes. Those who stay attached to me—and I to them—produce a lot of fruit; you're not able to achieve anything apart from me. [6]Those who don't remain attached to me are thrown away like dead canes: they are collected, tossed into the fire, and burned. [7]If you stay attached to me and my words lodge in you, ask whatever you want and it will happen to you. [8]My Father's honor consists of this: the great quantity of fruit you produce in being my disciples.

[9]"I loved you in the same way the Father loved me. Live in my love. [10]If you observe my instructions, you will live in my love, just as I have observed my Father's instructions and live in his love.

[11]"I have told you all this so you will be the source of my happiness and so you yourselves will be filled with happiness. [12]This is my order to you: You are to love each other just as I loved you. [13]No one can love to a greater extent than to give up life for friends. [14]You are my friends if you follow my orders. [15]I no longer call you slaves, since a slave does not know what his master is up to. I have called you friends, because I let you know everything I learned from my Father. [16]You didn't choose me, I chose you. And I delegated you to go out and produce fruit. And your fruit will last because my Father will provide you with whatever you request in my name. [17]This is my order to you: You are to love each other.

[18]"***If the world hates you,*** don't forget that it hated me first. [19]If you were at home in the world, the world would befriend ⟨you as⟩ its own. But you are not at home in the world; on the contrary, I have separated you from the world; that's why the world hates you. [20]Recall what I told

14:31 Cf. Mk 14:42, Mt 26:46
15:2–8 Ⓣ SJas 6:9–11
15:4 Ⓣ SJas 6:23
15:5–6 Cf. Th 40
15:6 Cf. Q 3:9, Mt 3:10, Lk 3:9
15:7 //Q 11:9–10, Mt 7:7–8, Lk 11:9–10; cf. Mk 11:24, Mt 21:22; Th 2, 92.1, 94; Ⓣ Jn 14:13–14, 16:24
15:13 Ⓣ Jn 10:15, 1 Jn 3:16
15:14 Cf. Mk 3:35, Mt 12:50, Lk 8:21
15:16 Cf. Jn 14:13–14, 16:24; Ⓣ GNaz 11
15:18 Cf. Mk 13.13, Mt 10:22, Lk 21:17
15:20 //Q 6:40, Mt 10:24–25, Lk 6:40, DSav 20:1; Ⓣ Jn 13:16

14:30 *the ruler of this world:* See the note on 12:31.
14:31 *Come on . . . :* Jesus' address to the disciples seems to end here, but evidently it has been extended after chap. 14 was completed.
15:1 *I am the . . . vine:* Another metaphor for Jesus' relation to the Father and to his followers.
15:13 *friends:* See the note on 13:34.
15:15 *no longer . . . slaves:* Contrast 8:33–34.
15:18–19 *the world:* See the note on 7:7.

Jesus departs

you: 'Slaves are never better than their masters.' If they persecuted me, they'll surely persecute you. If they observe my teaching, they will also observe yours. [21]Yet they are going to do all these things to you because of me, since they don't recognize the one who sent me.

[22]"If I hadn't come and spoken to them, they wouldn't be guilty of sin. But as it is, they have no excuse for their sin.

[23]"Those who hate me also hate my Father.

[24]"If I had not performed deeds among them such as no one else has ever performed, they would not be guilty of sin. But as it is, they have observed ⟨these deeds⟩ and come to hate both me and my Father. ([25]This has happened so the saying in their Law would come true: 'They hated me for no reason.')

[26]"When the advocate comes, the one I'll send you from the Father, the spirit of truth that emerges from the Father, it will testify on my behalf. [27]And you are going to testify because you were with me from the beginning.

16 ***"I've told you*** these things to keep you from being led astray. [2]They are going to expel you from the synagogue. But the time is coming when those who kill you will think they are doing God a service. [3]They are going to do these things because they don't recognize either the Father or me. [4]Yet I have told you all this so when the time comes you'll recall that I told you about them. I didn't tell you these things at first because I was with you then. [5]Now I am on my way to the one who sent me, and not one of you asks me, 'Where are you going?' [6]Yet because I have told you these things, you are filled with grief. [7]But I'm telling you the truth: you'll be better off to have me leave. You see, if I don't leave, the advocate can't come to you. But if I go, I'll send the advocate to you. [8]When the advocate comes, it will convince the world of its error regarding sin, justification, and judgment: [9]regarding sin because they don't believe in me; [10]regarding justification because I am going to the Father and you won't see me anymore; [11]regarding judgment because the ruler of this world stands condemned. [12]I still have a lot to tell you, but you can't stand it just now. [13]When ⟨the advocate⟩ comes, the spirit of truth, it will guide you to the complete truth. It will not speak on its own authority, but will tell

15:23 Cf. Q 10:16, Mt 10:40, Lk 10:16
15:25 ◊Ps 35:19, 69:4
15:26–27 Ⓣ Jn 14:16–17, 16:13
16:1–2 // Mk 13:9–13, Mt 24:9–12, Lk 21:12–19
16:2 Cf. Mt 10:17, Lk 21:16; ◊Is 66:5
16:4–5 Ⓣ Th 92:2, SJas 9:7–8
16:5 Ⓣ SJas 2:4
16:7 Ⓣ SJas 6:34
16:13 Ⓣ Jn 14:16–17, 15:26–27; DSav 7:4

16:4 Many mss read "their time" in place of *the time.*

16:4 The perspective of this Farewell Address, while given as if during Jesus' lifetime, is the future, when Jesus will no longer be present, and he speaks—as he does characteristically throughout this gospel—as if from heaven.

16:5 *not one of you asks me, 'Where are you going?':* The author here forgets, or is ignorant of, 13:36. See the note on 14:31.

16:8 *the world:* See the note on 7:7.

16:9–11 The logic, and therefore meaning, of these verses is notoriously difficult to understand.

16:11 *the ruler of this world:* See the note on 12:31.

only what it hears and will disclose to you what is to happen. [14]It will honor me because it will disclose to you what it gets from me. [15]Everything the Father has belongs to me; that's why I told you, 'It will disclose to you what it gets from me.' [16]After a time you won't see me anymore, and then again a little later you will see me."

[17]Some of his disciples remarked to each other, "What does he mean when he tells us, 'After a time you won't see me, and then a little later you will see me'? And what does he mean by, 'I'm going to return to the Father'?" [18]So they asked, "What does 'a little later' mean? We don't understand what he's talking about."

[19]Jesus perceived that they wanted to question him, so he said to them, "Have you been discussing my remark 'After a time you won't see me, and then a little later you will see me'? [20]I swear to God, you will weep and mourn, but the world will celebrate. You will grieve, but your grief will turn to joy. [21]A woman suffers pain when she gives birth because the time has come. When her child is born, in her joy she no longer remembers her labor because a human being has come into the world. [22]And so you are now going to grieve. But I'll see you again, and then you'll rejoice, and nobody can deprive you of your joy. [23]When that time comes you'll ask nothing of me. I swear to God, if you ask the Father for anything using my name, he will grant it to you. [24]You haven't asked for anything using my name up to this point. Ask and you'll get it, so your bliss will be complete.

[25]"I have been talking to you in figures of speech. The time is coming when I'll no longer speak to you in figures but will tell you about the Father in plain language. [26]When that time comes, you will make requests using my name; I'm not telling you that I will make requests on your behalf, [27]since the Father himself loves you because you have befriended me and believe that I came from God. [28]I came from the Father and entered the world. Once again I'm going to leave the world and return to the Father."

[29]His disciples respond, "Now you're using plain language rather than talking in riddles. [30]Now we see that you know everything and don't need anyone to question you. This is why we believe you have come from God."

[31]"Do you really believe now?" Jesus countered. [32]"Look, the time has come for all of you to scatter and return home; you'll abandon me. But I won't be alone, because the Father is with me. [33]I have told you all this so you can possess my peace. In the world you're going to have trouble. But be resolute! I now have the world under control."

16:16 Ⓣ SJas6:40
16:20 Ⓣ Q6:21, Mt5:4, 6, Lk6:21, DSav8, SJas6:31–32
16:23–24 Cf. Mk11:24, Mt21:21–22, Q11:9–10, Mt7:7–8, Lk11:9–10; Ⓣ Jn14:13–14; 15:7, 16
16:23 Ⓣ SJas6:37
16:25 Ⓣ SJas6:5
16:28 Ⓣ SJas2:4, 9:7
16:32 Cf. Mk14:27, Mt26:31; ◊ Zec13:7

16:16–19 *After a time . . . a little later:* These two phrases are synonymous; they translate the same Greek expression.
16:20 *the world:* See the note on 7:7.
16:21 *the world:* In contrast to its use in v. 20 and elsewhere, here the phrase has a positive, or at least neutral, meaning.
16:32 *you'll abandon me:* a prediction that is not fulfilled, unlike the synoptics, in this gospel.
16:33 *the world:* See the note on 7:7.

Final prayer

17 ***Jesus spoke these words,*** then he looked up and prayed: “Father, the time has come. Honor your son, so your son may honor you. [2]Just as you have given him authority over all humankind, so he can award real life to everyone you have given him. [3]This is real life: to know you as the one true God, and Jesus Christ, the one you sent. [4]I honor you on earth by completing the labors you gave me to do. [5]Now, Father, honor me with your own presence, the presence I enjoyed before the world ⟨began⟩.

[6]“I have made your name known to all those you gave me out of the world ⟨of humankind⟩. They were yours, you gave them to me, and they have kept your word. [7]They now recognize that everything you gave me is really from you. [8]I passed on to them the things you gave me to say, and they have been receptive ⟨to those things⟩ and have come to know truly that I have come from your presence; they have also come to believe you sent me. [9]I plead on their behalf; I am not pleading for the world but for those you turned over to me because they are yours. [10]Everything that belongs to me is yours, and everything that belongs to you is mine, so I have been honored by them. [11]I am no longer in the world, but they are to remain in the world, while I am going to return to you. Holy Father, keep them under your protection—all those you have given me, so they may be united just as we are united. [12]When I was with them, I kept them under your protection, and I guarded them; not one of them was lost, except the one destined to be lost, since scripture has to come true. [13]Now I'm returning to you, but I say these things while I'm still in the world, so they may fully share my elation. [14]I have passed on your instructions to them, so the world hated them because they are aliens in the world, as I am an alien in the world. [15]I do not ask to have them taken from the world but to have them rescued from evil. [16]They are aliens in the world, as I am. [17]Dedicate them to the service of truth. Your word is truth. [18]I sent them into the world as you sent me into the world. [19]And I now consecrate myself on their behalf, so they too may be consecrated by truth.

[20]“I am not pleading only on their behalf, but also on behalf of those who believe in me as a result of their word: [21]they should all be united, just as you, Father, are with me and I with you; may they be one in us, so the world will believe that you sent me. [22]The honor you granted me I passed on to them, so they may be one, as we are one, [23]I with them and you with me, so they may be perfectly united, so the world will know you sent me and loved them as much as you loved me. [24]Father, I want those you gave into my care to be with me wherever I am, so they may see my honor—the honor you bestowed on me because you loved

17:5
Ⓣ SJas6:13
17:6
Ⓣ GNaz11
17:20
Ⓣ SJas6:36

17:21 Many mss read merely “in us” in place of *one in us*.

17:9 *the world:* See the note on 7:7. Similarly in vv. 11, 14, 15 of this chapter, but in v. 5 and possibly vv. 6, 13 the phrase does not have this negative connotation.

me before the foundations of the world ⟨were laid⟩. [25]Noble Father, the world did not acknowledge you, but I acknowledged you, and these ⟨you gave into my care⟩ acknowledged that you sent me; [26]I also made your name known to them and will continue to make it known, so the kind of love you have for me may be theirs, and I may be theirs also."

Judas turns Jesus in

Before Annas

Peter's first denial

18 ***When he had said all this,*** Jesus went out with his disciples across the Kidron valley. There was a garden there where he and his disciples went. [2]But because Jesus had often gone there with his disciples, Judas, who was about to turn him in, knew the place too. [3]So it wasn't long before Judas arrives, bringing with him the detachment ⟨of Roman soldiers⟩ and some of the police from the ranking priests and the Pharisees, armed and with their lamps and torches.

[4]Jesus, of course, knew just what would happen to him, so he went right up to them and says, "Who is it you're looking for?"

[5]"Jesus the Nazarene," was their reply.

"That's me," says Jesus.

And all the while Judas, who was turning him in, was standing there with them. [6]But as soon as he said, "That's me," they all retreated and fell to the ground.

[7]So Jesus asked them again, "Who are you looking for?"

"Jesus the Nazarene," they said.

[8]"I told you that's me," Jesus answered, "so if it's me you're looking for, let the others go."

([9]This was so the prediction he had made would come true: "I haven't lost one—not one of those you put in my care.")

[10]Simon Peter had brought along a sword, and now he drew it, slashed at the high priest's slave, who was called Malchus, and cut off his right ear.

[11]"Put the sword back in its scabbard," Jesus told Peter. "Am I not to drink from the cup my Father has given me?"

[12]***Then the detachment*** and their captain, with the Judean police, arrested Jesus and put him under constraint. [13]They took him first to Annas. (Annas was the father-in-law of that year's high priest, Caiaphas. [14]It was Caiaphas, you'll remember, who had given the Judeans this advice: It's to ⟨your⟩ advantage that one man die for the people.)

[15]***Simon Peter*** and another disciple continued to trail along behind Jesus. This other disciple, somehow known to the high priest, went in

17:25–26 Cf. Q10:22, Mt11:27, Lk10:22
18:1–12 //Mk14:43–52, Mt26:47–56, Lk22:47–54
18:1 //Mk14:32, Mt26:36
18:11 Ⓣ Mk14:36, Mt26:39, Lk22:42
18:14 Ⓣ Jn11:50
18:15–18 //Mk14:66–68, Mt26:69–70, Lk22:54–57

18:1 *went out:* That is, from the place of the last supper, chapters 13–17.

Kidron valley: Separating Jerusalem and the Mount of Olives.

18:3 *detachment:* Strictly, a *cohort* of six hundred men; probably an exaggeration.

police: Or *deputies*, as in 7:32.

18:5 *That's me:* Literally, *I am*; see the note on 4:26.

18:6 *retreated and fell to the ground:* This unrealistic reaction is to be understood as the consequence of Jesus' words, reiterated from v. 5.

18:12 *put him under constraint:* literally, "bound him."

Trial before the high priest

Peter's second denial

Trial before Pilate

with Jesus to the high priest's court. [16]Peter was standing outside the door; so this other disciple, the one acquainted with the high priest, went out, had a word with the woman who kept the door, and got Peter in.

[17]The woman who kept watch at the door says to Peter, "You're not one of this man's disciples too, are you?"

"No, I'm not," he replies.

[18]Meanwhile, since it was cold, the slaves and police had made a charcoal fire and were standing around it, trying to keep warm. Peter was standing there too, warming himself.

[19]***Now the high priest*** interrogated Jesus about his disciples and about his teaching.

[20]"I have talked publicly to anyone and everyone," Jesus replied. "I've always taught in synagogues and in the temple area, in places where all Judeans gather. I've said nothing in secret. [21]Why are you asking me? Ask those who listened to what I told them—you'll find that they know what I said."

[22]No sooner had he said this than one of the police on duty there slapped Jesus. "So this is how you talk back to the high priest!" he said.

[23]"If I've said the wrong thing, tell me what's wrong with it," Jesus said in reply. "But if I'm right, why do you hit me?"

[24]At that Annas sent him, under constraint as before, to the high priest, Caiaphas.

[25]***Meanwhile,*** Simon Peter was still standing outside, keeping warm. The others there said to him, "You're not one of his disciples too, are you?"

He denied it: "No, I'm not," he said.

[26]One of the high priest's slaves, a relative of the one whose ear Peter had cut off, says, "I saw you in the garden with him, didn't I?"

[27]Once again Peter denied it. At that moment a rooster crowed.

[28]***They then take Jesus*** from Caiaphas' place to the governor's residence. By now it was early morning. They didn't actually go into the governor's residence; otherwise they would become unclean, and unable to eat the Passover meal. [29]Then Pilate came out and says to them, "What charge are you bringing against this man?"

[30]"If he hadn't committed a crime," they retorted, "we wouldn't have turned him over to you."

[31]"Deal with him yourselves," Pilate said to them. "Judge him by your own Law."

"But it's illegal for us to execute anyone," the Judeans said to him.

18:19–24 //Mk 14:55–65, Mt 26:59–68, Lk 22:66–71

18:20 Cf. Mk 14:49, Mt 26:55, Lk 22:53

18:25–27 //Mk 14:69–72, Mt 26:71–75, Lk 22:58–62

18:28–40 //Mk 15:1–15; Mt 27:1–2, 11–26; Lk 23:1–7, 13–25

18:28 *become unclean, and unable to eat the Passover meal:* Ritual purification before observing a sacred rite precluded associating too closely with any pagan, that is, unclean, person or thing.

18:29 Pilate begins to shuttle back and forth, between Jesus within the residence and the Judeans outside. The narrative evidently wants to show him at the mercy of two powers, each stronger than himself.

18:31 *it's illegal for us*: The accuracy of this claim is doubtful; it suggests that the Jewish authorities would have executed Jesus if they could (see the note on 19:16).

Trial before Pilate continues

([32]They said this so Jesus' prediction of how he would die would come true.)

[33]Then Pilate went back into his residence. He summoned Jesus and asked him, "*You* are 'the King of the Judeans'?"

[34]"Is this what you think," Jesus answered, "or what other people have told you about me?"

[35]"Am I a Judean?!" countered Pilate. "It's your own people and the ranking priests who have turned you over to me. What have you done?"

[36]To this Jesus responded, "Mine is not a secular government. If my government were secular my companions would fight to keep me from being turned over to the Judeans. But as it is, my government does not belong to the secular domain."

[37]"So you are a king!" said Pilate.

"You're the one who says I'm a king," responded Jesus. "This is what I was born for, and this is why I came into the world: to bear witness to the truth. Everyone who belongs to the truth can hear my voice."

[38]"What is the truth?" says Pilate.

When he had said this, he again went out to the Judeans. "In my judgment there is no case against him," he says to them. [39]"But it's your privilege at Passover to have me free one prisoner for you. So, do you want me to free 'the King of the Judeans' for you?"

[40]At this they shouted out again, "Not him, but Barabbas!" (Barabbas was a rebel.)

19 ***Only then did Pilate*** have Jesus taken away and beaten.

[2]And the soldiers wove a crown out of thorns and put it on his head; they also dressed him up in a purple robe. [3]They began marching up to him: "Greetings, 'King of the Judeans,'" they would say, as they slapped him in the face.

[4]Pilate went outside once more. "See here," he says, "I'm bringing him out to make it clear to you that in my judgment there is no case against him."

18.33–38
Cf. Mk 15:2, Mt 27:1, Lk 23:2–3
18:40
Cf. GNaz 9
19:1–3
//Mk 15:16–20, Mt 27:27–31, Pet 2:3b-3:4
19:4–16
//Mk 15:1–15; Mt 27:11–26; Lk 23:1–7, 13–25

18:32 *so Jesus' prediction of how he would die would come true:* The logic here seems to be that since Jesus has predicted he would be "lifted up" (3:14; 12:32–33), taken to refer to a crucifixion, he must be put to death by the Romans, not given a Jewish execution by stoning. The Jewish leaders' excluding themselves inadvertently determines that Jesus will be crucified.

18:36 *companions:* The Greek word, elsewhere translated *deputies* or *police* and used of servants to the Judean authorities, can hardly mean that here, since Jesus' authority is not one of *secular* power; on the contrary, as Jesus has just said.

18:38 *What is the truth?:* An expression of Pilate's bewilderment. He does not cynically raise a hopeless philosophical question, as it is often held, but simply despairs of getting to the bottom of the facts.

18:39 Outside the gospels there is no evidence for such a *privilege*.

18:40 *shouted out again:* or, *shouted back*, since as the narrative stands this is the first time they cry out for *Barabbas*.

5Now Jesus came outside, still wearing the crown of thorns and the
purple robe.
⟨Pilate⟩ says to them, "See for yourselves: here's the man."
6When the ranking priests and the police saw him, they screamed,
"Crucify him! Crucify him!"
"Deal with him yourselves," Pilate tells them. "You crucify him. I
have told you already: I don't find him guilty of any crime."
7"We have our Law," the Judeans answered, "and our Law says that
he ought to die because he has made himself out to be God's son."
8When Pilate heard their statement he was even more afraid. 9He
went back into his residence.
"Where are you from?" he asks Jesus.
But Jesus didn't answer him.
10"You won't speak to me?" says Pilate. "Don't you understand? I
have the power to free you, and I have the power to crucify you."
11"You would have no power of any kind over me," said Jesus,
"unless it was given to you from above. That is why the one who turned
me in to you has committed the greater sin."
12At this, Pilate began to look for a way to release him. But the
Judeans screamed at him, "If you free this man, you're not the emper-
or's friend! Every self-appointed king is in rebellion against the
emperor."
13Pilate heard all this, but still he brought Jesus out and sat him on
the judge's seat in the place called Stone Pavement (*Gabbatha* in
Hebrew). 14It was now the day of preparation for Passover, about twelve
noon. He says to the Judeans, "Look, here's your king."
15But they only screamed, "Get him out of here! Crucify him!"
"Am I supposed to crucify your king?" asks Pilate.
The ranking priests answered him, "The emperor's our king—we
19:9 Cf. Lk 23:9 have no other!"
16And so, in the end, ⟨Pilate⟩ turned him over to them to be cruci-
19:16 Cf. GHeb 1:6 fied.

19:5 *the man:* Or, *the ⟨true⟩ human being,* perhaps the author's irony.
19:11 *the one who turned me in to you:* Usually taken to refer to Judas (18:2–3) but possibly referring to the Judeans.
19:13 *sat him*: or, simply, *sat down.*
Hebrew: As in 5:2 and elsewhere the Semitic word, here of uncertain meaning, is actually in Aramaic.
19:14 *the day of preparation for Passover:* Or, *Friday in Passover*; see the note on v. 31.
19:15 *The emperor's our king—we have no other!:* The Jewish leaders are portrayed as rejecting all expectation of their messiah, a thoroughly unhistorical element in the story.
19:16 *to them to be crucified:* In the narrative as it stands, "them" can hardly mean anyone but "the Judeans" (unless this is a careless mistake and refers to the soldiers—see v. 23). The resulting implication that all the Jews/Judeans, or perhaps only some Jewish officials, crucified Jesus—as Pilate had suggested (v. 6)—is wholly inaccurate. In historical fact, whatever Pilate's view of Jesus' guilt, it was certainly he who saw to the execution (see v. 19); crucifixion was never practiced by Jews. The monstrous unreality of this half-verse, if it reads as intended, must be entirely a function of theological or political polemic. See Introduction on "Jews/Judeans."

So they took Jesus, [17]who carried the cross for himself, out to the place called Skull (known in Hebrew as *Golgotha*). [18]There they crucified him, and with him two others—one on each side, with Jesus in the middle.

Jesus is crucified

Jesus breathes his last

[19]Pilate also had a notice written and posted it on the cross; it read: "Jesus the Nazarene, the King of the Judeans." [20]Many of the Judeans saw the notice, since Jesus was crucified near the city and it was written in Hebrew, Latin, and Greek. [21]The ranking Judean priests tried protesting to Pilate: "Don't write, 'The King of the Judeans,' but instead, 'This man said, "I am King of the Judeans."'"

[22]Pilate answered them, "What I have written stays written."

[23]When the soldiers had crucified Jesus, they took his clothes and divided them into four shares, one share for each soldier. But his shirt was woven continuously without seam. [24]So they said to each other, "Let's not tear it, but toss to see who gets it."

(This happened so that the scripture would come true that says, "They divided my garments among them, and for my clothes they cast lots.")

So while the soldiers did this, [25]Jesus' mother, his mother's sister, Mary the wife of Clopas, and Mary of Magdala stood by his cross. [26]When Jesus saw his mother, and standing nearby the disciple he loved most, he says to his mother, "Woman, here is your son." [27]Then he says to the disciple, "Here is your mother." And from that moment the disciple considered her part of his own family.

[28]***Then, since Jesus knew*** that the course of events had come to an end, so the scripture would come true, he says, "I'm thirsty."

[29]A bowl of sour wine was sitting there, and so they filled a sponge with wine, stuck it on some hyssop, and held it to his mouth. [30]When Jesus had taken some wine, he said, "It's all over."

His head sank and he breathed his last.

[31]Since it was the day of preparation, the Judeans asked Pilate to have the legs of the three broken and the bodies taken away. Otherwise their bodies would remain on the cross during the sabbath day. (That sabbath was a high holy day.)

19:17–30 //Mk15:22–37, Mt27:33–50, Lk22:32–46, Pet4:1–5
19:24 ◊Ps22:18
19:28–30 Cf.Pet5:1–5
19:28–29 ◊Ps69:21
19:31 ◊Dt21:22–23

19:17 *Hebrew:* See the note on 5:2.

19:19 *notice:* At a crucifixion this sign (*titulus* in Latin) was customarily posted on the cross and indicated the crime deserving execution.

19:23–24 *But his shirt . . . to see who gets it:* This detail, not found in the other gospels, perhaps reflects the assumption that the passage from scripture would *come true* precisely as it is worded.

19:29 *hyssop:* Possibly an allusion to one of the uses of this plant in Jewish ceremonial, but here the word has often been regarded as an error and variously adapted. The precise species of plant must be uncertain, but the plant usually called hyssop is too delicate to support a sponge full of wine.

The offering of *sour wine* may be either a humane act (the soldiers sharing some of their ordinary wine) or—in view of Jesus' remark—a form of mistreatment like that described in Psalm 69:21.

19:31 *to have the legs of the three broken:* Perhaps a formality declaring the victim dead, or a practice designed to hasten death.

Otherwise their bodies would remain on the cross during the sabbath day: According to Jewish practice the dead must if possible be

Joseph buries Jesus

Mary of Magdala at the tomb

Two disciples at the tomb

32The soldiers came and broke the legs of the first man, and then of
the other who had been crucified with him. 33But when they came to
Jesus, they could see that he was already dead, so they didn't break his
legs. 34Instead, one of the soldiers jabbed him in the side with his spear,
and right away blood and water came pouring out. (35The one who
observed this has given this testimony and his testimony is true. He
knows he is telling the truth, so you too will believe.) 36This happened
so the scripture that says, "No bone of his shall be broken," would
come true, 37as well as another scripture that says, "They shall look at
the one they have pierced."

38***After all this,*** Joseph of Arimathea—a disciple of Jesus, but only
secretly because he was afraid of the Judeans—asked Pilate's permission to take Jesus' body down. Pilate agreed, so ⟨Joseph⟩ came and
took his body down. 39Nicodemus—the one who had first gone to him
at night—came too, bringing a mixture of myrrh and aloes weighing
about seventy-five pounds. 40So they took Jesus' body, and wound it up
in strips of burial cloth along with the spices, as the Judeans customarily do to bury their dead. 41Now there was a garden in the place
where he had been crucified, and a new tomb in the garden where no
one had yet been laid to rest. 42Since this tomb was handy and because
of the Judean day of preparation, it was here that they laid Jesus.

20 ***On Sunday,*** by the half-light of the early morning, Mary of
Magdala comes to the tomb—and sees that the stone has been moved
away. 2So she runs and comes to Simon Peter and the other disciple—
the one that Jesus loved most—and tells them, "They've taken the
Master from the tomb, and we don't know where they've put him."

3***So Peter and the other disciple*** went out, and they make their way
to the tomb. 4The two of them were running along together, but the
other disciple ran faster than Peter and was the first to reach the tomb.
5Stooping down, he could see the strips of burial cloth lying there; but
he didn't go in. 6Then Simon Peter comes along behind him and went
in. He too sees the strips of burial cloth there, 7and also the cloth they
had used to cover his head, lying not with the strips of burial cloth but
rolled up by itself. 8Then the other disciple, who had been the first to

19:36
◊Ps 34:20
19:37
◊Zec 12:10
19:38–42
//Mk 15:42–47; Mt 27:57–61; Lk 23:50–56; Pet 2:1–3a, 6:1–4
20:1–18
//Mk 16:1–8, Mt 28:1–15, Lk 24:1–11; cf. Pet 9:1–13:3

19:35 Some mss read "continue to believe" in place of *believe.*

buried before sundown; otherwise no later than the next day. But no such work could be done on the sabbath. This notice seems unaware of the requirement in Deut 21:22–23 that a hanged (including crucified) man must in any case be buried on the same day.

a high holy day: Being also Passover; *the day of preparation* (here and in v. 14) can mean either the day before Passover or simply Friday; in this case it is both.

19:35 This parenthetical remark, with its emphatic validation of the details in v. 34 and its insistence of historical accuracy, is puzzling. Some believe that it has been inserted by a later hand than the author's; if so, the puzzle remains.

19:39 *seventy-five pounds:* A wildly extravagant amount.

reach the tomb, came in. He saw all this, and he believed. [9]But since neither of them yet understood the prophecy that he was destined to rise from the dead, [10]these disciples went back home.

Mary meets Jesus

[11]***Mary, however,*** stood crying outside, and in her tears she stooped to look into the tomb, [12]and she sees two heavenly messengers in white seated where Jesus' body had lain, one at the head and the other at the feet.

[13]"Woman, why are you crying?" they ask her.

"They've taken my Master away," she tells them, "and I don't know where they've put him."

[14]No sooner had she said this than she turned around and sees Jesus standing there—but she didn't know that it was Jesus.

[15]"Woman," Jesus says to her, "why are you crying? Who is it you're looking for?"

She could only suppose that it was the gardener, and so she says to him, "Please, mister, if you've moved him, tell me where you've put him so I can take him away."

[16]"Mary," says Jesus.

She turns around and exclaims in Hebrew, "Rabbi!" (which means "Teacher").

[17]"Don't touch me," Jesus tells her, "because I have not yet gone back to the Father. But go to my brothers and tell them this: 'I'm going back to my Father and your Father—to my God and your God.'"

[18]Mary of Magdala goes and reports to the disciples, "I have seen the Master," and relates everything he had told her.

Behind locked doors

[19]***That Sunday evening,*** the disciples had locked the doors for fear of the Judeans, but Jesus came and stood in front of them and he greets them: "Peace."

[20]Then he showed them his hands and his side. The disciples were delighted to see the Master. [21]Jesus greets them again: "Peace," he says. "Just as the Father sent me, so now I'm sending you."

[22]And at this he breathed over them and says, "Here's some holy spirit. Take it. [23]If you forgive anyone their sins, they are forgiven; if you do not release them from their sins, they are not released."

Doubting Thomas

[24]***Now Thomas,*** the one known as "the Twin," one of the twelve, hadn't been with them when Jesus put in his appearance. [25]So the other disciples tried to tell him, "We've seen the Master."

20:14–18 Cf. Mary 7.1–2
20:17 Ⓣ SJas 6:13
20:18 //Mary 6:4
20:19–23 //Lk 24:33–49; cf. Mk 16:14–18
20:23 Cf. Mt 16:19, 18:18

20:17 Many mss read "my Father" in place of *the Father.*

20:16 *in Hebrew:* See the note on 5.2.
20:17 *touch:* or, *restrain, cling to.* The meaning of these words is much debated; see the next note.

because I have not yet gone back to the Father: It is not clear what this, together with the injunction that it seeks to explain, means: that Jesus must not be deterred from his destination? that he is in an intermediate or unclean state and must not be touched? that Mary's attempt is somehow, in her love for him, to try to draw him back into her world? or what?
20:24 *Twin:* See the note on 11:16.

Appearance by the Sea of Tiberias

But he responded, "Unless I see the holes the nails made, and put
my finger in them and my hand in his side, I'll never believe."
26A week later the disciples were again indoors, and Thomas was
with them. The doors were locked, but Jesus comes and stood in front
of them, and said, "Peace." 27Then he says to Thomas, "Put your finger
here, and look at my hands; take your hand and put it in my side. Don't
be skeptical but be a believer."
28Thomas responded, "My Master! My God!"
29"Do you believe because you have seen me?" asks Jesus. "Those
who can believe without having to see are the ones to be congratulated."
30Although Jesus performed many more miracles for his disciples to
see than could be written down in this book, 31these are written down
so you will come to believe that Jesus is the Anointed, God's son—and
by believing this have life in his name.

21 ***Some time after these events,*** Jesus again appeared to his disciples by the Sea of Tiberias. This is how he did it: 2When Simon Peter
and Thomas, the one known as "the Twin," were together, along with
Nathaniel from Cana, Galilee, the sons of Zebedee, and two other
disciples, 3Simon Peter says to them, "I'm going to go fishing."
"We're coming with you," they reply.
They went down and got into the boat, but that night they didn't
catch a thing.
4It was already getting light when Jesus appeared on the shore, but
his disciples didn't recognize that it was Jesus.
5"Lads, you haven't caught any fish, have you?" Jesus asks them.
"No," they replied.
6He tells them, "Cast your net on the right side of the boat and you'll
have better luck."
They do as he instructs them and now they can't haul it in for the
huge number of fish. 7The disciple Jesus loved most exclaims to Peter,
"It's the Master!"
When Simon Peter heard "It's the Master," he tied his cloak around
himself, since he was stripped for work, and threw himself into the

20:29 Cf. SJas 3:6–7; Ⓣ SJas 8:6
21:1–8 Cf. Lk 5:4–11

20:31 Some mss read "continue to believe" in place of *come to believe.*

20:30–31 These verses conclude the original gospel, in the view of most scholars, chapter 21 being a later addition, whether by the same author or (more likely) another.
21:2 *Twin:* See the note on 11:16.
21:7 *tied his cloak around himself, since he was stripped for work:* This sentence is usually rendered "put on his ⟨outer⟩ garment, for he was naked" or similarly; so understood it is highly anomalous in view of Peter's jumping into the water that follows. Peter's action means literally "girded himself" and the word for "naked" need mean only "not fully clad." As translated here the difficulty disappears. Peter was stripped to the waist for heavy work in the boat and so girded up the garments tied about his waist, so as to swim and wade ashore.

water. [8]The rest of them came in the boat, dragging the net full of fish. They were not far from land, only about a hundred yards offshore.

Meal on the shore

Jesus interrogates Peter

Peter & the disciple Jesus loved most

[9]***When they got to shore,*** they see a charcoal fire burning, with fish cooking on it, and some bread. [10]Jesus says to them, "Bring some of the fish you've just caught."

[11]Then Simon Peter went aboard and hauled the net full of large fish ashore—one hundred fifty-three of them. Even though there were so many of them, the net still didn't tear.

[12]Jesus says to them, "Come and eat."

None of the disciples dared ask, "Who are you?" They knew it was the Master. [13]Jesus comes, takes the bread and gives it to them, and passes the fish around as well.

[14]This was now the third time after he had been raised from the dead that Jesus appeared to his disciples.

[15]***When they had eaten,*** Jesus asks Simon Peter, "Simon, John's son, do you love me more than they do?"

"Of course, Master; you know I love you," he replies.

"Then keep feeding my lambs," Jesus tells him.

[16]⟨Jesus⟩ asks him again, for the second time, "Simon, John's son, do you love me?"

"Yes, Master; you know I love you," he replies.

"Keep shepherding my sheep."

[17]⟨Jesus⟩ says to him a third time, "Simon, John's son, do you love me?"

Peter was hurt that he had asked him for the third time, "Do you love me?" and he says to him, "Master, you know everything; you know I love you."

Jesus says to him, "Keep feeding my sheep. [18]I swear to God, when you were young you used to gather your cloak about you and go where you wanted to go. But when you've grown old, you'll stretch out your arms, and someone else will get you ready and take you where you don't want to go."

([19]He said this to indicate with what kind of death ⟨Peter⟩ would honor God.)

And after saying this, he adds, "Keep following me."

[20]***Peter turns*** and sees the disciple Jesus loved most following them—the one who had leaned over on Jesus' right at supper and asked, "Master, who is going to turn you in?" [21]When Peter saw this disciple ⟨following⟩, he asks Jesus, "Master, what about this fellow?"

[22]Jesus replies to him, "What business is it of yours if I want him to stay around till I come? You are to keep on following me."

21:18 Many mss read "others" in place of *someone else.*

21:11 *aboard:* or, *ashore,* the Greek word meaning either.

21:18 *you'll stretch out your arms:* Apparently a prediction that Peter is to be crucified (see the note on v. 19).

get you ready: or, *gird you,* that is, perhaps, "tie you ⟨to a cross⟩?"

21:19 With the parenthesis, compare 12:33.

Conclusion

([23]Because of this the rumor spread among the family of believers that this disciple wouldn't die. But Jesus had not said to him, "He won't die"; he said, "What business is it of yours if I want him to stay around till I come?")

[24]***This is the disciple*** who is testifying to all this and has written it down, and we know that his testimony is reliable.

[25]Jesus of course did many other things. If they were all to be recorded in detail, I doubt that the entire world would hold the books that would have to be written.

21:23 Some mss omit *What business is it of yours?*

21:23 Evidently it had been believed at one time in the Johannine community that "the disciple Jesus loved most" (13:23) would not die. (Was this disciple—mentioned first only in ch. 13—identified with Lazarus of chs. 11–12, "whom Jesus loved" and who had already died? Or does this disciple exemplify Jesus' promise in 8:51?) Presumably this figure, if a real person, had in fact died by the time this chapter was written, and the saying that would have given rise to the belief is shown to have been misunderstood.

21:24 *This is the disciple who is testifying to all this:* Possibly "the disciple Jesus loved most" had functioned as an authority standing at the beginning of the Johannine tradition. On the other hand, this assertion, together with the confidence that the evidence is *true*, may be either inadvertently inaccurate or even (some would claim) deliberately invented. It is widely thought unlikely that very much of the information in this gospel has historical accuracy (since that is what "true" here seems to mean).

and has written it down: This cannot be true. In its completed form this gospel, like the other three, was hardly written by an eyewitness to the events it records. And perhaps still less than the synoptic gospels does it contain tradition that would have stemmed from one of Jesus' disciples. It is interesting, nevertheless, that this gospel alone contains, as a brief epilogue to the appended chapter 21, a claim as to its authorship. The title at the work's beginning, "[The Gospel] according to John," as with the other gospels, was prefixed to the text only in the latter half of the second century. There is no suggestion in the text that "the disciple Jesus loved most" was named John.

21:25 This exaggerated observation seems to have been modeled on the earlier conclusion, 20:30–31.

Sayings Gospels

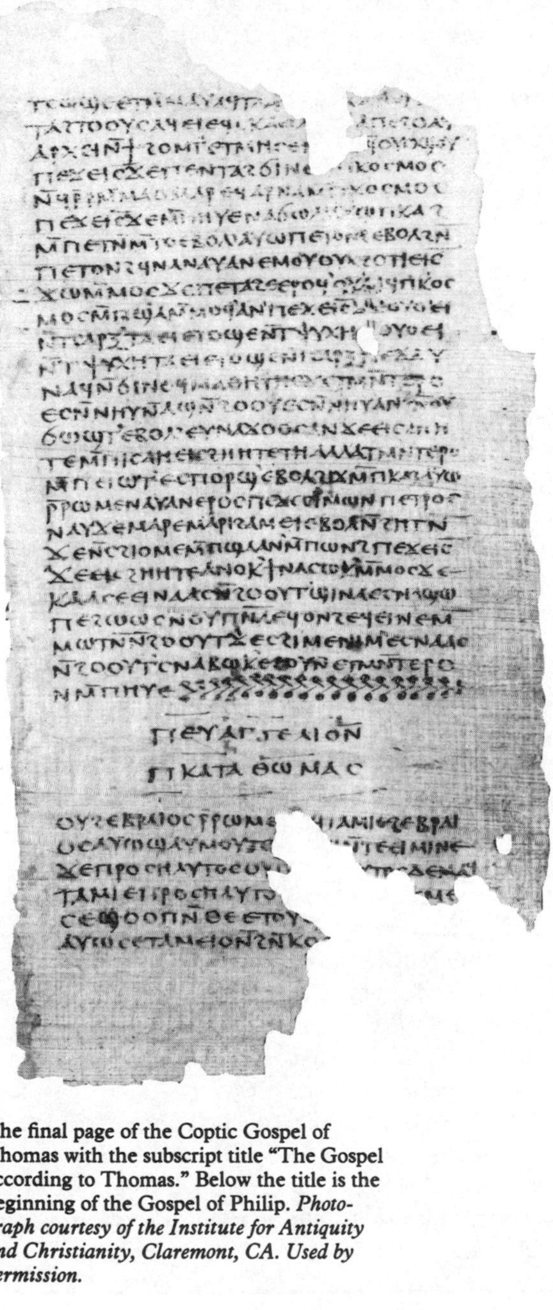

The final page of the Coptic Gospel of Thomas with the subscript title "The Gospel according to Thomas." Below the title is the beginning of the Gospel of Philip. *Photograph courtesy of the Institute for Antiquity and Christianity, Claremont, CA. Used by permission.*

Establishing the text of Q

Q no longer exists as a separate text so it must be reconstructed from Matthew and Luke. Two kinds of reconstruction are necessary: determining the sequence of the segments in Q, and establishing the wording of Q where Matthew and Luke diverge.

The *sequence* of Q is established by carefully analyzing the sequence of the material in Matthew and Luke, and then asking how one can account for differences between them. The main tool for doing this is knowledge of the editorial tendencies of Matthew and Luke.

For example, consider this sequence:

Matt 5:1–7:27	Luke 6:20–49	Jesus' Inaugural Sermon
8:5–13	7:1–10	Healing story
11:2–19	7:18–35	John and Jesus
8:19–22	9:57–60	Following Jesus

The location of the "John and Jesus" discourse varies in Matthew and Luke. The other items occur in the same relative order. Matthew has probably shifted the "Jesus and John" pericope to a later point in his gospel so that the miracles mentioned in 11:4–5 ("Go report to John what you have heard and seen") can first be described. In fact, Matt 8:5–13 becomes the first of a whole series of miracles reported in Matthew 8–9. By moving the "John and Jesus" segment, Matthew has narrated ample evidence for John's disciples to report to him.

Luke sensed the same problem. He solved it, however, by having Jesus perform many miracles on the spot (7:20–21) just before he has Jesus tell John's disciples to go and report to their master what they have seen and heard.

The *wording* of Q is established in a number of ways: simple logic, the study of the editorial tendencies of Matthew and Luke, comparison with Mark and with other independent traditions, and coherence with other Q materials.

In Q 7:35, for example, Matthew (11:19) reads, "Wisdom is vindicated by her deeds" while Luke 7:35 reads, "Wisdom is vindicated by all her children." While the word "children" in Luke could derive from the preceding parable (Luke 7:31–32), it is difficult to explain why Luke would have substituted the unusual "children" for "deeds," since "deeds" goes logically with "vindicated." It is more likely that Q had "children" both in 7:31–32 and 7:35. Moreover, Matthew introduced the whole discourse by referring to "the deeds of the Anointed" (11:2); he concludes the discourse by changing "children" to "deeds" to make the final reference agree with the first.

The process of establishing the text of Q, although highly conjectural at many points, can produce fairly reliable results in recreating the contours of what was probably the first gospel.

Introduction

A *hypothetical text*

"Q" is an abbreviation of the German word *Quelle*, meaning "source." It is used to designate a document which most scholars believe the authors of Matthew and Luke used in writing their gospels. These gospel writers, it is believed, also used the Gospel of Mark. While Mark is an extant text, Q is a hypothetical construct. No independent copy of it exists. But it is widely believed that the passages in Matthew and Luke that are almost the same, and that did not come from Mark, must have come from this lost source, Q. The non-Markan passages common to Matthew and Luke agree word-for-word so often that Q must have been a written document and not simply a body of material that Matthew and Luke took from oral tradition. The theory that Q and Mark were literary sources for the Gospels of Matthew and Luke is called the Two Source Theory; this theory was first proposed about 150 years ago. In recent years there has been a renewed interest in Q, and significant progress has been made in isolating and understanding it.

One convention of scholarship should be made clear at the outset. Since Q scholars hold the view that the sequence of sayings and their wording are best preserved in the Gospel of Luke, references to Q always indicate the chapter and verse of Luke. Accordingly, Q 3:7–9 refers to Luke 3:7–9.

Q texts are almost always printed in their Lukan order. The few exceptions should occasion no difficulty. However, since the author of Luke has scattered Q materials throughout the gospel, the Q references will not be continuous with the chapters and verses of Luke. The parallel references to Matthew, on the other hand, will rarely occur in their Matthean order. Since SV Q follows the Lukan order, the Luke text is printed on the left and the Matthean text on the right, reversing their canonical order. Verses printed in *italics* are passages attested in only one gospel but which, on literary or thematic grounds, have a strong probability of deriving from Q.

A sayings gospel

Q is a collection of the sayings of Jesus, similar in form to the Gospel of Thomas. Unlike the sayings in Thomas, however, most of the sayings in Q are gathered into discourses. One of these is the Sermon on the Mount (Matthew) or Plain (Luke). Other discourses focus upon John the Baptist (Q 7:18–35), mission instructions to the disciples (Q 10:2–16), prayer (Q 11:9–13), exorcism (Q 11:14–26), condemnation of Pharisees (Q 11:39–52), and other subjects. Not all of Q consists of sayings, however; it included at least two bits of narrative: the story of the temptation of Jesus in Q 4:1–13 and a miracle story in Q 7:1–10.

An early gospel

Q lacks many things one might expect in an early document dealing with Jesus: stories or even sayings that deal with Jesus' death and resurrection, the title "Anointed," named disciples, birth stories, and many miracle stories found elsewhere in the New Testament gospels. Compared with them, Q seems theologically underdeveloped. Q also seems quite provincial. It mentions only a few place-names: a few towns on the north shore of the Sea of Galilee (Capernaum in Q 7:1 and 10:15, and nearby Chorazin and Bethsaida in Q 10:13), Jerusalem (Q 13:34), and the Syrian towns of Tyre and Sidon (Q 10:13, 14). The theologically underdeveloped state of Q, its provincial character, and its use by Matthew and Luke are among the indications that Q must have been a very early document. Since Q lacks so many of the elements one finds in clearly Christian documents, one might even call it a pre-Christian gospel. Put differently, Q may be a kind of missing link between the Jewish world of Jesus and the early Christian church.

The language of Q

Q is not simply a transcript of the words of Jesus. One sign of this is the language in which Q was probably written. Most scholars assume that the first language of Jesus and his followers was Aramaic, though they may also have spoken Greek. In any case, Q was apparently written in Greek. The frequent word-for-word agreements between Matthew and Luke are impossible to account for if both were independently translating from Aramaic. Furthermore, most of Q's quotations or allusions to the Old Testament depend upon the Septuagint, the Greek version of the Hebrew Bible.

Wisdom and prophecy in Q

Q has some other rather unusual features. For example, in Proverbs 1–9 and elsewhere in Jewish writings we find Wisdom personified as a woman who has intimate knowledge of God. This figure appears in Q 7:35 and 11:49. Both passages imply that Q understood Jesus to be a messenger of Wisdom. Q 11:31 says that Jesus' wisdom exceeds that of the greatest of the wise, Solomon. It is no accident that many of Jesus' sayings have a proverbial character.

According to Q 11:49, Wisdom sent prophets to Israel. Here we have another unusual feature of Q—the linking together of traditions we often think of as distinct—wisdom and prophecy. Prophets, in fact, play a significant role in Q. Q 6:23 likens troubles of the Q audience to those of the prophets, indicating that the people who used Q compared themselves to the prophets. From the sayings about the persecution of the prophets (Q 11:47, 49; 13:34) we get the impression that the Q people thought of themselves as ones who, like their prophetic predecessors, were being persecuted.

The people who used Q made use of a tradition according to which Israel persistently disobeyed God, rejecting God's servants, the prophets, and refusing to obey God's commandments, thereby incurring God's wrath. This is a tradition prominent in the deuteronomic history of Israel (see especially 2 Kgs 17:7–20); it is also found in the work of the Chronicler (Ezra 9:6–15; Neh 1:5–11; 9:6–37), and in other writings too (e.g., Ps 106:6–46; Dan 9:4b–19). In Q, it is most clearly attested in Q 11:49–51 and 13:34–35. Jesus' death was understood in terms of this tradition; that is, Jesus died like the prophets before him. His death demonstrated how resistant Israel was to the divine message Jesus brought. There is nothing in Q to suggest that Jesus' death had a positive or redemptive significance. This is probably why Q has no story of Jesus' arrest, trial, and execution. The use of the deuteronomistic tradition also provides the context for understanding why the denunciations in Q are so violent (e.g., Q 3:7–9; 10:13–15).

Q's audience

One gets the impression from Jesus' Sermon (Q 6:20–49) that the Q people thought of themselves as an oppressed group—poor, hungry, weeping, persecuted (Q 6:20–23). This situation required them to reflect on how to respond to their enemies (Q 6:27–38). But they also had a need to maintain internal cohesion and commitment—something demanded in Q 6:39–49 (see also 11:34–36; 12:2–12). The marginal situation of these people is reflected in the concern about food and clothing in Q 12:22–31.

The mission charge in Q 10:2–16 provides another glimpse into the life of the people who composed and used Q. Their mission was exceedingly demanding—and apparently unsuccessful, as we can gather from Q 10:13–15 (see also 7:31–35; 11:29–32, 39–52; 13:34–35). This theme of being rejected occurs over and over again in Q. The Q people must have suffered a deeply traumatic experience which divided families (Q 12:51–53; cf. 16:18) and left painful memories of being shunned and excluded by their own people (Q 6:23). This pain can be sensed behind the vivid threats depicting how Israel will be punished for rejecting Jesus and the Q preachers (10:13–15; 11:31–32, 49–51; 13:28–29, 34–35). Some members of the group were apparently lured into messianic groups (Q 17:23; see also 7:24–25). And clearly there were sharp tensions with the "establishment" (Q 11:39–52).

It is difficult to know how many of the sayings ascribed to Jesus were uttered by him. We are probably safe in assuming that the selection of the sayings, their composition into discourses, and much of the wording reflect the Q people more than Jesus himself. But even if this is so, it is no loss. For the people who wrote and used Q were an extraordinarily interesting group. And careful readers will be able to read between the lines and recreate in their imaginations some of the earliest followers of Jesus.

The Sayings Gospel Q

John's preaching
Luke 3:7–9 / Matt 3:7–10

Luke	Matt
	[7]When he saw that many of the
	Pharisees and Sadducees were
	coming for baptism,
[7]So ⟨John⟩ would say to the	⟨John⟩ said to them,
crowds that came out to get	
baptized by him,	
"You spawn of Satan!	"You spawn of Satan!
Who warned you to flee from	Who warned you to flee from
the impending doom?	the impending doom?
[8]Well then, start producing fruits	[8]Well then, start producing fruit
suitable for a change of heart,	suitable for a change of heart,
and don't even start saying	[9]and don't even think of saying
to yourselves,	to yourselves,
'We have Abraham for our father.'	'We have Abraham for our father.'
Let me tell you,	Let me tell you,
God can raise up children for	God can raise up children for
Abraham right out of these rocks.	Abraham right out of these rocks.
[9]Even now the axe is aimed	[10]Even now the axe is aimed
at the root of the trees.	at the root of the trees.
So every tree not producing	So every tree not producing
choice fruit gets cut down	choice fruit gets cut down
and tossed into the fire."	and tossed into the fire."

The Coming One
Luke 3:16–17 / Matt 3:11–12

Luke	Matt
[16]"I baptize you with water	[11]"I baptize you with water
	to signal a change of heart,
but someone more powerful	but someone more powerful
than I	than I
is coming.	will succeed me.
I am not fit	I am not fit
to untie his sandal straps.	to carry his sandals.

3:7
//Mt 23:33;
cf. Mt 12:34;
Ⓣ SJas 6:28–29

3:8
Ⓣ Mt 7:16–20,
12:33–35;
Lk 13:6–9;
Ⓘ Acts 13:24;
◊ Is 51:1–2

3:9
//Mt 7:19;
cf. Jn 15:6, Th 40;
◊ Is 10:33–34,
Jer 22:7

3:16
//Mk 1:7–8,
Jn 1:26–27;
cf. Acts 13:25;
Ⓣ Acts 1:5, 11:16,
19:1–7

3:7 The *impending doom* is the day of the Lord (Yahweh) spoken of by the prophets, e.g., Isa 13:6–13; Mal 3:2; also Rom 2:5.

3:8 *Children for Abraham* is a self-designation for Israel; see Gen 15:1–5; also Rom 4:11b–12.

3:16 The Greek word for *spirit* (*pneuma*) also means "wind." The original Q wording may have been, "he will baptize you with wind and fire," which would fit well with Q 3:7.

He'll baptize you with holy spirit
and fire.
[17]His pitchfork is in his hand,
to make a clean sweep
of his threshing floor
and to gather his wheat into
the granary,
but the chaff he'll burn in a fire
that can't be put out."

He'll baptize you with holy spirit
and fire.
[12]His pitchfork is in his hand,
and he'll make a clean sweep
of his threshing floor,
and gather his wheat into
the granary,
but the chaff he'll burn in a fire
that can't be put out."

Jesus tested

Luke 4:1–4, 9–12, 5–8, 13 / Matt 4:1–11

[1]Jesus departed from the Jordan
full of the holy spirit
and was guided
by the spirit into the wilderness,
[2]where he was put to the test
by the devil
for forty days.
He ate nothing that whole time;
and when it was all over,
he was famished.
[3]The devil said to him,
"To prove you're God's son,
order this stone to turn into
bread."
[4]Jesus responded to him,
"It is written,
'Human beings are not to live
on bread alone.'"
[9]Then he took him
to Jerusalem,
set him on the pinnacle
of the temple,
and said to him,

[1]Then Jesus was guided
into the wilderness by the spirit
to be put to the test
by the devil.
[2]And after he had fasted
'forty days and forty nights,'
he was famished.
[3]And the tester confronted him
and said,
"To prove you're God's son,
order these stones to turn into
bread."
[4]He responded,
"It is written,
'Human beings are not to live
on bread alone,
but on every word that comes
out of God's mouth.'"
[5]Then the devil conducts him
to the holy city,
sets him on the pinnacle
of the temple,
[6]and says to him,

4:1–13
◊Wis 1:1–5, 2:12–18
4:1–2
//Mk 1:12–13; ◊Ex 34:28, Dt 9:9
4:4
◊Dt 8:3

NOTE: Text-critical notes for Q refer to the Lukan text, unless a Matthean text is specified.

4:1–2 Evil spirits were believed to lurk in the wilderness; see Lev 16:10; Isa 13:21; 34:14; Q 12:43.
4:3 *God's son*: the Greek lacks the article, and may also be translated "a son of God."
4:9 The *pinnacle* (literally, "wing") of the temple was an unidentified high point on the temple; early tradition says James, the brother

"To prove you're God's son,
jump off from here;
[10]remember, it is written,
'To his heavenly messengers
he will give orders about you,
to protect you,'
[11]and 'with their hands
they will catch you,
so you won't even stub your toe
on a stone.'"
And in response
[12]Jesus said to him,
"It is said,
'You are not to put the Lord
your God to the test.'"
[5]Then he took Jesus up,
and in an instant of time
showed him all the empires
of the civilized world.

[6]The devil said to him,
"I'll bestow on you authority over
all this and the glory that comes
with it; understand, it has been
handed over to me, and I can give
it to anyone I want.
[7]So, if you will pay
homage to me,
it will all be yours."
[8]Jesus responded,

"It is written,
'You are to pay homage
to the Lord your God,
and you are to revere him alone.'"
[13]So when the devil had tried
every kind of test,
he let him alone
for the time being.

"To prove you're God's son,
jump off;
remember, it is written,
'To his heavenly messengers
he will give orders about you,'

and 'with their hands
they will catch you,
so you won't even stub your toe
on a stone.'"

[7]Jesus said to him,
"Elsewhere it is written,
'You are not to put the Lord
your God to the test.'"
[8]Again the devil takes him
to a very high mountain
and shows him all the empires
of the world
and their splendor,
[9]and says to him,
"I'll give you all these,

if you will kneel down and pay
homage to me."

[10]Finally Jesus says to him,
"Get out of here, Satan!
Remember, it is written,
'You are to pay homage
to the Lord your God,
and you are to revere him alone.'"

[11]Then the devil leaves him,

and heavenly messengers
arrive out of nowhere
and look after him.

4:10–11 ◊Ps91:11–12
4:12 ◊Dt6:16
4:8 ◊Dt5:9

4:8 A few mss add "Get behind me, Satan" after *Jesus responded to him.*

of Jesus, was killed by being pushed off this "pinnacle."

4:6 The devil's claim to control the whole world is implicit in Matt 4:9 but expressly stated only in Luke 4:6.

Inaugural sermon

Luke 6:12, 17, 20 / Matt 5:1–2

Luke	Matt
	5 1 Taking note of the crowds,
12 During that time, it so happened that he went out to the mountain to pray, and spent the night in prayer to God.	he climbed up the mountain,
17 On the way down with them, Jesus stopped at a level place. There was a huge crowd of his disciples and a great throng of people from all Judea and Jerusalem and the coast of Tyre and Sidon.	
	and when he had sat down, his disciples came to him.
20 Then he would look squarely at his disciples	2 He then began to speak, and
and say:	this is what he would teach them:

Congratulations

Luke 6:20–26 / Matt 5:3, 6, 4, 11–12

Luke	Matt
"Congratulations, you poor!	3 "Congratulations to the poor in spirit!
God's domain belongs to you.	Heaven's domain belongs to them.
21 Congratulations, you hungry!	6 Congratulations to those who hunger and thirst for justice!
You will have a feast.	They will have a feast.
Congratulations, you who weep now!	4 Congratulations to those who grieve!
You will laugh.	They will be consoled.
22 Congratulations to you when people hate you, and when they ostracize you	11 Congratulations to you
and denounce you	when they denounce you and persecute you
and scorn your name as evil,	and spread malicious gossip about you
because of the son of Adam!	because of me.
23 Rejoice on that day,	12 Rejoice
and jump for joy!	and be glad!
Just remember, your compensation is great in heaven.	Your compensation is great in heaven.
Recall that their ancestors treated	Recall that this is how they

6:20b //Th 54; cf. Lk 6:24
6:21a //Th 69:2; cf. Lk 6:25a
6:21b Cf. Lk 6:25b
6:22–23 Cf. Lk 6:26
6:22 //Th 68, 1 Pet 4:14; cf. Th 69:1, 1 Pet 3:14; ◊ Is 66:5
6:23 Cf. Q 11:47–51, 13:34–35; 1 Pet 4:13; Ⓣ Acts 7:52

the prophets the same way.	persecuted the prophets who preceded you.
[24]*Damn you rich!* *You already have your consolation.* [25]*Damn you who are well-fed now!* *You will know hunger.* *Damn you who laugh now!* *You will learn to weep and grieve.* [26]*Damn you when everybody* *speaks well of you!* *Recall that their ancestors treated* *the phony prophets the same way.*	

Love of enemies
Luke 6:27–36 / Matt 5:44, 39–42; 7:12; 5:46–47, 45, 48

[27]But to you who listen I say, love your enemies, do favors for those who hate you, [28]bless those who curse you, pray for your abusers.	[44]But I tell you: Love your enemies and pray for your persecutors.
[29]When someone strikes you on the cheek, offer the other as well. If someone takes away your coat don't prevent that person from taking your shirt along with it.	[39]When someone slaps you on the right cheek, turn the other as well. [40]If someone is determined to sue you for your shirt, let that person have your coat along with it. [41]*Further, when anyone conscripts* *you for one mile, go along an extra* *mile.*
[30]Give to everyone who begs from you; and when someone takes your things, don't ask for them back.	[42]Give to the one who begs from you; and don't turn away the one who tries to borrow from you.
	7 [12]Consider this:
[31]Treat people the way you want them to treat you.	Treat people in ways you want them to treat you. This sums up the whole of the Law and the Prophets.

6:28b
//GOxy 1224 6:1,
Rom 12:14;
cf. 1 Pet 3:9

6:29a
◊Prv 19:11, 20:22,
24:29; Lam 3:30

6:30
Cf. Lk 6:34, Th 95;
◊Prv 25:21

6:31
Cf. Th 6:3,
Rom 13:10,
Tob 4:15

6:27=Matt 5:44 Some mss add "bless those who curse you, do good to those who hate you" after *love your enemies*.

6:31 The "Golden Rule" is based on, but reverses, the ancient principle of retaliation. The Golden Rule antedates Jesus, and is found in various forms in Chinese, Indian, Greek, Persian, Jewish and Arabic sources.

Luke	Matt
	5 46 Tell me,
32 "If you love those who love you, what merit is there in that?	if you love those who love you, why should you be commended for that?
After all, even sinners love those who love them.	Even the toll collectors do as much, don't they?
33 And if you do good to those who do good to you, what merit is there in that?	47 And if you greet only your friends, what have you done that is exceptional?
After all, even sinners do as much.	Even the pagans do as much, don't they?
34 If you lend to those from whom you hope to gain, what merit is there in that? Even sinners lend to sinners, in order to get as much in return.	
35 But love your enemies, and do good, and lend, expecting nothing in return. Your reward will be great, and you'll be children of the Most High.	45 You'll then become children of your Father in the heavens.
As you know, he is generous to the ungrateful and the wicked.	⟨God⟩ causes the sun to rise on both the bad and the good, and sends rain on both the just and the unjust.
36 Be as compassionate as your Father is."	48 To sum up, you are to be as liberal in your love as your heavenly Father is."

On judging

Luke 6:37–38 / Matt 7:1–2

Luke	Matt
37 "Don't pass judgment, and you won't be judged;	1 "Don't pass judgment, so you won't be judged. 2 Don't forget, the judgment you hand out will be the judgment you get back.

6:35c ◊Sir 4:10
6:36 ◊Dt 18:13(LXX), Lv 19:2
6:37 //Mary 9:12

6:35 Several mss have "despairing of no one" instead of *expecting nothing in return.*

6:32 *Sinner* was used for Jews who disregarded OT Law; they were thus the practical equivalent of Gentiles (non-Jews).

don't condemn,
and you won't be condemned;
forgive, and you'll be forgiven.
[38]Give, and it will be given to you:
they will put in your lap
a full measure, packed down,
sifted and overflowing.
For the standard you apply will
be the standard applied to you."

And the standard you apply will
be the standard applied to you."

Blind guides
Luke 6:39–40 / Matt 15:14; 10:24–25

[39]"Can one blind person
guide another?
Won't they both end up
in some ditch?
[40]Students are not above
their teachers.

But those who are fully taught
will be like their teachers."

[14]"They are blind guides
of blind people!
If one blind person
guides another,
both will end up
in some ditch.
10 [24]Students are not above
their teachers,
nor slaves above their masters.
[25]It is appropriate for students
to be like their teachers and
slaves to be like their masters."

On pretense
Luke 6:41–42 / Matt 7:3–5

[41]"Why do you notice the sliver
in your friend's eye,
but overlook the timber in
your own?
[42]How can you say to your
friend,
'Friend, let me get the sliver
in your eye,'
when you don't notice
the timber in your own?
You phony, first take the
timber out of your own eye,
and then you'll see well enough
to remove the sliver in your
friend's eye."

[3]"Why do you notice the sliver
in your friend's eye,
but overlook the timber in
your own?
[4]How can you say to your
friend,
'Let me get the sliver out
of your eye,'
when there is
that timber in your own?
[5]You phony, first take the
timber out of your own eye
and then you'll see well enough
to remove the sliver from your
friend's eye."

6:38b
//Mk 4:24;
◊Sir 35:10
6:39
//Th 34
6:40
Cf. Jn 13:16a,
15:20; DSav 20:1c
6:41–42
//Th 26

6:38b A common Jewish saying.

Tree & fruit

Luke 6:43–45 / Matt 7:16–20; 12:33–35

Luke	Matt
v. 44	16 "You'll know who they are by what they produce. Since when do people pick grapes from thorns or figs from thistles?
43 "A choice tree does not produce rotten fruit, any more than a rotten tree produces choice fruit;	17 Every healthy tree produces choice fruit, but the rotten tree produces spoiled fruit.
	18 A healthy tree cannot produce spoiled fruit, any more than a rotten tree can produce choice fruit.
	19 Every tree that does not produce choice fruit gets cut down and tossed on the fire.
	20 Remember,
44 for each tree is known by its fruit.	you'll know who they are by what they produce.
Figs are not gathered from thorns, nor are grapes picked from brambles.	v. 16
v. 43a–b	12 33 If you make the tree choice, its fruit will be choice; if you make the tree rotten, its fruit will be rotten.
v. 44a	After all, the tree is known by its fruit.
	34 You spawn of Satan, how can your speech be good when you are corrupt?
v. 45c	As you know, the mouth gives voice to what the heart is full of.
45 The good person produces good from the fund of good in the heart,	35 The good person produces good things out of a fund of good;
and the evil person produces evil from the evil within.	and the evil person produces evil things out of a fund of evil."
As you know, the mouth gives voice to what the heart is full of.	v. 34b

6:43–45
//Th 45;
Ⓣ Mt 3:7–10,
12:33–35,
21:33–43

6:44a
◊ Sir 27:6

6:44b
//Jas 3:12

6:45
Cf. Mt 12:37,
1 Sm 24:14,
Prv 12:14

Foundations

Luke 6:46–49 / Matt 7:21, 24–27

Luke	Matt
[46]"Why do you call me 'Master, master,'	[21]"Not everyone who addresses me as 'Master, master,' will get into Heaven's domain— only those who carry out the will of my Father in heaven.
and not do what I tell you?	
[47]Everyone who comes to me and pays attention to my words and acts on them— I'll show you what such a person is like:	[24]Everyone who pays attention to these words of mine and acts on them
[48]That one is like a person building a house, who dug deep	will be like a shrewd builder
and laid the foundation on bedrock;	who erected a house on bedrock.
	[25]Later the rain fell,
when a flood came,	and the torrents came, and the winds blew
the torrent slammed against that house,	and pounded that house,
but could not shake it, because it was well built.	yet it did not collapse, since its foundation rested on bedrock.
[49]But the one who listens ⟨to my words⟩ and doesn't act ⟨on them⟩ is like a person who built a house on the ground without a foundation;	[26]Everyone who listens to these words of mine and doesn't act on them will be like a careless builder, who erected a house on the sand.
	[27]When the rain fell,
when the torrent slammed against it,	and the torrents came,
	and the winds blew and pounded that house,
it collapsed immediately. And so the ruin of that house was total."	it collapsed. Its collapse was colossal."

6:46
//EgerG 3:5
6:47–49
◊Ps 1; Jer 17:5–8;
Sir 22:16, 27:3

6:47–49 Like some other Jewish sayings collections, the Q Sermon on the Mount/Plain concludes with a comparison with a ruined house; see also Job 3–27; Prov 1–9; 22:17–24:22.

Officer's slave

Luke 7:1–10 / Matt 7:28; 8:5–10, 13

Luke	Matt
	[28]And so,
[1]After he had completed all he had to say to his audience,	when Jesus had finished speaking, the crowds were astonished at his teaching.
he went into Capernaum.	8 [5]When he had entered Capernaum, a Roman officer approached him and pleaded with him: [6]"Sir, my servant boy was struck down with paralysis and is in terrible pain."
[2]A Roman officer had a slave he was very fond of but who was sick and about to die. [3]So when he heard about Jesus, the Roman officer sent some Jewish elders to him, and asked him to come and cure his slave.	[7]And he said to him, "I'll come and cure him."
[4]When they came to Jesus, they pleaded with him urgently, saying, "He deserves to have you do this for him. [5]As you probably know, he loves our people, and even built a synagogue for us." [6]So Jesus went with them. When he got close to the house,	
the Roman officer dispatched friends to say to him,	[8]And the Roman officer replied,
"Don't trouble yourself, sir,	
for I don't deserve to have you in my house;	"Sir, I don't deserve to have you in my house,
[7]that's why I didn't presume to come to you in person.	
Just say the word, and let my boy be cured.	but only say the word and my boy will be cured.
[8]After all, I myself am under orders, and I have soldiers under me.	[9]After all, I myself am under orders, and I have soldiers under me.
I order one to go, and he goes;	I order one to go, and he goes;

7:1–10 //Jn 4:46–53

7:1–10 Though this is a narrative, its emphasis lies on the word of Jesus, and thus does not seem out of place in a sayings collection.

7:1 *Capernaum* was a village on the north shore of the Sea of Galilee; it was where Jesus lived (see Matt 4:13).

I order another to come,
and he comes;
and ⟨I order⟩ my slave
to do something,
and he does it."
9As Jesus listened to this
he was amazed at him.
He turned
and said to the crowd
that followed,
"Let me tell you,
not even in Israel have I
found such trust."

10And when the emissaries
returned to the house,
they found the slave
in good health.

I order another to come,
and he comes;
and ⟨I order⟩ my slave
to do something,
and he does it."
10As Jesus listened
he was amazed

and said to those
who followed,
"I swear to you,
I have not found such trust
in a single Israelite!"
13And Jesus said to the Roman
officer, "Be on your way.
Your trust will be the measure
of the results."

And the boy was cured
at that precise moment.

John's inquiry
Luke 7:18–20, 22–23 / Matt 11:2–6

18The disciples of John brought
reports of all these things to him.
19John summoned a couple of his
disciples
and sent them to the Lord
to ask:
"Are you the one who is to come
or are we to wait for someone
else?"
20And when the men came to
⟨Jesus⟩, they said, "John the
Baptist sent us to you to ask: 'Are
you the one who is to come, or are
we to wait for someone else?'"

2While John was in prison
he heard about what the
Anointed had been doing

and he sent his disciples
3to ask,
"Are you the one who is to come
or are we to wait for another?"

7:9=Matt 8:10 Some mss have "not even in Israel have I found such trust," instead of *I have not found such trust in a single Israelite.*

At the end of this verse, several mss add "and returning to his house in that hour, the Roman officer found the slave in good health."

7:19
① Q3:16, 13:35; Mt21:9; Lk19:38; ◊Mal3:1, 4:5

7:18 John the Baptist also had disciples; e.g., Mark 6:29; Luke 5:33; John 4:1.

7:19 The *one who is to come* cannot be identified with any particular messianic figure.

[22]And so he answered them,
"Go report to John what you
have seen and heard:
the blind see again,
the lame walk,
lepers are cleansed,
the deaf hear,
the dead are raised,
and the poor have the good news
preached to them.
[23]Congratulations to those
who don't take offense at me."

[4]And so Jesus answered them,
"Go report to John what you
have heard and seen:
[5]The blind see again
and the lame walk;
lepers are cleansed
and the deaf hear;
the dead are raised,
and the poor have the good news
preached to them.
[6]Congratulations to those
who don't take offense at me."

Jesus praises John
Luke 7:24–28 / Matt 11:7–11

[24]After John's messengers
had left,
⟨Jesus⟩ began to talk about John
to the crowds:
"What did you go out to the
wilderness to gawk at?
A reed shaking in the wind?
[25]What did you really go out
to see?
A man dressed in fancy clothes?
But wait!
Those who dress fashionably
and live in luxury are found in
palaces.
[26]Come on, what did you go out
to see?
A prophet?
Yes, that's what you went out
to see,
yet someone more than a prophet.
[27]This is the one
about whom it was written:
Here is my messenger,
whom I send on ahead of you
to prepare your way before you.

[7]After ⟨John's disciples⟩
had departed,
Jesus began to talk about John
to the crowds:
"What did you go out to the
wilderness to gawk at?
A reed shaking in the wind?
[8]What did you really go out
to see?
A man dressed in fancy ⟨clothes⟩?
But wait!
Those who wear fancy ⟨clothes⟩
are found in regal quarters.
[9]Come on, what did you go out
to see?
A prophet?
Yes, that's what you went out
to see,
yet someone more than a prophet.
[10]This is the one
about whom it was written:
Here is my messenger,
whom I send on ahead of you
to prepare your way before you.

7:22
Ⓘ Q6:20b, 10:23–24; Mt 15:30–31; Lk 4:18–19; ◊ Is 29:18–19, 35:5–6, 61:1
7:24–25
//Th 78; Ⓘ Q3:7
7:27
Cf. Mk 1:2; Ⓘ Mt 3:3, Lk 1:17; ◊ Ex 23:20, Mal 3:1

7:24 Depending on the punctuation, the Greek word *ti* may also be translated "why": "Why did you go out to the wilderness? To gawk at a reed. . .?"

7:26 The "more than" comparison occurs several times in Q; see also Q 11:31, 32; 12:23.

[28]I tell you,	[11]I swear to you,
among those born of women	among those born of women
	no one has arisen
none is greater than John;	who is greater than John
	the Baptist;
yet the least in God's domain	yet the least in Heaven's domain
is greater than he."	is greater than he."

Law & prophets
Luke 16:16 / Matt 11:12–13

[16]"Right up to John's time	[12]"From the time of John
	the Baptist
	until now Heaven's domain has
v. 16d	been breaking in violently,
	and violent men are attempting
	to gain it by force.
	[13]You see,
you have the Law and	the Prophets and even
the Prophets;	the Law
	predicted everything that was to
	happen prior to John's time."
since then God's domain has	
been proclaimed as	
good news and everyone	
is breaking into it violently."	v. 12d

Children in the marketplace
Luke 7:31–35 / Matt 11:16–19

[31]"What do members of this	[16]"What does this
generation remind me of?	generation remind me of?
What are they like?	
[32]They are like children sitting	It is like children sitting
in the marketplace	in marketplaces
and calling out to one another:	who call out to others:
'We played the flute for you	[17]'We played the flute for you,
but you wouldn't dance;	but you wouldn't dance;
we sang a dirge,	we sang a dirge
but you wouldn't weep.'	but you wouldn't mourn.'
[33]Just remember, John	[18]Just remember, John
the Baptist	
appeared on the scene,	appeared on the scene
eating no bread	neither eating

7:28
//Th 46

16:16
Ⓣ SJas 6:2–4

7:31
◊Nm 32:13;
Ps 78:8, 95:8–11

7:33–34
Cf. Mk 1:6;
Ⓘ Mt 3:4, Lk 1:15;
Ⓣ Mt 9:10–11,
Lk 5:30

7:31 The epithet, *this generation*, is used in Q as a derisive designation for those Jews with whom the Q group was in conflict; see Q 11:29, 31, 32, 51.

and drinking no wine,	nor drinking,
and you say,	and they say,
'He is demented.'	'He is demented.'
[34]The son of Adam appeared	[19]The son of Adam appeared
on the scene	on the scene
both eating and drinking,	both eating and drinking,
and you say,	and they say,
'There's a glutton and a drunk,	'There's a glutton and a drunk,
a crony of toll collectors	a crony of toll collectors
and sinners!'	and sinners!'
[35]Indeed, wisdom is vindicated	Indeed, wisdom is vindicated
by all her children."	by her deeds."

Foxes have dens

Luke 9:57–62 / Matt 8:19–22

[57]As they were going	[19]And one scholar came
along the road,	forward
someone said to him,	and said to him,
"I'll follow you	"Teacher, I'll follow you
wherever you go."	wherever you go."
[58]And Jesus said to him,	[20]And Jesus says to him,
"Foxes have dens,	"Foxes have dens,
and birds of the sky have nests;	and birds of the sky have nests,
but the son of Adam has nowhere	but the son of Adam has nowhere
to rest his head."	to rest his head."
	[21]Another of his disciples
	said to him,
v. 59	"Master, first let me go
	and bury my father."
[59]To another he said,	[22]But Jesus says to him,
"Follow me."	"Follow me,
But he said, "First let me go	v. 21
and bury my father."	
[60]Jesus said to him,	
"Leave it to the dead to	and leave it to the dead to
bury their own dead."	bury their own dead."

7:34 ▷Dt 21:20
9:58 //Th 86
9:61–62 ▷1 Kgs 19:19–21

7:35=Matt 11:19 Some mss have "her children" instead of *her deeds*.

7:34 *Toll collectors* are lumped with "sinners" (see Q 6:33) because both were especially despised, both socially and religiously.
7:35 *Wisdom* (*sophia*) is personified as a female divine figure in Jewish tradition; see Prov 1:20–33; 8:1–31; Wis 6:12–16; Sir 24:1–22; Bar 3:9–4:4.

Wisdom is shown to be in the right by the *children* who respond affirmatively to her messengers, John and Jesus.
9:59 The burial of one's parents was a duty taking precedence over all other duties, including commands of the Law.

61 Another said, "I'll follow you, Sir; but let me first say goodbye to my people at home."

62 Jesus said to him, "No one who puts his hand to the plow and looks back is qualified for God's imperial rule."

The Mission Speech

Luke 10:2–12 / Matt 9:37–38; 10:7–16

Luke	Matt
2 He would say to them,	37 Then he said to his disciples,
"Although the crop is good,	"Although the crop is good,
still there are few to harvest it.	still there are few to harvest it.
So beg the harvest boss	38 So beg the harvest boss
to dispatch workers to the fields.	to dispatch workers to the fields.
3 Get going;	10 7 Go and announce:
v. 9	'Heaven's imperial rule is closing in.'
	8 Cure the sick, raise the dead, cleanse the lepers, drive out demons. You have received freely, so freely give.
look, I'm sending you out like lambs into a pack of wolves.	v. 16
	9 Don't get gold or silver or copper coins for spending money,
4 Carry no purse,	
no knapsack,	10 don't take a knapsack for the road,
	or two shirts,
no sandals.	or sandals,
	or a staff,
Don't greet anyone on the road.	
v. 7b	for the worker deserves to be fed.
v. 8a	11 Whichever town or village you enter,
	find out who is deserving;
v. 7a	stay there until you leave.
5 Whenever you enter a house,	12 When you enter a house,
first say,	
'Peace to this house.'	greet it.
6 If peaceful people live there,	13 And if the house is deserving,
your peace will rest on them.	give it your peace blessing,
But if not,	but if it is unworthy,
it will return to you.	withdraw your peace blessing.
7 Stay at that one house, eating and drinking whatever they provide,	v. 11b

10:2–12
//Mk 6:6b-13, Lk 9:1–6

10:2
//Th 73; cf. Jn 4:35

10:3 (Mt 10:16b)
//Th 39:3

10:4
Ⓘ Lk 22:35–36; ▷ 2 Kgs 4:29

10:6
Cf. 1 Pet 4:14

10:7–9
//Th 14:4

10:7
//1 Tm 5:17, DSav 20:1b; cf. 1 Cor 9:14

for workers deserve their wages.	v. 10b
Do not move from house to house.	v. 11b
8 Whenever you enter a town and they welcome you, eat whatever is set before you.	v. 11a
9 Cure the sick there and tell them,	v. 8a
'God's imperial rule is closing in.'	v. 7
10 But whenever you enter a town	14 And if anyone does not welcome you,
and they do not receive you,	or listen to your words,
go out into its streets	as you are going out of that house or town
and say,	
11 'Even the dust of your town that sticks to our feet,	
we wipe off against you.	shake the dust off your feet.
But know this: God's imperial rule is closing in.'	
12 I tell you,	15 I swear to you,
on that day Sodom	the land of Sodom and Gomorrah
will be better off	will be better off on judgment day
than that town."	than that town.
	16 Look, I'm sending you out
v. 3	like sheep in a pack of wolves." *Therefore you must be sly as a snake and as simple as a dove.*

Damn you Chorazin

Luke 10:13–15 / Matt 11:21–24

13 "Damn you, Chorazin!	21 "Damn you, Chorazin!
Damn you, Bethsaida!	Damn you, Bethsaida!
If the miracles done in you	If the miracles done in you
had been done in Tyre and Sidon,	had been done in Tyre and Sidon,
they would have sat in	they would have ⟨sat⟩ in
sackcloth and ashes	sackcloth and ashes
and changed their ways long ago.	and changed their ways long ago.

10:9 //Mk 1:14; Mt 3:2, 4:17; Lk 17:21
10:11 ① Acts 13:51, 18:6
10:12 //Mt 11:24

10:10=Matt 10:14 Several mss add "of the village" after *dust.*
10:11 Some mss add "on you" after *closing in.*

10:8 The command to *eat whatever is set before you* may imply that food laws should be suspended; see 1 Cor 10:27.
10:12 *Sodom and Gomorrah* were destroyed by God because of their wickedness (Genesis 18–19), and became proverbial (see Rom 9:29 [Isa 1:9]; 2 Pet 2:6; Jude 7).
10:13 *Chorazin* and *Bethsaida* were villages on the north shore of the Sea of Galilee, near Capernaum. *Tyre and Sidon* were cities in Syria (now Lebanon), to the northwest of Galilee (see Matt 15:21). Wearing *sackcloth*

[14]But Tyre and Sidon will be
better off
at the judgment than you.
[15]And you, Capernaum,
you don't think you'll be
exalted to heaven, do you?
No, you'll go to Hell."

[22]So I tell you,
Tyre and Sidon will be
better off
on judgment day than you.
[23]And you, Capernaum,
you don't think you'll be
exalted to heaven, do you?
No, you'll go to Hell.
Because if the miracles done among
you had been done in Sodom,
Sodom would still be around.
[24]*So I tell you, the land of Sodom*
will be better off on judgment day
than you."

Rejecting the sender
Luke 10:16 / Matt 10:40

[16]"Whoever hears you hears me,
and whoever rejects you
rejects me,
and whoever rejects me
rejects the one who sent me."

[40]"The one who accepts you
accepts me,
and the one who accepts me
accepts the one who sent me."

Father & son
Luke 10:21–22 / Matt 11:25–27

[21]At that moment
Jesus was overjoyed
by the holy spirit and said,
"I praise you, Father,
Lord of heaven and earth,
because you have hidden
these things from the wise
and the learned
but revealed them
to the untutored;
yes indeed, Father, because
this is the way you want it.
[22]My Father has turned
everything over to me.
No one knows who the son is
except the Father,

[25]At that point,
Jesus responded:

"I praise you, Father,
Lord of heaven and earth,
because you have hidden
these things from the wise
and the learned
but revealed them
to the untutored;
[26]yes indeed, Father, because
this is the way you want it.
[27]My Father has turned
everything over to me.
No one knows the son
except the Father,

10:15
◊ Is 14:11–15,
Ez 28:1–8
10:16
Cf. Mk 9:37;
Mt 18:5; Lk 9:48;
Jn 5.23, 13:20,
12:44–45, 15:23
10:21
Ⓣ Lk 9:45, 18:34,
19:42;
◊ Is 29:14
(1 Cor 1:19),
Wis 10:21
10:22
Cf. Mt 28:18;
Jn 3:35; 13:3;
17:1b-2, 25;
Th 61:3; Eph 1:22;
Ⓣ Q 4:6,
SJas 6:24–26

10:21 Many mss read "by the spirit" instead of *by the holy spirit.*

---

and ashes was a sign of repentance and grief; see Isa 58:5; 1 Macc 3:47.
10:15 *Hell* here translates the Greek word *Hades*, which refers to the abode of the dead, not to a place of punishment. *Heaven* is simply where God lives (see Matt 5:34).

or who the Father is
except the son—
and anyone to whom the son
wishes to reveal him."

nor does anyone know the Father
except the son—
and anyone to whom the son
wishes to reveal him."

Privileged eyes
Luke 10:23–24 / Matt 13:16–17

[23]Turning to the disciples
he said privately,
"How privileged are the eyes
that see what you see!

[24]I tell you,
many prophets
and kings wanted
to see what you see,
and didn't see it,
and to hear what you hear,
and didn't hear it."

[16]"How privileged are your eyes
because they see,
and your ears because they hear.
[17]I swear to you,
many prophets
and righteous ones have longed
to see what you see,
and didn't see it,
and to hear what you hear,
and didn't hear it."

Lord's prayer
Luke 11:2–4 / Matt 6:9–13

[2]"When you pray,
you should say:
Father,
your name be revered.
Impose your imperial rule.

[3]Provide us with the bread
we need day by day.
[4]Forgive our sins,
since we too
forgive everyone in debt to us.

[9]"Instead, you should pray
like this:
Our Father in the heavens,
your name be revered.
[10]Impose your imperial rule,
enact your will on earth
as you have in heaven.
[11]Provide us with the bread
we need for the day.
[12]Forgive our debts
to the extent that we have
forgiven those in debt to us.

10:23 Cf. Sir 48:11
10:24 //Th 38
11:2b ◊Is 29:23, Ez 36:23
11:3 //GNaz 3
11:4a //Mk 11:25; Mt 6:14–15, 18:35; ◊Sir 28:2

11:2 Some mss have "our Father in heaven" instead of *Father*. After *impose your imperial rule*, many mss add "enact your will in heaven and on earth".
11:4 At the end of this verse, many mss add "but rescue us from the evil one" and some mss add "for yours is the imperial rule and the power and the glory, forever. Amen".

11:2b It is unclear whether God is to make his name holy, or whether people are to do this.
11:2c *Impose your imperial rule* is a common petition in Jewish prayers, though the date of these prayers is uncertain.
11:4a *Debts* usually means simply financial debts or social obligations, but can also have the religious meaning, "sins."

Luke	Matthew
And please don't subject us to test after test."	[13]And please don't subject us to test after test, but rescue us from the evil one."

Ask, seek, knock
Luke 11:9–13 / Matt 7:7–11

Luke	Matthew
[9]"Ask—it'll be given to you; seek—you'll find; knock—it'll be opened for you. [10]Rest assured: everyone who asks receives; everyone who seeks finds; and for the one who knocks it is opened.	[7]"Ask—it'll be given to you; seek—you'll find; knock—it'll be opened for you. [8]Rest assured: everyone who asks receives; everyone who seeks finds; and for the one who knocks it is opened.
	[9]Who among you would hand a son a stone when it's bread he's asking for?
[11]Which of you fathers would hand his son a snake when it's fish he's asking for?	[10]Again, who would hand him a snake when it's fish he's asking for?
[12]Or a scorpion when it's an egg he's asking for?	
	Of course no one would!
[13]So if you, worthless as you are, know how to give your children good gifts, isn't it much more likely that the heavenly Father will give holy spirit to those who ask him?"	[11]So if you, worthless as you are, know how to give your children good gifts, isn't it much more likely that your Father in the heavens will give good things to those who ask him?"

Beelzebul controversy
Luke 11:14–23 / Matt 12:22–30

Luke	Matthew
[14]Jesus was driving out a demon that was mute,	[22]Then they brought to him a blind and mute person who was demon-possessed,
and when the demon had departed	and he cured him

11:4b //SJas 4:2; cf. Mk 14:38
11:9–10 //Jn 15:7, 16:23–24; Th 2:1–2; 92:1; 94; cf. Mk 11:24; Mt 18:19, 21:22; Jn 15:16; 1 Jn 3:22; ◊ Prv 8:17
11:10 //Mary 4:7; GHeb 6b; cf. DSav 7:2, 11:5
11:14–23 //Mk 3:22–27

11:13 Instead of *holy spirit,* a few mss have "a good gift" or "good gifts" or "a good spirit".

11:11 Bread and fish were staples of the Jewish diet.

the mute man spoke.	so the mute was able both to speak and to see.
And the crowds were amazed.	23 And the entire crowd was beside itself and would say, "This fellow can't be the son of David, can he?" 24 But when the Pharisees heard of it,
15 But some of them said, "He drives out demons in the name of Beelzebul, the head demon."	they said, "This fellow drives out demons only in the name of Beelzebul, the head demon."
16 Others were testing him by demanding a sign from heaven.	
17 But he knew what they were thinking, and said to them: "Every government divided against itself is devastated,	25 But he knew how they thought, and said to them: "Every government divided against itself is devastated, and every town or household divided
and a house divided against a house falls.	against itself won't survive.
18 If Satan is divided against himself —since you claim I drive out demons in Beelzebul's name—	26 So if Satan drives out Satan,
	he is divided against himself.
how will his domain endure?	In that case, how will his domain endure?
19 If I drive out demons in Beelzebul's name, in whose name do your own people drive ⟨them⟩ out? In that case, they will be your judges.	27 Even if I drive out demons in Beelzebul's name, in whose name do your own people drive ⟨them⟩ out? In that case, they will be your judges.

11:14–15 //Mt9:32–34

11:15 At the end of this verse, several mss add "and answering, he said to them, 'How can Satan drive out Satan?'" (see Mark 3:23).

11:15 *Beelzebul* is a title whose exact meaning is unknown. "Beel-" is "Baal," meaning "lord" or "master," and used in the OT for various Canaanite deities. Matthew apparently assumed Beelzebul meant "master of the house" (Matt 10:25). It was not uncommon to use the name of an opponent's deity as a term for a demon or, as here, the prince of demons.

As a supernatural spirit, a demon could be evicted from its human host only at the command of a higher-ranking spirit, whether good (God) or evil (Satan).

11:18 Jesus treats Satan as the equivalent of Beelzebul.

11:19 *Your own people* are other Jewish exorcists; see Acts 19:13–16.

20 But if by God's finger
I drive out demons,
then for you God's imperial rule
has arrived.
21 When a strong man
is fully armed
and guards his courtyard,
his possessions are safe.

22 But when a stronger man
attacks and overpowers him, he
takes the weapons on which he
was relying and divides up his
loot.
23 The one who isn't with me
is against me,
and the one who doesn't gather
with me scatters."

28 But if by God's spirit
I drive out demons,
then for you God's imperial rule
has arrived.
29 Or how can someone enter
a powerful man's house

and steal his possessions,
unless he first ties him up?
Only then does he loot his house.

30 The one who isn't with me
is against me,
and the one who doesn't gather
with me scatters."

Return of an unclean spirit
Luke 11:24–26 / Matt 12:43–45

24 "When an unclean spirit
leaves a person,
it wanders through waterless
places in search of a resting place.
When it doesn't find one,
it says,
'I will go back to the home I left.'
25 It then returns
and finds it swept
and refurbished.
26 Next, it goes out
and brings back seven
other spirits more vile than itself,
who enter
and settle in there.
So that person ends up worse off
than when he or she started."

43 "When an unclean spirit
leaves a person,
it wanders through waterless
places in search of a resting place.
When it doesn't find one,
44 it then says,
'I will return to the home I left.'
It then returns
and finds it empty, swept,
and refurbished.
45 Next, it goes out
and brings back with it seven
other spirits more vile than itself,
who enter
and settle in there.
So that person ends up worse off
than when he or she started.
That's how it will be for
this perverse generation."

11:20
◊ Ex 8:12–15
11:21–22
// Th 35
11:23a
// Mk 9:40,
GOxy 1224 6:2
11:24–26
Ⓣ 2 Esd 7:78–80
11:26b
Ⓣ 2 Pet 2:20

11:24 The *home* is the person from whom the demon was exorcised.

Congratulations to the womb
Luke 11:27–28

[27]*And so just as he was making*
these remarks, a woman from the
crowd raised her voice and
addressed him, "Congratulations to
the womb that carried you and the
breasts that nursed you!"
[28]*"Congratulations are due*
instead," he replied, "to those who
hear the word of God and keep it."

Request for a sign
Luke 11:16, 29–32 / Matt 12:38–42

Luke	Matt
	[38]Then some of the scholars and Pharisees responded to him,
[16]Others were testing him by demanding a sign from heaven.	"Teacher, we would like to see a sign from you."
[29]As more and more people were crowding around him,	
he began to say,	[39]In response he said to them,
"This generation is an evil generation.	"An evil and immoral generation
It insists on a sign,	insists on a sign,
but it will be given no sign	and no sign will be given it,
except the sign of Jonah.	except the sign of Jonah the prophet.
[30]You see, just as Jonah became a sign for the Ninevites,	[40]You see, just as 'Jonah was in the belly of a sea monster for three days and three nights,'
so the son of Adam will be a sign for this generation.	so the son of Adam will be in the bowels of the earth for three days and three nights.
v. 32	[41]At judgment time, the citizens of Nineveh will come back to life along with this generation and condemn it, because they had a change of heart in response to Jonah's message.

11:29
Cf. Mk8:11–12; Mt16:1, 4

11:29 *This generation*: see note to Q 7:31.
The *sign of Jonah* is probably the call by John and Jesus for Israel to repent.
11:30 Jonah was sent to Nineveh, the capital of Israel's enemy, the Assyrians, to call for repentance; much to Jonah's consternation, they repented (Jonah 3).

[31]At judgment time,
the queen of the south will
be brought back to life
along with members of
this generation,
and she will condemn them,
because she came from the ends
of the earth
to listen to Solomon's wisdom.
Yet take note: what is right here
is greater than Solomon."
[32]At judgment time,
the citizens of Nineveh will come
back to life
along with this generation
and condemn it,
because they had a change
of heart
in response to Jonah's message.
Yet take note: what is right here
is greater than Jonah.

Yet take note: what is right here
is greater than Jonah.
[42]At judgment time,
the queen of the south will
be brought back to life
along with
this generation,
and she will condemn it,
because she came from the ends
of the earth
to listen to Solomon's wisdom.
Yet take note: what is right here
is greater than Solomon."
v. 41

Lamp & bushel
Luke 11:33 / Matt 5:15

[33]"No one lights a lamp
and then puts it in a cellar
or under a bushel basket,
but rather on a lampstand
so that those who come in
can see the light."

[15]"Nor do people light a lamp

and put it under a bushel basket
but rather on a lampstand,
where it sheds light for everyone
in the house."

Eye & light
Luke 11:34–36 / Matt 6:22–23

[34]"Your eye is the body's lamp.

When your eye is clear,
your whole body is flooded
with light.
When your eye is clouded,

[22]"The eye is the body's lamp.
It follows that
if your eye is clear,
your whole body will be flooded
with light.
[23]If your eye is clouded,

11:31
◊1 Kgs 10:1–13
11:33
//Mk 4:21, Lk 8:16, Th 33:2–3
11:34
//Th 24:3, 61:5; DSav 6:1–2; Mary 7:4

11:31 The *queen of the south* is the queen of Sheba, a kingdom in southern Arabia.
11:34 The condition of the eye is described by a word (*haplous*) whose meaning is unclear; it can be "single," "simple," "sincere," "generous," or "sound."

your body is shrouded
in darkness.
35 Take care, then, that the light
within you is not darkness.

36 If then your whole body is flooded with light, and no corner of it is darkness, it will be completely illuminated as when a lamp's rays engulf you."

your whole body will be shrouded
in darkness.
If, then, the light
within you is darkness,
how dark that can be!"

On tithing
Luke 11:42 / Matt 23:23

42 "Damn you, Pharisees!
You pay tithes on mint
and rue and every herb,
but neglect
justice
and the love of God.
You should have attended
to the last
without neglecting the first."

23 "You scholars and Pharisees,
you impostors!
Damn you!
You pay tithes on mint
and dill and cumin too,
but ignore the really
important matters of the Law,
such as justice
and mercy and trust.
You should have attended
to the last
without ignoring the first."

On washing vessels
Luke 11:39–41 / Matt 23:25–26

39 "You Pharisees
clean the outside of cups
and dishes,
but inside you are full
of greed and evil.
40 You fools!
Did not the one
who made the outside
also make the inside?

25 "You scholars and Pharisees,
you impostors!
Damn you!
You clean the outside of cups
and plates,
but inside they are full
of greed and dissipation.
26 You blind Pharisee,

11:35 Cf. Jn 11:10, Th 70:2
11:42 ◊ Mi 6:8
11:39–40 //Th 89
11:39 Cf. GOxy 840 2:8

11:42 Pharisees were laymen dedicated to the application of the OT Law, including rules of purity, to the details of daily life.

The *tithe* was a tax (10%) for the support of the temple, but tithing was also part of dietary law; produce needed to be tithed before it could be consumed.

41 Still, donate what is inside to charity, and then you'll see how everything comes clean for you."

first clean the inside of the cup and then the outside will be clean too."

On seeking honors

Luke 11:43 / Matt 23:6–7

43 "Damn you, Pharisees!	
You're so fond of	6 "They love the best
	couches at banquets
the prominent seat	and prominent seats
in synagogues	in synagogues
and respectful greetings	7 and respectful greetings
in marketplaces."	in marketplaces."
	and they like to be called 'Rabbi'
	by everyone."

Unmarked graves

Luke 11:44 / Matt 23:27–28

	27 "You scholars and Pharisees,
	you impostors!
44 "Damn you!	Damn you!
You are like unmarked graves	You are like whitewashed tombs:
	on the outside they look beautiful,
	but inside they are full of dead
	bones and every kind of decay.
	28 So you too look like decent
	people on the outside, but on the
	inside you are doing nothing but
	posturing and subverting the
	Law."
that people walk on	
without realizing it."	

Heavy burdens

Luke 11:46 / Matt 23:4

46 And he said,	
"Damn you legal experts too!	
You load people down with	4 "They invent
crushing burdens,	heavy burdens
	and lay them on folks' shoulders,

11:41=Matt 23:26 Many mss add "and the dish" after *cup*.

11:43 //Mk12:38–40

11:44 Contact with the dead rendered one ritually unclean; see Num 19:11–13, 16.

Luke	Matt
but you yourselves don't lift a finger to help carry them."	but they themselves won't lift a finger to move them."

Prophet's tombs

Luke 11:47–48 / Matt 23:29–32

Luke	Matt
	[29]"You scholars and Pharisees, you impostors!
[47]"Damn you! You erect monuments to the prophets	Damn you! You erect tombs to the prophets and decorate the graves of the righteous [30]and claim: 'If we had
whom your ancestors murdered.	lived in the days of our ancestors, we wouldn't have joined them in spilling the prophets' blood.'
[48]You are therefore witnesses to	[31]So, you witness against yourselves:
and approve of the deeds of your ancestors: they killed ⟨the prophets⟩	You are descendants of those who murdered the prophets, [32]and you're the spitting image of your ancestors."
and you erect ⟨monuments⟩ to them."	

Wisdom's oracle

Luke 11:49–51 / Matt 23:34–36

Luke	Matt
[49]"That is why the wisdom of God has said,	[34]"Look, that is why
'I will send them prophets and apostles, and some of them they are always going to kill	I send you prophets and sages and scholars. Some you're going to kill and crucify, and some you're going to beat in your synagogues
and persecute.	and hound from town to town.
[50]So this generation will have to answer for the blood	[35]As a result, there will be on your heads all the innocent blood

11:47–48
Cf. Acts 7:51–53; Ⓣ Q6:23
11:49–52
Cf. 1 Thes 2:14–16
11:49–51
Ⓣ Q13:34–35, Mk 12:1–12

11:47–51 The OT portrays God as having sent prophets to Israel who refused to heed them (Jer 7:25–26; 44:4–5; Zech 1:4; 7:12; Bar 1:21–22), even killing the prophets (Neh 9:26; 1 Kgs 19:10, 14). This persistent refusal to hear the prophets leaves Israel under the continuing threat of God's wrath (Bar 1:15–22).

11:49 *Wisdom*: see note to Q 7:35.

of all the prophets
that has been shed
since the world was founded,
[51]from the blood of Abel
to the blood of Zechariah,

who perished
between the altar
and the sanctuary.'
Yes, I tell you,
this generation will have
to answer for it."

that has been shed
on the earth,
from the blood of innocent Abel
to the blood of Zechariah,
son of Barach,
whom you murdered
between the temple
and the altar.
[36]I swear to you,
all these things are going
to rain down on this generation."

Blocking the way
Luke 11:52 / Matt 23:13

[52]"You legal experts,

damn you!
You have taken away the key
of knowledge.

You yourselves haven't entered
and you have blocked the way
of those trying to enter."

[13]"You scholars and Pharisees,
you impostors!
Damn you!
You slam the door
of Heaven's domain
in people's faces.
You yourselves don't enter,
and you block the way
of those trying to enter."

Veiled & unveiled
Luke 12:2–3 / Matt 10:26–27

[2]"There is nothing veiled
that won't be unveiled,
or hidden
that won't be made known.
[3]And so whatever you've said
in the dark
will be heard in the light,
and what you've whispered
behind closed doors
will be announced from the
rooftops."

[26]"So don't be afraid of them.
After all, there is nothing veiled
that won't be unveiled,
or hidden
that won't be made known.
[27]What I say to you
in the dark,
say in the light,
and what you hear ⟨whispered⟩
in your ear,
announce from the rooftops."

11:52 //Th 39:1–2; cf. Th 102; Ⓣ Mt 21:31–32
12:2 //Mk 4:22; Lk 8:17; Th 5:2, 6:5–6; cf. 1 Cor 4:5; ◊ 2 Kgs 6:12, 2 Mc 12:41
12:3 //Th 33:1

11:52 Several mss read "hidden" instead of *taken away*.

11:51 The *blood of Abel*, the first person in the OT to be killed, cried out to God from the ground for vengeance (Gen 4:10). The *Zechariah* referred to here is probably the Zechariah in 2 Chr 24:17–22, who was murdered and, in death, called on God to avenge his death. Neither Abel nor Zechariah was a prophet.

God & sparrows
Luke 12:4–7 / Matt 10:28–31

Luke	Matt
4“I tell you, my friends,	
don’t fear those	28“Don’t fear those
who kill the body,	who kill the body
and after that can do no more.	but cannot kill the soul;
5I’ll show you	
whom you ought to fear:	
fear the one who can kill	instead, you ought to fear
	the one who can destroy
and then has authority to	both the soul and the body
cast into Gehenna.	in Gehenna.
Believe me,	
that’s the one you should fear!	
6What do sparrows cost?	29What do sparrows cost?
A dime a dozen?	A penny apiece?
Yet not one of them is overlooked	Yet not one of them will fall
by God.	to the earth without the consent
	of your Father.
7In fact,	30As for you,
even the hairs of your head	even the hairs on your head
have all been counted.	have all been counted.
Don’t be so timid:	31So, don’t be so timid:
You’re worth more	you’re worth more
than a flock of sparrows.”	than a flock of sparrows.”

12:5 ◊Ps 119:120
12:7a // Lk 21:18, Acts 27:34b; cf. 1 Sm 14:45, 2 Sm 14:11, 1 Kgs 1:52
12:7b Ⓣ Mt 12:12
12:8–9 Cf. 1 Jn 2:23; Ⓣ 1 Sm 2:30
12:8 Cf. Jn 12:26, Rv 3:5
12:9 // Mk 8:38, Lk 9:26, 2 Tm 2:12b

Before the father
Luke 12:8–9 / Matt 10:32–33

Luke	Matt
8“I tell you,	
everyone who acknowledges	32“Everyone who acknowledges
me in public,	me in public,
the son of Adam	I too
will acknowledge	will acknowledge
in front of God’s messengers.	before my Father in the heavens.
9But whoever disowns me	33But the one who disowns me
in public	in public,
will be disowned in the	I too will disown before my
presence of God’s messengers.”	Father in the heavens.”

12:5 A warning to fear God, who has power to cast one into *Gehenna*, the valley of fire (see Matt 5:22; Jas 3:6). Gehenna is Greek for Valley of Hinnom, south of Jerusalem; probably because of Jer 19:1–10, it became a metaphor for the place God would punish the wicked.

Blasphemies
Luke 12:10 / Matt 12:32

10 And everyone who utters
a word against the son of Adam
will be forgiven;
but whoever blasphemes
against the holy spirit
won't be forgiven."

32 And the one who speaks
a word against the son of Adam
will be forgiven;
but the one who speaks a word
against the holy spirit
won't be forgiven,
either in this age
or in the one to come."

Spirit under trial
Luke 12:11–12 / Matt 10:19

11 "And when they make you
appear in synagogues
and haul you up
before rulers and authorities,
don't worry about how
or in what way
you should defend yourself
or what you should say.
12 The holy spirit will teach you
at that very moment
what you ought to say."

19 "And when they lock you up,
don't worry about how
you should speak,
or what you should say.
It will occur to you
at that moment
what to say."

Disputed inheritance
Luke 12:13–14

13 *Someone in the crowd said to
him, "Teacher, tell my brother to
divide the inheritance with me."*
14 *But Jesus said to him, "Mister,
who appointed me your judge or
arbiter?"*

Rich farmer
Luke 12:16–21

16 *Then he told them a parable:
"There was a rich man whose
fields produced a bumper crop.*
17 *'What do I do now?' he asked
himself, 'since I don't have any
place to store my crops.* 18 *I know!'
he said, 'I'll tear down my barns
and build larger ones so I can store*

12:10
//Mk 3:28–29,
Th 44;
cf. 1 Sm 2:25;
Ⓣ Wis 1:6
12:11–12
//Mk 13:9, 11;
cf. Lk 21:14–15

all my grain and my goods. 19 *Then*
I'll say to myself, "You have plenty
put away for years to come. Take it
easy, eat, drink, enjoy yourself."'
20 *But God said to him, 'You fool!*
This very night your life will be
demanded back from you. All this
stuff you've collected—whose will
it be now?' 21 *That's the way it is*
with those who save up for
themselves, but aren't rich where
God is concerned."

On anxieties

Luke 12:22–31 / Matt 6:25–33

Luke	Matt
22 He said to his disciples,	
"That's why I tell you:	25 "That's why I tell you:
Don't fret about life	Don't fret about your life
—what you're going eat—	—what you're going eat
or about your body	and drink—or about your body
—what you're going wear.	—what you're going wear.
23 Remember,	
there is more to living	There is more to living
than food and clothing.	than food and clothing,
	isn't there?
24 Think about the crows:	26 Take a look at the birds
	of the sky:
they don't plant or harvest,	they don't plant or harvest,
they don't have storerooms	or gather into barns.
or barns.	
Yet God	Yet your heavenly Father
feeds them.	feeds them.
You're worth a lot more	You're worth more
than the birds!	than they, aren't you?
25 Can any of you add	27 Can any of you add
an hour to life	one hour to life
by fretting about it?	by fretting about it?
26 So if you can't do a little thing	
like that,	
why worry about the rest?	28 Why worry about clothes?
27 Think about	Notice
how the lilies grow:	how the wild lilies grow:
they don't slave	they don't slave
and they never spin.	and they never spin.

12:22 //Th 36
12:24a Ⓣ Jb 12:7–8; ◊Ps 147:9, Jb 38:41
12:24b Ⓣ Q 12:6–7
12:25 //GrTh 36:3–4
12:27 //GrTh 36:2

12:27 A few mss add "or weave" after *never spin*.

Yet let me tell you,
even Solomon at the height
of his glory
was never decked out like
one of them.
[28]If God dresses up the grass
in the field,
which is here today
and tomorrow is tossed
into an oven,
it is surely more likely
⟨that God cares for⟩ you,
you who don't take anything
for granted!

[29]And don't be constantly
on the lookout for
what you're going to eat
and what you're going to drink.

Don't give it a thought.
[30]These are all things
the world's pagans seek,
and your Father
is aware
that you need them.
[31]Instead, you are to seek
⟨God's⟩ domain,

and these things will come
to you as a bonus."

[29]Yet let me tell you,
even Solomon at the height
of his glory
was never decked out like
one of them.
[30]If God dresses up the grass
in the field,
which is here today
and tomorrow is thrown
into an oven,
won't ⟨God care for⟩ you
even more,
you who don't take anything
for granted?
[31]So don't fret.
Don't say,

'What am I going to eat?'
or 'What am I going to drink?'
or 'What am I going to wear?'

[32]These are all things
pagans seek.
After all, your heavenly Father
is aware
that you need them.
[33]You are to seek
⟨God's⟩ domain,
and his justice first,
and all these things will come
to you as a bonus."

On possessions
Luke 12:33–34 / Matt 6:19–21

[33]"Sell your belongings,
and donate to charity;

make yourselves purses
that don't wear out,
with inexhaustible wealth
in heaven,
where no robber can get to it
and no moth can destroy it.

[19]"Don't acquire possessions
here on earth,
where moths
and insects eat away
and where robbers break in
and steal.

[20]Instead, gather your nest egg
in heaven,

where neither moths nor
insects eat away

12:29
Ⓣ Q10:4
12:30
Ⓣ Q11:13
12:31
Cf. Rom 14:17;
Ⓣ Mt 19:29,
Lk 18:29b-30
12:33
//Th 76:3;
cf. Mk 10:21,
Mt 19:21,
Jas 5:2–3;
Ⓣ Lk 12:16–21,
18:22; Tob 4:9,
12:8–9

and where no robbers break in
or steal.

34 As you know,
what you treasure
is your heart's true measure."

21 As you know,
what you treasure
is your heart's true measure."

Homeowner & burglar
Luke 12:39–40 / Matt 24:43–44

39 "Mark this well:
if the homeowner had known
what time the burglar
was coming,
he would not have let anyone
break into his house.
40 You too should be prepared.
Remember,
the son of Adam is coming
when you least expect it."

43 "Mark this well:
if the homeowner had known
when the burglar
was coming,
he would have been on guard
and not have allowed anyone
to break into his house.
44 By the same token,
you too should be prepared.
Remember,
the son of Adam is coming
when you least expect it."

Unexpected return
Luke 12:42–46 / Matt 24:45–51

42 The Lord said,
"Who then is the reliable
and shrewd manager
to whom the master assigns
responsibility
for his household staff,
to dole out their food allowance
at the right time?
43 Congratulations to the slave
who's on the job
when his master arrives.
44 I'm telling you the truth:
he'll put him in charge of
all his property.
45 But suppose that slave
says to himself,
'My master is taking his time
getting here,'
and begins to beat

45 "Who then is the reliable
and shrewd slave
to whom the master assigns
responsibility
for his household,
to provide them with food
at the right time?
46 Congratulations to the slave
who's on the job
when his master arrives.
47 I swear to you,
he'll put him in charge of
all his property.
48 But suppose that worthless slave
says to himself,
'My master is taking his time,'
49 and begins to beat

12:39
//Th21:5; 103
12:44
Ⓣ Q19:17, 22:28–30; Mt25:21, 23
12:45–46
Cf. Mk13:35; Ⓣ Lk21:34

12:39 The arrival (*parousia*) of the son of Adam (or of the Lord) is frequently compared to the arrival of a thief: 1 Thess 5:2; Rev 3:3.

12:45–46 Many horror stories were told in antiquity of the misbehavior of slaves when their master was gone.

the servants and the maids,	his fellow slaves,
and to eat	and starts eating
and drink	and drinking
and get drunk,	with drunkards,
[46]that slave's master	[50]that slave's master
will show up on the day	will show up on the day
he least expects	he least expects
and at an hour he doesn't suspect.	and at an hour he doesn't suspect.
He'll cut him to pieces	[51]He'll cut him to pieces,
and assign him a fate fit	and assign him a fate fit
for the faithless."	for the other impostors.
	⟨Those who share this fate⟩
	will moan and grind their teeth."

Peace or conflict
Luke 12:49, 51–53 / Matt 10:34–36

[49]*"I came to set the earth on fire,*	
and how I wish it were already	
ablaze!	
[51]Do you suppose	[34]"Don't get the idea
I came here to bring peace	that I came to bring peace
on earth?	on earth.
No, I tell you,	I did not come to bring peace
on the contrary: conflict.	but a sword.
[52]As a result, from now on in any given house there will be five in conflict, three against two and two against three.	[35]After all, I have come
[53]Father will be pitted against son	to pit
and son against father,	a man against his father,
mother against daughter	
and daughter against mother,	a daughter against her mother,
mother-in-law	
against daughter-in-law	
and daughter-in-law	and a daughter-in-law
against mother-in-law."	against her mother-in-law.
	[36]Your enemies live under your own roof."

Knowing the times
Luke 12:54–56 / Matt 16:2–3

[54]He would also say to the crowds,	[2]In response he said to them,
	"When it's evening, you say, 'It'll
	be fair weather because the sky

12:54–56 Some mss omit the Matthean parallel (Matt 16:2–3).

12:49 //Th10; cf. Th82; Ⓣ Q3:16; Lk9:54–55, 17:28–30
12:51–53 //Th16; Cf. GNaz11
12:53 //Mk13:12; Ⓣ Q14:26; ◊Mi7:6

Luke	Matthew
	looks red.' [3]Early in the morning,
	⟨you say,⟩ 'The day will bring
	winter weather because the sky
	looks red and dark.'
"When you see a cloud rising in	
the west, right away you say that	
it's going to rain; and so it does.	
[55]And when the wind blows from	
the south, you say we're in for	
scorching heat; and we are.	
[56]You phonies!	
You know the lay of the land	You know
and can read the face	how to read the face
of the sky,	of the sky,
so why don't you know how	but you can't
to interpret the present time?"	discern the signs of the times."

Before the judge

Luke 12:57–59 / Matt 5:25–26

Luke	Matthew
[57]"Why can't you decide for	
yourselves what is right?	
[58]When you are about	[25]"You should come to terms
to appear with your opponent	quickly with your opponent
before the magistrate,	
do your best to settle with him	while you are both
on the way,	on the way ⟨to court⟩,
or else he might drag	or else your opponent will hand
you up before the judge,	you over to the judge,
and the judge turn you over	and the judge ⟨will turn you over⟩
to the jailer,	to the bailiff,
and the jailer throw you in prison.	and you are thrown in jail.
[59]I tell you,	[26]I swear to you,
you'll never get out of there	you'll never get out of there
until you've paid	until you've paid
every last red cent."	the last dime."

Mustard seed & leaven

Luke 13:18–21 / Matt 13:31–33

Luke	Matthew
[18]Then he would say:	[31]He put another parable
	before them
	with these words:

12:56
//Th91:2

12:58 Some mss read "condemn you" instead of *drag you up*.

12:58 The *opponent* is a creditor demanding payment of a debt (see Matt 18:23–34).

"What is God's imperial rule like? What does it remind me of? 19It is like a mustard seed that a man took and tossed into his garden.	 "Heaven's imperial rule is like a mustard seed that a man took and sowed in his field. 32Though it is the smallest of all seeds, yet, when it has grown up, it is the largest of garden plants,
It grew and became a tree, and the birds of the sky roosted in its branches." 20He continued:	and becomes a tree, so that the birds of the sky come and roost in its branches." 33He told them another parable:
"What does God's imperial rule remind me of? 21It is like leaven that a woman took and concealed in fifty pounds of flour until it was all leavened."	 "Heaven's imperial rule is like leaven that a woman took and concealed in fifty pounds of flour until it was all leavened."

Two gates

Luke 13:24–27 / Matt 7:13–14, 22–23

24"Struggle to get in through the narrow door;	13"Try to get in through the narrow gate. Wide and smooth is the road that leads to destruction.
I'm telling you, many will try to get in, but won't be able.	Many are taking that route.
	14Narrow and rough is the road that leads to life. Only a minority discover it.
25*Once the master of the house gets up and bars the door, you'll be left standing outside and knocking at the door: 'Sir, open up for us.'* *But he'll answer you, 'I don't know where you come from.'*	
26Then you'll start saying,	22On that day many will address me:

13:18–19 //Mk 4:30–32, Th 20; cf. Mt 13:24; Ⓣ DSav 36:1
13:19c ◊Ez 17:23, 31:6
13:20–21 //Th 96
13:21 Cf. 1 Cor 5:6
13:24 Ⓣ 2 Esd 7:6–8
13:25–26 Ⓣ Q 6:46
13:25 //Mt 25:12

13:19 Some mss read "a great tree" instead of *a tree.*

13:21 The *leaven* here is sourdough.

Luke	Matt
	'Master, master, didn't we use your name when we prophesied? Didn't we use your name when we exorcised demons? Didn't we use your name when we performed all those miracles?'
'We ate and drank with you, and you taught in our streets.'	
27But he'll reply, 'I don't know where you come from;	23Then I will tell them honestly: 'I never knew you;
get away from me, all you evildoers!'"	get away from me, you subverters of the Law!'"

Dining with patriarchs

Luke 13:28–30 / Matt 8:11–12; 20:16

Luke	Matt
28There'll be weeping and grinding teeth out there when you see Abraham and Isaac and Jacob and all the prophets in God's domain and yourselves thrown out.	v. 12
29"And people will come from east and west, from north and south,	11"I predict that many will come from east and west
and dine	and dine with Abraham and Isaac and Jacob
in God's domain.	in Heaven's domain,
	12but those who think Heaven's domain belongs to them will be thrown where it is utterly dark.
v. 28	There'll be weeping and grinding of teeth out there.
30And remember, those who will be first are last, and those who will be last are first."	20 16So the last will be first and the first last."

Jerusalem indicted

Luke 13:34–35 / Matt 23:37–39

Luke	Matt
34"Jerusalem, Jerusalem, you murder the prophets and stone those sent to you!	37"Jerusalem, Jerusalem, you murder the prophets and stone those sent to you!

13:27 ◊Ps6:9
13:28–29 Ⓣ Q14:16–24
13:28 Ⓣ Mt13:42, 22:13, 24:51, 25:30; ◊Hos9:17
13:29 Ⓣ 2Esd1:38–40; ◊Ps107:3; Is25:6–8, 43:5–6; Mal1:11; Bar4:36–37
13:30 //Mk10:31; Mt19:30, 20:16; Th4:2; cf. Mk9:35

13:34–35 The speaker here is probably Wisdom.

13:34 On prophets sent and killed, see the note to Q 11:47–51

Luke	Matt
How often I wanted to gather your children as a hen ⟨gathers⟩ her own chicks under her wings, but you wouldn't let me. 35Can't you see, your house is being abandoned?	How often I wanted to gather your children as a hen gathers her chicks under her wings, but you wouldn't let me. 38Can't you see, your house is being abandoned as a ruin?
I tell you, you certainly won't see me	39I tell you, you certainly won't see me from now on
until the time comes when you say, 'Blessed is the one who comes in the name of the Lord.'"	until you say, 'Blessed is the one who comes in the name of the Lord.'"

Promotion & demotion

Luke 14:11, 18:14 / Matt 23:12

Luke	Matt
11"Those who promote themselves will be demoted, and those who demote themselves will be promoted. 18 14For those who promote themselves will be demoted, but those who demote themselves will be promoted."	12"Those who promote themselves will be demoted, and those who demote themselves will be promoted."

The feast

Luke 14:16–24 / Matt 22:1–10

Luke	Matt
	1Jesus again responded to them
16Jesus told him:	and told them parables: 2"Heaven's imperial rule is like a secular ruler
"Someone was giving a big dinner and invited many guests. 17At the dinner hour	who gave a wedding celebration for his son.

13:34–35 Cf. 2 Esd 1:28–34; Ⓣ Q6:23, 11:47–51, 14:16–24, 20:9–18; Mt21:33–43; ◊ 1 Kgs 9:6–9, Jer 26:4–6

13:34a ◊ Dt 32:11, Ps 91:4, Is 31:5

13:35a ◊ Tob 14:4, Is 49:14

13:35b // Mk 11:9, Mt 21:9, Lk 19:38; ◊ Ps 118:26

14:11, 18:14 Cf. Mt 18:4; Phil 2:8–9; 1 Pet 5:6; Jas 4:10; Prv 29:23; Sir 10:14; Ez 17:24, 21:31; 2 Esd 8:48–49

13:35 Some mss add "as a ruin" after *abandoned*.

13:35a The *house* is probably the temple, the dwelling place of God.

the host sent his slave to tell the guests:	3Then he sent his slaves to summon those who had been invited to the wedding, but they declined to attend. 4He sent additional slaves with the instructions: 'Tell those invited, "Look, the feast is ready, the oxen and fat calves have been slaughtered,
'Come, it's ready now.'	and everything is ready. Come to the wedding!"'
18But one by one they all began to make excuses.	5But they were unconcerned
	and went off,
The first said to him, 'I just bought a farm, and I have to go and inspect it; please excuse me.'	one to his own farm,
19And another said, 'I just bought five pairs of oxen, and I'm on my way to check them out; please excuse me.'	one to his business,
20And another said, 'I just got married, and so I cannot attend.'	
	6while the rest seized his slaves, attacked and killed them.
21So the slave came back and reported these ⟨excuses⟩ to his master.	
Then the master of the house got angry	7Now the king got angry and sent his armies to destroy those murderers and burn their city.
and instructed his slave:	8Then he tells his slaves: "The wedding celebration is ready but those we've invited didn't prove deserving.
'Quick! Go out into the streets and alleys of the town,	9So go to the city gates
and usher in the poor, and crippled, the blind, and the lame.'	and invite anybody you find to the wedding.'
22And the slave said, 'Sir, your orders have been carried out, and there's still room.'	

14:16–24
//Th64;
Ⓣ Prv9:1–6
14:17
Ⓣ Q13:34
14:20
◊ Dt24:5
14:21–23
Ⓣ Q13:28–29
14:21
Ⓣ Lk14:13

[23]And the master said to the slave,
'Then go out
into the roads
and the country lanes,
and force people to come in
so my house will be filled.

[24]Believe you me, not one of those
who were given invitations will
taste my dinner.'"

[10]Those slaves then went out
into the streets
and collected everybody
they could find,
the good and bad alike.
And the wedding hall was full
of guests."

Hating one's family
Luke 14:26–27, 17:33 / Matt 10:37–39

[26]"If any of you comes to me
and does not hate your own
father and mother
and wife and children
and brothers and sisters
—yes, even your own life—
you're no disciple of mine.
[27]Unless you carry
your own cross
and come along with me—
you're no disciple of mine.
17 [33]Whoever tries
to hang onto life,
will forfeit it,
but whoever foreits life
will preserve it."

[37]"If you love your
father and mother more than me,
you're not worthy of me,
if you love your
son or daughter
more than me,
you're not worthy of me.
[38]Unless you take
your cross
and come along with me,
you're not worthy of me.
[39]By finding your life,
you'll lose it,
and by losing your life
for my sake
you'll find it."

Saltless salt
Luke 14:34–35 / Matt 5:13

[34]"Salt is good ⟨and salty⟩.
But if salt loses its zing,
how will it be renewed?

[13]"You are the salt
of the earth.
But if salt loses its zing,
how will it be made salty?

14:26–27 //Th 55
14:26 //Th 101; cf. Mk 10:29–30, Mt 19:29, Lk 18:29b-30; ◊ Dt 33:8–9
14:27 //Mk 8:34, Mt 16:24, Lk 9:23
17:33 //Mk 8:35, Mt 16:25, Lk 9:24, Jn 12:25

14:26=Matt 10:37 A few mss omit the second half of Matt 10:37.

35 It's no good for
either earth or manure.
It just gets thrown away.

Anyone here with two good ears
had better listen!"

It then has no further use

than to be thrown out
and stomped on."

Lost sheep & coin

Luke 15:4–10 / Matt 18:12–13

4 "Is there any one of you
who owns a hundred sheep
and one of them gets lost,
who wouldn't leave the
ninety-nine in the wilderness,
and go after
the one that got lost
until he finds it?
5 And when he finds it,
he lifts it up on his shoulders,
happy. 6 Once he gets home, he
invites his friends and his
neighbors over, and says to them,
'Celebrate with me, because I
have found my stray sheep.'
7 I'm telling you
it'll be just like this in heaven:
there'll be more celebrating
over one sinner
who has a change of heart
than over ninety-nine
virtuous people
who have no need to change their
hearts.
8 Or again, is there any woman
with ten silver coins, who if she
loses one, wouldn't light a lamp
and sweep the house and search
carefully until she finds it? 9 When
she finds it, she invites her friends
and neighbors over and says,

12 "What do you
think about this?
If someone
has a hundred sheep
and one of them wanders off,
won't that person leave the
ninety-nine in the hills
and go look for
the one that wandered off?

13 And if he should find it,

You can bet

he'll rejoice
over it

more than over the ninety-nine

that didn't wander off."

14:34 //Mk 9:50
14:35 Ⓣ Q 3:9
15:4–7 //Th 107
15:4 ◊ Ez 34:11–12, 15–16; Ps 119:176
15:7 Ⓣ Mk 2:17, Mt 9:13, Lk 5:32, 19:10, 2 Esd 7:59–60

15:8 The woman's coins are called *drachmas*, a Greek term probably used for the common Roman silver *denarius* which apparently was what a day-laborer could earn in a day (Matt 20:9).

'Celebrate with me, because I have found the silver coin I had lost.' [10]I'm telling you, it's just like this among God's messengers: they celebrate when one sinner has a change of heart."

Two masters
Luke 16:13 / Matt 6:24

Luke	Matt
[13]"No servant can be a slave to two masters. No doubt that slave will either hate one and love the other, or be devoted to one and disdain the other. You can't be enslaved to both God and a bank account!"	[24]"No one can be a slave to two masters. No doubt that slave will either hate one and love the other, or be devoted to one and disdain the other. You can't be enslaved to both God and a bank account!"

God's rule & violence
Luke 16:16 / Matt 11:12–13

Luke	Matt
[16]"Right up to John's time	[12]"From the time of John the Baptist until now
⟨you have⟩ the Law and the Prophets;	v. 13
since then God's imperial rule has been proclaimed as good news and everyone is	Heaven's imperial rule
breaking into it violently."	has been breaking in violently, and violent men are attempting to gain it by force. [13]You see, the Prophets and even the Law predicted everything that was to happen prior to John's time."

16:13
//Th 47:1–2; cf. Jas 4:4; Ⓣ Q 12:34
16:16
Ⓣ SJas 6:2–4
16:17
Cf. Mk 13:31, Mt 24:35, Lk 21:33, Th 11:1

Not one serif
Luke 16:17 / Matt 5:18

Luke	Matt
	[18]"I swear to you,
[17]"But it is easier for the world to disappear	before the world disappears,

---

16:16 The *Law* is the first five books of the Hebrew Bible; the *Prophets* are the prophetic writings.

than for one serif of one letter
of the Law to drop out.”

not one iota,
not one serif,
will disappear from the Law,
until that happens.”

On divorce

Luke 16:18 / Matt 5:32

18“Everyone who divorces his wife

and marries another
commits adultery;
and the one who marries a
woman divorced
from her husband
commits adultery.”

32“But I tell you:
Everyone who divorces his wife

(except in the case of infidelity)

makes her the victim of adultery;
and whoever marries a
divorced woman

commits adultery.”

Millstone award

Luke 17:1–2 / Matt 18:6–7

1He said to his disciples,
“It’s inevitable
that snares will be set;
nevertheless, damn the one
who sets them!

2You’d be better off
if you had a millstone hung
around your neck
and were dumped
into the sea
than to mislead
one of these little ones.”

v. 1

v. 7

6“Any of you who misleads one
of these little souls who trusts me
would be better off
to have a millstone hung
around your neck
and be drowned
in the deepest part of the sea!

7Damn the world
for the snares it sets!
Even though it’s inevitable
for snares to be set,
nevertheless damn the persons
who set such snares.”

16:18
//Mk 10:11–12;
Ⓓ Mt 19:9;
◊ Dt 24:1–4
17:1–2
Cf. Mk 9:42, 14:21;
Mt 18:6, 26:24;
Lk 22:22

16:18 The “exception” in Matthew is based on an interpretation of Deut 24:1 (“some indecency”).

Scold & forgive
Luke 17:3–4 / Matt 18:15, 21–22

[3]“If some companion
does wrong,
scold that person;

if there is a change of heart,
forgive the person.

[4]If someone wrongs you seven
times a day, and seven times
turns around and says to you,
‘I’m sorry,’ you should forgive
that person.”

[15]“And if some companion
does wrong,
go have it out privately
between the two of you.
If that person listens to you, you
have won your companion over.
[21]Then Peter came up and asked
him, ‘Master, how many times
can a companion wrong me
and still expect my forgiveness?
As many as seven times?’
[22]Jesus replies to him,
‘My advice to you
is not seven times,

but seventy-seven times.’”

Mountains into the sea
Luke 17:6 / Matt 17:20

[6]And the Lord said,
“If you had trust no larger
than a mustard seed,
you could tell this mulberry tree,
‘Uproot yourself
and plant yourself in the sea,’
and it would obey you.”

[20]“I swear to you,
even if you have trust no larger
than a mustard seed,
you will say to this mountain,
‘Move from here to there,’

and it will move.
And nothing will be beyond you.”

Coming of son of Adam
Lk 17:22–24, 26–30, 34–35, 37 / Mt 24:26–28, 37, 39–41

[22]*And he said to the disciples,*
“There’ll come a time when you
will yearn to see one of the days of
the son of Adam, and you won’t see
it.

[23]“And they’ll be telling you,
‘Look, there it is!’
or ‘Look, here it is!’

[26]“In fact,
if they should say to you,
‘Look, he’s in the wilderness,’

17.3b
Ⓣ Gal 6:1,
Jas 5:19–20

17:4
//GNaz 5:1;
Ⓣ Q 11:4

17:6
//Mk 11:23,
Mt 21:21;
cf. Th 48;
Ⓣ Mk 9:23,
1 Cor 13:2

17:23
//Mk 13:21,
Mt 24:23,
Th 113:2;
Ⓣ Lk 17:20–21,
2 Esd 13:52

17:23 The wilderness (Matt 24:26) was often
seen as the place of salvation.

Don't rush off;

don't pursue it.
[24]For just as
lightning flashes
and lights up the sky
from one end to the other,
that's what the son of Adam
will be like in his day.
v. 37

[26]And just as it was
in the days of Noah,
that's how it will be
in the days of the son of Adam.

[27]They ate, drank,
got married, and were given
in marriage, until the day
'Noah boarded the ark.'

Then the flood came
and destroyed them all.
[28]*That's also the way it was in the days of Lot. Everyone ate, drank, bought, sold, planted, and built.*
[29]*But on the day Lot left Sodom, fire and sulphur rained down from the sky and destroyed them all.*
[30]It will be like that on the day
the son of Adam is revealed.
[34]I tell you, on that night
there will be two
on one couch:
one will be taken
and the other left.
[35]There will be two women
grinding together:
one will be taken
and the other left."
[37]Then they asked him,

don't go out there;
'Look, he's in one of the secret rooms,'
don't count on it.
[27]For just as
lightning comes out of the east
and is visible
all the way to the west,
that's what the coming of
the son of Adam will be like.
[28]For wherever there's a corpse,
that's where vultures gather.
[37]The son of Adam's coming

will be just like
the days of Noah.
[38]This is how people behaved
then before the flood came:
they ate and drank,
got married and were given
in marriage, until the day
'Noah boarded the ark,'
[39]and they were oblivious
until the flood came
and swept them all away.

That's how it will be when
the son of Adam comes.

[40]Then two men will be
in the field;
one will be taken
and one will be left.
[41]Two women will be
grinding at the mill;
one will be taken
and one left."

17:24
◊Ps77:18, 97:4
17:34–35
//Th61:1

17:24 Several mss omit *in his day.*

"Taken where, Lord?" And he said to them, "Vultures collect wherever there's a carcass."	v. 28

Entrusted money

Luke 19:12–26 / Matt 25:14–30

12 So he said: "A nobleman went off to a distant land intending to acquire a kingship for himself and then return.	14 "You know, it's like a man going on a trip
13 Calling ten of his slaves, he gave them each one hundred silver coins,	who called his slaves and turned his valuables over to them. 15 To the first he gave thirty thousand silver coins, to the second twelve thousand, and to the third six thousand, to each in relation to his ability,
and told them: 'Do business with this while I'm away.'	
	and he left.
14 His fellow citizens, however, hated him and sent a delegation right on his heels, with the petition: 'We don't want this man to rule us.'	
	Immediately 16 the one who had received thirty thousand silver coins went out and put the money to work; he doubled his investment. 17 The second also doubled his money. 18 But the third, who had received the smallest amount, went out, dug a hole, and hid his master's silver.
15 As it turned out, he got the kingship and returned.	19 After a long absence, the slaves' master returned to settle accounts with them.
He had those slaves summoned	

17:35 After v. 35, a few mss add a v. 36: "There will be two in a field; one will be taken and the other left."

17:37 ◊Jb 39:30b

17:37 The bird referred to here could also be an eagle, which may be an allusion to the standards of the Roman legions, and by extension, to the legions themselves.

to whom he had given the money, in order to find out what profit they had made.	
16 The first	20 The first, who had received thirty thousand silver coins,
came in	came and produced an additional thirty thousand,
and reported, 'Master, your investment has increased ten times over.'	with this report: 'Master, you handed me thirty thousand silver coins; as you can see, I have made you another thirty thousand.'
17 He said to him, 'Well done, you excellent slave! Because you have been trustworthy in this small matter, you are to be in charge of ten towns.'	21 His master commended him: 'Well done, you competent and reliable slave! You have been trustworthy in small amounts; I'll put you in charge of large amounts. Come celebrate with your master!'
18 The second came in	22 The one with twelve thousand silver coins also came
and reported, 'Master, your investment has increased five times over.'	and reported: 'Master, you handed me twelve thousand silver coins; as you can see, I have made you another twelve thousand.'
19 And he said to him,	23 His master commended him: 'Well done, you competent and reliable slave! You have been trustworthy in small amounts;
'And you are to be in charge of five towns.'	I'll put you in charge of large amounts. Come celebrate with your master!'
20 Then the last	24 The one who had received six thousand silver coins also
came in and said, 'Master, here is your money. I kept it tucked away safe in a handkerchief. 21 You see, I was afraid of you,	came and reported: 'Master,
	I know

because you're a demanding man:
you withdraw what you
didn't deposit,
and reap what you didn't sow.'

[22]He said
to him,
'You incompetent slave!

Your own words convict you. So
you knew I was demanding, did
you? That I withdraw what I
didn't deposit

and reap what I didn't sow?

[23]So why didn't you put
my money in the bank?

Then I could have collected it
with interest when I got back.'
[24]Then he said to his attendants,
'Take the money away
from this fellow
and give it to the one
who has ten times as much.'
[25]'But my lord,' they said to him,
'he already has ten times as
much.'
[26]He replied,
'I tell you,
to everyone who has,
more will be given;

and from those who don't have,
even what they do have
will be taken away.'"

that you drive a hard bargain,

reaping where you didn't sow
and gathering where you didn't
scatter.
[25]Since I was afraid, I went out
and buried your money in the
ground. Look, here it is!'
[26]But his master replied
to him,
'You incompetent
and timid slave!

So you knew
that I reap where I didn't sow
and gather where I didn't scatter,
did you?
[27]Then you should have taken
my money to the bankers.
Then when I returned
I would have received my capital
with interest.

[28]So take the money away
from this fellow
and give it to the one
who has the greatest sum.

[29]In fact,
to everyone who has,
more will be given
and then some;
and from those who don't have,
even what they do have
will be taken away.
[30]And throw this worthless slave

19:26
//Mk4:25,
Mt13:12, Lk8:18,
Th41

19:25 Several mss omit this verse.

where it is utterly dark. Out there they'll weep and grind their teeth.'

On twelve thrones
Luke 22:28–30 / Matt 19:28

Luke	Matt
28"You are the ones who have stuck by me in my ordeals.	28"You who have followed me,
	when the son of Adam is seated on his throne of glory in the renewal ⟨of creation⟩,
29And I confer on you the right to rule, just as surely as my Father conferred that right on me,	
30so you may eat and drink at my table in my domain,	
and be seated	you also will be seated on
on thrones	twelve thrones
and sit in judgment on the twelve tribes of Israel."	and sit in judgment on the twelve tribes of Israel."

22:29 Ⓣ Q10:22
22:30 Cf. 1 Cor 4:8; Rv 2:26, 3:21; Ⓣ Mt 20:21; ◊ Wis 3:8, Sir 4:15

Introduction

The Gospel of Thomas is a sayings gospel. It consists, for the most part, of sayings attributed to Jesus, listed serially and presented using simple stock phrases such as "Jesus said." It thus has virtually no narrative element, a characteristic which distinguishes it from the better known canonical examples of early Christian gospel literature, Matthew, Mark, Luke, and John. As such, it does not purport to give an account or interpretation of Jesus' life, but focuses instead on Jesus' words, his preaching.

Discovery

Though scholars had known for years of the existence of a certain Gospel of Thomas in the early Christian period, it was thought that no copy of it had survived antiquity. This changed in 1945, when a copy of the lost gospel was discovered as part of a large collection of ancient religious texts known as the Nag Hammadi Library, so called after the Egyptian city near which the collection was found. The copy of Thomas discovered at Nag Hammadi is actually a Coptic (the common language of Egypt during the Christian period) translation of the original, which was probably written in Greek. Although fragments of the Greek text of Thomas were actually discovered some 45 years before the sensational find at Nag Hammadi, until scholars had the Coptic text of Thomas in hand, the identity of those fragments could not be ascertained with any certainty. The three Greek fragments are known as Papyrus Oxyrhynchus (POxy) 1, 654, and 655.

The Gospel of Thomas as a sayings collection

The Gospel of Thomas is a collection of sayings presented serially, and organized primarily around the principle of catchword association. Such collections were common in antiquity. The students of famous philosophers, such as Epicurus or Epictetus, often collected the wise and witty sayings of their tradition into *gnomologia*, or "words of insight," which they might then use as they evangelized the public in the marketplaces and streets of the ancient world. Jews and other ethnic groups of the eastern empire also gathered the aphoristic wisdom of their sages into collections of *logoi sophon*, or "sayings of the wise," such as one finds, for example, in the book of Proverbs. The gathering of Jesus' sayings into such a collection places him among the sages of the past, the prophets of Sophia (the feminine personification of wisdom in Jewish lore) sent into every generation with her saving words of wisdom (see Wis 7:27).

Authorship and provenance

As with all early Christian gospels, the ascription of the Gospel of Thomas to an apostolic figure probably derives from an urge to guarantee the reliability of the tradition rather than from accurate historical memory. Thus, we simply do not know who originally assembled this collection.

It is noteworthy, however, that the opening line of the gospel reads: "These are the secret sayings that the living Jesus spoke and Didymos Judas Thomas recorded." Didymos Judas Thomas seems to have been a popular legendary figure from apostolic times, especially in Syria. In fact, it is only in eastern Syria that we find precisely this form of the name, where it occurs in the Acts of Thomas. In early Christianity the names of particular apostles often acquired special significance within specific geographical areas. For example, Peter is associated with Rome, John with Asia Minor, and James with Jerusalem. We cannot be certain whether such associations are grounded in historical memories of the evangelization of these areas, or are purely legendary. Thomas, or Didymos Judas Thomas, was apparently the patron apostle for Syria. As such, most scholars now assume that the Gospel of Thomas, in more or less its present form, came originally out of Syria. It is certainly possible, however, that an earlier version might have originated in Palestine. Saying 12 in this gospel, after all, appeals not to the authority of Thomas, but to that of James, who was associated in early Christianity with the Jerusalem church (see Gal 1:19).

Date

The date for the compilation of a sayings collection such as Thomas may be given only in rough approximation. One must assume that as a sayings collection, this text would have enjoyed much greater flexibility of content than is generally true of narrative texts. In each new appropriation of the collection, new sayings could easily be added, even as older, outmoded sayings were sloughed away. Still, several factors point to a date sometime in the latter decades of the first century C.E.: First, the collection belongs to a time when individual Christian communities were still appealing to the authority of particular apostles (not to "the twelve" as a whole) as the guarantor of their traditions. In this respect it is comparable to Mark, which dates to around 70 C.E. Second, the genre of Thomas, the sayings collection, seems to have fallen into disuse among Christians by the end of the first century. Later church fathers revived the form, but always took care to cite the sources for their material, usually the canonical gospels. This is quite different from Thomas, which derives its material not from the canonical gospels, but from the same oral traditions on which these gospels themselves rely. This in turn suggests a third factor: Thomas was assembled before Matthew, Mark, Luke, and John had attained the ascendency which the later church codified in the form of a "canon," a process which began in the second century. All of these factors place Thomas approximately in the same period as the canonical gospels (ca. 70–100 C.E.).

Theology

As an example of the genre *logoi sophon* ("sayings of the wise") the Gospel of Thomas belongs to a lively tradition in first century Judaism: Wisdom. This Wisdom tradition produced collections such as one finds in Proverbs, Ecclesiastes, or the Wisdom of Solomon. Many of Thomas' sayings seem quite at home in this tradition: they speak of what is true about people, about life and the world. They speak about what is worthwhile in the world, and what is wrong with it, about human wisdom and human foolishness.

The Wisdom tradition, on the whole, is rather conservative. It tends toward the conventional, the tried and true. By contrast, Thomas frequently offers a rather uncommon wisdom, a wisdom that is "not of this age" (1 Cor. 2:6), to quote a contemporary of Thomas. Thomas' sayings can speak of renouncing the world (Thom 110); they can ridicule prudence (Thom 76); they can exclude the savvy of the world from God's realm (Thom 64); and they can undermine conventional values such as home and family (Thom 55 and 99, and 101), traditional piety (Thom 14), and respect for community leaders (Thom 3 and 102). The wisdom one finds in Thomas is hardly conventional. In fact, if one is to recognize any common wisdom at all in Thomas' outlook, one must first, it seems, cultivate a way of thinking that subverts dominant cultural values.

The theological underpinnings for Thomas' decidedly counter-cultural bent also go somewhat beyond those of standard Wisdom theology. The truth Thomas reveals about human nature extends beyond the rather ordinary observations that people tend to be selfish (Thom 41), vain (Thom 36), judgmental (Thom 26), foolish, and easily led astray (Thom 34). People are this way because they have forgotten who they are, where they have come from. In Thom 28 Jesus speaks as one who has come from God to remind the "children of humanity" of whence they have come and to where they shall ultimately return:

> [1]Jesus said, "I took my stand in the midst of the world, and in the flesh I appeared to them. [2]I found them all drunk, and I did not find any of them thirsty. [3]My soul ached for the children of humanity, because they are blind in their hearts and do not see, for they came into the world empty, and they also seek to depart from the world

empty. [4]But meanwhile they are drunk. When they shake off their wine, then they will repent." (Thom 28)

The religious background of this way of thinking is to be found in Gnosticism, a religious movement which flourished during the period of Christianity's rise. Gnosticism as a movement was very diverse, but its theological orientation may be described generally as anti-cosmic. Gnostics believed that the world (*kosmos*) is evil, a mistake in the divine order. Gnostics themselves, consequently, did not see themselves as part of the evil world. Having originally descended from God, their presence in the world is itself the result of a tragic error, a fall, an entrapment. Over time, however, the world had worked its anesthetizing powers on them, so that they had forgotten their origins, their God, until such time as a savior, a revealer, came to remind them of their heavenly origins.

Of course, not all of this is found in Thomas. Nor are there elaborate descriptions of the origin of the world, of humanity's fall, or the journey back to the divine realm, so typical of later Christian Gnosticism. Still, the rudiments of this type of thinking are present throughout Thomas: the deprecation of the world and the flesh (Thom 56 and 80); the tendency to remove oneself from the world (Thom 21:6); even perhaps a primitive catechism for the return home (Thom 49 and 50). In Thomas, one sees an early Christian community taking its first steps in the direction of Gnosticism, its countercultural wisdom a blossom of the anti-cosmic gnostic orientation that would reach its full flowering among Christians only in the second century. Thomas shares with Gnosticism a basic concern for personal identity within a world which was widely perceived as brutal and mean. Thomas presents us with a Jesus whose words call one from out of the chaos into a quest, to seek and to find (Thom 2, 92, and 94), and finally to discover one's true identity as a child of God (3:4).

Interpretation

The interpretation of the Gospel of Thomas is still in its infancy. This gospel, unlike those of the New Testament, has only been available for study for a few decades. Its interpretation is complicated by the fact that the only surviving complete text of Thomas is in Coptic, a language which few scholars have mastered. Finally, there is the troubling issue of esotericism in Thomas. Even a cursory reading of Thomas will reveal that many of its sayings are quite obscure, some perhaps intentionally so, often using paradox or obtuse metaphors to make their point. Some of the more difficult problems are addressed in the notes to the text, but the reader should be aware that such explanations are tentative at best. There is still much work to be done before this text is fully understood.

The Gospel of Thomas

Prologue These are the secret sayings that the living Jesus spoke and
Didymos Judas Thomas recorded.

1 And he said, "Whoever discovers the interpretation of these sayings will not taste death."

2 Jesus said, "Those who seek should not stop seeking until they
find. 2When they find, they will be disturbed. 3When they are disturbed, they will marvel, 4and will rule over all."

3 Jesus said, "If your leaders say to you, 'Look, the ⟨Father's⟩ imperial rule is in the sky,' then the birds of the sky will precede you. 2If they
say to you, 'It is in the sea,' then the fish will precede you. 3Rather, the
⟨Father's⟩ imperial rule is inside you and outside you. 4When you
know yourselves, then you will be known, and you will understand that
you are children of the living Father. 5But if you do not know yourselves, then you live in poverty, and you are the poverty."

4 Jesus said, "The person old in days won't hesitate to ask a little
child seven days old about the place of life, and that person will live.
2For many of the first will be last, 3and will become a single one."

Prologue
Cf. GHeb 5; Ⓣ Th 37:3; 59; 111:2

1
Cf. Jn 8:51; Ⓣ Th 18:3, 19:4, 85:2 111:2; Mk 9:1; Mt 16:28; Lk 9:27

2:1
Ⓓ Th 92:1, 94; //Mt 7:8; Lk 11:10; Mary 4:7, GHeb 6b

3
Ⓣ Th 113, 51

3:1–2
Cf. Mk 13:21–23; Mt 24:23 28; Lk 17:20–25; ◊ Jb 28:12–14, 20–22 (LXX); Bar 3:29 32, 35 37; Dt 30:11–14 (LXX); Sir 1:1–3

3:3a
//Lk 17:21b; cf. DSav 9:2–4; Mary 4:5

4:1
Cf. Q 10:21; Mt 11:25; Lk 10:21; Ⓣ Th 22:1–3, 46:2; Ⓣ DSav 14:1

4:2
//Mk 10:31; Mt 19:30, 20:16; Lk 13:30

4:3
Ⓣ Th 22:5, 23:2

2:3–4 GrThom has a different version of these verses: "[When they are] disturbed, they will rule, and [when they rule], they will [rest]."

Prologue *Didymos Judas Thomas:* This name appears in this form elsewhere only in the Syrian *Acts of Thomas* (ch. 1), although the name Judas Thomas occurs in some Syrian manuscripts of John 14:22 and in the prologue of *Thomas the Contender*, also of Syrian origin. Of the three names only Judas is a bona fide name; Didymos and Thomas are the Greek and Semitic words for *Twin*, respectively, although Thomas does function as a given name elsewhere. The title, which occurs at the end of the gospel, ascribes it to the apostle Thomas, who was thought by the early church to have evangelized eastern Syria and India. Whether Judas Didymos Thomas and the apostle Thomas were originally two different figures, melded together in the lore of Syrian Christianity, is a matter for further investigation.

3:1 *the ⟨Father's⟩ imperial rule:* The Coptic (*tmntero*) is conventionally rendered "kingdom," but as elsewhere in Scholars Version translations, here also this archaism has been abandoned. Normally, Scholars Version renders this term "imperial rule," as it is here. Often, however, the term is used with a spatial connotation, as, for example, when persons are said to 'enter' the Kingdom. In such cases Scholars Version translates the word using "Domain," capturing this spatial dimension. Often in the Gospel of Thomas the term is used without predication, that is, without specifiying 'of God,' 'of Heaven,' 'of the Father,' etc. To render these technical uses of *tmntero* more clearly for the modern reader, the translators have supplied ⟨Father's⟩, the most common predication for this term found in Thomas.

4:3 *and will become a single one:* This phrase

5 Jesus said, "Know what is in front of your face, and what is hidden from you will be disclosed to you. [2]For there is nothing hidden that won't be revealed."

6 His disciples asked him and said to him, "Do you want us to fast? How should we pray? Should we give to charity? What diet should we observe?"

[2]Jesus said, "Don't lie, [3]and don't do what you hate, [4]because all things are disclosed before heaven. [5]After all, there is nothing hidden that won't be revealed, [6]and there is nothing covered up that will remain undisclosed."

7 Jesus said, "Lucky is the lion that the human will eat, so that the lion becomes human. [2]And foul is the human that the lion will eat, and the lion still will become human."

8 And he said, "The human one is like a wise fisherman who cast his net into the sea and drew it up from the sea full of little fish. [2]Among them the wise fisherman discovered a fine large fish. [3]He threw all the little fish back into the sea, and easily chose the large fish. [4]Anyone here with two good ears had better listen!"

9 Jesus said,

> Look, the sower went out, took a handful (of seeds), and scattered (them). [2]Some fell on the road, and the birds came and gathered them. [3]Others fell on rock, and they didn't take root in the soil and didn't produce heads of grain. [4]Others fell on thorns, and they

5:2 //Mk4:22; Lk8:17, 12:2; Mt10:26; Ⓓ Th6:5–6
6:1 Ⓣ Th14:1–3
6:3 ↄTob 4:15
6:5–6 //Mk4:22; Lk8:17, 12:2; Mt10:26; Ⓓ Th5:2
8 //Mt13:47–50
9 //Mk4:2–9, Mt13:3–9, Lk8:4–8

5 GrThom adds a third verse: "and ⟨nothing⟩ buried that [will not be raised]."

is opaque, but occurs more than once in Thomas (22:5; 23:2). Here, as in 23:2, it designates a kind of soteriological status without further explanation. In 22:5, however, it is associated with the notion of androgyny. Some Gnostic groups held that the origin of human sin was the creation of woman as distinct from man, a departure from the sexually non-differentiated first human, Adam. Thus, the ultimate human destiny was to return to a primordial state of androgyny, the state of divine perfection before the fall.

7 The meaning of this saying is obscure. In antiquity the lion often symbolizes feelings of passion and pathos. To eat the lion may be to overcome such feelings. Likewise, to be consumed by the lion (7:2a) is to be overcome by them. 7:2b, however, may hold out hope. By one reading this clause indicates that though the passions may temporarily dominate a person, ultimately he/she will overcome them. But the phrase is very obscure.

7:1 *Lucky:* The Greek, *makarios*, is conventionally rendered "blessed." SV has replaced this archaism with a number of alternatives, which better reflect the versatility of this word. Here the lion's fate is viewed as good fortune, for in being consumed it has become part of the human.

8:1 *The human one:* Literally, *The person* (Coptic: *prome*) *is like* . . . The referent is unclear. There is a figure in some Gnostic systems known as *Anthropos*, or *Person*, who is a kind of primordial figure, the first person. It may be that Thomas' text intends to render this title in Coptic.

choked the seeds and worms ate them. 5And others fell on good soil, and it produced a good crop: it yielded sixty per measure and one hundred twenty per measure.

10 Jesus said, "I have cast fire upon the world, and look, I'm guarding it until it blazes."

11 Jesus said, "This heaven will pass away, and the one above it will pass away. 2The dead are not alive, and the living will not die. 3During the days when you ate what is dead, you made it come alive. When you are in the light, what will you do? 4On the day when you were one, you became two. But when you become two, what will you do?"

12 The disciples said to Jesus, "We know that you are going to leave us. Who will be our leader?"

2Jesus said to them, "No matter where you are, you are to go to James the Just, for whose sake heaven and earth came into being."

13 Jesus said to his disciples, "Compare me to something and tell me what I am like."

2Simon Peter said to him, "You are like a just angel."

3Matthew said to him, "You are like a wise philosopher."

4Thomas said to him, "Teacher, my mouth is utterly unable to say what you are like."

5Jesus said, "I am not your teacher. Because you have drunk, you have become intoxicated from the bubbling spring that I have tended."

6And he took him, and withdrew, and spoke three sayings to him.

7When Thomas came back to his friends, they asked him, "What did Jesus say to you?"

10
//Lk12:49; cf.Th16:1–2, Mt10:34
11:1
Cf.Mk13:31; Mt5:18, 24:34–35, Lk16:17, 21:33; Th111:1–2; ◊Ps102:25–27, Is34:4
11:4
Ⓣ Th22:4–7
13
Cf.Mk8:27–30, Mt16:13–20, Lk9:18–22
13:5
Ⓣ Th28:2; cf.Jn4:13–15, 7:38

9:5 It is often asserted that the yields of sixty and one hundred twenty per measure are extraordinarily large. But if the reports of contemporary historians (Pliny, Herodotus) are any indication, they are quite average.

10 *fire:* The image of fire is chosen here for its provocative and threatening effect. Fire was a constant menace in antiquity. Though apocalyptic visions often involve fiery conflagration, this need not be the sense in which it is used here.

11:1 *This heaven . . . and the one above it:* Ancient cosmology presupposed the existence of a number of heavenly spheres suspended above the earth's surface, enclosing it like thick layers of ethereal paint. Paul presupposes this notion in 2 Cor 12:2–4, where he refers to the esoteric rabbinic mystical tradition of ascending through these heavenly realms, eventually to come into the presence of God. These multiple heavenly spheres were considered as part of the created order. Hence, their transitory nature here is used to emphasize the transitory nature of the entire created order.

11:4 *when you were one, you became two:* The phrase, though obscure, may refer to the fall from primordial undifferentiated unity, an original perfection to which the Gnostic anticipates returning. For this concept, see the note on Thom 4:3.

12:2 *James the Just:* James the brother of Jesus (Mark 6:3; Matt 13:55; Gal 1:19) was known as James the Just in antiquity (Eusebius, *Ecclesiastical History II*, xxiii, 4–7).

13:5 *I am not your teacher. Because you have drunk, you have become intoxicated:* Or, "I am not your teacher, for you have drunk and have become intoxicated."

[8]Thomas said to them, "If I tell you one of the sayings he spoke to me, you will pick up rocks and stone me, and fire will come from the rocks and devour you."

14 Jesus said to them, "If you fast, you will bring sin upon yourselves, [2]and if you pray, you will be condemned, [3]and if you give to charity, you will harm your spirits. [4]When you go into any region and walk about in the countryside, when people take you in, eat what they serve you and heal the sick among them. [5]After all, what goes into your mouth won't defile you; what comes out of your mouth will."

15 Jesus said, "When you see one who was not born of woman, fall on your faces and worship. That one is your Father."

16 Jesus said, "Perhaps people think that I have come to cast peace upon the world. [2]They do not know that I have come to cast conflicts upon the earth: fire, sword, war. [3]For there will be five in a house: there'll be three against two and two against three, father against son and son against father, [4]and they will stand alone."

17 Jesus said, "I will give you what no eye has seen, what no ear has heard, what no hand has touched, what has not arisen in the human heart."

18 The disciples said to Jesus, "Tell us, how will our end come?"

[2]Jesus said, "Have you found the beginning, then, that you are looking for the end? You see, the end will be where the beginning is. [3]Congratulations to the one who stands at the beginning: that one will know the end and will not taste death."

19 Jesus said, "Congratulations to the one who came into being before coming into being. [2]If you become my disciples and pay attention to my sayings, these stones will serve you. [3]For there are five trees in Paradise for you; they do not change, summer or winter, and their leaves do not fall. [4]Whoever knows them will not taste death."

14:1–3
Ⓣ Th 6:1
14:4
//Q 10:8–9; Lk 10:8–9; Mt 10:5–8; cf. Mk 6:8–13; Mt 10:5–15; Lk 9:2–6, 10:1–12; Ⓣ 1 Cor 10:27
14:5
//Mk 7:15, Mt 15:11
15
Cf. DSav 23:2
16
//Q 12:51–53; Mt 10:34–39; Lk 12:51–53; cf. GNaz 11
16:2
Cf. Th 10, Lk 12:49
16:3
◊ Mi 7:5–6
16:4
Ⓣ Th 49:1; 75
17
//1 Cor 2:9; cf. Q 10:23–24; Mt 13:16–17; Lk 10:23–24; DSav 22:2–4; ◊ Is 64:4
18:3
Ⓣ Th 1, 19:4, 85:2, 111:2
19:4
Ⓣ Th 1, 18:3, 85:2, 111:2

14:4 *heal:* or, "care for."

countryside: The Greek word here translated as countryside is ambiguous. Literally it means "places," but the places in question could be either the rural areas in between small towns or the towns themselves.

16:4 *alone:* In other texts this Greek loan word (*monachos*) may indicate a unique, solitary, or lonely one, and unmarried one, or (later, as a technical term) a monk. It may have similar connotations here. Though this is far too early to think of Christian "monks" per se, discipleship of this order in Thomas probably involves the solitary life of the wandering ascetic.

18:2 *the end will be where the beginning is:* The phrase makes sense in terms of Gnostic notions of creation. Basic to most forms of Gnosticism is the notion that the world is evil, the result of a rebellious angel (demiurge) attempting to create something apart from God. The goal (*end*) of the Gnostic's existence is to escape the created world and return to the state of perfection that existed in the *beginning*, before the creation of the world.

20 The disciples said to Jesus, "Tell us what Heaven's imperial rule is like."

2He said to them,

It's like a mustard seed. 3 ⟨It's⟩ the smallest of all seeds, 4but when it falls on prepared soil, it produces a large branch and becomes a shelter for birds of the sky.

21 Mary said to Jesus, "What are your disciples like?"

2He said,

They are like little children living in a field that is not theirs. 3When the owners of the field come, they will say, "Give us back our field." 4They take off their clothes in front of them in order to give it back to them, and they return their field to them. 5For this reason I say, if the owners of a house know that a thief is coming, they will be on guard before the thief arrives, and will not let the thief break into their house (their domain) and steal their possessions. 6As for you, then, be on guard against the world. 7Prepare yourselves with great strength, so the robbers can't find a way to get to you, for the trouble you expect will come. 8Let there be among you a person who understands. 9When the crop ripened, he came quickly carrying a sickle and harvested it. 10Anyone here with two good ears had better listen!

22 Jesus saw some babies nursing. 2He said to his disciples, "These nursing babies are like those who enter the ⟨Father's⟩ domain."

3They said to him, "Then shall we enter the ⟨Father's⟩ domain as babies?"

4Jesus said to them, "When you make the two into one, and when you make the inner like the outer and the outer like the inner, and the upper like the lower, 5and when you make male and female into a single one, so that the male will not be male nor the female be female, 6when you make eyes in place of an eye, a hand in place of a hand, a foot in place of a foot, an image in place of an image, 7then you will enter [the ⟨Father's⟩ domain]."

20
//Mk 4:30–32, Mt 13:31–32, Lk 13:18–19

20:4
◊ Dn 4:20–21 (LXX), Ez 17:23 (LXX)

21:1–4
Ⓣ Mary 10:11

21:4
Cf. Th 37:2–3

21:5
//Q 12:35–40; Mt 24:42–44; Lk 12:35–40; Ⓣ Th 103

21:9
//Mk 4:29; ◊ Joel 3:13 (LXX)

22:2
Cf. Mk 10:14–15, Mt 18:3, Lk 18:16–17; Ⓣ Th 46

22:5b
Cf. Gal 3:27–28, Ⓣ Th 114

22:6
◊ Dt 19:21 (LXX)

21:4 *They take off their clothes:* The phrase is obscure. Clues from later literature suggest several alternatives for understanding the concept. 1) Removal of one's clothing may indicate one's sexual indifference, sexual desire having been overcome through asceticism. 2) The phrase could refer to a baptismal ritual, wherein the participants disrobe. Early Christian initiates were usually baptized in the nude. 3) It could refer symbolically to the Platonic and later Gnostic notion that upon death, the soul sheds the body (metaphorically referred to as one's "clothing") and proceeds upward to the heavenly realm from whence it came (see Thom 29, 87, and 112).

22:4–5 For the notion of primordial unity, especially androgyny, see the note on 4:3.

22:5 *and when you make:* or, "in order that you may make".

23 Jesus said, "I shall choose you, one from a thousand and two from ten thousand, [2]and they will stand as a single one."

24 His disciples said, "Show us the place where you are, for we must seek it."

[2]He said to them, "Anyone here with two ears had better listen! [3]There is light within a person of light, and it shines on the whole world. If it does not shine, it is dark."

25 Jesus said, "Love your friends like your own soul, [2]protect them like the pupil of your eye."

26 Jesus said, "You see the sliver in your friend's eye, but you don't see the timber in your own eye. [2]When you take the timber out of your own eye, then you will see well enough to remove the sliver from your friend's eye.

27 "If you do not fast from the world, you will not find the ⟨Father's⟩ domain. [2]If you do not observe the sabbath day as a sabbath day, you will not see the Father."

28 Jesus said, "I took my stand in the midst of the world, and in flesh I appeared to them. [2]I found them all drunk, and I did not find any of them thirsty. [3]My soul ached for the children of humanity, because they are blind in their hearts and do not see, for they came into the world empty, and they also seek to depart from the world empty. [4]But meanwhile they are drunk. When they shake off their wine, then they will change their ways."

29 Jesus said, "If the flesh came into being because of spirit, that is a marvel, [2]but if spirit came into being because of the body, that is a marvel of marvels. [3]Yet I marvel at how this great wealth has come to dwell in this poverty."

30 Jesus said, "Where there are three deities, they are divine. [2]Where there are two or one, I am with that one."

23:2 Ⓣ Th4:3, 22:5
24:1 Ⓣ Jn14:1–6, DSav30
24:3 //Q11:34–35, Mt6:22–23, Lk11:34–35; cf. Mt5:14–16; DSav6, 8; Ⓣ 2Cor4:6
25:1 //Mk12:31; Mt22:39, 19:19; Lk10:27; Ⓣ Rom 13:8, Jas 2:8; ◊ Lv19:18(LXX)
26 //Q6:41–42, Mt7:3–5, Lk6:41–42
27:1a Ⓣ Th110, 14:1
28:1a Ⓣ Jn1:14
28:1b ◊ Prv1:20–33, Bar3:37
29 Ⓣ Th87; 112; Gal5:16–18
30 //Mt18:20

30 The Coptic version of this saying is deficient, based perhaps on a scribal error. The Greek version is closer to the original: "Where there are [three, they are without] God, and where there is only [one,] I say, I am with that one." Also, in GrThom the saying continues with the words: "Lift up the stone, and you will find me there. Split a piece of wood, and I am there." The additional verses are found in the Coptic version at Thom 77:2–3.

23:2 On the term *single one* see the note on 4:3.
24:3 *it:* or, "he."
27:2 *observe the sabbath day as a sabbath day:* The Coptic phrase is difficult. It probably intends observing the sabbath with integrity. Criticism of contemporary sabbath observance is, of course, not unknown in the Jesus tradition (see Mark 2:27–28).

31 Jesus said, "No prophet is welcome on his home turf; [2]doctors don't cure those who know them."

32 Jesus said, "A city built on a high hill and fortified cannot fall, nor can it be hidden."

33 Jesus said, "What you will hear in your ear, in the other ear proclaim from your rooftops. [2]After all, no one lights a lamp and puts it under a basket, nor does one put it in a hidden place. [3]Rather, one puts it on a lampstand so that all who come and go will see its light."

34 Jesus said, "If a blind person leads a blind person, both of them will fall into a hole."

35 Jesus said, "One can't enter a strong man's house and take it by force without tying his hands. [2]Then one can loot his house."

36 Jesus said, "Don't fret, from morning to evening and from evening to morning, about what you're going to wear."

37 His disciples said, "When will you appear to us, and when will we see you?"

[2]Jesus said, "When you strip without being ashamed, and you take your clothes and put them under your feet like little children and trample them, [3]then [you] will see the son of the living one and you will not be afraid."

38 Jesus said, "Often you have desired to hear these sayings that I am speaking to you, and you have no one else from whom to hear them. [2]There will be days when you will seek me and you will not find me."

39 Jesus said, "The Pharisees and the scholars have taken the keys of knowledge and have hidden them. [2]They have not entered, nor have they allowed those who want to enter to do so. [3]As for you, be as sly as snakes and as simple as doves."

33:1 *in the other ear:* This difficult phrase may well represent an instance of dittography—that is, a scribe's inadvertent duplication of words already transcribed. Otherwise, it may indicate the ear of another, or perhaps one's own *inner* ear. **36** GrThom has a longer version. After "morning" add: "[about] your [food], what [you're going to] eat, or about [your clothing], . . ." At the end add: [2]"[You're much] better than the lilies, which don't card and never [spin]. [3]As for you, when you have no garment, what [are you going to put] on? [4]Who could add to your life span? That same one will give you your garment."

31
//Mk6:4–6a, Mt13:57–58, Lk4:23–24, Jn4:44

32
//Mt5:14; ◊Is2:2–3, Mi4:1–2

33:1
//Q12:3, Mt10:27, Lk12:3

33:2–3
//Mk4:21; Lk8:16, 11:33; Mt5:15

34
//Q6:39, Mt15:14, Lk6:39

35
//Mk3:27; Mt12:29, Lk11:21–22

36
//Q12:22, Mt6:25, Lk12:22

36:2–4
(POxy655) Ⓣ DSav19:8–12, 34:1–5

37:2
Ⓣ Th21:2–4, DSav34; ◊Gn2:25 (3:1LXX)

38:2
//Jn7:33–36

39:1–2
//Q11:52, Mt23:13, Lk11:52; Ⓣ Th102

39:3
//Mt10:16

37:2 For the concept of removing one's clothes in Thomas see the comment on 21:4.

40 Jesus said, "A grapevine has been planted apart from the Father. [2]Since it is not strong, it will be pulled up by its root and will perish."

41 Jesus said, "Those who have something in hand will be given more, [2]and those who have nothing will be deprived of even the little they have."

42 Jesus said, "Be passersby."

43 His disciples said to him, "Who are you to say these things to us?"

[2]"You don't understand who I am from what I say to you. [3]Rather, you have become like the Judeans, for they love the tree but hate its fruit, or they love the fruit but hate the tree."

44 Jesus said, "Whoever blasphemes against the Father will be forgiven, [2]and whoever blasphemes against the son will be forgiven, [3]but whoever blasphemes against the holy spirit will not be forgiven, either on earth or in heaven."

45 Jesus said, "Grapes are not harvested from thorn trees, nor are figs gathered from thistles, for they yield no fruit. [2]Good persons produce good from what they've stored up; [3]bad persons produce evil from the wickedness they've stored up in their hearts, and say evil things. [4]For from the overflow of the heart they produce evil."

46 Jesus said, "From Adam to John the Baptist, among those born of women, no one is so much greater than John the Baptist that his eyes should not be averted. [2]But I have said that whoever among you becomes a child will recognize the ⟨Father's⟩ imperial rule and will become greater than John."

47 Jesus said, "A person cannot mount two horses or bend two bows. [2]And a slave cannot serve two masters, otherwise that slave will honor the one and offend the other.

[3]"Nobody drinks aged wine and immediately wants to drink young wine. [4]Young wine is not poured into old wineskins, or they might

40 Cf. Mt 15:13, Jn 15:5–6
41 //Mk 4:24–25; Mt 13:10–13, 25:29; Lk 8:18, 19:26
43:3 Cf. Mt 12:33
44 //Mk 3:28–30, Mt 12:31–32, Lk 12:10
45 //Mt 7:15–20, 12:33–35; Lk 6:43–45; Ⓣ Jas 3:12
46 //Q 7:28, Mt 11:11, Lk 7:28
46:2 //Mk 10:15, Mt 18:3, Lk 18:17; Ⓣ Th 22:2
47:2 //Q 16:13, Mt 6:24, Lk 16:13
47:3–5 //Mk 2:21–22, Mt 9:16–17, Lk 5:36–39

---

42 The saying may be taken literally, as a call to take up the itinerant life of the disciple. Some, however, have seen in it a call to the Gnostic to pass through this world without becoming mired in it.

43:2 The sentence may be read as a question as well: "Don't you understand who I am . . .?"

43:3 The critical treatment of "the Judeans" here is typical of early Christian writing, which reflects the point of view of a small, sectarian group securing its identity over against the majority culture. Since there is no reason to think that Thomas Christians were themselves not Jewish (see Thom 27), one should refrain from interpreting the saying in an anti-Semitic vein.

46:1 *averted:* literally, "broken." The Coptic idiom is obscure.

break, and aged wine is not poured into a new wineskin, or it might spoil. [5]An old patch is not sewn onto a new garment, since it would create a tear."

48 Jesus said, "If two make peace with each other in a single house, they will say to the mountain, 'Move from here!' and it will move."

49 Jesus said, "Congratulations to those who are alone and chosen, for you will find the ⟨Father's⟩ domain. For you have come from it, and you will return there again."

50 Jesus said, "If they say to you, 'Where have you come from?' say to them, 'We have come from the light, from the place where the light came into being by itself, established [itself], and appeared in their image.' [2]If they say to you, 'Is it you?' say, 'We are its children, and we are the chosen of the living Father.' [3]If they ask you, 'What is the evidence of your Father in you?' say to them, 'It is motion and rest.'"

51 His disciples said to him, "When will the rest for the dead take place, and when will the new world come?"

[2]He said to them, "What you are looking forward to has come, but you don't know it."

52 His disciples said to him, "Twenty-four prophets have spoken in Israel, and they all spoke of you."

[2]He said to them, "You have disregarded the living one who is in your presence, and have spoken of the dead."

53 His disciples said to him, "Is circumcision useful or not?"

[2]He said to them, "If it were useful, their father would produce children already circumcised from their mother. [3]Rather, the true circumcision in spirit has become profitable in every respect."

48a Cf. Mt 18:19
48b Ⓓ Th 106; cf. Mk 11:22–23; Mt 21:21, 17:20b; Lk 17:5–6; Ⓣ 1 Cor 13:2
49 Ⓣ Th 16:4, 75; DSav 1–2
50:1 Ⓣ Th 83, 84
50:3 Ⓣ GrTh 2; Th 51:1; 60:6; 90; Mt 11:28–29; DSav 25; ◊Sir 51:26–27, 6:23–31
51:1 Ⓣ GrTh 2; Th 50:3; 60:6; 90; Mt 11:28–29; DSav 25; ◊Sir 51:26–27, 6:23–31
51:2 Ⓣ Th 3, 113; Lk 17:20–21; Mk 9:12–13; Mt 17:11; 2 Tm 2:17–18
52 Ⓣ EgerG 1:2–6, 3:2; Jn 5:39–40
53 Ⓣ Rom 2:29, Phil 3:3, 1 Cor 7:19, Gal 6:15, Col 2:11–12

---

49 *alone:* For the significance of this term in Thomas see the note on Thom 16:4.

49–50 Together these sayings form a kind of primitive Gnostic catechism. Jesus here instructs the disciples in the technique of ascending to a heavenly domain. The interlocutors of whom Jesus warns the disciples are no doubt guardians of the way heavenward; the precisely communicated responses of the disciples are intended to placate those who guard the way.

50:3 *motion and rest:* The phrase is obscure. It has the ring of code language, and thus may be intentionally opaque. On *rest* see the note on GrThom 2:4. *Motion* may refer to the movement of the Thomas Christian up through the heavenly spheres to the heavenly domain.

51:1 *rest:* On this term see the note on GrThom 2:4.

52:1 *twenty-four:* The number twenty-four is most intriguing. It is the number of books in the Hebrew scriptures (see 2 Esdr 14:45). See also Rev 4:4, as well as ancient magical texts, where twenty-four elders appear.

of you: literally, "in you."

53:2 *children:* The Coptic text reads simply "them;" the translator has supplied the noun object (*children*) for clarity's sake.

54 Jesus said, "Congratulations to the poor, for to you belongs Heaven's domain."

55 Jesus said, "Whoever does not hate father and mother cannot be my disciple, [2]and whoever does not hate brothers and sisters, and carry the cross as I do, will not be worthy of me."

56 Jesus said, "Whoever has come to know the world has discovered a carcass, [2]and whoever has discovered a carcass, of that person the world is not worthy."

57 Jesus said,

> The Father's imperial rule is like a person who had [good] seed. [2]His enemy came during the night and sowed weeds among the good seed. [3]The person did not let the workers pull up the weeds, but said to them, "No, otherwise you might go to pull up the weeds and pull up the wheat along with them." [4]For on the day of the harvest the weeds will be conspicuous, and will be pulled up and burned.

58 Jesus said, "Congratulations to the person who has toiled and has found life."

59 Jesus said, "Look to the living one as long as you live, otherwise you might die and then try to see the living one, and you will be unable to see."

60 ⟨He saw⟩ a Samaritan carrying a lamb and going to Judea. [2]He said to his disciples, "⟨. . .⟩ that person ⟨. . .⟩ around the lamb."

[3]They said to him, "So that he may kill it and eat it." [4]He said to them, "He will not eat it while it is alive, but only after he has killed it and it has become a carcass."

[5]They said, "Otherwise he can't do it."

[6]He said to them, "So also with you, seek for yourselves a place for rest, or you might become a carcass and be eaten."

61 Jesus said, "Two will recline on a couch; one will die, one will live."

54
//Q6:20b, Mt5:3, Lk6:20b
55
//Q14:26–27, Mt10:37–38, Lk14:26–27; Ⓓ Th101
56
Ⓓ Th80
57
//Mt13:24–30
58
Cf. Q6:22–23, Mt5:10–13, Lk6:22–23, Mt11:28–30; Ⓣ Jas1:12; 1Pet3:14a, 4:13–14; ◊Sir 51:26–27
59
Cf. Th38:2, Jn7:33–36
60
Ⓣ Th7, 11:3
60:6
Ⓣ GrTh2; Th50:3; 51:1; 90; Mt11:28–29; DSav25; ◊Sir51:26–27, 6:23–31
61:1
//Q17:34–35, Mt24:40–41, Lk17:34–35

60:1 *He saw:* Or, "They saw." Neither phrase occurs in the manuscript; the translator has emended the text on the assumption that the scribe erred in omitting it. **60:2** Scribal error has created a defective text here. Perhaps it once read: "⟨Why does⟩ that person ⟨carry⟩ around the lamb?" It may also be read literally: "That person is around the lamb," but it is unclear what such a statement would mean.

57:3 *workers:* The Coptic text simply reads "them"; the translator has supplied the noun object (*workers*) for clarity's sake.

58 *toiled:* or, "suffered."

59 *living one:* Perhaps Jesus (see the Prologue).

60:6 *rest:* On this term see the note on GrThom 2:4.

[2]Salome said, "Who are you, mister? You have climbed onto my
couch and eaten from my table as if you are from someone."
[3]Jesus said to her, "I am the one who comes from what is whole. I
was granted from the things of my Father."
[4]"I am your disciple."
[5]"For this reason I say, if one is ⟨whole⟩, one will be filled with
light, but if one is divided, one will be filled with darkness."

62 Jesus said, "I disclose my mysteries to those [who are worthy] of
[my] mysteries. [2]Do not let your left hand know what your right hand is
doing."

63 Jesus said,

> There was a rich man who had a great deal of money. [2]He said, "I
> shall invest my money so that I may sow, reap, plant, and fill my
> storehouses with produce, that I may lack nothing." [3]These were the
> things he was thinking in his heart, but that very night he died.
> [4]Anyone here with two ears had better listen!

64 Jesus said,

> Someone was receiving guests. When he had prepared the dinner,
> he sent his slave to invite the guests. [2]The slave went to the first and
> said, "My master invites you." The first replied, [3]"Some merchants
> owe me money; they are coming to me tonight. I have to go and give
> them instructions. Please excuse me from dinner." [4]The slave went
> to another and said, "My master has invited you." [5]The second said
> to the slave, "I have bought a house, and I have been called away for
> a day. I shall have no time." [6]The slave went to another and said,
> "My master invites you." [7]The third said to the slave, "My friend is
> to be married, and I am to arrange the banquet. I shall not be able to
> come. Please excuse me from dinner." [8]The slave went to another
> and said, "My master invites you." [9]The fourth said to the slave, "I
> have bought an estate, and I am going to collect the rent. I shall not
> be able to come. Please excuse me." [10]The slave returned and said to
> his master, "Those whom you invited to dinner have asked to be
> excused." [11]The master said to his slave, "Go out on the streets and
> bring back whomever you find to have dinner."
>
> [12]Buyers and merchants [will] not enter the places of my Father.

61:3b //Q10:22, Mt11:27, Lk10:22; cf. Jn3:35, 13:3–4
62:1 Ⓣ Mk4:10–11, Mt13:10–11, Lk8:9–10
62:2 //Mt6:3
63 //Lk12:16–21; ◊Sir11:18–19
64 //Q14:16–24, Mt22:1–10, Lk14:16–24; ◊Dt20:5–7
64:7 ◊Dt24:5
64:12 ◊Sir26:29–27:2, Zec14:13

61:5 *if one is whole:* The translator has emended the text here. Without the emendation the text reads: "if one is desolate."

61:2 *Salome:* In the NT Salome appears only in Mark (15:40; 16:1). Elsewhere in early Christian literature she is to be found in the Infancy Gospel of James, the Secret Gospel of Mark, the Gospel of the Egyptians, as well as several Gnostic works (Pistis Sophia, First Apocalypse of James, Manichaean Psalm-Book).

as if you are from someone: The meaning of the Coptic is unclear. It could mean "as if you are someone special," or perhaps "as if you are a stranger."

65 He said,

> A [. . .] person owned a vineyard and rented it to some farmers, so they could work it and he could collect its crop from them. [2]He sent his slave so the farmers would give him the vineyard's crop. [3]They grabbed him, beat him, and almost killed him, and the slave returned and told his master. [4]His master said, "Perhaps he didn't know them." [5]He sent another slave, and the farmers beat that one as well. [6]Then the master sent his son and said, "Perhaps they'll show my son some respect." [7]Because the farmers knew that he was the heir to the vineyard, they grabbed him and killed him. [8]Anyone here with two ears had better listen!

66 Jesus said, "Show me the stone that the builders rejected: that is the keystone."

67 Jesus said, "Those who know all, but are lacking in themselves, are utterly lacking."

68 Jesus said, "Congratulations to you when you are hated and persecuted; [2]and no place will be found, wherever you have been persecuted."

69 Jesus said, "Congratulations to those who have been persecuted in their hearts: they are the ones who have truly come to know the Father. [2]Congratulations to those who go hungry, so the stomach of the one in want may be filled."

70 Jesus said, "If you bring forth what is within you, what you have will save you. [2]If you do not have that within you, what you do not have within you [will] kill you."

71 Jesus said, "I will destroy [this] house, and no one will be able to build it [. . .]."

65
//Mk12:1–9, Mt21:33–41, Lk20:9–16

66
//Mk12:10–11, Mt21:42–43, Lk20:17–18; Ⓣ Acts4:11–12, 1 Pet2:4–8; ▷Ps118:22

67
Cf. Mk8:36–37, Mt16:26, Lk9:25

68
//Q6:22–23, Mt5:11–12, Lk6:22–23; Ⓣ Jas1:12

69:1
//Q6:22–23, Mt5:11–12, Lk6:22–23; Ⓣ Jas 1:12

69:2
//Q6:21a, Mt5:6, Lk6:21a

71
//Mk14:58, 15:29; Mt26:61, 27:40; Jn2:19; cf. Mk13:2, Acts6:14

65:1 A lacuna in the papyrus makes the Coptic here uncertain; the hole might be filled in to read either "good person" or "usurer." **65:4** *Perhaps he didn't know them:* Some scholars have suggested that the text be emended here to read: "Perhaps they didn't know him."

68:2 The second half of this saying is obscure. *Place* may refer to that seat of knowledge in the heart of the Gnostic. Thus, no such place is found where the Thomas Christians have been persecuted. Alternatively, the text could be corrupt (a displaced negative) such that the original text would have read: "a place will be found in which you will not be persecuted."

69:1 *in their hearts:* The phrase probably refers to the inner struggle for insight in which the Thomas Christian is invited to engage (see Thom 2).

69:2 *so that the stomach of the one in want may be filled:* or, "for the stomach of the one who desires will be filled."

71 *house:* It is noteworthy that Thomas' "temple" saying makes no direct reference to

72 A [person said] to him, "Tell my brothers to divide my father's possessions with me."

[2]He said to the person, "Mister, who made me a divider?"

[3]He turned to his disciples and said to them, "I'm not a divider, am I?"

73 Jesus said, "The crop is huge but the workers are few, so beg the harvest boss to dispatch workers to the fields."

74 He said, "Lord, there are many around the drinking trough, but there is nothing in the well."

75 Jesus said, "There are many standing at the door, but those who are alone will enter the bridal suite."

76 Jesus said,

> The Father's imperial rule is like a merchant who had a supply of merchandise and then found a pearl. [2]That merchant was prudent; he sold the merchandise and bought the single pearl for himself.

[3]"So also with you, seek his treasure that is unfailing, that is enduring, where no moth comes to eat and no worm destroys."

77 Jesus said, "I am the light that is over all things. I am all: from me all came forth, and to me all attained. [2]Split a piece of wood; I am there. [3]Lift up the stone, and you will find me there."

78 Jesus said, "Why have you come out to the countryside? To see a reed shaken by the wind? [2]And to see a person dressed in soft clothes, [like your] rulers and your powerful ones? [3]They are dressed in soft clothes, and they cannot understand truth."

72 //Lk 12:13–14
73 //Mt 9:37–38, Lk 10:2
75 Ⓣ Th 16:4, 49:1; DSav 19:7
76:1–2 //Mt 13:44–46
76:3 //Q 12:33–34, Mt 6:19–21, Lk 12:33–34
77:1a Cf. Jn 8:12; ◊ Wis 7:24–30
77:1b Ⓣ Rom 11:36, 1 Cor 8:6
78 //Q 7:24–26, Mt 11:7–9, Lk 7:24–26

---

74 *drinking trough:* Some scholars think that the Coptic here has been misspelled, and should read "well." The present translation assumes that the word is spelled correctly. *Well:* The Coptic here makes no sense; most scholars assume that the word has been misspelled by a scribe and emend the text to read "well." **77:2–3** In GrThom this saying is preceded by the words: [Jesus says], "Where there are [three, they are without] God, and where there is only [one], I say, I am with that one," which in the Coptic version are found in Thom 30:1–2.

---

the temple. Of course, *house* could here refer obliquely to the temple. It could also invite a number of other referents: the ruling (Herodian) house; a family household; or metaphorically, the body as the house of the soul.

74 *He:* Curiously, the saying is not explicitly attributed to Jesus. It may be that Saying 74 forms a dialogue together with Saying 73 and/or 75.

75 *alone:* For the significance of this term in Thomas see the note on Thom 16:4.

78:3 *They:* The Coptic here is ambiguous. This could also be the relative pronoun "who," the antecedent for which would be "rulers and your powerful ones."

79 A woman in the crowd said to him, "Lucky are the womb that bore you and the breasts that fed you."

[2]He said to [her], "Lucky are those who have heard the word of the Father and have truly kept it. [3]For there will be days when you will say, 'Lucky are the womb that has not conceived and the breasts that have not given milk.'"

80 Jesus said, "Whoever has come to know the world has discovered the body, [2]and whoever has discovered the body, of that one the world is not worthy."

81 Jesus said, "The one who has become wealthy should reign, [2]and the one who has power should renounce ⟨it⟩."

82 Jesus said, "Whoever is near me is near the fire, [2]and whoever is far from me is far from the ⟨Father's⟩ domain."

83 Jesus said, "Images are visible to people, but the light within them is hidden in the image of the Father's light. [2]He will be disclosed, but his image is hidden by his light."

84 Jesus said, "When you see your likeness, you are happy. [2]But when you see your images that came into being before you and that neither die nor become visible, how much you will have to bear!"

85 Jesus said, "Adam came from great power and great wealth, but he was not worthy of you. [2]For had he been worthy, [he would] not [have tasted] death."

79:1–2
//Lk 11:27–28; cf. Jn 13:17
79:3
//Lk 23:28–29
80
Ⓓ Th 56
81
//Th 110; Ⓣ Mk 10:23, Mt 19:23, Lk 18:24, 1 Cor 4:8
81:2
Cf. DSav 11

---

82 This saying, known also from Origen, among others, may be based loosely upon a proverb of Aesop: "Whoever is near to Zeus is near the thunderbolt." The gist of the saying is the risk that comes with enjoying the god's favor. Likewise, in our saying the risks of discipleship are explored.

83 *Image* is probably used here in its Platonic sense, referring to material things (as opposed to ideas). Thus, the saying speaks on the one hand of the light dwelling undetected within each person (83:1), and on the other of the inaccessibility of the Father's substance, hidden behind his overwhelming light. Though the light of the Father may become manifest, his substance may not.

83:2 *He:* or, "It."

84 Like Thom 83, the saying features the term *image.* But here, it is set in contrast to *likeness*, which seems to refer to the material nature, the substance of a person. *Image* here then has a different meaning than in 83. It seems to derive from the Gnostic notion that each person has a heavenly twin, or image, which never perishes, but awaits the moment of death, when the Gnostic's soul is reunited with it. The saying speaks of the astonishment one experiences when one discovers this concealed world.

86:2 *human beings:* The Coptic here reads literally "son of man." But most scholars seem to agree that it is not intended here as a title for Jesus, but rather the Semitic idiom meaning simply "human being." Occasionally, however, the phrase may be used self-referentially as a circumlocution for "I."

86 Jesus said, "[Foxes have] their dens and birds have their nests, [2]but human beings have no place to lie down and rest."

87 Jesus said, "How miserable is the body that depends on a body, [2]and how miserable is the soul that depends on these two."

88 Jesus said, "The messengers and the prophets will come to you and give you what belongs to you. [2]You, in turn, give them what you have, and say to yourselves, 'When will they come and take what belongs to them?'"

89 Jesus said, "Why do you wash the outside of the cup? [2]Don't you understand that the one who made the inside is also the one who made the outside?"

90 Jesus said, "Come to me, for my yoke is comfortable and my lordship is gentle, [2]and you will find rest for yourselves."

91 They said to him, "Tell us who you are so that we may believe in you."

[2]He said to them, "You examine the face of heaven and earth, but you have not come to know the one who is in your presence, and you do not know how to examine the present moment."

92 Jesus said, "Seek and you will find. [2]In the past, however, I did not tell you the things about which you asked me then. Now I am willing to tell them, but you are not seeking them.

93 "Don't give what is sacred to dogs, for they might throw them upon the manure pile. [2]Don't throw pearls [to] pigs, or they might . . . it [. . .]."

94 Jesus [said], "One who seeks will find, [2]and for [one who knocks] it will be opened."

86
//Q9:58, Mt8:20, Lk9:58

87
Ⓓ Th112, Ⓣ Th29, Gal5:16–18

89
//Q11:39–40, Mt23:25–26, Lk11:39–40; Ⓣ GOxy840 2:8

90
//Mt11:28–30; Ⓣ GrTh2; ◊Sir51:26–27, 6:23–31

91:2
//Mt16:1–3, Lk12:54–56

92:1
Ⓓ Th2:1; 94; //Q11:9–10; Mt7:7–8; Lk11:9–10; DSav7:2, 11:5; Mary4:7; cf. GHeb6b

92:2
Ⓣ Th38, Jn16:4–5

93
//Mt7:6

94
Ⓓ Th2:1, 92:1; //Q11:9–10; Mt7:7–8; Lk11:9–10; DSav7:2, 11:5; Mary4:7; Cf. GHeb6b

---

93:2 The text is deficient here. Among proposals for its restoration are the following: "bring it [to naught]" and "grind it [to bits]."

---

87 The obtuse saying seems to comment on two levels of depravity, one in which one becomes mired in corporeal existence, and yet another in which even the soul fails to realize its freedom over against the body.

88:1 *messengers:* The Coptic here could also mean "angels" in the sense of heavenly *messengers* (see Mark 8:38). But as in Greek, it may simply mean *messengers* in the ordinary sense as well (see Luke 9:51–52). Here it has been rendered in the latter sense because it is paired with *prophets*, an early Christian title for its itinerant preachers (see Didache 11:3–6).

90 *rest:* On this term see the note on GrThom 2:4.

95 [Jesus said], "If you have money, don't lend it at interest. [2]Rather, give [it] to someone from whom you won't get it back."

96 Jesus [said],

The Father's imperial rule is like [a] woman [2]who took a little leaven, [hid] it in dough, and made it into large loaves of bread. [3]Anyone here with two ears had better listen!

97 Jesus said,

The [Father's] imperial rule is like a woman who was carrying a [jar] full of meal. [2]While she was walking along [a] distant road, the handle of the jar broke and the meal spilled behind her [along] the road. [3]She didn't know it; she hadn't noticed a problem. [4]When she reached her house, she put the jar down and discovered that it was empty.

98 Jesus said,

The Father's imperial rule is like a person who wanted to kill someone powerful. [2]While still at home he drew his sword and thrust it into the wall to find out whether his hand would go in. [3]Then he killed the powerful one.

99 The disciples said to him, "Your brothers and your mother are standing outside."

[2]He said to them, "Those here who do what my Father wants are my brothers and my mother. [3]They are the ones who will enter my Father's domain."

100 They showed Jesus a gold coin and said to him, "The Roman emperor's people demand taxes from us."

[2]He said to them, "Give the emperor what belongs to the emperor, [3]give God what belongs to God, [4]and give me what is mine.

101 "Whoever does not hate [father] and mother as I do cannot be my [disciple], [2]and whoever does [not] love [father and] mother as I do cannot be my [disciple]. [3]For my mother [. . .], but my true [mother] gave me life."

95 //Q6:30, 34–35; Mt5:42; Lk6:30, 34–35
96:1–2 //Q13:20–21, Mt13:33, Lk13:20–21
96:2 Ⓣ Th8:2, 20:4
99 //Mk3:31–35, Mt12:46–50, Lk8:19–21, GEbi5
99:2 //GHeb4a
100 //Mk12:13–17, Mt22:15–22, Lk20:20–26, EgerG3:1–6
101 //Q14:26–27, Mt10:37–38, Lk14:26–27; Ⓓ Th55

97:2 *While she was walking along [a] distant road:* The text is deficient here; an alternative rendering is: "While she was walking on [the] road, still far off."
101:3 The lacuna cannot be filled in with certainty. One proposal: "For my mother [gave me falsehood]."

97:3 *she hadn't noticed a problem:* or, "she had not understood how to toil."
98:2 The parable probably envisions a modest peasant home of mud brick, whose walls would serve well as a surface on which to practice one's thrust.

102 Jesus said, "Damn the Pharisees! They are like a dog sleeping in the cattle manger: the dog neither eats nor [lets] the cattle eat."

103 Jesus said, "Congratulations to those who know where the rebels are going to attack. [They] can get going, collect their imperial resources, and be prepared before the rebels arrive."

104 They said to Jesus, "Come, let us pray today, and let us fast."
[2]Jesus said, "What sin have I committed, or how have I been undone? [3]Rather, when the groom leaves the bridal suite, then let people fast and pray."

105 Jesus said, "Whoever knows the father and the mother will be called the child of a whore."

106 Jesus said, "When you make the two into one, you will become children of Adam, [2]and when you say, 'Mountain, move from here!' it will move."

107 Jesus said,

> The ⟨Father's⟩ imperial rule is like a shepherd who had a hundred sheep. [2]One of them, the largest, went astray. He left the ninety-nine and looked for the one until he found it. [3]After he had toiled, he said to the sheep, "I love you more than the ninety-nine."

108 Jesus said, "Whoever drinks from my mouth will become like me; [2]I myself shall become that person, [3]and the hidden things will be revealed to him."

102
Cf. Th 39:1–2, Q11:52, Mt 23:13, Lk 11:52

103
(T) Th 21:5–7, Q12:39–40, Mt 24:42–44, Lk 12:39–40

104:3
//Mk 2:19–20, Mt 9:15, Lk 5:34–35; (T) Th 6:1; 14:1; 27

106
(D) Th 48

106:1a
(T) Th 22:4

106:2
//Mk 11:22–23; Mt 17:19–20, 21:21; cf. Lk 17:5–6; (T) 1 Cor 13:2

107
//Q15:4–7, Mt 18:12–14, Lk 15:4–7

108:1
(T) Th 13:5; Jn 4:13–14, 7:37–39; ◊Sir 24:21

---

103 *collect their imperial resources:* The phrase is obscure. If an invasion is in view, the injunction may be for a ruler to muster his forces.

105 *child of a whore:* The saying is obscure. Of possible relevance may be the charge, common in early Jewish-Christian debate, that Jesus was the illegitimate child of Mary and a certain Roman soldier.

106:1 *children of Adam:* The Coptic reads literally "sons of men." If making the two one has to do with returning to some primordial state of non-differentiated perfection (for example androgyny, a frequent notion among Gnostic groups), the expression may have originally read "sons of the Anthropos." Some early Christians believed that Adam was androgynous before the fall; a return to the perfection of the created order would then involve a return to androgyny, hence "sons of Adam." As it is, the expression is difficult.

107:3 *toiled:* or, "suffered." See the similar note to Thom 58.

108:1 Comparing revelation to water, from which the recipient drinks to satisfaction is common in wisdom and Gnostic texts. The reference here to Jesus' mouth as the source of this satisfying drink is no doubt related to Thomas' presentation of Jesus as one who *speaks* words of revelation. In principle, the concept is the same as that presupposed in John 4:13–14.

109 Jesus said,

The ⟨Father's⟩ imperial rule is like a person who had a treasure hidden in his field but did not know it. [2]And [when] he died he left it to his [son]. The son [did] not know ⟨about it either⟩. He took over the field and sold it. [3]The buyer went plowing, [discovered] the treasure, and began to lend money at interest to whomever he wished.

109
//Mt 13:44

110 Jesus said, "The one who has found the world, and has become wealthy, should renounce the world."

110
//Th 81;
Ⓣ Mk 10:23, Mt 19:23, Lk 18:24, DSav 11:4

111 Jesus said, "The heavens and the earth will roll up in your presence, [2]and whoever is living from the living one will not see death." [3]Does not Jesus say, "Those who have found themselves, of them the world is not worthy"?

111
Ⓣ Th 11:1–2
111:1
Ⓣ Mk 13:30–31; Mt 5:18, 24:34–35; Lk 16:17, 21:32–33; ◊ Is 34:4; Ps 102:25–27
111:3
Ⓣ Th 56, 80

112 Jesus said, "Damn the flesh that depends on the soul. [2]Damn the soul that depends on the flesh."

112
Ⓓ Th 87;
Ⓣ Th 29, Jn 3:6, Gal 5:16–18

113 His disciples said to him, "When will the ⟨Father's⟩ imperial rule come?"

[2]"It will not come by watching for it. [3]It will not be said, 'Look, here!' or 'Look, there!' [4]Rather, the Father's imperial rule is spread out upon the earth, and people don't see it."

113
//Lk 17:20–21; cf. Th 3:1–3; Mary 4:4–5;
Ⓣ Th 51, Mk 13:21, Mt 24:23, Lk 17:23

114 Simon Peter said to them, "Make Mary leave us, for females don't deserve life."

[2]Jesus said, "Look, I will guide her to make her male, so that she too may become a living spirit resembling you males. [3]For every female who makes herself male will enter the domain of Heaven."

114:2–3
Ⓣ Th 22:5; Mary 5:8

109:1 Wisdom is sometimes likened to *hidden treasure* (Prov 2:1–5; Sir 20:30–31).
113:3 *It will not be said:* or, "They will not say."
114:1 The Petrine tradition is not notably kind to women. In the NT the Petrine epistles place women in a subordinate role (1 Pet 3:1–6). In the extra-canonical tradition Peter is portrayed as critical of Mary in particular (e.g., in the Gospel of Mary and the Pistis Sophia). While some Gnostic groups were egalitarian with respect to gender, many were somewhat misogynist, identifying the origin of evil and sin in the world with the feminine.
114:2–3 The theological rationale for Jesus' reply is similar, but not identical to the notion elsewhere in Thomas that salvation consists in returning to the state of primordial, androgynous perfection (Thom 4:3; 22:5). Here, of course, the ideal is not to become androgynous, but to "become male." In other texts dealing with ideas from Gnosticism or speculative wisdom the transition from male to female is used as a metaphor for translation from earthly to heavenly existence, from mortality to immortality. There may also be a practical side to the saying, as women philosophers often disguised themselves as men.

The Greek Fragments of Thomas

Introduction

In addition to the copy of the Gospel of Thomas found in the Coptic Nag Hammadi library, there are several small fragments of this gospel in Greek. These fragments comprise all or parts of the Prologue, sayings 1–7, 24, 26–33, 36–39, and 77:2–3. They should be studied alongside the more complete Coptic version, though they merit attention in their own right.

Discovery and Rediscovery

The Greek fragments of Thomas were actually discovered half a century earlier than their better-known Coptic cousins. They first came to light shortly before the turn of the century, when the English archaeological team of Bernard P. Grenfell and Arthur S. Hunt came across the first of the known fragments while sifting through the debris of an ancient trash heap at the site of Oxyrhynchus, a Roman-era city in upper Egypt. They published this remarkable find in 1897 under the descriptive title *Logia Iēsou, Sayings of Our Lord.* Eventually two similar texts would show up at the same site. They were published by Grenfell and Hunt as *New Sayings of Jesus and Fragments of a Lost Gospel from Oxyrhynchus* in 1904. As these titles indicate, Grenfell and Hunt did not yet know that they had discovered remnants of the Gospel of Thomas, thought to have been lost forever. They knew only that they had discovered an as yet unknown gospel, a gospel quite unlike those found in the New Testament. For these new texts contained only sayings of Jesus; no narratives, no deeds of the Lord. They were catalogued along with the hundreds of other papyri recovered from Oxyrhynchus and were known for the next fifty years simply as POxy 1, 654, and 655.

With the discovery of a complete text of the Gospel of Thomas in 1945 a new chapter in the fate of these fragments was opened. While studying this newly discovered gospel, the French scholar Henri-Charles Puech realized that its Prologue and first seven sayings corresponded to the contents of POxy 654. He also found the contents of POxy 1 in sayings 26–33 and POxy 655 in sayings 36–39. In an article published in 1958 he announced his findings: the three Oxyrhynchus papyri were actually Greek fragments of the newly discovered Gospel of Thomas. The complete contents were as follows:

POxy 1	Thom 26–33 and 77:2–3
POxy 654	Thom Prologue and 1–7
POxy 655	Thom 24 and 36–39

Three Manuscripts, Not One

The three Greek Thomas fragments from Oxyrhynchus are not all from the same manuscript, but in fact from three different copies of Thomas. POxy 1 comes from an ancient codex, that is, a manuscript resembling a modern book, with pages, a binding, and other book-like features. The handwriting in this manuscript can be dated to the late second or early third century. POxy 654, on the other hand, is a fragment of a papyrus roll, the more common way of producing texts in this period. Its handwriting enables us to date it slightly later than POxy 1, in about the middle of the third century. POxy 655 originally consisted of eight small fragments (two are missing), only four of which bear any identifiable text. These fragments are also from a papyrus roll, but not the same scroll from which POxy 654 derives. The handwriting in these fragments is less formal than that in POxy 654, and slightly earlier in date.

These distinct manuscripts may indicate that the Gospel of Thomas was present at Oxyrhynchus in at least three different copies. The differing formats of these copies also raises points of interest. The book form of POxy 1 was probably the most expensive way of producing a text in this period. A papyrus roll was also an expensive item, but an economical alternative was to write on the unused back side of a scroll originally used for some other purpose. This is the case with POxy 654. It was written on the back of a discarded survey list. So it may well be that a number of people from a variety of social and economic backgrounds were interested in the Gospel of Thomas during this period in Oxyrhynchus.

A Greek "Version" of Thomas?

When the Greek fragments of Thomas are compared with the complete text from Nag Hammadi one finds a number of differences. For example, the Coptic version from Nag Hammadi claims its writer was Didymos Judas Thomas, or the Twin, Judas Thomas. POxy 654 simply calls him Judas Thomas. Again, POxy 1 attaches Thom 77:2–3 to Thom 30. Other significant differences are given in the notes to the text below. Together they raise the question of whether the Greek Oxyrhynchus text of Thomas was different enough from the Coptic text to warrant consideration as a distinct version of the Gospel of Thomas. Unfortunately, there is not enough extant text in the Greek fragments to answer this question with any certainty. However, many scholars have pointed out that we should not assume that ancients shared the modern concern that all texts with the same title should read exactly alike. Scribes in different places are known to have taken liberties in copying texts, altering them to suit their own needs and situations. This may also have been the case with the Gospel of Thomas.

The Greek fragments of

The Gospel of Thomas

POxy 654

Prologue These are the [secret] sayings [that] the living Jesus spoke, [and Judas, who is] also ⟨called⟩ Thomas, [recorded].

POxy 654

1 And he said, "[Whoever discovers the interpretation] of these sayings will not taste [death]."

POxy 654

2 [Jesus says], "Those who [seek] should not stop [seeking until] they find. [2]When they find, [they will be disturbed. [3]When they are] disturbed, they will rule, [4]and [when they rule], they will [rest]."

POxy 654

3 Jesus says, "[If] your leaders [say to you, 'Look,] the ⟨Father's⟩ imperial rule is in the sky,' then the birds of the sky [will precede you. [2]If they say] that it is under the earth, then the fish of the sea [will

Prologue
Ⓣ Th 37:3; 59; 111:2

1
Cf. Jn 8:51; Ⓣ Th 18:3, 19:4, 85:2, 111:2; Mk 9:1; Mt 16:28; Lk 9:27

2:1
Ⓓ Th 92:1; 94; //Mt 7:8, Lk 11:10, Mary 4:7

2:4
//GHeb 6; Ⓣ Th 50:3, 51:1, 60:6, 90; Mt 11:28–29; DSav 11:5; ◊Sir 51:26–27, 6:23–31

3
Ⓣ Th 113, 51

3:1–2
Cf. Mk 13:21–23, Mt 24:23–28, Lk 17:20–25; ◊Jb 28:12–14, 20–22 (LXX); Bar 3:29–32, 35–37; Dt 30:11–14 (LXX); Sir 1:1–3

Prologue *Judas Thomas*: The Coptic version reads "Didymos Judas Thomas," or "the Twin, Judas Thomas." This particular form of the name makes Syria the likely place for the origins of the Gospel of Thomas. The name appears in this form elsewhere only in the Syrian *Acts of Thomas* (ch. 1). The simpler form of the name, Judas Thomas, occurs in some Syrian manuscripts of John 14:22 and in the prologue of *Thomas the Contender*, also of Syrian origin. The shorter version of the name probably derives from the fact that Didymos and Thomas are the Greek and Semitic words for "twin," respectively; in dropping Didymos the redundancy is eliminated. The shorter version assumes that the proper name is Judas and "the Twin" is his nickname.

2 The wording of the Greek and Coptic versions differs at many points. The Coptic version reads as follows: "[1]Jesus said, 'Those who seek should not stop seeking until they find. [2]When they find, they will be disturbed. [3]When they are disturbed, they will marvel, [4]and will rule over all.'"

2:4 *rest*: This term is quite common in Thomas. Its soteriological significance is clear: to find rest is tantamount to salvation. Here its association with the quest for insight reflects its roots in the wisdom tradition (see Sir 51:26–27 and 6:23–31). In Thomas, one achieves rest through insight in the present, not a future existence (Thom 51). By contrast, later Gnostic groups spoke of the hoped for reunion of the Gnostic soul with the God of heavenly remove as achieving "rest." In the New Testament "rest" is also associated with a future hope (e.g., Rev 14:13).

3:1 *the ⟨Father's⟩ imperial rule*: The Greek *basileia* is conventionally rendered "kingdom," but here, as elsewhere in Scholars Version, this archaism has been abandoned. Normally, SV renders this term "imperial rule." Often, however, the term is used with a spatial connotation, for example, when persons are said to 'enter' the kingdom. In such

precede] you. 3And [the ⟨Father's⟩ imperial rule] is inside you [and outside ⟨you⟩. 4You who] know [yourselves] will find this. [And when you] know yourselves, [you will understand that] you are [children] of the [living] Father. 5[But if] you do [not] know yourselves, [you live] in [poverty], and you are [poverty]."

POxy 654

4 [Jesus says], "A [person old in] days won't hesitate to ask a [little child seven days] old about the place of [life, and] that person will [live]. 2For many of the [first] will be [last, and] the last first 3and [will become one]."

POxy 654

5 Jesus says, "[Know what is in front of] your face, and [what is hidden] from you will be disclosed [to you. 2For there is nothing] hidden that [wo]n't [become] exposed, 3and ⟨nothing⟩ buried that [won't be raised]."

POxy 654

6 [His disciples] ask him [and] say, "How [should we] fast? [How should] we [pray]? How [should we give charity]? What [diet] should [we] observe?" 2Jesus says, "[Don't lie, 3and] don't do [what] you [hate, 4because all things are apparent before] truth. 5[After all, there is nothing] hidden [that won't be exposed]."

POxy 654

7 [. . . "Lucky] is [the lion that the human will eat, so that the lion] will become [human. 2And foul is the human] that [the lion will eat . . .]."

3:3a
//Lk17:21b; Cf.DSav9:3, Mary4:5
4:1
Cf.Q10:21, Mt11:25, Lk10:21; Ⓣ Th22:1–3, 46:2; DSav14:1
4:2
//Mk10:31; Mt19:30, 20:16; Lk13:30
4:3
Ⓣ Th22:5, 23:2
5:2
//Mk4:22; Lk8:17, 12:2; Mt10:26; Ⓓ Th6:5
6:1
Ⓣ Th14:1–3, Mt6:1–18
6:3
▷Tob4:15
6:5
//Mk4:22; Lk8:17, 12:2; Mt10:26; Ⓓ Th5:2

---

cases SV translates the word "domain," capturing this spatial dimension. Often in Thomas the term is used without predication, that is, without specifiying 'of God,' 'of Heaven,' 'of the Father,' etc. To render these technical uses of *basileia* more clearly for the modern reader, the translators have supplied ⟨Father's⟩, the most common specification for this term found in Thomas.

4:3 *and will become one*: The Coptic has "and will become a single one." See the note to Thom 4:3.

5:3 The text breaks off, leaving the completion of this final phrase in doubt. The present text is a reconstruction based upon a similar saying from a fifth- or sixth-century burial shroud from Oxyrhynchus. Since Thomas does not directly speak of the resurrection anywhere else, this may well represent a later addition to the text, a probability reinforced by the absence of this verse in the Coptic version.

7 The Greek is too fragmentary to permit reconstruction by itself. The Coptic version, which serves as the basis for this reconstruction, reads as follows: "1Jesus said, 'Lucky is the lion that the human will eat, so that the lion becomes human. 2And foul is the human that the lion will eat; and the lion still will become human.'" The meaning of this say-

POxy 655

24 [3][. . .] "There [is light within a person] of light, [and it shines on the whole] world. [If it does not shine], it is [dark]."

POxy 1

26 [2][. . .] "then you will see well enough to remove the sliver from your friend's eye."

POxy 1

27 Jesus says, "If you do not fast from the world, you will not find God's domain. [2]If you do not observe the sabbath day as a sabbath day, you will not see the Father."

POxy 1

28 Jesus says, "I took my stand in the midst of the world, and I appeared to them in flesh. [2]I found them all drunk, and I did not find any of them thirsty. [3]My soul aches for the children of humanity, because they are blind in their hearts and [do not] see, [for . . .]."

POxy 1

29 [3]"[. . . comes to dwell in this] poverty."

24:3
//Q11:34–35, Mt6:22–23, Lk11:34–35; Cf.Mt5:14–16; DSav6, 8; Ⓣ 2Cor4:6
26
//Q6:41–42, Mt7:3–5, Lk6:41–42
27:1a
Ⓣ Th110, 14:1
28:1a
Ⓘ Jn1:14
28:1b
◊Prv1:20 33, Bar3:37
29
Ⓣ Th87, 112; Gal5:16–18

---

ing is obscure. See the notes to Thom 7.

24 The Oxyrhynchus version of the saying is very fragmentary. In the Coptic version the complete saying reads as follows: "[1]His disciples said, 'Show us the place where you are, for we must seek it.' [2]He said to them, 'Anyone here with two ears had better listen. [3]There is light within a person of light, and it shines on the whole world. If it does not shine, it is dark.'"

24:3 *it*: or, "he."

26 The first part of the saying is missing in the Greek version. The complete Coptic text reads as follows: "[1]Jesus said, 'You see the sliver in your friend's eye, but you don't see the timber in your own eye. [2]When you take the timber out of your own eye, then you will see well enough to take the sliver out of your friend's eye.'"

27:2 See the note to Thom 27:2.

28:3 The text breaks off in the middle of the verse. In the Coptic version the saying is completed as follows: ". . . for they came into the world empty, and they also seek to depart from the world empty. [4]But meanwhile they are drunk. When they shake off their wine, then they will change their ways."

29 The Oxyrhynchus version of the saying is very fragmentary. In the Coptic version the complete saying reads as follows: "[1]Jesus said, 'If the flesh came into being because of spirit, that is a marvel, [2]but if spirit came into being because of the body, that is a marvel of marvels. [3]Yet I marvel at how this great wealth has come to dwell in this poverty.'"

POxy 1

30 [Jesus says], "Where there are [three, they are without] God, [2]and where there is only [one], I say, I am with that one. [3]Lift up the stone, and you will find me there. [4]Split a piece of wood, and I am there."

POxy 1

31 Jesus says, "No prophet is welcome on his home turf; [2]doctors don't cure those who know them."

POxy 1

32 Jesus says, "A city built on top of a high hill and fortified can neither fall nor be hidden."

POxy 1

33 Jesus says, "⟨What⟩ you hear in one of your ears [proclaim . . .]."

POxy 655

36 [Jesus says, "Don't fret], from morning [to evening nor] from [evening to] morning, [about] your [food]—what [you're going] to eat, [or] about [your clothing], what you [are going] to wear. [2][You're much] better than the lilies, which don't card and never [spin]. [3]As for you, when you have no garment, what [are you going to put] on? [4]Who could add to your life span? That same one will give you your garment."

30
//Mt18:20
31
//Mk6:4–6a, Mt13:57–58, Lk4:23–24, Jn4:44
32
//Mt5:14; ◊Is2:2–3, Mi4:1–2
33:1
//Q12:3, Mt10:27, Lk12:3
36:1
//Q12:22, Mt6:25, Lk12:22
36:2
//Q12:27, Mt6:28, Lk12:27
36:3–4
//Q12:25, Mt6:27, Lk12:25; Ⓣ DSav19:8–12; 34

30:1 The Greek text of 30:1 as reconstructed probably gives a reading superior to that currently found in the Coptic. The Coptic reads as follows: "[1]Jesus said, 'Where there are three deities, they are divine. [2]Where there are two or one, I am with that one.'" This peculiar wording of the Coptic probably derives from a scribal error.

30:3–4 In the Coptic version of Thomas these verses are omitted here, but included at Thom 77:2–3.

33 The Oxyrhynchus version of the saying is very fragmentary. In the Coptic version the complete saying reads as follows: "[1]Jesus said, 'What you will hear in your ear, in the other ear proclaim from your rooftops. [2]After all, no one lights a lamp and puts it under a basket, nor does one put it in a hidden place. [3]Rather, one puts it on a lampstand so that all who come and go will see its light.'"

36 The Coptic version of this saying is much shorter. It reads as follows: "Jesus said, 'Don't fret, from morning to evening and from evening to morning, about what you're going to wear.'" Scholars are divided as to which represents the more original text. The brevity of the Coptic version may mean that it is prior. However, others have argued that shortening the saying to refer only to clothing is related to Thomas' concern elsewhere with clothing (see, e.g., Thom 21:4 and 37:2–3). This, however, seems unlikely in view of 36:3–4, which is absent in the Coptic.

36:3–4 These verses at first appear obscure. The *garment* in question may refer to a baptismal garment, a simple linen overlay given to the initiate for use in the ceremony. In Thomas it may also have more abstract

POxy 655

37 His disciples say to him, "When will you be revealed to us, and when shall we see you?" [2]He says, "When you strip without being ashamed, [3][. . . and you will not be afraid]."

POxy 655

38 [Jesus says, "Often you have desired to hear these sayings of mine], and [you have no one else from whom to hear ⟨them⟩]. [2]And [there will come days when you will seek me and you will not find me]."

POxy 655

39 [Jesus says, "The Pharisees and the scholars] have [taken the keys] of [knowledge; they themselves have] hidden [them. [2]Neither] have [they] entered, [nor] have they [allowed those who want to] enter [to do so. [3]As for you, be as sly] as [snakes and as] simple [as doves]."

37:2 Ⓣ Th 21:2–4, DSav 34; ◊Gen 2:25 (3:1 LXX)
38:2 //Jn 7:33–36
39:1–2 //Q 11:52, Mt 23:13, Lk 11:52; Ⓣ Th 102
39:3 //Mt 10:16

---

theological connotations. Some early Christian groups believed that at death the soul flees the body only to be clothed in a new, heavenly body suitable for the transcendent world (see 1 Cor 15:35–50). This idea was common in Jewish theology as it developed in the Greek world during the period of Christian origins. Sometimes the metaphor of clothing is used to describe this mystery: the old garments are shed, the new garments of immortality are put on. This is probably the subject matter of Thom 36:3–4.

37:2 The phrase *when you strip* is obscure. See the notes to GrThom 36:3–4 and Thom 21:4.

37:3 The Oxyrhynchus version of the saying is very fragmentary. In the Coptic version the complete saying reads as follows: "[3]then [you] will see the son of the living one and you will not be afraid."

38 The Greek version of the saying is very fragmentary and must be reconstructed on the basis of the Coptic, which reads as follows: "[1]Jesus said, 'Often you have desired to hear these sayings that I am speaking to you, and you have no one else from whom to hear them. [2]There will be days when you will seek me and you will not find me.'"

39 The Greek version of the saying is very fragmentary and must be reconstructed on the basis of the Coptic, which reads as follows: "[1]Jesus said, 'The Pharisees and the scholars have taken the keys of knowledge and have hidden them. [2]They have not entered, nor have they allowed those who want to enter to do so. [3]As for you, be as sly as snakes and as simple as doves.'"

Emendation and restoration

Not one ancient text survives in the original copy, or "autograph," written by its author. The texts that have come down to us are the result of several centuries of copying and editing by hand, and the destructive forces of history and climate. Most ancient documents have not survived exactly as they were first written, but only in (a) diverse copies that are often riddled with mistakes of grammar or spelling (in addition to scribes' attempts to "improve" the text), or (b) copies that clearly show the signs of aging and decay, with letters, words, sentences, or whole sections missing.

Modern scholars, as a consequence, are faced with the task of correcting the mistakes or changes made by the scribes who copied or recopied the ancient manuscripts, and/or of filling in the lacunae (literally, "gaps") left by the wear and tear of heavy use or natural disintegration. These two tasks are known as *emendation* and *restoration*.

In the case of scribal error (the surviving text is nonsense because a scribe has misunderstood or wrongly transcribed a previous copy of the text), the modern scholar is forced to *emend* the spelling or wording of the surviving text, by changing, adding or deleting letters or words. In some places this emendation is virtually certain, as when a word or phrase is accidentally repeated (dittography), for example in Thom 33:1 (see the note to this verse). In other places a word or phrase has been accidentally left out because nearby words end with the same or similar letters (haplography). For example, in Thom 60:1 "He saw" (Coptic *afnau*) or "They saw" (Coptic *aunau*) is missing from the text, probably because a scribe's eye skipped ahead from the last word in Thom 59, "to see" (Coptic *enau*). In still other places the scribe has simply written the wrong letter. For example, the Coptic text of Thom 74 ends with the word *shōne*, a masculine noun meaning "disease." This cannot be correct. Not only does it make no sense, it is grammatically wrong, for the manuscript has the feminine article preceding this masculine noun. Since the first line of the saying ends with *jōte* ("drinking trough"), the best guess is that *shōne* should be changed to the feminine noun *shōte* ("well"). With this emendation the second line is grammatically correct and both lines end in words that are closely related in meaning, and which sound nearly identical.

In the case of a lacuna (gap), either the context (the sense of the surrounding words) or the presence of distinct letters on either side of the gap is usually enough to permit the specialist to suggest some *restoration* of the text: the original letters or words most likely to have been in the manuscript before its corruption. In such cases, restoration is indicated in modern editions and translations by the use of square brackets—[and]—around the restored text. For example, in DialSav 4 it is obvious that the speaker's name is "Matthew," even though only the second half of his name is actually preserved in the manuscript.

Needless to say, in many places scholars have been unable to emend or restore a satisfactory or readable text—passages where even the specialists have not worked out what was probably in the original text. In such cases, modern editions and translations either print a question mark (?) after an attempted emendation, or print square brackets with periods—[. . .]—to show that a gap cannot be filled with any confidence.

These instances are a sober reminder that when we read ancient documents we are always at the mercy of scribal mistakes, historical accidents, and geographical fortune or misfortune. This is especially so when dealing with documents not included in the New Testament. The fact that the New Testament writings themselves require relatively little emendation or restoration is due to the victory that Christianity won over the Roman empire: in the fourth and later centuries many copies of the Greek Bible were made by imperial decree, thus ensuring that at least some of the best manuscripts from the fourth and later centuries would be widely used, repeatedly copied, and protected as the official text of these "canonical" writings.

Introduction

The Secret Book of James relates that 550 days after his resurrection and immediately prior to his ascension, Jesus imparted a private revelation to James and Peter. The account of this revelation is a "secret book" (*apocryphon*, 1:2, 5), which James introduces in the framework of a letter.

Even though Secret James makes no claim to be a gospel, it still deserves to be included in a collection of early Christian gospels. It makes use of various sayings traditions, some of which appear in the New Testament gospels, while others are preserved only in Secret James. In addition, the figures of James and Peter lend authority to the "revealed" (1:2, 5) status of Jesus' teaching, a device also used in the composition of the New Testament gospels (see, e.g., Peter in Matt 16:15–19; the eleven in Luke 24:48). Finally, the term "remembering" (2:1) was widely used to preface the quotation of oral sayings material (e.g., Acts 20:35). The dialogue and discourse are essentially a collection of sayings, some relatively primitive in form (e.g., 8:3), others substantially reworked (e.g., 6:9–11), and still others clearly late formulations (e.g., 6:17).

Character and origins of the papyrus text

There is but a single extant manuscript of Secret James; it has survived in the collection of bound documents (codices) discovered near Nag Hammadi, Egypt, in 1945. The text, inscribed on papyrus, is a Coptic (native Egyptian) translation of a lost Greek original. Though the manuscript is untitled, the text derives its modern name from its introductory material, in which an unknown author appropriates and speaks through the person of James, the brother of the Lord. Pseudonymity of this type was conventional in Antiquity, and is well-represented within the Nag Hammadi library itself.

It is difficult to date Secret James. Since it deals with martyrdom (5:3–5) it probably was not written after 313 C.E., when the emperor Constantine officially ended the persecution of Christians. Indeed, several factors point to a much earlier date. Its witness to the compiling or "remembering" of sayings traditions, the conspicuous deference to James and Peter, and the primitiveness of much of its content suggest that it may well have been written in the first half of the second century.

Message to an ancient audience

Its enthusiasm for martyrdom (5:3–5) is part of a vigorous exhortation to earnestness (4:3–5:6; 9:1)—likely a challenge to complacency within the community to which it is addressed (4:5–7). The Savior dwells with the believer (6:23) and urges him or her to participate in the realization of salvation (e.g., 6:7, 39; 7:3). Salvation consists of the knowledge or "fullness" (8:3–4) of "heaven's domain" (8:4, 11) or the spirit (3:18).

James himself assures his readers of their connection with and superiority to the broader church. It is James who transmits the private revelation (and, ostensibly, a previous one, 1:5) and narrates it in the first person. During the dialogue, Peter speaks twice (3:12; 9:1) but misunderstands Jesus; James alone is addressed directly by name (6:20), and he maintains the more dominant voice. It is significant that as James and Peter return to the other disciples after the ascension, it is James who sends "each one" on his way (10:9), travels to Jerusalem (10:9), and prays for inclusion among those for whose sake James has received the promise of salvation (10:7, 9).

A wedding of religious ideas

In Secret James, traces of Gnosticism blend with concepts that are more expressly Christian. Entrance into the heaven's domain, for example, presupposes not childlikeness (e.g., Mark 10:15) but being "full," a term associated in gnostic sources with knowledge and salvation ("fill" or "full" occurs fifteen times in Secret James; see, e.g., 2:6–7; 3:13–18). Similarly, heaven's domain is discovered through knowledge (6:18), the means of salvation in Gnosticism. The gnostic elements in Secret James, however, do not constitute a special system or doctrine; they are expressed through particular vocabulary and by association with other Christian notions (e.g., 9:4).

The structure

Although the document contains a minimum of narrative detail, it has a discernible literary pattern:

1. Introductory letter (1:1–7).
2. Secret book (2:1–10:9).
   a. Post-resurrection appearance (2:1–3:1).
   b. Dialogue and Discourse (3:2–9:13).
   c. Ascension (10:1–9).
3. Postscript (11:1–4).

The revelatory portion (2:1–10:9), which occupies most of the work, concludes with not only Jesus' ascension but also with the attempt of his companions, James and Peter, to follow. They are thwarted by the inquisitiveness of their fellow disciples (10:6).

Literary unity of the text

There are abrupt changes and inconsistencies between major sections of Secret James. Three theories, all of them plausible, have been advanced to explain this feature of the book. The first regards the letter (1:1–7) and the secret book as originally separate. The unity of the two sections, therefore, would be the work of a redactor, who in the process of editing embellished the material by enhancing the position of James. Another considers the passages on martyrdom (4:1–5:6) and prophecy (6:1–4) as secondary additions; their omission leaves a conceivably earlier document consisting of shorter sayings. A third theory views the document as the work of one author, for both the letter segment and the secret book use a rare grammatical feature, the beatitude with the verb in the future tense (1:4; 7:3; 8:3, 9). However, this could also be the work of a redactor attempting to harmonize the two sections.

Jesus through the community of Secret James

Secret James is an important witness to the diversity of forms in which sayings of Jesus were preserved in the early Church. Parables (e.g., 6:10, 17; 8:3), prophecies (e.g., 6:28–30), and wisdom sayings (e.g., 2:4, 6; 8:5) are easily identifiable within the discourse and dialogue. In Secret James, therefore, we can see how traditional sayings of Jesus were handed down and transposed in response to communal requirements, a process that continued until the widespread adoption of the 'Fourfold Gospel.' The most ancient of the sayings absorbed into Secret James may well belong to the earliest period of collected sayings traditions.

The cross as a symbol of Jesus' suffering is present in Secret James, though the brief account of his condemnation, imprisonment, death, and burial (4:6) has no direct literary relationship to the New Testament passion narratives. The treatise affirms the redemptive value of the crucifixion: belief in Jesus' "cross and death" leads to life and God's domain (4:11–5:2). Still, the death of Jesus is not a major concern of the document. Its interest, rather, lies in Jesus' teaching and in the furnishing of a foundational revelation for a community of gnostic Christians. In order to accomplish this, Secret James assembles and transforms sayings of Jesus, selectively preserving fragments of the Savior's salvific teaching "in parables" (6:5; Mark 4:2).

The Secret Book of James

1 [James, writing] to [—]thos. Peace [to you from] peace, [love from]
love, [grace from] grace, [faith] from faith, life from holy life!
2Since you asked me to send you a secret book that was revealed to
Peter and me by the Lord, I could neither refuse you nor dissuade you;
so [I have written] it in Hebraic letters and have sent it to you—and to
you alone. 3Nevertheless, you should do your best, as a minister of the
salvation of the saints, to take care not to disclose this book to many—
the things the Savior did not wish [to] disclose to all of us, his twelve
disciples. 4Still, congratulations to those who will be saved through the
trustworthiness of this text.
5Ten months ago I sent you another secret book that the Savior
revealed to me. 6However, that one you are to regard in this way, as
revealed to me, James. 7And this one [. . . revealed . . .] those who [. . .
], therefore, and seek [. . .] so it is [. . .] salvation [. . .].

2 Now the twelve disciples [used to] sit all together at the [same
time], remembering what the Savior had said to each one of them,
whether secretly or openly, and setting it down in books. 2I was writing
what went in [my book]—suddenly, the Savior appeared, [after] he had
departed from [us, and while we were watching] for him. 3And so, five
hundred fifty days after he rose from the dead, we said to him, "You
went away and left us!"
4"No," Jesus said, "but I shall go to the place from which I have
come. If you wish to come with me, come on!"
5They all replied, "If you bid us, we'll come."
6He said, "I swear to you, no one will ever enter heaven's domain at
my bidding, but rather because you yourselves are full. 7Let me have
James and Peter, so that I may fill them."

2:1 Ⓣ Th Prologue
2:3 Ⓣ Acts 1:3
2:4 Ⓣ Jn 7:33; 13:36; 14:3–5; 16:5, 16–20, 28; Pet 13:2
2:6–3:1 Ⓣ Jn 3:3–5
2:6 Ⓣ Mk 10:15; Mt 18:3; Lk 18.17

1:1–7 Along with 10:8–11:1, this is probably the final major addition in the composition of Secret James. (See the Introduction.)
1:1 Lists of virtues are frequent in early Christian literature. See Gal 5:22–23; Eph 6:23–24; 2 John 3.
1:3 The title *Savior* is applied to Jesus only in the later phases of the document's composition (see also 1:5; 2:1, 2; 11:3). *Lord* is the preferred address in the secret revelation itself (2:1–10:7). Also, it appears that the disciples as *twelve* (see 2:1) is a standard formula.
2:1 John 14:25–26; 15:20, 27; and 16:4 all associate the notion of *remembering* with the departure of Jesus.
2:3–4 Other writings of the period provide differing accounts of the length of time between Jesus' resurrection and his ascension: in Acts 1:3, he remains for 40 days; in the Ascension of Isaiah 9:16, for 545 days; in Irenaeus *Against Heresies* 1.3.2, for 18 aeons; *Against Heresies* 1.30.14, for 18 months.
2:6 The term *full* (and its related forms) is

3 And when he called these two, he took them aside, and commanded the rest to carry on with what they had been doing.
2The Savior said, "You have received mercy [. . .] become [. . .]
they wrote [. . .] book, as [. . .] to you [. . .] and just as [. . .] they [. . .]
hear and [. . .] they [. . .] understand. 3So don't you want to be filled?
And is your heart drunk? So don't you want to be sober? 4You ought,
then, to be ashamed! 5And now, waking or sleeping, remember that
you have seen the son of Adam, and with him have you spoken, and to
him have you listened. 6Damn those who have seen the son [of] Adam.
7Congratulations to those who have not seen that man, and who have
not associated with him, and who have not spoken with him, and who
have not listened to a thing from him. Yours is life! 8Know, therefore,
that he treated you when you were sick, so that you might reign.
9Damn those who have been relieved of their sickness, for they will
relapse again into sickness. 10Congratulations to those who have not
been sick, and have experienced relief before they became sick. God's
domain belongs to you! 11Therefore, I say to you, become full and leave
no place within you empty, or else the one who is coming will be able
to mock you."
12Then Peter responded, "Look, three times you have told us,
'Become [full,' but] we are full."
13The [Lord replied], "This [is why I told] you, ['Become full,' so]
that [you] might not [be lacking; those who are lacking] will not [be
saved]. 14For fullness is good [and lacking], bad. 15Therefore, inasmuch
as it's good for you to lack but bad for you to be filled, whoever is full
tends to be lacking. 16One who lacks is not filled in the same way that
another who lacks is filled; but whoever is full receives his just deserts.
17Therefore, it's fitting to lack while it's possible to fill yourselves, and
to be filled while it's possible to lack, so that you may be able [to fill]
yourselves the more. 18Therefore, [become] full of the spirit but
lacking in reason. For reason is of the soul; indeed, it is soul."

3:3–5
Ⓣ 1 Thes 5:4–8; Th 28
3:5–7
Cf. SJas 8:5–6; Jn 20:29

---

common in gnostic writings, where it usually indicates the attainment of knowledge or the virtue gained by knowledge. In both gnostic and apostolic literature, it also represents present or eventual salvation, the possession of grace, or the indwelling of the Spirit. For the sense here, see the note to 9:4.

3:6–7 The curse in v. 6 would be most unusual in the NT gospels, but here serves a polemical function for its intended audience of gnostic Christians. In v. 5 being an eyewitness is positive and desirable. Verse 7, on the other hand, denigrates the belief among mainstream apostolic Christians as compared to the faith transmitted (ostensibly by James) to gnostic Christians via a secret revelation.

3:14–15 The seeming conflict between the statements about being *filled* with those about *lacking* is explained by v. 18. See further the note to 7:6–8.

3:18 In Secret James, *spirit* is prized above both *reason* and *soul*. See the note at 7:6–8.

4 And I responded, "Lord, we can obey you if you wish, for we have
forsaken our fathers and our mothers and our villages and have
followed you. [2]Give us the means, [then], not to be tempted by the evil
devil."

[3]The Lord replied, "If you do the Father's will, what credit is that to
you—unless he gives you, as part of his gift, your being tempted by
Satan? [4]But if you are oppressed by Satan, and are persecuted, and you
do his will, I [say] that he will love you, and will make you equal with
me, and will regard [you] as having become [beloved] through his
providence according to your own choice. [5]So won't you cease being
lovers of the flesh and afraid of suffering? [6]Or don't you realize that you
have not yet been abused and have not yet been accused unjustly, nor
have you yet been locked up in prison, nor have you yet been
condemned unlawfully, nor have you yet been crucified ⟨without⟩
reason, nor have you yet been buried in the sand, as I myself was, by the
evil one? [7]Do you dare to spare the flesh, you for whom the spirit acts as
an encircling wall? [8]If you think about the world, about how long it
existed ⟨before⟩ you and how long it will exist after you, you will
discover that your life is but a single day, and your sufferings but a
single hour. [9]Accordingly, since what is good will not enter this world,
[10]you should scorn death and be concerned about life. [11]Remember my
cross and my death, and you will live!"

5 And I answered him, "Lord, don't proclaim the cross and death to
us, for they are far from you."

[2]The Lord replied, "I swear to you, none will be saved unless they
believe in my cross; [for] God's domain belongs to those who have
believed in my cross. [3]Become seekers of death, therefore, like the dead
who are seeking life, for what they seek is manifest to them. So what
can be of concern to them? [4]When you inquire into the subject of
death, it will teach you about election. [5]I swear to you, none will be
saved who are afraid of death; for ⟨God's⟩ domain belongs to those
who are dead. [6]Become better than I; be like the son of the holy spirit!"

4:1
Cf. Mk 10:28; Mt 19:27; Lk 18:28

4:2
Cf. Q 11:4; Mt 6:13; Lk 11:4

4:4
Ⓣ Jn 14:23

4:10–5:3
Ⓣ Mk 8:34–35; Mt 10:38–39; 16:24–25; Lk 9:23–24

4:4 *Providence according to your own choice* refers to the tension between predestination and the exercise of one's free will. Other hints of predestination are in 6:38 and 9:13.

4:6 This is the closest Secret James comes to describing the suffering and death of Jesus. *Buried in the sand* differs from the general tradition about the death of Jesus. The author was probably ignorant of first-century Judean burial practices and familiar with specific local interment methods, in Egypt for example.

4:9 *what is good will not enter this world:* Put another way, suffering is inevitable for all those who enter the world. Similar ideas are stated in 7:8 and 8:8.

5:5 *Belongs to those who are dead* can be translated "those who put themselves to death," i.e., offer themselves for martyrdom.

5:6 *Become better than I* is mediated by the second half of the verse, *be like the son of the holy spirit*, i.e., like Jesus himself, or at least like another man filled with the spirit. The emphasis is on facing death fearlessly, not on

6:2 Cf. Mk 6:14–29; Mt 14:1–12
6:2–4 (T) Q16:16; Mt 11:12–13; Lk 16:16; Eph 4:15–16
6:5–6 Cf. Mk 4:10–13; 4:33–34; Mt 13:10–17; 13:34–35; Lk 8:9–10; Jn 10:6; 16:25; ◊Ps 78:2; Is 6:9–10
6:7 (T) Jn 14:21–23
6:9–11 (T) Jn 12:24; 15:2–8; Jas 5:7
6:13 (T) Jn 17:5, 20:17
6:15a //Q15:3–7; Mt 18:12–14; Lk 15:3–7; Th 107; Jn 10:11–17
6:15b //Mk 4:3–9, 26–29; Mt 13:1–13; Lk 8:4–10; Th 9
6:15c //Q6:47–49; Mt 7:24–27; Lk 6:47–49
6:15d //Mt 25:1–13
6:15e //Mt 20:1–16
6:15f //Lk 15:8–10
6:15g //Q13:20–21; Mt 13:33; Lk 13:20–21
6:16 (T) 1 Cor 13:13
6:17 Cf. Mk 4:13–20; Mt 13:18–23; Lk 8:11–15

6 Then I asked him, "Lord, how will we be able to prophesy to those who ask us to prophesy to them? For there are many who inquire of us, and who look to us to hear an oracle from us."

2 The Lord replied, "Don't you realize that the head of prophecy was severed with John?"

3 But I said, "Lord, it's not possible to remove the head of prophecy, is it?"

4 The Lord said to me, "When you comprehend what 'head' means, and that prophecy issues from the head, understand what 'Its head was removed' means. 5 I first spoke with you parabolically, and you did not understand. Now I am speaking with you openly, and you do not perceive. 6 Nevertheless, for me you were a parable among parables, and the disclosure of openness.

7 "Be eager to be saved without being urged. Instead, become zealous on your own and, if possible, surpass even me. For that is how the Father will love you.

8 "Become haters of hypocrisy and evil intent. For intent is what produces hypocrisy, and hypocrisy is far from the truth.

9 "Don't let heaven's domain wither away. 10 For it is like a date palm shoot whose fruit fell down around it. It put forth buds, and when they blossomed, its productivity was caused to dry up. 11 So it also is with the fruit that came from this singular root: when it was picked, fruit was gathered by many. Truly, this was good. 12 Isn't it possible to produce new growth now? Can't you discover how?

13 "Since I was glorified in this way before now, why do you detain me when I am eager to go? 14 For after my [labors] you have constrained me to stay with you eighteen more days for the sake of parables. 15 It was enough for some people ⟨to⟩ pay attention to the teaching and understand 'the shepherds,' and 'the seed,' and 'the building,' and 'the lamps of the virgins,' and 'the wage of the workers,' and 'the silver coins,' and 'the woman.'

16 "Become eager for instruction. For the first prerequisite for instruction is faith, the second is love, the third is works; now from these comes life. 17 For instruction is like a grain of wheat. When they sowed it they had faith in it; and when it sprouted they loved it, because they envisioned many grains in place of one; and when they worked they were sustained, because they prepared it for food, then kept the rest in

---

surpassing Jesus as a goal.

6:10 The parable of the date palm shoot is unique to Secret James, occurring nowhere else in the early gospel traditions. The basic comparison between the shoot and heaven's domain could be quite early, but the remainder of the saying is a second-century expansion.

6:11 *This singular root* refers to *heaven's domain* in v. 9. The *fruit* in question may represent the gnostic Christian believer or the knowledge which she or he possesses.

6:15 This parable list would seem to prove that the NT gospels were familiar to the audience of Secret James, but it is the only such instance. As the list does not relate to the parables which precede and follow it, it is probably a later insertion into the text.

reserve to be sown. [18]So it is possible for you, too, to receive for yourselves heaven's domain: unless you receive it through knowledge, you will not be able to discover it.

[19]"Therefore, I say to you, be sober; don't go astray. [20]Moreover, I have often said to you all together—and also to you alone, James, have I said—be saved. [21]I have commanded you to follow me, and I have taught you how to respond in the presence of the rulers. [22]Observe that I have descended, and have spoken, and have expended myself, and have won my crown, so as to save you. [23]For I descended to dwell with you so that you might also dwell with me. And when I found your houses to be without roofs, I dwelt instead in houses that could receive me at the time of my descent.

[24]"Therefore, rely on me, my brothers; understand what the great light is. [25]The Father does not need me. For a father does not need a son, but it is the son who needs the father. [26]To him do I go, for the Father of the Son is not in need of you.

[27]"Pay attention to instruction, understand knowledge, love life. And no one will persecute you, nor will any one oppress you, other than you yourselves.

[28]"You wretches! You unfortunates! You pretenders to the truth! You falsifiers of knowledge! You sinners against the spirit! [29]Do you even now dare to listen, when you should have spoken from the beginning? Do you even now dare to sleep, when you should have been awake from the beginning, so that heaven's domain might receive you? [30]I swear to you, it is easier for a holy one to descend into defilement, and for an enlightened person to descend into darkness, than for you to reign—or even not to!

[31]"I have remembered your tears and your grief and your sorrow; they are far from us. [32]Now, then, you who are outside the Father's inheritance, weep where it's called for, and grieve, and proclaim what is good: how the Son is ascending, as he should. [33]I swear to you, were I sent to those who would listen to me, and were I to have spoken with them, I would never have come down to earth. From now on, then, be ashamed for them.

[34]"See, I shall leave you and go away; I don't wish to stay with you any longer—just as you have not wished it either. Now, then, follow me eagerly. [35]Therefore, I say to you, for your sake I descended. [36]You are the beloved; it is you who will become the cause of life for many. [37]Invoke the Father, pray to God frequently, and he will give to you. [38]Congratulations to whoever has envisioned you along with him when he is proclaimed among the angels and glorified among the saints.

6:19 Ⓣ Mt 24:4; Gal 6:7; 1 Thes 5:8; Jas 1:16
6:23 Ⓣ Jn 1:11, 14a; 14:3, 23; 15:4
6:24–26 Ⓣ Q 10:22; Mt 11:27; Lk 10:22; Jn 5:19–20
6:28–30 Ⓣ Q 3:7–9; Mt 3:7–10; Lk 3:7–9
6:31–32 Ⓣ Jn 16:20
6:33 Ⓣ Jn 8:47; 10:25–26
6:34–40 Cf. Jn 14:3–28
6:34 Ⓣ Jn 16:7
6:36 Ⓣ Jn 17:20
6:37 Ⓣ Jn 16:23
6:38 Ⓣ 1 Tm 3:16

6:21 The Coptic word for *rulers*, borrowed from Greek, refers either to heavenly rulers or to earthly ones. Most scholars tend toward the latter, though hostile heavenly rulers or powers are hinted at in 10:3.

6:22 *Crown* is often used to denote salvation after martyrdom.

6:23 *Without roofs* could be translated "unable to hold [me]," which would suggest the disciples' inability to receive the revealed word.

6:25–26 Rejection of the Son is not the point; v. 25 broadly illustrates the declaration of v. 26.

Yours is life! [39]Rejoice and exult as children of God. Keep [his] will, so that you may be saved. Accept reproof from me and save yourselves. [40]I am pleading for you with the Father, and he will forgive you much."

7 When we heard these things, we became elated, for we had despaired over what we recounted earlier. [2]But when he saw us rejoicing, he said, "Damn you who require an intercessor. Damn you who stand in need of grace. [3]Congratulations to those who have spoken out fearlessly, and have obtained grace for themselves. [4]Compare yourselves to foreigners: how are they regarded by your city? Why abandon your home on your own, making it available for those who wish to live in it? You outcasts and runaways! Damn you, for you will be caught. [5]Or perhaps you think that the Father is a lover of humanity? Or that he is persuaded by prayers? Or that he grants favors to one on behalf of another? Or that he bears with someone who seeks? [6]For he knows about desire, as well as what the flesh needs: does it not long for the soul? [7]For without the soul the body does not sin, just as the soul is not saved without the spirit. But if the soul could be saved from evil, and the spirit were also saved, then the body would become sinless. For the spirit is what animates the soul, but the body is what kills it—in other words, it is the soul which kills itself. [8]I swear to you, he will never forgive the sin of the soul, nor the guilt of the flesh; for none of those who have worn the flesh will be saved. [9]Do you think, then, that many have found heaven's domain? Congratulations to those who have envisioned themselves as the fourth one in heaven."

8 When we heard these things, we became distressed. [2]But when he saw that we were distressed, he said, "This is why I say this to you, that you may know yourselves. [3]For heaven's domain is like a head of grain which sprouted in a field. And when it ripened, it scattered its fruit and, in turn, filled the field with heads of grain for another year. [4]You also: be eager to reap for yourselves a head of the grain of life, so that you may be filled with the domain.

[5]"As long as I am with you, pay attention to me and obey me; but when I take leave of you, remember me. Remember me because I was with you, though you did not know me. Congratulations to those who have known me. [6]Damn those who have heard and have not believed. Congratulations to those who have not seen [but] have [had faith].

[7]"Once again do I [appeal] to you. For I am made known to you building a house of great value to you, since you take shelter in it;

6:40
Ⓣ Jn 14:16
7:7
Ⓣ Jn 6:63
8:3
Cf. Mk 4:3–9; 4:26–29; Mt 13:3–9; Lk 8:4–8; Th 9
8:5–6
Ⓣ SJas 3:5; Jn 12:35–36; 20:29
8:7
Ⓣ Mt 7:27; Jn 14:2

7:5 The precise intention of these rhetorical questions is difficult to gauge. But see the note to 6:25–26.

7:6–8 The conceptual division of the person into *body*, *soul*, and *spirit* was common in Antiquity. *Spirit* is the highest nature of the three, governing the *soul* and the *body* (or *flesh*) which the *soul* inhabits. The *soul* encompasses the non-physical capacities of a person (e.g., reason), and can be oriented toward good or toward evil; the *spirit*, which is from faith in the divine, guides the *soul* in its choices (see the note to 3:18).

7:9 *fourth one in heaven:* There is no general agreement among scholars as to the meaning, identification, or status of such a figure.

likewise, it can support your neighbors' house when theirs is in danger
[of] collapsing. [8]I swear to you, damn those for whose sake I was sent
down here. [9]Congratulations to those who are on the way to the Father.
[10]Again I admonish you. You who exist, be like those who do not exist,
so that you may dwell with those who do not exist.

[11]"Don't let heaven's domain become desolate among you. [12]Don't
be arrogant about the light that enlightens. [13]Rather, behave toward
yourselves in the way that I have toward you: I placed myself under a
curse for you, so that you might be saved."

9 To this Peter responded, "Sometimes you urge us on toward
heaven's domain, yet at other times you turn us away, Lord. Sometimes
you make appeals, draw us toward faith, and promise us life, yet at
other times you drive us away from heaven's domain."

[2]The Lord replied to us, "I have offered you faith many times;
moreover, I have made myself known to you, James, and you have not
understood me. [3]On the other hand, now I see you rejoicing again and
again. And even though you are elated over [the] promise of life, you
still despair and become distressed when you are taught about
⟨heaven's⟩ domain. [4]But you, through faith [and] knowledge, have
received life. [5]Accordingly, disregard rejection when you hear [it], but
when you hear about the promise, exult all the more. [6]I swear to you,
whoever receives life and believes in the domain will never leave it—
not even if the Father wishes to banish him!

[7]"This is all I shall tell you at this time. Now I shall ascend to the
place from which I have come. [8]But you, when I was eager to go, have
rebuffed me; and instead of accompanying me, you have chased me
away. [9]Still, pay attention to the glory that awaits me and, having
opened your hearts, listen to the hymns that await me up in heaven.
[10]For today I must take my place at the right hand of my Father. I have
spoken my last word to you; I shall part from you. [11]For a chariot of
spirit has lifted me up, and from now on I shall strip myself so that I

9:2 Ⓣ Jn 14:9
9:6 Ⓣ Jn 6:37
9:7–8 Ⓣ Jn 16:4–5
9:7 Ⓣ Jn 14:25; 16:28; Pet 13:2
9:11 Ⓣ Th 37

8:7 The author's rendering of the parable of the building (6:15; see Matt 7:24–27) uses the term *house* as an image of the spiritual constitution of the believer. How it can function to *support your neighbors' house* is unclear, though the spread of knowledge or faith may be envisioned here.

8:8 For a fuller account, see 6:33–34. Consider *Epistula Apostolorum* 39: "Whoever has kept my commandments shall be a son of light. But because of them that corrupt my words do I come down from heaven."

8:10 In gnostic and Christian writings, a tension is often established between true and false or illusory being. Those *who exist* are identified with the former. However, to not exist is a positive value in this verse, and the implication is that *those who do not exist* really do, but on another level (they *dwell*). Perhaps they are believers who have reached a fullness of knowledge. Notice as well the stylistic resemblance to 3:13–18.

8:13 *Under a curse* refers either to Christ becoming human, or to the fulfillment of OT law (Deut 21:23; quoted in Gal 3:13).

9:1–2 Peter asks the question, but Jesus answers James.

9:4 *Faith* and *knowledge* are virtually equated. Knowledge (*gnosis*) is highly valued in Gnosticism.

9:11 *I shall strip myself so that I may clothe myself*—i.e., in glory. The notion of stripping off to be clothed anew can be baptismal, but *from now on* precludes that once-for-all-time possibility.

may clothe myself. [12]So pay attention: congratulations to those who proclaimed the Son before he descended, so that, having come, I might ascend. [13]Congratulations three times over to those who [were] proclaimed by the Son before they existed, so that you might have a share with them."

10 When he said this, he went away. [2]So Peter and I knelt down, gave thanks, and sent our hearts up to heaven. [3]We heard with our ears and saw with our eyes the sound of battles and a trumpet's blast and utter turmoil.

[4]And when we passed beyond that place, we sent our minds up further. We saw with our eyes and heard with our ears hymns and angelic praises and angelic rejoicing. Heavenly majesties were singing hymns, and we ourselves were rejoicing.

[5]After this, we also desired to send our spirits heavenward to the majesty. [6]And when we went up, we were not permitted to see or hear a thing. For the rest of the disciples called to us and asked us, "What did you hear from the Teacher?" and, "What did he tell you?" and, "Where has he gone?"

[7]We answered them, "He has ascended. He has given us a pledge, and promised all of us life, and disclosed to us children who are to come after us, having bid [us to] love them, since we will [be saved] for their sake."

[8]And when they heard, they believed the revelation, yet were angry about those who would be born. [9]So, not wishing to give them an occasion to take offense, I sent each one to a different place. And I myself went up to Jerusalem, praying that I might obtain a share with the beloved who are to appear.

11 Now I pray that a beginning may take place with you. For this is how I can be saved—since they will be enlightened through me, through my faith and through another's that is better than mine, for I wish for mine to be more lowly. [2]Do your best, therefore, to be like them, and pray that you may obtain a share with them. [3]For, apart from what I have recounted, the Savior did not disclose revelation to us. [4]For their sake do we proclaim a share with those for whom this has been proclaimed, those whom the Lord has made his children.

10:1–3 //Lk 24:51; Acts 1:9–11
10:4 Cf. Rv 14:2–3
10:7 Ⓣ Mt 28:16–20
10:8–9 Ⓣ Th 12

9:13 *They who [were] proclaimed by the Son before they existed* are those chosen for salvation even before their earthly existence. Alternately, the phrase could indicate that those same chosen individuals existed before their own human births (see 6:38; 11:4).

10:7 *We will [be saved] for their sake* refers to Jesus' declaration in 9:13, and later, to James' advice in 11:2. Each of these verses likely has gnostic Christians in mind.

10:8–9 The disciples' anger is not fully explained in the narrative, but it probably points to the historical conflict between the main apostolic church and the gnostic Christians. With the dispersal of the twelve and the decisive action by James, the gnostic Christian community for whom the document was originally written understands its origins through James' association with the twelve. By virtue of his privileged relationship with the Lord, the community believes its foundation to be rooted in Jesus.

Introduction

A *gospel about baptism*

The Dialogue of the Savior is a dialogue between "the Lord" and several disciples composed in its final form probably around 150 C.E. It was originally written in Greek, but now survives only in one fragmentary Coptic manuscript from Nag Hammadi. The central theme of the Dialogue is a process of salvation described in GrTh 2: "Those who [seek] should not stop [seeking until] they find. When they find, [they will be disturbed. When they are] disturbed, they will rule, and [when they rule], they will [rest]" (see DialSav 11:5). This theme supports an invitation to baptism (1–3). It is even likely that the author intended the writing as a discussion of baptism, and in particular of the question: do baptized persons belong in heaven, or should they continue their struggle in the flesh, i.e., on earth?

The author answers the question as follows. First, the writing looks backwards—it describes a moment in the past, when Jesus and his disciples were together. But the reader sees the disciples not only as historical people; he or she finds that they stand for the community's "catechumens" (converts in training) being instructed by their "teacher" (34:1). In this way, the instructions to the disciples in the Dialogue are probably addressed to those in the author's community who are preparing for baptism.

Baptism and the destiny of the soul

The disciples are invited to watch the journey of a soul. What they see is also the journey of their own souls, for which this "single soul" stands as an example: along with its "consort" (5:3), the soul is transported to the height and given garments of light. The critical stage of the journey is described in 1:5: "the passage by which (the elect and the solitary) will pass." This process is probably the same as the "little" becoming one with the "great" (5:1; 17:18; 25:3). The disciples are amazed by what they see, and accept the vision and its interpretation "in faith" (17:11; cf. 29:2).

According to the Dialogue of the Savior, the purpose of baptism is not to make this heavenly journey unnecessary, for example by bringing about a spiritual "rebirth." In fact, discussion of any type of birth other than that from a woman is ruled out (37:4). The believer's soul, which is "from the truth" (23:2), needs no second birth. Instead baptism stands for the journey that the believer's soul will make in the future, at the time of death. Therefore baptism does not involve receiving future rewards ahead of time, but the instruction, by word and by ritual, about the nature of the world. The baptized do not yet *see* the *All*, but only *know* their true selves (14:1–4); they do not yet rule over the archons (or heavenly rulers), but at "the time of dissolution" (3:1) they will (19:1–6).

Therefore in the Dialogue three 'eras' are described. The first is the pictured, fleeting history of a believer's soul being redeemed. The second is the climax in the history of the Lord and his disciples, mentioned in the dialogue's opening and long in the past by the time of the reader. The third is the future of the author's community, whom the author hopes to convince that death, and life, may now be faced without fear.

Sources and composition

Several things about this document make it almost certain that the final author combined various written sources to produce the present Dialogue of the Savior. First, a series of long speeches of the Lord seem to belong together, in terms of subject-matter and style (see especially 1–3; 8:2–8; 12:2–11; 15:4–16:8; 38; 41:3–7). Second, several of the speeches have transitions that interrupt the flow of the dialogue (see especially in 12:12; 17:1–12, 14–21). Third, there are some abrupt changes of subject-matter, as if the author switched from one source to another and back again.

Because of these features, it is now widely held that the author of the Dialogue made use of four sources: (1) a *dialogue* between the Lord and his disciples; (2) a *creation myth*; (3) a *wisdom list* (or catalog of elementary substances); and (4) an *apocalyptic vision* (or heavenly revelation). To these the author added an introduction (1–3), concluding instructions (41:6), and various other sentences that enable the Dialogue of the Savior to be read as a continuous whole.

The *dialogue* (4–8; 11; 13:1–15:10; 18:4–41:7) consists of short speeches; in each of these a traditional saying of Jesus is quoted, or reflections on a traditional saying. Although numerous similar sayings are found in the synoptic gospels and in the Gospel of Thomas, it is unlikely that the author ever quotes the New Testament gospels. A wide range of topics is covered, and individual questions and answers are frequently linked by 'catchwords' (words or phrases in two or more adjacent lines); but the dialogue does not follow a particular pattern of questions and answers. The author does not even state whether the Lord is speaking before or after the resurrection.

The chapters that include the *creation myth* (9–10; 12) do not give a complete "myth." They are pieces of a mythic drama, based on ideas in Genesis 1–2, presumably known to the readers in a fuller form.

In quoting from a *wisdom list* (15:11–16:8), the author quotes a pattern of negative conditions ("If not . . .") and their consequences ("then . . .") built on a well known list of cosmic elements: earth, air, fire, and water. This list is made specifically Christian; it is also expanded with a statement of belief concerning the Son and the Father.

Finally, the *apocalyptic vision* (17) is unique in the Dialogue of the Savior, because it includes a lengthy descriptive narrative and someone identified as "the son of Adam." This "son of Adam," distinct from "the Lord" conversing with the disciples, directs and describes the journey of "a single soul" (17:16) from the abyss to the heights of heaven. Meanwhile the author tells us that the disciples see this drama in a vision, which they witness from "the edge of heaven and earth" (17:1).

Title

The final author or editor is probably responsible for the work's title, because after his first speech the Lord is identified simply as "the Savior" in the introductions to only two speeches (4:2; 6). Everywhere else the revealer is called "the Lord" (39 times) or simply identified as "he/him" (7 times, in introductions to speeches). His conversation partners, in order of appearance, are (1) Matthew (10 speeches); (2) Judas (18 speeches, including three addressed not to the Lord but to Matthew [17:4; 34:1; 37:7]); (3) "(all) his disciples" (7 speeches, including "his disciples, twelve in number" [32:1]); and (4) Mary (13 speeches). In addition, (5) "the son of Adam" has two speeches (17:8–10, 17).

Similarity to other gospels

The Dialogue of the Savior is obviously different in style and tone from the New Testament gospels or the Gospel of Thomas. But the differences are more in degree than in kind. For example, the combination of several older sources is similar to the composition of Matthew or Luke, each of whom used Q, Mark, and other materials. Similarly, the concern of the Dialogue with baptism, and more generally with the support of young believers, is not so unlike what we find in Matthew, a gospel often thought of as "catechetical." Again, the lack of narrative—stories about what Jesus did—shows that the Dialogue continues the tradition of "sayings gospels," like Q and Thomas.

Above all, what the Dialogue of the Savior shares with all the other gospels is an interest not only in what Jesus said, but in what he meant. And for the Dialogue, as for the other gospels, the meaning of Jesus' sayings was to be applied to the community's actual experience and concerns. The distinctive feature of the Dialogue of the Savior, its dialogue form, recognizes how such meaning might be sought and presented: by the written imitation of conversation between the Lord and his disciples.

The Dialogue of the Savior

1 The Savior said to his disciples, "The time has now come, (my)
brothers, for us to leave our labor and rest, for the one who rests will
rest forever. 2And I say to you, be always in heaven [. . .] time [. . .] you
[. . .] afraid [. . .] to you. 3I [say to you,] anger [is] to be feared [. . .] who
stirs up anger [. . .]. 4But when you had [. . .] they received these words
concerning it in fear and trembling, and it set them among archons, for
nothing came from it. 5But when I came, I opened the way and taught
them, the chosen and the solitary, the passage by which they will
pass—those who know the Father, since they have believed the truth,
and all the praises with which you ⟨are to⟩ give praise."

2 "So when you give praise, do it in this way: 2'Hear us, Father, as
you heard your only-begotten Son and received him to yourself, ⟨and⟩
gave him rest from many [labors. 3You] it is whose power [. . .] your
armor [. . .] light [. . .] living [. . . who] cannot be touched [. . .] the word
of [. . .] repentance of life [. . fr]om you. 4You are the solitary's purpose
and freedom from all care.' 5Again: 'Hear us, as you heard your elect,
those ⟨who⟩ through your sacrifi[ce] are to enter by their good works,
whose souls have been saved from these blind limbs so that they might
remain forever. Amen.'"

3 "I will teach you: When the time of dissolution comes, the first
power of darkness will come upon you. 2Do not fear and say, 'Look, the
time has come!' 3But when you see a single staff [which . .] this [. . .]
[. . .] you [. . .] understand that [. . .] from the work [. . .] and the archons
[. . .] come upon you [. . .] 4Now, fear is the pow[er . .] 5If then you fear
what is to come upon you, it will swallow you up, since there is not one

1:1 Ⓣ Heb4:10–11; Rv14:13
1:5 Ⓣ 2 Thes2:12; Th49:1
2:2 Ⓣ Jn1:14, 3:16, 18
2:3 Ⓣ Eph6:11–17
2:5 Ⓣ Eph5:2; Heb10:10, 14; 1Pet1:9; Jas1:21
3:1 Ⓣ 2Tm4:6; Col1:13

1:1 *Savior:* In the NT gospels this title is used of Jesus only in Luke 2:11 and John 4:42.

rest: a term for reaching heaven.

1:4 *concerning it: it* is the noun *anger*; so too the subject of the next verb.

archons: literally, "rulers," i.e., hostile heavenly forces.

1:5 *chosen and solitary:* These terms, used also in Thom 37:2, describe those considered to be among God's elect.

2:1 Probably a liturgical rubric; see the late first- or early second-century Did 9:1–2 and 10:1–2: "Give thanks in this way: 'We give thanks to you, Holy Father . . .'"

2:2 With this prayer compare another prayer from the Nag Hammadi writings, in the *Epistle of Peter to Philip* 133:121–26: "Father . . . hear us just as [. . .] in thy holy child Jesus Christ."

2:5 *by their good works:* The Coptic can also be translated "into their good things" (i.e., their heavenly reward). A comparable statement is found in Clement of Alexandria, *Excerpts from Theodotus* 86.3: "who . . . did not enter into the good things which have been prepared."

3:1–4 This fragmentary chapter appears to

among them who will spare you or have mercy on you. 6But in this way
look at [the . .] in it, for you have been victorious over every word that is
upon earth. 7It [will] take you up to the pl[ace . .] in which there is no
rule [. . ty]rant. 8When you [. . .] you will see the things that [. . .] and
also [. . .] tell you that [. . .], the design [. . .] design which is [. . . pla]ce of
truth [. . .] but [. . .] 9But you [. . .] of the truth, this [. . .] living [mind]
because of [. . .] your joy [. . .] 10So then, [. . .] so that [. . .] your souls [. . .]
lest it [. . .] the word [. . .] lift up [. . .] they did not [. . .] your [in]side [and
your outside] [. . .] 11For the crossing place is to be feared be[fore . .]
12But as for you, [with a] single mind pass it by, for its depth is great
⟨and⟩ [its] height very great [. . .] a single mind [. . .] and the fire
wh[ich . .] is [. . .] [. . .] all the powers [. . .] you, they will [. . .] and the
pow[ers . . .] they [. . .] 13I te[ll you . . .] this soul [. . .] become a [. . .] in
everyone [. . .] you are t[he . . .] and that [. . .] forgetfulness [. . .] children
of [. . .] and you [. . .] you [. . .]."

4 [Mat]thew said, "How [. . .] [. . .]?"
2The Savior said, "[. . .] the things that are in you [. . .] will remain,
[but] you [. . .]."

5 Judas [said], "Lord, [. . .] the works [. . . th]ese souls, these [. . .]
these little ones, when [. . .] where will they be? [. . .] the spirit [. . .]."
2The Lord [said], "[. . .] [. . .] recei[ve th]em. 3These do not die [. . .]
they do not perish, for they have known [their] consorts and the one
who will re[cei]ve them. 4For the truth seeks [after] the wise and the
righteous."

6 The Savior s[aid], "The lamp [of the b]ody is the mind. 2As long as
[the things that are] in you are rightly ordered, that is, [. . .] your bodies
are [light]. As long as your heart is da[rk], your light which you await
[. . .]. 3I have call[ed . . .] that I shall go [. . .] my word [. . .] I send to
[. . .]."

7 His discipl[es said, "Lord,] who is the one who seeks and [. . .]
reveals?"
2[The Lord] sai[d to them,] "The one who seeks [is also the one who]
reveals [. . .]."
3Matt[hew said to him, "Lord, wh]en I [hear . . .] and [when] I speak,
who is the one who [speaks, and who] the one who hears?"
4The [Lord] said, "The one who speaks is also the one who h[ears],
and the one who sees is also [the one who] reveals."

3:12
Ⓣ Th 42
6:1
//Q11:34; Mt6:22–23; Lk11:34
7:2
Cf. Q11:10, Mt7:8; Lk11:10; Th92:1, 94:1
7:4
Ⓓ DSav31:2; Ⓣ Jn16:13

---

summarize the soul's journey after death.
3:5 *not one among them:* i.e., among the archons (see 1:4).
5:3 *consort:* The Greek word *suzugos*, literally "yoke-fellow," occurs only once in the NT (Phil 4:3). In gnostic theology it often stands for the pairing of aeons (heavenly beings or realms).
7:3 The same question is found in another Nag Hammadi writing, the *Testimony of Truth* 42:3–4: "Who is the one who speaks? And who is the one who hears?"

8 M[ar]y said, "Lord, tell me, from where [do I] carry the body [when I] weep, and from where (do I carry it) when I [laugh]?"

[2]The Lord said, "[. . .] weep because of its works [. . .] remain and the mind laughs [. . .] [. . .] spirit. [3]If you do not [. . . the] darkness, you will [not] be able to see [the light]. [4]So then, I tell you [. . of the] light is the darkness. [5][And if you do not] stand in [the darkness, you will] not [be able] to see the light. [6][. . .] the lie [. . .] were brought by [. . .] [7]You will give [. . . lig]ht and [. . . b]e forever. [. . .] in the [. . .] one [. . .] forever. [8]Then [all] the powers will [. . .] you, those that are above and those [that] are below, in the place where [there will] be weeping and gnashing of teeth concerning the end of a[ll] these things."

9 Judas said, "Tell [us, L]ord, what [there was] before heaven and earth came into being."

[2]The Lord said, "There was darkness and water and a spirit upon ⟨the⟩ wa[ter.] [3]And I say to [you, . . .] what you seek [and] search for, lo[ok, it is wi]thin you, and [. . .] the power and the mys[tery . .] spirit, because from [. . .] wickedness comes [. . .] the mind and [. . .]. [4]Look, [. . .] [. . .]."

10 [. . .] said, "Lord, tell us where [the soul st]ands, and where the true m[ind] is."

[2]The Lord said, "The fire of [the] spirit came into being in [. . .] both of them. [3]Because of this the [. . .] came into being, ⟨and⟩ the true mind came into being wi[thin] them [. . .]. [4]If you se[t your so]ul on high, the[n you will be] exalted."

11 And Matthew asked him, "[. . .] took it, namely [. . .] those who [. . .]."

[2]The Lord said, "[. . .] stronger than him who [. . .] you [. . .] him to follow [yo]u and all the works [. . .] your heart. [3]For just as your hearts [. . .], [. . in this] way you shall be victorious over the powers that are [abo]ve and those that are below [. . .]. [4]I say to you, those [who have] power should deny [it and] change their ways. [5]And those who [. . .] seek and find and rejo[ice]."

8:1 Ⓣ DSav 16:4; Lk 6:21; Jn 16:20
8:3 Ⓣ Jn 12:35
8:8 Ⓣ Mt 8:12, 13:42, 50; Q 13:28, Mt 8:12, Lk 13:28; ▷Ps 112:10
9:1–4 ▷Gn 1:1
9:2 ▷Gn 1:2
9:3 Cf. Lk 17:21; Th 3:3
11:4 //Th 81:1–2; Ⓣ Mk 8:34
11:5 Cf. Q 11:10; Mt 7:8; Lk 11:10; Jn 16:24; Th 2, 92:1, 94:1; GHeb 6

8:5 The saying is reconstructed from DialSav 15:11.

8:1 *To carry the body* means to live a mortal human life.
8:5 The same topic is discussed in the Nag Hammadi *Teachings of Silvanus* 102:23–26: "Understand . . . that those who are in darkness will not be able to see anything unless they receive the light and recover (their) sight by means of it."
8:8 *concerning the end:* or "until the end" (see 1 Cor 1:8).
10:1 *The true mind* may indicate composure or "rest" (see 1:1) or the higher part of human existence.
11:3 The *powers* above and below are supernatural forces (e.g., archons) and earthly authorities.
11:5 This saying, in various forms, is widespread in early Christian literature; in addi-

12 Judas said, "Look! See that everything is [. . .] just like these signs that are over [the earth]. Because of this they came to be so."

[2]The Lord [said], "When the Fa[ther establi]shed the world, he [gathered] water from it, [and the] Word came forth from it. [3]He appeared in many [. . .], and was higher than the pa[th of the stars which surround] the whole earth. [4]They [. . .], for the water that was gather[ed . . .] was beyond them [. . .] of the water, a great fire [surr]ounding them like a wall. [5]And [. . .] time, when many things were separated from [what] was inside. [6]When the [Word] was set in place he looked at [. . .] and said to it, 'Go and [. . .] from you, so that [. . .] in want from generation to gene[ration an]d from age to age.' [7]Th[en it] cast forth from itself [spr]ings of milk and spri[ngs of] honey and oil and w[ine] and go[od] fruit and sweet taste and good roots, s[o that] it might lack nothing from generation [to] generation and from age to age.

[8]"And it is above [. .] [. . .] set, namely [. . .] its beauty [. . .] [9]And beyond [. . .] was a great light, [more] powerful [than] the one like it, for this is [the one which] rules over the aeons that are [abo]ve and that are below. [10][The light was] taken from the fire and was scattered over the [pler]oma that is above and that is [be]low. [11]On them all things depend."

[12]When Judas heard these things he bowed down and [worshi]ped, and praised the Lord.

13 [Ma]ry asked her brothers, "Where will you set down [the things] about which you ask the son of [Adam]?"

[2]The Lord [said] to her, "Sister, [no one] will be able to inquire about these things ex[cept one] who has a place to set them down in the heart. [3][. . .] to come forth [. . .] and enter [. . .] so that they might not be bound [to] this miserable world."

14 [Matt]hew said, "Lord, I wish [to see] that place of life [. . .] where there is no wickedness [but only] pure [li]ght."

12:6 *Word:* all that is certain is that this word is masculine.

12:1 ◊Gn 1:14

---

tion to the references above see, e.g., *The Book of Thomas the Contender* 140:40–141:2: "[Blessed are] the wise who [sought after the truth, and] when they found it, they rested upon it forever and were unafraid of those who wanted to disturb them"; 145:10–16: "As you pray, you will find rest, for you have left behind the suffering and the disgrace. For when you have come forth from the sufferings and passions of the body, you will receive rest from the good one, and you will reign with the king . . . ."

12:2 *from it:* The pronoun *it* refers back to *water,* or *cosmos,* or *him.*

12:3 *He appeared:* or "it appeared."

12:10 *pleroma:* the "fullness" of the heavenly realm.

12:12 *Judas:* Probably Judas (the same name as "Jude," literally "Jew") the apostle (see Luke 6:16); much less likely he is the brother of Jesus (see Mark 6:3; Matt 13:55).

13:2 *Sister:* i.e., sister in the faith (see "brothers" in 13:1).

2The Lord said, "Brother Matthew, you will not be able to see it as
l[ong as you] bear flesh."
3[Mat]thew said, "Lord, ev[en if I will not be able to] see it, let me
[know it]."
4The Lord said, "Those who have known themselves have seen [it
in] everything that is given them to do [for them]selves, and they have
come to be [. . .] it in their goodn[ess]."

15 Judas responded, "Tell me, Lord, as for the shak[ing] that
moves the earth—how does it move?"
2The Lord took a sto[ne and] held it in his hand, [saying, "What] is
this that I am holding in my hand?"
3He said, "[It is] a stone."
4He said to them, "That which supports the ear[th] is that which
supports the heaven. 5When a word comes forth from the Majesty, it
will come upon that which supports the heaven and the earth. 6For the
earth ⟨itself⟩ does not move—if it moved it would fall—but ⟨it does
not fall⟩ so that the first word might not be nullified. 7For that is the
one who established the world and came to be in it and received
⟨sweet⟩ fragrance from it. 8For [. . .] thing that does not move I [. . .]
you, all of humankind, for you are from that place: you are in the heart
of those who speak from jo[y] and truth. 9Even if it comes forth among
humankind from the body of the Father and is not received, it returns
again to its place. 10The one who knows [. . thi]ng⟨s⟩ of perfection
kno[ws] nothing. 11If you do not stand in the darkness, you will not be
able to see the light."

16 "If you do not [understand] how fire came to be, you will burn in
it, because you do not know its root. 2If you do not first understand
water, you know nothing; for what ⟨then⟩ is the use of your receiving
baptism in it? 3If you do not understand how the wind that blows came
to be, you will fly away with it. 4If you do not understand how the body
which you bear came to be, you will perish with it. 5And if you do not
know [the S]on, how will you know the [Father]? 6And you will not
know the root of all things; they are hidden from you. 7Those who will
not know the root of wickedness are not strangers to it. 8Those who will

14:4 Cf. Th 3:4
15:8 Ⓣ Th 50:1
16:4 Ⓣ DSav 8:1
16:5 Ⓣ Mt 11:27; Jn 14:7–9
16:7 Ⓣ 1 Tm 6:10

15:4 *That which:* or "The one who."
15:6 This verse affirms the truth of God's creative word ("and God said . . .") in Genesis 1.
15:9 *it comes forth:* probably a reference back to the "word" in 15:5.
the body of the Father: A curious expression, not found in other early Christian literature. The early fourth-century heretic Arius suggested that God having "body" was implied by the orthodox Nicene Creed.
16:7 *root of wickedness:* This phrase, familiar from 1 Tim 6:10, appears twice in a short treatise on hidden things in the Nag Hammadi *Gospel of Philip* 82:30–84:13, where the author states: "[Most things] in the world, as long as their [inner parts] are hidden, stand upright and live. . . . So with the tree: while its root is hidden it sprouts and grows. If its root is exposed, the tree dries up. So it is with every birth that is in the world, not only with the revealed but with the hidden. For so long

not understand how they came will not understand how they will go; and they are no strangers to this world which will [. . and] which will be humbled."

17 Then he [took] Judas and Matthew and Mary [. . .] the end of heaven [and] earth. 2[An]d when he placed his [hand] upon them, they hoped that they might [see] it. 3Judas lifted his eyes and saw a place of great height, and he saw the place of the abyss below. 4Judas said to Matthew, "Brother, who will be able to go up to this height, or down below to the abyss? For there is a great fire there, and great terror."

5At that instant a word came forth from it. 6As he stood there he saw how it came [do]wn.

7Then he said to it, "Why have you come down?"

8And the son of Adam greeted them and said to them, "A seed from a power was deficient, and went down below to the earth's abyss. 9And the Majesty remembered [it], and sent the wo[rd to] it. 10It brought it up into [his pre]sence, so that the first word might not fail."

11T[hen] hi[s dis]ciples marveled at [ever]ything that he had told them, and received them in [tr]ust. 12And they understood that there is no need to endure the sight of wickedness.

13Then he said to his disciples, "Did I not tell you that just like a visible flash of thunder and lightning, so will the good be taken up to the light?"

14Then all his disciples praised him and said, "Lord, before you appeared here, who was there to give you praise—for from you all praises come to be? 15Or who was there to bless [you]—for from you comes all blessing?"

17:11 Ⓣ DSav 29:2

---

as the root of wickedness is hidden, it is strong. But when it is recognized, it is dissolved. When it is revealed, it perishes . . . ."

16:8 Clement of Alexandria quotes the classic gnostic formula, part of which seems to be reflected here: "It is not the bath alone that makes us free, but also the knowledge of who we were and what we have become; where we were, into what we have been cast; to what we are hastening, from where we are redeemed; what is birth, what rebirth" (*Excerpts from Theodotus* 78).

17:5 *from it:* i.e., from the great height (see 17:3 and 17:6).

17:6 *he stood:* i.e., Judas (see 17:3, 4).

17:8 *the son of Adam:* This figure acts as an *angelus interpres*—a heavenly being who interprets a vision (see Rev 7:13–17). The title "son of Adam" is commonly used of Jesus in the NT gospels, but it is also used to refer to a heavenly agent of God (see Dan 7:13–14).

deficient: Gnostic theology commonly referred to a defective or sinful element in the heavenly realm that "fell" to earth.

17:10 *so that . . . fail:* or "because the first word was abrogated"; but see 15:6.

17:14–15 These verses show early Christian reflection on the 'double presence' of the Lord (in earth and on heaven); see, e.g., Melito, *Passover Homily* frag. 14: "He was seen as a lamb, but remained a shepherd; . . . treading the earth, and filling heaven"; Hippolytus, *Against Noetus* 4:11: "Who, then, was he in heaven but the fleshless Word—he who was sent for the purpose of showing that he who is on earth is in heaven too?"; and esp. *Gospel of Bartholomew* 31–32: "Bartholomew asked: 'Lord, when you lived among us, did you receive the sacrifices in paradise?' Jesus answered: 'I swear to you, I sat at the right hand of the Father and received the sacrifices in paradise.'"

[16]As they stood there, he saw two spirits bearing a single soul with them in a great flash of lightning. [17]And a word came forth from the son of Adam, saying, "Give them their garments."

[18][And] the small one became just like the great one. [19]They were [. . .] those who received them. [20][. . .] each other. [21]Then [. . .] disciples, those whom he [. . .]

18

Mary [said, " . . .] see the evil [. . .] them from the beginning [. . .] each other."

[2]The Lord said [to her], "When you see them [. . .] become great, they will [. . .]. [3]But when you see the One who is forever, that is the great vision."

[4]Then they all said to him, "Make it known to us."

[5]He said to them, "How do you wish to see it—[in] a vision that will pass or in an eternal vision?" [6]Again he said, "Strive to save the one who is able to follow [you], and seek him and speak with him, so that as you seek him everything may be in harmony with you. [7]For I say to you, truly, the living God [is] in you [. . .] in him."

19

Judas [said], "Truly I wish [. . .]."

[2]The L[ord] said to him, "[. . .] living [. . .] is [. . .] whole [. . .] of the deficiency."

[3]Judas [said], "Who is it [. . .]?"

[4]The Lord said, "[. . .] all the works which are [. . .] the remainder, it is they over which you [shall rule]."

[5]Judas said, "Look, the archons are above us; so, then, it is they who will rule over us!"

[6]The Lord said, "It is you who will rule over them. [7]But when you remove envy from you, then you will clothe yourselves with light and enter the bridal suite."

[8]Judas said, "How will our garments be brought to us?"

[9]The Lord said, "There are some who will bring ⟨them⟩ to you, and others who will receive [them], for it is they [who will give] you your garments. [10]For who [will] be able to reach that place [which is th]e reward? [11]But the garments of life were given to such people because they know the way by which they will go. [12]Indeed, for me too it is a burden to reach it."

19:6
Ⓣ 1 Cor 6:3
19:7
Ⓣ 1 Pet 2:1; Th 75

18:6 This *striving* probably includes missionary work, however understood (see DialSav 24:1–2).

19:11 Unless *such people* are examples of the *single soul* in 17:16, this statement may be proverbial: "The garments of life are given to humankind . . . ."

19:12 The Savior too must bear the burden of the journey (see 1:5) to the place of reward; the importance of this assertion is suggested by its repetition in 38:8 (and see 38:7).

20 Mary said, "Just so: 'The wickedness of each day ⟨is sufficient⟩,' and 'Laborers are worthy of their food,' and 'Disciples resemble their teachers.'" [2]She spoke this word as a woman who fully understood.

21 The disciples said to him, "What is the pleroma and what is the deficiency?"

[2]He said to them, "You are from the pleroma and you are in the place where the deficiency is. [3]And look, his light has ⟨been⟩ poured out upon me."

22 Matthew said, "Tell me, Lord, how the dead die and how the living live."

[2]The Lord said, "[You have] asked me about a saying [. . that] which eye has not seen, nor have I heard it, except from you. [3]But I say to you that when that which moves a person is drained out, that person will be called dead; [4]and when what is living leaves what is dead, ⟨it⟩ will be called alive."

23 Judas said, "Why then, in truth, do ⟨the living⟩ die and ⟨the dead⟩ live?"

[2]The Lord said, "Whatever is from the truth does not die; whatever is from woman dies."

24 Mary said, "Tell me, Lord, why have I come to this place—to gain or to lose?"

[2]The Lord said, "⟨You have come⟩ to reveal the greatness of the revealer."

[3]Mary said to him, "Lord, is there then a place that [. . .] or lacks the truth?"

[4]The Lord said, "The place where I am not."

[5]Mary said, "Lord, you are fearful and marvelous, and [. . .] those who do not know you."

25 Matthew said, "Why do we not together take ⟨our⟩ rest?"

[2]The Lord said, "When you leave behind these burdens."

[3]Matthew said, "How does the small unite with the great?"

[4]The Lord said, "When you leave behind the things that cannot follow you, then you will rest."

20:1a
//Mt6:34
20:1b
//Q10:7, Mt10:10, Lk10:7
20:1c
//Q6:40, Mt10:24, Lk6:40; Jn13.16
24:3–4
Ⓣ Th24:1
25:2
Ⓣ Mt11:28; Th37:2, 90:1–2

20:1 Three abbreviated aphorisms are given, as if the full form of each is familiar to the reader.
20:2 That Mary *fully understood* (see DialSav 26) may indicate that Mary can supply the missing (and essential) elements in the aphorisms in 20:1.
21:1 *the pleroma:* the 'fullness' of the heavenly realm.
21:3 *and*: perhaps with the sense "yet": the paradox of the disciples' condition.
22:4 *leaves:* or "sets free"; the Coptic verb can also mean: appoint, make, esteem, admit.
24:1 *this place:* i.e., earth.
25:1 *together:* literally, "at once." The translation *together* suggests the meaning: "Why

26 Mary said, "I wish to understand everything—[just how] it comes into being."
2 The Lord said, "Those who seek life—this indeed is their wealth. 3 For this world's [re]st is [false], and its gold and its silver are error."

27 His disciples said to him, "What shall we do, that our work may be perfect?"
2 The Lord [said] to them, "Be [re]ady before the whole ⟨creation⟩. 3 Congratulations to those who have found [. . .] the struggle with their eyes [. . .]. 4 They have not killed, nor have [they] been killed, but they came forth victorious."

28 Judas said, "Tell me, Lord, what is the beginning of the way."
2 He said, "Love and goodness. 3 For if one of these had been among the archons, wickedness would never have come to be."

29 Matthew said, "Lord, without wearying you have spoken about the end of the whole ⟨creation⟩."
2 The Lord said, "Everything that I have said to you you have understood and received in faith. 3 If you know them, then they are yours; if not, then they are not yours."

30 They said to him, "What is the place to which we shall go?"
2 The Lord said, "[Stand in] the place that you can reach."

31 Mary said, "Everything that endures in this way is seen."
2 The Lord said, "I have told you [that] the one who sees is the one who reveals."

32 His disciples, twelve in number, asked him, "Teacher, [. . .] freedom from ca[re . . .] teach us [. . .]."
2 The Lord said, "[. . .] everything that I have [told you], you will [. . .] you [. . .] everything."

33 Mary said, "There is but one word that I shall [sp]eak to the Lord concerning the mystery of truth, this one in which we stand and ⟨in which⟩ we appear to the worldly."

26:3 Ⓣ Jas 5:3
28:1 Ⓣ Jn 14:5
29:2 Ⓣ DSav 17:11
31:2 Ⓓ DSav 7:4

26:3 *[re]st:* This word (*a[nap]ausis*) may also be reconstructed *a[pol]ausis*, "enjoyment."

---

do we ⟨disciples⟩ not rest ⟨now⟩ together ⟨with you, the Lord⟩?" The question is not fully answered until 25:4.

27:2 *Be ready:* readiness, i.e., preparedness and eager expectation, was highly valued in early Christianity.

34 Judas said to Matthew, "We wish to understand what kind of
garments we are to be clothed with when we come forth from the
corruption of the [fle]sh."
2The Lord said, "The archons and the administrators have garments
that are given ⟨only⟩ for a while and that are impermanent. 3[But] you,
as children of truth, are not to clothe yourselves with these garments
that are impermanent. 4Rather, I say to you that you will be blessed
when you strip yourselves. 5For it is not a great thing [. . .] beyond."

35 [. . .] said [. . , " . . .] speak, I am [. . .]."
2The Lord said, "[. . .] your Father [. . .]."

36 Mary said, "[Of wha]t kind is this mustard seed? 2Is it from
heaven or from earth?"
3The Lord said, "When the Father established the world for himself,
he left many things with the Mother of All. 4Because of this he speaks
and acts."

37 Judas said, "You have told us this from the mind of truth. When
we pray, how are we to pray?"
2The Lord said, "Pray in a place where there is no woman."
3Matthew said, "He tells us, 'Pray in the place where there is no
woman,' that is, 'Destroy the works of the female'; 4not because there is
another birth but because they will cease [giving birth]."
5Mary said, "They will never be destroyed."
6The Lord said, "Who is it that knows that they will [not] dissolve
and [the works] of [the female] be [destroyed in this pl]ace [too]?"
7Judas said [to Matt]hew, "The works of the [female] will dissolve
[. . .] the archons will [. . . 8 . . .] shall we become ready for them in this
way?"

38 The Lord said, "Certainly not. They see yo[u and they] see
those who receive [yo]u. 2But look, a true word is coming forth from
the Father [to the] abyss in silence, with a flash of lightning. 3Do they

34:4 Cf.Th37
36:1 Ⓣ Mk4:30–32; Mt17:20; Q13:18–19; Mt13:31–32; Lk13:18–19; Th20
36:2 Cf.Mk11:30; Mt11:25; Lk20:4
37:1–2 Cf.Th6:1

34:2 *administrators:* another class of heavenly powers.
34:3 *not:* The Coptic word *an* (or emended to *on*) is either a negative ("not") or an adverb ("also," "too"; see 7:4; 19:12).
36:3 *Father* and *Mother:* A basic pairing of heavenly beings.
37:3–4 Clement of Alexandria (*Miscellanies* 3:63) quotes from the Gospel of the Egyptians: "The Savior himself said, 'I am come to undo the works of the female,' by the female meaning lust, and by the works meaning birth and decay"; and (*Miscellanies* 3:45): "When Salome asked, 'How long will death have power?' the Lord answered, 'So long as you women bear children'—not as if life was something bad and creation evil, but as teaching the sequence of nature."
37:4 The concept of rebirth is rejected; see John 3:6.
38:1–8 The Savior assures the disciples that they know the way they will travel, and cautions them to avoid the false way of the archons.

see it or over[power] it? 4⟨No, they do not,⟩ but you know better [the wa]y, that which neither [ang]el nor [authority . . .]. 5Rather it is the Father's and the So[n's, be]cause [the]y are both a single [. . .]. 6A[nd] you will travel the [wa]y that you have come to know. 7Even if the archons become great they will not be able to reach it. 8Bu[t lo]ok! For me too it is a burden to reach it."

39 [Mary] said to the Lord, "When the works [. . . which] dissolves a w[ork]."

2[The Lo]rd [said], "Now you know [. . .] if I dissolve [. . .] will go to his pla[ce]."

40 Judas said, "In what does the sp[irit] appear?"

2The Lord said, "In what does the sword [appear]?"

3Judas said, "In what does the light appear?"

4The Lord said, "[. . .] in it forever."

41 Judas said, "Who is it who forgives the works of whom? 2As for the works which [. . .] the world, [. . . wh]o forgives the works."

3The Lord [said], "Who is it [. . . ? 4 . . .] who have understood the works, it is for them to do the [wi]ll of the Father. 5But as for you, [st]rive to remove an[ger] and [en]vy from yourselves, and strip yourselves of your [. . .], and not to [. . . *ca. 13 lines missing or incapable of restoration*]. 6For I say to you, [. . .] you take the [. . .] you [. . .] who have inquired [. . .] this, will [. . .] they will live for[ever. 7But] I say to you, [. . .] that you not lead astray [your] spirits and your souls."

41:4
Cf. Mk 3:35; Mt 12:50; Lk 8:21; Ⓣ Jn 6:28–29; 14:10–11

41:6
Ⓣ Jn 8:32; Th 1, 2

41:7
Ⓣ Wis 17:1

The Gospel of Mary

Introduction

To those familiar with the canonical New Testament stories of Jesus, much will seem familiar in the Gospel of Mary. Some of the words and most of the characters evoke memories of Matthew, Mark, Luke, and John. In other matters, the reader may well agree with Andrew's complaint that Mary's teachings are strange. Strange to us, perhaps. But in the first and second centuries, they were firmly embedded in Christian debates about the meaning of Jesus' teaching, the roles of women, and how to attain salvation. The Gospel of Mary reproduces the contours of those debates, most especially in the contention among the disciples themselves about whether Mary Magdalene's teaching is valid and true. Moreover, the gospel's interpretation of early traditions about Jesus shows some of the fluidity and some of the passion with which such matters were engaged.

Story

As the text opens, the Savior is engaged in dialogue with his disciples, answering questions they have about the end of the world and the nature of sin. The Savior teaches them that salvation is achieved by seeking the true spiritual nature of humanity within oneself and overcoming the entrapping material nature of the body and the world. He warns them against those who would lead them astray by telling them to follow some heroic leader or a set of rules and laws. After commissioning them to go forth and preach the gospel, he departs.

At the Savior's departure, a controversy erupts. All the disciples except Mary Magdalene and Levi have failed to comprehend the Savior's teaching. Rather than seek peace within, they are distressed at their leader's absence and worried about their own deaths. When Mary tries to comfort them and give them further instruction, Andrew and Peter turn on her. Mary has recounted to them a vision she had in which the Savior described to her how to win the battle against the Powers of the world that seek to keep the soul imprisoned in the body and ignorant of its spiritual nature. But their false pride, awakened because Jesus seems to have preferred a woman to them, makes it impossible for Andrew and Peter to comprehend the truth of her teaching. When the gospel concludes, the controversy is far from resolved. Peter, Andrew, and the others have not understood the Savior's teaching. The reader must wonder what kind of good news such proud and ignorant men will announce.

A debate over who can speak for Jesus

Many early Christian writings affirm that Jesus gave superior teaching to his disciples in private or in visions and appearances after the resurrection (for example, Mark 4:10–11; 1 Cor 2:7; 3:1–3; 15:3–8). Indeed, Mary Magdalene's vision of the Savior in the Gospel of Mary probably reflects the same tradition known to John 20:16–18. Yet Andrew's objection to Mary's teaching in the Gospel of Mary raises a core problem much debated in early Christian circles: how can the validity of such teaching be determined? For Andrew, Mary's words did not seem to conform to the Savior's teaching that he knew and which he was using as a standard for the truth. But Mary's teaching concords perfectly with that given by the Savior himself in the first part of the text. The Gospel of Mary clearly affirms the truth and authority of Mary's teaching and thus implicitly affirms the validity of visionary revelations.

Many early Christian writings also portray the disciples as often misunderstanding the import of Jesus' teaching. One of his disciples even betrays him. Often Peter is singled out for rebuke, as when Jesus accuses him of being in league with Satan (Mark 8:33), or when Peter denies Jesus during the trial. It comes as no surprise, then, that some Christians might question the reliability of such disciples' teaching. The Gospel of Mary clearly doubts the value of Andrew and Peter's witness, at the same time that it identifies the true apostolic witness with Mary Magdalene and Levi. The reliability of apostolic testimony was clearly a problematic issue.

The role of women

The preeminence of Mary Magdalene gives one example of the leadership roles of women in early Christianity, roles that came to be increasingly challenged. The Coptic version of this gospel in particular opposes this challenge in a forceful way. Peter was willing to admit that the Savior loved Mary "more than all other women," but he balks at the idea that the Savior may have preferred her, a woman, to the male disciples. Yet Levi states explicitly that this is the case. The issue is not simply one of sentimentality, however. At the Savior's departure, Mary takes over his role. She comforts the distressed disciples, turns their hearts toward thoughts about the Savior's words, and gives them special teaching that will allow them to overcome the sin of the world. In every way, the text affirms that her leadership of the other disciples is based upon superior spiritual understanding. Peter, however, cannot see past the superficial sexual differentiation of the flesh to Mary's true spiritual power. He again shows his ignorance of the Savior's true teaching, while the Gospel of Mary unreservedly supports the leadership of spiritually advanced women.

Theological outlook

In the end, the Gospel of Mary communicates a vision that the world is passing away, not toward a new creation or a new world order, but toward the dissolution of an illusory chaos of suffering, death, and illegitimate domination. The Savior has come so that each soul might discover its own true spiritual nature, its "root" in the Good, and return to the place of eternal rest beyond the constraints of time, matter, and false morality.

Toward the end of the second century, many of the views found in the Gospel of Mary came under sharp attack. Condemned by later Christians as heresy, these strands of early Christian theology receded from view. The rediscovery of the Gospel of Mary restores a fragment of this heritage from early Christian history and theology.

The rediscovery of the Gospel of Mary

Unlike the canonical gospels, each of which is attested by hundreds of manuscripts, no complete copy of the Gospel of Mary exists. Indeed, for centuries, the Gospel of Mary remained completely unknown. Only three fragmentary manuscripts are known to have survived into the modern period, two third-century Greek fragments (P. Rylands 463 and P. Oxyrhynchus 3525) published in 1938 and 1983, and a longer fifth-century Coptic translation (Berolinensis Gnosticus 8052,1) published in 1955.

State of the text

The two earlier and shorter fragments are written in the original language of the Gospel of Mary, Greek. The most complete manuscript of the text, however, is the translation into Coptic (the form of native Egyptian language written during the Roman period). But even this more complete text is fragmentary. Six pages of the manuscript are missing at the beginning and four more in the middle. In all, perhaps half of the total text is still lost.

There are, moreover, some important variations between the Greek and Coptic manuscripts. The translation which follows gives preference to the Greek fragments over the Coptic because they are earlier and are written in the original language of the text, and also because the Coptic variants reflect theological tendencies that arguably belong to a later time. For example, the Greek fragments seem to presume that the leadership of Mary Magdalene *as a woman* is not under debate; only her teaching is challenged. Changes in the Coptic version, however, point toward a situation in which women's leadership *as such* is being challenged and requires defense. The changes in the text may reflect the historical exclusion of women from their earlier leadership roles in Christian communities.

Date and place of composition

Nothing is known about the author or provenance of the original text, although both Egypt and Syria have been suggested. Dating is also highly tentative, but the Gospel of Mary may arguably have been written sometime in the late first or early second centuries.

The Gospel of Mary

1 *(Six manuscript pages are missing.)*

The nature of matter

The nature of sin and the Good

2 [1]"... ***Will matter*** then be utterly destroyed or not?"

[2]The Savior replied, "Every nature, every modeled form, every creature, exists in and with each other. [3]They will dissolve again into their own proper root. [4]For the nature of matter is dissolved into what belongs to its nature. [5]Anyone with two ears capable of hearing should listen!"

3 [1]***Then Peter said*** to him, "You have been expounding every topic to us; tell us one further thing. [2]What is the sin of the world?"

[3]The Savior replied, "There is no such thing as sin; [4]rather, you yourselves are what produces sin when you act according to the nature of adultery, which is called 'sin.' [5]For this reason, the Good came among you approaching what belongs to every nature. [6]It will set it within its root."

[7]Then he continued. He said, "This is why you get sick and die, [8]for [you love] what de[c]ei[ve]s you. [9]Anyone with a mind should use it to think!

2:5
//Mk 4:23 par;
Ⓓ Mary 3:14
3:2
Ⓣ Jn 1:29

2:1 Whether matter is pre-existent (and therefore eternal) or created (and therefore subject to destruction) was an issue debated among philosophers.
2:1–5 While everything material is interconnected, in the end all things will dissolve back into their constituent natures. *Anyone with two ears* should realize that the material world is temporary and therefore has no ultimate spiritual value. Compare *Gospel of Philip* 53:14–23: "Light and darkness, life and death, right and left, are brothers of one another. It is not possible to separate them from each other. For this reason, neither are the good good, nor the evil evil, nor is life life, nor death death. This is why each one will dissolve into its original source. But those who are exalted above the world will not be dissolved, for they are eternal." Or compare the description of the end of the world in *Origin of the World* 127:3–5: "And the deficiency will be pulled by its root down into the darkness. And the light will go back up to its root."
3:3–4 *Sin* is not a matter of wrong acts, but rather has the *nature of adultery*. It means joining things that do not belong together, specifically the spiritual nature of the Good with material nature.
3:5–6 Like the Savior, the Good has come to separate what is improperly joined by placing the spiritual nature of humanity within its proper spiritual root and separating it from attachment to the body and the material world.
3:7–8 Confusing the natures of matter and the Good is fatal. A person gets sick and dies from loving the mortal, material nature since their own bodies deceive them.
3:9 To *think* is to understand one's spiritual nature and live accordingly, and so overcome one's ignorant love of mortal nature.

The commission

Mary comforts the other disciples

3:12 Cf. Lk 24:38; Jn 14:27
3:14 //Mk 4:23 par; (D) Mary 2:5
4:1 //Jn 20:19, 21, 26
4:2 Cf. Jn 14:27
4:3 //Mk 13:5; Mt 24:4; Lk 21:8
4:4 //Mk 13:21; Mt 24:23; Lk 17:21, 23; Th 113:3
4:5 Cf. Lk 17:21; Th 3:3, 113:4
4:7 //Q 11:10; Mt 7:8; Lk 11:10; Th 2:1, 92:1, 94:1; GHeb 6b
4:8 (T) Mk 13:10, 16:15; Mt 4:23, 9:35, 24:14
4:9–10 (T) Rom 7:4–6, 8
5:1 (T) SJas 6:31–32
5:2 (T) Mt 16:28
5:8 (T) Th 114

10“[Ma]tter gav[e bi]rth to a passion which has no ⟨true⟩ image
because it derives from what is contrary to nature. 11Then a disturbing
confusion occurred in the whole body. 12This is why I told you, ‘Be
content of heart.’ 13And do not conform ⟨to the body⟩, but form yourselves in the presence of that other image of nature. 14Anyone with two
ears capable of hearing should listen!”

4 1***When the Blessed One*** had said this, he greeted them all. “Peace
be with you!” he said. 2“Acquire my peace within yourselves!

3“Be on your guard so that no one deceives you by 4saying, ‘Look
over here!’ or ‘Look over there!’ 5For the seed of true humanity exists
within you. 6Follow it! 7Those who search for it will find it.

8“Go then, preach the good news of the domain. 9Do not lay down
any rule beyond what I ordained for you, 10nor promulgate law like the
lawgiver, or else it will dominate you.”

11After he said these things, he left them.

5 1***But they were*** distressed and wept greatly. 2“How are we going to
go out to the rest of the world to preach the good news about the
domain of the seed of true humanity?” they said. 3“If they didn’t spare
him, how will they spare us?”

4Then Mary stood up. She greeted them all and addressed her
brothers: 5“Do not weep and be distressed nor let your hearts be
irresolute. 6For his grace will be with you all and will shelter you.
7Rather we should praise his greatness, 8for he has joined us together
and made us true human beings.”

9When Mary said these things, she turned their minds [to]ward the
Good, 10and they began to [as]k about the wor[d]s of the Savi[or].

5:8 Coptic: “he has prepared us.”

3:10–11 Everything which is true and good is an Image of the divine reality above. *Matter has no Image* means that it does not have a heavenly origin and is contrary to the true nature of spiritual Reality. *Matter* is the formless, chaotic “stuff,” devoid of all qualities such as life and mind, out of which all things have been formed. Matter is thus the cause of passion, suffering, and confusion of the whole body. The body is a false image of the human self, one that leads people away from the truth of their own spiritual natures by keeping them absorbed with thinking falsely that the body is their true self.

3:12–13 True contentment comes from conforming not to the demands of the body, but to the spiritual Image of the true heavenly nature, the Good.

4:3–7 The disciples must search within themselves, to find the *seed of true humanity* that is within each person. They must guard against those who try to lead them astray by requiring that a person conform to what is outside, a leader who is *over here* or *over there*.

4:5 *seed of true humanity:* This term is translated elsewhere in SV as “son of Adam.” It is rendered differently here because it has a different connotation in the Gospel of Mary: it refers to the archetypal Image of humanity within each person.

4:9–10 The false view of the Savior’s teaching, against which he warns them, sees it as a set of rules and laws. These laws are intended to dominate the soul by preventing it from focussing on its own inner truth and spiritual freedom.

5:3 *If they didn’t spare him:* a reference to the death of Jesus.

Peter asks Mary to teach

6 [1]***Peter said to Mary,*** "Sister, we know that the Savior loved you
more than any other woman. [2]Tell us the words of the Savior that you
know, but which we haven't heard."
[3]Mary responded, "I will rep[ort to you as much as] I remember that
you don't know." [4]And she began to speak these words to them.

Mary's teaching on vision and mind

7 [1]***She said,*** "I saw the Lord in a vision [2]and I said to him, 'Lord, I
saw you today in a vision.'
[3]"He said to me, 'Congratulations to you for not wavering at seeing
me. [4]For where the mind is, there is the treasure.'
[5]"I said to him, 'Lord, how does a person who sees a vision see it—
[with] the soul [or] with the spirit?'
[6]"The Savior answered, 'The ⟨visionary⟩ does not see with the soul
or with the spirit, but with the mind which exists between these two—
that is [what] sees the vision and that is w[hat . . .]'

On the ascent of the soul

8 *(Four manuscript pages are missing.)*

9 [1]"'. . . ***it.***'
[2]"And Desire said, 'I did not see you go down, yet now I see you go
up. [3]So why do you lie since you belong to me?'
[4]"The soul answered, 'I saw you. You did not see me nor did you
know me. [5]You ⟨mis⟩took the garment ⟨I wore⟩ for my ⟨true⟩ self.
[6]And you did not recognize me.'
[7]"After it had said these things, ⟨the soul⟩ left rejoicing greatly.

6:4 //Jn 20:18
7:1–2 Cf. Jn 20:14–18
7:4 //Q12:34; Mt 6:21; Lk 12:34

6:3 Coptic: "I will inform you about what is hidden from you."

6:1–4 John 20:14–18 also preserves a tradition that Mary was the first disciple to see the resurrected Jesus, and that she subsequently reported his words to the disciples.
7:3 The term *wavering* carries important connotations in ancient thought, where it is contrasted with stability. Mary's stability illustrates her conformity to the spiritual state of God who is eternal and unchanging. It is one more indication of her spiritual superiority.
7:4 Compare Clement of Alexandria: "For where a person's mind is, his treasure is there too" (*Who is the Rich Man that shall be saved?* 17:1).
7:6 *Soul, spirit*, and *mind* are the three components of human consciousness. The *soul* is directed toward what is lower, the *spirit* toward what is higher. The *mind*, mediating between the two, allows the soul in the world to perceive a vision of the higher spiritual Reality.
8 Four pages are missing from the Coptic manuscript of the Gospel of Mary at this point. There are no parallel Greek fragments so we can only speculate about the contents.
9:1 The manuscript continues in the middle of Mary's account of the ascent of the soul out of its bondage to the material realm, represented symbolically by four *Powers*. These Powers probably represent the four elements of the material world: earth, water, fire, and air. The soul has just overcome the first Power, whose name probably was Darkness, and is now moving on to the second Power, *Desire*.
9:2–3 Desire did not see the soul descend from the heavens above, so it assumes that the soul belongs to the world below and is falsely trying to escape.
9:4–7 The soul unmasks the blindness of Desire and shows its own superior knowledge. The Power did not see it (9:2), but it sees the Power. To *see* is a metaphor for understanding the true nature of a thing. The

8“Again, it came to the third Power, which is called ‘Ignorance.’ 9[It]
examined the soul closely, saying, ‘Where are you going? 10You are
bound by fornication. 11Indeed you are bound! 12Do not pass judgment!’

13“And the soul said, ‘Why do you judge me, since I have not passed
judgment? 14I am bound, but I have not bound. 15They did not recognize me, but I have recognized that the universe is to be dissolved, both
the things of earth and those of heaven.’

16“When the soul had overcome the third Power, it went upward
and it saw the fourth Power. 17It had seven forms. 18The first form is
Darkness; 19the second, Desire; 20the third, Ignorance; 21the fourth,
Zeal for Death; 22the fifth, the Domain of the Flesh; 23the sixth, the
Foolish Wisdom of the Flesh, 24the seventh is the Wisdom of the
Wrathful Person. 25These are the seven Powers of Wrath.

26“They interrogated the soul, ‘Where are you coming from,
human-killer, and where are you going, space-conqueror?’

27“The soul replied, ‘What binds me has been slain, and what sur-
rounds me has been destroyed, and my desire has been brought to an
end, and my ignorance has died. 28In a world, I was set loose from a
world and in a type, from a type which is above, and ⟨from⟩ the chain
of forgetfulness that exists in time. 29From now on, for the rest of the

9:12 //Q6:37; Mt7:1; Lk6:37
9:23 Ⓣ 1 Cor3:18–19; 2 Cor1:12
9:24 Ⓣ Rom4:15

Power was able to perceive only the material, bodily husk which the soul wore like a *garment*, obscuring its own spiritual nature from view.

The text exploits the double meaning of the word *see* to ridicule the ignorant Power. It sees but does not understand. The soul both sees and understands the Power's true nature as well as its own. The joke is on the sinister but weak Power; the soul moves on in glee.

9:8–12 Again the soul's insight into its own true identity allows it the discernment to overcome the illegitimate domination of the third Power, *Ignorance.* Ignorance challenges the soul's ascent. It judges the soul, pointing out its *fornication* (adulterous union with the flesh). Because of this sin, in the Power's view, the soul has no power of discernment: *Do not pass judgment!*

9:13–15 The soul rejects the Power's judgment, knowing it to be ignorant. The soul proclaims the injustice committed against it (that it has been *judged* and *bound* to the material world) and it proclaims its own innocence (that it has not *passed judgment* or *bound* another). The soul recognizes that the material universe, both the earth and the planetary heavens along with its Powers, will come to an end. Again, the conversation of the soul shows considerable wit in pointing out that the Power itself has acknowledged that the soul's knowledge is true: sin *is* due to the domination of the flesh. Without the flesh, there is no sin, judgment, or condemnation; this insight frees the soul.

9:16–25 The seven names of the fourth Power, *Wrath,* indicate that the world below is opposed to the world above. The upper world is light, peace, knowledge, love, and life; the lower world is ruled by darkness, desire, ignorance, and death (vv. 18–21). The lower domain of the flesh is opposed to the heavenly domain of the seed of true humanity (vv. 22–23). The foolish wisdom of the flesh and wrath below is opposed to the true wisdom above (v. 24).

9:26 Again the Powers challenge the right of the soul to pass. *Human-killer* refers to the soul having cast off the flesh. *Space-conqueror* refers to the spheres of the Powers that it has overcome.

9:27 *What binds me:* the material elements and the body.

9:28–29 The soul contrasts the world from which it was freed with that to which it goes. It distinguishes the deceitful image (*type*) below from the true Image of Reality above, and mortality (the chain of time) from immortality (*rest in silence*).

course of the [due] measure of the time of the age, I will rest i[n] silence.'"

The disciples argue about Mary's teaching

[30]When Mary said these things, she fell silent, [31]since it was up to this point that the Savior had spoken to her.

10 [1]***Andrew sai[d,*** "B]rothers, what is your opinion of what was just said? [2]I for one don't believe that the S[a]vior said these things, be[cause] these opinions seem to be so different from h[is th]ought."

[3]After reflecting on these ma[tt]ers, [Peter said], "Has the Sa[vior] spoken secretly to a wo[m]an and [not] openly so that [we] would all hear? [4][Surely] he did [not wish to indicate] that [she] is more worthy than we are?"

[5]Then Mary wept and said to Peter, "Peter, my brother, what are you imagining about this? [6]Do you think that I've made all this up secretly by myself or that I am telling lies about the Savior?"

[7]Levi said to Peter, "Peter, you have a constant inclination to anger and you are always ready to give way to it. [8]And even now you are doing exactly that by questioning the woman as if you're her adversary. [9]If the Savior considered her to be worthy, who are you to disregard her? [10]For he knew her completely ⟨and⟩ loved her devotedly.

10:1–2 Coptic: "Then Andrew answered, addressing the brothers, 'Say what you will about the truth of the things she has said, but I do not believe that the Savior said these things. For indeed these teachings are strange ideas!'"
10:3–4 Coptic: "Peter answered, bringing up similar concerns. He questioned them about the Savior, 'Did he, then, speak with a woman in private without our knowing about it? Are we to turn around and listen to her? Did he choose her over us?'" **10:7** Coptic: "Peter, you have always been a wrathful person." **10:8** Coptic: "Now I see you contending against the woman like the Adversaries." **10:10** Coptic: "Assuredly the Savior's knowledge of her is completely reliable. Because of this he loved her more than ⟨he loved⟩ us."

10:2 Cf. Lk 24:10–11
10:3 Cf. Jn 4:27
10:5 Cf. Jn 20:11

9:30 Mary's *silence* symbolizes the perfect rest of the soul set free.
10:7–8 In the Coptic version, Levi calls Peter a *wrathful person* and then accuses him of acting like one of the Adversaries (Powers) by opposing Mary. *Wrathful person* is also the name of the seventh form of the Powers of Wrath (9:24). The Coptic version clearly aligns Peter with the Powers that try to entrap the soul, much as Jesus in the Gospel of Mark calls Peter "Satan" (Mark 8:33).
10:9 The Greek term translated here as *considered* also can mean "to guide." Compare Thom 114, where the second meaning is used in a similar context: "Simon Peter said to them, 'Let Mary leave us, for females are not worthy of life.' Jesus said, 'Look, I will *guide* her to make her male, so that she too may become a living spirit resembling you males. For every female who makes herself male will enter the domain of heaven.'" That Jesus *guides* Mary (Thom 114) implies that he *considers* her to be worthy (Mary 10:9). In both texts, her worthiness is based on her having achieved a supreme spiritual state, metaphorically expressed in Thom 114 as "being male" or in the Gospel of Mary as "truly human" (5:8).
10:9–10 Compare *Gospel of Philip* 63:34–64:5: "And the companion of the S[avior . . .] Mary Magdalene [. . . loved] her more than [all] the disciples [and used to] kiss her [often] on her [. . .]. The rest of [the disciples . . .]. They said to him, 'Why do you love her more than all of us?' The Savior answered them, 'Why do I not love you like her?'"

[11]"Instead, we should be ashamed and, once we clothe ourselves with perfect humanity, we should do what we were commanded. [12]We should announce the good news as the Savior ordered, [13]and not be laying down any rules or making laws."

[14]After he said these things, Levi left ⟨and⟩ and began to announce the good news.

10:11 The Coptic version adds: "and acquire it (perfect humanity) for ourselves as he commanded us." **10:13** The Coptic version adds: "that differ from what the Savior said." **10:14** Coptic: "And they began to go forth [to] teach and to preach."

10:11
Ⓣ Gal 3:27; Th 21:1–4

10:11 The passage may have a baptismal reference. Compare *Gospel of Philip* 75:21–24: "The living water is a body. It is necessary that we put on the living human being. For this reason, when people are about to go down into the water, they unclothe themselves, so that they might put on ⟨the living human being⟩."

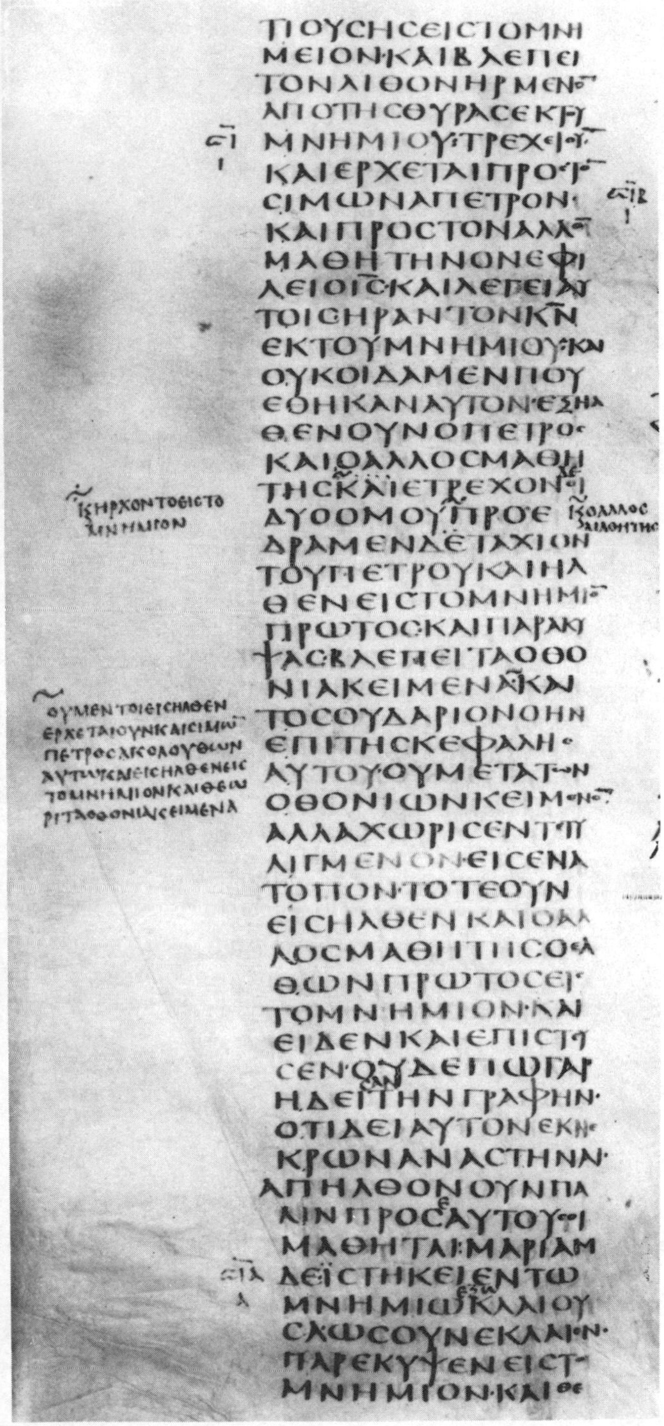

Codex Sinaiticus was discovered at St. Catherine's monastery in the Sinai peninsula in 1844. At left is the left column of New Testament folio 60 containing John 20:1–11. The Greek text is written all in capital letters without word breaks or punctuation, and contains numerous marginal corrections. See page 368 (over) for an English representation of the passage. *Photograph courtesy of the British Library. Used by permission.*

&THEYMAKETHEIR
WAYTOTHETOMB

BUTHEDIDNTGOINTHEN
SIMONPETERCOMESALONG
BEHINDHIMANDWENTINHE
TOOSEESTHESTRIPSOF
BURIALCLOTHTHERE

An English representation of column one of New Testament folio 60 of Codex Sinaiticus containing John 20:1–11. Like the Greek (see photograph on page 367), the English text is written here all in capital letters, without word breaks or punctuation. In the margin are corrections by the original scribe or by one of three later correctors. *English text courtesy of Daryl D. Schmidt, Texas Christian University.*

COMESTOTHETOMBANDSE
ESTHESTONEHASBEENMO
VEDAWAYSOSHERUNSAND
COMESTOSIMONPETERAND
THEOTHERDISCIPLETHEONE
THATJESUSLOVEDMOSTAND
TELLSTHEMTHEYVETAKEN
THEMASTERFROMTHETOMB
ANDWEDONTKNOWWHERETH
EYVEPUTHIMSOPETERAND
THEOTHERDISCPLEWENT
OUTANDTHETWOOFTHEM
WERERUNNINGALONGTOG
ETHERHERANFASTER &THEOTHER
THANPETERANDWASTHE DISCIPLE
FIRSTTOREACHTHETOMB
STOOPINGDOWNHECOULD
SEETHESTRIPSOFBURIAL
CLOTHLYINGTHEREANDAL
SOTHECLOTHTHEYHADUS
EDTOCOVERHISHEADLYING
NOTWITHTHESTRIPSOFBUR
IALCLOTHBUTROLLEDUPBY
ITSELFTHENTHEOTHERDIS
CIPLEWHOHADBEENTHEFIR
STTOREACHTHETOMBCAME
INHESAWALLTHISANDHEBE
LIEVEDBUTSINCENEITHER
OFTHEMYETUNDERSTOOD
THEPROPHECYTHATHEWAS
DESTINEDTORISEFROMTHE
DEADTHESEDISCIPLESWENT
BACKHOMEMARIAMHOWEVER
STOODCRYINGOUTSIDEAND
INHERTEARSSHESTOOPED
TOLOOKINTOTHETOMBAND

Introduction

Story and structure

The Infancy Gospel of Thomas belongs to the popular genre of legends about the youthful years of Jesus. Such legends developed in the early centuries of the Christian movement and were constantly elaborated and expanded from late antiquity through the middle ages for purposes of edification and instruction.

The Infancy Gospel of Thomas attempts to fill the gap between Jesus' birth and his visit to Jerusalem recorded in Luke 2:41–52. It consists of a series of loosely connected episodes recording events at various intervals of Jesus' youth. The text notes certain stages in Jesus' development, his actions at age five (2:1), six (11:1), eight (12:4), and twelve (19:1). Apart from these temporal markers there are no other overt indications of structure.

The initial episodes portray a petulant Jesus at play, a sometimes hot-tempered lad ready to use his remarkable abilities in destructive or self-serving ways, and a prodigy at school, impatient with the limitations of his merely human teachers. As time progresses, he becomes a child devoted to his parents and siblings, finally eager to use his powers to help and to heal those in need.

Origins of the gospel

The Infancy Gospel of Thomas survives in various forms in a number of languages, including Syriac, Greek, Latin, and Slavonic. The earliest extant is a Syriac manuscript dating to the sixth century. The variations among these versions make it difficult to reconstruct the earliest form of the work. The earliest clear attestation of an episode from the gospel is in the work of the church father Irenaeus, bishop of Lyons in the late second century. In his treatise *Against Heresies*, written around 185 C.E., he mentions "spurious and apocryphal writings" that include a "tale which tells that when the Lord was a child learning the alphabet, the teacher, as is customary, said to him 'Say Alpha,' and he replied, 'Alpha.' When the teacher next told him to say Beta, the Lord answered, 'Tell me first what Alpha is, and then I shall tell you what Beta is.'" This is obviously an allusion to the episode found in chaps. 6–8 and 14–15.

Patristic testimonies continue in the late second early third century with Hippolytus (*Refutation of all Heresies* 5.7) and Origen (*Homily I in Luke*), who mention the existence of a Gospel of Thomas of uncertain contents. Some of these testimonies may refer not to a narrative of Jesus' childhood but to the Gospel of Thomas, the collection of sayings of Jesus found in Nag Hammadi in Egypt in 1945.

The evidence provided by Irenaeus indicates that a version of Infancy Thomas was in circulation in the second century. Nothing certain, however, can be said about the place or circumstances of its composition.

Aims and themes

The orthodox Christian writers of the late second century associated this infancy gospel with circles that they considered heretical, particularly with groups of gnostic Christians. Scattered evidence confirms that such Christians did know the work. This evidence takes the form of allusions to stories reminiscent of Infancy Thomas in certain gnostic works such as the Gospel of Truth (19:19–20). While Gnostics may have been able to interpret stories in Infancy Thomas for their own ends, it is unlikely that they originally composed the work with the aim of propagating their theological positions.

Some scholars have argued that certain features of the work, especially its christology, are heterodox. All versions of the work obviously consider Jesus to be endowed from his earliest years with remarkable power, and some explicitly affirm that he is the incarnation of a divine being. These christological beliefs were hardly confined to Gnostics. They were present from the earliest generations of the Christian movement and were widespread in the second century. Hints have also been found of a "docetic" christology, tendencies, that is, to suggest that the humanity of Jesus is merely a matter of "appearance." Yet these elements too have been overemphasized. Although endowed with supernatural power, Jesus is, in many episodes, all too human.

There may be a certain naiveté in the portrait of Jesus in the work, but its understanding of Christ is what one would expect to find in the popular traditions of the Christian movement in the late first or second century. This gospel affords us a view of how Jesus was regarded in the unsophisticated religious imaginations of ordinary early Christians, rather than in the more abstract theological affirmations of Christian intellectuals.

The translation

The present translation is based on a new critical Greek text prepared especially for the *Scholars Version.*

The Infancy Gospel of Thomas

Boyhood deeds of our Lord Jesus Christ. *Prologue*

Jesus and the sparrows

The curse on Annas' son

1 ***I, Thomas*** the Israelite, am reporting to you, all my non-Jewish
brothers and sisters, to make known the extraordinary childhood deeds
of our Lord Jesus Christ—what he did after his birth in my region.
This is how it all started:

2 ***When this boy, Jesus,*** was five years old, he was playing at the ford
of a rushing stream. [2]He was collecting the flowing water into ponds
and made the water instantly pure. He did this with a single command.
[3]He then made soft clay and shaped it into twelve sparrows. He did this
on the sabbath day, and many other boys were playing with him.

[4]But when a Jew saw what Jesus was doing while playing on the
sabbath day, he immediately went off and told Joseph, Jesus' father:
"See here, your boy is at the ford and has taken mud and fashioned
twelve birds with it, and so has violated the sabbath."

[5]So Joseph went there, and as soon as he spotted him he shouted,
"Why are you doing what's not permitted on the sabbath?"

[6]But Jesus simply clapped his hands and shouted to the sparrows:
"Be off, fly away, and remember me, you who are now alive!" And the
sparrows took off and flew away noisily.

[7]The Jews watched with amazement, then left the scene to report to
their leaders what they had seen Jesus doing.

3 ***The son of Annas the scholar,*** standing there with Jesus, took a 3:2–3 Cf. Mk11:12–14, Mt21:18–19
willow branch and drained the water Jesus had collected. [2]Jesus, how-

---

Prologue 1 In the synoptic gospels Thomas is regularly linked with Matthew (Mark 3:18; Matt 10:3; Luke 6:15). In John (11:6; 14:5; 20:24–28; 21:2) Thomas is known as Didymus, "the twin." This is presumably the same apostle as the Didymus Judas Thomas who figures in the Gospel of Thomas and the Judas Thomas, the Twin of Jesus, who is the hero of the *Acts of Thomas*.

2:2 For the power of Jesus' command over the elements, see Mark 4:41; Matt 8:27; Luke 8:25.

2:3, 6 This miracle is also attested in the Quran: "Jesus will say, 'I bring you a sign from your Lord. From clay I will make for you a likeness of a bird. I shall breathe into it and, by God's leave, it shall become a living bird'" (3:49, also 5:113, Dawood translation).

2:4 Profaning the sabbath, usually by an act of healing, frequently occasions controversy in the gospel tradition. See Mark 2:23–28; 3:1–6; Matt 12:1–12; Luke 6:1–11; 13:10–17; 14:2–6; John 5.

3:1 Annas the scribe also appears in the Infancy Gospel of James 15. In the canonical gospels, Annas is a high priest. See Luke 3:2; John 18:13, 24; Acts 4:6.

Curse on a clumsy child

ever, saw what had happened and became angry, saying to him, "Damn you, you irreverent fool! What harm did the ponds of water do to you? From this moment you, too, will dry up like a tree, and you'll never produce leaves or root or bear fruit."

[3]In an instant the boy had completely withered away. Then Jesus departed and left for the house of Joseph. [4]The parents of the boy who had withered away picked him up and were carrying him out, sad because he was so young. And they came to Joseph and accused him: "It's your fault—your boy did all this."

4 ***Later he was going*** through the village again when a boy ran by and bumped him on the shoulder. Jesus got angry and said to him, "You won't continue your journey." [2]And all of a sudden he fell down and died.

[3]Some people saw what had happened and said, "Where has this boy come from? Everything he says happens instantly!"

[4]The parents of the dead boy came to Joseph and blamed him, saying, "Because you have such a boy, you can't live with us in the village, or else teach him to bless and not curse. He's killing our children!"

5 So Joseph summoned his child and admonished him in private, saying, "Why are you doing all this? These people are suffering and so they hate and harass us." [2]Jesus said, "I know that the words I spoke are not my words. Still, I'll keep quiet for your sake. But those people must take their punishment." There and then his accusers became blind.

[3]Those who saw this became very fearful and at a loss. All they could say was, "Every word he says, whether good or bad, has became a deed—a miracle, even!" [4]When Joseph saw that Jesus had done such a thing, he got angry and grabbed his ear and pulled very hard. [5]The boy became infuriated with him and replied, "It's one thing for you to seek and not find; it's quite another for you to act this unwisely. [6]Don't you know that I don't really belong to you? Don't make me upset."

4:3
◊Ps 33:9; 148:5
5:5
Cf. Q 11:9–10; Mt 7:7–8; Lk 11:9–10; Th 38:2, 92, 94; Jn 7:33–34

3:1 Some versions of this gospel place the curse on Annas' son (chap. 3) before the scene of Jesus and the sparrows (chap. 2).

3:2–3 The withering of the child may recall the episode of the withered fig tree. See Mark 11:12–14; Matt 21:18–19.

4:1–2 The punishment meted out to a clumsy child might have been remotely inspired by the punishment of the malicious children who abused a prophet. See 2 Kgs 2:23–35.

5:5–6 The response by Jesus to Joseph's rebuke is obscure. The command to seek and find (or receive) is common in gospel sources. See Matt 7:7; Luke 11:9–13; John 16:24; Gospel of Thomas 1, 92, 94. The remark to Joseph that he may seek but not find may parallel the critical remarks about Jesus' earthly kindred at Mark 3:31–35, Matt 12:47–50. Joseph may seek to discipline Jesus but not be able to find the means to do so.

Jesus and the teacher

6 ***A teacher*** by the name of Zacchaeus was listening to everything Jesus was saying to Joseph, and was astonished, saying to himself, "He is just a child, and saying this!" [2]And so he summoned Joseph and said to him, "You have a bright child, and he has a good mind. Hand him over to me so he can learn his letters. I'll teach him everything he needs to know so as not to be unruly."

[3]Joseph replied, "No one is able to rule this child except God alone. Don't consider him to be a small cross, brother."

[4]When Jesus heard Joseph saying this he laughed and said to Zacchaeus, "Believe me, teacher, what my father told you is true. [5]I am the Lord of these people and I'm present with you and have been born among you and am with you. [6]I know where you've come from and how many years you'll live. I swear to you, teacher, I existed when you were born. If you wish to be a perfect teacher, listen to me and I'll teach you a wisdom that no one else knows except for me and the one who sent me to you. [7]It's you who happen to be my student, and I know how old you are and how long you have to live. [8]When you see the cross that my father mentioned, then you'll believe that everything I've told you is true."

[9]The Jews who were standing by and heard Jesus marveled and said, "How strange and paradoxical! This child is barely five years old and yet he says such things. In fact, we've never heard anyone say the kind of thing this child does."

[10]Jesus said to them in reply, "Are you really so amazed? Rather, consider what I've said to you. The truth is that I also know when you were born, and your parents, and I announce this paradox to you: when the world was created, I existed along with the one who sent me to you."

[11]The Jews, once they heard that the child was speaking like this, became angry but were unable to say anything in reply. [12]But the child skipped forward and said to them, "I've made fun of you because I know that your tiny minds marvel at trifles."

[13]When, therefore, they thought that they were being comforted by the child's exhortation, the teacher said to Joseph, "Bring him to the classroom and I'll teach him the alphabet."

[14]Joseph took him by the hand and led him to the classroom. [15]The teacher wrote the alphabet for him and began the instruction by repeating the letter alpha many times. But the child clammed up and did not answer him for a long time. [16]No wonder, then, that the teacher got angry and struck him on the head. The child took the blow calmly and replied to him, "I'm teaching you rather than being taught by you: I already know the letters you're teaching me, and your condemnation is great. To you these letters are like a bronze pitcher or a clashing

6:1–7:11 Cf. Jn 3:1–14
6:6 Cf. Jn 8:58; Q 10:21–22, Mt 11:25–27, Lk 10:21–22
6:8 Cf. Jn 8:28
6:10 Cf. Jn 1:1–2
6:16 Cf. 1 Cor 13:1

6:1 Zacchaeus is also the name of the tax collector in Luke 19.

cymbal, which can't produce glory or wisdom because it's all just noise. [17]Nor does anyone understand the extent of my wisdom." [18]When he got over being angry he recited the letters from alpha to omega very quickly.

[19]Then he looked at the teacher and told him, "Since you don't know the real nature of the letter alpha, how are you going to teach the letter beta? [20]You imposter, if you know, teach me first the letter alpha and then I'll trust you with the letter beta." [21]He began to quiz the teacher about the first letter, but he was unable to say anything.

[22]Then while many were listening, he said to Zacchaeus, "Listen, teacher, and observe the arrangement of the first letter: [23]How it has two straight lines or strokes proceeding to a point in the middle, gathered together, elevated, dancing, three-cornered, two-cornered, not antagonistic, of the same family, providing the alpha has lines of equal measure."

7 After Zacchaeus the teacher had heard the child expressing such intricate allegories regarding the first letter, he despaired of defending his teaching. [2]He spoke to those who were present: "Poor me, I'm utterly bewildered, wretch that I am. I've heaped shame on myself because I took on this child. [3]So take him away, I beg you, brother Joseph. I can't endure the severity of his look or his lucid speech. [4]This child is no ordinary mortal; he can even tame fire! Perhaps he was born before the creation of the world. [5]What sort of womb bore him, what sort of mother nourished him?—I don't know. [6]Poor me, friend, I've lost my mind. [7]I've deceived myself, I who am wholly wretched. I strove to get a student, and I've been found to have a teacher. [8]Friends, I think of the shame, because, although I'm an old man, I've been defeated by a mere child. [9]And so I can only despair and die on account of this child; right now I can't look him in the face. [10]When everybody says that I've been defeated by a small child, what can I say? And what can I report about the lines of the first letter which he told me about? I just don't know, friends. For I don't know its beginning or its end. [11]Therefore, I ask you, brother Joseph, take him back to your house. What great thing he is—god or angel or whatever else I might call him—I don't know."

6:19
Cf. Q6:42, Mt7:5, Lk6:42
7:5
Cf. InJas3:2

6:18 *Alpha* and *omega* are the names of the first and last letters of the Greek alphabet. Other versions of the gospel use the names of the letters of the native alphabets.

6:22–23 The point of the story in all of its forms is that Jesus finds a deep symbolic significance in the shape of the first letter of the alphabet. The Greek version suggests that the letter A is symbolic of the Trinity.

6:23 *How it has two straight lines:* These are the only words of this most difficult and undoubtedly corrupt sentence that make sense. The rest of the translation is guesswork or simply a translation of words, if they are known at all. Some words are not even listed in Greek dictionaries. No wonder Zacchaeus despairs of taking on Jesus as a student.

7:4 The remark that Jesus can even subdue fire may allude to a lost episode. Zacchaeus unwittingly makes a christological confession when he speculates that Jesus may have been begotten before the creation of the world. See John 1:1–3; Heb 1:2–3.

A fallen child raised

Jesus heals a cut foot

8 While the Jews were advising Zacchaeus, the child laughed loudly and said, "Now let the infertile bear fruit and the blind see and the deaf in the understanding of their heart hear: 2I've come from above so that I might save those who are below and summon them to higher things, just as the one who sent me to you commanded me."

3When the child stopped speaking, all those who had fallen under the curse were instantly saved. 4And from then on no one dared to anger him for fear of being cursed and maimed for life.

9 ***A few days later*** Jesus was playing on the roof of a house when one of the children playing with him fell off the roof and died. When the other children saw what had happened, they fled, leaving Jesus standing all by himself.

2The parents of the dead child came and accused Jesus: "You troublemaker you, you're the one who threw him down."

3Jesus responded, "I didn't throw him down—he threw himself down. He just wasn't being careful and leaped down from the roof and died."

4Then Jesus himself leaped down from the roof and stood by the body of the child and shouted in a loud voice: "Zeno!"—that was his name—"Get up and tell me: Did I push you?"

5He got up immediately and said, "No, Lord, you didn't push me, you raised me up."

6Those who saw this were astonished, and the child's parents praised God for the miracle that had happened and worshiped Jesus.

10 ***A few days later*** a young man was splitting wood in the neighborhood when his axe slipped and cut off the bottom of his foot. He was dying from the loss of blood.

2The crown rushed there in an uproar, and the boy Jesus ran up, too. He forced his way through the crowd and grabbed hold of the young man's wounded foot. It was instantly healed.

3He said to the youth, "Get up now, split your wood, and remember me."

9:3 Jesus' denial that he pushed the boy off the roof is not found in this Greek version, but has been supplied from the Syriac and Slavonic versions.

8:2
Cf. Jn 16:28, 17:2

8:1–3 The combination of cursing and saving is awkward. As the text stands it suggests that Jesus would ascend into heaven where he could curse his enemies, but then call them upward. When he ceases speaking, those who had been afflicted by his potent words are healed. Yet the crowds remain fearful that they might be cursed. This sequence may reflect the fact that people who transmitted the story were uncomfortable with the notion that Jesus would curse and maim.

8:1 For the blind to receive sight is characteristic of the activity of Jesus. See Mark 10:46; Matt 11:5; 21:14; Luke 7:21–22; John 9.

9:4 The name Zeno, well attested in Greek culture, is not found in the canonical gospels.

10:2–3 The episode perhaps echoes the saying preserved in the Gospel of Thomas 77: "Split a piece of wood: I am there."

Jesus fetches water

A miraculous harvest

Miraculous woodworking

New instructors

[4]The crowd saw what had happened and worshiped the child, saying, "Truly the spirit of God dwells in this child."

11 ***When he was six years old,*** his mother sent him to draw water and bring it back to the house. [2]But he lost his grip on the pitcher in the jostling of the crowd, and it fell and broke. [3]So Jesus spread out the cloak he was wearing and filled it with water and carried it back to his mother.

[4]His mother, once she saw the miracle that had occurred, kissed him; but she kept to herself the mysteries that she had seen him do.

12 ***Again, during the sowing season,*** the child went out with his father to sow their field with grain. While his father was sowing, the child Jesus sowed one measure of grain. [2]When he had harvested and threshed it, it yielded one hundred measures. [3]Then he summoned all the poor in the village to the threshing floor and gave them grain. Joseph carried back what was left of the grain. [4]Jesus was eight years old when he did this miracle.

13 ***Now Jesus' father*** was a carpenter, making ploughs and yokes at that time. He received an order from a rich man to make a bed for him. [2]When one board of what is called the crossbeam turned out shorter than the other, and Joseph didn't know what to do, the child Jesus said to his father, "Put the two boards down and line them up at one end."

[3]Joseph did as the child told him. Jesus stood at the other end and grabbed hold of the shorter board, and, by stretching it, made it the same length as the other.

[4]His father Joseph looked on and marveled, and he hugged and kissed the child, saying, "How fortunate I am that God has given this child to me."

14 ***When Joseph saw*** the child's aptitude, and his great intelligence for his age, he again resolved that Jesus should not remain illiterate. So he took him and handed him over to another teacher. [2]The teacher

---

13:4 One Greek ms ends here with the comment: "When they had returned to town, Joseph told Mary. When she had heard and seen the wondrous deeds of her son, she rejoiced, glorifying him along with the Father and the Holy Spirit now and forever and ever. Amen."

11:4
Ⓣ Lk 2:19, 51; InTh 19:11

11:1–4 A single story about Jesus at age six. Jesus' mother plays a relatively minor role in this gospel, appearing only here and at 14:5; 19:1–2.

12:1–17:4 A series of stories about Jesus at age eight (12:4; cf. 18:1).

12:2 The yield is perhaps inspired by Mark 4:8; Matt 13:8; Luke 8:8.

13:1 For Joseph's trade, see Mark 6:3; Matt 13:55. In *Acts of Thomas* 3, Jesus' "twin," Judas Thomas, indicates that he knows how to make such implements as plows and yokes.

14:1 The stories in this and the following chapter are doublets of the account in chaps. 6–7.

said to Joseph, "First I'll teach him Greek, then Hebrew." This teacher, of course, knew of the child's previous experience ⟨with a teacher⟩ and was afraid of him. Still, he wrote out the alphabet and instructed him for quite a while, though Jesus was unresponsive.

[3]Then Jesus spoke: "If you're really a teacher, and if you know the letters well, tell me the meaning of the letter alpha, and I'll tell you the meaning of beta."

[4]The teacher became exasperated and hit him on the head. Jesus got angry and cursed him, and the teacher immediately lost consciousness and fell facedown on the ground.

[5]The child returned to Joseph's house. But Joseph was upset and gave this instruction to his mother: "Don't let him go outside, because those who annoy him end up dead."

15 After some time another teacher, a close friend of Joseph, said to him, "Send the child to my schoolroom. Perhaps with some flattery I can teach him his letters."

[2]Joseph replied, "If you can muster the courage, brother, take him with you." And so he took him along with much fear and trepidation, but the child was happy to go.

[3]Jesus strode boldly into the schoolroom and found a book lying on the desk. He took the book but did not read the letters in it. Rather, he opened his mouth and spoke by ⟨the power of⟩ the holy spirit and taught the law to those standing there.

[4]A large crowd gathered and stood listening to him, and they marveled at the maturity of his teaching and his readiness of speech—a mere child able to say such things.

[5]When Joseph heard about this he feared the worst and ran to the schoolroom, imagining that this teacher was having trouble with Jesus.

[6]But the teacher said to Joseph, "Brother, please know that I accepted this child as a student, but already he's full of grace and wisdom. So I'm asking you, brother, to take him back home."

[7]When the child heard this, he immediately smiled at him and said, "Because you have spoken and testified rightly, that other teacher who was struck down will be healed." And right away he was. Joseph took his child and went home.

Jesus and the viper

16 ***Joseph sent his son James*** to tie up some wood and carry it back to the house, and the child Jesus followed. While James was gathering the firewood, a viper bit his hand. [2]And as he lay sprawled out on the ground, dying, Jesus came and blew on the bite. Immediately the pain stopped, the animal burst apart, and James got better on the spot.

15:3–4
Ⓓ InTh 19:4–5
Ⓣ Lk 2:46–47
16:1–2
Cf. Acts 28:1–6

16:2 For another split serpent, see *Acts of Thomas* 33.

Raising a dead infant

Raising a dead laborer

Jesus in the temple

17 ***After this incident*** an infant in Joseph's neighborhood became
sick and died, and his mother grieved terribly. Jesus heard the loud
wailing and the uproar that was going on and quickly ran there.
2When he found the child dead, he touched its chest and said, "I say
to you, infant, don't die but live, and be with your mother."
3And immediately the infant looked up and laughed. Jesus then said
to the woman, "Take it, give it your breast, and remember me."
4The crowd of onlookers marveled at this: "Truly this child was a
god or a heavenly messenger of God—whatever he says instantly
happens." But Jesus left and went on playing with the other children.

18 ***A year later,*** while a building was under construction, a man
fell from the top of it and died. There was quite a commotion, so Jesus
got up and went there. 2When he saw the man lying dead, he took his
hand and said, "I say to you, sir, get up and go back to work." And he
immediately got up and worshiped him.
3The crowd saw this and marveled: "This child's from heaven—he
must be, because he has saved many souls from death, and he can go on
saving all his life."

19 ***When he was twelve years old*** his parents went to Jerusalem, as
usual, for the Passover festival, along with their fellow travelers. 2After
Passover they began the journey home. But while on their way, the
child Jesus went back up to Jerusalem. His parents, of course, assumed
that he was in the traveling party. 3After they had traveled one day, they
began to look for him among their relatives. When they did not find
him, they were worried and returned again to the city to search for him.
4After three days they found him in the temple area, sitting among
the teachers, listening to the law and asking them questions. 5All eyes
were on him, and everyone was astounded that he, a mere child, could
interrogate the elders and teachers of the people and explain the main
points of the law and the parables of the prophets.
6His mother Mary came up and said to him, "Child, why have you
done this to us? Don't you see, we've been worried sick looking for
you."
7"Why are you looking for me?" Jesus said to them. "Don't you know
that I have to be in my father's house?"
8Then the scholars and the Pharisees said, "Are you the mother of
this child?"

17:1–4
Cf. Mk 5:21–24, 35–43; Mt 9:18–19, 23–26; Lk 8:40–42, 49–56
19:1–11
// Lk 2:41–52
19:4–5
Ⓓ InTh 15:3–4
19:5
Ⓣ Mk 1:22, Mt 7:28–29

17:3 The concern to feed the resuscitated child resembles Mark 5:43.
18:2 For the command to arise, see Mark 5:41 and Luke 7:14.
19:1 *twelve years old:* Twelve years of age meant one thing for a girl, quite another for a boy. The former was considered ready for marriage and motherhood, the latter was still regarded as a child for two more years. Jesus at twelve engaging the teachers in the temple area further underscores how precocious he was. He is referred to as *a mere child* in v. 5.

9She said, "I am."

10And they said to her, "You more than any woman are to be
congratulated, for God has blessed the fruit of your womb! For we've
never seen nor heard such glory and such virtue and wisdom."

11Jesus got up and went with his mother, and was obedient to his
parents. His mother took careful note of all that had happened. 12And
Jesus continued to excel in learning and gain respect.

13To him be glory for ever and ever. Amen.

19:10 //Lk1:42; cf. InJas11:1, Lk11:27, Th79:1
19:11 //Lk2:40; Ⓣ InTh11:4
19:12 Ⓣ Lk2:19, 51

Purity and virginity

Why was Mary allegedly chosen by God to be the mother of Jesus? The Infancy Gospel of James was written to provide an answer. Mary remained pure throughout her childhood, both at home and in the temple. She maintained her virginity after becoming a woman, and even after giving birth to Jesus.

The emphasis on purity and virginity clearly develops in part out of the characterization of Mary in the canonical gospels. There it is her obedience that qualifies her to bear Jesus (so Luke 1:30), and Joseph marries her even if he does not have relations with her until after Jesus is born (Matt 1.24–25).

The increased focus on purity and virginity derives from one of the cultural trends of the period. In both philosophical and more popular literary sources there is an increasing value placed on the cardinal virtue of *sophrosyne*, self-control of the tongue, the belly, and, to use the euphemism of the day, the things below the belly. It was clearly control of what is below the belly that was most admired.

Mary is very like the heroines of the romance, the most popular literature of that day. The romance featured characters who preserved their chastity against all odds. But even in the romances the heroines remain chaste only outside of marriage. In this respect Mary exceeds them and remains always a virgin, and thus perfectly pure.

The Infancy Gospel of James

Introduction

Contents

The earliest Christian traditions—say, the credo of 1 Cor 15:3–5 or the hymn of Phil 2:6–11—focus attention on the end of Jesus' life, on his death and resurrection. By the end of the first century, Christians show interest in the beginning of Jesus' life, in the circumstances of his birth, as is evident from the birth stories that open the gospels of Matthew and Luke (Matthew 1–2; Luke 1–2). This interest continues into the second and later centuries and in fact prompts a new genre of Christian writing, the infancy gospel, or narratives that focus exclusively on the birth or on the childhood of Jesus.

One such gospel is the Infancy Gospel of James. This gospel ends with the birth of Jesus and its immediate aftermath in Herod's murder of the infants, but the ending is not the culmination or goal of the narrative. For the birth story comprises at most one-third of the narrative. The real narrative interest is in Mary; it is her story—the circumstances of her birth, the years of her infancy and childhood, the announcement of her conception—that is central to the narrative as a whole.

The story of the Infancy Gospel of James falls into three roughly equal parts. The first eight chapters narrate the miraculous circumstances of Mary's birth and the unusual circumstances of her childhood. The story opens with the plight of the wealthy, righteous, but childless couple, Joachim and Anna. Their childlessness is particularly grievous, but their laments and prayers to God are eventually heard, so that Anna becomes pregnant. Their gratitude is so great that they promise their offspring to the Lord, and so at age three, Mary is sent to serve the Lord in the temple in Jerusalem.

The second eight chapters begin with the crisis posed by Mary's becoming a woman and thus her imminent pollution of the temple. The priests resolve the crisis by turning her over to a divinely chosen widower, the carpenter Joseph, who agrees to be her guardian, but refuses to marry her. While he is out of town plying his trade, Mary is visited by an angel and told of her favor with the Lord. By the time Joseph returns she is visibly pregnant. A priest suspects that Joseph is responsible and accuses them both. The two are put to a test, but pass and are publicly exonerated.

The last eight chapters begin with Augustus' edict of enrollment that requires Joseph to register in Bethlehem. Here the story has reached the point where it begins to follow the accounts in the opening chapters of Matthew and

Luke. But the infancy gospel, while recalling the canonical stories, does not hesitate to go its separate way. Thus Joseph and Mary go to Bethlehem (see Luke 2:1), but are now accompanied by his grown sons from his previous marriage (17:5). Mary gives birth to Jesus (see Luke 2:7) but is visited, though not helped, by local midwives (19:1–20:12), who testify to the miraculous nature of the birth—Mary, though she has given birth, is still a virgin (19:18). The astrologers trick Herod, who responds by murdering the infants (see Matt 2:16), but now Jesus is saved by being hidden in a feeding trough (22:4) and even the infant John is threatened by Herod but saved by his father Zechariah's martyrdom and by Elizabeth's hiding in the hills with him (22:5–23:8).

The infancy gospel ends with the author, James, claiming that he has written his account shortly after the death of Herod (25:1).

Authorship and dating

The claim that a certain James wrote this infancy gospel and did so shortly after the death of Herod in 4 B.C.E. would, if true, imply that the narrative was composed by the James known in the New Testament as "James the Lord's brother" (Gal 1:19; see Mark 6:3), but here as only one of the sons of Joseph from a previous marriage. But, whatever the relation, James is thereby an eyewitness of the birth of Jesus and of Mary's life, at least from the time she became Joseph's ward. Thus the claim to authorship by James functions to establish the credibility and truth of the account.

But is the claim true? The answer is no. The claim falls on the following argument. The gospels of Matthew and Luke both narrate the birth of Jesus, but they do so quite differently. One difference is that only Matthew's account includes the visit of the astrologers and the subsequent murder of the infants by Herod (see Matt 2:1–12, 16–18), and only Luke's account includes the parallel story of the birth of John the Baptist to Zechariah and Elizabeth (see Luke 1:5–25, 39–80). An observant reader of both gospels, however, might ask: How did John, born only months apart from Jesus, escape Herod's soldiers?

The Infancy Gospel of James answered this question by having Zechariah choose death rather than tell of John's whereabouts and by having Elizabeth flee to the hills with John. The author thereby shows that he knew of the canonical accounts, and since Matthew and Luke were written toward the end of the first century, well after James's death in 62 C.E., the author of the infancy gospel could not have been James.

Just who wrote the infancy gospel can no longer be determined, but whoever did write it wrote after Matthew and Luke and probably around the middle of the second century, when evidence of this document begins to show up in other Christian writings.

Origins and thematic focus

The origins of the Infancy Gospel of James probably lie in a trajectory that begins with the Gospel of Mark, written about 70 C.E. This gospel opens with the simple claim that Jesus is the son of God (Mark 1:1). This claim may then have prompted Matthew and Luke, writing independently of each other a decade or two later, to explain how it was that Jesus came to be the literal son of God (Matthew 1–2; Luke 1–2).

In many ways, the Infancy Gospel of James is dependent on the traditions preserved in the Matthean and Lukan accounts, as evidenced by the numerous quotations, phrases, and echoes in the infancy gospel from these accounts, not to mention other portions of the New Testament and the Septuagint (see the cross references). In fact, the infancy gospel expands on the canonical traditions, developing their logic, for example, by solving the problem of John's fate during the murder of the infants.

And yet, in other ways, the Infancy Gospel of James is not simply a development of the New Testament birth stories. For, despite all the bits and pieces taken from these stories and other Christian literature, the infancy gospel also shows an independence from this literature and a unity of its own. This independence is evident in the various narrative deviations from the stories in Matthew and Luke. But more important are the changes in characterization. Thus Joseph, who in the Matthean and Lukan accounts was engaged to Mary and later married to her (Matt 1:18, 24–25; Luke 2:5), is now turned into an old man, a widower with grown sons who is embarrassed to accept Mary even as a ward (9:11) and becomes at most only her protector (13:1; 14:1; 16:7). Similarly, Mary, the central character, is no longer a virgin in the ordinary sense of a young woman of marriageable age, but a virgin of extraordinary purity and unending duration.

Indeed, Mary's purity is so emphasized that it becomes thematic and thus answers the fundamental question which guides the narrative: why Mary, of all the virgins in Israel, was chosen to be the mother of the son of God. The answer: no one could have been any purer. Thus Anna transforms Mary's bedroom into a sanctuary where she receives no impure food and is amused by the undefiled daughters of the Hebrews (6:5). When she turns three years of age, these young women escort her to the temple in Jerusalem where she spends the next nine years in absolute purity and is even fed by the hand of an angel (7:4–8:2). When, at age twelve, she is made the ward of Joseph, she spends her time spinning thread for the temple with the other virgins from Israel (10:1–12:1). When she is later suspected of impurity, she passes a test and has her innocence proclaimed by the high priest (15:1–16:7). Finally, when she gives birth to Jesus, two midwives certify that she remains a virgin (19:18–20:11). In short, it is through her purity that Mary fulfills the blessing which the priests made when she was only one year old: that she might be blessed with a blessing that could not be surpassed (6:9).

The Infancy Gospel of James

1 ***According to the records*** of the twelve tribes of Israel, there once was a very rich man named Joachim. [2]He always doubled the gifts he offered to the Lord, [3]and would say to himself, "One gift, representing my prosperity, will be for all the people; the other, offered for forgiveness, will be my sin-offering to the Lord God."

Childless Joachim

Childless Anna

[4]Now the great day of the Lord was approaching, and the people of Israel were offering their gifts. [5]And Reubel confronted Joachim and said, "You're not allowed to offer your gifts first because you haven't produced an Israelite child."

[6]And Joachim became very upset and went to the book of the twelve tribes of the people, saying to himself, "I'm going to check the book of the twelve tribes of Israel to see whether I'm the only one in Israel who hasn't produced a child." [7]And he searched ⟨the records⟩ and found that all the righteous people in Israel did indeed have children. [8]And he remembered the patriarch Abraham because in his last days the Lord God had given a son, Isaac.

[9]And so he continued to be very upset and did not see his wife but banished himself to the wilderness and pitched his tent there. [10]And Joachim fasted 'forty days and forty nights.' [11]He would say to himself, "I will not go back for food or drink until the Lord my God visits me. Prayer will be my food and drink."

2 ***Now his wife Anna*** was mourning and lamenting on two counts: "I lament my widowhood and I lament my childlessness."

[2]The great day of the Lord approached, however, [3]and Juthine her slave said to her, "How long are you going to humble yourself? Look, the great day of the Lord has arrived, and you're not supposed to mourn. [4]Rather, take this headband which the mistress of the workshop gave to me, but which I'm not allowed to wear because I'm your slave and because it bears a royal insignia."

[5]And Anna said, "Get away from me! I won't take it. The Lord God has greatly shamed me. Maybe a trickster has given you this, and you've come to make me share in your sin."

1:1
◊ Sus 4
1:8
◊ Gn 21:1–7
1:10
Ⓣ Q 4:2, Mt 4:2, Lk 4:2; ◊ Ex 24:18, 1 Kgs 19:8
2:1
Ⓢ 1 Sm 1:2
2:5
◊ Is 64:12

1:4 In the OT and NT *the great day of the Lord* usually refers to the day of judgment, but here (and in 2:2) a festival seems more likely. The Feast of Sukkoth has been suggested, but the vagueness of the reference precludes any more precise determination.

2:4 The words *headband* and *mistress of the workshop* are obscure, and no solution has been achieved.

2:5 The word translated *trickster* is obscure, but may refer to a clever young man with whom Juthine has had an affair.

Anna laments

Anna's vision

[6]And Juthine the slave replied, "Should I curse you just because you haven't paid any attention to me? The Lord God has made your womb sterile so you won't bear any children for Israel."

[7]Anna, too, became very upset. She took off her mourning clothes, washed her face, and put on her wedding dress. [8]Then, in the middle of the afternoon, she went down to her garden to take a walk. She spied a laurel tree and sat down under it. [9]After resting, she prayed to the Lord: "O God of my ancestors, bless me and hear my prayer, just as you blessed our mother Sarah and gave her a son, Isaac."

3 ***And Anna looked up*** toward the sky and saw a nest of sparrows in the laurel tree. [2]And immediately Anna began to lament, saying to herself: "Poor me! Who gave birth to me? What sort of womb bore me? [3]For I was born under a curse in the eyes of the people of Israel. And I've been reviled and mocked and banished from the temple of the Lord my God.

[4]"Poor me! What am I like? I am not like the birds of the sky, because even the birds of the sky reproduce in your presence, O Lord.

[5]"Poor me! What am I like? I am not like the domestic animals, because even the domestic animals bear young in your presence, O Lord.

[6]"Poor me! What am I like? I am not like the wild animals of the earth, because even the animals of the earth reproduce in your presence, O Lord.

[7]"Poor me! What am I like? I am not like these waters, because even these waters are productive in your presence, O Lord.

[8]"Poor me! What am I like? I am not like this earth, because even the earth produces its crops in season and blesses you, O Lord."

4 ***Suddenly a messenger*** of the Lord appeared to her and said: "Anna, Anna, the Lord God has heard your prayer. You will conceive and give birth, and your child will be talked about all over the world."

[2]And Anna said, "As the Lord God lives, whether I give birth to a boy or a girl, I'll offer it as a gift to the Lord my God, and it will serve him its whole life."

[3]And right then two messengers reported to her: "Look, your husband Joachim is coming with his flocks." [4]You see, a messenger of the Lord had come down to Joachim and said, "Joachim, Joachim, the

2:6 ◊ 1 Sm 1:6
2:9 ◊ Gn 17:16, 21:1–3
4:1 Ⓢ Lk 1:26–31, Jgs 13:2–7
4:2 ◊ 1 Sm 1:11, 28
4:4 Ⓢ Lk 1:8–13

2:6 Childlessness was understood, not as having a natural cause, but as a sign of divine punishment (see Gen 16:2; 20:18; and especially 1 Sam 1:5–6).
2:7 Putting on her *wedding dress* suggests that Anna is anticipating the outcome of her plea to God for a blessing similar to that which God gave Sarah, that is, for the blessing of offspring.

Birth of Mary

Lord God has heard your prayer. Get down from there. Look, your
wife Anna is pregnant."
5And Joachim went down right away and summoned his shepherds
with these instructions: "Bring me ten lambs without spot or blemish,
and the ten lambs will be for the Lord God. 6Also, bring me twelve
tender calves, and the twelve calves will be for the priests and the
council of elders. 7Also, one hundred goats, and the one hundred goats
will be for the whole people."
8And so Joachim came with his flocks, while Anna stood at the gate.
9Then she spotted Joachim approaching with his flocks and rushed out
and threw her arms around his neck: "Now I know that the Lord God
has blessed me greatly. This widow is no longer a widow, and I, once
childless, am now pregnant!"
10And Joachim rested the first day at home.

5 ***But on the next day,*** as he was presenting his gifts, he thought to
himself, "If the Lord God has really been merciful to me, the polished
disc on the priest's headband will make it clear to me." 2And so
Joachim was presenting his gifts and paying attention to the priest's
headband until he went up to the altar of the Lord. And he saw no sin
in it. 3And Joachim said, "Now I know that the Lord God has been
merciful to me and has forgiven me all my sins." 4And he came down
from the temple of the Lord acquitted and went back home.
5And so her pregnancy came to term, and in the ninth month Anna
gave birth. 6And she said to the midwife, "Is it a boy or a girl?"
7And her midwife said, "A girl."
8And Anna said, "I have been greatly honored this day." Then the
midwife put the child to bed.
9When, however, the prescribed days were completed, Anna
cleansed herself of the flow of blood. 10And she offered her breast to the
infant and gave her the name Mary.

4:5–7 ◊Jgs 13:15–20
5:1 ◊Ex 28:36–38
5:4 Ⓢ Lk 18:14
5:8 Ⓢ Lk 1:46
5:9 ◊Lv 12:1–8

4:9 The mss differ over whether Anna *is pregnant* or will be pregnant. The future tense would be more likely if the word *rested* in the next sentence were a euphemism for sexual intercourse, but since this word is used of Joseph in much the same circumstances (see 15:2) and no such euphemism is intended there, it is probably better to prefer the literal meaning and so the present tense (*is pregnant*). Thus, Anna's conceiving a child becomes as much a miracle as later Mary's will be.

5:2 A metal *disc* was part of the high priest's garb and was attached to his headband (Exod 28:36), but its use here, to reveal sin, is otherwise unattested. The disc may have been a mirror, and mirrors were used to obtain revelations.

5:9 Childbirth rendered a woman ritually unclean, unable to touch anything holy or enter the temple. For the regulations on how and when a woman *cleansed herself* after childbirth, see Lev 12:1–8.

Mary's first birthday

Mary at the temple

6 ***Day by day*** the infant grew stronger. [2]When she was six months old, her mother put her on the ground to see if she could stand. She walked seven steps and went to her mother's arms. [3]Then her mother picked her up and said, "As the Lord my God lives, you will never walk on this ground again until I take you into the temple of the Lord."

[4]And so she turned her bedroom into a sanctuary and did not permit anything profane or unclean to pass the child's lips. [5]She sent for the undefiled daughters of the Hebrews, and they kept her amused.

[6]Now the child had her first birthday, and Joachim gave a great banquet and invited the high priests, priests, scholars, council of elders, and all the people of Israel. [7]Joachim presented the child to the priests, and they blessed her: "God of our fathers, bless this child and give her a name which will be on the lips of future generations forever."

[8]And everyone said, "So be it. Amen."

[9]He presented her to the high priests, and they blessed her: "Most high God, look on this child and bless her with the ultimate blessing, one which cannot be surpassed."

[10]Her mother then took her up to the sanctuary—the bedroom—and gave her breast to the child. [11]And Anna composed a song for the Lord God: "I will sing a sacred song to the Lord my God because he has visited me and taken away the disgrace attributed to me by my enemies. [12]The Lord my God has given me the fruit of his righteousness, single yet manifold before him. [13]Who will announce to the sons of Reubel that Anna has a child at her breast? 'Listen, listen, you twelve tribes of Israel: Anna has a child at her breast!'"

[14]Anna made her rest in the bedroom—the sanctuary—and then went out and began serving her guests. [15]When the banquet was over, they left in good spirits and praised the God of Israel.

7 ***Many months passed,*** but when the child reached two years of age, Joachim said, "Let's take her up to the temple of the Lord, so that we can keep the promise we made, or else the Lord will be angry with us and our gift will be unacceptable."

[2]And Anna said, "Let's wait until she is three, so she won't miss her father or mother."

[3]And Joachim agreed: "Let's wait."

[4]When the child turned three years of age, Joachim said, "Let's send for the undefiled Hebrew daughters. [5]Let them each take a lamp and light it, so the child won't turn back and have her heart captivated by things outside the Lord's temple." [6]And this is what they did until the time they ascended to the Lord's temple.

6:1
Ⓢ Lk 2:40
6:6
◊Gn 21:8
6:11
Ⓢ Lk 1:25; ◊Gn 21:1, 30:23
6:13
◊Gn 21:7
7:1
◊1 Sm 1:22; Ⓘ InJas 4:2

6:12 The meaning of *single yet manifold before him* is obscure.

Mary at twelve

Joseph accepts Mary

7The priest welcomed her, kissed her, and blessed her: "The Lord God has exalted your name among all generations. 8In you the Lord will disclose his redemption to the people of Israel during the last days."

9And he sat her down on the third step of the altar, and the Lord showered favor on her. 10And she danced, and the whole house of Israel loved her.

8 ***Her parents left*** for home marveling and praising and glorifying the Lord God because the child did not look back at them. 2And Mary lived in the temple of the Lord. She was fed there like a dove, receiving her food from the hand of a heavenly messenger.

3When she turned twelve, however, there was a meeting of the priests. "Look," they said, "Mary has turned twelve in the temple of the Lord. 4What should we do with her so she won't pollute the sanctuary of the Lord our God?" 5And they said to the high priest, "You stand at the altar of the Lord. Enter and pray about her, and we'll do whatever the Lord God discloses to you."

6And so the high priest took the vestment with the twelve bells, entered the Holy of Holies, and began to pray about her. 7And suddenly a messenger of the Lord appeared: "Zechariah, Zechariah, go out and assemble the widowers of the people and have them each bring a staff. 8She will become the wife of the one to whom the Lord God shows a sign." 9And so heralds covered the surrounding territory of Judea. The trumpet of the Lord sounded and all the widowers came running.

9 ***And Joseph, too,*** threw down his carpenter's axe and left for the meeting. 2When they had all gathered, they went to the high priest with their staffs. 3After the high priest had collected everyone's staff, he entered the temple and began to pray. 4When he had finished his prayer, he took the staffs and went out and began to give them back to each man. 5But there was no sign on any of them. Joseph got the last staff. 6Suddenly a dove came out of this staff and perched on Joseph's head. 7"Joseph, Joseph," the high priest said, "you've been chosen by lot to take the virgin of the Lord into your care and protection."

8But Joseph objected: "I already have sons and I'm an old man; she's only a young woman. I'm afraid that I'll become the butt of jokes among the people of Israel."

7:7
Ⓢ Lk 1:48
7:8
◊ 1 Sm 18:16
8:1
Ⓢ Lk 2:39–40
8:7
Ⓢ Lk 1:11;
◊ Nm 17:1–11

8:4 Mary would *pollute the sanctuary* when she began to menstruate. The Law considered a woman ritually unclean during her period. See Lev 15:19–24.

9:7 This is the first occurrence of the word *virgin,* which plays a prominent role in Mary's characterization for the remainder of the story.

9:8 That Joseph has *sons* and is an *old man* marks a significant change in the portrayal of

Virgins & temple veil

Mary's vision

[9]And the high priest responded, "Joseph, fear the Lord your God and remember what God did to Dathan, Abiron, and Kore: the earth was split open and they were all swallowed up because of their objection. [10]So now, Joseph, you ought to take heed so that the same thing won't happen to your family."

[11]And so out of fear Joseph took her into his care and protection. [12]He said to her, "Mary, I've gotten you from the temple of the Lord, but now I'm leaving you at home. I'm going away to build houses, but I'll come back to you. The Lord will protect you."

10

Meanwhile, there was a council of the priests, who agreed: "Let's make a veil for the temple of the Lord."

[2]And the high priest said, "Summon the true virgins from the tribe of David." [3]And so the temple assistants left and searched everywhere and found seven. [4]And the high priest then remembered the girl Mary, that she, too, was from the tribe of David and was pure in God's eyes. [5]And so the temple assistants went out and got her.

[6]And they took the maidens into the temple of the Lord. [7]And the high priest said, "Cast lots for me to decide who'll spin which threads for the veil: the gold, the white, the linen, the silk, the violet, the scarlet, and the true purple."

[8]And the true purple and scarlet threads fell to Mary. And she took them and returned home. [9]Now it was at this time that Zechariah became mute, and Samuel took his place until Zechariah regained his speech. [10]Meanwhile, Mary had taken up the scarlet thread and was spinning it.

11

And she took her water jar and went out to fill it with water. [2]Suddenly there was a voice saying to her, "Greetings, favored one! The Lord is with you. Blessed are you among women." [3]Mary began looking around, both right and left, to see where the voice was coming from. [4]She became terrified and went home. After putting the water jar down and taking up the purple thread, she sat down on her chair and began to spin.

[5]A heavenly messenger suddenly stood before her: "Don't be afraid, Mary. You see, you've found favor in the sight of the Lord of all. You will conceive by means of his word."

[6]But as she listened, Mary was doubtful and said, "If I actually

9:9 ◊Nm 16:25–33
9:11 Ⓢ Mt 1:24
10:7 ◊Ex 26:31, 36, 35:25; 2 Chr 3:14
10:9 Ⓢ Lk 1:20–22, 64
11:2 //InThom 19:4; Ⓢ Lk 1:28
11:5 Ⓢ Lk 1:30–33

Joseph from that in the canonical accounts.

9:11 That *Joseph took her* recalls Matt 1:24, but with this significant difference: there it is as his wife, here merely as his ward.

10:2 Strictly speaking, there was no *tribe of David.* According to Luke, Mary is related to Elizabeth, who belongs to the tribe of Aaron (Luke 1:5, 36).

10:9 The *time that Zechariah became mute* reflects an attempt on the part of the author to place his narrative in the context of the canonical account (see Luke 1:20–22, 64).

Mary & Elizabeth

Joseph accuses Mary

conceive by the Lord, the living God, will I also give birth the way
women usually do?"
7And the messenger of the Lord replied, "No, Mary, because the
power of God will overshadow you. Therefore, the child to be born will
be called holy, son of the Most High. 8And you will name him Jesus—
the name means 'he will save his people from their sins.'"
9And Mary said, "Here I am, the Lord's slave before him. I pray that
all you've told me comes true."

12 ***And she finished*** ⟨spinning⟩ the purple and the scarlet thread
and took her work up to the high priest. 2The high priest accepted
them and praised her and said, "Mary, the Lord God has extolled your
name and so you will be blessed by all the generations of the earth."
3Mary rejoiced and left to visit her relative Elizabeth. 4She knocked
at the door. Elizabeth heard her, tossed aside the scarlet thread, ran to
the door, and opened it for her. 5And she blessed her and said, "Who
am I that the mother of my Lord should visit me? You see, the baby
inside me has jumped for joy and blessed you."
6But Mary forgot the mysteries which the heavenly messenger
Gabriel had spoken, and she looked up to the sky and said, "Who am I
that every generation on earth will congratulate me?"
7She spent three months with Elizabeth. 8Day by day her womb kept
swelling. And so Mary became frightened, returned home, and hid
from the people of Israel. 9She was just sixteen years old when these
mysterious things happened to her.

13 ***She was in*** her sixth month when one day Joseph came home
from his building projects, entered his house, and found her pregnant.
2He struck himself in the face, threw himself to the ground on
sackcloth, and began to cry bitterly: "What sort of face should I present
to the Lord God? 3What prayer can I say on her behalf since I received
her as a virgin from the temple of the Lord God and didn't protect her?
4Who has set this trap for me? Who has done this evil deed in my
house? Who has lured this virgin away from me and violated her? 5The
story of Adam has been repeated in my case, hasn't it? For just as Adam
was praying when the serpent came and found Eve alone, deceived her,
and corrupted her, so the same thing has happened to me."
6So Joseph got up from the sackcloth and summoned Mary and said
to her, "God has taken a special interest in you—how could you have
done this? 7Have you forgotten the Lord your God? Why have you
brought shame on yourself, you who were raised in the Holy of Holies
and fed by a heavenly messenger?"

11:6 Ⓢ Lk 1:34
11:8 Ⓢ Lk 1:35, Mt 1:21
11:9 Ⓢ Lk 1:38
12:2 Ⓢ Lk 1:42, 48
12:3–6 Ⓢ Lk 1:39–44
12:6 Ⓢ Lk 1:48
12:7 Ⓢ Lk 1:56
12:8 Ⓢ Lk 1:24
13:5 ▷ Gn 3:1–13
13:6 ▷ Gn 3:13
13:7 Ⓘ InJas 8:2

12:3 The author assumes that readers will know who *Elizabeth* is. She is the wife of Zechariah and mother of the future John the Baptist (see 22:5; Luke 1:5).

Joseph's vision

Mary & Joseph accused

[8]But she began to cry bitter tears: "I'm innocent. I haven't had sex with any man."

[9]And Joseph said to her, "Then where did the child you're carrying come from?"

[10]And she replied, "As the Lord my God lives, I don't know where it came from."

14 ***And Joseph became*** very frightened and no longer spoke with her as he pondered what he was going to do with her. [2]And Joseph said to himself, "If I try to cover up her sin, I'll end up going against the law of the Lord. [3]And if I disclose her condition to the people of Israel, I'm afraid that the child inside her might be heaven-sent and I'll end up handing innocent blood over to a death sentence. [4]So what should I do with her? ⟨I know,⟩ I'll divorce her quietly."

[5]But when night came a messenger of the Lord suddenly appeared to him in a dream and said: "Don't be afraid of this girl, because the child in her is the holy spirit's doing. [6]She will have a son and you will name him Jesus—the name means 'he will save his people from their sins.'" [7]And Joseph got up from his sleep and praised the God of Israel, who had given him this favor. [8]And so he began to protect the girl.

15 ***Then Annas*** the scholar came to him and said to him, "Joseph, why haven't you attended our assembly?"

[2]And he replied to him, "Because I was worn out from the trip and rested my first day home."

[3]Then Annas turned and saw that Mary was pregnant.

[4]He left in a hurry for the high priest and said to him, "You remember Joseph, don't you—the man you yourself vouched for? Well, he has committed a serious offense."

[5]And the high priest asked, "In what way?"

[6]"Joseph has violated the virgin he received from the temple of the Lord," he replied. "He had his way with her and hasn't disclosed his action to the people of Israel."

[7]And the high priest asked him, "Has Joseph really done this?"

13:8 Ⓢ Lk 1:34; Ⓓ InJas 15:13
14:1–6 Ⓢ Mt 1:19–24
14:2 ▷ Dt 22:23–24
14:3 Ⓢ Mt 27:3–4

13:10 That Mary is unable to say *where it came from* is surprising, given the explicit announcement (see 11:7). Presumably Mary forgot, as also in her conversation with Elizabeth (see 12:6).

14:3 That there could be *a death sentence* derives from Deut 22:23–24.

14:4 That Joseph should *divorce her quietly* makes little sense here because they are neither engaged nor married. The author is clearly dependent on Matt 1:19.

14:5 The command here, *Don't be afraid of this girl*, differs significantly from the parallel account in Matt 1:20 ("Do not be afraid to take Mary as your wife"). This difference is deliberate, reflecting the very different relationship between Joseph and Mary in this gospel.

15:6 That Joseph should be held responsible for having *violated* Mary and made her pregnant is odd because, when he had left to build, she was twelve years old (see 8:3) but now she is sixteen (see 12:9).

The drink test

On the way to Bethlehem

[8]And he replied, "Send temple assistants and you'll find the virgin
pregnant."
[9]And so the temple assistants went and found her just as Annas had
reported, and then they brought her, along with Joseph, to the court.
[10]"Mary, why have you done this?" the high priest asked her. "Why
have you humiliated yourself? [11]Have you forgotten the Lord your
God, you who were raised in the Holy of the Holies and were fed by
heavenly messengers? [12]You of all people, who heard their hymns and
danced for them—why have you done this?"
[13]And she wept bitterly: "As the Lord God lives, I stand innocent
before him. Believe me, I've not had sex with any man."
[14]And the high priest said, "Joseph, why have you done this?"
[15]And Joseph said, "As the Lord lives, I am innocent where she is
concerned."
[16]And the high priest said, "Don't perjure yourself, but tell the truth.
You've had your way with her and haven't disclosed this action to the
people of Israel. [17]And you haven't humbled yourself under God's
mighty hand, so that your offspring might be blessed."
[18]But Joseph was silent.

16 ***Then the high priest*** said, "Return the virgin you received from
the temple of the Lord."
[2]And Joseph, bursting into tears. . . .
[3]And the high priest said, "I'm going to give you the Lord's drink
test, and it will disclose your sin clearly to both of you."
[4]And the high priest took the water and made Joseph drink it and
sent him into the wilderness, but he returned unharmed. [5]And he
made the girl drink it, too, and sent her into the wilderness. She also
came back unharmed. [6]And everybody was surprised because their sin
had not been revealed. [7]And so the high priest said, "If the Lord God
has not exposed your sin, then neither do I condemn you." And he
dismissed them. [8]Joseph took Mary and returned home celebrating and
praising the God of Israel.

17 ***Now an order came*** from the Emperor Augustus that everybody
in Bethlehem of Judea be enrolled in the census. [2]And Joseph wondered, "I'll enroll my sons, but what am I going to do with this girl?

15:11 Ⓘ InJas 8:2
15:13 Ⓓ InJas 13:8
15:17 Ⓢ 1 Pet 5:6
16:3 Ⓞ Nm 5:11–31
16:7 Ⓢ Jn 8:11
16:8 Ⓢ Lk 5:25
17:1–11 Ⓢ Lk 2:1–7

16:2 There is probably a lacuna here, for no finite verb accompanies the participle *bursting*. How much has dropped out is difficult to tell, but perhaps nothing more than "said nothing" is missing.

16:3 *The Lord's drink test* reflects a similar, yet far from identical, test described in Num 5:11–31. For another such test, outside the biblical tradition, see Achilles Tatius, *Cleitophon and Leucippe*, 8.3.3; 6.1–15; 13.1–14.2.
17:1 With the *order from the Emperor Augustus* the gospel begins to follow the sequence of events narrated in Luke 2:1–39, with some attention to Matt 1:16–2:16. Note, however, that Augustus' order here extends only to *Bethlehem of Judea*, not to the whole world, as in Luke 2:1.

Time stands still

How will I enroll her? 3As my wife? I'm ashamed to do that. As my daughter? The people of Israel know she's not my daughter. 4How this is to be decided depends on the Lord."

5And so he saddled his donkey and had her get on it. His son led it and Samuel brought up the rear. 6As they neared the three mile marker, Joseph turned around and saw that she was sulking. 7And he said to himself, "Perhaps the baby she is carrying is causing her discomfort." 8Joseph turned around again and saw her laughing and said to her, "Mary, what's going on with you? One minute I see you laughing and the next minute you're sulking."

9And she replied, "Joseph, it's because I imagine two peoples in front of me, one weeping and mourning and the other celebrating and jumping for joy."

10Halfway through the trip Mary said to him, "Joseph, help me down from the donkey—the child inside me is about to be born."

11And he helped her down and said to her, "Where will I take you to give you some privacy, since this place is out in the open?"

18 ***He found a cave*** nearby and took her inside. He stationed his sons to guard her 2and went to look for a Hebrew midwife in the country around Bethlehem.

3"Now I, Joseph, was walking along and yet not going anywhere. 4I looked up at the vault of the sky and saw it standing still, and then at the clouds and saw them paused in amazement, and at the birds of the sky suspended in midair. 5As I looked on the earth, I saw a bowl lying there and workers reclining around it with their hands in the bowl; 6some were chewing and yet did not chew; some were picking up something to eat and yet did not pick it up; and some were putting food in their mouths and yet did not do so. 7Instead, they were all looking upward.

8"I saw sheep being driven along and yet the sheep stood still; 9the shepherd was lifting his hand to strike them, and yet his hand remained raised. 10And I observed the current of the river and saw goats with their mouths in the water and yet they were not drinking. 11Then all of a sudden everything and everybody went on with what they had been doing.

17:9
Ⓢ Gn 25:23, Lk 2:34

18:3 From here on the earliest ms differs sharply from later mss in that it omits the vision of Joseph (18:3–11) and has shorter accounts of the incidents that follow.

17:4 *How this is to be decided:* literally, "this day of the Lord," an expression that implies a time of judgment or decision. "Day" might refer to some particular day, but, if so, it is not clear which one. Or it might refer simply to that day that Joseph travels, since every day belongs to the Lord. Or it might refer to the series of events culminating in the enrollment, which is how it is taken here.

17:5 No *Samuel* is mentioned among the brothers of Jesus in Mark 6:3.

18:1 That Jesus is born in a *cave* outside Bethlehem differs from Luke's stable at an inn there (Luke 2:7).

18:3–11 Joseph's vision, which begins with his claim to be *walking along and yet not*

A child is born

Salome's folly

19

"Then I saw a woman coming down from the hill country, and she asked, 'Where are you going, sir?'

2"I replied, 'I am looking for a Hebrew midwife.'

3"She inquired, 'Are you an Israelite?'

4"I told her, 'Yes.'

5"And she said, 'And who's the one having a baby in the cave?'

6"I replied, 'My fiancée.'

7"And she continued, 'She isn't your wife?'

8"I said to her, 'She is Mary, who was raised in the temple of the Lord; I obtained her by lot as my wife. 9But she's not really my wife; she's pregnant by the holy spirit.'

10"The midwife said, 'Really?'"

11Joseph responded, "Come and see."

12And the midwife went with him. 13As they stood in front of the cave, a dark cloud overshadowed it. 14The midwife said, "I've really been privileged, because today my eyes have seen a miracle in that salvation has come to Israel."

15Suddenly the cloud withdrew from the cave and an intense light appeared inside the cave, so that their eyes could not bear to look. 16And a little later that light receded until an infant became visible; he took the breast of his mother Mary.

17Then the midwife shouted: "What a great day this is for me because I've seen this new miracle!"

18And the midwife left the cave and met Salome and said to her, "Salome, Salome, let me tell you about a new marvel: a virgin has given birth, and you know that's impossible!"

19And Salome replied, "As the Lord my God lives, unless I insert my finger and examine her, I will never believe that a virgin has given birth."

20

The midwife entered and said, "Mary, position yourself for an examination. You are facing a serious test."

2And so Mary, when she heard these instructions, positioned herself, and Salome inserted her finger into Mary. 3And then Salome cried aloud and said, "I'll be damned because of my transgression and my disbelief; I have put the living God on trial. 4Look! My hand is disappearing! It's being consumed by the flames!"

19:13 ◊Ex 16:10
19:14 Ⓢ Lk 2:30
19:19 Ⓢ Jn 20:25

---

going anywhere, seems to describe an experience in which everything—the winds, birds, workers, herds, herders, and himself—are momentarily frozen in whatever activity they were engaged in. This moment would seem to be the time when, back at the cave, Jesus was born.

19:6 That Joseph should refer here to Mary as his *financée* is odd, given the author's deliberate attempt elsewhere to depict their relationship as that of merely guardian and ward.

19:19 Salome inserting her *finger* recalls the language and story of doubting Thomas in John 20:24–25.

Visit of the astrologers

[5]Then Salome fell on her knees in the presence of the Lord, with these words: "God of my ancestors, remember me because I am a descendant of Abraham, Isaac, and Jacob. [6]Do not make an example of me for the people of Israel, but give me a place among the poor again. [7]You yourself know, Lord, that I've been healing people in your name and have been receiving my payment from you."

[8]And suddenly a messenger of the Lord appeared, saying to her, "Salome, Salome, the Lord of all has heard your prayer. [9]Hold out your hand to the child and pick him up, and then you'll have salvation and joy."

[10]Salome approached the child and picked him up with these words: "I'll worship him because he's been born to be king of Israel." [11]And Salome was instantly healed and left the cave vindicated.

[12]Then a voice said abruptly, "Salome, Salome, don't report the marvels you've seen until the child goes to Jerusalem."

21 ***Joseph was about ready*** to depart for Judea, but a great uproar was about to take place in Bethlehem in Judea. [2]It all started when astrologers came inquiring, "Where is the newborn king of the Judeans? We're here because we saw his star in the East and have come to pay him homage."

[3]When Herod heard about their visit, he was terrified and sent agents to the astrologers. [4]He also sent for the high priests and questioned them in his palace: "What has been written about the Anointed? Where is he supposed to be born?"

[5]They said to him, "In Bethlehem, Judea, that's what the scriptures say." [6]And he dismissed them.

[7]Then he questioned the astrologers: "What sign have you seen regarding the one who has been born king?"

[8]And the astrologers said, "We saw a star of exceptional brilliance in the sky, and it so dimmed the other stars that they disappeared. Consequently, we know that a king was born for Israel. And we have come to pay him homage."

[9]Herod instructed them: "Go and begin your search, and if you find him, report back to me, so I can also go and pay him homage."

[10]The astrologers departed. And there it was: the star they had seen in the East led them on until they came to the cave; then the star stopped directly above the head of the child. [11]After the astrologers saw him with his mother Mary, they took gifts out of their pouches—gold, pure incense, and myrrh.

20:11 Ⓢ Lk 18:14
21:1–12 Ⓢ Mt 2:1–12
21:5 ◊ Mi 5:1
21:11 ◊ Is 60:6

20:12 The author seemingly refers to Joseph's and Mary's last trip *to Jerusalem*, which is narrated in Luke 2:22–39.

21:1 *Judea:* Here and in v. 12 "Judea" must refer to the city of Jerusalem.

21:5 It is remarkable that after the words *what the scriptures say* the quotation from Mic 5:1, 3, which follows these very words in Matt 2:6, is omitted here.

[12]Since they had been advised by the heavenly messenger not to go into Judea, they returned to their country by another route.

Slaughter of the infants

Murder of Zechariah

22 ***When Herod realized*** he had been duped by the astrologers, he flew into a rage [2]and dispatched his executioners with instructions to kill all the infants two years old and younger.

[3]When Mary heard that the infants were being killed, she was frightened [4]and took her child, wrapped him in strips of cloth, and put him in a feeding trough used by cattle.

[5]As for Elizabeth, when she heard that they were looking for John, she took him and went up into the hill country. [6]She kept searching for a place to hide him, but there was none to be had. [7]Then she groaned and said out loud, "Mountain of God, please take in a mother with her child." You see, Elizabeth was unable to keep on climbing because her nerve failed her. [8]But suddenly the mountain was split open and let them in. This mountain allowed the light to shine through to her, [9]since a messenger of the Lord was with them for protection.

23 ***Herod, though,*** kept looking for John [2]and sent his agents to Zechariah serving at the altar with this message for him: "Where have you hidden your son?"

[3]But he answered them, "I am a minister of God, attending to his temple. How should I know where my son is?"

[4]So the agents left and reported all this to Herod, who became angry and said, "Is his son going to rule over Israel?"

[5]And he sent his agents back with this message for him: "Tell me the truth. Where is your son? Don't you know that I have your life in my power?"

[6]And the agents went and reported this message to him.

[7]Zechariah answered, "I am a martyr for God. Take my life. [8]The Lord, though, will receive my spirit because you are shedding innocent blood at the entrance to the temple of the Lord."

[9]And so at daybreak Zechariah was murdered, but the people of Israel did not know that he had been murdered.

22:1–2 Ⓢ Mt 2:16–18
22:4 Ⓢ Lk 2.7
23:1–9 Ⓢ Mt 23:35, Lk 1:5–25
23:7–8 Ⓢ Mt 23:35, Acts 7:59

22:4 The *strips of cloth* and *feeding trough* recall Luke 2:12, but here these items are used in the Matthean context of Herod's threat to Jesus' life. By having Mary wrap Jesus up and hide him in a trough, the author can dispense with Joseph's, Mary's and Jesus' escape to Egypt, which is Matthew's solution to the threat (Matt 2:3–15).
22:5 For the significance of why Elizabeth took John and *went up into the hill country*, see the Introduction.
22:8 The translation of the phrase *This mountain allowed the light to shine through to her* is very tentative, for the Greek is opaque and probably corrupt.
23:2 Zechariah's presence at the *altar*, where he will be killed, shows that the author has apparently identified this Zechariah, the father of John, with another Zechariah, mentioned in Matt 23:35, who did die at the altar.

Zechariah mourned

Author

24 ***At the hour of formal*** greetings the priests departed, but Zechariah did not meet and bless them as was customary. 2And so the priests waited around for Zechariah, to greet him with prayer and to praise the Most High God.

3But when he did not show up, they all became fearful. 4One of them, however, summoned up his courage, entered the sanctuary, and saw dried blood next to the Lord's altar. 5And a voice said, "Zechariah has been murdered! His blood will not be cleaned up until his avenger appears."

6When he heard this utterance he was afraid and went out and reported to the priests what he had seen and heard. 7And they summoned up their courage, entered, and saw what had happened. 8The panels of the temple cried out, and the priests ripped their robes from top to bottom. 9They didn't find a corpse, but they did find his blood, now turned to stone. 10They were afraid and went out and reported to the people that Zechariah had been murdered. 11When all the tribes of the people heard this, they began to mourn; and they beat their breasts for three days and three nights.

12After three days, however, the priests deliberated about whom they should appoint to the position of Zechariah. 13The lot fell to Simeon. 14This man, you see, is the one who was informed by the holy spirit that he would not see death until he laid eyes on the Anointed in the flesh.

25 ***Now I, James,*** am the one who wrote this account at the time when an uproar arose in Jerusalem at the death of Herod. 2I took myself off to the wilderness until the uproar in Jerusalem died down. 3There I praised the Lord God, who gave me the wisdom to write this account.

4Grace will be with all those who fear the Lord. Amen.

24:1
Ⓣ Lk1:21
24:8
Ⓣ Mk15:38, Mt27:51
24:14
Ⓢ Lk2:25–26

24:9 *They didn't find a corpse* presumably because the murderers carried the body away and buried it without a name.

25:1 For the historical problems raised by having *James* compose this gospel after *the death of Herod* see the Introduction.

Fragmentary Gospels

Papyrus Köln, discovered and published in 1987, has been identified as a piece of the Egerton Gospel *Used by permission of the Institut für Altertumskunde der Universität zu Köln.*

Gehenna / Hades / Hell

The Greek (and Hebrew) terms for places under the earth—the underworld or nether world—are especially difficult to distinguish in English since the term Hell is in general use for them all.

Gehenna comes from a Hebrew phrase meaning "valley of Hinnom," a ravine running along the west and south of Jerusalem. In Jeremiah's day it was known as a place of human sacrifice to the gods Baal and Molech. Later it became a trash dump and so was perpetually on fire.

Gehenna came to symbolize the place where the dead were punished because of their sins. It is always used in this symbolic sense in the gospels.

In order to avoid associations with the term Hell, the translators have retained the Greek (Hebrew) word in English dress. The English transliteration appears in English for the first time around 1600.

Hades is the Greek equivalent of the Hebrew term *Sheol,* the place or abode of the dead, where wicked and righteous alike go. Hades is the name of the god of the underworld in Greek mythology; the name was later transferred to the place or domain of the god.

Hades is accessible by gates (Matt 16:18) since it is located under the earth, like Sheol. In Hades the dead lead a shadowy existence.

The translators have retained Hades in Matt 16:18 and in the parable of the rich man and Lazarus (Luke 16:23), but elsewhere have translated it "Hell" because it occurs in the phrase "go to Hell," which can scarcely be represented in idiomatic English by "go to Hades."

Hades was introduced into English as a word in its own right around 1600 in connection with controversies over the Apostles' Creed.

Hell can be used to represent either Gehenna or Hades in English. The term Hell is derived from Old Teutonic *Hel,* where it is the name for the goddess of the infernal regions. The Book of Revelation ("lake of fire," "the abyss"), Dante, and other authors have contributed to the associations connected with the term. The preaching of fire and brimstone sermons by Puritan divines and others have given the term a graphic life in American English.

Outer darkness: In ancient cosmology, the sky was thought to be held up by mountains at the ends of the earth. Beyond these mountains lay the regions of darkness. The Garden of Eden or Paradise was widely thought to lie in the east, the outer darkness in the extreme west. In rabbinic sources, Gehenna is equated with this darkness. In the New Testament, this particular phrase is used only by Matthew.

Introduction

In 1886 French archaeologists discovered a small papyrus codex in a monk's grave at Akhmim in Upper Egypt. On pp. 2–10 of this codex is a fragmentary gospel narrative containing significant portions of a passion story, a miraculous epiphany, an empty tomb story, and an introduction to what is probably a resurrection story. A small cross decorates the top middle of p. 2, while three small crosses stand above a knotwork interlacing at the bottom of p. 10. The presence of the surrounding ornamentation indicates that the writer was copying an already fragmented text. The cursive handwriting of the gospel narrative dates from the eighth or ninth century. This gospel fragment became known as the Gospel of Peter due to the fact that Simon Peter is presented as its author (14:3, 7:2).

Relationship to the canonical gospels

From its initial reception there has been scholarly controversy over whether the Gospel of Peter is independent of or dependent on the canonical gospels. Opposing positions were quickly established and maintained, but by the first quarter of this century most scholars agreed that Peter was dependent on the canonical gospels and composed no earlier than the first half of the second century. Associated with this debate was the contention that Peter presented "the Lord" as only appearing to suffer (4:1, 5:5). However, recent analysis of the document has found that what once appeared to be clear docetic indications are, at best, ambiguous elements. Finally, both sides of the longstanding debate agree that Peter comes out of a Syrian petrine tradition. This would account for its later association with the church at Rhossus (Eusebius, Eccl. Hist. 6.12.2–6) on the Syrian coast.

Modern reconsiderations

In recent years, however, two major developments have made us reconsider the position and significance of Gospel of Peter in the development of early Christianity.

First, the 1972 publication of Oxyrhynchus Papyrus 2949 introduced two tiny fragments into the discussion. While little can be made of the contents of the smaller fragment, the larger relates the story of Joseph of Arimathea's request to Pilate for the body of Jesus. This request appears to occur before the execution, contradicting the order of events in the canonical gospels, but closely resembling Pet 2:1–3a. These fragments date from the late second or the early third century.

Second, New Testament scholarship has long since undermined the basic assumption of the early interpreters of Peter. The arguments both for dependence and for independence assumed the existence of some historical (that is, factual) account. Depending on how one reads the relationship between Peter and the canonical gospels, one could maintain that one or the other preserves an earlier, historical kernel. But, since the canonical gospels are witnesses to a very complex interpretive enterprise, both oral and literary, and were subject to the various formats and patterns of ancient communication, they cannot be simple historical reports. This means that the extracanonical gospels, such as Peter, must also be reevaluated.

This rethinking has been based on the discovery that almost every sentence of the passion narrative of Peter appears to be composed out of references and allusions to the psalms and the prophets. In effect, "scriptural memory" may well have been a major influence in the formation of this early passion narrative. Furthermore, recent studies which are not interested in searching for some historical core have tentatively established an original compositional layer whose form and content was shaped by the Jewish tradition of the suffering righteous one.

The origins of the passion traditions

The most important result established by this research is that the original stage of Peter may well be the earliest passion story in the gospel tradition and, as such, may contain the seeds of subsequent passion narratives. In contrast to those early interpreters of Peter who assumed some sort of factual account at the core, the recent revisionists find something other than sheer historical report. They contend that the passion tradition begins not as a simple historical description but as an imaginative response to the trauma of Jesus' fate, expressed in the stock form of the Jewish tale of the righteous one who is unjustly persecuted and subsequently vindicated. The story pattern of this tale (see Wisdom 2–5) is as follows. The actions and claims of a righteous person provoke his opponents to conspire against him. This leads to an accusation (Pet 3:2?; 4:2?), trial (1:1), condemnation (2:3), and ordeal (3:1–4; 4:1; 5:2). In some instances this results in his shameful death (5:5). The hero of the story reacts characteristically (4:1), expressing his innocence, frustration, or trust in prayer (5:5), while there are also various reactions to his fate by characters in the tale (4:3–5). Either at the brink of death or in death itself the innocent one is rescued (5:5) and vindicated (5:6–6:1). This vindication entails the exaltation (5:5) and acclamation (8:1) of the hero as well as the reaction (8:1) and punishment (5:1, 3–4) of his opponents.

Beyond this basic narrative, there has been added a miraculous epiphany story, detailing a divine breakthrough and intensifying the vindication of the righteous sufferer. After an introduction (8:1–9:1), we find a visit by heavenly beings (9:2–3), the miraculous opening of the tomb (9:4), a supernatural appearance (10:2–3), and reaction by witnesses (11:3). One can also note further additions: an empty tomb story (12:1–13:3) and the probable beginning of a resurrection appearance story (14:1–3). On this analysis, the figure of Simon Peter (7:2; 14:3) appears only at the final stage of the gospel's composition. These findings not only move the date of the earliest stage of Peter to the middle of the first century, but also challenge basic assumptions about the historical development of early Christian literature.

The Gospel of Peter

Hand washing

Request for the body

Paying their respects

1 . . . ***but of the Judeans*** no one washed his hands, neither Herod nor
any one of his judges. Since they were [un]willing to wash, Pilate stood
up. [2]Then Herod the king orders the Lord to be [taken away], saying to
them "Do what I commanded you to do to him."

2 ***Joseph stood there,*** the friend of Pilate and the Lord, and when he
realized that they were about to crucify him, he went to Pilate and
asked for the body of the Lord for burial. [2]And Pilate sent to Herod and
asked for his body. [3]And Herod replied, "Brother Pilate, even if no one
had asked for him, we would have buried him, since the sabbath is
drawing near. For it is written in the Law, 'The sun must not set upon
one who has been executed.'" And he turned him over to the people
on the day before the Unleavened Bread, their feast.

3 ***They took the Lord*** and kept pushing him along as they ran; and
they would say, "Let's drag the son of God along, since we have him in
our power." [2]And they threw a purple robe around him and sat him

2:1 //Mk15:43–45; Mt27:57–58; Lk23:50–52; Jn19:38–42
2:3 ◊Dt21:22–23; //Mk15:15; Mt27:26; Lk23:24–25; Jn19:16
3:1 ◊Ps117:13 (LXX)
3:2–3 ◊Zec3:1–5; Is58:2; //Mk15:17; Mt27:28–29; Lk23:11; Jn19:2, 13
3:4 ◊Is50:6; //Mk14:65, 15:15, 19; Mt26:67–68, 27:26, 30; Jn19:1, 3

1:1 The text begins in the middle of a scene. The ornamentation at the beginning of the material indicates that the writer copied an already fragmented text. **1:2** The text is corrupt here. Either *taken away* or *escorted* is possible.

1:1 The text begins abruptly in a scene from the passion narrative. Evidently the Jewish officials have refused to join Pilate in a washing ritual which was accompanied by a declaration of innocence. In the canonical version this declaration occurs with the washing whereas in Peter it comes later (11:4).

1:2 In contrast to the canonical gospels, Herod assumes control of the trial of Jesus. See Luke 13:31–33. *Lord* is the principal title in Peter for Jesus. Others are *son of God* and *savior of humanity.*

2:1 In contrast to the canonical versions, Joseph asks for the body of the Lord before his crucifixion. Oxyrhynchus Papyrus 2949 (see Introduction) is either an independent witness to this tradition or an earlier version of Peter than the one we now have.

2:3 This quotation (see Deut 21:22–23) refers originally to the hanging of an executed criminal upon a tree. The law was apparently interpreted to include cases of crucifixion, which carried the stigma of social disgrace. The onset of the sabbath demanded the removal of such defilement. The *feast* of *Unleavened Bread* is the Passover.

3:1 *They* refers to the *people.* Unlike the canonical gospels, the people are in control of the fate of Jesus. Herod's control ends in 2:3.

3:1–4 Crucifixion was preceded by torture and scourging. Since this was an act of public humiliation, a royal mockery, involving a throne, crown, robe, sceptre, and title, was not uncommon. This may have had the important social function of diverting hatred of the dominating class onto scapegoats.

Crucifixion

On the cross

upon the judgment seat and said, "Judge justly, king of Israel." 3And
one of them brought a crown of thorns and set it on the head of the
Lord. 4And others standing about would spit in his eyes, and others
slapped his face, while others poked him with a rod. Some kept flogging him as they said, "Let's pay proper respect to the son of God."

4 ***And they brought*** two criminals and crucified the Lord between
them. But he himself remained silent, as if in no pain. 2And when they
set up the cross, they put an inscription on it, "This is the king of
Israel." 3And they piled his clothing in front of him; then they divided
it among themselves, and gambled for it. 4But one of those criminals
reproached them and said, "We're suffering for the evil that we've
done, but this fellow, who has become a savior of humanity, what
wrong as he done to you?" 5And they got angry at him and ordered that
his legs not be broken so he would die in agony.

5 ***It was midday*** and darkness covered the whole of Judea. They
were confused and anxious for fear the sun had set since he was still
alive. ⟨For⟩ it is written that, "The sun must not set upon one who has
been executed." 2And one of them said, "Give him vinegar mixed with
something bitter to drink." And they mixed it and gave it to him to
drink. 3And they fulfilled all things and brought to completion the sins
on their head. 4Now many went about with lamps, and, thinking that it
was night, they laid down. 5And the Lord cried out, saying, "My power,
⟨my⟩ power, you have abandoned me." When he said this, he was
taken up. 6And at that moment, the veil of the Jerusalem temple was
torn in two.

4:1 ◊Is 53:7; //Mk 15:27; Mt 27:38; Lk 23:32–33; Jn 19:18; cf. Mk 14:61, 15:5; Mt 26:63
4:2 //Mk 15:26; Mt 27:37; Lk 23:38; Jn 19:19
4:3 ◊Ps 22:18; //Mk 15:24; Mt 27:35; Lk 23:34; Jn 19:23–24
4:4 //Lk 23:39–41
4:5 Cf. Jn 19:31–37
5:1 ◊Dt 21:22–23; Am 8:9; //Mk 15:33; Mt 27:45; Lk 23:44; Jn 19:31
5:2 ◊Ps 69:21; //Mk 15:23, 36; Mt 27:34, 48; Lk 23:36; Jn 19:28–29
5:3 Ⓣ1 Thes 2:16
5:5 ◊Ps 22:1; //Mk 15:34, 37; Mt 27:46, 50; Lk 23:46; Jn 19:30; cf. Acts 1:2
5:6 //Mk 15:38; Mt 27:51; Lk 23:45

5:1 *For* is added to clarify the cause of confusion and anxiety. **5:4** The text is quite problematic here. Either *laid down* or *fell down* is possible. Some editors also add *and* before the term in question.

4:1 *As if in no pain* is modeled on Isa 53:7 and so does not imply docetism.
4:2 This *inscription* contrasts with the canonical version.
4:3 This is modeled on Ps 22:18.
4:5 Breaking the legs of the crucified was done in order to hasten death. See John 19:32–33.
5:1 Untimely *darkness* is a feature of apocalyptic narratives.
5:2 The *bitter* substance is probably myrrh (see Mark 15:23), which may have been given to crucified victims to dull the pain. This is likely an allusion to Ps 69:21.
5:3 The language suggests Jewish prophetic tradition where the actions of the people are criticized and understood to bring down divine wrath. See 1 Thess 2:16 and Matt 23:32.
5:5 *Taken up* may be a euphemism for death or it might refer to an ascension into heaven. The latter meaning would suggest a rescue combined with an exaltation of a suffering son of God.
5:6 Along with the apocalyptic darkness in 5:1, this event is part of a series of cataclysmic events (see 6:1). The *veil* is the curtain which separated the precincts of the temple from the inner sanctuary (see Exod 26:31–35, 40:21).

Burial

Regrets

Sealing the tomb

6 ***And then they pulled*** the nails from the Lord's hands and set him on the ground. And the whole earth shook and there was great fear. [2]Then the sun came out and it was found to be the ninth hour. [3]Now the Judeans rejoiced and gave his body to Joseph so that he might bury it, since ⟨Joseph⟩ had observed how much good he had done. [4]⟨Joseph⟩ took the Lord, washed ⟨his body⟩ and wound a linen ⟨shroud⟩ around him, and brought him to his own tomb, called "Joseph's Garden."

7 ***Then the Judeans*** and the elders and the priests perceived what evil they had done to themselves, and began to beat their breasts and cry out "Our sins have brought woes upon us! The judgment and the end of Jerusalem are at hand!" [2]But I began weeping with my friends. And quivering with fear in our hearts, we hid ourselves. After all, we were being sought by them as criminals and as ones wishing to burn down the temple. [3]As a result of all these things, we fasted and sat mourning and weeping night and day until the sabbath.

8 ***When the scholars*** and the Pharisees and the priests had gathered together, and when they heard that all the people were moaning and beating their breasts, and saying "If his death has produced these overwhelming signs, he must have been entirely innocent!", [2]they became frightened and went to Pilate and begged him, [3]"Give us soldiers so that ⟨we⟩ may guard his tomb for three [days], in case his disciples come and steal his body and the people assume that he is risen from the dead and do us harm." [4]So Pilate gave them the centurion Petronius with soldiers to guard the tomb. And elders and scholars went

6:1
//Mt27:51
6:2
//Mk15:33; Mt27:45; Lk23:44
6:3–4
//Mk15:43–47; Mt27:57–60; Lk23:50–53; Jn19:42
7:1
◊Is3:9b; Zec12:10–12; cf. Lk23:48
7:3
Cf. Mk16:10
8:1
Cf. Mk15:39; Mt27:19, 54; Lk23:47
8:2–6
//Mt27:62–66

6:1 This implies that the feet were not nailed. The procedure of crucifixion allowed for tying one set of the crucified's extremities while nailing the other. The shaking of the ground is a further apocalyptic feature.

6:2 *The ninth hour* would be three P.M.

6:4 Joseph prepares the corpse of Jesus in the usual Jewish manner. 12:3–4 suggests that the burial ritual is incomplete.

7:1 The Jewish officials are portrayed as repenting and as understanding that their deeds call for divine judgment. This may well be an allusion to the fall of Jerusalem in 70 C.E. Notice the apparent contradiction to their reaction in 11:6.

7:2 While this might reflect the tradition found in Mark 14:58; Matt 26:61; John 2:19; and Acts 6:13; it also might refer to the horrors of the burning of the temple (see Josephus, *The Jewish War* 6.250–280).

7:3 *Night and day* suggest that some time has passed (see 2:3). Yet 9:1–2 points to the sabbath mentioned in 2:3.

8:1 *Beating their breasts* indicates the people's repentance over their role in the death of a righteous one. This may have originally followed 6:1. The gospel seems to play the *people* off against the official leaders by contrasting their different reactions to the sign in 6:1. It also may be that 7:1 comes from a later version of Peter.

8:4 *Petronius*: Although the centurion is named here, he is not named again in 8:5; 10:1; 11:3, 5, 7. The name may indicate that 8:4 comes from a later version.

with them to the tomb. 5And all who were there ⟨with⟩ the centurion
and the soldiers helped roll a large stone against the entrance to the
tomb. 6And they put seven seals on it. Then they pitched a tent there
and kept watch.

Two from the sky

Three men & a cross

Report to Pilate

9 ***Early, at first light*** on the sabbath, a crowd came from Jerusalem
and the surrounding countryside to see the sealed tomb. 2But during
the night before the Lord's day dawned, while the soldiers were on
guard, two by two during each watch, a loud noise came from the sky,
3and they saw the skies open up and two men come down from there in
a burst of light and approach the tomb. 4The stone that had been
pushed against the entrance began to roll by itself and moved away to
one side; then the tomb opened up and both young men went inside.

10 ***Now when these soldiers*** saw this, they roused the centurion
from his sleep, along with the elders. (Remember, they were also there
keeping watch.) 2While they were explaining what they had seen,
again they see three men leaving the tomb, two supporting the third,
and a cross was following them. 3The heads of the two reached up to
the sky, while the head of the third, whom they led by the hand,
reached beyond the skies. 4And they heard a voice from the skies that
said, "Have you preached to those who sleep?" 5And an answer was
heard from the cross: "Yes!"

11 ***These men then consulted*** with one another about going and
reporting these things to Pilate. 2While they were still thinking about
it, again the skies appeared to open and some sort of human being
came down and entered the tomb. 3When those in the centurion's
company saw this, they rushed out into the night to Pilate, having left
the tomb which they were supposed to be guarding. And as they were
recounting everything they had seen, they became deeply disturbed

9:3–4 //Mk16:5; Mt28:2–4; Lk24:4; cf.Mk9:4; Acts1:10
10:4 Ⓣ1Pet3:18–20
11:3 //Mt27:54; cf.Mk15:39

8:5 The fact that the soldiers complete the burial of Jesus by *rolling a large stone* against the tomb may be evidence of a different burial tradition.
8:6 *seven seals*: the highest level of security.
9:2 *The night before the Lord's day dawned* is ambiguous. It can refer to the time either before sunrise on Sunday or after sunset on Saturday. The *noise from the sky* indicates a divine communication.
9:4 In contrast to *both young men* 13:1 mentions only one. The movement of the stone *by itself* indicates divine agency.
10:2–3 *The third* presumably refers to the *Lord.* The size of the figures symbolize their supernatural status.
10:4–5 *A voice from the skies* indicates a divine communication. Here a response *from the cross* turns this into a brief dialogue. Preaching *to those who sleep* suggests the mythical descent into the underworld. The speaking cross is unique in early Christian literature.
11:2 The return of a heavenly figure prepares for 13:1.

Mary at the tomb

and cried, "Truly, he was a son of God!" [4]Pilate responded by saying, "I am clean of the blood of the son of God; this was all your doing." [5]Then they all crowded around ⟨Pilate⟩ and began to beg and urge him to order the centurion and his soldiers to tell no one what they saw. [6]"You see," they said, "it is better for us to be guilty of the greatest sin before God than to fall into the hands of the Judean people and be stoned." [7]Pilate then ordered the centurion and the soldiers to say nothing.

Empty tomb

12 ***Early on the Lord's day,*** Mary of Magdala, a disciple of the Lord, was fearful on account of the Judeans and, since they were enflamed with rage, she did not perform at the tomb of the Lord what women are accustomed to do for their loved ones who die. [2]Nevertheless, she took her friends with her and went to the tomb where he had been laid. [3]And they were afraid that the Judeans might see them and were saying, "Although on the day he was crucified we could not weep and beat our breasts, we should now perform these rites at his tomb. [4]But who will roll away the stone for us, the one placed at the entrance of the tomb, so that we may enter and sit beside him and do what ought to be done?" [5](remember, it was a huge stone.) "We fear that someone might see us. And if we are unable ⟨to roll the stone away⟩ we should, at least, place at the entrance the memorial we brought for him, and we should weep and beat our breasts until we go home."

13 ***And they went*** and found the tomb open. They went up to it, stooped down, and saw a young man sitting there ⟨in⟩ the middle of the tomb; he was handsome and wore a splendid robe. He said to them, [2]"Why have you come? Who are you looking for? Surely not the one who was crucified? He is risen and gone. If you don't believe it, stoop down and take a look at the place where he lay, for he is not there. You see, he is risen and has gone back to the place he was sent from." [3]Then the women fled in fear.

11:4 Cf. Mt 27:24; Lk 23:4; Ⓣ Pet 1:1
11:7 //Mt 28:11–15
12:1–2 //Mk 16:1–2; Mt 28:1; Lk 24:1; Jn 20:1
12:4 //Mk 16:3
13:1–2 //Mk 16:4–7; Mt 28:2–7; Lk 24:2–5; Jn 20:11–13
13:3 //Mk 16:8; Mt 28:8; Lk 24:9

12:1 *Disciple of the Lord* may reflect the early tradition that women were equal to men in terms of the mission and message of Jesus. *Fearful on acount of the Judeans*: see 7:2 and 12:3.

12:3 The women are probably bringing burial spices for a final anointing. They intend to perform the customary rites of mourning (*weep and beat our breasts*).

13:1 The *young man* is an angelic interpreter whose function is to shed light on the situation.

13:2 The words of the heavenly interpreter are probably drawn from the common kerygma of the early Jesus movement.

13:3 The reaction of the women is typical of people experiencing a divine epiphany.

14 ***Now it was the last day*** of Unleavened Bread, and many began
to return to their homes since the feast was over. [2]But we, the twelve
disciples of the Lord, continued to weep and mourn, and each one, still
grieving on account of what had happened, left for his own home. [3]But
I, Simon Peter, and Andrew, my brother, took our fishing nets and
went away to the sea. And with us was Levi, the son of Alphaeus,
whom the Lord . . .

Departure

14:3 The text breaks off abruptly. The ms has ornamentation immediately following these words, which suggests that it was copied from an already fragmented text.

14:3 Cf. Mk 2:14; Lk 5:2-11; Jn 21:1-4

14:1 This indicates that seven days have passed since the beginning of the feast of Passover. See Exod 12:18.
14:2 This is the only mention of *twelve disciples* in Peter.
14:3 This may reflect early traditions about a post-Easter vision to Peter (see John 21:1-4; Luke 5:2 11; 1 Cor 15:5). The *sea* most likely refers to the Sea of Galilee. The use of *I* with *Simon Peter* is the basis for the title *Gospel of Peter*.

Introduction

The Secret Gospel of Mark is a version of the Gospel of Mark that was in use in Alexandria at least by the first quarter of the second century. It differs from the standard version of Mark in that it has additional passages, which were intended only for those who had attained a higher degree of initiation into the church than the common crowd. It was, apparently, a version of Mark intended only for insiders.

Discovery

Until 1958 the Secret Gospel of Mark was unknown to the modern world. In that year, while cataloguing manuscripts at the famous Mar Saba monastery near Jerusalem, Morton Smith discovered a fragment of a previously unknown letter of Clement of Alexandria (ca. 150–215 C.E.). This letter fragment mentions the Secret Gospel and contains two excerpts from the mysterious text. Were it not for this meager evidence, the Secret Gospel of Mark would have remained lost.

The Clementine fragment

The Clementine letter fragment was found in the back of an edition of the letters of Ignatius of Antioch published in 1646, copied hastily onto the final page and the inside back cover of the book. Learned monks traveling to distant monasteries and libraries commonly took notes in this manner, quickly recording unexpected discoveries on the unused pages of a book to be transported home, where they might be studied more carefully. The handwriting can be dated to around 1750. Smith published the letter in 1973. Early discussion of it was marred by accusations of forgery and fraud, no doubt owing in part to its controversial contents. Today, however, there is almost unanimous agreement among Clementine scholars that the letter is authentic.

The letter is addressed to a certain Theodore, unknown to us outside the letter. Apparently Theodore has come into contact with a group of Carpocratians from whom he has learned of a Secret Gospel of Mark containing teachings not found in the more public version known to Theodore. It seems that Theodore has even been shown a copy of this mysterious book, for Clement's letter intends to answer his inquiries about the veracity of some of its stories. Clement's response is most interesting. He begins with an account of how, after migrating from Rome to Alexandria following the death of Peter, Mark revised his gospel to include "whatever would be appropriate for those who are advancing with respect to knowledge (*gnosis*)," and "of which he knew that the interpretation would initiate the hearers into the shrine of the truth which is hidden by seven veils." This account is dependent partly on the legends about Mark communicated by Papias, and partly on local traditions about the origins of the Secret Gospel itself. However, it is important insofar as it indicates that the Alexandrian church did in fact have two versions of Mark in Clement's day, a "public Mark," thought to have been written in Rome with a more general audience in mind, and a revised version, a "Secret Mark," allegedly written in Alexandria for a narrow circle of initiates.

Clement goes on to say that not all of what Theodore has related to him concerning the book shown to him by the Carpocratians actually comes from the Secret Mark used in Clement's church. He therefore charges that Carpocrates must have added unauthorized material of his own, as Clement himself puts it: "mixing the immaculate and sacred words with most shameless lies." This is where the letter becomes most intriguing, for in order to prove his point to Theodore, Clement cites two of the added passages from the "real" Secret Gospel of Mark so that Theodore can compare them to the passages he has seen in the Carpocratian version and see the difference for himself.

The Secret Gospel fragments

The first passage is a story of how Jesus miraculously raises a young man (*neaniskos*) who has recently died, at the behest of his bereaved sister. According to Clement, the story was added to Mark between verses 10:34 and 10:35. The story bears a striking resemblance to the raising of Lazarus in the Gospel of John (John 11:1–44). However, since it shows none of the typical marks of Johannine redaction which so strongly color the story about Lazarus, it is unlikely that the Secret Mark story is directly dependent upon its Johannine parallel. For its part, the version of the story from Secret Mark has its own peculiarities not found in John, such as the initiation of the young man into the "mystery of God's domain." The basic story, however, probably derives from the common stock of miracle stories available to both Mark and John, or their sources.

The second fragment is extremely brief, but nonetheless interesting. First, it mentions Salome, who appears in the New Testament elsewhere only in Mark (see 15:40; 16:1). Secondly, when placed in the slot where Clement indicates it occurs in Secret Mark (between 10:46a: "Then they came to Jericho," and 10:46b: "As he was leaving Jericho . . .") it fills a well-known hole in the Markan narrative. The stop in Jericho now seems, in light of the Secret Gospel, at least a little less futile.

These two fragments do not tell us much about the overall character of the

Secret Gospel of Mark. Whether Secret Mark contained additional material not mentioned in Clement's letter is not known. If there was more to this gospel, for the present it is lost. Still, we may know more about the Secret Gospel of Mark that one would initially assume.

Secret Mark and canonical Mark

One question in the ongoing debate about the Secret Gospel of Mark is the relationship between what we have come to know as canonical Mark and the version of Mark known to Clement as the Secret Gospel of Mark. Now, it is clear that what we have come to know as canonical Mark did not reach its final form until relatively late, probably sometime in the second century. This may be deduced from the fact that although both Matthew and Luke made use of a version of Mark as a source in the composition of their respective versions of the gospel, occasionally one encounters an episode, or simply details, in the canonical Markan narrative which neither Matthew nor Luke have included. Rather than assume that by coincidence both Matthew and Luke, independently of one another, chose to alter Mark's story in precisely the same way, scholars have tended to argue that such differences arose when later editors changed the Gospel of Mark after Matthew and Luke had already made use of it. That is to say, Matthew and Luke did not use what we have come to know as the canonical Gospel of Mark, but rather an earlier version of it. Clement's account, which speaks of various versions of Mark known in the second century, generally confirms this view. But more than this, it raises the question of the possible relationship between our canonical Mark and Clement's Secret Gospel of Mark. For there are a number of affinities between later editorial developments in canonical Mark and the fragments of Secret Mark quoted by Clement. The most striking similarity concerns the mysterious figure of a young man (*neaniskos*) who appears in canonical Mark in the scene of Jesus' arrest in the Garden of Gethsemane, dressed only in a linen cloth draped about his naked body (14:51–52). (Neither Matthew nor Luke preserve any reference to this young man.) Since the role of this young man in the narrative of canonical Mark is utterly baffling, it is all the more significant that he is dressed in exactly the same way as the young man prepared for initiation in the first Secret Mark fragment. This and other similarities between canonical Mark and the Secret Mark fragments have led many to conclude that canonical Mark is not the direct descendent of that early version of Mark used by Matthew and Luke, but rather of the Secret Gospel of Mark. In other words, what moderns have come to know as the Gospel of Mark is in fact a version of Secret Mark from which some, but not all, of the esoteric passages have been removed. If this is true, then the Secret Gospel of Mark will have provided us with some rather striking new information about the early transmission history of the Gospel of Mark.

The Secret Gospel of Mark

Fragment 1: To be located between Mark 10:34 and 10:35. Clement to Theodore, Folio 1, verso, line 23–Folio 2, recto, line 11.

1 [1]And they come into Bethany, and this woman was there whose
brother had died. [2]She knelt down in front of Jesus and says to him,
"Son of David, have mercy on me." [3]But the disciples rebuked her.
[4]And Jesus got angry and went with her into the garden where the
tomb was. [5]Just then a loud voice was heard from inside the tomb.
[6]Then Jesus went up and rolled the stone away from the entrance to
the tomb. [7]He went right in where the young man was, stuck out his
hand, grabbed him by the hand, and raised him up. [8]The young man
looked at Jesus, loved him, and began to beg him to be with him.
[9]Then they left the tomb and went into the young man's house.
(Incidentally, he was rich.) [10]Six days later Jesus gave him an order;
[11]and when evening had come, the young man went to him, dressed
only in a linen cloth. [12]He spent that night with him, because Jesus
taught him the mystery of God's domain. [13]From there ⟨Jesus⟩ got up
and returned to the other side of the Jordan.

1:1 //Jn11:1
1:4 Ⓣ Jn11:33
1:6 Cf. Jn11:39
1:7a Ⓣ Mk14:51; 16:5
1:12 Ⓣ Mk4:11
2:1b Ⓣ Mk15:40; 16:1; Th61

Fragment 2: To be located between 10:46a ("Then they came to Jericho") and 10:46b ("As he was leaving Jericho . . ."). Clement to Theodore, Folio 2, recto, lines 14–16

2 The sister of the young man whom Jesus loved was there, along
with his mother and Salome, [2]but Jesus refused to see them.

1:7a This *young man* seems to play a rather important role in Mark. Most notably, his reappearance in the empty tomb announcing to the women Jesus' resurrection suggests that this story of his own resurrection serves to foreshadow Jesus'.

1:7b The action is comparable to that found in Mark 5:41; 9:27.

1:7c *Grabbed him by the hand* could be linked with what follows in v. 8, rather than with what precedes: "Grabbing him by the hand, the young man . . ."

1:10 *gave him an order*: The meaning of the Greek is obscure; it may imply that Jesus gave the young man instructions.

1:11 *dressed only in a linen cloth*: The text reads literally: "a linen cloth having been draped over the naked body." The Markan "young man" appears so dressed also in Mark 14:51. The significance of the linen cloth worn over a naked body is a long standing riddle in Markan scholarship. It may be some sort of early Christiam baptismal garb. Hippolytus, *Apostolic Tradition* 21.11, specifies that in the ceremony of baptism both the catechuman and the presbyter are to stand in the water naked.

2:1a The *young man* is the same one as in the first fragment.

Introduction

The remains of the Egerton Gospel, named after the Englishman who funded the purchase of the papyrus fragments on which it is preserved, were first published in 1935; one more small portion, Papyrus Köln 255, was discovered and published in 1987. The extant text includes miracle stories, controversy dialogues, and incidents of violence toward Jesus, none of which is wholly preserved. A story in which Jesus miraculously causes vegetative growth and some sayings are unparalleled in other early Christian texts.

Relationship with other gospels

The Egerton Gospel bears some resemblance to the Gospel of Peter and to the story of the adulteress found in late manuscripts of John and Luke, but its closest counterparts are the canonical gospels. The relationship of Egerton to the canonical gospels has long posed a problem for biblical scholars. On the one hand, some scholars have maintained that Egerton's unknown author composed by borrowing from the canonical gospels. This solution has not proved satisfactory for several reasons: The Egerton Gospel's parallels to the synoptic gospels lack editorial language peculiar to the synoptic authors, Matthew, Mark, and Luke. They also lack features that are common to the synoptic gospels, a difficult fact to explain if those gospels were Egerton's source.

The Egerton Gospel does have very close parallels to John, but because Egerton's versions of these parallels show less development than John's, Egerton may preserve earlier forms of the tradition.

On the other hand, suggestions that the Egerton Gospel served as a source for the authors of Mark and/or John also lack conclusive evidence. The most likely explanation for the Egerton Gospel's similarities to and differences from the canonical gospels is that Egerton's author made independent use of traditional sayings and stories of Jesus that also were used by the other gospel writers. The author combined these elements with other stories and speech material to compose an independent narrative gospel.

Egerton and the formation of the gospels

Although the document's fragmentary state does not permit scholars to determine its exact connection to similar texts, the Egerton Gospel can offer insight into ways the narrative gospels emerged. It provides significant evidence about early variations in the formulation and transmission of written or oral traditions about Jesus. As an analogue to the canonical gospels, Egerton offers independent documentation for the long-held scholarly view that evangelists preserved fairly fixed units of traditional material but freely arranged them into independent literary frameworks. Egerton's contents also suggest that there was early contact between Christian groups that preserved synoptic sources and those that preserved Johannine sources, conceivably before the divergence of these two branches in early Christianity.

Date and provenance

The lone papyrus manuscript of the Egerton Gospel comes from Egypt and probably was copied in the second half of the second century, making it one of the earliest extant Christian manuscripts. The original document perhaps was composed near Palestine/Syria in the second half of the first century, approximately at the same time that the related narrative gospels were being drafted. Like the Gospel of John, the Egerton Gospel probably circulated among Jewish followers of Jesus experiencing strong opposition from fellow Jews who rejected their claims about Jesus.

The Egerton Gospel

Because of the fragmentary condition of the Egerton papyrus, many of its Greek letters and words are not completely visible. However in the translation below, for the sake of readability, missing material is enclosed in square brackets only in those instances where scholars have expressed significant doubt about how the text should be restored.

Jesus & the scriptures

1 ***[. . .] to the legal experts*** [. . .] everyone who acts unjustly [. . .] and
not me [. . .] he does, how does he? [2]Turning to the rulers of the people,
⟨Jesus⟩ made this statement: "Pore over the ⟨sacred⟩ writings. You
imagine that in them there is life to be had. They do indeed give
evidence on my behalf. [3]Don't imagine that I have come to be your
accuser before my Father. The one accusing you is Moses—the one
you thought you could trust." [4]They say, "We know God spoke to
Moses. But you—we don't know [where you come from."] [5]Jesus
replied: "Now you stand accused for not trusting those who are [com-
mended by ⟨Moses⟩.] [6]If you had trusted Moses, you would have
trusted me, for he [wrote] about me to your ancestors." [. . . [7]. . .] stones

1:2 //Jn 5:39
1:3 //Jn 5:45
1:4 //Jn 9:29
1:5 Ⓣ Jn 12:31
1:6 //Jn 5:46
1:7 Cf. Jn 8:59, 10:31

1:4 *[where you come from]:* The Greek letters are completely lost, so the restoration is based on the parallel to John 9:29. **1:5** *Those who are [commended]* translates one possible restoration; "those who are [written about]" is another possible restoration. **1:6** *[wrote]* is a restoration based on the parallel to John 5.46; "spoke" is another possible restoration.

1:1 Although several words can be made out in these lines, the manuscript lacks sufficient legible material to connect them with much confidence. The lines seem to have contained a statement made by Jesus to legal experts.

1:3 Jesus ironically denies a role as accuser here just before he raises an accusation against his opponents. He attributes the accusation to Moses, who was understood by some Jews to play the role of a heavenly advocate for them before God. Jesus contends that Moses' role is more like that of a prosecutor than that of a defense attorney.

my father: The parallel verse in John has "the father," which is more characteristic of John (and Thomas) than Egerton's term. "My father" is found elsewhere in John, also in Q 10:22, Thom 99, and several times in Matthew and Luke. Matthew often embellishes the phrase as "my heavenly father" or the like. Mark has no instances of "my father."

1:5 The identity of *those commended by Moses* is uncertain. The phrase could refer to prophetic successors of Moses who are mentioned in Deut 18:15–22.

1:6 *he [wrote] about me to your ancestors:* Moses was thought to be the author of the Pentateuch, which Christians believed to contain predictive prophecies fulfilled in Jesus.

1:7 An indefinite number of lines is missing in the manuscript between 1:6 and 1:7. It is not certain that the threatened violence of 1:7–8 follows immediately upon the heated exchange of 1:2–6, but it is likely because Jesus' opponents are mentioned as *rulers* in both sections. Although several words can be made out in these lines, the manuscript lacks

together [. . .] him [. . .] 8[The rulers] laid their hands on him to arrest
him and [turn him] over to the crowd. 9But they couldn't arrest him
because the time for him to be turned over hadn't yet arrived. 10So the
master himself slipped through their hands and got away.

The leper

2 ***Just then a leper*** comes up to him and says, "Teacher, Jesus, in
wandering around with lepers and eating with them in the inn, I
became a leper myself. 2If you want to, I'll be made clean." 3The master
said to him, "Okay—you're clean!" And at once his leprosy vanished
from him. 4Jesus says to him, "Go and have the priests examine ⟨your
skin⟩. Then offer for your cleansing what Moses commanded—and no
more sinning." [. . .]

The tax test

3 ***They come to him*** and interrogate him as a way of putting him to
the test. 2They ask, "Teacher, Jesus, we know that you are [from God],
since the things you do put you above all the prophets. 3Tell us, then, is
it permissible to pay to rulers what is due them? Should we pay them or
not?" 4Jesus knew what they were up to, and became indignant. 5Then

1:8 Cf. Jn 7:30, 32; Mk 14:46; Mt 26:50; Lk 20:19
1:9 Cf. Jn 7:44, 8:20; Ⓣ Mk 14:41; 1 Cor 11:23
1:10 //Jn 10:39; Lk 7:30
2:1–4 //Mk 1:40–45; Mt 8:2–4; Lk 5:12–14; cf. Lk 17:12–19; ◊Nm 12:1–18; 2 Kgs 5:1–19
2:4 Cf. Lk 17:14; Jn 5:14; Jn 8:11
3:1–6 //Mk 12:13–17; Mt 22:16–22; Lk 20:21–26; Th 100
3:2 Cf. Jn 3:2

1:8 *[turn him] over:* The number of missing letters is uncertain and another suggested restoration is "throw him to." **3:2** *[from God]:* The letters are completely lost, so the restoration is based on the loose parallel to John 3:2.

sufficient legible material to connect them with much confidence. They probably contained a narrative description of an attempt to stone Jesus.

1:9 Jesus' *time* is a highly developed theme in John, referring to the decisive moment of history when the Son of God's crucifixion becomes his exaltation. But Egerton's use of the term *time* shows no such development and so does not suggest that a divine plan for salvation is at work. Popular notions about a proper time for a person's destiny may underlie Egerton's understanding of the time of Jesus' arrest here.

2:1 The man's social contact with lepers and indeed his approach to Jesus violate Jewish customs. According to Lev 13:45–46 lepers were supposed to be isolated for fear that their impurity was contagious. Unlike the accounts in Mark, Matthew, and Luke, in Egerton the leper makes no gesture of obeisance to Jesus when he approaches him.

Teacher Jesus: This term of address for Jesus is unique to the Egerton Gospel. See also 3:52.

2:2 *If you want to, I'll be made clean:* Egerton's wording of the request is different from that found in Mark, Matthew, and Luke all of whom have: "If you want to you can make me clean."

2:4 Jesus' series of instructions to the leper in Egerton are completely coherent with Jewish law. Rules for priestly examinations of lepers are found in Lev 13:1–59. Ritual offerings for purification are specified in Lev 14:1–32. Jesus' command for the man not to sin again implies that his mistake consists in not abiding by the Jewish custom of avoiding contact with unclean people such as lepers.

Egerton's account lacks the first command given in Mark, Matthew, and Luke in which Jesus tells the leper to speak to no one.

3:1 *They:* The identity of those who aproach Jesus is completely lost. They are no doubt Jewish and could be *rulers*, like those who argued with Jesus and tried to arrest him in the earlier episodes. Their way of engaging Jesus suggests that they are learned authorities with special interest in the Law.

3:2 In the context of the Egerton fragments it is a reasonable guess that *the things you do* refer to Jesus' miracles. The two that are mentioned are the healing of a leper and a miracle of growth at the Jordan.

Miracle at the Jordan

he said to them, "Why do you pay me lip service as a teacher, but not [do] what I say? [6]How accurately Isaiah prophesied about you when he said, 'This people honors me with their lips, but their heart stays far away from me; their worship of me is empty, [because they insist on teachings that are human] commandments [. . .]' "

4 ***[. . .] confined*** [. . .] has been subjected uncertainly [. . .] its weight unweighed [. . .] [2]As they were perplexed at this strange question, Jesus walked over and stood at the bank of the Jordan River. [3]He extended his right hand, [took water,] and scattered it over the [. . .] [4]And then [. . .] [scattered] water [. . .] the [. . .] and it [became full] before their eyes and produced fruit [. . .] [much] [. . .] into [. . .] [them]

5 [. . .] if [. . .] him [. . .] knowing [. . .]

3:5 *[do]:* Another possible restoration is "hear." **4:3–4** The text of the story about miraculous fruit has been restored in various ways, none of which is entirely convincing. Some reconstructions are translated here.

MILNE: ". . . and stretching out his right hand, he took grain and sowed it on the river and then, taking water that had been sown, he cast it down on the ground and it was filled before them and and brought forth fruit."

DODD: ". . . and stretching out his right hand, he filled it with water and sprinkled it upon the shore; and thereupon the sprinkled water made the gound moist, and it was watered before them and brought forth fruit."

LAGRANGE: ". . . stretching out his right hand he filled it with soil and sowed wheat on the soil. And then he poured over it flowing water. The seed penetrated the ground and was raised up before them and it produced fruit."

DANIELS: ". . . and after stretching out his right hand, he took water and sprinkled it upon the tree. And then accordingly he anointed the dry fig tree with the water that had been sprinkled, and it became full before them and he brought forth a fruit."

[took water] is an uncertain restoration. Another possible restoration of the verb is "filled." What Jesus took or filled is lost but the most common suggestion besides *water* is "seed."

4:4 *[scattered] water* is an uncertain restoration. *[became full]:* Other possible restorations are "was watered" and "rose up." . . . *[much]* . . . *into* . . . *[them]* . . . *:* The fragmentary condition of these lines permits no satisfactory restoration. **5:1** . . . *if* . . . *him* . . . *knowing* . . . *:* The fragmentary condition of these lines permits no satisfactory restoration.

3:5
//Q6:46; Mt7:21; Lk6:46
3:6
◊Is29:13; //Mk7:6–8; Mt15:7–8
4:2
◊2Kgs2:13
4:4
◊Nm17:1–11

4:1 Although several words can be made out in these lines, the manuscript lacks sufficient legible material even to guess at how they should be connected. They probably contained the *strange question* which perplexes unidentifiable people in the next verse.

4:3–4 The verbs in the story are fairly well preserved; what is missing are nouns that would permit one to see what is taking place. It is clear that Jesus approached the Jordan, stood at the water's edge, stretched out his hand, took something, and scattered something. What he took and what he scattered must be guessed at. One more action of Jesus is unclear, but in the end something, probably one or more plants, became full and produced fruit. Whatever he has done in the story, Jesus appears to have produced instantaneous growth.

4:3 *Scattered* could be translated more literally as "sowed."

6 [. . .] we are one [. . .] I stay [. . .] stones into [. . .] they kill [. . .] says [. . .]

---

6 *. . . we are one . . . I stay . . . stones into . . . they kill . . . says . . . :* The fragmentary condition of these lines permits no satisfactory restoration.

6
Cf. Jn 10:30

---

6 It is possible that Jesus makes a controversial statement parallel to John 10:30 which is followed by threatened violence, perhaps an attempt to stone him, as above in 1:7–8.

Introduction

Nature of the fragment

Gospel Oxyrhynchus 840 is an excerpt from an otherwise unknown narrative gospel that is quite similar to the New Testament gospels in its style and tone. Jesus is shown in Jerusalem with his disciples, arguing over issues of purity in a manner familiar to readers of Matthew 15 or Mark 7, though there the case centers on rituals connected with eating, rather than the need for cleansing before approaching the temple. There is very little in the fragment to help us place it historically or to label it theologically. It is a bit unusual that Jesus is called "savior" instead of "master" or "teacher" (the Samaritan converts of John 4:42 call Jesus "savior of the world"). An educated guess for the date of composition is sometime before 200 C.E.; a more precise dating may be impossible unless the fragment could be identified with another known text.

Contents of the fragment

Most of the fragment involves a dispute over true purity held in the temple precincts of Jerusalem between Jesus and a leading priest. At the top of the first page, however, we begin with the conclusion of a preceding episode, where Jesus is exhorting his followers to avoid doing evil and thus escape divine judgment. Then he takes his disciples somewhere within the temple precincts, into an area called the "purification," provoking a rebuke from a priest, since his group had not cleansed themselves before entering this sacred court. Jesus' partner in the dispute is both a Pharisee and a leading priest—an historically unusual combination, to be sure, but not unlike the typical sort of generic opponent of Jesus found in the New Testament stories. Jesus counters by questioning whether the priest has himself really been made clean by ritual bathing—after all, thoroughly unclean people (called dogs and swine, prostitutes and entertainers) do this same sort of external washing. Only the "waters of eternal life" can truly cleanse.

Circumstance of discovery

British archaeologists uncovered this fragment nearly a century ago at Oxyrhynchus in Upper Egypt—the same place that the famous "Sayings of the

Lord" were found, now known to be part of the Gospel of Thomas. The fragment consists of a single small leaf of vellum, measuring 8.8 by 7.4 cm., with a writing surface barely two inches wide. A total of 45 lines survives more or less complete on the two sides of the page. The script used dates most likely to the fourth century C.E. The writing was decorated with red ink, used to outline the first letters of sentences, punctuation marks, and strokes used to mark the abbreviation of sacred names. The book itself likely served as an amulet for some ancient Egyptian Christian before this single page became detached. A few other books of similar size have been found from late antiquity that are thought to have been intended for some such magical use.

Gospel Oxyrhynchus 840

Planning ahead

Dispute over defilement

1 [1]*[. . .] before he commits* a crime, he plans carefully. [2]But you
should be on guard so that you don't suffer a similar fate. [3]After all,
those who commit crimes against humanity not only get ⟨their due⟩ in
this life, they also will have to endure punishment and repeated torture
⟨in the next life⟩.

2 [1]***And taking*** ⟨the disciples⟩ along, he led them into the inner
sanctuary itself, and began walking about in the temple precinct.

[2]This Pharisee, a leading priest, Levi by name, also entered, ran into
them, and said to the Savior, "Who gave you permission to wander
around in this inner sanctuary and lay eyes on these sacred vessels,
when you have not performed your ritual bath, and your disciples have
not even washed their feet? [3]Yet in a defiled state you have invaded this
sacred place, which is ritually clean. No one walks about in here, or
dares lay eyes on these sacred vessels, unless they have bathed
themselves and changed clothes."

1:3 The phrase *in this life* is a slight but significant correction of the ms, which reads literally "among the animals." **2:2** The name *Levi* is only partially preserved and may not be original.

1:1 We begin toward the end of a passage about an evildoer who plans ahead but will nonetheless be caught up in divine judgment. Presumably the point of the story lay somewhere between Jesus' parables of poor planning (such as the Two Builders in Q 6:48–49 or the Rich Farmer in Luke 12 and Thom 63) and those of the King Going to War and the Tower Builder (Luke 14) or the Assassin (Thom 98), where individuals are shown planning ahead to good effect.

2:1 The phrase used for the *inner sanctuary* (*hagneuterion*, "purification") is otherwise unattested and thus suggests that the gospel writer was unfamiliar with the details of the temple arrangement. In any case, what is meant is a large open court rather than any particular inner room, and more specifically a place that can be entered only in a state of ritual cleanliness. The most likely candidate is the area usually called the "Court of the Men of Israel." On the need for ritual purity see John 11:55; Josephus *War* 5.5 (227); *Apion* 2.8 (104).

2:2 The temple had a *leading priest* on duty charged with making sure that those who entered were ritually clean. The priest's further identity as *a Pharisee* connects him with other opponents of Jesus in the gospel tradition who dispute with him over questions of ritual.

The *sacred vessels* are the precious items used for libations in the temple service and kept in small rooms opening off of the Court of the Men of Israel. The *ritual bath* was required to achieve a state of levitical purity. *Washing the feet* seems to have been the minimal cleansing required if a Jewish male was otherwise in a state of levitical purity. See John 13:10: "People who have bathed need only wash their feet."

2:3 Priests on duty in the temple are known to have *changed their clothes* after bathing. This fragment is our only evidence that put-

[4]And the Savior stood up immediately, with his disciples, and replied, "Since you are here in the temple, I take it you are clean."

[5]He replies to ⟨the Savior⟩, "I am clean. I bathed in the pool of David, you know, by descending into it by one set of steps and coming up out of it by another. [6]I also changed to white and ritually clean clothes. Only then did I come here and lay eyes on these sacred vessels."

[7]In response the Savior said to him: "Damn the blind who won't see. You bathe in these stagnant waters where dogs and pigs wallow day and night. [8]And you wash and scrub the outer layer of skin, just like prostitutes and dance-hall girls, who wash and scrub and perfume and paint themselves to entice men, while inwardly they are crawling with scorpions and filled with all sorts of corruption. [9]But my disciples and I—you say we are unbathed—have bathed in lively, life-giving water that comes down from [. . .] But damn those [. . .]"

2:7
Ⓣ Mt7:6; Jn9:40–41; 2Pet2:22; Rv22:15

2:8
Ⓣ Mk7:1–23, Q11:39–40, Mt23:25–26, Lk11:39–40, Th89

2:9 Half a line is missing after the words *water that comes down from.*

---

ting on new clothes was required of laymen too. This may well indicate that the author is not well informed about temple regulations.

2:4 As is characteristic throughout the gospel tradition, Jesus answers a challenge with a challenge of his own.

2:5–6 The priest details the steps of his cleansing process. A large double *pool* found nearby the temple may have been used for this purpose (see "the pool of Bethesda" in John 5). The term *pool of David* is otherwise unattested.

2:7 *Stagnant waters* (as in artificial pools) need replenishment, unlike flowing or "living" streams. Jesus' reference to *dogs and pigs* is not meant literally, as though these animals were actually wallowing in the priests' ritual bathing pools! Instead Jesus is pointing to thoroughly unclean sorts of people, as in Matt 7:6; see further 2 Pet 2:22; Rev 22:15.

2:8 Jesus dismisses *washing and scrubbing* as mere external adornment, often covering up the evil inside. The sentiment is similar to that found in Mark 7:1–23, Q 11:39–40, and Thom 89.

Picturing moral corruption with *scorpions crawling inside* is reminiscent of invective addressed by Jesus elsewhere against the Pharisees (Matt 23:25). More commonly in biblical tradition, the presence or threat of scorpions suggests danger or unusually severe punishment (Deut 8:15; 1 Kgs 12:11, 14; Ezek 2:6; Luke 10:19; Rev 9:3, 5, 10).

2:9 Jesus contrasts ritual bathing with Christian baptism, called *lively, life-giving water from heaven.*

Introduction

Gospel Oxyrhynchus 1224 contains fragments of Jesus sayings. It was discovered in 1903 and published in 1914. It consists of two fragments from a Greek papyrus book whose handwriting dates to the early fourth or late third century.

Fragment 1 is very small, 3.5 × 4.3 cm., so that only three partial lines and three full words are visible on the front and two partial lines and one full word on the back. Fragment 2 is much larger, 6.3 × 13.1 cm., and has two columns on both sides. Judging from the page numbers on the two fragments, there are over thirty pages in between them. We cannot be certain, however, that both fragments are from the same work even though both were copied by the same scribe and we cannot presume that other works were not included before or even between those represented by the fragments.

The papyrus is badly mutilated with not even a single complete line anywhere extant. Restorations are therefore highly conjectural. The text does not seem to be dependent on the New Testament gospels since none of their redactional elements are discernible in its few verses. Furthermore, where New Testament parallels exist, it is hard to discern a reason for the papyrus' changes, if indeed those were its sources. As an independent gospel, it belongs, insofar as its fragmentary state allows us to see, not with discourse gospels involving the risen Jesus (e.g., the Secret Book of James and the Gospel of Mary), but with sayings gospels involving the earthly Jesus (e.g., Q and the Gospel of Thomas). But the vision in 3:2 and the debates in 4:1–2 and 5:1–2 indicate a position closer to Q than to Thomas. No opponents, for example, ever challenge Jesus in the few narrative situations in Thomas as they do here and in Q.

The date when the manuscript was copied tells little about the date of this gospel's composition. It could be as early as the 50s when Christians first began to create books about what Jesus had said and done.

Gospel Oxyrhynchus 1224

1 [. . .] in every [. . .] To you I swear [. . .]

2 [. . .] you [. . .]

3 [. . .] weighed me down. [2]And [standing] by Jesus [i]n a visio[n says:] Why are you d[iscouraged]? For it is not [. . .] [y]ou but the [. . .] gave [. . .]

4 [. . . you s]aid not answer[ing.] [2][What then do you re]nounce? What is the ne[w] teach[ing that they say] you te[ach] or new [procla-ma]tion [you proclaim? Answ]er and [. . .]

5 When the scholars an[d Pharise]es and priests observ[ed hi]m, they
were indignant [because he reclined ⟨at table⟩ in the com]pany of 5:1–2
sin[ners]. [2]But Jesus overheard [them and said,] Those who are we[ll //Mk2:15–17, Mt9:10–13,
don't need a doctor.] Lk5:29–32

1a The phrase *in every* . . . is found in the NT on the lips of Jesus only in Luke 21:36.
1b The phrase *To you I swear* is never found on the lips of Jesus in the NT in that form, but always as "I swear to you" (sixty times in the four gospels).
3:1 The verb *weighed down* is found in the NT in Matt 26:43; Luke 9:32; 21:34; 2 Cor 1:8; 5:4; 1 Tim 5:16. The first two cases involve being weighed down by sleep. The subject here is what: sleep? sorrow? fear?
3:2a Matt 17:9 describes the Transfiguration as a *vision.* The only other NT occurrences of the term are in Acts, three times in the phrase *in a vision.* Note that here the vision is given to the individual narrating the story.
3:2b The restoration of *discouraged* is little more than guesswork. The word is found in the NT only in Col 3:21.
4:2a *Renounce* occurs in the NT only in 2 Cor 4:2.
4:2b The restoration is highly conjectural with *ne[w] teach[ing]* suggested especially by the parallel in Mark 1:27.
4:2c The line can be restored with either *baptism* or *proclamation.* If *baptism* is adopted, then, on the analogy of Mark 1:4 = Luke 3:3 where John "proclaims a baptism," this excerpt would refer to the Baptist. If it referred to Jesus, it would be an independent witness to Jesus himself as a baptizer. SV adopts *proclamation* because it continues the redundancy of *teaching/teach* of the previous clause into the parallel *proclamation/proclaim.*
5:1 The triple designation *scholars and Pharisees and priests* does not occur in the NT. The word *[Pharise]es* is restored on analogy with Mark 2:16, which has *the scholars of the Pharisees* criticizing Jesus in a similar situation. An alternative word such as "[elder]s" is also possible. There might, therefore, have originally been an attempt to designate the three groups in the Sanhedrin: priests, elders, and scholars.
5:2 This verse is restored to match Luke 5:31 which has *well* rather than *able-bodied* as

6:1a
//Q6:27–28,
Mt5:44,
Lk6:27–28
6:1b
//Mk9:40, Lk9:50
6:2
Cf.Q11:23,
Mt12:30, Lk11:23

6 [A]nd p[r]ay for your [ene]mies. For the one who is not [against
y]ou is on your side. [2][The one who today i]s at a distance, tomorrow
will [b]e [near you,] and in [. . .] of the advers[ary]

---

in Mark 2:17 = Matt 9:12. But since only eight Greek letters remain on the page, very different restorations are possible, for instance, "hearing [that] the ph[onies were an]gry."

6:1a This aphorism appears as *love your enemies* in Q 6:27–28, 35. However, in versions of the sayings which depend on the NT gospels (Did 1:3 and Polycarp's Letter to the Philippians 12:3), it was changed to *pray for your enemies,* as here. The present form might be taken as a softening of a too-difficult injunction, but it probably is at least its equivalent, if not its more specific and practical intensification.

6:1b This aphorism appears, opening with a Greek participle, as *not on your side = against* in Q 11:23. It appears, opening with a Greek relative pronoun, as *not against = on your side* in Mark 9:40 = Luke 9:50. The GOxy 1224 version, however, has the participial opening, as in Q, and the *not against = on your side* as in Mark. This is an indication that GOxy 1224 did not use any of the NT gospels as a written source.

6:2 The aphorism in 6:1 has a two-verse formulation with *not on your side = against* and *not gathers = scatters* in Q 11:23. In Q the verses are parallel in form and content, and the second verse might have been created on the analogy of the first one. In GOxy 1224, however, this next verse is less equivalent. It speaks not of the simultaneity of *not against* and *on your side*, thereby excluding any neutral middle position, but of a future change to *at a distance/near* from a present posture of *against/on your side.* The restoration is highly conjectural.

Jewish-Christian Gospels

A gold coin from Rome
honoring the Emperor Constantine,
under whose patronage the Council
of Nicea was convened in 325 C.E.
Courtesy of Numismatic Fine Arts International, Inc., Los Angeles.

Jewish-Christian Gospels

Christian authors from the mid-second to the early fifth century refer to gospels that were used by Christians who understood themselves to be deeply rooted in Judaism. No copies of these gospels exist today, not even in independent manuscript fragments. Our sole source of information about the existence and contents of these gospels is the references to and quotations from them in the works of Christian authors.

The lack of any actual copies of these gospels makes our knowledge of them tentative and partial. The authors who transmit quotations from them seem to assume that all their quotations come from the same gospel. However, the literary characteristics and theological tendencies of the different quotations are so inconsistent that it is virtually certain that they derive from more than one gospel. After analyzing all the quotations and piecing together all the clues from all the sources, scholars have reached a consensus that there were three distinct Jewish-Christian gospels: 1) the Gospel of the Hebrews (GHeb), a gospel with gnostic tendencies and little relationship to the canonical gospels; 2) the Gospel of the Ebionites (GEbi), a gospel based on the synoptics; 3) the Gospel of the Nazoreans (GNaz), a gospel quite similar to Matthew.

Three problems further complicate our attempt to understand the Jewish-Christian gospels: 1) It is sometimes difficult to ascertain which gospel a given author is referring to; 2) the quotations from these gospels are quite fragmentary—some are extremely brief, a mere line or two; 3) these later authors are sometimes hostile witnesses, since they regard some of the ideas in these gospels as heretical. Information derived from opponents is not always reliable.

These quoted fragments are fraught with difficulties for our understanding of the lost gospels they represent. Still, were it not for these citations, we would know little or nothing about these interesting communities who continued for centuries to consider themselves both Jewish and Christian.

The Gospel of the Hebrews

Introduction

Gospel of the Hebrews (GHeb) is the title given most frequently by early Christian authors to what they took to be a single Jewish-Christian gospel. It is impossible, however, to reconcile all of the extant fragments into a single gospel and there is broad scholarly agreement that they derive from three gospels, though there is not always consensus on which fragment should be assigned to which gospel. Even when our Christian authors clearly state that a certain quotation comes from the Gospel of the Hebrews, this information cannot be trusted in every case. This gospel is the most widely attested of the three Jewish-Christian gospels. Direct citations are preserved by five authors and three more mention it without quoting from it.

Genre

The surviving fragments of the Gospel of the Hebrews do not give a clear indication of its genre, except that it contained narrative. We cannot tell whether GHeb 1 is a quotation or a summary, but if it is a quotation, it shows that its author worked extensive theological commentary into the narratives, which would make the Gospel of the Hebrews more like the Gospel of John than the synoptics. GHeb 4 takes the form of a first person report by Jesus himself, giving the reader a privileged insight into Jesus in much the same way as John does in presenting Jesus' final discourse (John 17).

Contents

The contents and structure of the gospel are impossible to determine. GHeb 1 deals with Jesus' pre-existence and birth, GHeb 2–3 with his baptism, and GHeb 4 probably with his temptation. The call of Levi-Matthias (GHeb 5) presumably fell near the beginning of the gospel. It is impossible to tell where GHeb 6–8 could have been found, or even whether they were simple sayings or parts of narratives. The appearance of the risen Lord to James (GHeb 9) came near the end. GHeb 9 presupposes three earlier stories that are nowhere recorded, but of which we can recover something: a last supper scene at which James vowed to fast until he saw the risen Jesus, a resurrection scene in which Jesus gave his shroud to the priest's slave, and, by inference, some sort of burial scene.

The existing pieces of this gospel are enough to indicate that it must have been quite different from other gospels. In a few places, it seems to have been influenced by the wording of passages in the canonical gospels, but for the most part it goes its own way. There is no reason to think that the Gospel of the Hebrews drew from the canonical gospels deliberately or directly, nor that it represents a development of synoptic or Johannine traditions.

Theology

The Gospel of the Hebrews has a distinctive christology. Christ and his mother both existed before their appearance on earth in human form (GHeb 1). At his baptism, Jesus is addressed as son, not by God, but by the spirit, which turns out to be his mother (GHeb 3, 4). Jesus is not merely led by the spirit (as in Luke's gospel). He is completely united with her: "the whole fountain of the holy spirit came down and rested on him" (GHeb 3).

This gospel's depiction of the holy spirit as female is striking. GHeb 4c, 4d, and 4e explain that the Semitic word for "spirit" is feminine in gender, but this way of portraying the spirit is due to more than a peculiarity of Hebrew grammar. This distinctive depiction of the spirit is rooted in Jewish speculation about divine Widsom, a female personification of one of God's attributes who was believed to dwell with "holy souls" (see the note to GHeb 3).

The "seek-find" and "rule-rest" language of GHeb 6 also comes from the wisdom tradition. This saying describes the stages on the way to salvation ("rest") and encourages the believer to imitate heavenly Wisdom and thus to share in her qualities.

The Gospel of the Hebrews gives prominence to James the Just by making him the first believer to see the risen Lord (GHeb 9). This James was not an apostle, but was known as the brother of the Lord in GHeb 9 and in the New Testament (Mark 6:3, Gal 1:19). Christian tradition remembered him as the leader of the Christian community in Jerusalem and a formidable advocate of Law-observant Christianity. However, the remains of the Gospel of the Hebrews give no indication that it advocated strict Torah observance.

Language

Jerome claims to have translated this gospel from Hebrew (GHeb 4c, 9), but there are good reasons to doubt this, the most important being the fact that his quotation in 4c corresponds so closely (even in word order) to that of Origen's in 4a that it seems certain that Jerome got his quotation from Origen, not from any Semitic document. There is no compelling reason to doubt that the Gospel of the Hebrews was composed in Greek.

The early Christian quotations of the Gospel of the Hebrews are preserved in Coptic (1), Greek (4a, 4b, 5, 6), and Latin (2, 3, 4c, 4d, 4e, 7, 8, 9).

Date and place of origin

Since this gospel seems to know the canonical gospels and since it was used by Christian authors in the mid-second century, it must have been written in the early second century.

We have no direct information as to where the Gospel of the Hebrews was written. Most of its citations come from, or can be traced to, Christians who lived in Egypt. Parallels to some of its teachings are found in Egyptian Christianity, so it may well have been written there, though this is only an educated guess.

The Gospel of the Hebrews

1 *Paraphrased by Cyril of Jerusalem (4th century),* Discourse on Mary the Mother of God

It is written in the Gospel of the Hebrews that

> [1]when Christ wanted to come to earth, the Good Father summoned
> a mighty power in the heavens who was called Michael, and en-
> trusted Christ to his care. [2]The power came down into the world,
> and it was called Mary, and Christ was in her womb for seven
> months. [3]She gave birth to him and he grew up and he chose the
> apostles who preached him everywhere. [4]He fulfilled the appointed
> time that was decreed for him. [5]The Jews grew envious of him and
> came to hate him. They changed the custom of their law and they
> rose up against him and laid a trap and caught him. [6]They turned
> him over to the governor, who gave him back to them to crucify.
> [7]And after they had raised him on the cross, the Father took him up
> into heaven to himself.

1:6 Cf.Mt27:2, Jn19:16
1:7 Ⓣ Phil2:8–9
2 //GNaz2
2:1 Ⓣ Mk1:4, Lk3:3

2 *Quoted by Jerome (4th–5th century),* Against the Pelagians *3*

In the Gospel of the Hebrews . . . the following story is told:

> [1]The mother of the Lord and his brothers said to him, "John the
> Baptist baptized for the forgiveness of sins. Let's go and get baptized
> by him."

1:1–2 According to the Gospel of the Hebrews, both Christ and his mother existed in heaven before coming to earth. Apparently, *Michael* is the name of a *mighty power in the heavens* that came to earth in the form of Mary. In GHeb 4 Michael/Mary is identified with the holy spirit.

1:2 *in her womb for seven months*: According to some Jewish, Greek, and Roman traditions, a number of ancient heroes were born after only seven months. Among them were Isaac, Moses, Samuel, Dionysus, Apollo, and Julius Caesar.

1:3 The Coptic for *he grew up* may reflect the Greek of Luke 2:52.

1:6 *They turned him over to the governor* may reflect the wording of Matt 27:2.

He gave him back to them to crucify recalls John 19:16 and makes the Jews, rather than the Romans, responsible for killing Jesus.

2 It cannot be determined with certainty whether this fragment belongs to the Gospel of the Nazoreans or to the Gospel of the Hebrews. Jerome mistakenly believes that all his quotations originate from one Jewish-Christian gospel, which in some cases makes it difficult to distinguish fragments of the Gospel of the Hebrews from those of Nazoreans.

[2]But he said to them, "How have I sinned? So why should I go and get baptized by him? Only if I don't know what I'm talking about."

3 *Quoted by Jerome,* Commentary on Isaiah *4 (commenting on Isa 11:2)*

In the Hebrew gospel that the Nazarenes read it says,

> [1]The whole fountain of the holy spirit comes down on him. For the Lord is the spirit and where the spirit is, there is freedom.

Later on, in the same gospel, we find the following:

> [2]And it happened that when the Lord came up out of the water, the whole fountain of the holy spirit came down on him and rested on him. [3]It said to him, "My Son, I was waiting for you in all the prophets, waiting for you to come so I could rest in you. [4]For you are my rest; you are my first-begotten Son who rules forever."

4a *Quoted and explained by Origen (3rd century),* Commentary on John *2*

Those who give credence to the Gospel of the Hebrews, in which the Savior says,

> "Just now my mother, the holy spirit, took me by one of my hairs and brought me to Tabor, the great mountain,"

2:2 Cf.Mt3:14 Ⓣ Heb4:15
3 //Mk1:9–11, Mt3:13–17, Lk3:21–22, Jn1:29–34, GEbi4
3:1–2 ◊Is11:2
3:1 //2Cor3:17
3:3 Cf.Wis7:27, Sir24:7
3:4 ◊Ps132:14, 2:7 Ⓣ Heb1:6, Col1.15, Lk1:33
4 Cf.Mk1:12–13, Lk4:1–2, Mt4:1–2, 8–10 ◊Ez8:3
4a //Mk3:35, Mt12:50, Lk8:21, Th99:2, GEbi5:3–4

2:2 Jesus' statements do not mean that he refused baptism. If they did, Jerome would have mentioned that this gospel lacked a baptism scene. The purpose of this passage is to avoid any implication that Jesus got baptized because he was seeking forgiveness of his sins. Matthew also deals with this problem, though in a different way (Matt 3:13–15). This fragment also seems to assume that Jesus' family was baptized along with him.

3 In this version of the baptism scene, the voice is that of the holy spirit, not of God as in the rest of the gospel tradition. Contrary to GEbi 4, Jesus' baptism here does not transform his status; he already was the divine son of the spirit.

3:3 *I was waiting for you in all the prophets*: Wisdom is similarly described in Wis 7:27: "In every generation she enters holy souls and makes them prophets and friends of God."

so I could rest: The holy spirit speaks like divine Wisdom: "I have acquired something among every people and nation. Among all of them I sought rest. I sought to make my home in someone's land" (Sir 24:6–7).

4 This seems to be an excerpt from a unique version of the story of Jesus' temptation, with the holy spirit taking Jesus up to the mountain, a role played by the devil in Matt 4:8. The event is here reported by Jesus himself, which may be the way the Gospel of the Hebrews explains how this private event came to be known publicly.

As in GHeb 1, the holy spirit is understood to be Jesus' mother. GHeb 4c,d,e attribute this unusual concept to the gender of the Hebrew word for "spirit." In SecJas 5:6 Jesus calls himself a "son of the holy spirit." Thom 101 may be referring to the holy spirit when Jesus says, "My true mother gave me life."

have to face the problem of explaining how it is possible for the "mother" of Christ to be the holy spirit which came into existence through the Logos. But those things are not difficult to explain. For if "whoever does the will of the heavenly father is his brother and sister and mother," and if the name "brother of Christ" applies not only to humans, but also to beings of a more divine rank, there is nothing absurd in the holy spirit being his mother, when anyone who does the will of the heavenly father is called "mother of Christ."

4b *Quoted by Origen,* Homily on Jeremiah *15*

If someone can accept this—

> "Just now my mother, the holy spirit, took me by one of my hairs and brought me to Tabor, the great mountain"

—one can see that she is his mother.

4c *Quoted and explained by Jerome,* Commentary on Micah *2 (commenting on Mic 7:6)*

Whoever has read the Song of Songs will understand that the word of God is also the bridegroom of the soul. And whoever gives credence to the gospel circulating under the title "Gospel of the Hebrews," which we recently translated, in which it is said by the Savior himself,

> "Just now my mother, the holy spirit, took me by one of my hairs,"

will not hesitate to say that the word of God proceeds from the spirit, and that the soul, which is the bride of the word, has the holy spirit (which in Hebrew is feminine in gender, RUA) as a mother-in-law.

4d *Quoted and explained by Jerome,* Commentary on Isaiah *11 (commentary on Isa 40:9)*

In the Gospel of the Hebrews that the Nazarenes read it says,

> "Just now my mother, the holy spirit, took me."

Now no one should be offended by this, because "spirit" in Hebrew is feminine, while in our language (Latin) it is masculine and in Greek it is neuter. In divinity, however, there is no gender.

4e *Quoted and explained by Jerome,* Commentary on Ezekiel *4 (commenting on Ezek 16:13)*

In the Book of Judges we read "Deborah," which means "bee." Her prophecies are the sweetest honey and refer to the holy spirit, who is called in Hebrew by a feminine noun. In the Gospel of the Hebrews that the Nazarenes read, the Savior indicates this by saying,

> "Just now my mother, the holy spirit, whisked me away."

5 *Reported by Didymus (4th century),* Commentary on the Psalms *184 (commenting on Psalm 33)*

Thomas is also called Didymus, and there are many other people with two names. Scripture seems to call Matthew "Levi" in the Gospel of Luke, but they are not the same person. Rather, Matthias, who replaced Judas, and Levi are the same person with a double name. This is apparent in the Gospel of the Hebrews.

6a *Quoted by Clement of Alexandria (2nd–3rd century),* Miscellanies *2*

In the Gospel of the Hebrews it is written,

> "Whoever marvels will rule and whoever rules will rest."

6b *Quoted by Clement of Alexandria,* Miscellanies *5*

"Those who seek should not stop until they find; when they find, they will marvel. When they marvel, they will rule, and when they rule, they will rest."

7 *Quoted by Jerome (4th–5th century),* Commentary on Ephesians *3 (commenting on Eph 5:4)*

We can read in the Hebrew gospel that the Lord, speaking to his disciples, said,

> "Never be glad except when you look at your brother or sister with love."

5
Cf.Th Prologue, Lk 5:27, Mk 2:14, Mt 9:9, Acts 1:15–26

6
//GrTh 2:4
Ⓣ Th 50:3, 51:1, 60:6, 90; Mt 11:28–29; DSav 11:5
Cf. Sir 51:26–27, 6:23–31

6b
//Th 2:1, 92:1, 94; Q 11:10; Mt 7:8; Lk 11:10; Mary 4:7

---

5 Matt 9:9 identifies Levi the toll collector of Mark 2:14 with Matthew. The Gospel of the Hebrews is unique in identifying Levi with Matthias, the apostle chosen after Jesus' death (Acts 1:15–26). The names "Matthew" and "Matthias" are nearly identical in Greek (*Matthaios* and *Matthias*).

6 GHeb 6b is the fullest form of this saying, found in different versions in Thom 2 and GrThom 2.

Whoever marvels will rule is a concept from the Jewish wisdom tradition: "The desire for wisdom leads to ruling" (Wis 6:20).

rest is salvation, the final attainment in the search for wisdom, as in Matt 11:28–29 and Thom 90 (see also Sir 51:26–27 and 6:26–28).

7–8 *brother or sister* probably refers to a fellow believer, as in GNaz 5 and Matt 18:21–22. In Naz 6 "brothers and sisters" refers to fellow Jews.

8 *Quoted by Jerome,* Commentary on Ezekiel *6 (commenting on Ezek 18:7)*

The Gospel of the Hebrews that the Nazarenes are used to reading listed this among the most serious crimes:

> Those who have saddened their brother's or sister's spirit.

9 *Quoted by Jerome,* On Famous Men *2*

I recently translated into Greek and Latin the gospel called the "Gospel of the Hebrews," the one that Origen also frequently uses. After the resurrection of the Savior, it says,

> [1]The Lord, after he had given the linen cloth to the priest's slave, went to James and appeared to him. [2](Now James had sworn not to eat bread from the time that he drank from the Lord's cup until he would see him raised from among those who sleep.)

[3]Shortly after this the Lord said,

> "Bring a table and some bread."

[4]And immediately it is added:

> He took the bread, blessed it, broke it, and gave it to James the Just and said to him, "My brother, eat your bread, for the Son of Adam has been raised from among those who sleep."

9:1 Cf. 1 Cor 15:7
9:2 Cf. Mk 14:25, Mt 26:29, Lk 22:18
9:4 Cf. Mk 14:22, Mt 26:26, Lk 22:19, 1 Cor 11:23–24

9:1 This account of the resurrection is unique in that James is the first believer to see the risen Jesus (see 1 Cor 15:7), not Peter or Mary of Magdala, as in the other gospels. It also presupposes that the tomb was guarded by the high priest's personnel rather than by Roman soldiers. Peter 8:1–4 has Pharisees, elders, scholars, and Roman soldiers at the tomb.

9:2–4 That James vowed to fast until the resurrection (see Luke 22:16, where Jesus makes this vow) lets him share sympathetically in Jesus' fate and makes James overcome the disciples' misunderstanding of Jesus' death, an important theme in the synoptic passion predictions and meal scenes. The transformation of James into a hero in this gospel is echoed in Thom 12, where Jesus pronounces James to be the chief authority among the disciples.

Introduction

All of our quotations from the Gospel of the Ebionites (GEbi) come from the church father Epiphanius of Salamis (ca. 315–403). If this gospel had a title, we do not know what it was. "Gospel of the Ebionites" is a modern title that reflects the fact that all of its citations come from Epiphanius' discussion of the Jewish-Christian group called the Ebionites and that some (though not all) of the gospel's fragments have theological traits that match what we know of the Ebionites from other sources.

Ebionites is a narrative gospel. It is closest to Matthew, but has clear connections also to Mark and Luke. Judging from the way Ebionites combines elements from all three of these gospels, it can best be characterized as a harmony of the synoptics, with various expansions and abridgements.

We possess only seven fragments of this gospel, so we cannot ascertain much about its contents or structure. The fragments have to do with John the Baptist, Jesus's baptism, his choice of the twelve apostles, and the last supper. Two more quotations preserve sayings of Jesus. Epiphanius informs us that Ebionites omitted the birth stories and genealogy of Jesus. This gospel therefore began, like Mark, with the appearance of John.

Theology

Three fragments point to a distinctive christology. The baptism of Jesus (GEbi 4) is told in a way that seems to emphasize that Jesus became God's son on this occasion. This belief, known as "adoptionism," held that Jesus was not divine by nature or by birth, but that God chose him to become his son, i.e., adopted him. According to Epiphanius' comments on GEbi 5 and 6, the Ebionites "deny that he was human" and assert that "he was not born of God the Father, but created like one of the archangels." Though these two beliefs may seem inconsistent when taken out of context, they are two aspects of a christology that made a distinction between the human Jesus before his baptism and the semi-divine Christ after his "adoption" by God. However, this specific christology cannot easily be reconciled with what writers prior to Epiphanius tell us about the Ebionites: that they believed Jesus to be merely human. This puzzling discrepancy raises the question whether this gospel was actually an Ebionite text. Unfortunately, its very fragmentary state and the often contradictory reports about the Ebionites make it impossible for us to answer this question with certainty.

Language

Epiphanius twice tells us that Ebionites was known as "the Hebrew gospel." Nevertheless, the quotations that he provides show that Ebionites closely followed the Greek text of the synoptic gospels, so there is little doubt that this gospel was originally composed in Greek.

Date and place of origin

Since the only quotations of Ebionites come from a work by Epiphanius in 375, this gospel had to be earlier than this, though how much earlier cannot be determined with certainty. However, there are several indications that give scholars confidence that Ebionites was composed in the first half of the second century.

Irenaeus (ca. 140–200) is probably the earliest witness to Ebionites. He reports that the Ebionites used only Matthew's gospel, but also that they deny the virgin birth. This means that they must have been using their own gospel and not canonical Matthew, which clearly attests to this belief. Irenaeus' remarks, then, presuppose that by about 175 the Ebionites had a gospel that could be confused with Matthew but that lacked the story of the virgin birth. This gospel was almost certainly Ebionites, which Epiphanius himself confused with Matthew and which does not contain an infancy narrative.

Ebionites' character as a harmony of the synoptic gospels makes it fit well into the early to mid-second century, since several other synoptic harmonies were composed in this period.

We cannot be sure where this gospel was written. A few early Christian writers indicate that the Ebionites lived in the area east of the Jordan, which is where Epiphanius found the gospel, though this does not mean it was composed there.

The Gospel of the Ebionites

All fragments are quoted by Epiphanius (4th century), Heresies *30*

1a Now the beginning of their gospel goes like this:

> 1 In the days of Herod, king of Judea, John appeared in the Jordan
> river baptizing with a baptism that changed people's hearts. 2 He was
> said to be a descendant of Aaron the priest, a son of Zechariah and
> Elizabeth. 3 And everybody went out to him.

1b By mutilating Matthew's genealogy, they make the beginning say, as we have already stated:

> In the days of Herod, king of Judea, during the high-priesthood of Caiaphas,

they say,

> this man named John appeared in the Jordan river baptizing with a baptism that changed people's hearts,

and so on.

2 At any rate, in the gospel that they call "According to Matthew," which is not complete but adulterated and mutilated—they call it the "Hebrew" gospel—is found the following:

> 1 There was this man named Jesus, who was about thirty years old,
> who chose us. 2 And when he came to Capernaum, he entered the
> house of Simon, who was nicknamed Peter. He then began to speak
> as follows:
> 3 "As I was walking along by the lake of Tiberias, I chose John and
> James, sons of Zebedee, and Simon and Andrew and Thaddeus and

1 Cf. Mk 1:4–5, Mt 3:5–6, Lk 3:1–3, 1:5

2:1 Cf. Lk 3:23

2:2 Cf. Mk 1:29, Mt 8:14, Lk 4:38

2:3 Cf. Mk 1:16–18, 3:16–19; Mt 4:18–20, 10:2–4; Lk 5:1–11, 6:14–16

---

1 Epiphanius makes it clear in both citations that Ebionites opens with this announcement of John's baptizing. Ebionites has no genealogy or infancy narrative, probably because the ones in Matthew and Luke attest to Jesus' virgin birth, a belief denied by the Ebionites.
1a:2 *descendant of Aaron, son of Zechariah and Elizabeth*: Even though Ebionites has no story of Jesus' birth, this phrase, copied from Luke 1:5, shows that the author knew at least Luke's infancy narrative.
2:1 *chose us*: the first person plural narration is unusual in a gospel.

Simon the Zealot and Judas the Iscariot. [4]Then I summoned you, Matthew, while you were sitting at the toll booth, and you followed me. [5]Therefore, I want you to be twelve apostles, to symbolize Israel."

3 And

[1]It so happened that John was baptizing, and Pharisees and all Jerusalem went out to him and got baptized. [2]And John wore clothes made of camel hair and had a leather belt around his waist. [3]His food,

it says,

consisted of raw honey that tasted like manna, like a pancake cooked with oil.

Thus they change the word of truth into a lie and instead of "locusts" they put "pancake cooked with honey."

4 After saying many things, it adds:

[1]When the people were baptized, Jesus also came and got baptized by John. [2]As he came up out of the water, the skies opened and he saw the holy spirit in the form of a dove coming down and entering him. [3]And there was a voice from the sky that said, "You are my favored son—I fully approve of you." [4]And again, "Today I have become your father."

[5]And right away a bright light illuminated the place. When John saw this,

2:4 Cf.Mt 9:9, Mk 2:14, Lk 5:27–28
3 //Mk 1:4–6, Mt 3:4–7
3:2 ◊2 Kgs 1:8
3:3 ◊Num 11:8, Ex 16:31
4 //Mt 3:13–17, Mk 1:9–11, Lk 3:21–22, GHeb 3
4:3–4 //Lk 3:22
4:3 //Mk 1:11 ◊Is 42:1
4:4 ◊Ps 2:7

2:4 *Matthew*: Mark lists Matthew among the twelve, but names the toll collector "Levi" (Mark 2:14). Matthew changes "Levi" to "Matthew" (Matt 9:9) and adds "the toll collector" to his name in the list of the twelve (Matt 10:3). Ebionites' version thus sides with Matthew.

2:5 It is odd that Ebionites specifies *twelve* apostles, while Epiphanius' quotation names only eight. Perhaps Epiphanius inadvertently skipped over four names, an easy enough mistake when copying a long list. The four missing apostles, according to Mark 3:8, Matt 10:3, and Luke 6:14–15 are Philip, Bartholomew, James the son of Alphaeus, and Thomas.

3:1–2 combines phrases from Matthew and Mark.

3:3 The omission of locusts from John's diet may indicate, along with GEbi 7, that the Ebionites were vegetarians.

The unusual description of the honey depends on Num 11:8 and Exod 16:31 and is unique to Ebionites. It confirms that this gospel was composed in Greek, for the connection between locusts (*akris*) and pancakes (*egkris*) could only be made in Greek.

4 This story combines phrases mostly from Matthew and Luke. The voice from heaven speaks three times, each time in words taken from a different gospel (Mark, Luke, then Matthew).

4:4 *Today I have become your father* could well reflect adoptionist christology, in which Jesus becomes son of God at his baptism.

it says,

> he said to him, "Who are you?" [6]And again a voice from the sky said to him, "This is my favored son—I fully approve of him."
> [7]And then,

it says,

> John knelt down in front of him and said, "Please, Lord, you baptize me."
> [8]But he stopped him and said, "It's all right. This is the way everything is supposed to be fulfilled."

5 They deny that he was human, I suppose because of what the Savior said when it was reported to him:

> [1]"Look, your mother and your brothers are outside."
> [2]"My mother and brothers—who ever are they?" [3]And he pointed to his disciples and said, "These are my brothers and mother and sisters, [4]those who do the will of my Father."

6 They say that ⟨Christ⟩ was not born of God the Father, but created like one of the archangels, and even more, that he rules over the angels and over everything that was made by the Almighty, and that he came and announced, as it says in the gospel, the one called "According to the Hebrews,"

> "I came to do away with sacrifices, and if you don't stop sacrificing, you won't stop experiencing wrath."

4:6 //Mt3:17
4:7–8 //Mt3:14–15
5 //Mk3.31–35, Mt12:46–50, Lk8:19–21, Th99
6 Cf.Mt5:17, 9:13, 12:7 ◊Hos6:6

4:7–8 These verses are derived from Matthew. They subordinate John to Jesus, even though it is John who does the baptizing, and therefore avoid any hint of rivalry between them. This may reflect a controversy between early Christians and the followers of John, who could claim that the Baptist was greater than the one he had baptized.

5 Epiphanius links the Ebionite belief that Jesus was not human to the saying in which he disowns his natural family. This probably presupposes the belief that, prior to his baptism, Jesus was merely human, whereas after it he was God's son and so no longer belonged to his earthly family. This would fit with the adoptionist character of GEbi 4 and the christology implicit in GEbi 6.

6 This saying seems odd in a Jewish-Christian gospel, even though animal sacrifice ceased to be an option after the destruction of the temple in 70 C.E.

This saying has no parallel in the gospel tradition. It may be loosely based on Jesus' quotation of Hos 6:6 in Matt 9:13 and 12:7 ("It's mercy I desire instead of sacrifice") although it directly contradicts Jesus' declaration in Matt 5:17–18. In what might be a reference to GEbi 6, a fourth century Jewish-Christian text makes the following comment: "In saying, 'I did not come to do away with the law,' and yet doing away with something, he indicated that what he did away with had not originally been part of the law" (Pseudo-Clement, *Homilies* 3.51.2).

According to Epiphanius, the Ebionites believed that Jesus was not born with a divine nature, but that he became the highest of all creatures, though still not equal to God. It is difficult to understand how *created like one of the archangels* fits into an adoptionist christology.

7 They take it on themselves to obscure the logic of the truth and to alter the saying, as is evident to everyone from the context, and make the disciples say:

> [1]"Where do you want us to get things ready for you to eat the Passover meal?"

And apparently they make him answer:

> [2]"I certainly have not looked forward with all my heart to eating meat with you at this Passover, have I?"

Anyone can detect their deceit because the sequence makes it obvious that the *mu* and the *eta* have been added. Instead of saying, "I have looked forward with all my heart" they add the additional word *mē* ("not"). Now in fact he said, "I have looked forward with all my heart to eating the Passover meal with you." However, they deceive themselves by adding the word "meat," and they do evil by saying, "I do not look forward to eating meat with you at this Passover."

7:1 //Mk14:12, Mt26:17, Lk22:8–9
7:2 Cf.Lk22:15

---

7 As Epiphanius points out, Ebionites adds the word *meat* to Jesus' statement. Apparently, Jesus objects to eating the Passover meal, not out of any objection to the festival itself, but because the meal includes meat (lamb). Other than GEbi 7 (and possibly GEbi 3), no other source reports that the Ebionites were vegetarians.

The Gospel of the Nazoreans

Introduction

The Gospel of the Nazoreans (GNaz) is a narrative gospel closely related to the Gospel of Matthew. Like the other Jewish-Christian gospels, it is preserved only in a few quotations and citations in the writings of early Christian authors. All the quoted passages show interesting differences between Nazoreans and Matthew. It seems that early Christian authors quote from Nazoreans only when they want to draw attention to passages in which this gospel is peculiar in some way or another. This characteristic of the quotations is an important clue to the overall character of this gospel, because it makes it likely that the rest of Nazoreans (the lost, unquoted material) was basically the same as Matthew. This is the reasoning that leads scholars to the conclusion that its contents were more or less identical to those of Matthew. Nazoreans seems to have diverged from Matthew only in minor ways, usually by slightly expanding Matthew's version and clarifying a few of its details. For example, GNaz 3 explains the meaning of a difficult word in the Lord's prayer, a word whose exact meaning still eludes us; GNaz 7 corrects a reference to a figure in the Hebrew Bible that Matthew seems to have gotten wrong; and GNaz 4 fills out the story of Jesus' healing of the man with the crippled hand by making it clear that the man's condition prevented him from making a living.

Nazoreans can be aptly characterized as a slightly reworked version of Matthew. The existing fragments show no familiarity with any other gospel, nor any contact with the gospel traditions prior to Matthew. Nazoreans does in a modest way to Matthew what Matthew had done in a more sweeping way to Mark and Q. Nazoreans is evidence that the process of clarifying, correcting, and expanding the written accounts of the words and deeds of Jesus continued beyond the writing of the canonical gospels. Since Nazoreans is a rewriting of a gospel rather than a new gospel altogether, it shows us that at least one community of Christians considered Matthew to be authoritative, but not beyond correction or alteration.

Language

The Christian authors who are our sources for Nazoreans (Hegesippus, Eusebius, Epiphanius, and Jerome) report that it was written in the Hebrew alphabet (GNaz 8, 10) and that it was known as the "Gospel of the Hebrews" (a title Christian authors apparently gave to any gospel they thought had been written in a Semitic language). Scholars are convinced that the original language of Nazoreans was Aramaic (which uses the same alphabet as Hebrew).

Because Nazoreans is based on Matthew and was written in Aramaic, some scholars have speculated that an Aramaic version of Matthew must have once been in circulation. This theory parallels a widespread rumor among early Christian writers that Matthew had originally been composed in Aramaic. However, close analysis of the quoted fragments of Nazoreans shows that this gospel is based on the Greek text of Matthew. Hence, Nazoreans is an Aramaic "translation" of Matthew, though of course not a literal or even necessarily an accurate translation.

The chain of translation between Nazoreans and the modern reader is a complex one. Early Christian authors translated its Aramaic (which was based on Matthew's Greek) into their own languages. GNaz 8 is preserved in Greek, GNaz 11 in Syriac, and the rest of the fragments in Latin. These excerpts are the basis for the Scholars Version of Nazoreans. Since every translation loses some of the original meaning, our English version of these fragments may in some places only approximate the original sense of this gospel.

Date and place of origin

Nazoreans had to have been written after Matthew and before the Christian writer Hegesippus first referred to it in 180. This means that it was probably written in the first half of the second century. In the fourth century, Jerome informs us that the Nazorean community was living in Beroea, a city in Syria. The gospel may have been composed there.

The Gospel of the Nazoreans

1 *Quoted by Jerome (4th–5th century),* On Famous Men *3*

Here are two of these ⟨citations from the gospel used by the Nazoreans, in which Matthew quotes the ancient scriptures, not following the Septuagint, but the original Hebrew text⟩:

> Out of Egypt I have called my son

and

> for he will be called a Nazorean.

2 *Quoted by Jerome,* Against the Pelagians *3*

In the Gospel of the Hebrews . . . the following story is told:

> [1]The mother of the Lord and his brothers said to him, "John the Baptist baptized for the forgiveness of sins. Let's go and get baptized by him."
>
> [2]But he said to them, "How have I sinned? So why should I go and get baptized by him? Only if I don't know what I'm talking about."

3a *reported by Jerome,* Commentary on Matthew *1 (commenting on Matt 6:11)*

In the so-called Gospel of the Hebrews ⟨in the Lord's prayer⟩, instead of "the bread we need for the day" I found "*mahar*," which means "for

1
//Mt 2:15, 23
◊Hos 11:1; Jgs 13:5
2
//GHeb 2
2:1
Ⓣ Mk 1:4, Lk 3:3
2:2
Cf. Mk 3:14
Ⓣ Heb 4:15
3
//Q 11:3, Mt 6:11, Lk 11:3

---

1 *He will be called a Nazorean* presupposes the Greek version of Judg 13:5 (LXX) as the basis for Matt 2:23; Jerome uses "Nazorean" in both places in his translation of the Bible. It is not, despite Jerome's assertion, a quotation from any passage in the Hebrew Bible. This, and several other of Jerome's misleading claims, makes him an unreliable source of information about the Jewish-Christian gospels. While it would be overly skeptical to dismiss everything he reports, the information he provides must be evaluated with great care.

2 It cannot be determined with certainty whether this fragment belongs to the Gospel of the Hebrews or to Nazoreans. Jerome mistakenly believes that all his quotations originate from one Jewish-Christian gospel, which in some cases makes it difficult for us to distinguish fragments of the Gospel of the Hebrews from those of Nazoreans.

2:2 Jesus' statements do not mean that he refused baptism. If they did, Jerome would have mentioned that this gospel lacked a baptism scene. The purpose of this passage is to avoid any implication that Jesus got baptized because he was seeking forgiveness of his sins. Matthew also deals with this problem, though in a different way (Matt 3:13–15). This fragment also seems to assume that Jesus' family was baptized along with him.

3 *Mahar* is an Aramaic translation of the

tomorrow," so that the sense is "Provide us today with the bread we need for tomorrow"—that is, for the future.

3b *Quoted by Jerome,* Tractate on Psalm 135

In the Hebrew Gospel of Matthew it reads thus:

"Provide us today with the bread we need for tomorrow,"

that is, give us today the bread that you will give us in your domain.

4 *Quoted by Jerome,* Commentary on Matthew *2 (commenting on Matt 12:13)*

In the gospel that the Nazoreans and Ebionites use ⟨in the story of the healing of the man with the crippled hand⟩, this man who had a crippled hand is described as a stonemason who called for help with words like this:

"I was a stonemason making a living with my hands. I plead with you, Jesus, give me back my health so that I won't have to beg for my food in shame."

5 *Quoted by Jerome,* Against the Pelagians *3*

In the same book ⟨Jesus⟩ said,

[1]"If your brother or sister has wronged you verbally and has made amends, welcome him or her seven times a day." His disciple Simon said to him, "Seven times a day?" The Lord answered him, "That's right; in fact, up to seventy times seven times. [2]The prophets themselves were capable of sinful talk, even after they were anointed with the holy spirit."

4 Cf.Mk3:1–6, Mt12:9–14, Lk6:6–11

5:1 //Q17:4, Mt18:21–22, Lk17:4

6 *Quoted by Origen (3rd century),* On Matthew *15 (commenting on Matt 19:16–30)*

It is written in a certain gospel called the "Gospel of the Hebrews"—if anyone will accept it, not as authoritative, but to shed light on the question at hand:

Greek *epiousios*, the meaning of which is disputed. Its only certain occurrence in the Greek language is in the Lord's Prayer (Matt 6:11//Luke 11:3). Origen, a Greek author of the third century and one of the greatest early Christian scholars, thought that the word had been coined by the evangelists. Possible translations of *epiousios* are "daily," "for subsistence," and "for the future." GNaz 3 is the earliest example of a Christian attempt to explain this difficult term.

4 In Matthew, Jesus heals this man in order to make a point about the sabbath law which provokes his opponents (Matt 12:9–14). By adding the man's request, Nazoreans transforms this healing into an act of compassion.

6 Three minor additions to Matthew's version of this scene (Matt 19:16–24) enhance its Jewish coloring: *sons and daughters of Abraham* (v 4) reinforces the meaning of *brothers*

[1]The second rich man said to him, "Teacher, what good do I have to do to live?"
[2]He said to him, "Mister, follow the Law and the Prophets."

He answered, "I've done that."

He said to him, "Go sell everything you own and give it away to the poor and then come follow me."

[3]But the rich man didn't want to hear this and began to scratch his head. And the Lord said to him, "How can you say that you follow the Law and the Prophets? In the Law it says: 'Love your
neighbor as yourself.' [4]Look around you: many of your brothers and sisters, sons and daughters of Abraham, are living in filth and dying of hunger. Your house is full of good things and not a thing of yours
manages to get out to them." [5]Turning to his disciple Simon, who
was sitting with him, he said, "Simon, son of Jonah, it's easier for a camel to squeeze through a needle's eye than for a wealthy person to get into heaven's domain."

7 *reported by Jerome,* Commentary on Matthew *4 (commenting on Matt 23:35)*

In the gospel that the Nazoreans use, we found "son of Joiada" written instead of "son of Baruch."

8 *paraphrased by Eusebius (4th century),* Theophany *4 (discussing Matt 25:19–30)*

The gospel written in the Hebrew alphabet that we have obtained has the threat being made not against the man who had hidden the money, but against the one who had behaved dissolutely. He (the master) had three slaves. One squandered his master's resources with prostitutes and dance hall girls, one multiplied his earnings, and one hid the money. One was later commended, one was merely criticized, and one was thrown into prison. This makes me wonder whether in Matthew the threat that is made after the statement against the man who did nothing might refer not to him, but rather, by the literary device of echoing, to the first man who had been eating and drinking with the drunks.

6 //Mk10:17–25, Mt19:16–24, Lk18:18–25

6:3 ◊Lv19:18

7 Cf.Mt23:35

8 Cf.Mt24:45–51, 25:14–30

---

and sisters as fellow-Israelites, and Jesus and Peter are *sitting* (v 5), i.e., in the posture of Jewish teachers. Nazoreans also embellishes Matthew's version by adding that giving away one's goods should be motivated by compassion for the poor.

7 Matt 23:35 refers to "Zechariah, son of Baruch," who was "murdered between the temple and the altar." According to 2 Chr 24:20, this prophet was not the son of Baruch but of Jehoiada. Matthew probably confused this Zechariah with the one mentioned in Zech 1:1. Nazoreans corrects Matthew on this point. Jerome's *Joiada* seems to be a Latin variant spelling of "Jehoiada" in 2 Chronicles.

8 Nazoreans is apparently dissatisfied with the harsh ending of the parable of the Entrusted Money in Matt 25:14–30. Nazoreans alters the parable so that it includes the opportunistic and abusive slave featured in a nearby parable (Matt 24:45–51). The master

9 *reported by Jerome,* Commentary on Matthew *4 (commenting on Matt 27:16)*

In the so-called Gospel of the Hebrews the name of the man who was to be condemned for sedition and murder is interpreted as "son of their teacher."

10a *reported by Jerome,* Epistle *120*

In the gospel that is written in the Hebrew alphabet we read not that the curtain of the temple was torn, but that the lintel of the temple, which was huge, collapsed.

10b *reported by Jerome,* Commentary on Matthew *4 (commenting on Matt 27:51)*

In the gospel that we have often mentioned we read that the lintel of the temple, which was immense, was fractured and broken up.

9
Cf.Mk15:7, Mt27:16, Lk23:18–19, Jn18:40
10a
Cf.Mk15:38, Mt27:51
11
Cf.Q12:51–53, Mt10:34–36, Lk12:51–53, Th16
Ⓣ Jn15:16, 17:6

11 *Quoted by Eusebius,* Theophany *4 (discussing Matt 10:34–36)*

⟨Christ⟩ himself taught the reason for the separation of souls that takes place in households, as we have found somewhere in the gospel that is spread abroad among the Jews in the Hebrew language, in which it is said:

> "I choose for myself the most worthy—the most worthy are those whom my Father in heaven has given me."

---

punishes him, not (as in Matthew) the slave who merely hid the master's money.

9 The man referred to is Barabbas (Matt 27:16). This interpretation of this Aramaic name is extremely puzzling. The name was common and its meaning ("son of the father") was obvious to Aramaic speakers. Why a gospel composed in Aramaic would need to "interpret" it is a mystery. Why it would give an erroneous explanation of it is even more mysterious. Perhaps Jerome mistook it for "Barrabban," which, if it were a name, would mean "son of the teacher." Perhaps also Jerome himself (or one of his sources) supplied *their* to make it clear that "the teacher" was not Jesus.

10 In a writing earlier than the one in which he discusses this passage, Jerome had attributed the report that the lintel of the temple collapsed to "some interpreters." Also, a few lines before his discussion of this passage, Jerome mentions an event reported to have happened in the temple at the time of its destruction in 70 C.E., but he mistakenly places it at the time of the crucifixion. All this raises a doubt as to whether Jerome personally found this report about the collapse of the lintel in Nazoreans.

11 There is no parallel to this saying in the gospels, though *whom my Father has given me* echoes a phrase in John (6:37, 39; 17:2, 6, 24).

This passage is extant only in a Syriac translation of an early Christian text composed in Greek. This quotation from Nazoreans, therefore, has gone from Aramaic to Greek to Syriac before being translated here into English. We can only hope it is close to the original.

Orphan Sayings and Stories

The Freer Logion, a fifth century C.E. Greek manuscript. The box shows the location of the logion in the manuscript. *Courtesy of the Freer Gallery of Art, Smithsonian Institution, Washington, D.C.*

Congratulations / Damn

The beatitudes take their name from the Latin term *beati,* used to translate the Greek word, *makarios.* The corresponding Hebrew word is *ashre.* What do these terms mean?

Congratulations: The traditional translation "blessed" lives on primarily in its connection with the Bible, apart from sayings like "bless you" when someone sneezes. In that context, "bless you" invokes God's care for the person coming down with a cold. In colloquial English, bless does not mean a declaration of God's favor.

The language of the beatitudes is performative: performative language means that the words accomplish what they say. When the minister says, "I now pronounce you husband and wife," that declaration makes it so. When the judge says, "I sentence you to six months in jail," that statement is the fact. Analogously, when Jesus says, "I declare you poor to be in God's special favor," that is a performative statement. In English we can achieve that sense by translating,

> Congratulations, you poor! / God's domain belongs to you.

"Blessed" is archaic language and now nearly empty of meaning. To translate "happy" or "fortunate" is to introduce connotations that are not present: the poor and the hungry are not "happy" or "fortunate." Further, "happy" or "fortunate" misses the performative character of the language.

Damn: The traditional translation of the Greek interjection *ouai* is "woe." As a noun, a woe refers to a state of intense hardship or suffering of the dimensions of calamities or catastrophes. In the Book of Revelation, woes are cataclysmic events that bring wholesale destruction and condemnation. Woes are more like curses than the mild distress suggested by the English word "woe."

When Jesus says, "Woe to you, Chorazin! Woe to you, Bethsaida!" he is condemning them to a state of intense hardship or suffering (Matt 11:21). The parallel pronouncement in the same passage addresses Capernaum: "And you, Capernaum, you don't think you'll be exalted to heaven, do you? No, you'll go to Hell." The translators of SV concluded that "woe" ought, in contexts like this, to be given its due weight in English by using the English word, "damn." SV reads: "Damn you, Chorazin! Damn you, Bethsaida!" to make it parallel to the assignment of Capernaum to Hell.

Traditional translations have avoided the word "damn" probably because it was unacceptable for liturgical use in the churches.

In Luke's version of the beatitudes, there follows a list of curses (Luke 6:24–25). In SV they read:

> Damn you rich! / You already have your consolation.
> Damn you who are well-fed now! / You will know hunger.
> Damn you who laugh now! / You will learn to weep and grieve.

Like the term "congratulations!," damn is performative language: it is like pronouncing sentence on a convicted criminal.

Orphan Sayings & Stories

Introduction

The sayings and anecdotes presented below are all fragments, which, over the course of the transmission and production of early gospel manuscripts, were introduced by various scribes into particular known copies of the canonical gospels. Their poor attestation in the broader manuscript tradition indicates that they do not belong to the original text of the gospels in which they are found in the odd manuscript. They are often found in only one or two manuscripts, or are missing from the earliest or best witnesses. For this reason, most scholars disregard them in the study of the canonical gospels, and they have been excluded from most modern editions and translations. The exceptions would be the story of the woman caught in adultery in John 7:53–8:11, and the traditional Longer Ending of Mark (16:9–20), which, for traditional or sentimental reasons, are often retained.

These stray fragments fall into the category of *agrapha*, that is, isolated sayings and stories of Jesus not written in the canonical tradition. Many known agrapha have survived antiquity. Most are found in the early church Fathers as brief quotations, sometimes taken from a gospel now lost, such as the Gospel of the Hebrews or the Gospel of the Nazoreans, sometimes given without reference to any source at all. Occasionally one finds an agraphon tucked into a later rabbinic story, there placed on the lips of a hapless Christian interlocutor engaged in debate with the rabbis. What follows is a not a complete list of the agrapha, but a selective sample. The texts associated with lost Jewish Christian gospels are available elsewhere in this volume. As for the anonymous agrapha, their provenance is too uncertain to warrant inclusion here. They might just as well derive from an apocryphal acts tradition (see Acts 20:35) or a lost epistolary tradition (see 1 Thess 4:15–17) as from the early Christian gospel tradition. In any event, a complete catalogue of all the known agrapha could easily occupy an entire volume in its own right. The small collection in this volume is limited to those agrapha which are found within the gospel tradition itself, and thus supply an episode to the overall history of the gospel tradition and contribute to its understanding.

The agrapha must be considered secondary with respect to the larger texts in which they are found and nothing certain is known about their age, provenance or authorship. Nonetheless, they deserve consideration in the study of the gospel tradition. Their chief value lies in the tale they can tell of the later transmission history of the gospels. They remind us how fluid the situation was with these texts well into the second and third centuries, a point often washed over in the quest for a single canonical text to which one might confidently appeal as authoritative. The problem of the New Testament canon involves not just the question of which books belong, but also in what form certain books were considered to bear authority for the early church. The fact that the ancient record is so "messy" suggests that interest in such a quest belongs more to the modern period than to the ancient.

But apart from what these vagabond sayings and stories tell us of the later transmission history of the gospels, we should not rule out the possibility that they might eventually tell us something about the earlier period as well, the early Jesus movement, perhaps even Jesus himself. Their origins, after all, are unknown, shrouded deeply in the folds of early Christian tradition. These sayings and stories are introduced here without judgments about where they might ultimately fit into the history of the gospel tradition.

Orphan Sayings & Stories

1 *A continuation of Matt. 6:13 (the end of the Lord's Prayer) found in several manuscripts: and in Didache 8:2:*

. . . for the imperial rule and the power and the glory are yours forever. Amen.

2 *A continuation of Mark 9:49 in several manuscripts:*

. . . and every sacrifice will be salted with salt.

3 *A saying found replacing Luke 6:5 in one important manuscript, Codex Bezae Cantabrigiensis:*

That day he saw someone working on the sabbath and said to him, "Mister, if you know what you're doing, you are to be congratulated, but if you don't, to hell with you; you are ⟨nothing but⟩ a lawbreaker.

4 *A saying found after Luke 9:55 in several manuscripts:*

And he said, "You don't know of what spirit you are. [For] the son of Adam did not come to destroy human life, but to save it.

5 *A saying found after John 6:56 in one important manuscript, Codex Bezae Cantabrigiensis:*

. . . just as the Father is in me and I am in the Father. I swear to you, if you do not receive the body of the son of Adam as the bread of life, you do not have life in him.

1 The text is preserved very irregularly; *imperial rule, power, glory,* and *Amen* are each missing in at least one of the mss. **4** Most mss read *destroy* here, but a few read "kill." **4** Codex Bezae Cantabriensis omits the second sentence.

3 *to hell with you:* The Greek is a curse (literally, "you are accursed").

5 *I swear to you:* Literally, "Amen, amen I say to you."
5 *in him:* or, "in it."

6 *A continuation of Matt 20:25–28 found in a few manuscripts:*

But you ⟨should⟩ seek to grow out of smallness, and from greatness to become less. For example, when you go in some place and are invited to eat, don't recline on one of the places of honor, in case someone more important than you comes in and the host has to come over and tell you, "Move further down," and embarass you. Rather, it will work to your advantage if you sit down in a lesser place, so that in case someone less important than you comes in, the host will say to you "Move further up."

7 *A story found following John 17:26 in the obscure Codex evangelii Johannei Parisii in sacro Templariorum tabulario asservatus:*

[1]Then, lifting up his hands, Jesus said to his students, "Look, the time has come for me to drink from the cup that my Father has given me to drink. [2]I am going up to my Father who sent me. [3]So I'll tell you once more: I am sending you; obey my instructions, teach ⟨others⟩ what I have taught you, so the whole world might learn it. [4]For this reason, receive the holy spirit; the sins of anyone you forgive are forgiven, and those of anyone you refuse to forgive are not forgiven. [5]Listen to what I have told you: I am not from this world. [6]The advocate is among you; teach with the help of the advocate. [7]Just as the Father sent me, so also I am sending you. [8]I swear to you, I am not from this world. [9]But your father will be John, until he comes with me to paradise." [10]Then he consecrated them with the holy spirit.

8 *A variant version of John 19:26–30 in the obscure Codex evangelii Johannei Templariorum:*

He says to his mother, "Don't cry. I am returning to my Father, and to eternal life. Here is your son! This man will take my place." Then he says to his disciple, "Here is your mother!" Then, bowing his head, he gave up his spirit.

6
//Lk14:8–10
7, v. 1
//Jn13:1, 17:1, 18:11
7, v. 2
//Jn16:5, 7, 10
7, v. 3
//Jn14:15
7, v. 4
//Jn20:22–23
7, v. 5
//Jn17:14, 16
7, v. 6
//Jn14:26
7, v. 7
//Jn20:21
7, v. 8
//Jn17:14, 16
7, v. 9
//Jn20:22

---

6 In the Syriac version there is a negation in the second clause of the first sentence: "and *not* from greatness to become less."

7, v. 6 *advocate:* This Greek word carries a number of related meanings, including witness, spokesperson (terminology associated with the courtroom setting), or one who encourages.

7, v. 8 *I swear to you:* Literally, "Amen, amen I say to you."

9 *A story found at various places in the manuscript tradition. In several manuscripts it is found after John 7:52. Many modern editions of the New Testament include it here, assigning it the versification John 7:53–8:11. Another important group of manuscripts includes it after Luke 21:38. In the Georgian tradition it was sometimes located after John 7:44, and in another group it is found after John 21:25:*

7 [53]Then everybody returned home, 8 [1]but Jesus went to the Mount of Olives. [2]Early in the morning he showed up again in the temple area and everybody gathered around him. He sat down and began to teach them.

[3]The scholars and Pharisees bring him a woman who was caught committing adultery. They make her stand there in front of everybody, [4]and they address him, "Teacher, this woman was caught in the act of adultery. [5]In the Law Moses commanded us to stone women like this. What do you say?" ([6]They said this to trap him, so they would have something to accuse him of.)

Jesus stooped down and began drawing on the ground with his finger. [7]When they insisted on an answer, he stood up and replied, "Whoever is sinless in this crowd should go ahead and throw the first stone at her." [8]Once again he squatted down and continued writing on the ground.

[9]His audience began to drift away, one by one—the elders were the first to go—until Jesus was the only one left, with the woman there in front of him.

[10]Jesus stood up and said to her, "Woman, where is everybody? Hasn't anyone condemned you?

[11]She replied, "No one, sir."

"I don't condemn you either," Jesus said. "You're free to go, but from now on no more sinning."

The endings of the Gospel of Mark

The ending of the Gospel of Mark is a classic problem in New Testament textual criticism. The scholarly consensus is that Mark originally ended with the abrupt stop at 16:8. The earliest Patristic evidence (Clement of Rome, Origen, Eusebius, and Jerome) gives no indication of any text beyond 16:8. In most

Jn 8:1–2 //Lk21:37–38
Jn 8:3 Ⓣ Mk4:1, 9:35; Mt5:1; Lk4:20
Jn 8:5 ◊Lv20:10, Dt22:22–24
Jn 8:6 Ⓣ Lk6:7
Jn 8:7 Ⓣ Rom2:1
Jn 8:11 Ⓣ Jn5:14; EgerG2:4

Jn 8:9 A few mss add "convicted by their conscience" to *his audience.*

Jn 8:3 *Scholars* are mentioned nowhere else in John.

What happened to the woman's lover?

Jn 8:6 The text provides no clue as to what Jesus was supposed to be writing, although a 10th century manuscript fills in the detail by having Jesus writing the sins of the accusers. The text may simply picture Jesus doodling, thereby showing his contempt for the whole situation.

Longer ending to Mark

Shorter ending to Mark

manuscripts, however, Mark comes with endings which extend beyond 16:8. These alternative endings are attempts to smooth out the abruptness of 16:8 and to harmonize Mark with the ending of the other gospels.

10 *A story appended to the end of Mark (16:8) in many manuscripts and versions. It is often referred to as the* Longer Ending of Mark, *and assigned the versification Mark 16:9–20:*

[[9***Now after he arose*** at daybreak on Sunday, he appeared first to Mary of Magdala, from whom he had driven out seven demons. 10She went and told those who were close to him, who were mourning and weeping. 11But when those folks heard that he was alive and had been seen by her, they did not believe it.

12A little later he appeared to two of them in a different guise as they were walking along, on their way to the country. 13And these two returned and told the others. They did not believe them either.

14Later he appeared to the eleven as they were reclining ⟨at a meal⟩. He reproached them for their lack of trust and obstinacy, because they did not believe those who had seen him after he had been raised. 15And he said to them: "Go out into the whole world and announce the good news to every creature. 16Whoever trusts and is baptized will be saved. The one who lacks trust will be condemned. 17These are the signs that will accompany those who have trust: they will drive out demons in my name; they will speak in new tongues; 18they will pick up snakes with their hands; and even if they swallow poison, it certainly won't harm them; they will lay their hands on those who are sick, and they will get well."

19The Lord Jesus, after he said these things, was taken up into the sky and sat down at the right hand of God. 20Those ⟨to whom he had spoken⟩ went out and made their announcement everywhere, and the Lord worked with them and certified what they said by means of accompanying signs.]]

11 *An episode offering a conclusion to the Gospel of Mark, usually found appended to the Longer Ending of Mark, and in at least one instance appended directly to Mark 16:8, without the Longer Ending. It is often referred to as the* Shorter Ending of Mark, *and sometimes assigned the versification 16:21:*

[[***All the instructions*** they had been given they promptly reported to Peter and his companions. Afterwards Jesus himself, using them as agents, broadcast the sacred and imperishable message of eternal salvation from one end of the earth to the other.]]

16:9 //Jn 20:11–18, Lk 8:2; cf. Pet 12:1

16:11 //Lk 24:11

16:13a //Lk 24:13–35

16:13b //Lk 24:11

16:14 //Lk 24:36–43, Jn 20:19–23, 26–29

16:15 //Mt 28:18–20; Ⓣ Mary 4:8

16:18a Cf. Lk 10:19

16:18c Cf. Mt 9:18

16:19 //Lk 24:51; cf. Mt 26:64

16:21 //Jn 20:2; Mt 28:18–20

12 *An episode to the story found in the Longer Ending of Mark, which is inserted directly after Mk. 16:14 in a single known manuscript, Codex Washingtonianus. It is sometimes known as the* Freer Logion, *after the codices' discoverer, Charles L. Freer:* ***Freer Logion***

[[***And they would apologize*** and say, "This lawless and faithless age is under the control of Satan, who by using filthy spirits doesn't allow the real power of God to be appreciated. So," they would say to the Anointed, "let your justice become evident now."

And the Anointed would respond to them, "The time when Satan is in power has run its course, but other terrible things are just around the corner. I was put to death for the sake of those who sinned, so they might return to the truth and stop sinning, and thus inherit the spiritual and indestructible righteous glory that is in heaven."]]

Son of Adam

The traditional translation, "the Son of Man," is apt to be misleading. In ordinary English, "man" refers primarily to males of the species. But the Greek word (*anthropos*) means "human," as distinct from beast or god. It is a generic term that can apply to any member of the human species. *Anthropology* is thus the study of the behavior of all humans, male and female.

In the Hebrew Bible, the phrase, Son of Adam, is used in three different senses.

1. Son of Adam: Insignificant Earthling

The phrase is employed to refer to the human species as insignificant creatures in the presence of God:

How can a human be right before God?
Look, even the moon is not bright,
  and the stars are not pure in his sight;
How much less a human, who is a maggot,
  and a *son of Adam*, who is a worm! Job 25:4–6

2. Sons of Adam: A Little Lower than God

The phrase was also used to identify human beings as next to God in the order of creation:

When I look at the heavens, the work of your fingers,
  the moon and the stars that you set in place;
what are humans that you should regard them,
  and *sons of Adam* that you attend them?
You made them a little lower than God
  and crowned them with glory and honor;
you gave them rule over the works of your hands
  and put all things under their feet. Ps 8:3–6

3. Son of Adam: the Apocalyptic Figure

The Jewish scriptures portray the human being as the agent to exercise control over every living creature (Gen 1:28). This ideal decisively shaped Jewish visions of the end of history:

As I looked on, in a night vision,
I saw one like a *son of Adam* coming with heaven's clouds.
He came to the Ancient of Days and was presented to him.
Dominion and glory and rule were given to him.
His dominion is an everlasting dominion that will not pass away,
and his rule is one that will never be destroyed. Dan 7:13–14

The phrase "son of Adam" is employed in three different senses in the gospels: (a) To refer to the heavenly figure who is to come; (b) To refer to one who is to suffer, die, and rise; (c) To refer to human beings.

(a) References to the figure who is to come in the future on clouds of glory to judge the world are found in Mark 8:38, 13:26, and 14:62 and parallels. This usage is derived from Daniel 7 (sense 3 above). On the lips of Jesus these references to the apocalyptic figure of the future are not self-references but allusions to a third person.

(b) References to the figure who is to suffer, die, and rise are scattered through the gospels. They refer to unique events in the story of Jesus' suffering and death, so that "son of Adam" seems to be only a roundabout way of saying "I."

(c) Two sayings highlight the authority of the "son of Adam" on earth, in one instance, to forgive sin (Mark 2:10), in a second, to "lord it" over the sabbath (Mark 2:28). These sayings appear to conform to the first two senses drawn from the Hebrew Bible mentioned earlier.

The confusion in how this phrase is to be understood owes to the fact that the Christian community tended to understand the phrase messianically or apocalyptically. The original senses derived from the Hebrew Bible were lost or suppressed.

Suggestions for Further Study

All the Gospels

Willis Barnstone, editor. *The Other Bible.* San Francisco: HarperSanFrancisco, 1984.

Ron Cameron. *The Other Gospels: Non-Canonical Gospel Texts.* Philadelphia: Westminster, 1982.

John Dominic Crossan. *Four Other Gospels.* Sonoma: Polebridge, 1993.

Helmut Koester. *Ancient Christian Gospels: Their History and Development.* Philadelphia: Trinity, 1990.

Gospel Parallels

Robert W. Funk. *New Gospel Parallels.* Vol. 1, 2: *Mark.* Sonoma: Polebridge, 1990.

Robert W. Funk. *New Gospel Parallels.* Vol 2: *John and the Other Gospels.* Philadelphia: Fortress, 1985.

E. P. Sanders and Margaret Davies. *Studying the Synoptic Gospels.* Philadelphia: Trinity, 1989.

David R. Cartlidge and David L. Dungan, editors. *Documents for the Study of the Gospels.* Minneapolis: Fortress, 1980, 1994.

Sayings Gospel Q

Arland Jacobson. *The First Gospel: An Introduction to Q.* Sonoma: Polebridge, 1992.

John S. Kloppenborg. *The Formation of Q: Trajectories in Ancient Wisdom Collections.* Studies in Antiquity and Christianity. Philadelphia: Fortress, 1987.

John S. Kloppenborg. *Q Parallels: Synopsis, Critical Notes, and Concordance.* Sonoma: Polebridge, 1988.

John S. Kloppenborg, editor. *The Shape of Q: Signal Essays on the Sayings Gospel.* Minneapolis: Fortress, 1994.

Burton Mack. *The Lost Gospel: The Book of Q and Christian Origins.* San Francisco: HarperCollins, 1993.

Gospel of Thomas

Stevan L. Davies. *The Gospel of Thomas and Christian Wisdom.* New York: Seabury, 1983.

John S. Kloppenborg, Marvin W. Meyer, Stephen J. Patterson, and Michael G. Steinhauser. *The Q–Thomas Reader.* Sonoma: Polebridge, 1990.

Stephen J. Patterson. *The Gospel of Thomas and Jesus.* Sonoma: Polebridge, 1993.

Gospel of Mark

Burton Mack. *A Myth of Innocence: Mark and Christian Origins.* Philadelphia: Fortress, 1988.

Daryl D. Schmidt. *The Gospel of Mark.* The Scholars Bible, Vol. 1. Sonoma: Polebridge, 1991.

Gospel of John

Raymond E. Brown. *The Community of the Beloved Disciple.* New York: Paulist, 1979.
Robert T. Fortna. *The Fourth Gospel and Its Predecessor.* Philadelphia: Fortress, 1989. Now Sonoma: Polebridge.

The Gnostic Gospels

Karen L. King and Charles D. Hedrick, editors. *A Reader's Guide to the Nag Hammadi Library in English.* Sonoma: Polebridge, 1995.
Elaine Pagels. *The Gnostic Gospels.* New York: Random House, 1979.
James M. Robinson. *The Nag Hammadi Library in English.* San Francisco: HarperSan Francisco, 1988.

Infancy Gospels

Ronald F. Hock. *The Infancy Gospels of James and Thomas.* Scholars Bible, Vol. 2. Sonoma: Polebridge, 1995.

Secret Gospel of Mark

Morton Smith. *The Secret Gospel. The Discovery and Interpretation of the Secret Gospel According to Mark.* New York: Harper & Row, 1973.

Jesus

W. Barnes Tatum. *In Quest of Jesus: A Guidebook.* Atlanta: John Knox, 1982.
Marcus J. Borg. *Jesus: A New Vision. Spirit, Culture, and the Life of Discipleship.* San Francisco: Harper & Row, 1987.
Marcus J. Borg. *Meeting Jesus Again for the First Time. The Historical Jesus and the Heart of Contemporary Faith.* HarperSanFrancisco, 1994.
John Dominic Crossan. *The Historical Jesus: The Life of a Mediterranean Jewish Peasant.* San Francisco: HarperSanFrancisco, 1991.
John Dominic Crossan. *Jesus: A Revolutionary Biography.* San Francisco: Harper SanFrancisco, 1994.
Robert W. Funk, Roy W. Hoover, and the Jesus Seminar. *The Five Gospels. The Search for the Authentic Words of Jesus.* New York: Macmillan, 1993.
Stephen Mitchell. *The Gospel According to Jesus: A New Translation and Guide to His Essential Teachings for Believers and Unbelievers.* New York: HarperCollins, 1991.
Thomas Sheehan. *The First Coming: How the Kingdom of God Became Christianity.* New York: Random House, 1986.
Geza Vermes. *The Religion of Jesus the Jew.* Minneapolis: Fortress, 1994.
Marcus J. Borg. *Jesus in Contemporary Scholarship.* Valley Forge: Trinity, 1994.
Hershel Shanks, editor. *The Search for Jesus: Modern Scholarship Looks at the Gospels.* Washington, DC: Biblical Archaeology Society, 1994.
Albert Schweitzer. *The Quest of the Historical Jesus: A Critical Study of Its Progress from Reimarus to Wrede.* New York: Macmillan, 1961. (Originally published in German in 1906.)

Glossary

Acts of Thomas: The legendary accounts of the deeds of the apostle Judas Thomas (probably the Judas Didymos Thomas of the Gospel of Thomas), telling of Thomas' missionary journeys east to Parthia and eventually to India. In these adventuresome tales, Thomas preaches the values of asceticism and gnosis as the path to salvation.

Androgyny: The state of being in which an individual possesses both male and female characteristics.

Aphorism: Aphorisms and proverbs are striking one-liners. An aphorism is a short, provocative saying that challenges the accepted view of things. A proverb embodies common sense. A proverb: "Early to bed, early to rise, makes one healthy, wealthy, and wise." An aphorism: "It's not what goes into a person that defiles, but what comes out" (Mark 7:15).

Apocalyptic: A type of religious thinking characterized by the notion that through an act of divine intervention, the present evil world is about to be destroyed and replaced with a new and better world in which God's justice prevails.

Aramaic: A Semitic language related to Hebrew which was spoken in Palestine at the time of Jesus.

Beatitudes: Literary or oral formulations that confer good fortune on the recipient. They usually begin with the expression "Congratulations to" (more traditionally translated as "blessed is"). The most famous beatitudes are said by Jesus at the opening of the Sermon on the Mount/Plain in Q 6:20–23.

Canon: An authoritative list or collection of books accepted as holy scripture. The canon was determined for Catholics at the Council of Trent (1546), which formally ratified the list of books in use since the fourth century. The canon has never been determined for Protestants, except by common consent.

Carpocratians: Followers of Carpocrates, a gnostic Christian teacher from Alexandria from the first half of the second century, whose teachings later came to be regarded as heretical.

Catchword: A word repeated in consecutive sayings which serves to link them together in the mind of the audience and so facilitate their memorization.

Catechesis: Religious instruction given to Christian initiates (catechumens) either as preparation for baptism or as a follow-up to it.

Christology: Teaching concerning the role or identity of Jesus.

Chronicler: A name designating the writer or writers responsible for the Old Testament books of 1 and 2 Chronicles, Ezra, and Nehemiah.

Clement of Alexandria: The head of an important Christian school for catechumens in Alexandria. Among his many works is the *Stromateis*, which deals extensively with the question of the relationship between Christian faith and Greek philosophy. It is a letter from Clement which contains the excerpts from the Secret Gospel of Mark.

Codex: An ancient manuscript in book form, as distinguished from a scroll, which is a book in roll form.

Coptic: The form of the Egyptian language in use at the time of the introduction of Christianity in Egypt.

Council: A Jewish high commission, presided over by the high priest, which met regularly in the temple to deliberate and rule on religious matters. Under the Roman occupation it had limited political jurisdiction. In Greek it was called the *Sanhedrin,* which means simply to "sit together."

Deuteronomic history: The Old Testament writings which tell of the history of Israel from the theological perspective of the book of Deuteronomy: obedience to God produces prosperity, disobedience trails disaster in its wake, to put it simplistically. The Deuteronomic history includes Joshua, Judges, 1 and 2 Samuel, and 1 and 2 Kings.

Didache: An early Christian compendium of instruction, an incipient catechism, also known as the *Teachings of the Twelve Apostles.* The final form of the Didache, which was discovered in 1875, dates from the early second century, but its main sections go back to the first century.

Docetism: The belief that Christ was not truly human, but only seemed to be so (from *dokeo*, "seem").

Epiphany: An English cognate term for the Greek *epiphaneia* meaning "manifestation," usually of a supernatural being.

Eschatology: Religious teaching about those events supposed to happen at the end of time.

Gehenna, see the Cameo Essay, p. 392.

Gnosticism: Gnosticism gets its name from the Greek word *gnosis*, meaning "knowledge" or "insight." It was a widespread religious movement in Antiquity, which in general terms focused on the world as a place of fallenness and evil, the illegitimate creation of a rebellious demi-god. Gnostics believed that their origin is not this world of evil, but in a higher realm in which dwells the one true God, who, through a messenger or redeemer, has seen fit to communicate to them the knowledge (*gnosis*) of their true heavenly home. Armed with this *gnosis*, the Gnostic seeks to break free from this world and its rebellious creator, to be reunited with the Godhead in the heavenly realm above. Gnosticism was very adaptable and manifested itself in numerous forms, attaching to and transforming older traditional religious systems, such as Judaism or Christianity.

Josephus: A Jewish historian from the late first century. His two principal works, the *Jewish War* and the *Jewish Antiquities*, are the most important ancient historical sources for Jewish history during the period 200 B.C.E.–100 C.E.

Judas (the brother of Jesus): Judas is named as a brother of Jesus in Mark 6:3 and Matt 13:55, along with James, Joses, and Simon. Judas (=Jude), "a servant of Jesus and brother of James" is named as the author of the Epistle of Jude. These two figures may be the same person, even though the author of the Epistle of Jude demures from claiming the status of "brother" of Jesus.

Judean, see the Cameo Essay, pp. 193–94.

Kerygma: A technical term of New Testament scholarship deriving from the Greek word for "preaching." It is used to refer to the earliest Christian proclamation about Jesus. Most scholars agree that the gospels were profoundly influenced by the early Christian kerygma, and thus are more a product of early Christian preaching than a desire to preserve history.

Lacuna: A gap in a manuscript caused by damage or deterioration.

Levites: Descendants of the tribe of Levi who had sacred duties in the Jerusalem temple, but who did not offer sacrifice or conduct worship, duties reserved for priests.

Nag Hammadi: The town in Egypt near which a collection of Christian and Gnostic documents, known as the Nag Hammadi library, was discovered in 1945.

Oxyrhynchus: An ancient village in Egypt where numerous papyri have been discovered. Among its most important treasures are Oxyrhynchus Gospels 840 and 1224, fragments of otherwise unknown gospels, and POxy 1, 654, 655, Greek fragments of the Gospel of Thomas.

Paleography: The study of ancient handwriting. Paleography can often determine the age of a manuscript by the style of its handwriting.

Papyrus: The predecessor to modern paper. Ancient works were written on animal skins, called parchment or vellum, or on papyrus, made from Egyptian reeds.

Parable: A brief narrative or picture. It is also a metaphor or simile drawn from nature or common life, arresting the hearer by its vividness or strangeness, and leaving the mind in sufficient doubt about its precise application to tease it into active thought.

Parousia: Literally "presence"; in the New Testament it refers to the arrival or coming of the Son of Adam, or the messiah, another name for which is the Anointed (Jesus), who will sit in cosmic judgment at the end of history. It is thus commonly understood to mean "second coming," as distinguised from the first coming or advent of the messiah.

Pericope: A Greek term literally meaning "something cut out." A discrete unit of discourse, such as a paragraph in an essay or a segment of a well-ordered story.

Pharisees: Jewish laymen dedicated to the exacting observance of religion, the rigorous application of the Law to everyday life, and the cultivation of a tradition of teaching not found in the Torah, sometimes called the "oral torah." The Pharisees are routinely parodied and condemned in the gospels. The polemic more accurately reflects conflicts between the synagogue and the Christian communities which produced the Gospels in the last quarter of the first century than it does the situation of the historical Jesus.

Redaction: The process of producing a new text by reworking an existing text with a particular purpose in mind. Redaction can include adding or deleting material, rearranging, and rewriting. Redaction criticism is a scholarly method of investigation that seeks to isolate an evangelist's purpose and perspective by analyzing the way he handles material derived from sources. A less technical name for redaction is editing.

Sanhedrin, see Council.

Son of Adam, see the Cameo Essay, pp. 428–29.

Sophia: Greek for "wisdom." Wisdom is often personified in early Jewish literature as a supernatural female figure. See, for example, Proverbs 8 and Sirach 1.

Synoptic: A term from the Greek *synoptikos*, "seeing together," meaning "having a common view of," referring to the Gospels of Mark, Matthew, and Luke, which are similar in form, outline, and contents.

Torah: The first five books of the Bible, often called simply "the Law."